QUALITY:
A CORPORATE FORCE

Managing for Excellence

QUALITY:
A CORPORATE FORCE
Managing for Excellence

C. Harold Aikens
The University of Tennessee

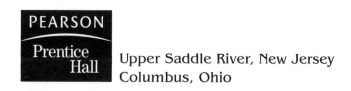

PEARSON
Prentice
Hall

Upper Saddle River, New Jersey
Columbus, Ohio

Library of Congress Cataloging-in-Publication Data

Aikens, C. Harold.
  Quality: a corporate force: managing for excellence / C. Harold Aikens.
    p. cm.
  Includes index.
  ISBN 0-13-119757-6
  1. Total quality management.   2. Quality control.   3. Quality assurance.   4. Six sigma
(Quality control standard)   I. Title.
  HD62.15.A395 2006
  658.4′013—dc22

                                                                              2005013503

Editor: Deborah Yarnell
Assistant Editor: Maria Rego
Editorial Assistant: ReeAnne Davies
Production Editor: Kevin Happell
Production Coordination: Karen Ettinger, TechBooks/GTS York, PA Campus
Design Coordinator: Diane Ernsberger
Cover Designer: Jason Moore
Cover art: Super Stock
Production Manager: Deidra Schwartz
Marketing Manager: Jimmy Stephens

This book was set in Times Ten by TechBooks/GTS York, PA Campus. It was printed and
bound by R. R. Donnelley & Sons Company. The cover was printed by Phoenix Color Corp.

Pearson Education Ltd.   Pearson Education Australia Pty. Limited
Pearson Education Singapore Pte. Ltd.   Pearson Education North Asia Ltd.
Pearson Education Canada, Ltd.   Pearson Educación de Mexico, S.A. de C.V.
Pearson Education—Japan   Pearson Education Malaysia Pte. Ltd.

10 9 8 7 6 5 4 3 2 1
ISBN 0-13-119757-6

This book is dedicated to the memory of my father,
Charles Harold Aikens, Jr. (1916–1985), and my father-in-law,
Albert Allan Maskell (1916–2004). Their values and personal ideals
live on through the concepts and principles expressed herein.

Brief Contents

Contents

CHAPTER 5:   Managing for Quality: Accountability and Implementation   113

SECTION IV: THE THIRD GENERATION: SIX SIGMA, LEAN, AND QUALITY-INSPIRED MANAGEMENT   315

CHAPTER 9:   Six Sigma and Continuous Improvement   315

Preface

THE VISION

Quality is more than the application of statistical tools, more than a team-based approach to continuous improvement, and more than measurements and standards. Quality goes beyond Six Sigma, black belts, supplier qualification, or ISO certification. Although all these features may be present, the key to a successful quality program lies, not so much in tools and techniques, but in values and attitudes. The tough lessons of total quality management (TQM) teach that quality is not merely defined by words, mandates, or acronyms. Quality is a state of mind—a pervasive driver that influences all business decisions. In short, *quality is a corporate force,* a message that is captured in the title and forms the theme for this work.

My purpose in writing this book was to provide a comprehensive resource that would help students and practitioners properly integrate decisions in the boardroom with activities on the shop floor. Reviewers advised that this goal would be best served through a two-volume series, so the decision was made to devote the first book to managerial issues. As the subtitle—*Managing for Excellence*—suggests, the emphasis is on issues that pertain to the formulation and execution of strategy. The second volume will build on these principles, adding the technical depth necessary for design, maintenance, operations, and logistics.

Two decades ago, the world rallied behind TQM and the doctrines of the great quality pioneers, including Shewhart, Deming, Juran, Crosby, and Ishikawa. Today, the winds have shifted to newer philosophies such as lean production, Six Sigma, and high-performing work practices. Despite labels, quality as a corporate force is broader than a single philosophy. While writing this book, it became obvious to me that a new term was needed—one that did not carry with it preconceptions. I decided to use *quality-inspired management* (QIM) to represent any corporate culture that relentlessly pursues excellence and that embraces shared values epitomizing the highest ideals of business, morality, respect, responsibility, ethics, and perfection. A QIM organization is goal driven, committed to its customers, and is a place of continual learning. QIM is third-generation quality, as described in Chapter 5.

HOW THE BOOK IS ORGANIZED

The book is organized in four major sections.

Section I, Quality and the Business System, is divided into three chapters designed to set the stage, provide a historical perspective, and develop the subject from the open systems view of management. Chapter 1 provides a short history of the quality movement, introduces the many and varied definitions of quality, and offers a working definition. Chapter 2 discusses open systems theory and describes how QIM requires a movement away from machine age thinking toward an open systems approach. Chapter 3 focuses on QIM as it relates to strategic planning, competition, and the development of trusting relationships up and down the supply chain.

Section II, Quality and Management Practices, contains three chapters that address issues important to management practice. Chapter 4 examines various organization models (mechanistic and organic), decision-making methodologies (programmed and nonprogrammed), and leadership qualities. Chapter 5 presents the use of the balanced scorecard as a framework for establishing accountability and measuring performance. Implementation approaches are discussed from the perspective of lessons learned and organizational readiness. Chapter 6 focuses on the human element, presenting the human resources function as an open subsystem that exists to support institutional purpose. A model for developing human capability and enhancing organizational readiness is presented.

Section III, Quality and Process Management, consists of two chapters that cover the process improvement toolkit. Chapter 7 presents the "soft" tools—those that can be applied to new idea creation, planning, process analysis, and problem solving. Chapter 8 introduces the "hard" tools—those that are based in statistics, such as control charts, measurement processes, and process capability.

Section IV, The Third Generation: Six Sigma, Lean, and Quality-Inspired Management, constitutes the final two chapters of the book. Chapter 9 discusses the advantages of Six Sigma and lean production, and how these complementary principles relate to former quality philosophies such as TQM. Chapter 10 covers topics that are important to supply chain management, including vendor selection and acceptance sampling.

PEDAGOGY

A motivating minicase is used to introduce each chapter, as well as to set the stage through contextual scenarios and issues. Next, a list of learning objectives and key outcomes defines the educational purpose of each chapter. These objectives again appear at the end of the chapter, with a brief discussion of key points to help with study and review.

Two continual study aids are provided throughout each chapter. In the margin, key ideas and key terms have been highlighted. At the end of each chapter, a section titled To Test Your Understanding provides some thought-provoking questions or problems to test the student's understanding of major concepts.

The final element is a case study, which follows most of the chapters. Each case provides an opportunity for discussion and debate, and to be able to take the content to a realistic level of practical application.

Many of the statistical illustrations in the text were developed using Minitab Release 14 software. There are numerous packages commercially available to support quality management. I have found that Minitab is user friendly, enables files to be easily exported to and from Excel, and generates reports of exceptional quality.

THE INTENDED AUDIENCE

Quality: A Corporate Force—Managing for Excellence treats quality broadly from a strategic open systems management view. I have tried to develop the business perspective without sacrificing the tools for quality improvement. Therefore, although this book would be an excellent text for graduate and undergraduate business courses, the content of Chapters 7 to 10 provides a depth of coverage suitable for teaching quality improvement to engineering students. This text can meet a wide range of needs—from simple awareness training to skills development—up to and including the level of Six Sigma black belt. The second book in this series will introduce some advanced topics consistent with the needs of Six Sigma master black belt training. The following examples indicate how the content can be distributed to meet various needs:

- A three-credit-hour core course in a baccalaureate degree program in business, strategy, or operations management, or an elective course supporting any undergraduate business major: all ten chapters
- A three-credit-hour graduate course in an MBA program or as an elective course in any business-related master's degree program (e.g., accounting, strategy, marketing, finance): all ten chapters
- A companion text for Six Sigma training and reference:
  - Champions/senior management: Chapter 9, with selected overview materials from Chapters 2 to 7
  - White belt: Selected overview materials from Chapters 1 and 9
  - Green belt: Selected materials for proficiency training from Chapters 1 and 7 to 9
  - Black belt: Chapters 7 to 9; selected materials for knowledge and proficiency from Chapters 1 to 6 and 10

For undergraduates, pedagogy should emphasize quality fundamentals and assess a student's ability to answer the questions presented at the end of each chapter. At the graduate level, more emphasis should be placed on integrating the material across chapters and students should be required to debate issues raised by the cases. Topics can include the differing perspectives of quality, which factors have contributed to successes or failures, and to what extent quality principles can be applied generically, given geographical, cultural, industrial, and organizational size differences.

ONLINE SUPPLEMENTS

A companion website (**http://www.prenhall.com/aikens**) is available online to both students and instructors using the text.

An online Instructor's Manual is also available to instructors. To access the online Instructor's Manual, go to **www.prenhall.com.** Instructors can search for a text by author, title, ISBN, or by selecting the appropriate discipline from the pull down menu at the top of the catalog home page. To access supplementary materials online, instructors need to request an instrutor access code. Go to **www.prenhall.com,** click the **Instructor Resource Center** link, and then click Register Today for an instructor access code. Within 48 hours of registering you will receive a confirming e-mail including an instructor access code. Once you have received your code, go to the site and log on for full instructions on downloading the materials that you wish to use.

Acknowledgments

I want to express my appreciation to those who have helped make this book a reality. A special thanks goes to the companies that have permitted me to observe firsthand their agonies and ecstacies, as they traveled the path of quality improvement. I would also like to acknowledge my students, who have provided continual inspiration and the tangible assurance that there is always a brighter future. Specific recognition goes to my friend and colleague, Tom Williams, who has always been a willing sounding board. The task cycle and variance tracking matrix tools would be absent were it not for Tom's counsel.

The following were especially helpful in providing suggestions on organizing the content: Vidyaranya Gargeya, The University of North Carolina at Greensboro; Rebecca Gregory, Palomar College; John Kelley, Villanova University; John Kobza, Texas Tech University; Pat LaPoint, McMurry University; and Dan Voss, Wright State University.

I am indebted to Samir Shrivastava, Bond University, Australia, who did much of the background research for Chapter 6, and to Hampton Liggett, The University of Tennessee, for contributions to Chapter 10.

I want to acknowledge my reviewers who made helpful suggestions that helped shape the content to its intended purpose Thomas M. Box, Pittsburg State University; Cyndi A. Crother, Cal Poly State University, San Luis Obispo; David Lemak, Washington State University; and Richard M. Miech, Fox Valley Technical College. I am also grateful to the companies who have graciously given permission to document some of their experiences as case studies so others may learn. These contributors include JetBlue Airways, Nissan Motor Company, Nestlé USA, Lincoln Electric Company, Starbucks Corporation, Sears, Roebuck and Co., GE Healthcare, and Harley-Davidson, Inc.

In addition, I want to acknowledge the support of Minitab, Inc., and to Christine Bayly, who kindly provided me with a copy of Minitab Release 14 for use during the development of this project.

The "moments of truth" story recounted in Chapter 1 is from pages 1 and 2 of *Moments of Truth* by Jan Carlzon, copyright © 1987 by Ballinger Publishing Company, and has been reprinted by permission of HarperCollins Publishers, Inc.

Finally, there are two persons who merit special recognition—my wife, Helen, who spent countless hours poring over manuscripts, and my daughter, Jocelyn, a former MBA student, who read the final proofs and made suggestions for improvement. Thank you both for your love and support.

SECTION I

Quality and the Business System

CHAPTER 1

Introduction to Quality: The Fundamentals

Quality is never an accident; it is always the result of high intention, sincere effort, intelligent direction, and skillful execution; it presents the wise choice of many alternatives, the cumulative experience of many masters of craftsmanship. Quality also marks the search for an ideal after necessity has been satisfied and mere usefulness achieved.

—WILLA A. FOSTER
THE QUALITY YEARBOOK

Koolewong Vineyards

Experience Life and Savor the Moment

Koolewong Vineyards is a privately owned winery situated on 1,500 hectares in New South Wales, Australia. Its staff of eighteen produce a variety of red and white wines. They are rapidly establishing a national reputation for their Shiraz, which the wine critics consistently rate highly for its distinctive spicy nose and dark fruits. To achieve quality, Koolewong's process is designed to encourage the release of color and flavor during the juice phase, and to minimize extraction during the alcohol phase. Mature grapes are harvested and delivered to the winery early in the day while the fruit is cool. They then go through a destemming process. Unlike other wine-making techniques, the grapes are not crushed; this can release bitter compounds found in grape seeds. Fermentation begins twenty-four to thirty-two hours after destemming and takes about seven days to complete; the temperature is maintained at 85°F. After fermentation, the wine is aged in casks made of French or American oak.

The owners of Koolewong Vineyards are striving to become a leader in the Australian red wine market and to begin exporting overseas within ten years. To accomplish this goal, they realize the need for an ambitious growth strategy to take market share from competitors. Koolewong reds are sold

1

under a premium label and are marketed to discerning customers who appreciate quality. The definition of quality, however, depends on one's point of view. At the process level, quality begins with soil testing and managing those agricultural factors necessary to ensure a healthy crop of grapes. As the grapes are converted into wine, batches are tested for proper pH levels, alcohol content, and other essential chemical concentrations. The product is tested at various stages of fermentation and again prior to bottling. Quality to the consumer means something entirely different. The consumer judges a wine's quality based on taste, which is subjective and therefore difficult to measure from the customer's viewpoint.

The company has launched a marketing campaign to introduce its reds to a broader customer base. Trying to get people to associate lifestyles with Koolewong reds, the company has adopted the slogan "Experience life, savor the moment." They have also employed expert wine tasters who can reliably represent consumer tastes, and detect and judge the subtle variances that occur among production batches. ∎

1.1 LEARNING OBJECTIVES AND KEY OUTCOMES

After studying the material in Chapter 1, you will be able to

1. Recognize that quality is a powerful corporate force that influences nearly every major decision, from the boardroom to the cutting room
2. Define quality from numerous perspectives
3. Understand the difference between quality as a function and quality as a core value
4. Develop your own working definition of quality
5. Demonstrate an understanding of the history of quality, and describe the three generations in the evolution of the quality movement
6. Identify the pioneers of the quality movement, and describe their respective contributions

1.2 WHAT IS QUALITY?

Quality Assurance

Total Quality Control

Customer-Driven Quality

Continuous Process Improvement

Zero Defects

Total Quality Management

Six Sigma

Quality is a corporate force influencing important decisions at all levels—from the boardroom to the shipping dock. Quality can be viewed from many different perspectives as evidenced by the multitude of books on the subject. Some authors have presented quality as a fundamental management principle—ingrained in the dispositions that drive managerial behaviors. This viewpoint is consistent with a management philosophy that has been known by many names. A few of the more common ones have been **quality assurance** (QA), **total quality control** (TQC), **customer-driven quality** (CDQ), **continuous process improvement** (CPI), **zero defects** (ZD), **total quality management** (TQM), and **Six Sigma**. Such programs vary widely in scope and implementation, but they all have one goal in common: the centricity of quality as a corporate value.

Other writers have chosen to present quality as a technical discipline of measurements, controls, mechanical processes, and probability theory. Both viewpoints are correct. On the technical side, methodologies should be employed to ensure quality is produced at the source. On the front end of the production value chain is the design function, and it is important that product designs meet customer needs and are manufacturable—that is, technical specifications should be compatible with production capabilities. The production processes, in contrast, should be designed so output is reliable and consistent. Above all, to control and improve quality, process operators should have a substantive knowledge of how their processes behave and why.

On the management side, an organization's leadership is responsible for

- Creating a culture where quality is a core value, characterized by customer centricity, value creation, management engagement, and an organizational structure that supports sustained improvement
- Understanding their markets so they can recognize and adapt to changes, and be able to anticipate customer needs
- Understanding their internal capabilities so resources can rapidly be redeployed to take advantage of new opportunities

In today's organizations, quality is the engine that drives all major decisions. Quality is the nucleus around which all dimensions of the business (structures, policies, strategies, decisions, planning, and operations) must orbit if the enterprise is to claim long-term success.

Contemporary quality management must be the embodiment of many and varied perspectives—all rolled up into a committed **corporate culture** with strong **knowledge-driven leadership**. For the sake of clarity, this text refrains from using any of the common and sometimes misused terms to refer to this new "quality-conscious" paradigm. To do so would be at the risk of readers confusing sound principles with preconceived biases that have arisen through bad experiences. For example, the term "TQM" is now considered by some to be either passé or ineffective. Although the validity of such claims could arguably be questioned, the wisest course is to avoid terms that motivate readers to take a stand (for or against). Behind each popularized approach are sound principles with lasting values, and research studies have indicated that most failures are due to poor or ill-conceived implementations, not to flaws in the concepts.

The old terms are used where appropriate, when making comparisons or historical references. However, when referring to a culture that is quality conscious, knowledge driven, participatory, and systems integrated (ideal traits), a new term is needed that does not suffer from any preexisting biases. Therefore, this book has adopted the term—**quality-inspired management** (QIM)—to represent quality cultures that possess the ideal traits.

1.2.1 Quality in 3D

We begin our study of quality by trying to define it. One of the earliest documented definitions dates to around 40 BC when the noted Roman engineer and architect, Marcus Vitruvius Pollio, known simply as Vitruvius, wrote a treatise entitled "The Ten Books on Architecture.[1]" As related to architectural structures, Vitruvius defined three dimensions of quality, which in Latin are *utilitas, firmitas,* and *venustas.*

1.2.1.1 **Utilitas**, or **commodity**, refers to how well a product fulfills its intended function. For example, a building is usually designed for a specific purpose. Anyone who has experienced converting a building for a new use—for example, using a garage for a bedroom or a warehouse for a home—understands the meaning of *utilitas.*

The U.S. pavilion at the 1982 Knoxville World's Fair was impressive, with wide expanses of steel and concrete and an attached multistory IMAX theater. At the conclusion

---

Sidebar notes (left margin):

Quality is fundamental to all major business decisions.

Quality is about relationships.

Corporate Culture

Knowledge-Driven Leadership

Quality-inspired management (QIM) is the integration of all quality perspectives into a cohesive management paradigm.

Quality-Inspired Management

Quality is function.

Function

Utilitas

Commodity

---

[1]Pollio, Marcus Vitruvius. "The Ten Books on Architecture," translated by Morris Hicky Morgan, Dover Publications, Inc., New York, 1960. 331 pages. Originally published by Harvard University Press in 1914.

Quality is structural
integrity.

of the fair, the General Services Administration was unable to sell the building. Apparently, the costs and modifications needed to transform the U.S. pavilion into a venue with a different purpose were excessive. The building was ultimately demolished, and a new multimillion dollar convention center occupies the site today.

Structural Integrity

Firmitas

Firmness

Durability

Reliability

1.2.1.2 Firmitas, or **firmness**, refers to the **structural integrity** of a building. Buildings should be designed so they withstand the test of tempest and time. They must also meet local building codes to ensure the safety of the occupants. Firmitas is a measure of **durability** and **reliability**.

1.2.1.3 *Venustas,* or **delight**, refers to a building's **aesthetics**. Delight is the most difficult of the three dimensions to define, and it changes with time and culture. It is easy to tell an architect, "we require three stories, twelve rooms, a live load of 150 pounds per square foot, and so on." These technical requirements may satisfy function and structural integrity, but how does one specify that the architect must also create something of beauty? Two houses can have identical square footages; one has curb appeal and the other does not. Can aesthetics be specified? Can it be measured? Who can be trusted to define it? Furthermore, changing tastes and technologies influence **perception**. Venustas is a measure of the human experience and **pleasure**.

Quality is delight.

Delight

Aesthetics

Perception

Pleasure

Architectural designs have evolved with the development of high-strength, load-bearing materials, and inventions such as the Otis elevator, which in 1852 launched an era of steel-framed, glass-gilded skyscrapers. Function and structure are utilitarian factors—what Juran had in mind when he defined quality as "**fitness for use**."[2] When delight is added to the mix, the quality issue goes well beyond simple metrics. Quality as the purveyor of pleasure is a fuzzy domain. There may be instances where customers are unable to clearly articulate a definition for quality, but they are steadfast in the confidence that they will know it when they see it. Hence, quality can be largely perceptual, reflecting personal feelings or attitudes. Quality is an individual **value judgment**, and at the end of the day, quality is simply what your customers say it is. If a customer ever perceives that a better deal is available from a competitor, you will lose the business. The "true" quality of the competitor is somewhat irrelevant. Subjective perception always overrules objective reality.

Perception is more
important than
reality.

Fitness for Use

Value Judgment

Quality is a value
judgment.

1.2.2 Moments of Truth and Spontaneous Value Judgments

Moments of truth
are instantaneous
contacts with
customers.

Any time a customer experiences a direct encounter with an employee, quality can be made or broken. Jan Carlzon, former president and chief executive officer (CEO) of Scandinavian Airlines (SAS), coined the term **moments of truth** to describe such casual, instantaneous, and even accidental contacts.[3]

Moments of Truth

This simple concept turned SAS around to become one of the most respected airlines in the industry. To illustrate, Carlzon relates the story[4] of an American businessman, Mr. Petersen, who was staying in a hotel in Stockholm and was booked on an SAS flight to Copenhagen. On arriving at the airport, Mr. Petersen discovered that he had

---

[2]Juran, Joseph M. *Juran on Leadership for Quality.* New York: The Free Press, 1989, 15.

[3]Carlzon, Jan. *Moments of Truth.* Reprint edition. New York: HarperCollins, 1989, 1–2.

[4]Excerpt from pp. 1–2 from *Moments of Truth* by Jan Carlzon. Copyright © 1987 by Ballinger Publishing Company. Reprinted by permission of HarperCollins.

Moments of truth in the airline business occur when customers

1. Call to make a reservation
2. Arrive at the airport, check their bags, and collect their boarding passes
3. Are greeted at the gate
4. Are served by the flight attendants aboard the aircraft
5. Need to make a change in their itinerary
6. Report lost or damaged luggage

---

inadvertently left his ticket in his hotel room. He was pleasantly surprised when the ticket agent cheerfully issued a temporary ticket and boarding pass. She phoned his Stockholm hotel, a bellhop promptly located the missing ticket, and an SAS limo was dispatched to retrieve it. Everyone acted so quickly that the ticket actually arrived before the flight left the gate, and the flight attendant was able to personally deliver the ticket to the passenger onboard the aircraft.

In a traditional scenario, the airline's response would have been "no ticket, no flight." At best, the agent would have referred the matter to a supervisor, but the passenger would in all likelihood have missed his flight. Which company is Mr. Petersen likely to choose for future air travel?

This story illustrates how a company can differentiate itself from its competition if it is willing to be flexible and to empower its frontline employees to act in the interest of customer service. Annually, SAS serves ten million customers, and each customer comes into contact with approximately five employees for an average of fifteen seconds. This generates fifty million opportunities for the company to prove to its customers that they made the right choice. It is important that frontline employees be empowered to effect a suitable response during the golden fifteen-second time interval. Having to seek authorizations up the chain of command can lose the opportunity to earn a loyal customer forever.

> Value is the difference between benefits and sacrifices.

1.2.2.1 A Value Judgment   *Value* is created when a customer perceives that the benefit derived from a product or service (e.g., pleasure, function, return) exceeds the personal sacrifices required (e.g., cost, inconvenience, time). The greater the difference between the benefits and sacrifices, the greater the value. This maxim is obvious during an auction where value is instantaneously established. On a more discreet level, it plays out millions of times per day as customers weigh the pros and cons of alternatives, trading off benefits with sacrifices, and ultimately making a choice based on a comparative value judgment.

1.2.3 Dynamic Quality Factors

> Quality is the difference between what is received and what is expected.
>
> **Principal of Neutral Awareness**

Quality is the difference between what the customer received and what the customer expected. The irony is that certain features (even if of high quality) may go unnoticed (and therefore not count as a quality measure) by the customer if those features were expected. It is when the customer fails to find certain features that the perception of quality is impacted—and then in a negative way. This idea is captured in the **principle of neutral awareness**.[5]

---

[5]Cusins, Peter. "Understanding Quality through Systems Thinking." *The TQM Magazine* 2, no. 5 (1994): 19–27.

Static quality factors
do not enhance a
customer's
perception of
quality.

Principle of Neutral Awareness   The presence of certain features, called *static quality factors,* may go unnoticed by the customer. However, if these factors are absent, quality will be perceived to be unsatisfactory. The provision of other features, called *dynamic quality factors,* is unanticipated. The perception of quality will be unaffected if dynamic quality factors are absent; however, if such factors are present, the positive affect on a customer's assessment of quality can be profound.

Static quality factors represent intrinsic features—such as meeting design specifications, on-time deliveries, and matching advertised features—things that are taken for granted by the customer. If static factors are absent, the customer will judge quality negatively. For example, if a delivery is expected within forty-eight hours as promised, early delivery (say within forty hours) might go unnoticed. However, a late delivery (say sixty hours) could result in damaging consequences for the customer and dissatisfaction to the extreme.

Dynamic quality factors, in contrast, are not particularly missed if they are not present, but can have a very positive affect on customer attitudes if they are. These are the difference makers that can move a customer's perception from mere satisfaction to the ideal state of *venustas.* If dynamic quality factors are present, the customer's expectations are clearly exceeded (and there is a desire to repeat the experience in the future). The inclusion of dynamic quality factors in the overall service experience can be an important key to competitive advantage. Dynamic factors include

- Providing an unexpected additional feature or service (e.g., complimentary champagne or a loaner vehicle)
- Responding to a special personal preference (going to extra lengths to cook a steak or mix a drink the way the customer likes it)
- Offering a culture-related courtesy (e.g., extra assistance with heavy parcels or home delivery)

Dynamic quality
factors are
difference makers.

**Static Quality
Factors**

1.2.4 Four Dimensions of Service Quality

Quality can relate to a tangible product *or* the delivery of a service, and the distinction can sometimes be arbitrary. Consider the difference between an auto dealership and an auto rental agency. Both exist to provide the transportation needs of their customers. The former would be considered a supplier of a product, whereas the latter would be regarded as a service provider. According to Rust, Zahorik, and Keiningham, a **physical product** is just one of four components involved in the provision of services. The other three are **service product**, **service environment**, and **service delivery**.[6] All supplier–customer relationships can be defined in terms of these four components and, depending on the nature of the business, some will be emphasized more than others.

Physical Product

Service Product

**Service
Environment**

Service Delivery

[6]Rust, Roland T., Anthony J. Zahorik, and Timothy L. Keiningham. *Return on Quality: Measuring the Financial Impact of Your Company's Quest for Quality.* Chicago: Probus, 1994.

TABLE 1-1 Components of Service: Some Industry Examples

Industry	Physical Product	Service Product	Service Environment	Service Delivery
Auto manu-facturing	Vehicle	Pricing	Showroom	Test drive and sales pitch
		Warranty	Workshop	Repair time and performance
		After-sale service		
Auto rental	Rental contract	Pricing policies	Check-in counter	Performance of check-in agent
		Insurance	Car lot	Cleanliness and maintenance of vehicle
		Transportation	Vehicle	Availability
Hotel	Room supplies	Pricing & quality	The room	Front desk and bellman performance
	Food and beverage service		Restaurant and bar	Chef, waitress, and bartender per-formance
		Shuttle	Pool and lobby	Promptness of room service
University	Diploma	Majors	Classrooms and library	Teaching quality
		Residence	Dormitories	Janitorial
		Placement	Sports fields	
Retail	Goods	Pricing	Sales floor	Knowledgeable
		Credit		Friendliness
		Inventory		Speed
Airline	Food and beverage service	Pricing	Airplane	Courtesy
	Ticket	Transportation	Airport facilities	Timeliness
		In-flight entertainment		Efficiency
		Baggage handling		Cleanliness of aircraft
				Safety
				In-flight service

SOURCE: Adapted from Roland T. Rust, Anthony J. Zahorik, and Timothy L. Keiningham. *Return on Quality: Measuring the Financial Impact of Your Company's Quest for Quality.* Probus, Chicago: 1994. Used by permission of authors.

A service orientation places customer needs ahead of organizational needs.

Table 1-1 provides examples of how the four dimensions of service quality apply to various industries, including the auto purchase versus auto rental example described previously. [7] In this context, a physical product is simply the medium used to facilitate the other services and a **service** rather than **product orientation** becomes the focus. Customers' needs take precedence over organizational needs. In contrast, when quality

[7]Ibid.

Service Orientation

Product Orientation

programs are product oriented, it is often the case that a higher priority is placed on process (and bottom-line) performance than on customer satisfaction. Trying to squeeze the last ounce of "performance" from its internal business processes, a company can lose touch with its customers and what they value.

How do customers make choices based on value judgments? Customers typically compare alternative service providers on the basis of value. Whether they are conscious of it or not, customers perform a gap analysis, awarding their business to the company that in their opinion provides the smallest gap between what they expect and what they perceive is the value received. This phenomenon is especially evident in service industries where a customer's satisfaction is often based on such intangible factors as assurance, empathy, reliability, and responsiveness.[8]

1.2.5 Big Q and Little q Quality: Various Perspectives

Little q Quality

Big Q Quality

Some have found it convenient to differentiate between **little q quality** and **big Q quality**[9, 10] to avoid confusion that can arise when an organization with an established quality control (QC) function tries to expand its program to incorporate the principles of QIM. Little q treats quality as an attribute of a product or process. Its scope is narrowly focused on specific tools, techniques, or QC procedures. Big Q is broad in scope and associated with an organization's overall quality culture. QIM is consistent with the big Q perspective. Table 1-2 illustrates seven different perspectives on quality.[11] The first five are little q definitions, and the last two fall in the big Q category.

1.2.6 The Value Stream and Its Customers

Value Stream

Internal Customer

External Customer

All the resources required to take production inputs (e.g., materials, capital, plant, human resources, energy) and transform them into a suitable mixture of products or services constitutes what is known as the **value stream**. A production system serves many customers, some internal and some external. The word "customer" can be used to describe anyone who benefits from goods or services anywhere along the value stream. An **internal customer** and its suppliers share the same production system, whereas an **external customer** and its suppliers are members of different systems. Internal customers are linked together through the design of the value stream, and the output of the value stream becomes an input to an external customer's system.

Quality is about *people.*

The value stream is a network of producer/customer subsystems linked together through technological, process, and material dependencies, and quality is repeatedly sourced across the subsystem boundaries. Reliable and rational measures are needed at each subsystem interface to gauge performance. These measures in turn can be

The value stream includes the steps necessary to produce a product or service.

---

[8]Parasuraman, A., Leonard L. Berry, and Valarie A Ziethaml. "Refinement and Reassessment of the SERVQUAL Scale." *Journal of Retailing* 27, no. 4 (1991): 420–50.

[9]Greene, Richard T. *Global Quality: A Synthesis of the World's Best Management Methods.* Homewood, IL: Business One Irwin, 1993; 771.

[10]Juran. *Juran on Leadership,* 47–49.

[11]Cameron, Kim S., and David A. Whetten. "Organizational Effectiveness and Quality: The Second Generation." In *Higher Education: Handbook of Theory and Research,* edited by J. R. Smart, 265–306. New York: Agathon, 1992.

TABLE 1-2 Various Definitions of Quality

Orientation	Source	Definition	Example
Transcendental	Persig, 1974	"Quality is neither mind nor matter, but a third entity independent of the two. . . . Even though Quality cannot be defined, you know what it is."	Excellence, beauty, appeal, preference
Product	Leffler, 1982	"Quality refers to the amounts of the unpriced attributes contained in each unit of the priced attribute."	Durability, extra unexpected features, provision of expected features
User	Juran, 1974	"Quality is fitness for use."	Satisfaction, performs required function, fulfills needs and expectations
	Edwards, 1968	"Quality consists of the capacity to satisfy wants."	
Production	Crosby, 1979	"Quality means conformance to requirements."	Reliability, conformance to specifications process
Value	Fiegenbaum, 1961	"Quality means best for certain conditions . . . (a) the actual use and (b) the selling price."	Performance consistent with price, value exceeds sacrifice, affordable excellence
System	Japanese Industrial Standard Z8101, 1981	"[Quality is] a system of means to economically produce goods or services which satisfy customers' requirements."	Operational definitions, Six Sigma processes, integrated approach
Cultural	Sashkin and Kiser, 1993	"Culture is what supports the driving aim of quality for the customer."	Management style, work practices, values, and attitudes

SOURCE: Adapted with permission from Cameron, Kim, and David Whetten. "Organizational Effectiveness and Quality: The Second Generation." In *Higher Education: Handbook of Theory and Research,* edited by J. R. Smart, 283, Table 3. Agathon, NY: Springer, 1996.

helpful in establishing realistic management priorities. The balanced scorecard approach, described in Chapter 4, is a tool that has been applied successfully to achieve these goals.

1.2.7 A Working Definition of Quality

Quality is a gap measure.

So far our discussion has been broad, examining the definition of quality from many different perspectives. Our attention now turns to an important operational issue. Is it possible to compose a working definition of quality that embodies the essence of all disparate viewpoints? The following working definition seems to satisfy that requirement.

Positive gaps reflect good quality, and negative gaps poor quality: the larger the gap the more favorable or unfavorable the measure. Good quality invokes positive (pleasurable) feelings and often the desire to repeat the experience. Poor quality, in contrast, engenders feelings of disappointment, sometimes anger, and the desire to find an alternative source in the future.

WORKING DEFINITION OF QUALITY

Quality is a gap measure that simultaneously considers two dimensions:

> **Expectations**
>
> *Gap 1:* The difference between a consumer's **expectations** and perception of *actual results*
>
> **Benefits**
>
> *Gap 2:* The difference between a consumer's perceived **benefits** and **sacrifices**
>
> **Sacrifices**

These comparisons form the basis for making personal judgments as to whether an experience is worth repeating.

1.3 QUALITY THROUGH THE AGES: HISTORY OF THE QUALITY MOVEMENT

1.3.1 Quality in Antiquity

In antiquity, quality was controlled through pride and close supervision.

The desire to produce something of value can be traced to ancient times. The pyramids of Egypt and the temples of Rome were extraordinary engineering feats. Each step of these mammoth construction projects had to be carefully planned and precisely followed, and the outputs had to be meticulously monitored. Quality took top priority, often ranking higher in importance than time, cost, or human safety.

Craft System

By the thirteenth century, the **craft system** had become standard manufacturing practice throughout western Europe. A master craftsperson was in charge of each craft guild, and a new recruit could enter the guild only after being indentured as an apprentice for a long period. A craftsperson could then only advance to the status of master by demonstrating a superior mastery of skills. The process was therefore held in the highest esteem, and quality was controlled mostly through pride in workmanship and close supervision as artisans combined dedication with talent while they worked their trades. Because items were produced one at a time (an early version of **job shop production**) quality was easy to monitor and control. No two items of output were identical, and there was no specialization of labor within the trade. Typically, the craftsperson would perform all tasks necessary to fashion a completed unit. This was the system of manufacture that existed throughout the Middle Ages.

Job Shop Production

1.3.2 Founders and Foundations

By the early twentieth century, techniques of mass production created the need for new analytical tools that could be used to predict process results by inspecting only a fraction of the outputs. In the 1930s, Walter A. Shewhart, a physicist at Bell Telephone Laboratories, pioneered the use of statistical methods in what later became formally known as QC.[12] In 1931, Shewhart published a book that introduced the world to control charts.[13] During this same era, two of Shewhart's colleagues at Bell Labs, Harold F. Dodge and his assistant, Harry Romig, developed statistical methods for acceptance sampling. The Dodge-Romig sampling inspection tables, published in 1940, were first applied to the inspection of rifle bullets during World War II. Much of the early work of these three pioneers still forms the basis for statistical QC methods in use today.

---

[12]Shewhart, Walter A. *Statistical Method from the Viewpoint of Quality Control.* Washington, DC: Graduate School, Department of Agriculture, 1939.

[13]Shewhart, Walter A. *Economic Control of Quality in Manufactured Product.* 1931 New York: Van Nostrand.

However, in the 1940s, the proven tools of quality were few, and the quality innovators of the day fought an uphill battle. Priorities were elsewhere. Juran is quoted as having said, "The top priority (during the war) was on meeting delivery schedules,[14] which too often were met at the expense of quality. Even after the war had ended, the emphasis was on securing market share, and this was often done at the expense of quality. Quality practitioners were desperately vying for management attention, but were doing so in vain.

In December 1949, Ralph **Wareham**, who pioneered QC at General Electric, wrote a feature article that proved to be a turning point that helped bolster QC as a profession.[15] For the first time an article was written in a language managers understood, published in a magazine highly respected by them, and illustrated the important contributions statistics could make to the overall success of business operations.

The American Society of Quality Control (ASQC), formed in 1942, was struggling for recognition. Each ASQC member was urged by the society to share the contents of Wareham's article with their respective managers. From that point quality control began to take off, gradually evolving into an independent discipline that principally existed to support mainstream production areas. QC departments were found mainly in manufacturing organizations and were staffed with highly skilled analysts, typically working in laboratory environments. These foundation blocks marked the beginning of QC in the modern era.

In the early 1950s, W. Edwards **Deming**, a physicist-turned-statistician and a protégé of Shewhart, was recruited to assist the Japanese with postwar reconstruction. Deming's approach was to focus attention on **management principles**, analyzing the production **system** first, and then using statistical tools to gain the necessary knowledge to improve performance. Deming insisted that problems were the fault of management and were not the workers' responsibility. Deming's celebrated **14 points**,[16] shown in Figure 1-1, later became a focal point for a number of TQM implementations.

Joe Juran, a contemporary of Deming and a mechanical engineer by trade, was also actively involved with the Japanese. Juran's approach stressed the need for hands-on management, better training, and CPI. Juran's structured approach called for management integration of three prongs of a trilogy: planning, control, and improvement.

Armand Feigenbaum, also a graduate engineer, pioneered the idea of **total quality management**. His book ***Total Quality Control***,[17] first published in 1951 under the title *Quality Control: Principles, Practice, and Administration,* has been printed in more than twenty languages, including Chinese, Japanese, French, and Spanish, and has become a global foundation reference for the practice of quality management.

By the 1950s, quality control was recognized as a profession.

Wareham

Deming introduced quality principles to management practice.

Deming

Management Principles

System

14 Points

Feigenbaum introduced the idea of total quality management.

Total Quality Management

Total Quality Control

---

[14]Juran, Joseph M. "A History of Managing for Quality in the United States—Part 1." *Quality Digest* 15, no. 11 (November 1995). Also available online at http://www.qualitydigest.com/nov95/html/histmang.html (Accessed March 25, 2005).

[15]Wareham, Ralph E. "Quality Control Is Among the Sharpest Management Tools Developed in a Half Century." *FORTUNE,* December 1949.

[16]Deming, W. Edwards. *Out of the Crisis.* Cambridge, MA: MIT Center for Advanced Engineering Study, 1982, 23–24.

[17]Feigenbaum, Armand V. *Total Quality Control.* 3rd ed., revised. New York: McGraw-Hill, 1991.

FIGURE 1-1 Deming's 14 Points

Point 1: *Create constancy of purpose*

Willingness to learn and change
Total commitment
Quality over quantity and bottom line
Long-range view

Point 2: *Adopt the new philosophy*

Cultural intolerance to errors
Decisions based on profound knowledge
No quick fixes to systemic problems
Any action not necessarily better than no action
Quality and total costs can be negatively correlated

Point 3: *Cease dependence on mass inspection*

Quality must be designed into products and processes
Quality must be built into products and services
System deficiencies must be identified and corrected
Inspection adds cost without value
Workers must become responsible for quality

Point 4: *End the practice of awarding business on the basis of price tag alone*

Vendors must be quality certified
Cheapest can be most costly
Reliability, durability, and variability are important

Point 5: *Continually improve systems*

Continual improvement = solving problems
Processes can only perform to capabilities of design
Only management can redesign systems

Point 6: *Institute modern methods of training*

Employees must clearly understand his or her job and be thoroughly trained to do it properly
Need for consistent methods
Need for formal and structured training program

Point 7: *Institute leadership*

Quality is built by leading, not driving
Good leadership understands importance of human factor
Need for knowledge of system capability vs. human impact
Need for clear and consistent messages

Point 8: *Drive out fear*

Fear is pervasive
Fear of supervisors, fear of failure, fear of change
Job insecurity, competition for raises, promotions
Performance ratings
Need for environment of trust and full disclosure
Good communication is key

Point 9: *Break down barriers among departments*

Cross-functional teamwork is a necessary ingredient to effective systems analysis
Rewards must support organizational rather than functional goals

Point 10: *Eliminate numerical goals, targets, and slogans*

Slogans and campaigns unfairly imply that the responsibility for quality is at the worker level
Quality cannot be "willed" or "mandated"
Setting unattainable goals can be counterproductive
If culture embraces quality principles, then slogans are irrelevant

Point 11: *Eliminate work standards and management by objectives (MBO)*

Management by the numbers does not consider quality implications
Production standards typically do not address causal systems or improvement issues
MBO programs are typically contests that feed internal competition between functional areas

Point 12: *Remove barriers that take away pride*

Management must treat people with respect: treat them as participants and not opponents
Three major inhibitors to quality: performance appraisal, daily production report, and financial management system
Management must recognize that most valuable assets are people, what they carry around in their heads, and their ability to work together

Point 13: *Institute a vigorous program of education and self-improvement*

An investment in people is good business sense
Exercising the mind is valuable and need not be job related
If intellectual input is sought on the job, then minds must be developed to their peak potentials

Point 14: *Put everyone to work on the transformation*

Requires an implementation strategy and careful planning
Cultural change and new paradigms cannot occur quickly
Everyone must be involved

SOURCE: Adapted with permission from W. Edwards Deming. *Out of the Crisis.* Cambridge, MA: MIT Center for Advanced Engineering Study, 1982, 23–24.

TABLE 1-3 Three Generations of Quality

Characteristics	Generation		
	First	*Second*	*Third*
Perspective on quality	Process	Holistic	Relational
Focus	Measurement	Assessment	Consensus
Type of action	Reactive	Proactive	Engagement
Criterion for success	Reliability	Efficiency and effectiveness	Accountability
Orientation	Production	Policy and planning	Relationships
Basic assumptions	Control	Manageability	Interconnectedness
Change	Improvement	Transformation	Transaction
Stakeholder relationships	Nonexistent	Peripheral and emerging	Embedded

SOURCE: Reprinted with permission from David Foster, and Jan Jonker. "Third Generation Quality Management: The Role of Stakeholders in Integrating Business in Society." *Managerial Auditing Journal* 18, no. 4 (2003): 327, Table II.

Crosby introduced the concepts of cost of quality and zero defects.

In 1979, Philip **Crosby** published a book entitled *Quality is Free: The Art of Making Quality Certain.*[18] The book was easy to read, using terminology that people could readily understand. Crosby is best known for the **cost of quality** concept—that is, knowing what it costs to do things poorly. Many of Crosby's ideas concerning zero defects actually foreshadowed the modern Six Sigma principles. Crosby believed that just coming close to requirements was not good enough and that **zero defects** is not something that originates on the assembly line. Crosby insisted that zero defects can only be achieved if management establishes the leadership and systems that enable the workers to succeed.

Crosby

Cost of Quality

Zero Defects

Ishikawa Diagram

Quality Circles

In the mid-1980s, Kaoru Ishikawa is credited with creating a version of TQM specifically for Japan.[19] Ishikawa believed in broad participation that permitted both bottom-up and top-down involvement, and he used quality circles as the vehicle to draw on the talents and expertise of frontline employees. Perhaps Ishikawa is best known for his cause-and-effect diagram (called the **Ishikawa diagram** or fishbone diagram), a powerful tool that **quality circles** of nonspecialists could use to effectively analyze and solve problems.

Kaizen

In 1986, Masaaki Imai introduced to the Western world the concepts, tools, and systems of a philosophy called **Kaizen**. Imai's best-selling book, *Kaizen: The Key to Japan's Competitive Success*[20] has been translated into seventeen languages. Loosely translated, Kaizen means "ongoing improvement involving everybody, without spending much money."

Ishikawa contributed the idea of using worker teams to help solve process problems.

1.3.3 Quality in the Modern Era: Three Generations

Including the work of the early pioneers, the quality movement has experienced three distinct stages (or generations) of development as depicted in Table 1-3.[21]

With Kaizen, Imai brought the idea of small incremental continuous improvements.

1.3.3.1 First Generation Pre-1980—Measurement and Control. First-generation quality was largely based on **measurements**, **controls**, and **detection**. The work involved periodically taking scientific measures from critical process stages and applying

Measurement

Controls

Detection

[18]Crosby, Philip B. *Quality Is Free: The Art of Making Quality Certain.* New York: McGraw-Hill, 1979.

[19]Ishikawa, Kaoru. *What Is Total Quality Control? The Japanese Way.* Upper Saddle River, NJ: Prentice Hall, 1985.

[20]Imai, Masaaki. *Kaizen: The Key to Japan's Competitive Success.* New York: McGraw-Hill/Irwin, 1986.

[21]Foster, David and Jan Jonkes. "Third Generation Quality Management: The Role of Stakeholders in Integrating Business into Society." *Managerial Auditing Journal* 18, no. 4 (2003), 323–28.

First-generation quality was based on measurements, controls, and detection.

Inspection

Incentives

Incentives

By the 1970s, there was a growing interest in prevention.

The Japanese introduced innovative work practices.

Quality Management

High-Performing Work Organizations

Productivity

statistical tools to predict process outputs. The primary focus of these early QC departments was to keep poor quality out of the hands of customers by sorting good quality from bad quality. The emphasis was on **inspection** of output rather than on process. Improvement was achieved mostly through remedial actions whenever the quality of outputs failed to meet minimum requirements. First-generation quality programs were internally focused and product oriented. The absence of a systems view generated little interest in cross-functional integration, networking with suppliers, or engaging the workforce.

Problem-solving efforts were limited to production lines or workstations with known problems, and the frontline workers were blamed when things did not go as planned. Management believed that improved quality could be achieved through **incentives** and controls. Formal efforts at controlling quality were mainly aimed at manufacturing enterprises, with little or no application to the service sector.

During the postwar expansion era, from the early 1950s to the 1960s, when markets were flush with products and demand was high, customers were not discriminating, and there was little incentive for manufacturers to provide tighter controls on quality.

By the 1970s, QA programs (in contrast to QC programs) began to divert attention from detection to prevention, but the interest was not widespread. By this time, some remarkable changes, largely transparent in the West, were occurring in Japan.

There is an adage that states "if you continue to do what you've always done, you will continue to get what you've always gotten." This could not have been truer than during the two decades following World War II. Like a Phoenix rising from the ashes, Japan was silently giving birth to a new empire, completely reinventing itself and rebuilding its manufacturing infrastructure. The Western world got its first glimpse of the transformation when a new breed of automobiles began arriving in foreign ports. Not only did customers notice the superior quality, but the Japanese vehicles were also more fuel efficient, a criterion of great importance during the energy crisis of the mid-1970s. Still, this did not arouse the interest of the chiefs of industry, who refused to believe that consumer loyalty would ever abandon the Western (predominantly American) automobile market.

It took a white paper entitled "If Japan Can, Why Can't We?" aired as a TV documentary by NBC in 1980, to focus widespread attention on the work of Deming and the imposing Japanese threat. This was the wake-up call to the Western industrialized world. In addition to pioneering new concepts of **quality management**, the Japanese introduced innovative work practices to the world and laid the groundwork for the **high-performing work organizations** (HPWOs) of today. Highly skilled Japanese workforces, loyal to their companies through guaranteed lifetime employment, used just-in-time production and knowledge-based QC systems to drive levels of **productivity** far beyond those attainable by Western counterparts. Meanwhile, changes were on the way that would irrevocably affect the business climate. The world was beginning to shrink. Spawned by jet air travel, computer technology, and satellite communications, domestic markets were rapidly becoming global markets. Led by corporate giants—companies such as General Motors, Ford, General Electric, Motorola, and Procter & Gamble—attention turned to the teachings of quality gurus such as Deming, Juran, and Crosby.

1.3.3.2 Second Generation   Post-1980—Reckoning and Reform, and the Emergence of Six Sigma. The second generation of the quality movement commenced around the

During the second generation, management accepts responsibility for poor quality.

mid-1980s when industry's senior leadership awakened to the realization that quality can be a major factor in gaining a competitive edge. This period marked a turning point in contemporary management practice.

Quality became a top management priority—a corporate force—and a minor industry was born. The 1980s saw the emergence of a growing army of consultants, academics, and a new breed of professionals who marched into battle armed with statistical tools, training aids, and implementation strategies. As companies committed significant resources to the cause, they had to face head-on the realities of past management practices and future threats. Quality ranked high on the list of corporate priorities. Standard business glossaries were expanded to include three-letter buzzwords, such as **statistical process control** (SPC) and TQM.

Statistical Process Control

Companies invested heavily in wholesale training until all employees were thoroughly indoctrinated in the teachings of the quality guru of choice. The attention turned from product orientation and quality of output to the overall management system responsible for producing the output. Under the mentorship of Deming and his contemporaries, industry leaders began to accept the idea that the root causes for poor quality were largely systemic. Because management owned the systems, the idea that inferior quality was management's responsibility and not the worker's fault became widely accepted.

Second-generation quality programs emphasize systems and empowerment.

With an expanded role, managers began to understand the holistic nature of their responsibilities and the need to reach out beyond organizational boundaries. Leadership teams were formed. The emphasis shifted from measurement to assessment, and from control to employee self-management. QC turned from detection to prevention and problem solving from reactive to proactive interventions. These concepts were often formally written into job descriptions and team charters.

Companies that subscribed to the new movement were often encouraged by the dramatic short-term results they observed. Continuous improvement became the cornerstone of cultural change. Companies soon learned that there were no quick fixes and that total commitment to quality meant to be in it for the long haul. Quality is a journey, not a destination.[22,23] The quest for improved quality, including the acquisition of process knowledge and learning how to effectively respond to it, became a process in itself.

Six Sigma was developed at Motorola as a disciplined approach for implementing TQM.

During this period, Bill Smith, an engineer working for Motorola, coined the term "Six Sigma" (a registered trademark of Motorola) to represent a statistical approach he developed for reducing defects. The idea behind Six Sigma is to achieve a process capability where production is near perfect. The name originates from the statistical idea that almost 100 percent of process output will be on spec if the nearest specification limit is a minimum of six standard deviations from the process average. For processes where this has been achieved, the number of defects are only significant when measured in parts per million—a condition that is nearly defect free.

Mikel Harry, a senior staff engineer at Motorola, and Richard Schroeder, an ex-Motorola executive, are responsible for transforming Smith's statistical measurement tools into a TQM spin-off philosophy—an integrated change management and data-driven culture that won Motorola the Malcolm Baldrige National Quality Award in 1988. The development of the Six Sigma movement had the benefit of support from such

---

[22]Cusins, "Understanding Quality," 19–27.

[23]Rhinehart, Emily. "Quality Management Is a Journey, Not Just a Destination." *Managed Healthcare* 10, no. 5 (2000): 52–55.

high-profile business leaders of the day as Bob Galvin, CEO of Motorola; Larry Bossidy, CEO of Allied Signal (now Honeywell); and Jack Welch, CEO of General Electric.

The appeal of Six Sigma is in its prescriptive approach to implementation and cultural change. The emphasis is on selecting high-leverage projects that offer clearly defined benefits to the bottom line—a concept that is sure to be a rallying point for top managers and shareholders. In completing these tasks, the program offers a clear delineation of responsibilities—top to bottom—as well as the articulation of training requirements, including a formal certification plan for credentialing all participants. Six Sigma is covered in detail in Chapter 9.

By the mid- to late 1990s, the competition was getting fiercer, management issues were more complex, and despite their best efforts in TQM, many corporations could not prevent downturns in performance.

During this second-generation period, the ASQC grew in stature and broadened its mission. It assumed the role of administering a number of major quality awards and of certifying the credentials of quality professionals. The organization's name was shortened in 1997 to the **American Society for Quality** (ASQ).

1.3.3.3 Third Generation Quality Maturity. By the late 1990s, some quality programs had reached a level that clearly set them apart from prior generations. Six Sigma increased in popularity as ASQC assumed the role of administering the tests leading to the various levels of Six Sigma certification. In the third generation, quality is not seen as a means to an end, but as a contributor to a strategic commitment to create sustained customer value. Third-generation quality represents an advanced stage of quality deployment and is discussed in more detail in Chapter 5.

1.3.4 The World Scene

While the United States and Europe were catching up, Japan was securing its leadership role on world markets, notably in automobiles, electronics, and steel. It was no longer accurate to specify a particular region of the globe (e.g., Western world) when making reference to the world's developed nations. The nations representing the most powerful and productive economies formed the **Organization for Economic Cooperation and Development** (OECD), sharing a common commitment to the principles of democratic government and the market economy. Further information on the OECD can be found at www.oecd.org.

Sidebar notes

The pursuit of quality is a journey, not a destination.

ASQ is responsible for certifying credentials and administering awards.

American Society for Quality

Third-generation quality recognizes the need for a strategic commitment.

Organization for Economic Cooperation and Development

OECD MEMBER NATIONS

Australia	France	Korea	Slovak Republic
Austria	Germany	Luxembourg	Spain
Belgium	Greece	Mexico	Sweden
Canada	Hungary	Netherlands	Switzerland
Czech Republic	Iceland	New Zealand	Turkey
Denmark	Ireland	Norway	United Kingdom
European Community	Italy	Poland	United States
Finland	Japan	Portugal	

The OECD plays a role similar to that of a referee, whose field of play is the global marketing arena. Representatives from the member nations meet to establish the rules that will govern international business and to develop international marketing standards. Globalization strategies have had positive spin-offs around the world, boosting standards of living that extend far beyond the boundaries of the OECD. Ironically, as the result of a closer net global community and a rise in world prosperity, there is a new threat on the horizon. Many of the OECD economies have found that they are now competing with forty-one developing economies in Asia and the Pacific Rim.[24] Four of these nations, known as the **newly industrialized economies** (NIEs), pose the greatest threat, and another nine have been designated **transition economies**.

Newly Industrialized Economies

Transition Economy

DEVELOPING ECONOMIES IN ASIA AND THE PACIFIC RIM

East Asia
- Peoples Republic of China
- Hong Kong, China[a]
- Republic of Korea[a]
- Mongolia[b]
- Taipei, China[a]

Southeast Asia
- Cambodia[b]
- Indonesia
- Lao People's Democratic Republic[b]
- Malaysia
- Myanmar
- Philippines
- Singapore[a]
- Thailand
- Viet Nam[b]

South Asia
- Afghanistan
- Bangladesh
- Bhutan
- India
- Maldives
- Nepal
- Pakistan
- Sri Lanka

Central Asia
- Azerbaijan[b]
- Kazakhstan[b]
- Kyrgyz Republic[b]
- Tajikistan[b]
- Turkmenistan[b]
- Uzbekistan[b]

The Pacific
- Cook Islands
- Fiji Islands
- Kiribati
- Republic of the Marshall Islands
- Federated States of Micronesia
- Nauru
- Papua New Guinea
- Samoa
- Solomon Islands
- Democratic Republic of Timor-Leste
- Tonga
- Tuvalu
- Vanuatu

[a] Newly industrialized economy (NIE).
[b] Transition economy.

---

[24] Asian Development Bank. *Asian Development Outlook 2003*. New York: Oxford University Press, 2003. Also available online at http://www.adb.org/Documents/Books/ADO/2003/ado2003.pdf (Accessed March 25, 2005).

ISO establishes and monitors international standards.

International Organization for Standardization

Lean Production

As early as the 1950s, interest had begun to focus on international standards and monitoring, and the **International Organization for Standardization** (ISO) was formed. ISO is a network of national standards institutes from member nations, and it has partnerships with international organizations, governments, industry, and consumer representatives. The current membership of ISO is 140 countries, and its primary mission is to form a bridge between public and private sectors. As the global economy expanded through the 1980s, ISO began administering a formal quality certification program called ISO 9000. Its standards were quick to become a benchmark, and indeed a prerequisite, for international trade. Then, in the 1990s, responding to world attention on the protection of the earth's natural resources, the ISO 14000 standards were implemented to establish standards regarding environmental issues.

During the 1980s, as interest in TQM intensified across America and Europe, companies turned to benchmarking to learn the secrets of the Japanese competitive advantage. This led to the discovery of **lean production**,[25–27] a philosophy that some have advocated as an alternative to TQM. At the same time, led by some U.S. companies such as IBM and Texas Instruments, a human resources model was developed that draws on organizational psychology to tie incentives and communications to human performance.

1.3.5 Human Relations

Reengineering

Rightsizing

Delayering

High-Performance Work Practices

With the twenty-first century approaching, faced with globalization issues and tougher competition, the opinion in many executive circles was that approaches such as **reengineering** and TQM were not enough. The spotlight more often than not came to rest on the most visible cost center—labor. Shedding labor, called downsizing and sometimes euphemistically referred to as **rightsizing**, became a popular boardroom activity. In some organizations, labor reductions were achieved through a process of **delayering**—that is, reducing the number of management levels. Delayering was actually reinforced by TQM and HPWO, both of which advocated pushing management responsibilities down to the front lines. With fewer personnel to do the work, multiskilling and work teams seemed a natural answer to improving efficiency. Thus, ironically, delayering actually promoted the cause of **high-performance work practices** (HPWPs).

As quality evolved, importance of the worker was emphasized.

Toward the end of the twentieth century, the interest in **quality of working life** (QWL)[28] and **employment involvement** (EI)[29, 30] gave further support to the importance of **high involvement organizations** (HIOs) and their successors HPWOs. Collectively, these programs symbolized a growing recognition of the importance of the worker and the tremendous potential of frontline employees—those with the best process knowledge—to bring about performance improvements.

[25]Ono, Taiichi. *Toyota Production System—Beyond Large-Scale Production.* Cambridge, MA: Productivity Press, 1988.

[26]Monden, Yusuhiro. *Toyota Production System—Practical Approach to Production Management.* Norcross, GA: Industrial Engineering and Management Press, 1983.

[27]Womack, James P., Daniel T. Jones, and Daniel Roos. *The Machine That Changed the World: The Story of Lean Production.* New York: Rawson Associates, 1990, 48–69.

[28]Ackoff, Russell L. *Democratic Corporation—A Radical Prescription for Recreating Corporate America and Rediscovering Success.* New York: Oxford University Press, 1994, 69–109.

[29]Sashkin, Marshall, and Kenneth J. Kiser. *Putting Total Quality Management to Work: What TQM Means, How to Use It, & How to Sustain It Over the Long Run.* Roseville, CA: Prima, 1993, 108–11.

[30]Hackman, J. Richard, and Greg R. Oldham. *Work Redesign.* Reading, MA: Addison-Wesley, 1980.

1.4 QUALITY AND MANAGEMENT SYSTEMS

Quality of Working Life

Employment Involvement

High Involvement Organizations

Quality is about large complex systems with many components that interact in complicated and unpredictable ways, and systems that involve people whose behavior is uncertain and inconsistent, and who collectively are called on daily to make unstructured decisions with incomplete information. Quality not only depends on how good these decisions are, but also on the ability to build consensus and create relationships built on trust and respect. Therefore, a study of quality requires a knowledge of systems. This forms the topic for Chapter 2.

SUMMARY OF LEARNING OBJECTIVES AND KEY OUTCOMES

1. *Recognize that quality is a powerful corporate force that influences nearly every major decision, from the boardroom to the cutting room.* Quality is fundamental to all major business decisions, including structures, policies, strategies, decisions, planning, and operations. Organizations exist because they have customers who depend on them for products or services. Customers will transact business with the organization that gives them the greatest perceived value, defined as the difference between benefits and sacrifices. For a company to sustain its position in the market, customer value must play a central role in all its major decisions and quality must be accepted as a core value.

2. *Define quality from numerous perspectives.* Quality can be defined from many perspectives: function in use, firmness, durability, and delight—all as perceived by customers. Quality is also an instantaneous value judgment made during a moment of truth, which may have more to do with the psychology of the experience than the substance of the service. Quality can be the absence of static factors or the presence of dynamic factors. Quality is personal and, in the end, is what customers say it is. Quality is a judgment call, made at the boundary of a system, and is based on perceived value and whether the perceived benefits meet or exceed customer expectations.

3. *Understand the difference between quality as a function and quality as a core value.* As a function, quality (designated "little q") is narrowly focused on specific tools, techniques, or quality control procedures. These tools are used to track and control quality attributes as they relate to individual processes along the value stream. As a core value, quality (designated "Big Q") is inculcated into an organization's culture and influences the management paradigm, which includes strategy, structure, problem solving and decision making, internal and external relationships, production philosophy and configuration, and personnel policies. QIM is a term that has been coined by this text to represent the embodiment of an integrated management paradigm with a committed culture and a strong knowledge-driven leadership.

4. *Develop your own working definition of quality.* It is important that each organization develop a working definition of quality. The definition should be communicable and understood the same way by everyone. This chapter provides an example of what a working definition might look like. The definition provided here treats quality as a two-dimensional gap assessment. The first gap is the perceived difference between what the customer receives and what the customer expected. The second gap is a measure

of perceived value (i.e., the difference between the benefits received and what the customer had to sacrifice to get them).

5. *Demonstrate an understanding of the history of quality, and describe the three generations in the evolution of the quality movement.* The concept of quality has been around since the time one person relied on another to provide a needed product or service. In antiquity, quality was controlled through pride and close supervision in craft guilds. Masters would provide apprentices with personalized on-the-job training over a period of many years. Production was slow, and skills were not specialized.

The twentieth century introduced mass production techniques, standardization, specialization of labor, and tools for predicting process output. By mid-century, statistical tools were being applied to acceptance sampling and process control. The evolution of the quality movement has consisted of three identifiable generations. The first generation, which lasted until about 1980, was a "little q" era concerned primarily with measurements, controls, and detection. The second generation, starting around 1980 and lasting two decades, marked an era when attention turned from detection to prevention.

The Big Q mind-set began to replace little q as quality became an important component in the paradigm of corporate governance. TQM became a rallying philosophy as companies by the multitudes tried to get on board. In time, the interest in TQM waned as companies turned to what they perceived as alternative strategies with greater appeal. Programs such as lean production, business process reengineering, high-performing work organizations, and Six Sigma entered the landscape.

Around the turn of the twentieth century, a third generation of quality emerged that placed more emphasis on structure, accountability, and management participation. Six Sigma has achieved widespread popularity because it has satisfactorily addressed many of the shortcomings of failed TQM programs. In the third generation, the focus is on continual improvement, resource leverage, management commitment from the top, and creating a culture that will sustain customer value.

6. *Identify the pioneers of the quality movement, and describe their respective contributions.* The earliest pioneers were Shewhart, Dodge, and Romig, who established the statistical foundations for the tools that are used today to control and improve quality. Deming and Juran had the opportunity to develop new tools and refine their application when they were called on to help Japan with its postwar reconstruction. Both saw the need for strong management leadership if the tools were to be effective. Feigenbaum was among the first to integrate the technical and management sides in a way that clarified management's responsibilities. His TQC was the forerunner to a philosophy that came to be known as TQM.

In advocating a participatory implementation strategy, Ishikawa introduced TQM to Japan. Building on Ishikawa's quality circles concept, quality improvement teams are now the norm. Ishikawa is best known for the fishbone diagram, a powerful tool that can be used by nonspecialists to analyze and solve process problems. Crosby was among the first to point out that quality is not defined by simply being close to a target and that there is a cost associated with missing a target, even if by a small amount. Crosby's goal of zero defects is consistent with the modern-day Six Sigma aspirations. Bill Smith is considered to be the father of the Six Sigma foundations, and Harry and Schroeder transformed the basics into an integrated management philosophy.

1-1   Place yourself in the top leadership position of a small manufacturing firm that produces a range of consumer goods. Describe the process that you would use to define quality for your business. How would your process differ if you were the manager of a large metropolitan hotel?

1-2   What are the characteristics of a QIM? Explain, in your own words, what it means for quality to be a corporate force?

1-3   How did contributions from the various quality eras throughout history shape the role of modern managers in the delivery of quality products and services?

JetBlue Airways
*Part I—The AntiAirline Airline**

When David Neeleman started JetBlue Airways in February 2000, his vision was to fill a niche market not satisfied by the major air carriers. He believed customers had become too accustomed to rude personnel and lackadaisical service, and was determined " to bring humanity back to air travel and make flying more enjoyable." With $130 million from financial backers, Neeleman purchased a small fleet of Airbus A320s that were fitted with such unconventional features as leather seats and seat-back satellite TV screens with DIRECTV programming. Based at New York's JFK International Airport, JetBlue offers one-class service to twenty-nine cities in the United States, Puerto Rico, the Dominican Republic, and the Bahamas.

Neeleman's formula for success has been due to the consistent application of four fundamental principles (1) the willingness to invest whatever capital is necessary to achieve quality goals; (2) maintaining a fleet of new airplanes; (3) hiring the best people, training them well, and giving them the tools they need to provide high-quality service; and (4) creating a culture that is customer focused.

JetBlue's marketing plan was designed to lure customers with service that was affordable and personalized, and that did not appear to compromise on comfort. The strategy worked. The company was soon turning a profit and beating industry performance standards. At 80%, its load factor was the highest of any U.S. airline, and its on-time performance was 7% higher than the industry average. During 2001, the company earned a profit of $38.5 million, while the industry as a whole logged billions of dollars in losses.

How did JetBlue do it? Part of the answer is effective cost management. The airline does not serve meals, and customers are enticed to book tickets online. By offering a $5 each-way discount on its fares sold on jetblue.com, the airline motivated customers to use the Web site over its toll-free number. Today, the airline sells 75 percent of its seats via jetblue.com, the cheapest and most efficient distribution mechanism. The choice of the Airbus A320 was also integral to JetBlue's overall strategy. The new aircraft, noted for superior fuel efficiency, gave the company instant credibility, while helping keep costs down and fares low. ∎

---

*Printed with the permission of JetBlue Airways.

QUESTIONS FOR THOUGHT

1. How can quality be defined for JetBlue Airways

    a. from the perspective of its passengers?

    b. from the perspective of its employees?

    c. from the perspective of its suppliers?

    d. from the perspective of its financial backers?

e. from the perspective of society?

f. from the perspective of Neeleman and senior management?

2. Suggest some static and dynamic factors that would affect JetBlue passengers' perceptions of quality. How could the Principle of Neutral Awareness be used by JetBlue to improve the airline's competitive position?

3. The minicase says that effective cost management was part of the reason for JetBlue's success? Given Neeleman's determination "to bring humanity back to air travel and make flying more enjoyable," what factors do you think have likely contributed to the success of this company?

CHAPTER 2

The Pursuit of Quality through Systems Thinking: A Business Imperative

Quality in a product or service is not what the supplier puts in. It is what the customer gets out and is willing to pay for.

—PETER F. DRUCKER

MicroMediform, Inc.

A Lasting Impression

MicroMediform, Incorporated, founded as a small family business in the early 1970s, specializes in placing patient records on microfilm and microfiche for hospitals, private medical practices, and health insurance carriers. Over several decades, the company grew and prospered and earned the reputation for being the best in the business at converting printed documents to microform media. During the 1980s, MicroMediform experienced annual growth at an average rate of 20% and typically produced double-digit returns for its investors.

In 1995, the tide started to turn, and for the first time in its history, the company's annual re-port showed a financial performance worse than the previous year. MicroMediform's board of directors were bewildered. The decision was made to invest more heavily in advertising and promotion, including a thirty-second commercial during the SuperBowl and increasing the sales force by 10%. These efforts appeared to help and revenues increased the following year. Nevertheless, by 1997, a decline in sales returned, starting an unrecoverable downward spiral that continued—with each quarter worse than the previous one—despite evasive actions taken by management to turn things around.

By March 2001, the future of the company looked bleak. This paragon of American enterprise found it necessary to file for Chapter 11 bankruptcy protection. After thirty years of success, MicroMediform faced $1 billion in debt and plummeting profits. Its shares of stock that had once traded on the New York Stock Exchange as high as $80 were suddenly worth 80 cents.

MicroMediform's story is not unique. Companies that have been the pillars of economic stability and seemingly stood the test of time can, without much warning, waver and crumble. How does this happen? What can go so wrong and cause a strong company to fail? In MicroMediform's case, the root cause can be attributed to poor forward planning and management's inability to see beyond the core business of microform. Success can create complacency and can become a form of self-reinforcing feedback that supports business as usual. As a result, the leadership does not recognize the need to look beyond itself and create vision. In cybernetics, this is called a viscous circle and can lead to behaviors that are self-validating and invariant. This was enough to keep MicroMediform prosperous for a long time. Nevertheless, as times changed, management failed to anticipate new digital technologies that were eroding its markets. While the company continued to promote capabilities in microfilm and microfiche, the market was migrating to images on compact discs with fully functional search engines. From a customer's perspective, the new technologies offer the following advantages:

- Imaging eliminates the need for outdated microfilm and microfiche readers.
- The time required to retrieve images is dramatically reduced.

- Space required for storage is greatly reduced: up to 15,000 images can be placed on a single CD.
- No special equipment is needed to read images—any PC with a CD-ROM drive and Windows operating system can be used.
- Instant access can be provided at the desktop to millions of images.
- Images can easily be printed, faxed, or e-mailed.
- Multiple users can access images at the same time over a network.
- Images can be viewed using a Web browser.
- Images can be easily converted to PDF file format for complete document portability.

Bankruptcy protection allows a firm to continue to operate while it tries to sort out its problems. During this period, MicroMediform's senior leadership, convinced that they still had the magic, continued to pin their hopes on the strengths of the past. Refusing to properly acknowledge a migrating market, they aggressively concentrated marketing efforts on expanding their customer base, and implemented lean Six Sigma to eliminate waste and improve their quality of service. However, efficiencies and good marketing could not prevent the inevitable. MicroMediform found it necessary to downsize and eliminate 2,000 jobs. The company was eventually sold, a deal that was devastating to stockholders and that cost retirees $150 million in lost stock and pensions. Under new ownership, the company survived and refocused. By 2005, the future of the company looked bright. Sadly, the toil on its stakeholders, who placed their faith in its leadership, is a legacy that will linger for many years to come. ■

2.1 LEARNING OBJECTIVES AND KEY OUTCOMES

After studying the material in Chapter 2, you will be able to

1. Describe the machine theory principle of management, and explain the shortcomings of machine theory as the basis for managing contemporary organizations
2. Describe the open systems theory view and how it supports the concepts of QIM
3. Differentiate between outputs and outcomes, and describe what makes an output or outcome undesirable
4. Define the major subcomponents of the value stream
5. Describe how relationship marketing influences system outcomes

6. Distinguish between positive and negative feedback

7. Discuss the differences between deviation-amplifying and deviation-correcting forms of feedback

8. Describe the significance of the funnel experiment to QIM

2.2 OPEN SYSTEMS THINKING AND THE EVOLUTION OF ORGANIZATIONAL DESIGN THEORY

2.2.1 Systems Theory—The First Step in the Quality Journey

MicroMediform is a solid company. In business for thirty years, it was unimaginable that the good times would not last. How could such a good company come so close to failure?

Sadly, MicroMediform is not an isolated case. Countless business failures can be attributed to a lack of a basic understanding of systems theory and the application of systems principles to organizational design and management. A systems view can help a company avoid the pitfalls and navigate around the minefields. Quality is about the performance of systems, and an understanding of systems theory is a necessary building block for learning to design effective quality programs.[1]

The word **system** is encountered frequently in many contexts, varying in scope and purpose. We know about the solar system, freeway systems, sound systems, sewage systems, education systems, the judicial system, and production systems, to name a few. What do these systems have in common? They all have component parts, but the collection of parts alone does not make a system. To become a system, the parts must be designed to work together in a manner that performs some intended **function**. The intricate and sometimes mysterious interactions that occur between its components are a system's defining features.

To illustrate system complexity, Deming has related in his seminars the story of a furniture manufacturer who decided to diversify by expanding into the high-end piano market. To better understand the proposed new line, a decision was made to purchase and reverse engineer a mature, time-tested brand currently on the market. The company acquired a Steinway and with great care dismantled the instrument. Each part was meticulously copied and its location carefully documented. Assembling the reproduced parts produced a prototype.

The copy was superb—it looked just like the original. There was only one downside. The engineers and craftsmen had succeeded in creating a fine-looking instrument, one that looked like a Steinway in every way, but when played it could not make music. A second prototype was then constructed with similar results. A third prototype proved no better. In desperation, the company decided to abandon the project, believing it could at least recover its original investment. However, after reassembly, despite using its original parts, the Steinway now functioned no better than the prototypes. The piano had lost its ability to make music.

To function as a musical instrument, a Steinway is a complex system, requiring all its parts to work together in synergy. If the system works as intended, it will produce

> For a system to function as intended, all parts must work together in harmony.

System

Function

> Understanding systems theory is essential to understanding quality.

---

[1]Harrington, H. James, Joseph J. Carr, and Robert P. Reid. "What's This 'Systems' Stuff, Anyhow?" *The TQM Magazine* 11, no. 1 (1999): 54–57.

Systems analysis
breaks a complex
system into small
pieces.

tone, pitch, and voice, as well as other quality attributes that attract discriminating musicians to the Steinway brand. Without a thorough understanding of the system, any **performance measures** and **improvement efforts** are meaningless. **Systems Knowledge** is required. It is essential for the system's purpose, function, design, operation, and value to be clearly understood.

Simple concepts can sometimes require complex systems. Complexity results from the intricate interrelationships that exist between a system's components and can affect the ability to predict and control system outputs. **Complexity** has been defined as a state where a delicate balance exists between **stability** and **chaos**.[2] Small influences can push the system in one direction or the other. A chaotic system is the antithesis of stability. Behavior is unpredictable, and consequences are unintended. Nevertheless, an interesting phenomenon is that even when a system erupts into chaos, it will tend to seek a new point of equilibrium so a new redefined and stable system can emerge. Researchers have referred to this observation as "order out of chaos." With no outside intervention, the new stable system can differ significantly from the purpose and goals of the original system.

In general, managers are not well equipped to deal with complexity. A popular approach to problem solving has been to use a form of **systems analysis** in which the system is broken down into its component parts and then each part is studied independently. The rationale is that it is much easier to analyze a small piece in detail rather than the behavior of the entire system. This approach is not new and has been effective in analyzing certain types of business systems. In particular, there was a time when business systems were less complex than they are today, and could be decomposed, studied, and improved in much the same way that industrial machines could be disassembled, diagnosed, and repaired. This historical period was called the "Machine Age."

2.2.2 The Machine Age and Machine Theory

Prior to the Industrial Revolution (circa 1790), the only organizations of any considerable size were the government, the military, and the church. Consequently, there was little interest in organized production methods. By the twentieth century, machines had made it possible to mass produce, and new workplace theories emerged. By dividing work into simple specialized tasks, low-skilled workers could be used to economically produce goods using **assembly line manufacturing**. These workers had to be closely supervised, and they were not held accountable for the quality of their work. Multilayered organizations became necessary to oversee work practices, and the modern concept of an organizational structure evolved. This was the beginning of the **Machine Age** and **machine theory**, a term that refers to the way organizations were designed, analyzed, and managed during this era.

Under machine theory, an organization, like a machine, was considered to be a collection of parts, and it was believed that the key to efficiencies was through standardization and tight central controls. Manufacturing systems were designed with an emphasis on specialized equipment and labor, and economies of scale. Industrialists such as Henry Ford perfected the model, and it became possible to produce high volumes at low cost. For the first time, products that had only been affordable by the upper class were now within reach of the masses. A new wave of consumerism was born.

---

[2]Ibid.

In the early twentieth century, the work of Frederick W. Taylor and the Gilbreths (Frank and Lillian) helped popularize machine theory. Out of this era came *scientific management* in which a cogent body of knowledge applied scientific principles to the study and improvement of human–machine work systems. Machine theory gained momentum as proponents of scientific management (later called industrial engineers or operations researchers) were able to achieve impressive production efficiencies. Large numbers of low-skilled people, trained in standard methods, were moved into the workplace. Their bosses were provided with tools for making better decisions and optimizing the use of limited resources. For more than fifty years, this analytical clockwork machine model worked well. Markets were stable, and individual fortunes could be made. Then, in the early 1960s, the world began to change.

Clearly defined and stable markets gave way to complexity, dynamics, and uncertainty. Although many of the ideas of the early proponents of scientific management still had relevance, the machine theory view could not adequately address many of the important issues that confronted organizations trying to compete in what had become a global technocracy.

Under machine theory, an organization is treated as a closed system, meaning it cannot adapt to a changing environment. Specifically, attributes that could limit the capability to readily respond to new conditions include standardization, specialization, lack of human uniqueness, centralized decision making, uniformity, and lack of feedback.

2.2.2.1 Standardization   *Standardization* can be a positive feature if it fosters more consistent results. However, it can also muzzle the power of the human (individual) component of the value stream. The various components of the value stream are discussed in the next section. Too much standardization can be dehumanizing, and counterproductive if work is **repetitious** and **boring**. It is important to note that there is a difference between a disciplined workplace and a standardized workplace. Discipline is an important principle for maintaining order and consistency in the way that work gets done. Where the quality of work and improvement depends on people, work practices need to be devised that can release creativity and capitalize on individual differences. A fundamental premise of machine theory was that the machine was the center of the workplace and all activity revolved around it. It was the supervisors, not the workers, who were responsible for production performance.

Repetitious

Boring

2.2.2.2 Specialization   Specialization starts at an early age. A football coach recognizes the potential in a young recruit and grooms him to take over as starting quarterback. A drama teacher casts the parts in a school play, giving the leading roles to talented and budding artists. When young people leave high school, they base career decisions on how they want to specialize. If they go to college, they are required to select a major. When they enter the workforce, they will be employed on the basis of their specializations.

Specialized skills are essential. Nevertheless, in QIM cultures, the emphasis is on unity of purpose and cross-functional teamwork. Loyalty to the organization must rank ahead of loyalty to a profession or department. Placing too much emphasis on specialization, as was the trend with machine theory organizations, can create the opposite effect—loyalties to disciplines over corporate goals.

Segregation

Isolationism

Vertical structures, such as the one depicted in Figure 2-1, can reinforce workforce **segregation** and create functional **isolationism**. Within the function, such structures do

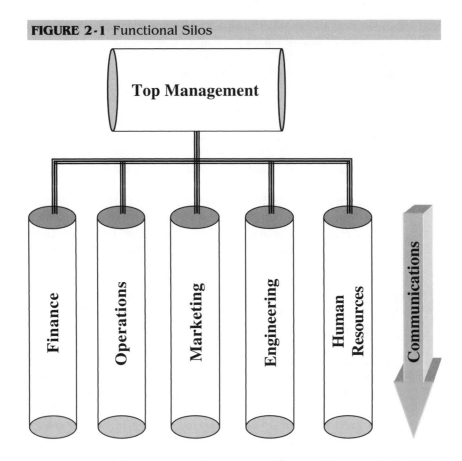

FIGURE 2-1 Functional Silos

have some appeal. Communications are rapid and easily controlled within the function. Personnel issues such as training, assignment of work, and rewards are also facilitated. However, on the downside, the boundaries between **functional silos** can become impenetrable barriers to communications, coordination, or cooperation. When improvement projects are conducted, they often produce **suboptimal results**. Interactions among functions are not considered because there is a conflict between the organizational view of work and the way work is actually performed. Such structures are not generally supportive of modern management practices, such as Six Sigma, that encourage teams with diverse memberships to put their combined talents to work on multifunctional value streams.

2.2.2.3 Human Uniqueness   The scientific approach has been based on the premise that, in any endeavor, there is one best way. This is still a sound principle, and QIM companies conduct extensive benchmarking to learn best practices. However, at the workplace level, too much emphasis on a standard method fails to take into account the uniqueness of individuals and the power of **human creativity**. The inventiveness of the human mind can often lead to innovations in work practices. What may work best for one person might not be the best for another.

2.2.2.4 Centralized Decision Making   In machine theory organizations, management made important decisions without consulting those further down the chain of command.

Functional Silos

Suboptimal Results

A functional-oriented organization can breed suboptimization.

Decision making should involve those with the most knowledge.

Human Creativity

Decision Maker

Knowledge

Under this centralized approach the **decision maker** is normally a person who does not have the most **knowledge** about a problem. QIM organizations have adopted knowledge-based decision making, delegating the decision to the level where there is the most knowledge and to those who have the greatest vested interest in the results.

Uniformity

Standard Operating Procedures

2.2.2.5 Uniformity   The **uniformity** principle is also inconsistent with modern organization design. Under machine theory, standard methods were documented using written **standard operating procedures** (SOPs). These SOPs covered almost everything and, ironically, constrained management's freedom to act. Managing by the book often became more important than serving customers.

2.2.2.6 Feedback   Perhaps the biggest limitation of machine theory is its lack of feedback mechanisms. If a system is to survive, it must continuously receive input from its environment and adapt to changing requirements. Just as humans draw nourishment and stimulation from their environments, an organization is an open system that also needs external inputs if it is to grow and prosper. Under machine theory, organizations were managed as closed systems.

To survive, systems need to be receptive to new ideas for improvement.

The second law of thermodynamics uses the concept of entropy to describe the self-destructive nature of closed systems. **Entropy** is energy that cannot be turned into a useful purpose—that is, entropy represents energy that is lost during a system's normal operating routine. The second law states that all systems will naturally move toward a state of increasing entropy, eventually causing a random rearrangement of system elements, a dissolution of structure, and a state of **chaos**. Because a closed system has no mechanism to **reenergize** itself from external stimuli, it will seek chaos and self-destruct.[3,4] An organized system will become less organized, and systems are incapable of organizing themselves (closed systems are irreversible). Even a highly effective system, without **continuous improvement**, will seek ineffectiveness. Because closed systems are doomed to failure, sustainability depends on an **open systems** approach, where the trend toward increasing entropy can be reversed.

Entropy

Chaos

Reenergize

Continuous Improvement

Open Systems

2.2.3 Quality from an Open Systems Perspective

2.2.3.1 The Information Age and Open Systems   During the last three decades of the twentieth century, computing and data processing eclipsed technological advances in mechanical processes, and the Machine Age yielded to an age of information. The proponents of machine theory could not in their wildest imaginations have conceptualized a world with personal computers, cellular telephones, satellite communications, and the Internet.

An open system can correct, rebuild, and redirect. Open systems can improve.

In parallel with these leaps in technology, open systems theory has emerged as an alternative model for explaining modern organizations.[5] The main distinction between open and closed systems is that open systems are capable of drawing new energy from

---

[3]Feynman, Richard P., Robert B Leighton, and Matthew Sands. *The Feynman Lectures on Physics*. Vol. 1. Reading, MA: Addison-Wesley, 1963, 44.10–44.13.

[4]Feynman uses examples from physical science to illustrate how, without the infusion of new energy, a system will eventually and irreversibly reach some new level of equilibrium. A measure of the energy expended in this transformation process is called entropy. In the case of organization systems, the idea of a virtual buildup of entropy can occur if there is no mechanism for reenergizing the system with feedback from the environment and the infusion of fresh ideas.

[5]Bertalanffy, Ludwig von. *General Systems Theory: Foundations, Development, Applications*. New York; George Braziller, 1968, 39–40.

FIGURE 2-2 The Business Organization as an Open System

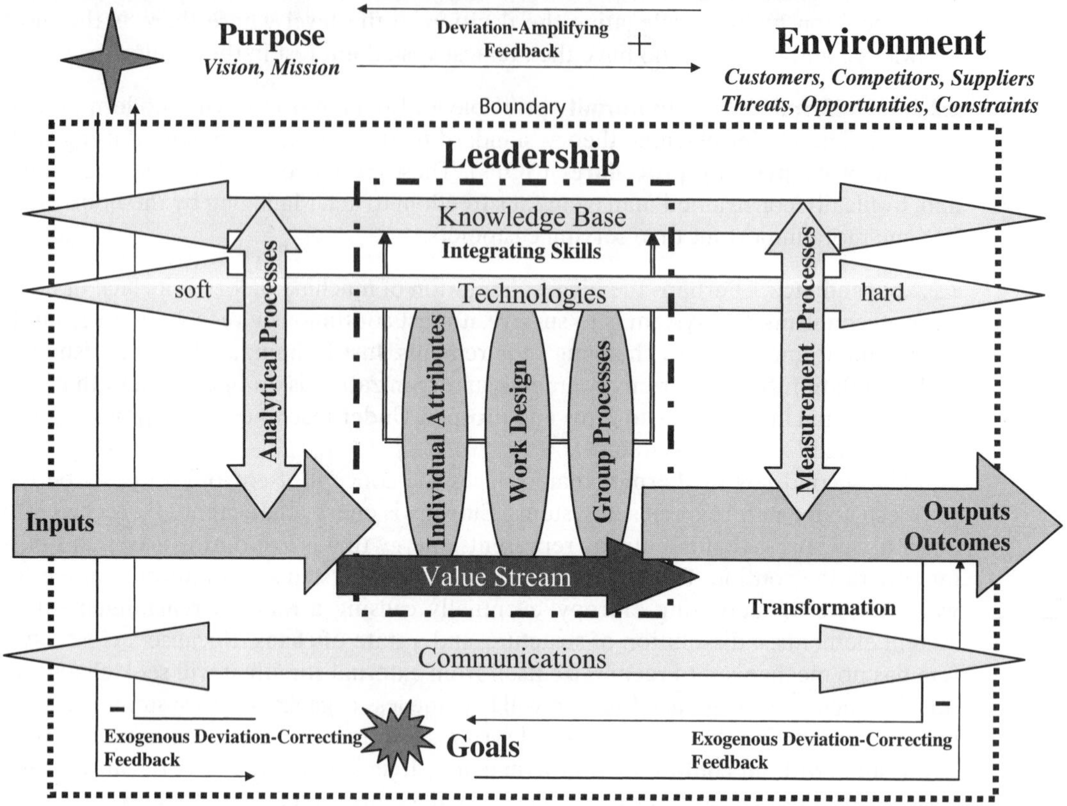

Negentropy

The open systems view recognizes the need for an organization to commune with its environment.

sources outside itself (i.e., its environment). Unlike closed systems, an open system can actually create negative entropy (called **negentropy**) by importing talents, ideas, and knowledge that exceeds what it already has. This ability to reenergize is the key to sustainability because the organization can use new sources of energy to correct, rebuild, and redirect. The open systems view gives special emphasis to the importance of communal relationships similar to those observed in biological systems, where systems dynamically engage on a personal level with coinhabitants of a shared environment.

Industrial systems such as biosystems depend on feedback for growth and for a sense of self-worth. In addition, organizations demonstrate the characteristics of wholeness, growth, differentiation, hierarchical order, dominance, control, and competition.[6] Just as nature will seek to place two conflicting forces in a state of equilibrium, forces within business systems will also seek a harmonious balance over time. Given time and the proper nourishment, open systems can grow. Growth can be reflected in several ways: through physical enlargement, through increased staffing, or through an expanded knowledge base.

Figure 2-2 illustrates the complexity and scope of the open systems model. Understanding its many components and relationships can provide the basis for designing and managing modern systems in a manner that will enhance the achievement of quality goals.

---

[6]Ibid, 46–47.

System Boundaries

2.2.3.2 System Boundaries   **System boundaries** separate what belongs to an organization from those things that are external. A boundary in an industrial system behaves much like a biosystem membrane, facilitating a two-way process of osmosis between the organization and its environment. It is essential for the boundary to be permeable so the system can interact across it. However, boundary interfaces should be carefully managed. Too little interaction can starve, and too much can bury the organization. In a data-rich world, there is always a dilemma between the perils of making decisions with incomplete or inaccurate information and paralysis by analysis.

2.2.3.3 Purpose   Every organization exists for a reason. Customers depend on it to measure up to their expectations. If the organization did not exist, its customers would have to do without, deal with a competitor, or become self-reliant. In committing to a **purpose,** an organization assumes an obligation—in effect saying to its customers: "You can trust us. We won't let you down." This constitutes a morally, if not legally, binding contract between the organization and its constituencies. Purpose is a defining element. Why a company exists, to whom it targets its services, where it is heading, and its core beliefs are all part of the purpose. These are normally stated in the firm's vision and mission statements.

Purpose

The purpose is a contract between the organization and its customers.

2.2.3.4 System Goals   Think of the purpose as the organization's intended destination. Its goals are the road maps for getting there. Internal goals steer the organization to improved levels of performance to help it achieve its purpose. At the highest levels, goals are usually expressed in aggregate terms and support the key performance indicators for the business. At each lower level of the structure, supporting subgoals are more specific, and the degree of specificity increases as the lower levels of the structure are reached. It is important that all subgoals are mutually supportive and consistent with the overall mission. A quality organization is one that has been able to inculcate, top to bottom, a sense of unity and commonality of purpose throughout its culture.

2.2.3.5 System Inputs   Organizations depend on many types of inflows from the environment, including personnel, information, energy, capital, and materials. Some inputs take the form of constraints that govern business conduct, such as legal, political, ethical, and bureaucratic controls.

In biosystems, there is much truth in the adage "you are what you eat." The industrial parallel is that quality of output begins with purity of input. Sources of supply are very important, and management attention should be directed to vendor's **critical to quality (CTQ)** characteristics. These are attributes that are key to the quality of internal process performances and value stream outputs. This can be a daunting task if the supplier network changes frequently. If left to random forces and not cultivated, suppliers will affiliate with whomever offers them the best deal. Suppliers play an essential role along the supply chain of the extended enterprise, and long-term trust relationships are essential. We discuss in detail how suppliers can be selected and certified in Chapter 10.

Critical to Quality (CTQ)

One form of input that is dynamic and unpredictable is the human element. By nature, individuals have divided loyalties, and will join or leave organizations based on personal priorities and the deals they are able to make.

2.2.3.6 The Value Stream   Michael Porter was the first to describe a sequence of interrelated process activities as a value chain (referred to here as the value stream).[7] The

---

[7]Porter, Michael E. *Competitive Advantage.* New York: The Free Press, 1985, 11–15.

value stream can also be thought of as a *transformation process,* and includes the tasks, skills, and knowledge required to convert a system's inputs into desirable outputs. When the value stream is expanded to include external supplier systems upstream and the customer's supply and distribution points downstream, the resulting network is called the **supply chain**. The **extended enterprise** is a collective term used to describe all organizational systems along the supply chain and their interdependencies. There are three critical subcomponents that work together to create the value stream:[8]

Supply Chain

Extended Enterprise

1. *Individual attributes* are the mix of skills and human traits that contribute to making each member of the workforce unique. Individual attributes include education, experience, attitudes, physical capabilities, preferences, wit, and intelligence.

2. The *group process* represents the human ability to work together—a propensity to cooperate, coordinate, and delegate. Teaming, social, and communications skills are important to the group process, even if formal team structures are not used.

3. *Work design* includes the task elements. These elements collectively define the work and prescribe the sequence that must be followed to create a product or service. When work design and group processes intersect, the value stream depends on teaming or interpersonal relations to get the work accomplished.

Five additional important system subcomponents impact the value stream.

1. *Technologies.* All transformations, no matter how primitive, use technologies to get things done. The word "technology" is defined in a broad sense, ranging from an abstract soft side (paradigms, procedures, and computer software) to a more complex and rigorous hard side (innovation, experimentation, and computer hardware). Incremental continuous improvements and quantum breakthroughs (a key to competitive superiority) can impact the soft side, the hard side, or both. Organizational effectiveness depends on integrating existing technologies and being able to identify, justify, and introduce new technologies as necessary.

2. *Knowledge.* The value stream is the defining framework for the **knowledge base** that has relevance to the value stream's processes. A knowledge base is the organization's collective wisdom concerning how processes behave and why they behave the way they do, including the complex interrelationships that exist between the technologies and work design. A **learning organization** is likely to be mature in its approach to quality as it continuously enriches its knowledge bases, and where decision making is based on fact. Senges has defined five disciplines that characterize the cultures of learning organizations: **systems thinking**, **team learning**, a **shared vision**, **mental models**, and **personal mastery**.[9] A QIM approach requires senior management to have **profound knowledge** of what it is doing and why. Decision makers must be sincere in seeking the truth and then be willing to act accordingly.

3. *Measurement.* An important lesson is that one usually gets what one measures. It is human nature to pay attention to those things that are measured and then ignore the rest. An important corollary to this rule is that one can measure what they expect to get. If one approaches a measurement with predisposed ideas of what the results should be, then the predisposition can influence the actual recorded

A learning organization has a knowledge base that is growing.

Knowledge Base

Learning Organization

Systems Thinking

Team Learning

Shared Vision

Mental Models

Personal Mastery

Profound Knowledge

[8]Hanna, David P. *Designing Organizations for High Performance.* Reading, MA: Addison-Wesley, 1988, 12–14.
[9]Senge, Peter M. *The Fifth Discipline: The Art and Practice of the Learning Organization.* London: Century Business, 1990, 5–11.

Measurement Process

Measurement Error

What is measured defines what is important.

numbers and bias the analysis. Every measured attribute in production has a shadow process—the tool and procedure used to obtain the measurements. This shadow or **measurement process** is only a simulation of the truth. How closely the measurements approximate the truth depends on the size of the **measurement error**, which depends on accuracy, bias, and precision. Neither process analysis nor improvements are meaningful unless there is a good understanding of measurement capabilities and the relevance of the data with respect to the issues at hand. As an example, the output from a process could be mischaracterized if data are only collected from the best process performers. Measurement is discussed in further detail in Chapter 8.

4. *Analytical Processes.* Analytical processes are required to convert raw measurement data into useful information. Numerous tools are available, ranging from soft unsophisticated tools, to some rather complex statistical hard tools. In Six Sigma programs, all participants in improvement projects, including champions, sponsors, black belts, green belts, master black belts, and team members, will be trained in soft tools. A rich variety of these tools are presented in Chapter 7. Only black belts and master black belts would be proficient in hard tools, such as those presented in Chapter 8. Under the category of hard, there are many other useful tools that are beyond the scope of this text.

5. *Integration and Communications.* The integrating skills of the workforce and the communications network provide the keys to transforming a collection of parts into a cohesive functioning system. The information technologies employed should be compatible and integrated in a way that provides relevant, timely, and reliable intelligence consistently to those who need it all along the value stream.

2.2.3.7 System Outputs and Outcomes   A customer's view of quality will be based on the outputs or outcomes of a value stream, or perhaps both. Outcomes differ from outputs. **Outputs** are seen from a vantage point of the production system, looking outward toward the customers' systems. Outputs are immediate and are the cumulative consequences of all the transformations that occur along the value stream up to the point where a unit of output is measured. As soon as all tasks along a value stream have been completed, the outputs can be observed. One can measure outputs from within a system, usually at the system boundary as the service or facilitating product is handed over to the customer.

Outputs

Outcomes

Outcomes are seen from an external perspective—from the environment looking back toward the producing system. An outcome can be thought of as the effect that outputs have on a subsequent system or systems. Outcomes can be beneficial or adverse and may occur several tiers removed from the original system (e.g., several stages down the supply chain). Although outputs can be observed immediately, outcomes may take considerable time to become apparent, if ever.

Undesirable outputs or outcomes are called *waste.*

Waste

Toxic Waste

Outcomes and outputs can be desirable or undesirable. Any output that cannot be used by the customer or outcome that negatively impacts the achievement of a customer's mission is called **waste**. As an output, waste may enter the customer's system where it cannot be used, enter another system by default (often the system of nature), or simply collect in the system where it was created. Waste that has a damaging effect on the system where it collects is called **toxic waste**. Damages from waste can be minor in the form of impaired efficiency, or severe, adding significant costs or leading to destructive consequences. The tools of lean production have as a primary goal the elimination of waste, no matter what form. Lean Six Sigma is a philosophy that combines the principles of lean thinking with Six Sigma to simultaneously increase efficiencies and effectiveness, thereby improving responsiveness to customers through increased quality and decreased lead time. This topic is discussed in detail in Chapter 9.

The following example shows how waste can be an unintentional consequence of well-intended management decisions. During the implementation of TQM, a certain automobile parts supplier required all employees to undergo SPC training. After the training, many employees were never given the opportunity, nor empowered, to apply the tools they had learned. This unintended consequence was a form of waste. Not only was the initial investment a waste of resources, but the waste also became toxic when some of the employees, resenting what they considered to be an invasion of their personal time through excessive training, vented their frustrations on the company. Absenteeism increased, morale declined, and deliberate subversion of quality standards occurred. The waste in this case was an outcome because it was an eventual consequence of the training, not a direct deliverable.

Outcomes can be used as the basis for selecting suppliers. A large minerals company once lost a customer to a competitor. To understand why the customer defected, the company obtained a supply of competitor's product and sent it to one of their QC labs for comparison with one of their own production batches. A battery of tests was used to compare the two samples with all industry-accepted standards. In test after test, there was simply no evidence that the competitor's product was superior. Interestingly, the customer could not provide a scientific explanation either. All the customer could say was, "the competitor's product works better in our processes." Good QC sometimes makes it essential to understand outcomes and outputs, as well as the correlation between the two.

Productivity

Productivity is a measure of the ratio of desirable (usable) outputs to inputs.

2.2.3.8 Productivity and Waste **Productivity** is a widely used measure of efficiency and is defined as the ratio of desirable outputs to inputs. Continuous improvement initiatives strive to get more for less by increasing productivity. This often requires closer attention to quality at the source, more efficient utilization of resources, and minimizing the occurrence of undesirable outputs.

The objective of lean production is to eliminate waste.

Pioneered by the Japanese, lean production[10] has become popular as a philosophy dedicated to the elimination of waste, which can occur anywhere in a primary or support value stream. Examples of waste in a primary product-producing stream are **scrap** (nonreworkable output), **rework**, and **line imbalances**. In a support value stream, waste can occur as inefficiencies, errors, and delays.

Scrap

Rework

Line Imbalances

Rework and line inefficiencies collect in the systems that create them. Scrap collects in its parent system if it can be recycled; otherwise, the scrap becomes input to one or more external systems. For example, it may become an input to a scrap recycler's input stream, or it may collect in the system of nature (becoming part of some landfill). The scrap is toxic waste if it is nonbiodegradable or if it contains poisonous pollutants.

Examples of waste are scrap, rework, and line imbalances.

2.2.3.9 Customer Loyalty Ultimately, it is customers who judge how well the outputs or outcomes fulfill a system's purpose. A satisfied customer will likely rate performance highly and reward the business with repeat patronage or **customer loyalty**. Conversely,

Customer Loyalty

---

[10]Womack, James P., Daniel T. Jones, and Daniel Roos. *The Machine That Changed the World: The Story of Lean Production*. New York: Rawson Associates, 1990.

a dissatisfied customer will give the performance a low score. Customer dissatisfaction can range from mild disappointment to anger. If feelings are strong enough, the customer may defect to a competitor.

Customer Defection

To prevent **customer defection**, some companies make customer cultivation a strategic priority. This then becomes part of the business plan, with customer loyalty as a key outcome. Competition is about attracting new customers, while retaining existing ones. However, assessing these goals can be difficult because there are no straightforward measures of customer loyalty. In the case of consumer goods, market share can be used as a rough indicator; however, share alone does not differentiate between new and repeat business. In service industries, loyalty can be measured by tracking the number of repeat customers, and in the case of investors, stock volatility, although an imperfect measure, can be considered. If the interest is internal customers (i.e., employees), one can get an approximate idea of loyalty by analyzing certain behavioral measures, such as retention, absenteeism, and grievances. These are nevertheless biased measures because factors other than disloyalty can cause behavioral trends.

Apostles

Terrorists

Certain marketing strategies strive to aggressively induce loyalty. Xerox Corporation uses the terms **apostles** and **terrorists** to define success and failure in deploying their strategy. Apostles are customers who are so delighted with service that they willingly spread the word and actively recruit other customers. Terrorists, in contrast, represent the other end of the scale. These are customers who are so unhappy that they not only defect themselves, but they also spread an unhealthy word and actively encourage other defections.[11]

Relationship Marketing

Relationship marketing is a tool that promotes the idea that the overall experience (as an outcome) is what customers care about most and is more important than the service itself (evaluated using output measures).[12] A departure from traditional marketing theory, relationship marketing emphasizes the importance of building trust relationships throughout the extended enterprise up and down the supply chain.

2.2.3.10 The Environment   Everything that is external to a system's boundaries constitutes its **environment**. The environment is where **competitors**, **suppliers**, and **customers** are found. Each competitor, customer, and supplier represents a unique

Environment

Competitors

Suppliers

Customers

COMMITMENT AND TRUST

When commitment and trust are present in a relationship, both parties will

1. Work at preserving the relationship
2. Resist attractive short-term alternatives in favor of remaining in the relationship long term
3. Engage in potentially high-risk actions in the belief that their partners in the relationship will not take advantage of the situation by acting opportunistically[13]

---

[11]Heskett, James L., Thomas O. Jones, Gary W. Loveman, W. Earle Sasser, Jr., and Leonard A. Schlesinger. "Putting the Service-Profit Chain to Work." *Harvard Business Review,* March/April 1994, 164–74.

[12]Bowen, John T., and Stowe Shoemaker. "Loyalty, a Strategic Commitment." *Cornell Hotel and Restaurant Administration Quarterly* 39 (February 1998): 12–25.

[13]Morgan, Robert M., and Shelby D. Hunt. "The Commitment-Trust Theory of Relationship Marketing." *Journal of Marketing* 58, no. 3 (1994): 20–38.

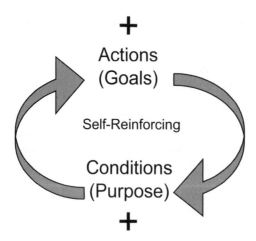

FIGURE 2-3 Positive Feedback Loop

open system that interacts with the mutually shared environment and with each other. Governmental and legal regulatory authorities are also part of the environment.

New knowledge, fresh opportunities, threats, constraints, and general economic conditions are also in the environment. To gain deeper insights into what makes customers tick, an organization can employ **environmental scanning**. Scanning can help the business take advantage of emerging trends, properly assess imposing threats from competitors, understand its markets, and forecast economic patterns. This topic is discussed in detail in Chapter 3.

Environmental Scanning

2.2.3.11 Feedback Feedback distinguishes a closed system from an open one. A closed system has no feedback loops, and once a process starts, it continues unaltered to completion. Feedback provides information on outputs or outcomes. Information is generated at some particular step and then fed back as an input into a previous step (or prior system). This knowledge can then be used to modify future system behavior. External, or **exogenous**, **feedback** loops capture information about system outcomes. When the information is about outputs, the feedback is internal, or **endogenous**.

Exogenous Feedback

Endogenous Feedback

Feedback can be positive or negative. A **positive feedback** loop is called a vicious or virtuous circle and, contrary to what its name might imply, positive feedback is not necessarily good. Positive loops amplify divergence, modifying the context of an action in such a way that the conditions favoring that action are reinforced. The consequence is that the action continues to be exerted, but with increasing fervor. The feedback then indicates even more favorable conditions so the action is accelerated repeatedly. The positive sign is simply a convention that describes the fact that all influences around the loop are positive as shown in Figure 2-3. The process feeds on itself with explosive consequences. The influences have an exponential effect and double in strength at periodic intervals. If the outcomes are favorable, the loop is a **virtuous circle**. However, the process can reverse itself and become a **vicious circle**, in which the outcomes are increasingly unfavorable. The causal system that had led to explosive growth can suddenly reverse and lead to extinction.[14]

Positive Feedback

Vicious Circle

Virtuous Circle

[14]Ballé, Michael. *Managing with Systems Thinking: Making Dynamics Work for You in Business Decision Making.* London: McGraw-Hill, 1994.

Deviation-amplifying feedback validates whether the purpose aligns with customer needs and expectations.

The dot-com phenomenon of the late 1990s is an example of a vicious circle at work. Fueled by a general hype on high-tech and a growing proficiency in society's use of the Internet, Wall Street favored tech stocks and values soared. Included in the mix were Internet companies called dot-coms—start-ups that were overvalued and under-capitalized, and had weak business plans. Encouraged by unparalleled short-term gains, investors increased their holdings, driving prices higher and higher. When the NASDAQ faltered and public confidence wavered, investors retreated. The management of many of the dot-coms had falsely placed their trust in emerging technologies instead of sound business plans. When investors began selling off their holdings, the value of tech stocks declined. Lower stock prices resulted in more defections, and stock prices declined even more—amplifying the retreat. With subsequent replications of this cycle and defective business plans that were ill conceived to avert the trends, share values eventually plummeted. Today, many of the dot-coms, once strongly recommended by reputable brokerage firms, no longer exist.

Refer again to Figure 2-2. The communications loop that informs the organization as to whether its purpose is in harmony with its environment is an example of positive feedback. Defining purpose is the responsibility of senior leadership, is at the heart of business strategy, and should be periodically revalidated. The annual planning cycle should attempt to answer the question, "Is the purpose on target with the needs and expectations of existing and potential customers, giving due consideration to the threats, constraints, and opportunities that exist at this point in time?" The answer to this question represents a type of positive feedback called **deviation-amplifying feedback**[15] and is what some call "the voice of the customer."

Deviation-Amplifying Feedback

MicroMediform is an example of a system that had adapted so perfectly to its environments that it had lost the ability to change (at least at a fast enough rate). According to the historian Arnold Toynbee, "a creature which has become perfectly adapted to its environment . . . can do what is necessary to survive without any conscious striving or unadapted movement. It can, therefore, beat all competitors in the special field; but equally, should the field change, it must become extinct."[16] MicroMediform had overevolved and become so proficient in the narrow field of instant photography that it failed to notice consumer interest was migrating to more attractive alternatives.

A virtuous circle is created when the purpose is consistently reinforced by signals from the environment, informing the organization that it is still on target, or better yet, acting as a homing mechanism, moving purpose closer to what the environment expects. As a result, the corporate ship stays its course and may even add a head of steam. If the ship veers off course and establishes a new heading, the virtuous circle could become vicious. Suppose after the ship changes its heading, the skipper realizes his ship is now on a collision course with an iceberg. A crisis reflex brings another course correction that places the vessel in a minefield, and then another right hard rudder takes the ship aground on a sand bar. Each action to get out of harms way results in placing the vessel in a worse situation than before.

Nelson Funnel

A good tabletop laboratory demonstration of positive feedback is the **Nelson funnel,** described in Deming's book, *Out of the Crisis,* and illustrated in Figure 2-4.[17]

---

[15]Hanna, *Designing Organizations,* 14–16.

[16]Ballé.

[17]Deming, W. Edwards. *Out of the Crisis.* Cambridge, MA: MIT Center for Advanced Engineering Study, 1986, 327–31.

FIGURE 2-4 Experiments with a Funnel and Marble

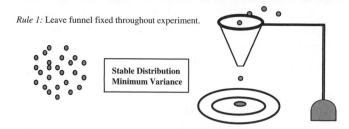

Rule 1: Leave funnel fixed throughout experiment.

**Stable Distribution
Minimum Variance**

Rule 2: Measure the distance z_k from the kth drop to the target.
Move the funnel a distance $-z_k$ from its *last position* for
the $k+1$ drop.

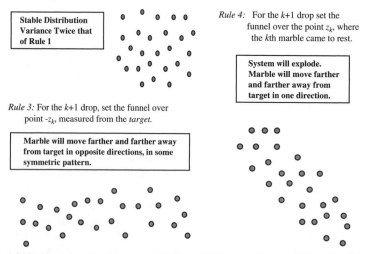

**Stable Distribution
Variance Twice that
of Rule 1**

Rule 4: For the $k+1$ drop set the
funnel over the point z_k, where
the kth marble came to rest.

**System will explode.
Marble will move farther
and farther away from
target in one direction.**

Rule 3: For the $k+1$ drop, set the funnel over
point $-z_k$, measured from the *target*.

**Marble will move farther and farther away
from target in opposite directions, in some
symmetric pattern.**

SOURCE: Adapted with permission from W. Edwards Deming. *Out of the Crisis.* Cambridge, MA: MIT Center for Advanced Engineering Study, 1986, 327–31.

A simple experiment can be set up using a funnel, marbles, a felt marker, and a ruler as follows:

1. A funnel is suspended above a table at a fixed location.
2. Marbles are dropped through the funnel one at a time. After each drop, the spot where the marble came to rest is carefully marked.
3. The funnel may then be relocated based on the selection of one of four rules stated in Figure 2-4 and illustrated in Figure 2-5.

As the funnel experiment is repeated, each rule will produce a distinctive pattern of points as shown in Figure 2-4. One can clearly see that the adjustment rules create more variability in outcomes than rule 1, which stipulates that no action should be taken.

Although rule 1 (funnel fixed for all drops) produces some variability in outcomes, the overall pattern of marble positions is stable and clustered randomly around the target. In contrast, rule 4 (which moves the funnel to where the last marble came to rest) produces a pattern that resembles a random walk (borrowing from operations research language).

Rule 4 is an example of adjusting a process based on the positive reinforcement from the last outcome. In applying such a rule, the original object of the game (the

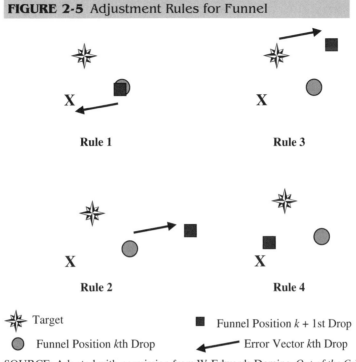

FIGURE 2-5 Adjustment Rules for Funnel

SOURCE: Adapted with permission from W. Edwards Deming. *Out of the Crisis.* Cambridge, MA: MIT Center for Advanced Engineering Study, 1986, 327–31.

target or goal), is all but forgotten. Successive application of rule 4 ironically leads the decision makers further and further from their goal. Imagine a process in which a number of boards must be cut to a specified length. If rule 4 is applied, the last board cut will be used as the template for the next board. By the time the last board is cut, it will likely not even be close to the original specification.

In his book, Deming provides another example of rule 4 in suggesting that this rule describes a common practice in which junior workers are called on to train new hires.[18] The most junior worker is given the task of training the next worker hired. As this procedure is repeated over time, the variability in work practices is magnified, and this significantly increases inconsistencies and diminishes quality of output.

Positive feedback cannot last indefinitely. An organization will eventually seek a state of equilibrium and will survive in the long term only if it can adapt to change. A stable system deals with change by creating mechanisms that either negate or cancel out the effects brought about by change.[19] This is the role of negative feedback.

As with positive feedback, the label is a little misleading. The word negative does not imply bad. Negative feedback balances a system, trying to return it to some stable state. Such feedback loops are characterized by a controller mechanism that continually measures the gap between existing and desired states, and then transmits instructions for corrective action to close the gap. This is illustrated in Figure 2-6.

> Negative feedback either negates change or employs countermeasures.

---

[18]Ibid, 330.

[19]Ballé, *Managing with Systems Thinking.*

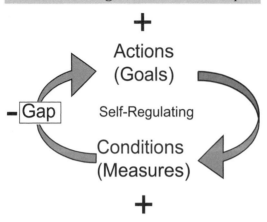

FIGURE 2-6 Negative Feedback Loop

A common example of negative feedback is the thermostat on a home's heating and air conditioning system. When the room temperature deviates from the preset (desired) temperature, the thermostat relays instructions to the switch to turn the system on. When the desired temperature in the room is restored, the thermostat instructs the system to shut down.

Negative feedback is called deviation-correcting feedback.[20] In an open system, negative feedback exists at two levels. At the endogenous level, the feedback is contained within system boundaries and attempts to answer the question, "Did we do what we intended?" That is, "how did the outputs compare with internal goals?" The organizational response to such feedback will be corrective actions aimed at closing the gaps between expectations and realities. When actual performance falls short of goals, a causal analysis can result in countermeasures to improve internal processes. This can result in enhanced performance, a modification of the goal, or both. **Endogenous deviation-correcting feedback** is relatively easy to obtain. What is not so simple is setting realistic attainable goals in the first place, or knowing what actions to take to close gaps between actual outputs and internal expectations.

The other type of negative feedback is **exogenous deviation-correcting feedback**, obtained by looking outward from the system—across its boundaries and into the environment to inquire, "How well do our goals align with our purpose?" An organization can become entrapped in its own introspectivity and lose sight of its mission. Purpose and mission should be the litmus tests used to validate each organizational goal. Planners should ask, "How does the achievement of this goal support our mission and purpose, and ultimately help to move us closer to our vision?"

2.2.3.12 Leadership   Deming's 14 points, which are summarized in Figure 1-1, represent a management paradigm that supports the open systems view.[21] Although the seventh point (Institute Leadership) specifically calls for strong **leadership**, leadership is implicit in all 14 points. The first criterion for the **Malcolm Baldrige National Quality Award** evaluates an organization's leadership system and its senior management's

Endogenous Deviation-Correcting Feedback

Exogenous Deviation-Correcting Feedback

Deming's 14 Points

Leadership

Malcolm Baldrige National Quality Award

---

[20]Hanna, *Designing Organizations,* 14–16.

[21]Deming, *Out of the Crisis,* 18–96.

**Total Quality
Leadership**

leadership qualities. The importance of leadership as a final, and arguably the most important, component in the open system is therefore well documented. Some organizations, notably the military, have implemented **total quality leadership** programs[22] to emphasize the importance of leadership qualities. We explore the traits pertaining to quality leadership more thoroughly in Chapter 4.

2.3 QUALITY AS A BOUNDARY JUDGMENT AND STRATEGIC INTENT

Quality is a
judgment made at
the boundary where
two systems
interface.

Quality is a judgment made at the boundary where two systems interface, and as previously discussed, can be assessed either in terms of a system's outputs or outcomes. As quality is defined as a **boundary judgment**, it is at the boundaries where improvement opportunities are often found. Thus, close management attention to the activities that occur at the system interfaces is crucial to good QC.

Boundary Judgment

Because quality determinations are made across system boundaries, quality plays a defining role in how a system interacts with parts of its environment. Quality is key to deciding what types of feedback to obtain and in designing intelligence-gathering mechanisms. Therefore, quality is central to business strategy, the topic that is discussed in Chapter 3.

SUMMARY OF LEARNING OBJECTIVES AND KEY OUTCOMES

1.   *Describe the machine theory principle of management, and explain the shortcomings of machine theory as the basis for managing contemporary organizations.* Under machine theory, an organization is considered to be like a machine—a collection of parts that should be standardized and centrally controlled. Machine theory favors specialization of labor and economies of scale. This style of organization worked well in manufacturing organizations based on mass production techniques.

The machine theory view has some shortcomings. The emphasis on standard methods minimizes the value of humans and specialization of labor can foster stronger loyalties to a discipline than to overall goals. Machine theory is nonparticipatory, and those that are the furthest removed from problems often make the decisions. Machine theory organizations are also procedure driven, and customers can take a back seat to managing by the book. Finally, the machine theory systems are closed and do not provide for feedback.

2.   *Describe the open systems theory view and how it supports the concepts of QIM.* To be competitive in today's marketplace, an organization must understand its environment and actively interact with it. It is important to understand customers, competitors, the supply chain, and all environmental forces that shape decisions and business strategy. Under open systems theory, feedback is used to adapt to changing conditions. To reach the level of maturity required by a QIM approach, it is essential that an organization be responsive to the needs of its constituencies. The open systems view drives a change management process that will ensure customer value is sustained over time.

[22]Houston, Archester, and Steven L. Dockstader, *Total Quality Leadership: A Primer.* Publication 97-02. Washington, DC: Total Quality Leadership Office, Department of the Navy, 1998, 35–53.

3. *Differentiate between outputs and outcomes, and describe what makes an output or outcome undesirable.* An output is measured from within a system. An outcome is an effect that an output has on another system and may take a period of time to show up. Outputs and outcomes can be desirable or undesirable. Any output that cannot be used by the customer or any outcome that negatively impacts the achievement of a customer's mission is called "waste." Waste is toxic if it has a damaging effect on the system where it collects.

4. *Define the major subcomponents of the value stream.* The value stream consists of human attributes, group processes, and work design. Five other system subcomponents impact the performance of the value stream. They are technologies, knowledge, measurement processes, analytical processes, and integration and communications.

5. *Describe how relationship marketing influences system outcomes.* Relationship marketing focuses on a supplier–customer relationship, and stresses commitment and trust. The idea is that a satisfactory experience is more important than the product or service received. The aim of relationship marketing is to induce loyalty and improve the incidence of repeat customers.

6. *Distinguish between positive and negative feedback.* Positive feedback amplifies either good or bad behavior. The consequence is that, as a result of the feedback, the behavior is continued, but with greater fervor. By comparison, negative feedback has a built-in adjustment mechanism that balances a system and returns it to some desired or stable state.

7. *Discuss the differences between deviation-amplifying and deviation-correcting forms of feedback.* Deviation-amplifying feedback is a type of positive feedback that attempts to validate whether a system's purpose is in alignment with customers' needs and expectations. Deviation-correcting feedback is negative feedback that either negates or employs countermeasures that cancel out the effects of change. Deviation-correcting feedback is the type of information that will evaluate whether an organization's goals were met and, if not, will trigger some corrective measures.

8. *Describe the significance of the funnel experiment to QIM.* The funnel experiment illustrates the perils of overadjusting a stable system and inadvertently adding variability. Rule 4 of the funnel specifically shows how positive feedback can take an organization down a destructive path, leading it further from the achievement of stated goals.

TO TEST YOUR UNDERSTANDING

2-1   Describe the differences between machine theory and open systems theory. Why is the open systems view a more appropriate basis for managing in the information age?

2-2   Describe the concept of a value stream. Why does quality depend on managing the entire value stream, rather than focusing on its component parts? Specifically, how could an improvement of part of a value stream, without considering the whole, result in an overall reduction in quality?

2-3   What are the differences between outputs and outcomes? How can these definitions be used to better satisfy customers?

2-4   What is the difference between positive and negative feedback? How can these types of feedback be useful in improving a company's competitive position?

———————————————◆◆◆———————————————

JetBlue Airways
*Part II—Post 9/11**

During the second quarter of 2001, David Neeleman, founder and CEO of JetBlue Airways, decided to take his company public. The date selected for filing with the Securities and Exchange Commission was September 11. Two hours before the scheduled time for filing, the first plane crashed into the World Trade Center.

The impact of September 11 on the airline industry was immediate. Nothing could possibly have prepared Neeleman for these events. Suddenly, he was faced with a crisis of enormous proportions. Because JetBlue operates out of JFK, the majority of its customers are New Yorkers—those most deeply affected by the tragic attack. While the country was still in shock, Neeleman instinctively knew that he had to talk to his customers and reassure them. What could he tell them?

Other domestic airlines were urging Americans not to give in to their fears, saying, "That is just what the terrorists want," or "Show the terrorists that America is not a country that can be intimidated, and that life will go on as usual." Such a message just did not seem right for New York. JetBlue simply ran a full-page ad that told its customers, "We know you need time to heal. JetBlue will be here when you are ready to fly again."

Americans did stop flying—for a while. The industry responded with personnel layoffs and cancelled flights. During this time Neeleman bucked the trend, ensuring the airline's 2,000 employees their jobs were secure, even though in the weeks following the attack, planes were traveling mostly empty. JetBlue flights took off and landed on schedule, while competitors were eliminating routes and cutting capacity.

Seizing the moment, Neeleman and his management team moved swiftly. Using the computerized reservation system, they identified flights that had been cancelled by the competition. Particular attention was focused on Florida where American Airlines, Delta Express, US Airways, and Metrojet had all reduced service. The decision was made to inaugurate seven new flights from JFK to Florida, representing an increase in capacity on those routes of 44%.

As for safety, JetBlue was the first airline to install bulletproof, dead-bolted cockpit doors on all aircraft, well ahead of Federal Aviation Administration mandates for such changes. Neeleman believed that it was important for his customers to learn that he was taking voluntary initiatives to protect their safety. Being small and nimble worked in the company's favor. JetBlue could upgrade its entire fleet of aircraft in a matter of weeks, where it would take larger carriers months. Neeleman's philosophy: "We do it first, because we think it is the right thing to do." To some, JetBlue's strategy may seem risky, but JetBlue believes the public will reward an airline that can move quickly, understands what needs to be done, and does it.

September 11 changed the airline industry forever. JetBlue was able to adapt quickly to the market dynamics and will likely need to revamp its strategy from time to time, continuing to respond to the changing concerns of the flying public. The following statement appears on JetBlue's Web site and summarizes the company philosophy: "At JetBlue, we're not perfect, but we do try to do things differently and work hard to be the best. But don't take our word for it. Ask someone who's flown us." ∎

———————————————◆◆◆———————————————

QUESTIONS FOR THOUGHT

1. Describe the small regional airline industry as an open system.
2. How did Neeleman and his management team employ the principles of open systems theory to cope with the crisis of September 11?
3. Suggest some important feedback mechanisms that would enable JetBlue to achieve its vision of bringing humanity back to air travel. How could the company go about collecting the feedback?
4. How can JetBlue simultaneously achieve the goals of giving exceptional customer service and of keeping costs and fares low? Are these goals in conflict?

CHAPTER 3

The Pursuit of Quality through Strategy

Think of these things, whence you came, where you are going, and to whom you must account.

—BEN FRANKLIN
POOR RICHARD'S ALMANAC

Nissan Motor Company
Winning through Strategy

Nissan Motor Company, Ltd., had been importing vehicles to the United States since 1958, originally under the Datsun nameplate. In the early days, it had built its image around a marketing theme that emphasized affordable pleasure, whereas its competitors were selling transportation. Datsun was the first to produce an economically priced, high-performance sports car, and its 240Z had been a boon to sales. The company's model 510 performance sedan and small pickup truck had also been well received in the American market.

In the 1990s, the auto industry was undergoing dramatic change. Economic downturns, competitive and cost pressures, environmental concerns, and heightened customer expectations were affecting manufacturers, suppliers, and dealers. Success became a measure of how rapidly a company could adapt to the dynamics of its environment. By 1999, Nissan was on the brink of collapse. With huge debt, declining market share, and vehicles that were uninspiring, the future looked bleak. Its strategy was not working, and if the company were to survive, it would need a major shake-up.

Renault came to Nissan's rescue, paying $5.4 billion for a controlling interest in the ailing automaker—an alliance that brought an infusion of much-needed resources and new leadership. Carlos Ghosn was sent to Tokyo to manage Nissan's worldwide operations and to lead the company in a turnaround.

Ghosn's approach involved three sequential and ambitious multiyear plans. The initial goal was to save the company, and the Nissan Revival Plan (NRP) was an aggressive three-year plan of how the automaker could return to profitability and restore its market image. The NRP reinvented Nissan by developing and executing a strategy that more clearly defined the business, how it was to position itself in the marketplace, and how it intended to compete. Costs were slashed, and the savings reinvested in new products that resonated better with customers. By engaging with suppliers and deeply integrating them into a concept called integrated manufacturing, Nissan has been able to produce the right mix of cars and trucks in response to changing demands in the marketplace.

One of the most important goals of the NRP was to trim the cost of purchased parts and materials, which at the time represented 80% of manufacturing costs. Other NRP goals included reducing purchasing costs by 20% and cutting the number of suppliers in half. The company met all the NRP goals in the first two years. Working in concert with its suppliers, entire systems were reengineered and working relationships were streamlined. Through bold and visionary leadership, the organization was able to focus on clear objectives and the realistic means for achieving them.

Ghosn could not have done this alone. However, it was his ability to inspire a willing and motivated workforce to do whatever had to be done, and to support top-level decisions, that probably made the difference. He brought with him new ways of tackling old problems, using cross-functional teams to carefully examine all areas of the company.

When NRP goals were achieved one year early, Ghosn launched a second three-year plan called the NISSAN180, aimed at making Nissan a global player. The three major "180" objectives were to increase global sales by one million units (by September 2005), achieve an operating profit margin of at least 8%, and eliminate debt. Half way through the planning period, the second and third objectives have already been achieved, and the first is clearly within Nissan's sights.

The gamble by a bold and resolute leadership has paid off. Profits for 2003 were $4.6 billion on $68 billion revenues, up 8% from the year before. At 11.1%, Nissan's operating margins are the best in the business, and its market capitalization is the second highest in the industry, just behind Toyota. The Nissan brand is hot again, with the reintroduction of the legendary Z-car, as well as vehicles such as the Murano crossover SUV, the Nissan Titan full-size pickup truck, the Infiniti G35, and the Altima and Maxima sedans. New products such as these have reenergized Nissan's customer base, capturing the excitement of consumers and industry critics.

Strategy is a moving target, and the job is never done. The third phase in Nissan's transformation, which will be launched in 2005, is a three-year initiative called NISSAN Value Up—a plan aimed at continuing to improve Nissan's competitive edge. Value Up also has three major goals: maintain a return on invested capital at 20%, increase global sales by an additional 17%, and maintain a 10% or better operating margin. In continuing to move forward, the company recognizes that its greatest enemy now is complacency. It must never let its guard down and must continuously strive for improvement as a way of life. That's a winning strategy.

SOURCE: Data used with permission of Nissan Motor Co. Ltd. ∎

3.1 LEARNING OBJECTIVES AND KEY OUTCOMES

After studying the material in Chapter 3, you will be able to

1. Describe the four steps of the strategic planning cycle
2. Demonstrate an understanding of how a SWOT analysis can help an organization establish its purpose
3. Describe the four types of competitive intelligence

4. Define vision, mission, and core values as they relate to the strategic planning process

5. Describe the seven disciplines of enterprise engineering and how each supports the strategic visioning process

6. Discuss how the four steps of the open systems planning model help an organization to address the interface issues between an organization and its environment

7. Describe the theory of constraints and how it can be used to improve relationships at system boundaries

8. Define vertical integration, deverticalization, outsourcing, and hollowing out, and discuss what these practices have to do with the formulation of strategy based on core competencies

9. Differentiate between order qualifiers and order winners and their relationship with competitive priorities, and describe how competitive priorities can be used to develop market strategies

10. Describe the significance of the sand cone model in explaining the sequence that an organization needs to follow in developing multiple capabilities

11. Describe the strategy canvas cycle and how it can be useful in the formulation of strategy

12. Discuss policy deployment as a methodology for executing strategy, including factors that are critical to success and some anticipated benefits

13. Describe a process for applying open systems thinking to the formulation of strategy

3.2 STRATEGIC PLANNING FOR QUALITY

Strategy requires strong leadership, vision, knowledge, commitment, and relationships.

A SWOT analysis can help an organization establish purpose by gaining a better understanding of itself and its environment.

Will Rogers once said, "even if you are on the right track, you'll get run over if you just sit there." Good strategic planning is knowing how and when to adapt to change. A strategy is not something that can be relegated to an individual or even a group. Strategy is not a task or end product. Strategy is dynamic. Over time, strategy emerges and is the consequence of a strong leadership with vision and a solid understanding of the business system. A good strategy covers a broad time continuum and takes into account short-, medium-, and long-range issues. Although there is no one best way for management to induce the emergence of strategy, the following eight themes appear to be critical to success.[1]

---

[1]Beckham, J. Daniel. "Hot Concepts in Strategy." *The Healthcare Forum Journal*, January/February 1997, 43–47.

COMMON THEMES THAT INDUCE STRATEGY

Theme 1: The business begins and ends with the customer.

Theme 2: Functional hierarchies surrender to carefully cultivated processes, capabilities, and competencies.

Theme 3: Organizations stretch beyond current assumptions, structures, and ambitions.

Theme 4: Financial performance as a measure of organizational success is insufficient.

Theme 5: Leadership inspires and articulates a vision, and then gains organizational commitment to it.

> ***Theme 6:*** Resources focus on creating market differentiation based on customer value, even if it means foregoing some opportunities.
>
> ***Theme 7:*** Leaders manage interactions, instead of actions, recognizing that the connections and interdependencies between internal and external components are increasing in number and complexity.
>
> ***Theme 8:*** Organizations must lead. Simply meeting the market is not an option.

Although there is no universally accepted best practice for strategic planning, most organizations employ some variation of the four-step process outlined in Figure 3-1, and discussed in detail in this section.

Strengths

3.2.1 Establishing Purpose

Weaknesses

Opportunities

Threats

A tool that is widely used during the first and second strategic planning steps is a **strengths-weaknesses-opportunities-threats** (SWOT) analysis. Although critical thinking should be applied to each of the four areas, a SWOT analysis does not necessarily

FIGURE 3-1 Strategic Planning Cycle

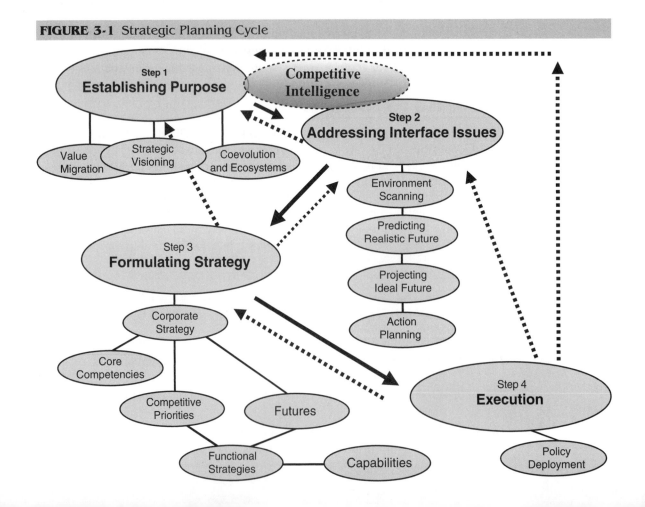

give them equal balance. There is a tendency to place greater emphasis on strengths and weaknesses (which are internal issues), and pay less attention to opportunities and threats (external issues). The reason for this is obvious for those who have been through the process. Obtaining information about one's own organization (the system) is usually less problematic than acquiring reliable intelligence on the competitive environment. However, the availability of new technologies has broadened access, and much of the information is available free of charge.[2] To improve the quality of external data, some organizations have established a formal **competitive intelligence** (CI) function. Short of breaking any laws, the CI staff compiles, analyzes, and assimilates information on competitors. Obtaining useful information on the competition is usually not a problem. Most of the information that would be helpful to strategic planning already resides in the public domain if one knows where to look.[3]

Competitive Intelligence

A CI group will concern itself with four types of intelligence. Each has an important role to play in the formulation of strategy and the definition of corporate purpose.[4]

TYPES OF COMPETITIVE INTELLIGENCE

1. *Strategy-oriented intelligence*—information that is harvested on the competitive, legal, economic, and political environments in which the firm and its competitors operate now and in the future
2. *Tactics-oriented intelligence*—sales and marketing experience that is tracked relative to competitors for the purpose of fine-tuning marketing efforts
3. *Technology-oriented intelligence*—information on relevant research and emerging technologies that will allow the firm to identify and exploit opportunities arising from technological and scientific change
4. *Target-oriented intelligence*—information that is gathered on competitors, including their capabilities, current activities, future plans, and strategic intentions

---

A strategy defines intended relationships with competitors.

Defining purpose is as much about competitors as it is about customers. A SWOT analysis helps an organization understand its uniqueness relative to the competition—features that should play prominently in market positioning. An organization's strategy defines its intended relationships with its competitors, which in turn will drive its marketing efforts. Marketing efforts will then have the effect of defining customer relationships. Therefore, formulating strategy can be viewed as a process of **competitive positioning** as opposed to customer cultivation.

Competitive Positioning

Strategic planning can be painfully slow, requiring patience and meticulous attention to detail. Experience and proficiency comes from due diligence and applying the lessons learned along the way to the continual improvement of future planning efforts.

Purpose can change as a result of new knowledge.

As each of the four steps in Figure 3-1 is executed, feedback is used to modify actions taken in prior steps, as appropriate. As the cycle repeats, a business strategy will emerge over time. The organization's purpose is clarified when all intelligence

---

[2]Lang, Eva M. "Using Competitive Intelligence as a Strategic Planning Tool." *CPA Consultant* 15, no. 4 (August/September 2001): 5–7.

[3]Curtis, James. "Behind Enemy Lines." *Marketing,* May 24, 2001, 28–29.

[4]McGonagle, John J., and Carolyn M. Vella. "A Case for Competitive Intelligence." *Information Management Journal* 36, no. 4 (July/August 2002): 35–40.

concerning markets, competitors, customers, and internal capabilities are assimilated and used to determine market positioning. Purpose can change as a result of planning activities further down the chain. For example, intelligence gathered through environmental scanning could reveal new information on competitive threats or opportunities. Alternatively, improvement initiatives such as business process reengineering (BPR), lean production, or Six Sigma could result in a reevaluation of core competencies.

Vision

Mission

Core Values

Vision and mission are closely tied to purpose. A **vision** is a projection of realistic aspirations matched to core strengths and emerging opportunities. The **mission** is a succinct statement of purpose.

> The mission is a succinct statement of purpose.

Although several pages may be needed to fully explain purpose, most firms attempt to communicate its purpose with a short statement of mission and vision. The mission statement pertains to the currently defined purpose, and the vision statement proclaims what the firm aspires to become. The vision and mission statements are sometimes accompanied by a statement of **core values** that serve as a self-imposed code of ethics under which the business will be managed.

> Vision is a proclamation of aspirations.

Strategy and internal capabilities are mutually supportive. The SWOT analysis is used to identify core competencies, and this knowledge can then be used to exploit the firm's strategic uniqueness. Conversely, as strategy emerges, management will establish priorities and set goals that may lead to the creation of additional capacity or the development of new competencies.

> Strategy and capabilities are linked.

There is no "best" approach for establishing purpose. **Strategic visioning**, **value migration**, and **coevolution** are three widely recognized methodologies. Because these differ fundamentally only in perspective, the discussion here is limited to describing the strategic visioning methodology.

Strategic Visioning

Value Migration

Coevolution

3.2.1.1 Strategic Visioning   The goal of strategic visioning is to develop strategists—individuals who are possibility thinkers, who can recognize new windows of opportunity, and who can spot potential. Strategic visioning is a comprehensive methodology that emphasizes the creation of visionaries and a building process called *enterprise engineering.*

Visionaries

1. *Creating Visionaries.* It is not necessary to recruit people with vision. **Visionaries** can be cultivated internally, provided individuals with potential can be identified and properly trained. The research suggests that people with vision are heretics, innovators, and empathetic. Such traits are attitudinal and can be taught. Training a visionary is more a process of conditioning than education, and would emphasize developing such viewpoints as skepticism, challenging existing orthodoxies, and becoming sensitized to the frustrations and unspoken needs of customers.[5]

Enterprise Engineering

2. *Enterprise Engineering.* The building block process of strategic visioning is a seven-discipline model called **enterprise engineering**. This model is shown in Figure 3-2 and provides an excellent framework for understanding how strategies and capabilities are linked.[6]

---

[5]LaBarre, Polly. "The New Strategic Paradigm: Getting to the Future First by Getting Different." *Industry Week* 243, no. 21 (November 21, 1994): 30–36.

[6]Martin, James. *The Great Transition: Using the Seven Disciplines of Enterprise Engineering to Align People, Technology, and Strategy.* New York: AMACOM, 1995.

FIGURE 3-2 Seven Disciplines of Enterprise Engineering

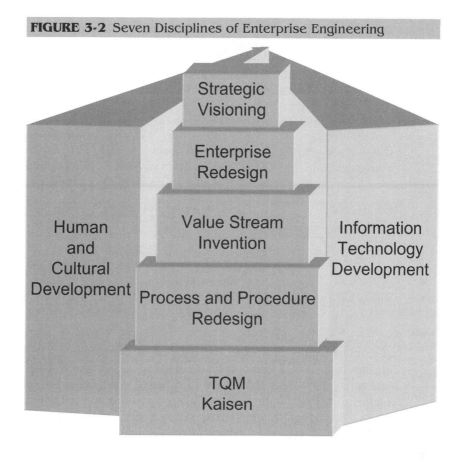

Enterprise engineering is grounded in the principles of Six Sigma, **TQM**, and **continuous improvement** (Kaisen), which are the foundations for the model. Although a capability at this level is necessary for competitiveness, it is not sufficient to sustain a long-term competitive advantage. Learning organizations have realized that incremental continuous improvement strategies must ultimately be supplemented with regular infusions of discontinuous breakthrough improvements. Significant step improvements can be achieved through initiatives such as **business process reengineering** (BPR)[7] or Six Sigma applied to process redesign. Breakthrough activities form the second tier of enterprise engineering, signifying that the business has reached a new level of capability—one of innovativeness. Table 3-1 shows a comparison between the capabilities of the first and second tiers.

When properly implemented, BPR or Six Sigma can result in quantum improvements; however, sustainability often depends on replacing existing structures with new ones. There is a difference between **initiative** and **innovation**, and care should be taken to avoid mistaking the two. In the zeal to improve scorecard metrics or to keep up with the times, managers may elect to automate when they should obliterate, downsize

---

[7]Hammer, Michael, and James A. Champy, *Reengineering the Corporation: A Manifesto for Business Revolution.* New York: HarperBusiness, 1993.

TABLE 3-1 Comparison of Incremental and Breakthrough Strategies

	Quality-Inspired Management	
	Six Sigma/Process Improvement	*Six Sigma Process Design/Redesign*
Objective	Incremental improvements, continuous, Kaizen	Radical breakthrough improvements, discontinuous, Kaikaku
Improvement targets	Key business processes	Clean slate value stream redesign
Skills required	Black belts, master black belts, green belts, effective work teams, committed leadership	Innovative leadership, creative possibility thinkers, strategists
Participation	Led from the top, improvements bottom up	Led from the top, Improvements top down
Change resistance	Low to moderate	Moderate to high
Toolkit	Data-driven, statistical analysis, SPC, consensus-building soft tools, creative tools	Information technologies driven, vision, innovation, risk evaluation, long-range forecasting
Risk of failure	Low to moderate	Moderate to high

Initiative should not be confused with innovation.

Working *in* the system should not be confused with working *on* the system.

when the work should be redesigned or the purpose redefined, reorganize when radically different structures are needed, and establish autonomous work teams when fundamental roles and lines of communication need to be redefined. True innovation requires working *on* the system, although, with initiative, managers are never forced to leave the comfort of working *in* the system. Taking a systems approach to reinventing the value stream links the second and third tiers of the model, and makes the company sustainable.

There are two types of value streams—primary and support. *Primary value streams* are those that add value to the product or service and directly serve customers. The core business processes that are essential to Six Sigma improvement efforts are primary value streams. All functions that are not part of a primary value stream belong to a secondary or *support value stream*. The cost of support functions usually shows up in overhead and is part of the organization's infrastructure. For example, a certain university's primary value streams (and core business processes) might include research, instruction, outreach/public service, development, student services, and athletics. Support value streams would include such areas as financial management, human resources, legal, facilities management, information technology, government relations, auxiliary enterprises, and procurement.

Value Stream Reinvention

Value stream reinvention attempts to shape a new future based on core competencies.

Value stream reinvention uses core competencies to shape a new future. The term "core competency" should not be confused with the term "core business process." The former defines those internal capabilities that provide a discernable competitive advantage. The latter are value streams that directly serve customers. Core competencies include strengths such as unique manufacturing technologies, human resource development, marketing, and innovation. Such factors are market differentiators because they are difficult for competitors to imitate. Core competencies are also typically extendible to new business opportunities, which Hamel and Prahalad call white-space opportunities.[8]

[8]Hamel, Gary, and Coimbatore K. Prahalad. *Competing for the Future: Breakthrough Strategies for Seizing Control of Your Industry and Creating the Markets of Tomorrow.* Boston: Harvard Business School Press, 1994, 84.

White-Space Opportunities

White-space opportunities is a term used to describe any emerging possibilities that represent applications of core competencies outside the current business unit structure, where the current mix of products and services are defined. If the future is narrowly focused on existing operations, white-space opportunities can easily be overlooked.

Reinventing a value stream requires a willingness to challenge paradigms and formulate subversive strategies.[9] The goal is to aim high—to achieve truly remarkable levels of improvement—such as increases of 1,000% rather than 10%. The Japanese word for **breakthroughs** of this magnitude is **kaikaku**. When a capability in kaikaku has been mastered, the organization advances another level to enterprise redesign.

Breakthroughs

Kaikaku

Enterprise Redesign

Enterprise redesign requires a committed and visionary leadership that is willing and able to fundamentally rethink the strategic vision. There must be sufficient management talent to deal with unanticipated and complex problems, as well as to understand the need for reforming the **information technologies** (IT) and **human resources** (HR) functions[10] to keep pace with organizational change. It is imperative that IT and HR be aligned to corporate goals as the strategic process goes forward. These two functions act as enablers, helping elevate the planning process from one tier to the next.

Information Technologies

Human Resources

Strategic visioning permits managers at the top to see their company differently.

Strategic visioning is the pinnacle. When the organization reaches this level, its top leadership share a vision. To get there, the top managers—the strategists—will have learned many things about their company, its environment, its people and processes, and themselves. They will have acquired powers of perception to think about the world, and the company's role in it, in new and dramatically different ways.

3.2.1.2 Alternative Approaches   Two approaches that were previously mentioned are Slywotsky's **value migration**,[11] and Moore's **co-evolution**.[12] The thinking behind these approaches is consistent with the principles that underlie strategic visioning. Value migration uses business models and operations research techniques, such as game theory, to track the migration of market values and to adjust corporate strategy accordingly. Whitespace opportunities can be identified through the following line of inquiry.[13]

Value Migration

Co-evolution

Value migration adjusts a strategy based on observed changes in market values.

> *1. What does the industry ask of customers that they may not want to do or may be inconvenient? (e.g. furniture stores may not be open after hours or on weekends when working couples wish to shop)*
>
> *2. How would new entrants into the industry, unencumbered by traditional sources of sales and service, successfully steal value from the incumbents?*
>
> *3. Can the strategic position be improved by expanding customers' purchasing options (e.g. creating a bundle of services), or by linking up with the markets of others (e.g. offering tax audit protection to the users of a particular tax preparation software).*

---

[9]Ibid.

[10]Grotevant, Susan M. *Business Engineering and Process Redesign in Higher Education: Art or Science?* Paper presented at CAUSE98, an EDUCAUSE conference, Seattle, WA, December 8, 1998. http://www.educause.edu/ir/library/html/cnc9857/cnc9857.html (Accessed Mar. 25, 2005).

[11]Slywotsky, Adrian J., *Value Migration: How to Think Several Moves Ahead of the Competition,* Harvard Business School Press, Boston, 1996 (327pp).

[12]Moore, James F. *The Death of Competition: Leadership and Strategy in the Age of Business Ecosystems,* HarperBusiness, 10 East 53rd Street, New York, 1996, (83).

[13]Donlon, J.P, "The Great Value Migration—Panel Discussion," *The Chief Executive,* 123, May, 1997. (64–73).

Co-evolution applies the principles of continuous improvement to the evolution and sustainability of the business system

Co-evolution takes the view that the environment is a business ecosystem in which survival depends on improving relationships with other members of the ecosystem (that are mutually co-evolving). The improvement process can be defined as four distinct stages of development:

1. Pioneering—creating value, developing relationships with supply chain partners, and encouraging and protecting new ideas;

2. Expansion—establishing a critical mass of support, strengthening supplier partnerships, and using competitive intelligence to increase market share;

3. Authority—becoming an industry innovator, unifying supply chain partners through common vision, and securing a dominant market position; and

4. Renewal—continuously improving, using input from visionaries armed with creative ideas, and using proactive means to bar new entries and discourage customer and partner defections.

3.2.2 Addressing Interface Issues

Scanning the Environment

Predicting the Future

Projecting an Ideal Future

Establishing Action Plans

During the second strategic planning step, strategists will address interface issues. An organization's relationship with its constituencies is like a contract under which the company has willingly assumed an obligation to do certain things on behalf of its customers. Fulfilling the terms of this defacto obligation, the business has to fully understand what its customers expect from it, how it is constrained in delivering its services, and any other parameters that will govern how it will interact with other participants in the marketplace. A useful methodology for answering these questions is the open systems planning (OSP) model,[14] which prescribes a four-step procedure: **scanning the environment**, **predicting the future** without intervention, **projecting an ideal future** with intervention, and **establishing action plans**.

3.2.2.1 Environmental Scan Scanning the environment helps an organization to determine where it will position itself in the marketplace and how it will compete. This information can come from data gathered through competitive intelligence sources or from a more informal procedure. An environmental scan attempts to answer questions similar to those shown in Figure 3-3.

The objective of an environmental scan is to determine whether an organization has strengths in cost or in differentiation, and if competitive advantage can be achieved industry-wide or only within a niche market segment. Acting on this information, Porter suggest that a company will adopt one of three generic strategies: focused, cost leadership, or product differentiation.[15]

If the object is to compete in a narrow market, a company will develop a focused strategy that targets specific customer needs. If the scope is broad, an organization must decide whether cost or product will be emphasized. If cost is the priority, then quality becomes secondary in importance. Cost-driven strategies will typically incorporate production and distribution efficiencies, concurrent engineering, lean production, design for manufacturability, supply chain management, and the use of process improvement teams.

---

[14]Jayaram, G. K. "Open Systems Planning." In *The Planning of Change*, 3rd ed., edited by Warren G. Bennis, Kenneth D. Benne, Robert Chin, and Kenneth E. Corey, 275–83. New York: Holt, Rinehart and Winston, 1976.

[15]Porter, Michael E., *Competitive Strategy: Techniques for Analyzing Industries and Competitors,* The Free Press, Collier Macmillan Publishers, 866 Third Ave, New York, 1980, (39–41).

FIGURE 3-3 Example Questions for Environmental Scanning

	Environmental Scan Questions			
	Customers and Suppliers	**Competitors**	**Social, Political, Legal, and Economic**	**Resources**
1	What do our customers and suppliers expect of us?	What is the competition planning and why?	What are the economic trends?	How available are critical resources?
2	What do we expect of them?	How do they plan to execute their plans?	How are they likely to impact our business in the short, medium, and long term?	Are supplies of any critical resources likely to be threatened in the future?
3	How do we interact with our customers and suppliers?	How do our competitors interface with our customers and suppliers?	What are the trends in technology?	Are substitutes available for any critical resources?
4	How do they interact with us?	What advantages do our competitors have over us that make them more attractive than us to their customers?	How are they likely to impact our business in the short, medium, and long term?	What is the availability of ready sources of supply?
5	How viable are our customers and suppliers?	How do our core competencies compare with our competitors'?	What political changes are possible and if they occur how will they impact our business?	
6	How likely are they to still be around in the future?	How can we leverage our core competencies to gain advantage in the marketplace?	What are the legal parameters that govern how we conduct business? E-market share?	
7	How do our customers and suppliers affect our performance metrics?		Are any of the laws likely to change, and if they do, how will the business be affected?	
8	How do we affect theirs?		What are the trends in social values and mores?	
9			How can our business take advantage of social trends to increase market share?	

In contrast, strategies based on differentiation will place primary emphasis on customer satisfaction. The objective is to produce products or services that are perceived by customers to be superior to those available from competitors. Product oriented strategies will concentrate on developing strengths in product development, quality management and control, marketing, sales force knowledge, and cooperation among supply chain partners.

3.2.2.2 Predicting the Future without Intervention   After assimilating the information collected during an environmental scan, planners will then project the present into the future, assuming all trends and current conditions will continue unabated. By asking questions similar to the following, scenarios can be created for specific future time points and the consequences of various generic strategies tested. "If nothing unforeseen happens and we continue to operate with our current business strategies, what will our business environment look like in three years? What will it look like in five years? Can we predict what the environment will look like in ten years?"

Theory of Constraints

3.2.2.3 Projecting an Ideal Future with Intervention   After predicting the future without intervention, the next step is to map an ideal future—the future that might be possible by intervening to alter the course of nature. The **theory of constraints** (TOC)[16] can help identify intervention opportunities. TOC is the quintessence of the work of Eliyahu M. Goldratt, whose research revealed that approximately 40% of untapped potential is locked within the constraints of the business system. The four-step TOC process is illustrated in Figure 3-4.

Identify

Breaking a constraint can often occur with little or no investment. During step one of the TOC cycle (**Identify** the Constraints), an organization will strive to identify factors that are inhibitors to success. These factors can be in the market, supply chain, internal value streams, organizational structure, capabilities, or culture. A constraint is something that, if not elevated (broken), would result in a less than desirable future. Once the constraints are identified, steps two through four of the TOC

---

[16]Goldratt, Eliyahu M., and Jeff Cox. *The Goal: A Process of Ongoing Improvement.* Great Barrington, MA: North River Press, 1992.

FIGURE 3-4 Theory of Constraints Cycle

Identify
What are the barriers to success?
What are the constraints?

Elevate
Break the constraint, and
then identify another one.

Exploit
Work to get the best performance
from the identified constraint.

Subordinate
Make constraint highest priority.
Everything else is subordinate.

Exploit

Subordinate

Elevate

cycle (**Exploit**, **Subordinate**, and **Elevate**) will focus attention on exploring intervention strategies that will shape a future more ideal than the one predicted. Options can include either removing (elevating) a constraint or effectively managing around it (exploiting and subordinating). This methodology can help the organization identify those constraints that are roadblocks to a chosen strategy. As an example, TOC could help management identify any new competencies that should be developed or any existing ones needing improvement. For each competency so identified, the next step is to determine the inhibitors—those factors that stand in the way of excellence.

To illustrate how this might work in practice, suppose an organization considered the following constraints to be key barriers to success:

1. Lack of ability to maintain cutting-edge technologies
2. Lack of agility due to an internal resistance to change
3. A passive-reactive response to an escalating public interest in protecting natural resources

The following thought process could possibly generate ideas to break one or more of the constraints.

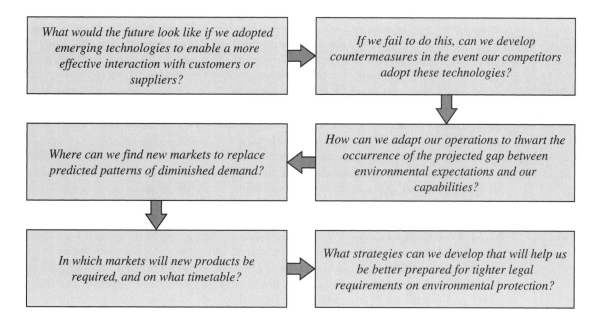

3.2.2.4 Establishing Action Plans   The final step of the OSP model is to develop

Action Plans

some **action plans** designed to create the ideal future. The action plan, which should balance the needs of the system with those of the environment, will determine how system interfaces will be managed.[17] Three types of actions typically result from this process:

1. Those that seek to change the way the business system interacts with an external system, or to change the service provided by an external system

---

[17]Hanna, David P. *Designing Organizations for High Performance.* Reading, MA: Addison-Wesley, 1988, 17.

2. Those that call for reengineering internal operations to better respond to the expectations of an external system

3. Those that seek to change the relationship with an external system by redefining work, expectations, purposes, or communication systems

3.2.3 Formulating Strategy

The challenge with good strategy is to make serendipity occur.

Circumstance

Cognition

Data

Desire

Serendipity

Passion

Is good strategy the result of brilliant foresight or luck? Both may be true. Hamel states that "**circumstance**, **cognition**, **data**, and **desire** converge, and a strategy insight is born. The fact that strategy has a significant element of **serendipity** should not be cause for despair."[18] The challenge is to try to make good fortune happen—to increase the odds of success. To quote Red Blaik, the legendary football coach who produced three Heisman trophy winners at West Point, "the champion makes his own luck." Shaping an organization's destiny—and creating its luck—requires visionary leadership.

The formulation of strategy requires new voices, conversations, passions, perspectives, and experiments.[19] Participation should be broad and diverse, slicing through the organization horizontally, vertically, and demographically. Fresh dialogues should be initiated across functional subsystem boundaries, kindling a **passion** for change. The key is people, and obtaining the commitment and buy-in across a broad base. To achieve this, the organization expects a considerable emotional investment on the part of the workforce companywide, from bottom to top. People are more likely to be receptive to change if they believe there is a chance that an exciting future will actually result, and most important, that they can personally share in the benefits.

Great strategies are focused, divergent, and have compelling tag lines.

Focused

Divergent

Tag Line

Core Competencies

Senior leadership should constantly be on the lookout for new and different perspectives. When a major change is considered, conducting a small-scale pilot study can often minimize risks by testing human reaction and trying to learn what may or may not work prior to a full-scale implementation.

A great strategy is **focused** (it cannot be all things to all people), **divergent** (it should identify some differentiating uniqueness), and should have a compelling **tag line** (a slogan that captures the essence of how the strategy wins against the competition).[20]

3.2.3.1 Core Competencies   We previously discuss the important role that **core competencies** play in strategic visioning. Once identified, core competencies can provide the basis for formulating a business strategy because they define how an organization will relate to the markets it serves. Some specific examples of core competencies are Six Sigma and e-business (General Electric); executive recruitment and retention (Coca-Cola and Microsoft); the creation of loyal customers (Dell Computer); fast response (Wal-Mart); miniaturization (Sony); knowledge of substrates, coatings, and adhesives (3M); small electrical motors and industrial design (Black & Decker); and engines and power trains (Honda).

There are two important strategic issues that relate to competencies. To what extent should the company vertically integrate? What products or services will be

---

[18]Hamel, Gary. "Strategy Emergence." *Executive Excellence* 15, no. 12 (December 1998): 3–4.

[19]Ibid.

[20]Kim, W. Chan, and Renee Mauborgne. "Charting Your Company's Future." *Harvard Business Review*, June 2002, 76–83.

Vertical Integration

Outsourcing

outsourced? **Vertical integration** and **outsourcing** are closer to Porter's cost leadership strategy than his differentiation strategy, since these practices result in some loss of control over quality and service.

Vertical integration means that the organization owns pieces of its supply chain outside the production system. Owning supplier systems is called *backward integration,* and owning distribution centers or points of sale is called *forward integration.* In theory, through vertical integration, a business gains greater control over its supply chain and can possibly add depth to its core competencies.

Deverticalization

The opposite of vertical integration is called **deverticalization**, which is the process of outsourcing all those functions that are not core competencies. If deverticalization is excessive, an organization can become hollowed out. A hollow organization is one with no core competencies. This can result from the **creeping breakeven phenomenon**—a vicious cycle where products appear to become more costly to produce in-house than to outsource. This phenomenon can sometimes be the result of poor cost accounting practices or too much emphasis on achieving cost reduction goals.

Creeping Breakeven Phenomenon

Defining core competencies effectively in the first place can be the best safeguard against unwittingly outsourcing those skills and tasks that are the defining elements of the organization. The ultimate consequence of **hollowing out** is that an organization loses its sustainability and can end up not producing any outputs.

Hollowing Out

3.2.3.2 Competitive Priorities   To become part of business strategy, core competencies must be matched to customers' needs. To do this, the organization should ask itself

Competitive priorities match core competencies to customers' needs.

- *What do our customers value that we can provide?*
- *Why do (would) our customers choose us over our competitors?*

Competitive Priorities

Cost

Quality

The answers to these questions form the basis for establishing **competitive priorities** and for designing a supportive production system. For example, if **cost**—the basis of cost leadership strategies—were selected as a competitive priority, the production system would be designed to efficiently generate outputs that can be sold at a price below what competitors charge. In contrast, if **quality** is a competitive priority—the basis of differentiation strategies—the production system would be designed for outputs with superior features, such as close tolerances; durability; maintainability; available, courteous, and knowledgeable service; convenient locations; or safety.

Time

In some markets, **time** is an important competitive priority. Specifically, for customers requiring just-in-time deliveries, short production cycles and delivery lead times are essential. For other customers, the need for short lead times is not so critical, but it is imperative that deliveries be made when promised. Time can also be important in terms of new product development. Competitiveness can sometimes mean getting new products to the market first, particularly if an organization has built its image on innovation.

Flexibility

Flexibility can also be a competitive priority. Increasingly, customers are demanding greater customization (accommodating their unique needs) or volume flexibility (the ability to order in small batch quantities and change the order on short notice). In 1997, the Next Generation Manufacturing Initiative published its study on the characteristics necessary for businesses to compete in the twenty-first

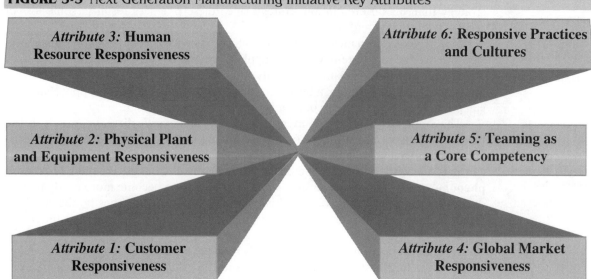

FIGURE 3-5 Next Generation Manufacturing Initiative Key Attributes

century.[21] Six key attributes for next generation organizations were identified and are shown in Figure 3-5. The word **responsiveness** appears in the names of five of them.

3.2.3.3 Market Strategies   Competitive priorities will help an organization determine market timing. As Figure 3-6 illustrates, a *first-to-market strategy* is consistent with the competitive priority of innovation, and requires a system that has depth and a commitment to ongoing research and development. A *second-to-market* strategy supports a competitive priority of new product improvement. Once a new product has been successful, the second-to-market firm must be able to understand the design and produce rapid imitations with improvements at a price that does not exceed that charged by the first-to-market organizations. Systems that support a second-to-market strategy must be designed to support rapid prototyping and short product development cycle times. A *late-to-market strategy* is patient, waiting until the market shows stability and maturity. Then the firm boldly enters the market, having to compete on both quality and price. The late-to-market organization wins business on cost, but must have quality that is equal to or surpasses that of other competitors. Late-to-market production systems are designed to produce outputs efficiently and with consistently high quality.

When competitive priorities include flexibility and response, some organizations use a **segmentation** strategy that targets **niche markets**. Internal systems can then be designed to match the firm's core competencies to the unique needs of these markets.

Market strategists draw a distinction between **order winners** and **order qualifiers**. An order winner is a quality attribute that will earn a customer's business; the absence of an order qualifier will drive a customer to the competition. Linking this to the

Segmentation

Niche Markets

Order Winners

Order Qualifiers

---

[21]*Next Generation Manufacturing—A Framework for Action.* Vol. 2. Bethlehem, PA: Agility Forum, 1997, 3.

FIGURE 3-6 Market Timing and Competitive Priorities

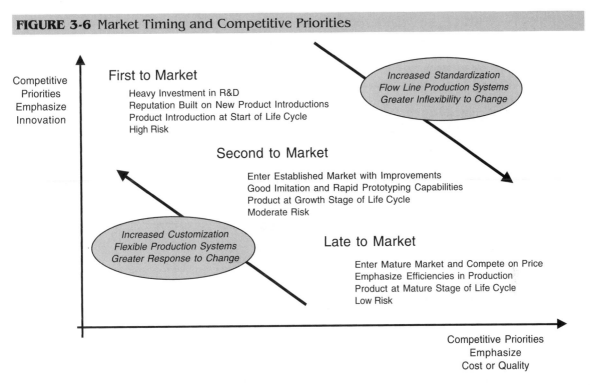

Competitive
Priorities
Emphasize
Innovation

First to Market

Heavy Investment in R&D
Reputation Built on New Product Introductions
Product Introduction at Start of Life Cycle
High Risk

*Increased Standardization
Flow Line Production Systems
Greater Inflexibility to Change*

Second to Market

Enter Established Market with Improvements
Good Imitation and Rapid Prototyping Capabilities
Product at Growth Stage of Life Cycle
Moderate Risk

*Increased Customization
Flexible Production Systems
Greater Response to Change*

Late to Market

Enter Mature Market and Compete on Price
Emphasize Efficiencies in Production
Product at Mature Stage of Life Cycle
Low Risk

Competitive Priorities
Emphasize
Cost or Quality

**Principle of Neutral
Awareness**

principle of neutral awareness, introduced in Chapter 1, static quality factors are order qualifiers. Order winners include any quality attribute that excites and delights the customer, including dynamic factors that take the customer by surprise. A firm's competitive priorities include those factors that have been identified as order winners and order qualifiers.

Customer expectations are constantly changing, so it is important that a strategy keeps abreast of what it takes to retain existing customers and lure new ones. The automobile industry is a good example of where the competitive bar has continually been raised over the last twenty years. In the early 1980s, quality, as measured by performance, reliability, and manufacturing integrity, was an order winner. By the beginning of the twenty-first century, all those traits must be present just to be in the race. What were once winning features are now qualifiers. Similarly, in other industries, quality and price are order qualifiers, and competition is fought and won on the basis of service and time. Because the goal is to design systems that can simultaneously satisfy both order qualifiers and winners, the question arises as to whether it is possible for any organization to develop multiple capabilities. It can be done, however, capabilities must be developed according to a critical sequence, which is illustrated using the sand cone model.

3.2.3.4 Sand Cone Model for Operational Capability   In the late 1960s, the
Focused Factory   **focused factory** required organizations to choose cost, quality, or customer satisfaction as a top priority. The underlying assumption was that an organization cannot simultaneously perform well in all areas.[22] This premise was refuted by some

---

[22]Skinner, Wickham. "Manufacturing—The Missing Link." *Harvard Business Review* 47, no. 3 (1969): 136–45.

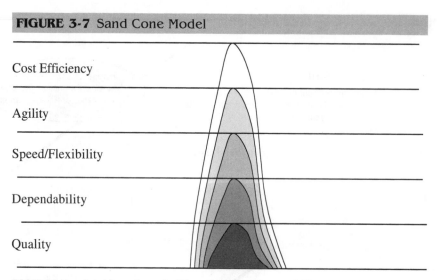

FIGURE 3-7 Sand Cone Model

Cost Efficiency

Agility

Speed/Flexibility

Dependability

Quality

SOURCE: Reprinted from *Journal of Operations Management,* 8, Kasra Ferdows and Arnoud DeMeyer, "Lasting Improvements in Manufacturing Performance: In Search of New Theory, pp. 168–84, Copyright 1990, with permission from Elsevier.

Sand Cone Model

Quality

important research studies that were conducted across a broad cross-section of industry.[23–25] It was discovered that cost is not the major driver that had previously been assumed. Conversely, cost was found to be a consequence that can only be achieved once quality levels have reached a fairly advanced stage. The term "**sand cone model**" was coined to illustrate what the researchers had observed in practice—that capability is a building process, and as each layer is added capability expands in both depth and breadth. This is illustrated in Figure 3-7. **Quality** is the foundation capability on which all other capabilities are built. Without quality, no further capabilities are possible.

Dependability

The sand cone metaphor demonstrates that early quality initiatives can be represented as a small initial mound of sand. As the quality program matures and the benefits of continuous improvement begin to take effect, management can begin working on a capability in **dependability**, which is defined as doing what you say you will do—the reliability of delivering on promises. Then, as the organization becomes more dependable, depicted by additional sand being poured onto the mound, the height of the sand hill grows. Interestingly, the breadth of the base also expands, showing that developing a capability in dependability has also strengthened the foundation capability in quality.

[23]Ferdows, Kas ra, and Arnoud DeMeyer. "Lasting Improvements in Manufacturing Performance: In Search of a New Theory." *Journal of Operations Management* 9, no. 2 (1990): 168–84.

[24]Nakane, Jinchiro. *Manufacturing Futures Survey in Japan: A Comparative Survey 1983–1986.* Tokyo: Waseda University, System Science Institute, May 1986.

[25]Vokurka, Robert J., and Gene Fliedner. "The Journey toward Agility." *Industrial Management and Data Systems* 98, no. 4 (1998): 165–71.

Flexibility

As dependability continues to grow, at some point attention can be directed toward building a capability in flexibility. The American Production and Inventory Control Society defines flexibility as the ability to "respond quickly to . . . changes." **Flexibility** is the ability to switch directions or tasks, using established procedures. A flexible organization is one that has systems in place that can rapidly respond to changing requirements. With increasing flexibility, more sand adds height and breath to the growing sand cone—not only further strengthening the capability in quality, but also improving the capability in dependability. It is clear that as each new capability tier is added, all capabilities on lower tiers become stronger as a result.

Agility

The idea is that each preceding capability contributes to the development of successive ones, and development of new capabilities can only be achieved by strengthening existing ones. Once high levels of flexibility are achieved, senior executives can move their organization toward a capability in agility. In contrast to flexibility, where formal systems are in place to respond to change, **agility** is defined as the capability of responding to unanticipated changes (often market conditions) where a predefined procedure to guide the response does not necessarily exist.

Cost

It is only after the organization has made sufficient strides in developing its capabilities in quality, dependability, flexibility, and agility that serious consideration can be given to **cost** efficiency—the final sand cone layer. As the capabilities on lower tiers continue to expand, cost efficiencies will become more sustainable. An enhancement of the sand cone model expands its use from the business system to the extended enterprise, defining the sequence for developing capabilities in the design and management of supply chains.[26] The impact of supply chain management on strategy is discussed in further detail in the next section.

Cost efficiencies will become sustainable as an organization becomes more capable.

3.2.3.5 The Strategy Canvas: A Graphical Process for Formulating Strategy

Once the necessary capabilities are in place, one further ingredient is required before strategy can emerge—performance metrics. A business needs benchmarks that it can use as the basis for comparisons with its competition. An internal CI group can be tasked with making these comparisons or a less formal methodology, such as the strategy canvas cycle proposed by Kim and Mauborgne[27] (and illustrated in Figure 3-8), can be used to communicate the message in graphical terms.

Strategy Canvas

Constructing a **strategy canvas** is a four-step procedure that can be used to impress the need for change, build consensus on what to change, and provide a reference point for decision making and resource allocation. The procedure does not produce a strategic plan. Instead, it provides a picture window view of an organization's strategic intent, making it easier to see how the pieces fit together and where the organization should be headed.

Competitive Factors

Value

A strategy canvas is a two-dimensional plot whereby the horizontal axis represents **competitive factors** relevant to the industry—not necessarily the firm's competitive priorities—and the vertical axis represents the degree to which the company is delivering value against the competitive factors. A series of these **value** curves can be drawn to

---

[26]Vokurka, Robert J., Gail M. Zank, and Carl M. Lund III. "Improving Competitiveness through Supply Chain Management: A Cumulative Improvement Approach." *Competitiveness Review* 12, no. 1 (2002): 14–25.
[27]Kim and Mauborgne, "Charting Your Company's," 76–83.

FIGURE 3-8 Strategy Canvas Cycle

Visual Awakening

• Draw your "as is" strategy
• Compare your business with competitors'
• Identify flaws in your strategy

Visual Exploration

• Go into the field
• Discover hurdles for noncustomers
• Observe distinctive advantages of alternative products and services
• Identify factors to eliminate, modify, or create

Visual Communication

• Distribute "before" and "after" strategies for comparison
• Support only those projects that support closing the gap

Visual Strategy Fair

• Draw your "to be" strategies
• Obtain feedback on alternative strategies from customers, lost customers, competitors' customers, and noncustomers
• Build the best "to be" strategy

SOURCE: Reprinted with permission from W. Chan Kim, and Renee Mauborgne. "Charting Your Company's Future." *Harvard Business Review,* June 2002. Copyright © 2002 by the Harvard Business School Publishing Corporation; all rights reserved.

form a composite of all the strategies being played out in the marketplace, including the business at hand, its major competitors, and all other industry participants.

To illustrate, Figure 3-9 is a strategy canvas that compares Southwest Airlines against their competitors in the short-haul airline industry. The canvas makes it clear that Southwest's intent is to compete on three factors: friendly service, speed, and frequent point-to-point departures. The strategists considered all competing airlines to be similar enough that they could be combined into a single value curve. It is not necessary to do this and, if warranted, separate plots could be constructed for each competitor or competitor grouping. An additional value curve has been constructed for an alternative competing form of transportation—driving.

The strategy canvas highlights three qualities Kim and Mauborgne consider to be essential to an effective strategy: focus, divergence, and a compelling tag line. To illustrate how this works, Southwest Airlines was able to price its services at a level comparable to automobile travel, using a strategy that emphasized service, speed, convenience, and no frills. The company's strategy specifically targets a niche market. The following tag line has been suggested to define Southwest's strategy: "The speed of a plane at the price of a car—whenever you need it."[28]

---

[28]Ibid.

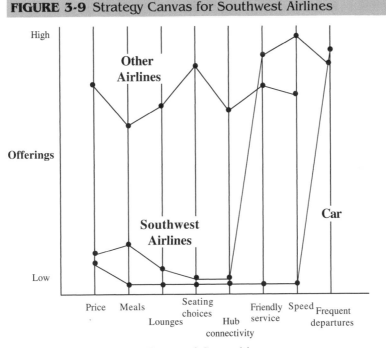

FIGURE 3-9 Strategy Canvas for Southwest Airlines

SOURCE: Reprinted with permission from W. Chan Kim, and Renee Mauborgne. "Charting Your Company's Future." *Harvard Business Review,* June 2002. Copyright © 2002 by the Harvard Business School Publishing Corporation; all rights reserved.

3.2.4 Execution: Policy Deployment

Originating in Japan, policy deployment, also called *hoshin kan*ri, has been widely used to execute strategy by such world class organizations as Canon, Toyota, Procter & Gamble, Hewlett-Packard, AT&T, DEC, DuPont, Nissan, 3M, Xerox, Intel, Alcoa, and Texas Instruments.[29] The word "policy" is defined as the collection of strategic objectives that are vital if a business system is to move in the direction prescribed by its senior leadership. Policy deployment has four key elements:

Targeted Policies

Manager Participation

Policy Attainment

Progress Reviews

Feedback

1. Discretionary resources are directed to a few **targeted policies**, while encouraging continuous incremental improvements.
2. **Manager participation**, called "catchball," is emphasized.
3. Progress toward **policy attainment** and deployment is systematically reviewed.
4. **Progress reviews** create **feedback** for the next planning cycle, validating policies selected and facilitating learning.

3.2.4.1 The Policy Deployment Process   Policy deployment relies on the linking pin team structure shown in Figure 3-10. At the top of the structure is a senior management team responsible for planning and implementing business strategies. Members of the

---

[29]Norton, Brian R. "Breaking the Constraints to World Class Performance." *Accountancy SA*, June 2000, 5–7.

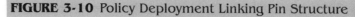

FIGURE 3-10 Policy Deployment Linking Pin Structure

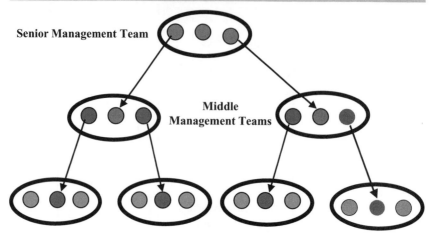

Senior Management Team

Middle Management Teams

Process Improvement Teams

senior team will sit on other teams consisting of middle managers. Middle managers will in turn sit on departmental teams that are working on continuous improvement issues. At the middle management level, one of the teams is responsible for direction setting, prioritizing needs, and rolling out change initiatives as required. At the departmental level, the improvement teams provide feedback up the chain so progress can be benchmarked against strategic goals. The linking pin structure is set up so each member of the team on one level leads a team at the next lower level.

Figure 3-11 illustrates how the linking team structure works in practice. Because the emphasis is on cross-functional collaboration and vertical linkages, policy deployment clarifies and enhances the role of management. For senior managers, the planning activity now consumes the majority of their time and, for middle managers, planning and operational control are proportionately balanced. For departmental team leaders, a small amount of time is devoted to planning, with a majority of the effort being spent on control and improvements.

Policy deployment broadens participation and facilitates learning.

3.2.4.2 Why Policy Deployment   A research study of eight manufacturing organizations indicated that there are some factors that may be critical to the success of a policy deployment approach.[30] The demographic of the subject companies were diverse: four were subsidiaries of American companies, three were Japanese owned, and one was British. All produced consumer products that were manufactured for inventory, and the companies ranged in size from 346 to 5,000 employees. All had been committed to TQM for similar lengths of time, but the time periods during which policy deployment had been in use varied from one to eight years. Most were single-facility operations. The research focused on four issues:

1. *Why did your organization choose policy deployment?*
2. *What were the organizational preconditions for success?*

[30]Marsden, Neal. "The Use of Hoshin Kanri Planning and Deployment Systems in the Service Sector: An Exploration," *Total Quality Management* 9, no. 4/5 (July 1998): S167–71.

FIGURE 3-11 Policy Deployment Process

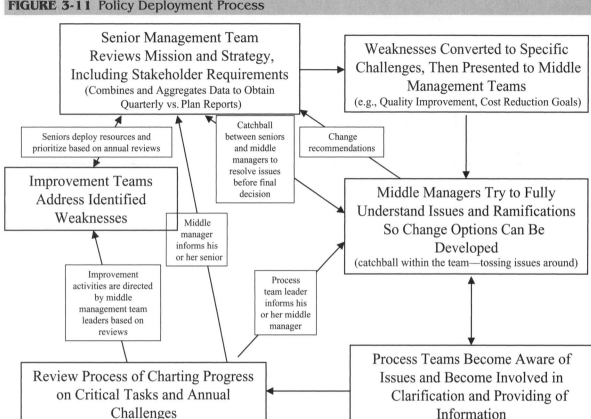

3. *What systemic features contribute to successful implementations?*

4. *What were the benefits?*

Participation

Learning

Priorities

Improvement

Duplication

Bottlenecks

Inconsistencies

Discontinuities

Management by Fact

Process Control

Statistical Tools

The research concluded that companies implemented policy deployment primarily as a means for increasing the level of **participation** in the planning process, eliciting a wider understanding of corporate goals, promoting more effective organizational **learning**, encouraging people to begin thinking about **priorities**, and improving existing planning processes. As for **improvement**, the companies studied saw policy deployment as a process that can help eliminate **duplication**, **bottlenecks**, **inconsistencies**, and **discontinuities**. Policy deployment can therefore support a TOC initiative, particularly in the step that deals with the elevation of constraints.[31]

3.2.4.3 Preconditions for Success   The research also produced another important finding. The companies studied placed a high priority on using its knowledge base for decision making. Instinct, relationships, and power had been replaced with **management by fact**. Other success factors included a widespread understanding of **process control**; the broad application of **statistical tools** and management tools during the

[31]Goldratt and Cox, *The Goal.*

Success in executing strategy depends on knowledge, commitment, empowerment, and culture.

Empowerment

Management Commitment

Supportive Culture

catchball phase; **empowerment** of staff who are receptive and willing to set realistic goals; **management commitment** at the top; and finally, a **supportive culture** that treats mistakes as opportunities. These are some of the same factors that are often cited as keys to success in TQM. This topic is explored in detail in Chapter 5.

3.2.4.4 System Features Systems should be designed to enable success, which means that policies selected for deployment should contribute to long-term breakthroughs. It is also important that implementations be approached in bite-size chunks. The research findings conclude that a maximum of two breakthrough objectives should be selected for deployment at any one time. For an organization new to policy deployment, starting with a single policy is usually a good idea. It is also imperative that policy deployment incorporate the catchball feature, which will force a top-to-bottom participatory process and include feedback that can be used for organizational learning.

3.2.4.5 Anticipated Benefits The following benefits can be expected from using a policy deployment approach:

1. An increase in employee commitment to strategic goals
2. The identification and improvement of critical business processes
3. Improved response to changes through greater flexibility
4. More clarity in vision and mission, and improved communications
5. Improved decision making
6. More effective use of teams through empowerment and cross-functional composition

3.3 STRATEGY AND THE SUPPLY CHAIN

3.3.1 The Supply Chain and Extended Enterprise

Extended Enterprise

Supply Chain

The **extended enterprise** is a term that is used to describe the open systems that form links along a company's **supply chain**. This is illustrated in Figure 3-12. The supply chain is comprised of all those systems that contribute either directly or indirectly to providing a product or service to a customer. This includes the manufacturer, all suppliers (sometimes there are several tiers of them), transportation companies, warehouses and distribution centers, wholesalers and retailers, and customers.

The supply chain links together the strategies of all participating organizations.

The supply chain is the structure that joins the strategies of all the organizations up and down the chain. All supply chain participants have a common objective—to maximize value to the customer while maximizing supply chain profitability. We previously defined value to be the difference between the customer's perceived benefits (e.g., quality, delivery, service) and sacrifices (e. g., cost, lead time, inconvenience). Success in delivering value requires the strategic alignment of all participants up and down the chain.

Supply chain profitability, which is shared among all participants, is the difference between revenues generated, at the point of use, and the accumulation of all costs required to get the product or service to market. Costs are generated as information, materials, and capital flow from one entity to the next along the chain.

3.3.1.1 Cycle Processes As Figure 3-12 illustrates, each link in the supply chain interacts with upstream and downstream systems through a connecting process known as a

FIGURE 3-12 Supply Chain

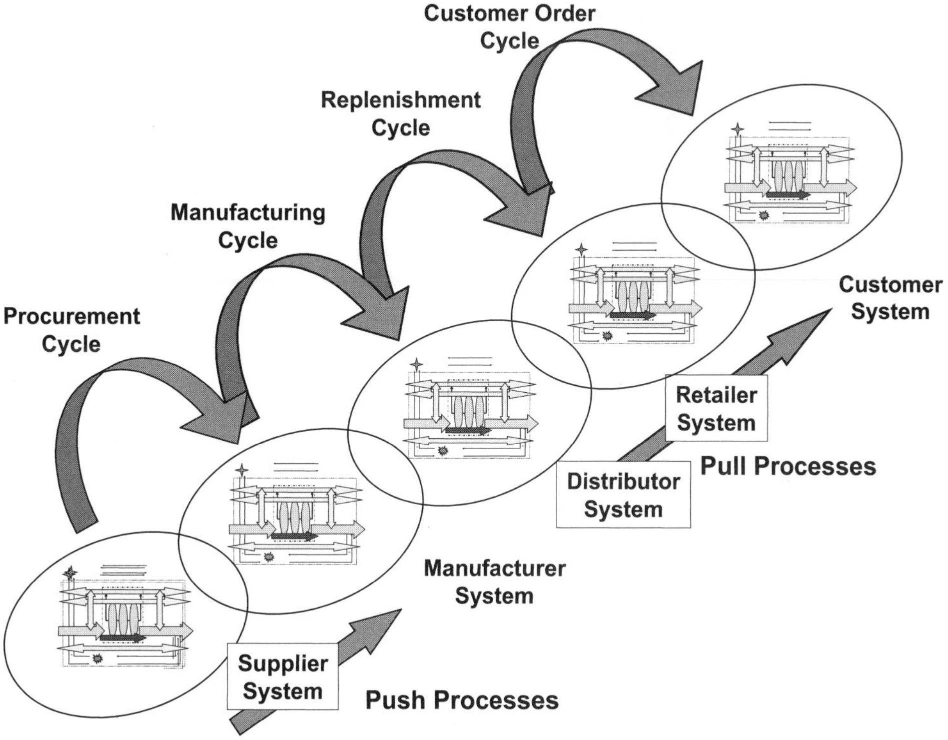

cycle. The **procurement cycle** is the process that operates between a manufacturer and its suppliers. The **manufacturing cycle** is the process that represents the interactions that occur between a manufacturer and its distribution channels, particularly its distributors and intermediate inventory stocking points. The **replenishment cycle** represents the interface between the retailer and the entities that it relies on for stock replenishments. This includes all intermediate inventory stocking points such as distributors. Replenishment can be direct from the manufacturer. The final cycle is the interface between the retailer and the customer. This is called the **customer order cycle** and includes the activities required to receive and fulfill a customer's requirement.

3.3.1.2 Push versus Pull   The flow of materials along a supply chain is managed in one of two ways—push or pull. In push, activities are performed in anticipation of customer demand. Under a push philosophy, customer demand is not known with certainty and must be forecast. Inventory levels and safety stock are maintained to buffer against forecasting errors, uncertainty, and variability in demand patterns. With a **push scheduling system**, there is always the trade-off between the costs of maintaining inventories, damage, obsolescence, and overproduction, with the costs of stockouts, long lead times, lost sales, and possible loss of good will.

In a pull process, the triggering mechanism is a customer order. Therefore, at the time of execution, a **pull scheduling system** responds to known demand. Pull systems remove much of the uncertainty from the system, so inventory buffers can be significantly reduced. Pull systems are often implemented because of a

Procurement Cycle

Manufacturing Cycle

Replenishment Cycle

Customer Order Cycle

Push processes trigger activities in anticipation of demand.

Push Scheduling System

Pull Scheduling System

customer mandate, and upstream suppliers are required to make just-in-time deliveries, with timings and quantities that match the rate of consumption. It is not uncommon to find both push and pull relationships among a specific company's many suppliers.

3.3.2 Supply Chain Design: Ensuring a Strategic Fit

To be competitive, an organization's supply chain must support its strategy. It is essential that strategic alignment be achieved all along the supply chain. Conflicts can arise if entities are not united in their goals and if individual strategies are formulated with differing competitive priorities. In seeking a **strategic fit**, the most important consideration in supply chain design is the trade-off between the degree to which the supply chain can respond to customer needs and the cost of providing service.

Strategic Fit

A **responsive supply chain** is one that has the following capabilities:

Responsive Supply Chain

- Ability to respond to a large variety of products or features
- Ability to accommodate varied sizes of orders
- Ability to deliver with short lead times
- Capability of providing a high level of customized service
- Ability to accommodate changes in orders on short notice
- Ability to deliver exceptionally high levels of quality

By comparison, an **efficient supply chain** has the following characteristics:

Efficient Supply Chain

- Standardized work processes, long production runs, low product variety, and automation
- High utilization of plant capacity
- Low inventories
- Lean with minimum waste

To ensure a strategic fit, efficient supply chains are best suited to environments where product variety is minimal, new product introductions are infrequent, and profit contributions are low. Competitive priorities consistent with an efficient supply chain would include low cost, consistent quality, or on-time deliveries. Responsive supply chains are best suited to environments that are characterized by high variety, frequent new product introductions, and high profit margins. Competitive priorities consistent with responsive supply chains include short product development cycles, fast and variable delivery times, customization of products or services, flexible volumes, or exceptionally high quality.

Demand predictability is also a factor. Efficient supply chains work best when demand is predictable with relatively low forecast errors. Responsive supply chains can accommodate demand uncertainties with large forecast errors.

Figure 3-13 compares those features that differentiate a supply chain design on the basis of production design, capacity, inventories, lead times, supplier selection, and transportation. To be effective, it is essential that all organizations along the supply chain adopt consistent strategies. The manufacturer will often take the lead and work closely with suppliers and distributors to ensure a good strategic fit. Once achieved,

FIGURE 3-13 Supply Chain Design

	Efficient	Responsive
Production Design	Production lines, high volume, standardized products	Flexible flow lines, cellular manufacturing, low volume, product variety
Capacity	High utilization, relatively inflexible	Flexibility more important than utilization
Inventories	Low, high inventory turns	As needed to buffer against variabilities in the supply chain and to enable fast deliveries
Lead Times	Costs more important than lead times	Lead times should be shortened aggressively
Supplier Selection	Certify on the basis of cost, consistent quality, and dependability	Certify on the basis of fast delivery, volume flexibility, customization, and high quality
Transportation	Reliance on lowest-cost modes	Reliance on fastest and most reliable modes

retaining alignment may necessitate modifying the supply chain design from time to time. Over the product life cycle, competitive priorities may have to be altered to respond to changing expectations or to reenergize demand.

3.3.3 Supply Chain Performance

3.3.3.1 How Supply Chain Performance Affects Financial Performance   The overall performance of a supply chain is ultimately measured by its profitability—that is, how much revenue it earns minus the costs associated with making a product or service available. How well a particular supply chain is performing can best be evaluated by understanding how supply chain measures directly impact a firm's financial measures. Refer to Figure 3-14. If inventories can be reduced or turned over more frequently, the demands on **working capital** are reduced and money that might otherwise be reflected on a balance sheet as **current assets** would possibly instead appear on the equity side of the ledger.

Working Capital

Current Assets

Better supplier relations can result in reduced and more reliable lead times and a reduced need for raw materials inventories, freeing up working capital for other purposes. Reductions in materials and production costs can show up either as increased **revenues** (where low cost is a competitive priority) or improved **profit margins**. Improved quality can result in an increased **market share** or improved profitability. Decreasing the product development cycle and increasing delivery responsiveness can translate to new business if the supply chain has been designed to be responsive.

Revenues

Profit Margins

Market Share

FIGURE 3-14 Supply Chain Performance

Supply Chain Measures		Financial Measures
Decrease in	**Results in**	**Decrease in**
Inventory Investment		Current Assets
Inventory Levels	⟶	Working Capital
Supplier Lead Times		Working Capital
Decrease in		**Increase in**
Costs of Production		Profit Contribution Margin
Material Costs	⟶	Profit Contribution Margin
Defects, Rejects, and Returns		Profit Contribution Margin
Product Development Cycle		Sales and Revenue
Increase in		**Decrease in**
Inventory Turns	⟶	Working Capital
Increase in		**Increase in**
On-Time Deliveries	⟶	Sales and Revenue

FIGURE 3-15 Illustration of Bullwhip Effect

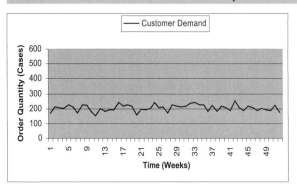

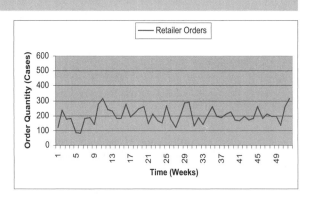

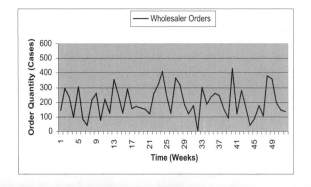

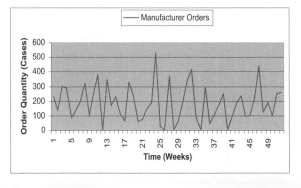

Bullwhip Effect

3.3.3.2 The Bullwhip Effect   A phenomenon that many firms have observed is called the **bullwhip effect**, in which demand fluctuations increase as information flows up the supply chain from the ultimate point of use (at the retail level), through wholesalers and distributors to manufacturers and suppliers. As illustrated in Figure 3-15, the bullwhip effect distorts demand information within the supply chain. The "true" independent demand pattern occurs at the retailer–customer interface. Depending on the industry, demand at this level usually occurs in unitary or small increments. Other demand up the supply chain is dependent on the perceived demand pattern at the retail level. Orders upstream of retail are typically expressed in batch quantities instead of units.

Ordering decisions at each level up the chain are based on three factors: (1) how much is currently on hand, (2) the expected replenishment lead time, and (3) the estimated demand that will occur during that lead time. Cost considerations also influence ordering decisions. Trade-offs are carefully balanced between the fixed costs of placing a replenishment order, the cost of holding excess inventory that has not yet been sold, and the costs of being out of stock and therefore unable to fill an order.

Supply Chain Coordination

The bullwhip effect occurs through lack of **supply chain coordination** and sharing of information up and down the supply chain, and is the consequence of inadequate supply chain integration. Supply chain profitability is reduced because the increased (internally induced) variability adds costs and reduces product availability.[32]

The bullwhip effect drives up supply chain costs.

Because of the bullwhip effect, manufacturing costs are increased as suppliers try to respond to the ebbs and flows of orders that tend to be much more variable than actual customer demand. As a result, intermediaries often have to either build excess capacity (with reduced utilization) or carry more inventories, both of which add costs. The bullwhip phenomenon also drives up average inventory levels that are needed to smooth out the increased variability in demand.

In addition, lead times increase because scheduling order replenishments is more difficult when demand varies widely. Variation also corrupts the ability to gain efficiencies in transportation and labor utilization across the various distribution points. Ultimately, product availability suffers, and the number of stockouts can be expected to increase.

Bullwhip variability can be dampened through improved coordination across the supply chain. Senior managers should incorporate an extended enterprise (nested chain of open systems) perspective as part of their strategic thinking. Coordination requires an alignment of goals and incentives all along the supply chain to prevent the local optimization of benefits by a single entity at the expense of optimum performance of the supply chain as a whole. It is important that all participants freely share information, trying to ensure communications are timely and accurate. Other proactive measures, such as lead time reduction, reduced lot sizes, product rationing (to discourage artificially inflated orders when shortages occur), and pricing strategies (to discourage forward buying and encourage small lots) can also help achieve a better match between independent demand and the orders reverberating up the supply chain. The most important factor is the building of partnerships based on **trusting relationships**.

Trusting Relationships

---

[32]Chopra, Sunil, and Peter Meindl. *Supply Chain Management: Strategy, Planning and Operation.* Upper Saddle River, NJ: Prentice Hall, 2001, 360–61.

FIGURE 3-16 Strategy and Open Systems Thinking

Leadership	Planning Feedback, Decisions Communications, Group Processes Analytical and Measurement Processes	Managing and Doing Feedback, Decisions, Communications Transformation Process Analytical Processes Measurement Processes Integrating Skills
Goal Setting — What new performance standards and measures do I want?	What corporate initiatives and directions do I need to pay attention to?	Specifically, what am I going to pursue?
Execution — What capacity changes am I considering?	What are the key components (initiatives) of my business portfolio?	What assumptions and principles will guide me?
Visioning — How do I build understanding, ownership, and support for what I want to do?	How do I think through and integrate what I want to achieve from where I am now?	What specifically do I intend to do—what, how, and why? What is the plan (strategy)?
Outputs and Outcomes — What exists, and what are the possibilities for improvement within my current organization?	What competitive, external factors do I need to pay attention to?	Therefore, what do I need to plan for and put into place?
Technologies — What capabilities and attitudes are in place? What needs to be changed?	What internal issues and restraints might I have to deal with now and in the future?	Therefore, what approaches will I have to build into my plans and activities?
Knowledge Base — What resources, tools, information, and help do I have? What must I provide?	How do I move forward, keeping activities balanced and integrated, and meeting desired targets?	How do I build the desired changes into my operations and systems? How do I sustain new levels of performance?

Left margin labels: *What Might Be and Change Management* (Goal Setting, Execution); *Strategy* (Visioning); *What Is and Current State* (Outputs and Outcomes, Technologies, Knowledge Base). Vertical arrows labeled *Integration*.

☐ External (Environmental) Focus   ☐ Internal (Systems) Focus

Courtesy of Thomas R. Williams, Consultant.

3.4 STRATEGIC PLANNING AND OPEN SYSTEMS THINKING

Strategic planning requires open systems thinking and the ability to see the organization as an extended enterprise consisting of numerous systems linked together. Figure 3-16 is a tool that can help senior planners focus on those internal and external issues that are strategic to the organization's competitive position, and to identify any organizational changes that may be warranted.

Moving through the matrix from bottom to top, the analysis first focuses on the current state (What is?)—clearly an internal issue. At this stage, it is important to determine what is known about the current state, the relevant technologies, and the desirable outputs and outcomes. Management then moves to an external focus and a visioning cycle of possibility thinking. This is the stage where relationships with the environment and the extended enterprise will develop. The final phase is to establish a vision (What might be?) and a change strategy for achieving it.

At each tier, the management team applies a critical thought process involving three steps—defining the leadership issues, planning, and taking action.

SUMMARY OF LEARNING OBJECTIVES AND KEY OUTCOMES

1. *Describe the four steps of the strategic planning cycle.* The four steps are establishing purpose, addressing interface issues, formulating strategy, and execution. Establishing purpose is a step in which an organization gathers as much intelligence

as it can on its competitors and decides how it intends to position itself in the marketplace. Because the marketplace is ever changing, it is important that the firm have people of vision contribute to the statement of purpose, which is normally succinctly communicated through a company's vision and mission statements. In addressing the interface issues, the organization strives to understand its environment, including customer expectations, constraints, and other parameters that govern how the firm will operate.

2.   *Demonstrate an understanding of how a SWOT analysis can help an organization establish its purpose.* A SWOT analysis is a process by which an organization assesses its strengths, weaknesses, opportunities, and threats. The first two of these are based on an internal self-assessment. The latter two are external to the firm and come from the application of an effective competitive intelligence effort. When done well, a SWOT analysis can help the organization identify its uniqueness as compared with its competitors. A clear purpose statement can emerge from what is learned as a result of this exercise.

3.   *Describe the four types of competitive intelligence.* CI can be oriented toward strategy, tactics, technology, or targets. Strategy-oriented intelligence gathers information about the environment that is coinhabited by the business at hand and its competitors. Intelligence aimed at tactics tracks information on how well customer acquisition systems (e.g., marketing, sales, promotions) are working as compared with the competition. Technology intelligence tracks emerging opportunities that arise due to research and changing societal values. Finally, target intelligence gathers information on specific competitors.

4.   *Define vision, mission, and core values as they relate to the strategic planning process.* A vision is the projection of what an organization aspires to be. The mission is a statement that reflects the status quo—that is, a statement of current mission. Core values are a code of ethics under which the management governs.

5.   *Describe the seven disciplines of enterprise engineering and how each supports the strategic visioning process.* The foundation of enterprise engineering is a solid capability in continuous improvement, such as Six Sigma or TQM. The next level is the development of capabilities in discontinuous breakthrough improvement strategies, such as BPR or the use of Six Sigma to redesign core business processes. This leads to the next tier, value stream reinvention, which in turn enables the enterprise to reinvent itself. Each level is supported by evolutionary changes in the HR and IT systems. The final level of the model is strategic visioning that enables a firm to spot and exploit new opportunities, and is only possible when all tiers are in place.

6.   *Discuss how the four steps of the open systems planning model help an organization to address the interface issues between an organization and its environment.* The four steps of the OSP model are scanning the environment, predicting the future without intervention, projecting an ideal future with intervention, and establishing action plans. These steps help an organization understand its environment, identify new opportunities, and determine what changes need to take place.

7.   *Describe the theory of constraints and how it can be used to improve relationships at system boundaries.* The TOC involves these four steps: identify, exploit, subordinate,

and elevate. TOC can help an organization identify and remove those factors that are inhibitors to success. Constraints can be found internally within the system or externally in the environment.

8.   *Define vertical integration, deverticalization, outsourcing, and hollowing out, and discuss what these practices have to do with the formulation of strategy based on core competencies.* Vertical integration can be the means by which an organization builds competencies by expanding beyond its own system boundaries to include one or more of the components of its supply chain. This can include suppliers or parts of its distribution channels. Deverticalization is the opposite of vertical integration and is the process of outsourcing all functions that are not core competencies. If the organization goes too far, and outsources all its core competencies, it is said to have hollowed out. In this case, the organization may have nothing left on which to develop a differentiating strategy.

9.   *Differentiate between order qualifiers and order winners and their relationship with competitive priorities, and describe how competitive priorities can be used to develop market strategies.* An order winner is a quality attribute that wins the business. An order qualifier will not win the business but is a prerequisite for being in the game. Market strategies must determine the difference and develop competitive priorities that determine how the organization will compete, and how its supply chain and production systems will be designed.

10.   *Describe the significance of the sand cone model in explaining the sequence that an organization needs to follow in developing multiple capabilities.* The sand cone model asserts that an organization can develop multiple capabilities, but they must be developed in a prescribed sequence. First, a fundamental capability in quality must be established. Then, an organization can work on dependability, followed by flexibility and agility. It is only after these capabilities are in place that an organization can be capable in terms of cost management.

11.   *Describe the strategy canvas cycle and how it can be useful in the formulation of strategy.* The strategy canvas cycle is a four-step graphical procedure that can help an organization visualize strategy through its construction. The strategy canvas is used to impress the need for change, build consensus on what to change, and provide a ready reference point for decision making and resource allocation.

12.   *Discuss policy deployment as a methodology for executing strategy, including factors that are critical to success and some anticipated benefits.* Policy deployment has four defining features: targeted use of resources, management participation, systematic reviews, and feedback. The critical factors for success are similar to some of the factors that contribute to successful quality programs, such as knowledge-based decision making, an empowered staff, committed management, and a supportive culture.

13.   *Describe a process for applying open systems thinking to the formulation of strategy.* Strategic planning requires open systems thinking. This entails being able to view the organization as a system where continual interchanges at the system boundaries, together with feedback, shape structure, strategic intent, and management practices. Each business can also be viewed as an extended enterprise, consisting of numerous systems linked together by a common purpose. In developing and executing strategy,

management should focus on those internal and external issues that effect the organization's competitive position and initiate changes that will move it closer to the strategic intent.

TO TEST YOUR UNDERSTANDING

3-1   How does a SWOT analysis help an organization establish purpose? What is CI, and how does it support the establishment of purpose? Why is it easier to obtain information on strengths and weaknesses than on opportunities and threats?

3-2   What do operational capabilities have to do with business strategy? How does the sand cone model help an organization develop these capabilities?

3-3   Define the advantages and disadvantages to vertical integration. What does business strategy have to do with vertical integration or outsourcing?

3-4   Why is the open systems view critical to the formulation of competitive business strategies?

3-5   Why is fact-based decision making essentially good strategy? How can a process be designed in which strategic planning is based on knowledge?

3-6   What does good business strategy have to do with quality? How does a good business plan support QIM?

◆●◆

Nestlé USA

*A Web Strategy for an Old Company**

When Joe Weller became CEO and chairman of Nestlé USA in 1995, he inherited a fragmented company that was a subsidiary of the world's largest food company, Nestlé S.A., based in Vevey, Switzerland. The company relied on established brands—Nescafé® and Nestea®, Purina® Friskies® and Purina® Alpo®, Nestlé® Toll House®, and Stouffer's® Lean Cuisine®—to maintain its century-long record of success. Weller found that the culture had become risk averse and was too slow to adapt to change. One of his first initiatives was a document titled "Blueprint for Success," designed to unify the company under a common set of objectives that he hoped would transform Nestlé into a fast-moving organization.

The company needed to become leaner and more responsive. This would require some radical reengineering. The Internet was seen to be the most significant catalyst for change, so it became the epicenter of the corporate redesign effort. "Make e-business the way we do business" became the official company slogan. Nevertheless, old habits die hard and Nestlé personnel were slow to embrace the Web. It took three years before the first brand Web site, CarnationBaby.com, was operational.

In June 1997, Nestlé was part of the World Wide Web but it did not have a focused strategy. Each of its eight divisions was given free reign to design its own Web site and develop whatever unique Web strategy its division leader thought was appropriate. As a result, each division simply took its brand names, put "dotcoms" at the end of them. These new brand Web sites bore names like TollHouse.com, Stouffers.com, and LibbysPumpkin.com.

---

*Printed with kind permission of Nestlé USA.

Management had assumed Nestlé could market its brands over the Internet in much the same way they were marketed using conventional means. Brand managers were given responsibility over the Web-based marketing; however, expectations were not high. It was perhaps no surprise when the brand managers assigned low priorities to their Internet projects.

It soon became obvious that something was awry. The anticipated volume of Web site hits had not materialized. Conceding that they did not know what had gone wrong, the top leaders sought counsel from employees, customers, retailers, and respected Web heavyweights—experts from companies like America Online and Yahoo. The feedback was enlightening.

First, Nestlé learned that Web surfers find brandcentric Web sites abrasive and obtrusive. Online consumers value trust and reliability, and are turned off by what they perceive as yet another form of advertising. Second, the Internet offers the potential for a direct conversation between consumers and manufacturers. Net-savvy consumers have grown to expect the opportunity to use the Internet to engage interactively.

Nestlé decided to revolutionize its Web approach. Instead of placing the brand first, it would place the consumer first, treating the brand only as a Web resource. A new Net strategy, designed to help and inform consumers, was rolled out in the form of a number of "Very Best" sites. VeryBestBaking.com provided recipes and cooking tips. VeryBestPet.com offered advice on grooming and nutrition for dogs and cats. VeryBestBaby.com and VeryBestKids.com provided answers to myriad questions concerning babies and contained creative ideas and fun activities that parents could experience with their children. The brand was deemphasized on these sites, appearing just once, often portrayed as the site sponsor, on the home page and with a reduced logo.

When logging on to a Very Best site, a consumer can receive helpful hints, subscribe to e-newsletters, or ask a question of subject-matter experts. The Web strategy is aimed at replacing "return on investment with return on trust" thereby creating a different objective than conventional marketing. Developing credibility and building a relationship with consumers is the first priority. When Web sites focus on consumer needs, the company is wagering that consumers will develop a bonded relationship with the brand. Then, when it comes time to make a purchase it is hoped that these consumers will not even consider a brand other than the one they have come to trust as a source of reliable and helpful information.

Since its inception Nestlé's Web strategy has taken on some new dimensions. During 2001, Nestlé EZOrder.com, one of the first e-commerce sites to be launched by a major food company, linked the company directly to its retailers, making it easy for small mom-and-pop shops to do business with Nestlé. For one thing, using the site eliminates the need for customers to place orders by phone or fax. This not only improves service to small retailers, but also saves high transaction costs associated with manually processing orders.

In addition, Nestlé is using the Internet for internal training and communications. It estimates that millions of dollars in travel expenses will be saved per year by simply converting 10% of all meetings to interactive Web-based events. A series of two-hour training modules have been created that employees can complete at their convenience rather than having to fly to corporate offices in California to attend training sessions as part of an organized group.

Nestlé is determined that its Net strategy will change the company's DNA, and intends to stick with it until they get it right, which means changing a culture that took a century to build and that involves 21,000 employees. Training in e-business technologies has permeated the organization and most employees are familiar with the jargon. Changes in behavior—going from conservative and safe to risk taking and innovative—takes much longer. Cultural revolutions must be led from the top, and during 2000, senior executives vacated offices on the top floor of the corporate headquarters building in favor of more modest surroundings throughout the building, where they could work alongside front-line personnel. ■

QUESTIONS FOR THOUGHT

1. Why were Nestlé's first attempts at a Web strategy unsuccessful? What went wrong? Why is the new Net strategy approach more likely to succeed?

2. How could the disciplines of enterprise engineering be used to help Nestlé maintain its market dominance?

3. How would you define Nestlé's competitive priorities? How does its Net strategy support those priorities? What key capabilities are essential for Nestlé to compete in its chosen markets?

4. Nestlé's strategy for change can at best be described as a work in progress. How do you think the company could use the strategy canvas and policy deployment approaches to help facilitate cultural change?

SECTION II

Quality and Management Practices

CHAPTER 4

Managing for Quality: Organization, Leadership, and Decision Making

Knowledge unused is like a torch in the hand of a blind person.
—ADAPTED FROM INDIAN (KASHMIRI)

Lincoln Electric Company

The Actual Is Limited, The Possible Is Immense

With $200 in capital, John C. Lincoln started Lincoln Electric Company in 1895 to manufacture electric motors to his designs. He later expanded the business to include battery chargers for electric-powered automobiles. John's younger brother James joined the firm in 1907 as a salesman. Unlike John, who was a technical wizard, James' forte was management.

In 1911, the company pioneered the world's first variable-voltage, single-operator, portable arc welding machine. Arc welding was in its infancy, and the Lincoln brothers were quick to recognize the alternative market for the automobile generators the company was producing to recharge batteries. John applied his genius toward research and development,

and the company soon became the market leader in arc welding equipment. In 1914, John Lincoln decided to concentrate on science and other interests, and placed James in charge of managing the company.

James' management style was reminiscent of his earlier college days at Ohio State, where he had been a football standout and learned that it takes the effort of an entire team to get a job done. This became a core value that James applied as manager throughout the rest of his life because he often found himself playing different roles—coach, cheerleader, quarterback, and even at times, chaplain. Like most successful leaders, he surrounded himself with creative and talented people, and Lincoln Electric flourished.

James operated with a simple and effective management philosophy. Growing up in a family that stressed Judeo-Christian values and a strong work ethic, he believed that if these values "did control our acts, the savings in the cost of distribution would be tremendous . . . (and) competition . . . would be in improving the quality of products and increasing efficiency in producing and distributing them; not in deception, as is now too customary."[1] James firmly believed that the key to success was to continually find ways to help and encourage employees to put forth their best efforts.

To help motivate his personnel, James established an Advisory Board—a forum of employee-elected representatives to facilitate communications between the workforce and the management. The board members met with Mr. Lincoln twice per month to discuss employee relations, productivity improvements, and new product developments. James believed that, through competition and adequate incentives, every person could develop to their maximum potential. From the beginning, employees were rewarded handsomely for cost reduction ideas and individual contributions.

Lincoln Electric continued to prosper with solid growth in all markets. By 1922, the production of welders exceeded that of motors, making welding the company's primary business. The key to success was rooted in a simple strategy—build a quality product at a cost below that of competitors. The slogan "The Actual Is Limited, The Possible Is Immense"[2] could be found conspicuously displayed throughout Lincoln's facilities. The company believed that it could continually make progress on lowering costs if it was diligent in focusing on the needs of its employees. The theory was that if management took care of employees, the employees would take care of the company—and productivity would continue to improve. The strategy called for sharing a portion of cost savings with customers in the form of lower prices—thus improving market share—and returning a portion to the employees who made the savings possible.

By 1915, all employees were covered by group life insurance, a progressive move for the time, and in 1923, Lincoln Electric became one of the first companies in the United States to provide its employees with paid vacations. An employee stock ownership plan was initiated in 1925, and in 1929, a formal employee suggestion program was launched. An incentive bonus program was implemented in 1934, creating substantial end-of-year bonuses that have typically averaged 25 to 100% of regular compensation. Taken collectively, these progressive measures became the foundation of incentive management.

During World War II, the business expanded dramatically because the U.S. Navy created an enormous demand for welded ship hulls. Lincoln workers who were drafted into the armed forces were replaced with large numbers of women and minority workers for the first time.

During the 1960s, James Lincoln continued to enhance the concept of incentive management, adding a cost-of-living multiplier, a formal merit rating system, and a guarantee of employment (no layoffs). The company was one of the early adopters of an organic-style organization structure aimed at facilitating internal communications and maximizing flexibility.

James Lincoln was a believer in the concept of niche marketing, and throughout his career the company focused on a narrow product line consisting of electric welding machines, metal electrodes, and electric motors. Being a rugged individualist, he refused to consider new product ideas that might target expanded markets. When James passed away in 1965, his successor, William Irrgang, maintained the same business perspective, so little changed with respect to marketing strategy. Irrgang controlled the company and its destiny until his retirement in 1985. In 1972, Lincoln entered a new era of professional management with the appointment of George Willis to president and Irrgang to chairman.

---

[1]Lincoln, James F. *A New Approach to Industrial Economics.* New York: The Devin-Adair Company, 1961, 64.
[2]Berg, Norman A., and Norman D. Fast. *Lincoln Electric Company.* Harvard Case Study No. 9-376-028. Boston: Harvard Business School Publishing, August 1975 (Revised July 1983), 10.

By the early 1980s, due to an economic recession, Lincoln Electric experienced a 40% drop in sales. This period proved to be an ultimate test of the guaranteed continuous employment policy, but to Lincoln's credit, during this trying time not one worker was laid off.

When Irrgang retired, Donald Hastings became president and George Willis was elevated to chairman. Lincoln Electric embarked on an ambitious plan for global expansion. Eventually, the company obtained controlling interest in sixteen countries, but things had not gone well. In 1992, the company found itself with large corporate losses and substantial debt, necessitating substantial cutbacks in the year-end incentive bonuses. The workers countered with hostility and resentment. Since the U.S. operations were producing strong profits, employees did not believe they were responsible for creating the international problems and did not see why they should have to suffer the consequences. However, under Hastings' leadership, the company used its credit to borrow money to pay U.S. employees their bonuses.

In 1992, Fred Mackenbach assumed the office of president, and Donald Hastings became chairman. Mackenbach brought a leadership style that was able to turn the company around—to rally the workforce, motivating them to achieve record levels of production and sales, and to rebuild trust and loyalty. For example, capacity was so strained in 1993 that the workforce voluntarily postponed 614 weeks of vacation in order to meet commitments to customers. In 1996, Anthony A. Massaro was appointed president and chairman a year later. In 1998, the company distributed its sixty-fifth consecutive bonus to employees. Then, in 2004, John M. Stropki continued the tradition as he took over as chairman, president, and CEO.

Lincoln Electric Company is regarded as a paragon of social innovation, and one of the rare examples of a company that has sincerely strived to practice Douglas McGregor's Theory Y[3] participatory-style management. It is also a clear example that high standards of excellence and high ethical standards are compatible.[4] By placing a high value on human resources, permitting employees to have a voice, and sharing ownership, Lincoln Electric has a financial history of breaking records and achieving majestic goals.

SOURCE: Data used with permission of the Lincoln Electric Company. ■

4.1 LEARNING OBJECTIVES AND KEY OUTCOMES

After studying the material in Chapter 4, you will be able to

1. Differentiate between mechanistic and organic organization structures, and understand some theories that underlie organizational design
2. Discuss the importance of value stream ownership in the context of being able to produce quality at the source
3. Define a lattice structure
4. Discuss how structure supports continuous and breakthrough improvements
5. Define good leadership
6. Differentiate between analytical and naturalistic decision making
7. Demonstrate an understanding of naturalistic decision making, and differentiate between good and poor decisions
8. Describe the essential elements for effective team building

---

[3]McGregor, Douglas. *The Human Side of Enterprise*. New York: McGraw-Hill, 1960, 45–57.

[4]American National Business Hall of Fame. "James F. Lincoln. Lincoln Electric Company." http://www.anbhf.org/laureates/lincoln.html. (Accessed March 25, 2005).

4.2 ORGANIZING FOR QUALITY

4.2.1 Organization Structures

In March 2002, Fujitsu Limited announced a major restructuring. The new organic company, shown in Figure 4-1, would be guided by only seven directors (down from thirty-two) and managed by a cross-functional management committee. The Fujitsu action typifies a growing trend, as companies look to innovative structuring as a vehicle for change. [5, 6] Structural reform can also be the means for achieving a more responsive management style and superior quality because flatter and delayered structures can foster more productive cross-functional relationships and provide greater flexibility in the distribution of resources.

Mechanistic Structures

Organic Structures

Figure 4-2 illustrates the two fundamental types of organizational designs: **mechanistic structures** and **organic structures**.[7] Most organizations will not be totally

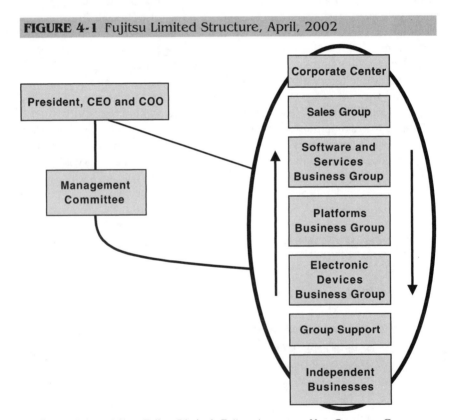

FIGURE 4-1 Fujitsu Limited Structure, April, 2002

SOURCE: Adapted from Fujitsu Limited. *Fujitsu Announces New Corporate Governance, Business Management Structures.* Press release dated March 7, 2002. Also available online at http://pr.fujitsu.com/en/news/2002/03/7.html (Accessed March 26, 2005).

---

[5]Shea, Christine M., and Jane M. Howell. "Organizational Antecedents to the Successful Implementation of Total Quality Management." *Journal of Quality Management* 3, no. 1 (1998): 3–24.

[6]Waldman, David P., and Mohan Gopalakrishnan. "Operational, Organizational, and Human Resource Factors Predictive of Customer Perceptions of Service Quality." *Journal of Quality Management* 1, no. 1 (1996): 91–107.

[7]Zaltman, Gerald, Robert Duncan, and Jonny Holbek. *Innovations and Organizations.* New York: Wiley, 1973, 130–31.

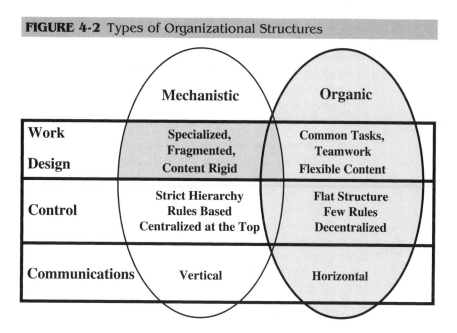

FIGURE 4-2 Types of Organizational Structures

	Mechanistic	Organic
Work Design	Specialized, Fragmented, Content Rigid	Common Tasks, Teamwork Flexible Content
Control	Strict Hierarchy Rules Based Centralized at the Top	Flat Structure Few Rules Decentralized
Communications	Vertical	Horizontal

An organic structure is flat, has few rules, is flexible, and emphasizes teamwork.

on one side or the other, but somewhere in between. Nevertheless, for our purposes, if the predominance of attributes fall on the right of Figure 4-2, the organization will be said to have an organic-style structure; if the predominance is on the left side, the structure will be said to have a mechanistic-style structure.

Although organizations date back to ancient civilizations, the idea of an "organizational theory" is normally credited to the works of Frederick W. Taylor[8] and Max Weber.[9] Taylor and Weber developed models from different perspectives (Taylor from factory management, Weber from sociological impacts), but both had some common threads. These were the earliest of the mechanistic models, relying on standardization with highly defined tasks, broken down into specialized work elements, and governed by numerous rules and a strict hierarchy of authority and central control.

Probably one of the first advocates of an organic structure was Herbert A. Simon,[10] but even Simon's model viewed the organization as a closed system with all-important issues to be dealt with internally. A true organic structure is flexible, has few rules, vests control where the work is performed, and emphasizes the use of teams performing broad tasks. An organic company is one that takes the open systems view and is able to adapt to its changing environment.

4.2.2 Mechanistic Structures

Most machine age structures were mechanistic. These mechanistic (also referred to as silo and bureaucratic designs) were formal, nonparticipative, hierarchical, tightly controlled, and inflexible.

---

[8]Taylor, Frederick W. *The Principles of Scientific Management.* New York: Harper Bros., 1911.

[9]Weber, Max. *Economy and Society: An Outline of Interpretive Sociology.* Edited by Guenther Roth and Claus Wittich. Berkeley: University of California Press, 1978.

[10]Simon, Herbert A. *Administrative Behavior.* 3rd ed. New York: The Free Press, 1976, 220–47.

Some modern organizations still use mechanistic designs, which appear to work well for certain types of production technologies. The correlation between structure and technology is based on volume and variety considerations. One is more likely to find mechanistic structures in mass flow and process industries, and organic structures in small batch or make-to-order settings.[11, 12] Structure is important in the design of a quality program and can be an enabler or an inhibitor. Mechanistic structures in general have some features that can act as inhibitors. We suggest two principal ones here:

- When a business is organized with a clearly defined vertical chain of command, and divided and subdivided along functional lines, a fundamental contradiction arises between the structure of work and the execution of work. Figure 4-3 shows how internal value streams engage with the functional structure to get work accomplished. Value streams are defined by these cross-functional linkages. As work is handed off from workstation to workstation down the value stream it must cross the boundaries of numerous functional subsystems. Mechanistic structures, although providing the prospect for excellent within-function control and communications, do not provide the participants with a vantage point of the entire process. It is difficult to achieve quality at the source when no one has overall process responsibility. Managing the entire value stream requires lateral leadership, and there must be a value stream owner.

  In mechanistic systems, each worker is responsible for a small individual component of the work, and no one is responsible for the integrated whole. As in a relay, the baton gets passed from workstation to workstation, and there is no single person who is accountable for the quality of the entire chain of events. Normally,

Managing the value stream requires cross-functional leadership and ownership.

[11]Clegg, Stewart R. *Modern Organizations: Organization Studies in the Postmodern World.* London: Sage, 1990.

[12]Mintzberg, Henry. *The Structuring of Organizations: A Synthesis of the Research.* Upper Saddle River, NJ: Prentice Hall, 1979, 249–56.

FIGURE 4-3 Cross-Functional Nature of Work

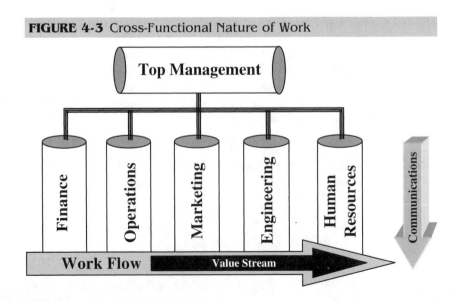

each worker is oblivious to how his or her contributions affect the performance of the entire system. One department's goals can conflict with another's, and solving a problem for one can unwittingly create problems for others. Even optimizing just a piece of the value stream, without taking a systems approach, can lead to suboptimization or worse—a decrease in overall system performance.

Mechanistic structures are inflexible.

- The second problem with mechanistic structures is that they are intrinsically inflexible. A responsive organization is capable of rapidly adapting to change. In contrast, vertical organizations partitioned by function, can sometimes develop a myopic view of what is required, and change is approached solely from a disciplinary perspective. The merits of change are often based on the size of the threat rather than the magnitude of the benefit. In a mechanistic structure, it is difficult at best and impossible at worst to stimulate the need for change, let alone elicit a timely and effective response.

4.2.3 The Effect of Social Values on Organizational Structure

Change is not always driven by market dynamics or technology. Social factors can also influence the way a business operates. An editor of a popular business publication cites an 1890 survey in which parents responded that what they valued most in their children was obedience. A similar survey administered 100 years later reported that parents now valued above all else independence. People populate systems, and changes in social values impact the way they judge the world around them. Core values influence management styles and management–employee relationships. "The generation that was brought up before the Second World War used military-style management. The baby boomers generation was in the middle: they did not like hierarchy, but they do like control. . . . The newer generations of workers, however, neither respond to authority nor exhibit sustained loyalty to organizations."[13]

Society is continually defining and redefining markets. This phenomenon is called *value migration,* and reflects fundamental changes in attitudes and expectations over time. An organization's structure must have the capability to detect (better yet anticipate) and respond to major changes as they occur. To illustrate, Aughton and Brien[14] cite the following example.

In the 1980s, Australian brewing companies invested heavily, adding capacity to meet a perceived growth in the demand for beer. During the ensuing decade, however, social pressures caused beer consumption to decline. Special interest groups were successful in raising public awareness of the industry's negative side. Social demands for tougher standards resulted in new legislation covering drunk driving. Legal blood alcohol limits were lowered, and enforcement was strengthened through the use of breathalyzers and random checking. The industry's forward planning, as carefully thought out as it was, had failed to account for a fundamental change in societal attitudes. Ironically, over the same period, another set of social factors caused the demand for red wine to increase. No one seems to know the reasons why. Solving that mystery would provide this industry a better understanding of market behavior.

---

[13]James, David. "The Need for Persuasion." *Australian Business Review Weekly* November 3, 1997.

[14]Aughton, Peter, and Neville Brien. "Applying Open Systems Theory for Dramatic Improvements in Business Performance." In the Sixth European Ecology of Work Conference, Bonn, Germany, May 1999, 9.

4.2.4 Organic Structures

Addressing complex issues requires open systems thinking, the management of system interfaces (as described in Chapter 2), and most of all, organization structures that are capable of adapting to the requirements of their changing environments.[15, 16] Organic structures are flexible and responsive, informal with decentralized controls, and stress open communications.[17] However, even organizations that have adopted an organic-type structure can still be hampered by mechanistic thinking when it comes to managing uncertainties. It is human nature to look for panaceas, and invest heavily in programs that promise flexible and right-sized organizations—and to do so faster than the competition. However, if changes are introduced for the wrong reasons, valuable resources can be wasted and nothing actually improves. Sometimes conditions get worse.

Active Adaptation

Certain features, if present, can make an organic structure more effective. The following elements, called **active adaptation** by Aughton and Brien,[18] are found in most QIM organizational structures such as Six Sigma:

1. Self-managed work teams
2. Measurable team goals that are monitored, negotiated, and renegotiated
3. High levels of training and development
4. Rewarding employees, not for simply "doing their jobs," but for having the business skills to achieve business goals

4.2.5 Contingency Theory

Contingency Theory

Contingency theory (CT), a term originally coined by Lawrence and Lorsch,[19] broadens the scope of structural design. Under CT, a business can base its decisions on its dependencies with the environment. According to Scott,[20] business organizations are open systems that are intrinsically responsive. As challenges and opportunities arise, an organization draws on a survival instinct to make whatever changes are necessary to differentiate themselves from their competitors. Interestingly, CT acknowledges that organizations need access to the full range of options, including the use of mechanistic designs when appropriate.

Organizations adapt their structures to respond to the challenges and opportunities around them.

Under CT, contingencies are major factors such as strategy and technology, which will determine how a business organizes. Contingency theory acknowledges that organizations are unique—that one shoe size will not fit all—and that it is highly unlikely that a similar combination of contingencies and circumstances will result in the same type of organizational structure.

---

[15]Miles, Morgan P., Jeffrey G. Covin, and Michael B. Heeley. "The Relationship between Environmental Dynamism and Small Firm Structure, Strategy, and Performance." *Journal of Marketing Theory and Practice* 8, no. 2 (Spring 2000): 63–78.

[16]Mintzberg, Henry. *The Structuring of Organizations: A Synthesis of the Research.* Upper Saddle River, NJ: Prentice Hall, 1979, 270–85.

[17]Khandwalla, Pradip N. *The Design of Organizations.* New York: Harcourt Brace Jovanovich, 1977.

[18]Aughton and Brien, "Applying Open Systems Theory," 9–10.

[19]Lawrence, Paul R., and Jay W. Lorsch. *Organization and Environment: Managing Differentiation and Integration.* Homewood, IL: Irwin, 1967, 156–58, 185–210.

[20]Scott, *Organizations,* 79–81.

4.2.6 Structures Based on Knowledge Content

Macrostructure

Strategic Structure

Work Process
Structure

Knowledge content also has an effect. According to Maccoby,[21] a structure *can be examined* at three levels: **macrostructure, strategic structure**, and **work process structure**. How much knowledge employees are expected to use in the performance of their duties will influence how a business organizes to get work done.

4.2.6.1 Macrostructure   The macrostructure is the level of corporate governance, and may have little to do with the knowledge base. The reorganization of Futjitsu illustrates how a company can use a combination of product and function to create macrostructure. It is not unusual for a company to employ a mixture of criteria in this way. Some corporations divide themselves into numerous companies based on specific brand identities. Then each company can be further divided according to markets, products, regions, functions, and processes. This can result in a highly complex matrix structure.

Futures

Operations

Doing

4.2.6.2 Strategic Structure   The strategic structure provides the operating framework for each business unit and supports three levels of activity: **futures** (strategic planning), **operations** (tactical planning), and **doing** (execution). Mechanistic structures have generally failed to adequately model the knowledge hierarchy. Top-down control and strict adherence to the chain of command makes sense only if the boss has more knowledge than the subordinates. This may have been the case in the craft guilds where masters oversaw the work of journeymen, who in turn supervised apprentices. Even up to the post–World War II era, it was common for someone to begin a career at the bottom and rise through the ranks, with a chance of ultimately reaching the senior management echelons. However, in modern times, companies typically recruit raw management talent from college campuses or fill vacant positions on the open market. Internally, personnel are moved around so frequently that managers never remain in one job long enough to develop a depth of technical knowledge, that parallels their subordinates. This problem has been further aggravated by the rise of management as a profession. Over the last 50 years, management became a specialty, emphasizing a skills set that included planning, communicating, executing, and decision making. Business curricula taught that management skills could generically be applied and that technical skills are subordinate—that is, they can be acquired on delegated. As a result, it is often the doers who know more about the technologies they operate than their bosses.

The information age has created a new breed of employee—the knowledge worker. Each level in the hierarchy owns a unique piece of the knowledge base, and it is important that what has been learned be shared across all boundaries, both vertical and horizontal. Learning is a two-way street. Senior managers should acknowledge that they can learn from lower levels. In contrast, seniors should be willing to mentor and teach their subordinates. A responsive strategic structure will formally recognize the importance of bottom-up learning. The strategic planners (futurists) need to learn from tactical planners (operationists), and both futurists and operationists need to learn from the doers (executionists) who are in direct contact with customers.

An approach that has worked for some is the formation of a planning council, consisting of representatives from the operations and execution levels. Council members are required to attend training sessions where they learn about pressing business concerns. Regular meetings are then used to discuss the ideal future, the state of the current

---

[21]Maccoby, Michael. "Knowledge Workers Need New Structures." *Research Technology Management* 30, no. 3 (January/February 1996): 56–58.

FIGURE 4-4 The Structure of Work Processes

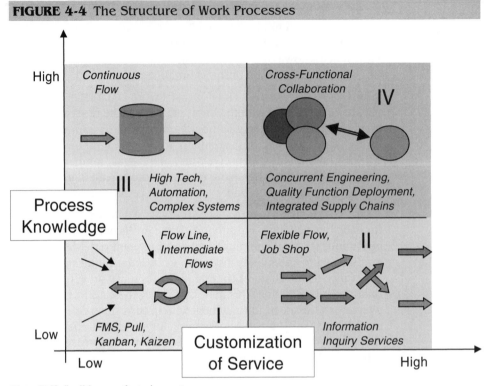

Note: FMS, flexible manufacturing systems.

system, and possible actions that would narrow the gap between the two. The futurists on the council use those decisions to modify business strategy.

In the information age, the distinction between operations and executions is blurred at best. Organic structures depend on *teaming,* a concept popularized in the 1980s as companies began emulating Japanese experiences with quality circles, and more recently, as an essential component in the formation of work cells in flexible manufacturing. Teaming is an empowering strategy that gives workers greater autonomy in how their work is performed and evaluated. How individual work is designed constitutes the lowest level—the microstructure, which is the fabric of the value stream.

4.2.6.3 Work Process Structure   Work design depends on such factors as volume, variety, capital intensity, the degree of customer involvement, and the knowledge requirement of workers. Figure 4-4 illustrates how knowledge and customization requirements are related to the structure of work. The need for more complex structures parallels an increase in either requirement. The lower left-hand region of Figure 4-4, or quadrant I, depicts a work domain with standardized products and low intellectual capital. This quadrant typifies a broad range of production scenarios and can be further refined by mapping customization against knowledge within the cell.

Standardized Flow   At the extreme left-hand position are highly **standardized flow** processes, such as assembly-line operations, characterized by low skill (knowledge) levels, repetitive work, low product variety, and large batch quantities. Processes located here

Make to Stock

Make to Assembly

Intermediate Flow

Cellular Manufacturing

Just in Time

Flexible Flow

Job Shops

Continuous Processes

Automation

High-Tech Services

are typically **make-to-stock** or **make-to-assembly** applications, or in the case of pure services, jobs with few tasks such as ticket takers and carwash attendants.

Progressing to the right in quadrant I, toward quadrant II, one would find **intermediate flow** configurations, such as **cellular manufacturing** and **just-in-time** pull scheduling systems. Some cellular designs would be positioned in the upper right-hand corner of the quadrant, where the knowledge requirement is somewhat higher to accommodate increased flexibility and multitasking. Teamwork is sometimes encouraged, either as a means to improve processes as with quality circles, or as an integral part of the work design, such as flexible work cells.

Quadrant II includes **flexible flow** and process-oriented work, where the knowledge content is typically low, customization is high, volume is low, capital intensity is minimal, and flexibility is high. Examples are telephone order takers, customer service representatives, and **job shops**. Employees in this domain must know how to deal effectively with small variations in customer needs.

Quadrant III represents work that is low in customization and high in knowledge content. This domain includes **continuous processes** and those dependent on **automation**, such as pulp and paper mills, oil refineries, and food processing plants. **High-tech services** such as airline pilots, heart surgeons, and attorneys are classified in quadrant III. Such knowledge-intensive workers must have a thorough understanding of their particular technologies and be able to respond quickly to changing requirements so as not to jeopardize quality, investment, or safety. When teams are employed, they are usually self-managed and consult with external specialists as the need arises.

Quadrant IV is representative of the most complex structures. This is where experts from different functional areas work together in close coordination with peers who represent customers' interests. Work in this region is highly customized and knowledge intensive. Examples are concurrent engineering, customized telecommunications services, and quality function deployment. To illustrate activity in this quadrant, Aughton and Brien[22] described a case in which the new CEO of a rural hospital engaged the local community in the hospital's strategic planning process. Key individuals from the hospital and community leaders were invited to participate in a search conference to determine future directions geared to customer concerns. As an example, the search conference revealed that many residents wanted treatment in their own homes. After a home care program was underway, the CEO got a pleasant surprise. Overheads decreased, patient loyalty improved, and patient leakage—an industry measure of defections—was significantly reduced.

4.2.7 Lattice Structure

Lattice Structure

Array

A lattice structure matches resources with needs.

With a lattice structure, customers can pull services from providers.

A **lattice structure** matches resources with needs, using a business array framework similar to Figure 4-5.[23] An **array** is a matrix in which the rows represent customer needs and the columns represent the providers of services. This is the marketing analogue of a pull system in manufacturing. The idea is to shift the focus from a product orientation (pushing services at customers) to a market orientation (permitting customers to pull services from providers). The pull philosophy is introduced by consolidating the outputs from several suppliers into bundles. In the process, the system boundaries of individual suppliers become blurred as these systems merge into larger complex supersystems. Setting up and

---

[22] Aughton and Brien, "Applying Open Systems Theory," 9–10.

[23] Mills, D. Quinn, and G. Bruce Friesen. "Emerging Business Realities: Organizing for Value in a Wired World (Part Two)." *Consulting to Management* 11, no. 1 (May 2000): 3–17.

FIGURE 4-5 A Business Array

Customer Intention	Bankers			Brokers		Agents
	Accounts	**Credit**	**Mortgages**	**Advice**	**Mutual Funds**	**Insurance**
Managing for retirement	X	X	X	X	X	X
Moving to a new city	X	X	X	X	X	X
Starting a business	X	X		X	X	X
Raising a family	X	X	X	X	X	X
Managing daily life	X	X		X	X	

X, relevant to the intention; ▮, bundle of services.

Traditional Product Markets

SOURCE: Reprinted with permission from D. Quinn Mills, and G. Bruce Friesen. "Emerging Business Realities: Organizing for Value in a Wired World (Part Two)." *Consulting to Management* 11, no. 1 (May 2000): p. 5.

managing this monolithic structure so customers can seamlessly get one-stop shopping requires dramatically different customer–supplier and supplier–supplier relationships.

To show how this concept might work in practice, Figure 4-5 is an example of a business array for the finance industry. This array was constructed by first considering the types of customers and their needs, and second, the services required to fill each need. Each column represents a different company (or companies), and each row depicts a unique bundle of services or products that have been designed specifically to fill the need. Managing the delivery of these bundles requires a new kind of organization— a lattice structure—that enables companies to work together with unity of purpose.

Structure does not guarantee quality.

4.2.8 Structure and Quality

In Chapter 3, we discussed how the sand cone model explains a prescribed sequence that companies must follow to build capabilities. This model teaches that a capability in cost cannot be established until other capabilities (quality, dependability, flexibility, and agility) are in place first. Therefore, making efficiencies that stress a management priority is unlikely to succeed until all personnel have been given the knowledge and encouragement to work together to improve those capabilities that must be built first.

The key to effectiveness is through people.

Structure does not guarantee quality. Once capabilities are in place, value becomes a design issue and, if flawed, trying to make a value stream operate at peak efficiency will only result in intensifying the creation of waste. Thomas Edison once said, "Being busy does not always mean real work. . . . Seeming to do is not doing." Management

Efficiency

Effectiveness

Roving Leadership

should ensure busy people are doing the right things. According to Peter Drucker, **efficiency** is doing the thing right, but effectiveness is doing the right thing.

DePree advised that the key to **effectiveness** is through people, and it can be achieved by enabling others to reach their full potential and by encouraging **roving leadership**.[24] A roving leader is a person whom others will follow in abnormal situations. Different situations demand different talents, so one person may emerge as the leader in one situation, and someone else in another. In a particular crisis, the one who rises to the challenge and takes charge may be a surprise to everyone.

DePree's principles can be applied by setting up a supportive structure that enlists the workforce to help improve the effectiveness of work. In most organizations, incremental improvements occur through the use of a team structure to solve problems at the work interface. This is a bottom-up approach to improvement, and often relies on the emergence of roving leadership to do much of the fact finding and trouble shooting. In Six Sigma companies, improvement teams are formalized, goal driven, and accountable to management for changes that will improve effectiveness and efficiencies at the same time.

Breakthrough Improvements

Improvement takes place in small increments or as quantum breakthroughs. The enterprise engineering model, discussed in Chapter 3, makes the case that competitive organizations will do both. **Breakthrough improvements** normally originate from the top, and therefore, require a structure that will enable fresh thinking of the type embodied in Hammer and Champy's business process reengineering (BPR) methodology.[25] Incremental improvements occur by working *in* the system, whereas breakthroughs require working *on* the system. As we discussed in Chapter 3, reinventing value streams, taking advantage of white-space opportunities, and having a vision for the future are responsibilities of top management who formulate strategy and draft business plans. The structure to facilitate this must support a strong strategic planning cycle and the top leadership should be willing to accept that their primary role is forward planning, not current operations.

BPR is a revolutionary approach and once changes are implemented, the effects can be immediate, whereas continuous improvements are steady and slow. The organization structure should be able to effectively integrate and enable bottom-up and top-down change inducers. Patell[26] warns that tension between continuous improvement (a foundation capability) and radical reengineering (BPR) can potentially sabotage a company's entire quality effort. There are eight key ideas behind BPR:

1. Discard organizational and operational principles and procedures, and create entirely new ones.
2. Start from scratch with a clean sheet of paper.
3. Forget how work was done.
4. Old job titles and organizational arrangements no longer matter.
5. How people and the company did things yesterday is irrelevant.
6. Reengineering cannot be evolutionary—it must be revolutionary.
7. The process cannot be carried out in small, cautious steps.
8. Reengineering is an all-or-nothing proposition.

---

[24]DePree, Max. *Leadership Is an Art.* New York: Doubleday, 2004 (45–52), 1989.

[25]Hammer, Michael, and James Champy. *Reengineering the Corporation: A Manifesto for Business Revolution.* New York: HarperBusiness, 1993.

[26]"The Straining of Quality." Economist 334 (1897), January. 14, 1995, London (55–56).

4.3 QUALITY LEADERSHIP

Management commitment and leadership are both important to the success of QIM. Although sometimes used interchangeably, the two attributes are not the same. Every quality leader needs to be totally committed, but every committed manager is not necessarily a leader. A committed manager can establish priorities, distribute resources, and start new programs. However, doing those things does not invoke loyal followers. A leader is able to influence feelings, provoke creativity, arouse enthusiasm, build consensus, strike compromise, negotiate buy-in, communicate effectively, and create a team spirit.

Commitment

Deming understood the difference between **commitment** (points 1 and 2) and leadership (point 7), but in practice the distinction is not always clear. For example, some formal quality assessment schemes include leadership as an important criterion, but then use broad measures, ranging from commitment to corporate citizenship, and only indirectly try to assess leadership skills through employee feedback.

Responsibilities

According to Peter Scholtes,[27] poor leadership accounts for more than 95% of an organization's problems. Substantial improvements are therefore possible if those who are in charge can be helped to do a better job at leading. The primary **responsibilities** of a business leader, as depicted in Figure 4-6, are

- To provide energy and continuing momentum to the organization
- To create, promote, and defend a set of corporate values

FIGURE 4-6 Responsibilities of a Business Leader

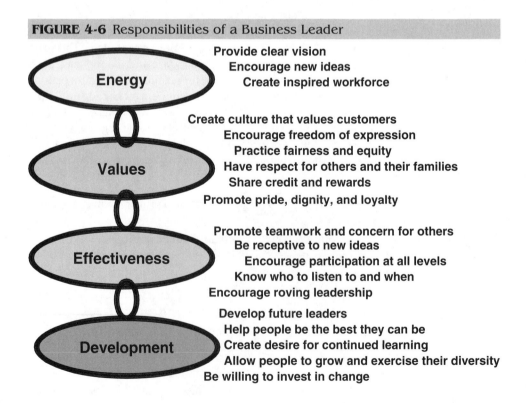

Energy
- Provide clear vision
- Encourage new ideas
- Create inspired workforce

Values
- Create culture that values customers
- Encourage freedom of expression
- Practice fairness and equity
- Have respect for others and their families
- Share credit and rewards
- Promote pride, dignity, and loyalty

Effectiveness
- Promote teamwork and concern for others
- Be receptive to new ideas
- Encourage participation at all levels
- Know who to listen to and when
- Encourage roving leadership

Development
- Develop future leaders
- Help people be the best they can be
- Create desire for continued learning
- Allow people to grow and exercise their diversity
- Be willing to invest in change

---

[27]Scholtes, Peter R., *The Leader's Handbook: Making Things Happen, Getting Things Done,* New York: McGraw-Hill, 1997 (ix, 83).

FIGURE 4-7 FedEx Leadership Attributes

Criteria Used for Management Selection

Charisma	The ability to instill in others a sense of mission, faith, respect, and trust
Consideration	A genuine interest in his or her followers—coaching, advising, and teaching people who need it; ready and willing to give assistance to newcomers; **active listening skills**
Stimulation	The ability to encourage others to think about old problems in new ways, and to use reasoning and evidence, supported by hard data
Courage	A willingness to stick to his or her beliefs and convictions, even if unpopular
Dependability	Keeps commitments, and accepts responsibility for actions taken and mistakes made
Flexibility	Ability to work in a changing environment; ability to deal with more than one problem at once
Integrity	A consistent role model, doing what is morally and ethically right, and never abusing management privileges
Judgment	The capacity to reach sound and objective decisions using logic, analysis, and analytical comparison
Respect for Others	Respect for the opinions or work of others, regardless of their status or position

SOURCE: Row, Heath. "The Nine Faces of Leadership." Copyright © 2005 Gruner and Jahr US Publishing, first published in *Fast Company Magazine* page 52, February 1998. Reprinted with permission.

- To ensure the organization is effective in carrying out its mission and operates in the best interest of its stakeholders
- To promote an environment that creates growth opportunities for the business and for each employee

It is the leadership who sets the tone, establishes priorities, creates the culture, and engenders morale. Recognizing the importance of good leadership, some companies are now using attributes, such as the ones for FedEx shown in Figure 4-7,[28] as criteria to screen applicants for senior management positions.

What does it take to be a good leader? To try and understand this, we first turn to a related question—Why do people follow a leader?

4.3.1 Why People Follow a Leader

Guillen and Gonzalez[29] suggested that all human motivation is based on a quest for outcomes that are good and that dimensions of leadership arise from three different definitions of the word "good:" useful, pleasant, and moral. This is illustrated in Figure 4-8.

---

[28]Row, Heath. "The 9 Faces of Leadership." *Fast Company, Magazine* no. 13 (February 1998): 52.

[29]Guillen, Manuel, and Tomas F. Gonzalez. "The Ethical Dimension of Managerial Leadership: Two Illustrative Case Studies in TQM." *Journal of Business Ethics* 34, no. 3/4 (December 2001): 175–89.

FIGURE 4-8 Why People Follow a Leader

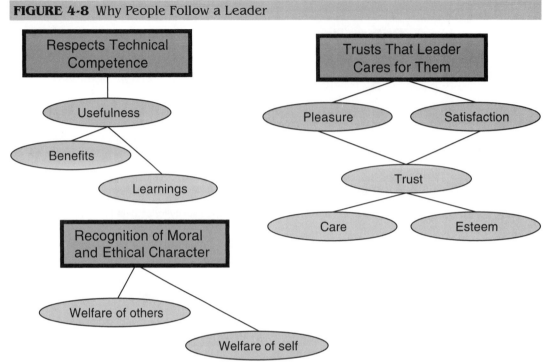

SOURCE: Information based on Manuel Guillen, and Tomas F. Gonzalez. "The Ethical Dimension of Managerial Leadership: Two Illustrative Case Studies in TQM." *Journal of Business Ethics,* 34, no. 3/4, December 2001: 175–189.

People follow a charismatic leader because the association makes them feel good.

Pleasure Trust

Psychoemotive Motivations

Self-Realization

Self-Esteem

Social Needs

People follow a leader due to superior skills and knowledge.

Ethics

Fairness

Defining good as useful, some people follow a leader because they trust the leader's technical competence. The follower does not have to admire the leader, but will follow their lead due to an acknowledgment that the leader possesses superior skills and knowledge. The leader may be seen as the source for useful personal gain, such as learning or rewards. These good-as-useful benefits fit the basic and security needs of Maslow's hierarchy.

When people follow a leader for the purpose of **pleasure**, personality traits, such as charisma, are important. The followers' motivations are sometimes described as **psychoemotive motivations,** meaning that the followers sincerely believe the leader cares about them and will genuinely work to build a relationship based on trust. Motivation based on pleasure satisfies Maslow's **self-realization, self-esteem,** and **social needs**.

The third reason why people follow someone is that they recognize in the leader a moral authority. Morality has to do with right, good, and **ethics**—and includes such virtues as **fairness, integrity, loyalty, determination, courage,** and **responsibility**. Other virtues, such as **generosity, humility,** and **humor**, could also be added to the list. This class of followers cares deeply about outcomes that are consistent with their personal moral standards, even when they conflict with the **useful** and pleasant. Moral virtues are not found on Maslow's scale of **basic and security needs** because morality focuses not only on self, but also on the welfare of others. A manager who possesses attributes at all three levels—**technical competence**, psychoemotive traits, and moral virtues—is capable of inspiring trustworthiness and loyalty. This explains why one person can achieve remarkable improvements in

Integrity

Loyalty

Determination

Courage

Responsibility

Generosity

Humility

Humor

Useful

Basic and Security
Needs

Technical
Competence

People follow a
leader because of
moral authority.

---

productivity using the same workforce that was only mediocre under the direction of another.

4.3.2 Leadership Skills

A research study investigated the leadership styles of 1,200 managers from companies, institutions, governments, military commands, and professional associations.[30] It was concluded that the critical leadership skills can be taught through proper training and experience. The research found that leadership skills fall into the following categories:

- *A Sense of Timing.* Leaders know when and how to decisively intervene in a problem situation.
- *Ability to Enable.* Leaders can bring the best out in people. They know how to offer encouragement, create opportunities, and be a mentor. Leaders can motivate others to set and reach lofty goals.
- *Advocate for Change.* Leaders are good listeners, knowing where and when to seek advice. They are receptive to new ideas and know how to adapt decision options to changing situations.
- *Vision.* Leaders can recognize potential and spot opportunities. They have the ability to champion a cause and persuade others to buy-in. Leaders have a positive outlook; they see problems as merely stumbling blocks or as challenges to be overcome in the quest for greatness.
- *Empathy.* Leaders are sensitive to opposing viewpoints. They have the ability to focus in complex situations, to build consensus, and to resolve conflicts.

An excellent summary of quality leadership was given by Jo Ann Brumit, CEO and Chairman of KARLEE, a recipient of the Malcom Baldrige National Quality Award: "Anyone can be a leader if he or she chooses to serve others first, is humble, and has a heart full of thanksgiving." Brumit explained that these values enable a leader to provide encouragement, to recognize value in others, and to deeply care about those who look to him or her for direction.[31]

4.4 QUALITY DECISION MAKING

4.4.1 Decision Making Is a Process

Decision making is a
process that can be
analyzed and
improved.

What constitutes a "good" decision? How can one tell a good (as in quality) decision from a bad (defective) one? Everyone makes decisions. Some are critical and the outcomes can mean the difference between life or death, war or peace, fortune or poverty, and success or failure. Others are not so significant, but the outcomes are still important to the purpose of the decision—such as, What will I have for breakfast? Where will my kids attend school? Who should be promoted to fill the new position at the plant? Decision making is a process and can be analyzed using many of the same tools

---

[30]Smith, August W. "Leadership Is a Living System. Learning Leaders and Organizations." *Human Systems Management* 16, no. 4 (1997): 277–84.

[31]Baldrige National Quality Program. *Baldrige: Recognizing Role Model Practices of World Class Organizations.* CEO Issue Sheet. Gaithersburg, MD: National Institute of Standards and Technology, Technology Administration, U.S. Department of Commerce, Fall 2001. Also available online at www.quality.nist.gov/Issue _Sheet_Model.htm (Accessed March 25, 2005).

FIGURE 4-9 The Anatomy of Decision Making

Analytical

- Balancing a checkbook
- Computing safety stock
- Solving a linear program
- Computing internal rate of return
- Calculating fuel consumption
- Ordering replenishment stock using reordering rules
- Producing a forecast using time-series techniques

Naturalistic

Programmed

- Navigating the route from home to work
- Phoning a friend or colleague
- Driving a car or riding a bicycle
- Operating a machine
- Administering CPR

Nonprogrammed

- Selecting a new piece of equipment
- Troubleshooting a problem
- Performing a cause–effect analysis
- Making a major purchase
- Administering CPR
- Planning a vacation
- Making strategic choices
- Disciplining an employee
- Producing a forecast based on judgment and qualitative factors

- Repairing a machine
- Setting up a process
- Designing a part
- Running a meeting

- Collecting and analyzing data sets
- Applying and interpreting SPC tools
- Conducting a design of experiment
- Hiring, dismissing, and evaluating staff

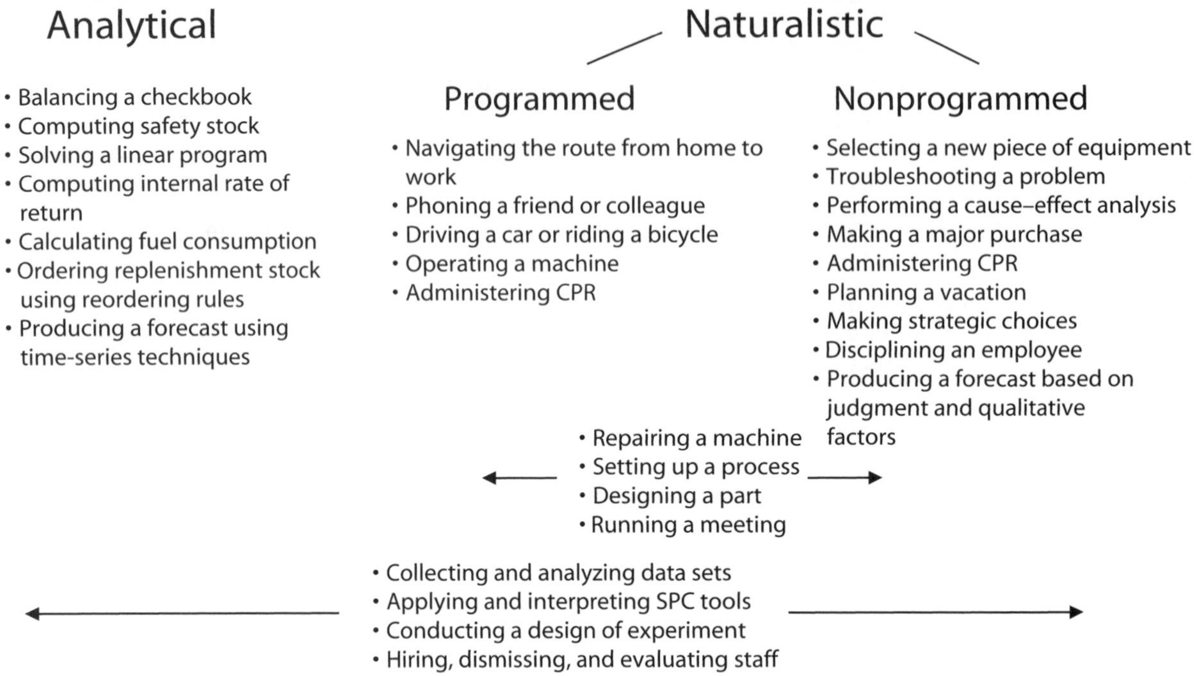

Decision making capabilities can be developed with practice.

Cognitive Process

Learning

Expertise

employed to improve production processes. How people make decisions is a **cognitive process** and not well understood because human behavior is variable and unpredictable, and the outcomes are difficult to measure. Relying on individual expertise and beliefs, decisions are personal. Unlike most production processes, decision making has a built-in improvement mechanism called **learning**. This takes place as experience grows. Eventually, learning becomes **expertise**, which in turn improves decision making. These skills can also be developed with practice.

Experienced decision makers such as Yoshihide Nakamura, deputy president of Sony Corporation's Core Technology and Network Company, have developed guiding principles to help them make important business decisions. Mr. Nakamura asks himself, Is it good for the customer? Is it ethical? Does it make money? Does it help to improve Sony's brand name? Is it legal?[32] Rotarians the world over are taught to apply the four-way test to decision making: Is it the truth? Is it fair to all concerned? Will it build good-will and better friendships? Is it beneficial to all concerned? Principles such as these provide a framework that should lead to consistency and more predictable outcomes. Individual skills necessary to follow the guidelines are the quintessence of good decision making. Many of these skills can be taught.

4.4.2 The Anatomy of Decision Making

Figure 4-9 illustrates the anatomical breakdown of the decision process, with examples of everyday decisions made in the business and personal lives of individuals. Decisions

---

[32]Beamish, Paul W. "Sony's Yoshihide Nakamura on Structure and Decision Making." *The Academy of Management Executive* 13, no. 4 (November 1999): 12–16.

Analytical decision making is important to management by fact.

Managing by Fact

Analytical Decision Making

Satisficing

occur at two levels: analytical and naturalistic. At the analytical level, decisions are based on deductive reasoning, probability theory, and the application of formulae. Grounded in solid mathematical and statistical theories, analytical models can help the decision maker reach objective conclusions using data relevant to the issues at hand. Such methodologies are very important to **managing by fact**. At the operations level, the analytical tool alone is sometimes sufficient provided the data collection is reliable, consistent, and answers the right questions. For example, an investment opportunity might be justified on the basis of a well-executed engineering economic analysis, or a targeted level of service might be sustained by consistently applying a set of inventory replenishment rules.

This text only peripherally covers tools that assist in **analytical decision making**. For in-depth coverage, the student is advised to consult the abundant literature available in operations research and statistics. Analytical tools include simulation, queuing theory, linear programming, Markov processes, analysis of variance, and design of experiments. These can help the decision maker better understand the decision environment, and analyze hypothesized scenarios, perform "what if?" analyses, and develop optimum policies.

Most important decisions in quality management are naturalistic. With naturalistic decision making, the object is to reach a decision that is good enough rather than one that is optimal. This is called *satisficing*. Even when deterministic outcomes result from the use of analytical tools, converting the information into effective actions often requires some decisions in the naturalistic domain. Although a mathematical or statistical model can be invaluable for working on a process, it cannot identify which process to study, how to study it, or by whom, or even how to interpret information in a changing context of the work environment. The analytical model cannot provide guidance on how to select from a number of alternatives or how to evaluate the trade-offs. Making decisions in complex, unstructured, or pressure situations requires naturalistic capabilities, such as perception, judgment, and intuition. There are two types of naturalistic decisions—programmed and nonprogrammed.

4.4.3 Programmed Decision Making

Programmed decisions are actions that are predetermined.

Programmed decisions are actions that are taken in circumstances where the outcomes have been predetermined. When certain situations arise, the decision maker has been programmed, through repetition, training, familiarity, and experience, to respond in a certain way. As an example, by the time an operator has followed the assembly steps for the 10,000th production unit, little conscious thought is given to what needs to be done and in what order. The steps occur naturally. When the whistle blows, the worker heads for home, practically unaware of all the little decisions that must be made—which street, whether to stop on red lights, and so on—to arrive safely home. However, a number of subliminal decisions (programmed responses) had to occur for the person to succeed in navigating the desired route. Programmed decision making is a product of training and experience. As a result of expertise, the decision maker is often unaware that decisions are being made.

4.4.4 Nonprogrammed Decision Making

Capabilities can be learned to help make better nonprogrammed decisions.

Klein[33] conducted research over a twenty five-year period to learn how people make nonprogrammed decisions in crisis situations such as firefighting, police work, and emergency rooms. From these studies, Klein identified the nine capabilities (which he called powers) shown in Figure 4-10, and described on the following pages.

---

[33]Klein, Gary. *Sources of Power: How People Make Decisions.* Cambridge, MA: The MIT Press, 1998, 330 pages.

FIGURE 4-10 How People Make Nonprogrammed Decisions

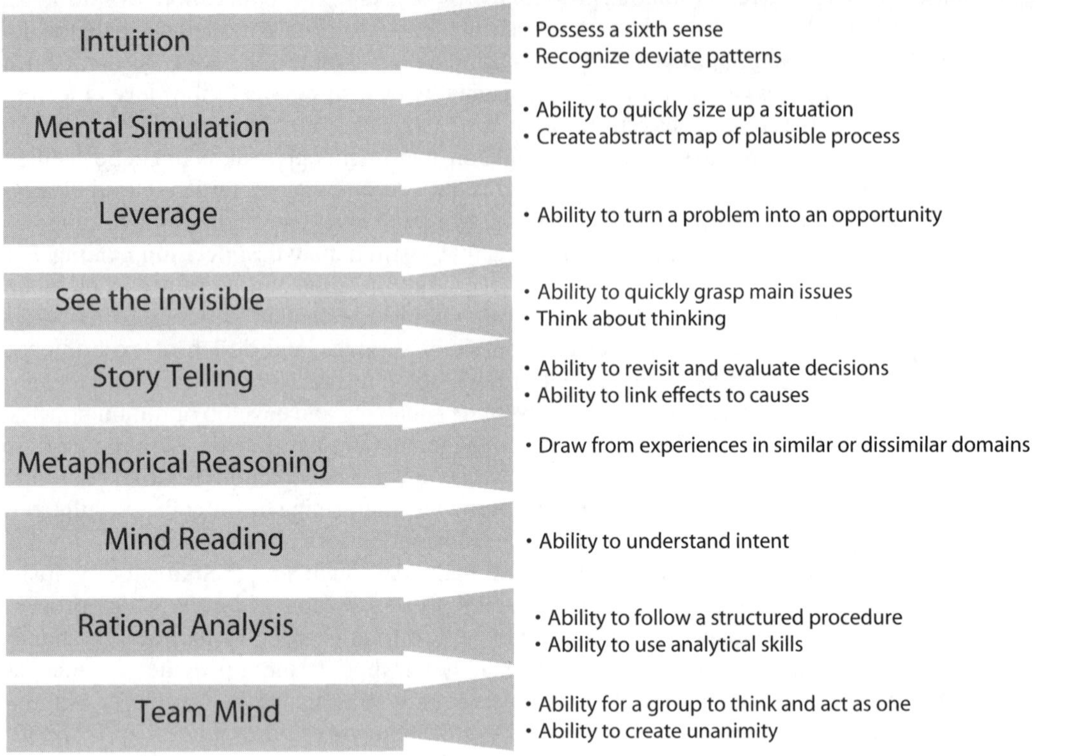

Intuition	• Possess a sixth sense • Recognize deviate patterns
Mental Simulation	• Ability to quickly size up a situation • Create abstract map of plausible process
Leverage	• Ability to turn a problem into an opportunity
See the Invisible	• Ability to quickly grasp main issues • Think about thinking
Story Telling	• Ability to revisit and evaluate decisions • Ability to link effects to causes
Metaphorical Reasoning	• Draw from experiences in similar or dissimilar domains
Mind Reading	• Ability to understand intent
Rational Analysis	• Ability to follow a structured procedure • Ability to use analytical skills
Team Mind	• Ability for a group to think and act as one • Ability to create unanimity

Intuition

Sixth Sense

Pattern Matching

4.4.4.1 Intuition   **Intuition** is what some call the **sixth sense**. People are not born with intuition. It develops with experience. An intuitive person has mastered the art of recognizing a pattern, without being able to explain why or how. For example, a person who does a repetitive job will, over time, develop a sixth sense for how the process should behave. If something out of the ordinary occurs, the experienced employee will sense it long before the change shows up in process output. **Pattern matching** is based on the ability to recognize what is familiar. These skills can be taught by expanding a person's experience base. Training programs that expose participants to problems of increasing complexity, presented in the context of realistic scenarios, have proven to be effective in building intuitive skills. Intuition is an important decision making skill for quality improvement. For example, properly interpreting and acting on process control charts depends on the intuitive ability to spot patterns that deviate from the norm.

Mental Simulation

Abstract Thinking

Plausibility

Mental Imagery

4.4.4.2 Mental Simulation   **Mental simulation** is a type of **abstract thinking**. The decision maker imagines people and objects in a certain way, and then transforms them to a final picture that places them in a different context from the start. Mental simulation is the ability to quickly size up a situation, place it in a familiar context, and then draw on skill and experience to test its **plausibility** by using **mental imagery** to visualize a sequence of events that could have led to the current situation or to some future condition. In this process, the decision maker is mentally ferried from a known starting state to some future target state.

As an example of how mental simulation works, suppose a quality problem shows up in a food processing plant: contaminants are found in the product at the packaging line. The process engineer creates mental images of all the steps in the process leading up to the packaging operation. He tries to get a mental picture of where the contaminants could have been introduced. As a result, the problem is quickly traced to a leak in an upstream hydraulic system.

There is a major weakness of mental simulation. Humans have a tendency to ignore contradictory evidence. The mind can conveniently argue against anything that challenges an interpretation or conclusion. Another limitation is that mental simulation cannot deal with complexity. When the pieces of a puzzle get too complicated, the human brain has trouble creating a reliable action sequence.

Leverage

Choke Points

4.4.4.3 Leverage   Leverage is the ability to take something small and turn it into something big, and perhaps invent an ingenious solution on the spot. Leverage is knowing how to exploit a situation, capitalize on strengths, turn problems into opportunities, and spot weaknesses. Using leverage, a decision maker can sometimes identify **choke points**—factors that inhibit good decisions. By knowing the choke points, decision makers can often anticipate trouble before it occurs and take timely preventative action.

The following is an example of leverage in action. In a certain plant, the rumor mill has been spreading stories of downsizing and possible layoffs. Management can elect to do nothing and take the risk of reinforcing fears that are growing daily, or the issue could be defused by meeting with employees in small groups to reassure them and communicate the truth about any future plans.

4.4.4.4 Ability to See the Invisible   Decision making is about selecting the best from a choice of alternatives. Experts can sometimes see things others cannot, and readily size up a situation. They are capable of recognizing patterns and also anomalies—something that is conspicuous by its absence. Being able to see the invisible means detecting fine discriminations, understanding personal limitations, and possessing the

Metacognition

power of what psychologists refer to as **metacognition**—the ability to think about thinking. A metacognitive person is a deep thinker who looks beyond the obvious.

Judgment

Tacit Knowledge

The power to see the invisible is a skill that can be taught, yet is rarely emphasized in company training courses. In-house training usually focuses on tools and procedures, and pays little attention to perception and **judgment**. Training programs that only stress the one-way communication of knowledge from instructor to student miss out on the potential of tapping into **tacit knowledge** that resides in the head of a seasoned employee.

Deming claimed that tacit knowledge is an organization's most valuable resource. The irony is that many organizations either fail to recognize it or choose to ignore it. Sadly, when layoffs, resignations, or retirements occur, it is common for companies to let personnel walk out the door taking decades of expertise with them. No one bats an eyelid, but if any one of those employees tried to carry a company-owned computer off the premises, that person would get no further than the security gate!

Knowledge Engineering

Fortunately, technology provides a solution. An emerging discipline called **knowledge engineering**, a spin-off from computer science, provides the framework for capturing untapped tacit knowledge. Knowledge engineers can codify the organization's knowledge base in a form that can be easily integrated into internal training programs.

Knowledge engineering can capture and codify an organization's tacit knowledge.

Story Telling

4.4.4.5 Story Telling   Story telling can provide a vicarious experience for someone who was not present when an actual event occurred. A story can teach a lesson, preserve values, and help people understand situations and relationships. Stories can improve decision making by broadening the experience base. This especially works well in a team environment. Recounting an experience takes the decision maker back to the situation, where the decision can be analyzed and its effects can possibly be linked to causes. Through the medium of a story, the human mind can analyze events using such questions as, "what could I have done differently?" and, "if I had acted differently, what would the consequences have been?"

4.4.4.6 Metaphors and Analogues An **analogue** is an example that is similar to the decision at hand. A company wanting to predict the demand for a new service may rely on its history with a similar-type service and customers with comparable demographics to those in the proposed market. The existing (known) service as an analogue can be the basis for predicting demand in the future (unknown) environment.

Analogue

The following analogue has been used to emphasize why training is important to empowerment programs such as job enrichment.[34] Suppose a task requires the physical loading of 50-pound bags onto pallets. It would be unreasonable to expect an unfit 120-pound worker to be productive wielding heavy bags, and certainly not on a sustained basis. However, the benefits of sending that person to a gym for the proper exercise regimen are obvious. Eventually, the worker's physical capabilities can match job requirements. Similarly, when job responsibilities are expanded intellectually, the mental capabilities of personnel filling those jobs need to be conditioned to match the new requirements.

Metaphor

A **metaphor** is drawn from a domain that is dramatically different from the situation at hand. Metaphorical reasoning structures one's thinking and creates a situational awareness. Suppose a team is not working well due to one team member who is particularly difficult. To suggest a remedy, the section manager might use a metaphor such as we should remove the bad apple before it spoils the bunch.

In another example, a human resources director was promoting a revised policy requiring the use of across-the-board standard performance measures. In defense of a more equitable policy, he explained that the existing practice might be like the engine telling the caboose that the train's performance will be measured by which of them reaches the station first!

A person receiving instructions must know the intent to properly carry them out.

4.4.4.7 Mind Reading Whenever anyone tries to communicate with another person, whether to implement a new procedure, or assign a task, the person on the receiving end must interpret the intent of the communiqué. The receiver must read the sender's mind; how well depends on his or her listening skills. What a person hears is not necessarily the same as what the sender intended. **Mind reading** is not easy, and it does not come naturally. However, both parties to the communication can facilitate a **meeting of the minds**. The person initiating a request can help by trying to explain clearly why the request is being made and the expected outcomes. The person receiving the request can listen intently, trying to understand what that person really wants.

Mind Reading

Meeting of the Minds

Intent

In communicating **intent**, there are seven types of information that are important.[35] All seven are not necessarily relevant to every situation, but the list can be useful in providing a mental checklist. This is particularly helpful for good teamwork.

---

[34]Job enrichment gives the employee greater autonomy by adding decision-making responsibilities.

[35]Klein, Gary A. "A Script for the Commander's Intent Statement." In *Science of Command and Control: Part III: Coping with Change,* edited by A. H. Levis and I. S. Levis. Fairfax, VA: AFCEA International Press, 1994.

> ## INFORMATION RELEVANT TO COMMUNICATING INTENT
>
> **1.** The purpose of the task or request
> **2.** The objective of the task or request
> **3.** The sequence of steps to be followed in the action plan
> **4.** The rationale for the plan or decision
> **5.** The key decisions that may have to be made in following the plan or performing the task
> **6.** Unwanted outcomes and their consequences
> **7.** Any constraints and other considerations

The ability to read one's mind depends on familiarity with that person, as well as the clarity with which that person has been successful in communicating intent. When someone issues an order or makes a request, they cannot anticipate every possible contingency. However, the person expected to carry out the instructions must know the intent to properly adjust to any changing conditions that might arise.

Rational Analysis

4.4.4.8 Rational Analysis **Rational analysis** is a systematic approach to decision making, also known as the scientific method. There are many forms of rational analysis in practice. The ones most widely used to solve quality-related problems are the PDCA cycle, which is discussed in Chapter 7, and the DMAIC tactics, discussed in Chapter 9. The skills used in rational analysis combine naturalistic and analytical decision making to make realistic improvements that can be implemented.

4.4.4.9 Acquiring a Team Mind Team decision making differs from the process a person goes through when making a decision alone. To be effective, teams need to act and think as an entity—to develop a **team mind**. The following characteristics distinguish a team mind from the mind of an individual:

Team Mind

Working Memory

- A team has the ability to store and process information for short periods of time in a **working memory**. When the team moves on to a new topic, the previous information is promptly discarded and replaced with information relevant to the current issue.

Long-Term Memory

- There are certain types of information that a team needs to retain permanently in **long-term memory** and be able to retrieve as required. Because a team's membership can be transient, it is important that more than one individual on the team possesses the knowledge and that there is a way to pass it on so knowledge is not lost.

Limited Attention Span

- Teams have a **limited attention span**, and they can typically focus well on one item at a time. Because a team is comprised of individuals with diverse opinions, it is sometimes a challenge to reach consensus on what topics are worthy of consuming valuable time.

Perceptual Filtering

- Information that is processed by teams passes through a **perceptual filtering** process. Teams usually act on secondhand information rather than through direct experience. This can introduce inaccuracies in the way the team members hear and process the information received.

Learning

- Like individuals, teams learn. Unlike individuals, the **learning** takes place in a mutually supportive environment where the group grows together. Teams learn such things as how to become more effective as a team, how to improve procedures, and how to increase its collective wisdom about some problem of mutual interest.

4.4.5 What Is a Poor Decision?

Poor consequences are different from poor decisions. Given the knowledge available, a high-quality decision can lead to a less than satisfactory result. Quality management terminology can be used to define a defective (poor) decision. A decision is defective if what is learned as a consequence of the decision would result in a different decision in a future similar situation. That is, a decision is the output of the decision process, and negative corrective feedback in the form of experiential learning is an outcome. If feedback results in a different decision (output) in the future, then the decision is a poor one. As in any process, if one can identify and remove the cause of poor decisions, the process will be improved and higher-quality decisions can be expected in the future.

Decision Bias

———

Decision makers are prone to use information that supports what they think they know.

———

4.4.5.1 Decision Bias   Why do people make poor decisions? In analytical decision making, poor decisions may be due to **decision biases** in either the way the decision makers think or the way they process the available information. Khaneman et al.[36] demonstrate that decision makers are prone to use available information that represents a problem situation, starting with what they think they know and then making adjustments, rather than approaching the problem objectively seeking the truth. When confronted with a problem, a decision maker will often formulate a hypothesis (i.e., form an opinion) based on personal expertise. Efforts will then be directed toward collecting data that will confirm the hypothesis, when perhaps more could be learned about the problem by seeking evidence that would refute it.

In this regard, we can learn from statistics. Good statistical practice favors designed experimentation leading to the rejection of hypotheses. In conducting such experiments, the risk of being wrong (that the hypothesis is actually true) is tightly controlled. This is what statisticians refer to as the type I or alpha error. In the alternative scenario (seeking support for the hypothesis), the risk of being wrong when the hypothesis is actually false is much more elusive and difficult to quantify. This is called the type II or beta error. In a well-conceived experiment, when the hypothesis is rejected, the decision maker has faith in the results, knowing that there is only the small alpha error risk of being wrong.

Latent Pathogens

———

Latent pathogens make the creation of errors inevitable.

———

4.4.5.2 Latent Pathogens   A second source of poor decision making is what Reason[37] calls **latent pathogens**. These are inherent flaws in the system that make the creation of errors inevitable. When a process error is made, the operator can receive the blame even though the error was actually brought about by such systemic factors as poor design, training, or procedures. Deming suggested that the percentage of errors due to systemic flaws could be as high as 96% and, because management owns the system, correcting its flaws are clearly management's responsibility.

4.4.5.3 Other Explanations   Klein[38] performed an extensive study to discover the reasons behind poor decision making. The conclusions were that poor decision outcomes

---

[36]Kahneman, Daniel P., Slovic, and Amos Tversky, eds. *Judgement under Uncertainty: Heuristics and Biases.* Cambridge: Cambridge University Press, 1982.

[37]Reason, James. *Human Error.* Cambridge: Cambridge University Press, 1990, 197–99.

[38]Klein, Gary. "Sources of Error in Naturalistic Decision Making Tasks." In Proceedings of the 37th annual meeting of the Human Factors and Ergonomics Society, 368–71 (1993).

were often due to one of three factors: lack of experience, lack of data, or de minimus error.

Lack of Experience

- **Lack of experience**. Experience does not always translate into expertise. For example, the decision domain can be so dynamic (e.g., the stock market) that there is not enough repetition to build typicality, human behavior is involved (which by nature is unpredictable), there is little chance for feedback, or the scope of the experience base is too small.[39]

Lack of Data

- **Lack of data**. It might seem surprising that poor decisions can result from lack of information because most organizations operate in a data-rich environment. Nevertheless, decision makers can be deprived of information that is relevant and timely. Filtering out the information that is pertinent to the problem, and doing so in a time frame that suits the urgency of the situation, can be challenging.

De Minimus Error

- The **de minimus error**. The de minimus error is the human tendency to explain away or minimize symptoms so they do not have to be taken seriously. It is human weakness to dismiss evidence that is inconvenient, to ignore early warning signs, to fail to recognize anomalies, or to not fully appreciate a sense of urgency.

4.5 TEAM BUILDING

4.5.1 Teaming Effectiveness

A *team* is a group of people working together to achieve a common goal. Using teams to make decisions, manage operations, and effect improvements has become the norm as a means for broadening participation and empowering the workforce. However, simply placing people in a group and calling it a team does not ensure it will work as one. Teamwork is a building process, and if it is to be productive, teaming must be a part of internal training. However, training alone is insufficient. Team building is the process of enabling the group to effectively and efficiently reach a common goal. It is a management issue, and as such, the most effective environment for team building is one in which management plays an active role, taking a genuine interest in and guiding activities. Applying this principle has proved to be one of the keys to success in Six Sigma companies.

Figure 4-11 depicts a team-building model based on developmental psychology.[40] Klein has expanded this model to include the following four dimensions of team development.[41]

Team effectiveness is the ability to manage an uninterrupted flow of ideas.

1. *Team Competencies.* Teams must rely on shared practices and routines. As teams mature, they develop the ability to work as one and become automatic in performing basic procedures.
2. *Team Identity.* Inexperienced teams have fragmentary identities, with each team member focusing on individual tasks rather than team requirements. In contrast, a mature team has an integrated identity, where the members identify themselves in relationship to the whole team.

---

[39]Maccoby, "Knowledge Workers," 56–58.
[40]Klein, Gary A., Caroline E. Zsambok, and Marvin L. Thordsen. "Team Decision Training: Five Myths and a Model," *Military Review* April 1993: 36–42.
[41]Klein, 1998 pages 240–246.

3. *Team Cognition.* As teams become more effective, they develop conceptual skills at four levels:

CONCEPTUAL SKILLS FOR TEAMS

1. How teams describe their goals and intents
2. To what degree the team shares a common understanding of a particular situation
3. The amount of effort a team spends looking ahead and anticipating problems
4. How the team manages uncertainty and is able to reconcile opposing viewpoints

---

4. *Team Metacognition.* The ability to manage the flow of ideas is a characteristic that differentiates a mature team from an immature one. A team does not know in advance who is going to show up at a meeting, who will be alert, what ideas will be presented, and how the ideas will coalesce. The team mind makes the whole greater than the sum of its parts, creates new and unexpected outcomes from all individual contributions, manages the flow, and keeps the discussion relevant.

5. *Team Self-Analysis.* It is important that during the building process teams periodically evaluate themselves to determine how well they are working together. In the early stages of team building, this step may require some assistance from an external expert. The following guidelines can help identify areas needing improvement:

Guidelines for Team Improvement

1. *Team Goals.* Are goals developed through a group process that ensures broad interaction and buy-in from each team member?

FIGURE 4-11 Team-Building Development Model

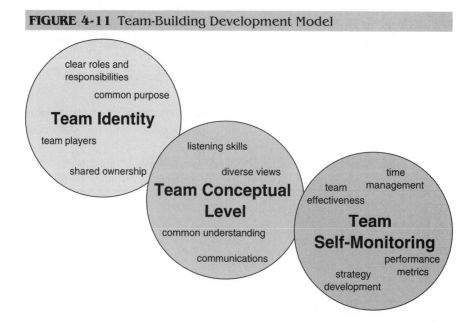

2. *Broad Participation.* Do all team members actively participate in the accomplishment of tasks, and are roles within the team equitably shared? Do all members actively participate in team decision making?

3. *Feedback.* Is feedback frequently asked for and freely given in the spirit of evaluating the team's performance and clarifying individual feelings and interests?

4. *Leadership.* Is leadership shared among team members, or do a few strong personalities dominate?

5. *Enthusiasm.* Do members willingly and enthusiastically contribute to team requirements?

6. *Problem Solving.* Are members encouraged to solve problems, critique the team effectiveness, and freely discuss team issues?

7. *Conflict Resolution.* How does the team deal with conflict? Are members encouraged to express negative feelings and to confront others within the group? Are opposing views welcome and dealt with in a sincere and respectful manner?

8. *Exploitation of Individual Potential.* Has the team fully recognized and used the resources that each member is capable of contributing to team goals. These include talents, skills, knowledge, and experiences.

9. *Risk Taking and Creativity.* Does the team encourage risk taking and creativity? When mistakes are made, and are they treated as a source of learning or reprimand?

4.5.2 Team-Building Culture

Team building is a process of creating a climate that encourages and values the contributions of all members. The combined energies of individual members are directed toward problem solving, task effectiveness, and the achievement of the team's goals. The team recognizes that it is not possible to separate the performance of one individual member from the performance of others. To maximize effectiveness the team must strive to meet the following conditions:[42]

1. Teamwork must be highly interdependent. Members must be committed to their goals and recognize that the only way to achieve them is by working together.

2. The team leader must have good people skills and be committed to the group. Team management should be a shared function, and each member should have the opportunity to exercise leadership when the needs of the group require their particular skills or experiences.

3. Each member is committed to the team and is willing to contribute.

4. A climate exists in which members feel relaxed, and can participate in open and direct communications.

5. Team members have mutual respect for each other.

6. Members are prepared to take risks, and are permitted to develop individual skills and abilities.

7. The team has clear goals that are understood by everyone and sets ambitious but achievable performance targets.

8. The roles of individual members are well defined.

---

[42]Francis, Dave, and Don Young, *Improving Work Groups: A Practical Manual for Team Building.* San Diego: University Associates, 1979, 261 pages.

9. Members can examine group and individual weaknesses and errors without engaging in personal attacks. This enables the team to learn from its experiences.

10. The team frequently evaluates its own performance to determine how it can improve.

11. The team has the capacity to create new ideas. This can come from within the group through interaction or by seeking input from outside sources. Good ideas are followed up. Creativity and risk taking are rewarded.

12. Each member believes they can influence the team's agenda. The feeling of trust and equality facilitates a culture of open and honest communications.

Team building occurs naturally when members work together on a task that all agree is important (e.g., when a crisis occurs). When a group organizes to achieve a common purpose, working relationships will emerge. An effective team will develop either formal or informal operating guidelines that will govern how the team will function, serve as a benchmark for evaluating performance, and facilitate individual cooperation and productivity. The team will learn how to manage conflict, critique itself without personal attack or anyone taking offense, and provide feedback that encourages individual commitment and participation.

SUMMARY OF LEARNING OBJECTIVES AND KEY OUTCOMES

1. *Differentiate between mechanistic and organic organization structures, and understand some theories that underlie organizational design.* A mechanistic structure is standardized with highly defined tasks, broken down into specialized work elements, and governed by numerous rules and a strict hierarchy of authority and central control. In comparison, an organic structure is flat, has few rules, is flexible, and emphasizes teamwork and worker participation in decision making. Contingency theory states that an organization will respond to contingencies and will go into a survival mode, adapting its structure to fit the situation. An alternative theory suggests that structures occur at three different levels and are influenced by the knowledge content of the work performed. Another theory ties changing societal values to organizational structures.

2. *Discuss the importance of value stream ownership in the context of being able to produce quality at the source.* A value stream represents the sequence of work activities required to convert a set of raw inputs into a product or service that satisfies a customer's need. To produce the product or service, the value stream usually requires contributions from numerous functional departments and support areas. Under a traditional vertical organization structure, no one person has management responsibility for the entire system (i.e., value stream). When individual departments try to maximize quality in their areas, the focus is narrow, and there is no way of assessing how their "improvements" will impact workstations further down the value stream. Quality needs to be integrated throughout the value chain if it is to be built into a product or service. This requires integrated leadership, which can best be achieved if one person is in charge—a system owner.

3. *Define a lattice structure.* A lattice structure matches resources with demand by offering one-stop shopping to customers. A customer is offered a bundle of services by consolidating the output from numerous suppliers.

4. *Discuss how structure supports continuous and breakthrough improvements.* To sustain competitiveness, an organization must achieve incremental continuous improvements and breakthrough improvements. The team structure at the bottom of the organization is normally used to generate incremental improvements. Breakthrough improvements are driven from the top and are often the result of achieving strategic objectives. Breakthroughs occur from initiatives that a company takes to reinvent itself, such as BPR or DFSS (Design for Six Sigma).

5. *Define good leadership.* One way to define leadership is from the perspective of those who choose to follow. There are three main reasons why people follow a leader: they might perceive benefits by following someone with acknowledged superior technical skills, they may trust that the leader genuinely cares for their well-being, or they may recognize the leader's moral authority. A good leader is an enabler, a change advocate, a visionary, empathetic, and has a sense of timing.

6. *Differentiate between analytical and naturalistic decision making.* Decisions are based on either analytical or naturalistic skills. Analytical decisions are based on deductive reasoning, probability theory, and the application of formulae that are usually designed to produce an optimal solution. Naturalistic decisions are made in complex situations where the aim is to produce a satisficing solution that is workable and, rather than being the best, is good enough.

7. *Demonstrate an understanding of naturalistic decision making, and differentiate between good and poor decisions.* Naturalistic decision making is a cognitive process with a built-in improvement mechanism called "learning" that can be divided into programmed and nonprogrammed decisions. Programmed decisions are made at the subconscious level, and result from experience in making routine repetitive decisions. Nonprogrammed decisions can be improved through the development of skills in nine capability areas: intuition, mental simulation, leverage, being able to see the invisible, story telling, using analogues and metaphors, mind reading, rational analysis, and acquiring a team mind. A poor decision is defined retroactively. If what was learned as a result of the decision would lead to a different one in the future, the decision is said to have been defective. Decision makers should be guarded against the penchant to use information that supports what they think they know, rather than honestly and actively seeking the truth. Poor decisions can result from too little experience, data that lacks relevance or timeliness, or application of the de minimus principle.

8. *Describe the essential elements for effective team building.* Team building is a process through which a climate is created that encourages and values the contributions of all members. Individuals on a team must learn to function as one—to develop a team mind. Team effectiveness can be achieved by emphasizing unity, conceptual skills, and the ability to manage an uninterrupted flow of ideas regardless of who attends meetings.

TO TEST YOUR UNDERSTANDING

4-1   Why do you think it is important for one person to be assigned ownership of a value stream? Do you think that this is more likely to happen in a mechanistic structure or an organic one? Explain.

4-2   How can contingency theory lead to an organizational structure that is mechanistic? Can a mechanistic structure support the goals of a QIM company? Explain.

4-3   Are there any differences between the attributes of a good leader who is in a senior management position and a good leader of a process improvement team? If so, what are they? If not, why not?

4-4   How can analytical and naturalistic decision making be applied together to improve quality and service? What role does feedback play in improving the quality of decisions made?

4-5   How can one know if a team is working well? How can the effectiveness of team building be measured? What can be done to improve group outcomes?

◆●◆

Starbucks Corporation

Just Say Yes

Company legend has it that Starbucks was named after the coffee-loving first mate in Herman Melville's *Moby Dick*. The company began in the early 1970s as a shared vision of Jerry Baldwin, Zev Siegel, and Gordon Bowker. What they had in common was a love for fine coffees and exotic teas. The three partners believed they might be successful by opening a store that specialized in selling imported coffees and teas, dark roasting its own coffee beans the European way to enhance the full flavor, and advising its customers on how to grind beans and brew their own coffee at home. The first Starbucks store was at Pike Place Market in Seattle, a location frequented by tourists.

The Pike Place store was modest, and in keeping with a nautical theme, one wall contained shelves of whole bean coffees, another contained coffee products, and a few shelves were devoted to teas. The store did not offer coffee by the cup, although free samples were sometimes available for tasting. The business was an immediate success, and sales exceeded all expectations. A second store was opened in 1972, and by 1980, a total of four stores were operating in the Seattle area.

In 1981, Howard Schultz, a vice president and general manager at Hammerplast, a Swedish kitchenwares manufacturer, noticed that his company was receiving an unusually large number of orders for a certain type of drip coffeemaker from Starbucks. He decided to go to Seattle and investigate. When he reached the store, Schultz was greeted at the door by a violinist playing Mozart. As he entered, the pleasing aroma of coffee was overpowering. The person

behind the counter scooped out some Sumatran coffee beans, ground them, placed them in a cone filter, slowly poured boiling water through the cone, and handed Schultz a porcelain mug of some of the best coffee he had ever tasted. Schultz was impressed. It seemed like this insignificant coffee shop had successfully created a customer experience; sales seemed of secondary importance.

Schultz was hooked, and convinced Baldwin to hire him as the head of marketing, with responsibilities over the retail store operations. During the first few months, he spent most of his time learning the coffee business—taking turns working behind the counter in each of the four Seattle stores, talking with customers, tasting and learning about different coffees, educating himself about the retail aspects of selling coffee, and finally, familiarizing himself with different roasting techniques.

In 1983, Starbucks sent Schultz to Milan to attend an international housewares show, where he became acquainted with Italian coffee bars. When not at the conference, he would walk the streets of Milan, discovering and comparing the different bars and what they offered. He found that they seemed to tailor their services to the needs that were specific to their particular clientele. Some were upmarket and stylish, whereas others were more basic and blue collar. For Schultz, this was an epiphany. Starbucks had missed the point. He decided the company should expand its current operations and create an atmosphere where people could escape from reality—a place where they could meet with friends to unwind after a stressful day. Starbucks could create for its customers an experience in pleasure. Like the Italian coffee bars, Starbucks would have to begin serving fresh-brewed coffee, preferably espresso, and cappucino.

Schultz's idea met with strong opposition from Starbucks owners, so in 1985, he left Starbucks and started his own company, which he called Il Giornale (pronounced *ill jor-nahl-ee*). Il Giornale featured Italian décor, menus containing Italian words, and Italian background music. Customers had to stand because no seating was provided. Although the concept worked well on most fronts, some customers objected to the incessant opera music, others did not like the menu in Italian, and many wanted a place to sit down. Once known, these problems were quickly solved without compromising on the overall concept. The business had grown to three stores by 1987 and boasted annual sales of $1.5 million. In March of that year, Schultz had the opportunity to purchase Starbucks, and the two companies were combined under the new name Starbucks Corporation.

As the CEO and chairman of this new corporation, Schultz had a vision to provide the most respected brand in coffee and to be admired for corporate responsibilities—to the community and also to its employees. This was not going to be easy. He was quick to learn that morale was low. The workers felt unappreciated and largely abandoned by the previous owners. Building a solid management–labor relationship built on trust was a top priority.

Schultz believed the formula for success was simple: ensure customers are served by skillful employees who consistently deliver good service, have a high energy level and an eagerness to communicate the company's passion for coffee, and who pay attention to the details of pleasing customers. In other words, the key to quality is through people, and the most important challenge was how to attract, motivate, train, reward, and retain good staff. Schultz committed to make Starbucks a place where people would want to work.

One of the first reforms was to expand health care coverage to include part-time employees who worked at least 20 hours per week. By 1991, the company was able to offer all employees a stock option plan, and at that time, the term "partner" was substituted for "employee." In 1995, the employee stock ownership program was expanded to include a stock purchase plan. In addition to good fringe benefits, Starbucks paid attractive wages. Company policy was to ensure that the lowest paid employees earned well above the industry average. The strategy worked. Starbucks annual personnel turnover rate dropped to around 65%, compared with an industry average of 150% to 400%. For store managers, the turnover rate was 25%, half of the industry average. Schultz's rationale was simple. If you treat your employees well, they will in turn treat your customers well.

During the building years, Schultz and his key executives worked hard to instill core values into the evolving culture, building a company with soul, meaning that Starbucks would never stop pursuing the perfect cup of coffee. Quality was to never be sacrificed. Artificially flavored coffee would not be sold, and high-quality coffee beans would never be polluted with chemical additives. Pleasing customers had become a passion—and employees were trained to do whatever was necessary, even taking heroic or unprecedented measures, to ensure customers were satisfied. All employees were trained to "just say yes."

In June 1992, Starbucks became a public company and commenced an ambitious expansion program. A Stores-of-the-Future project team was formed in 1995 to come up with the design of the next generation of Starbucks stores. Howard Schultz surrounded himself with a top management team, selecting people with extensive experience in managing and growing retail businesses. He continued to emphasize the importance of hiring good employees, and expansion meant a new focus on hiring practices. In screening applicants, the company sought passion, a love for coffee, and a type of diversity that mirrored the community being served. Intensive and comprehensive training programs were implemented, ranging from "How to Brew the Perfect Cup" to the three "Star Skills" in interpersonal relations: (1) maintaining self-esteem, (2) listening and acknowledging, and (3) asking for help if required.

By 1998, Starbucks was serving 5 million customers per week, spending little on advertising, relying instead on word of mouth and storefront appeal. The company had built its brand literally cup by cup.

Starbucks had begun entering into licensing agreements with companies such as Marriott and Aramark, and had started a mail order business. Joint venture arrangements were in place with PepsiCo and Dreyer's to create new products.

Meanwhile, the competitive environment had toughened. By 1997, there were an estimated 8,000 specialty coffee outlets in the United States. It was no longer enough for the company to aspire to be the most recognized and respected brand of coffee in the world. Schultz believed sustaining the company's growth objectives required a willingness to take risks, to challenge the status quo, and to realign its vision with current conditions.

SOURCE: Printed with the kind permission of Starbucks Corporation. ■

QUESTIONS FOR THOUGHT

1. How would you describe Howard Schultz's leadership style? When he acquired Starbucks in 1987, he found low employee morale. Workers believed they had been betrayed by the former owners and were skeptical concerning the new owner. How do you think Schultz used his leadership skills to turn this situation around and rebuild a trusting relationship with the workforce?

2. Based on what you read, would you say that Starbucks has a mechanistic- or organic-style organization structure? How do you think that Starbucks has adapted its structure to fit the requirements of its environment? Defend your answer.

3. A key to Starbucks' success has been empowering store employees to make decisions on the spot to please customers. In keeping with the spirit of "just say yes," if you were the HR Director of Starbucks, how would you organize a training program to teach employees not only how to make decisions, but also how to make good decisions? How would this training differ for store managers? How would the training differ for senior executives?

CHAPTER 5

Managing for Quality: Accountability and Implementation

Those who know how to win are much more numerous than those who know how to make proper use of their victories.

—POLYBIUS, GREEK HISTORIAN, 205–118 BC

Falk Power Systems[1]

Power Solutions Through People and Technology

Falk Power Systems (FPS), a multinational corporation with facilities in Asia, Europe, and the United States, produces power supplies for a diverse industry mix, including data processing, industrial controls, instrumentation, and telecommunications. In 1991, FPS management pledged to become the undisputed leader of quality power supply systems. TQM was piloted at the Hong Kong factory, and the company became ISO9001 certified.

The FPS implementation plan focused on six goals:

1. Standardizing work procedures
2. Developing ISO9000-compliant documentation systems
3. Establishing a company policy on quality
4. Conducting training for all employees in ISO9001 certification preparation and TQM problem-solving tools

---

[1]Further information on this case can be Found in Gurnani, Haresh. "Pitfalls in Total Quality Management Implementation: The Case of a Hong Kong Company." *Total Quality Management* 10, no. 2 (March 1999): 209–28.

5. Establishing a steering committee to oversee the implementation

6. Setting up quality circles of experts to meet regularly to identify, analyze, and solve quality problems

Two years into the implementation, FPS hired a consultant to study and evaluate progress. Although most employees were united in the belief that they were personally responsible for quality and most trusted that management was genuinely committed, the consultant observed some problems. First, the company had no formal system for evaluating TQM progress. Second, FPS had failed to incorporate TQM into its rewards and recognitions system, and consequently, there was no incentive for employees to participate.

The consultant also discovered problems with training. The training course designed to build problem-solving skills was largely ineffective, and there was no follow-up or attempt to evaluate training effectiveness.

Finally, even though employees placed their trust in management, the consultant found a diversity of management styles and widespread inconsistencies. Workers throughout the factory were confused and the consultant observed numerous behaviors that were counterproductive. ∎

5.1 LEARNING OBJECTIVES AND KEY OUTCOMES

After studying the material in Chapter 5, you will be able to

1. Demonstrate an understanding of the balanced scorecard as an integrated performance metric and how to apply its principles to develop some realistic measures for an industrial organization

2. Demonstrate an understanding of some of the major reasons why TQM programs fail and discuss what steps companies can take to improve the chances for success

3. Discuss the three myths that may be responsible for many TQM failures and defend TQM against its critics

4. Discuss the phases necessary for a successful QIM implementation plan

5. Describe the characteristics of a third-generation (QIM) quality culture and how to recognize a company with this level of quality maturity

6. Describe the sand cone model of organizational change capability and how it supports a QIM culture

5.2 PERFORMANCE MEASUREMENT AND THE BALANCED SCORECARD

A company can have all the outward trappings of quality and still not be committed.

Employees hear and respond to what they perceive their bosses care about.

Management can only achieve what it rewards, and it can only reward what it measures. Performance standards are implemented from the top, and the measures used will determine performance priorities. Behaviors at all levels of the organization will be based on what employees perceive their bosses genuinely care about. A company can have all the outward trappings of a commitment to total quality—a Web site pledge to customers, promotional declarations, and slogans posted in the workplaces. Nevertheless employees hear a different message if their supervisors seldom inquire about quality, respond to quality measures, or track progress against quality goals.

Financial measures (e. g., return on assets, earnings per share) worked well under machine theory, where the primary focus was maximizing profitability and containing costs. However, financial metrics alone are inadequate in the open systems model. Kaplan and Norton collaborated with twelve top performance measurement companies and combined

FIGURE 5-1 Balanced Scorecard Performance Metrics

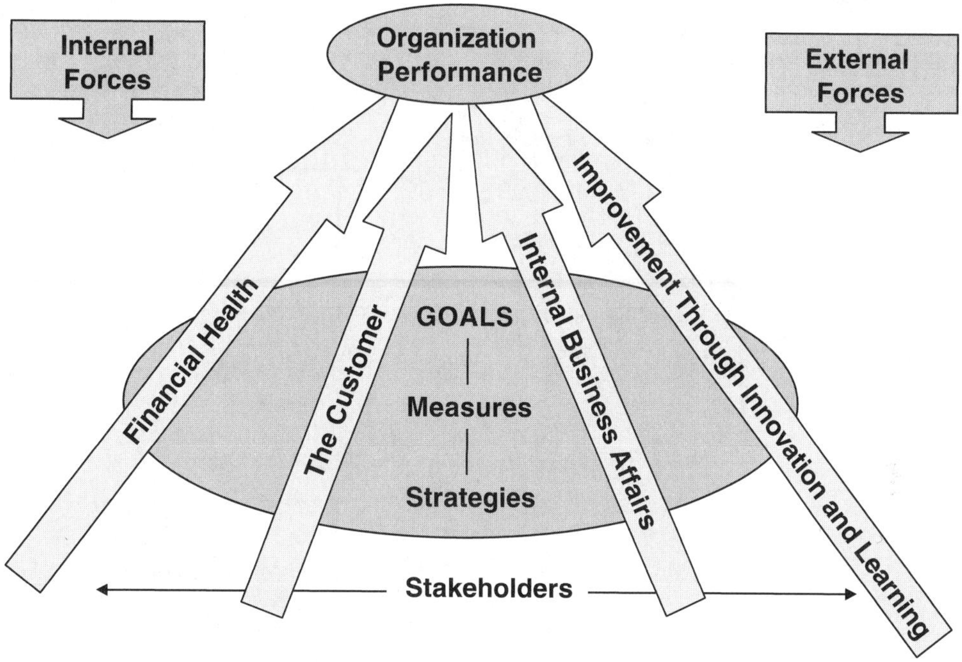

Balanced Scorecard

Metrics

best practices into an approach known as the **balanced scorecard**.[2] Illustrated in Figure 5-1, the balanced scorecard emphasizes four critical operational perspectives: the customer, internal business affairs, improvement through innovation and learning, and financial health. It is a departure from the conventional wisdom of using financial **metrics** alone to determine success. Using the scorecard, a company can achieve superior performance if its leadership can learn to effectively manage the trade-offs that arise among the four areas. Sometimes improvement in one area can only be achieved at the expense of another, so keeping the four perspectives in a state of balance presents a challenge.

5.2.1 Customer Perspective

Customer Perspective

The **customer perspective** measures business performance in those areas that matter most to them. The aim is to try to see the organization through the eyes of its customers and ask such questions as the following:

> *"What do our customers think of us? What do they think of the job we are doing? Have we built a solid relationship with them? Can they trust us?"*

The customer perspective measures performance through the eyes of the customer.

As Figure 5-2 depicts, pleasing customers is the centerpiece of a mature QIM culture. In a QIM organization, everything is subordinate to satisfying customer needs. Focusing on competitive priorities is a good starting point. As Figure 5-3 illustrates, the balanced scorecard process is to set goals, identify specific attributes relative to each goal, and

---

[2]Kaplan, Robert S., and David P. Norton. "The Balanced Scorecard—Measures That Drive Performance." *Harvard Business Review,* January/February 1992, 71–79.

FIGURE 5-2 The Wheel of Quality-Inspired Management

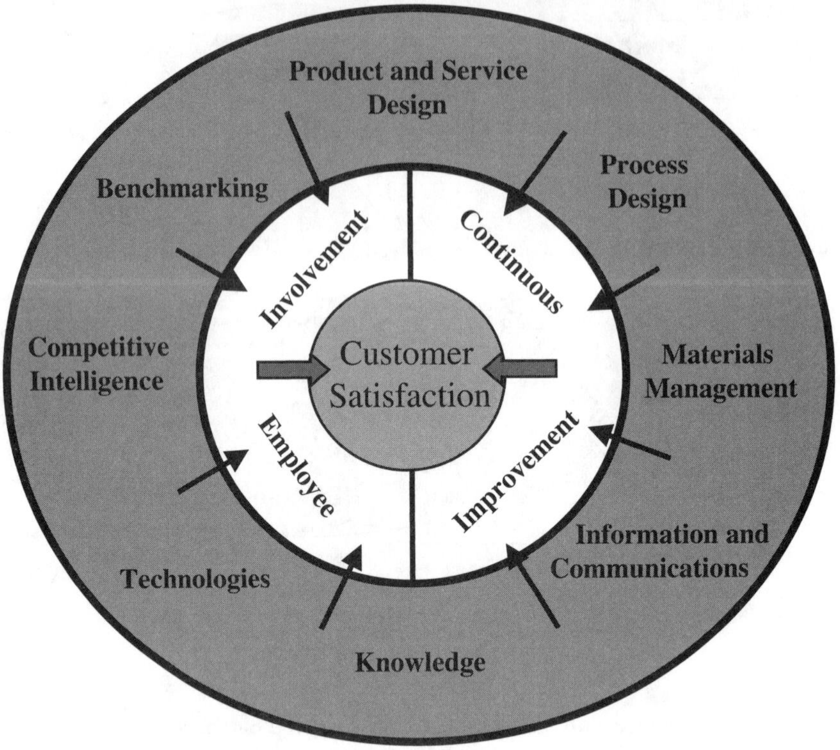

Quality measures should be selected that reflect the customer's point of view.

establish measures for each attribute. What customers value can usually be listed under one of four major headings: quality, time, flexibility, or dependability. A fifth category, customer loyalty, is sometimes added to address success at building relationships.

5.2.1.1 Quality Quality measures should reflect the customer's point of view. For example, instead of using the measure—percentage of defective items shipped—it is better to use numbers that customers generate, such as the percentage of on-time deliveries. It is important to resist the temptation to use measures that are convenient, rather than those that are an accurate reflection of customer satisfaction.

Design Issues

Service Features

Consistency

Appropriate measures can focus on **design issues** such as superior features, tolerances, durability, reliability, and safety; **service features** such as availability, courtesy, knowledgeable staff, convenience, and location; or **consistency** (low variability).

Time is a measure that reflects how long it takes to deliver expected services.

Lead Time

Time

5.2.1.2 Time Usually called **lead time**, this measure is defined as the total time from the receipt of an order (realization of demand) to when the finished product or service is available to the customer. In the case of new product development, lead time is the time it takes from product definition through design, prototyping, tooling, production, and shipping, and finally to making the product available for purchase.

Time can also be a measure of an organization's responsiveness to changes in customer requirements.

Flexibility

Customization

5.2.1.3 Flexibility and Dependability **Flexibility** is the capability to handle a large variety of products, small batch sizes, and mass **customization**. This is a measure of how

FIGURE 5-3 Balanced Scorecard Process

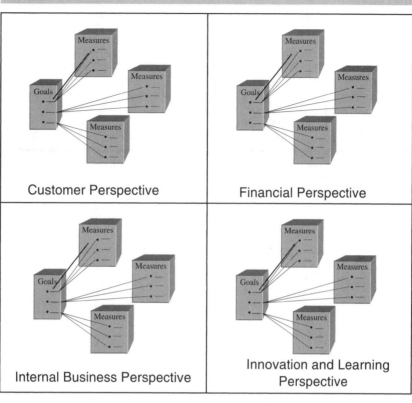

Customer Perspective

Financial Perspective

Internal Business Perspective

Innovation and Learning Perspective

Flexibility is a measure of the ability to change.

Dependability

Customer Loyalty

Dependability is a measure of how well the organization delivers on its promises.

Internal Business Perspective

Quality at the source means quality of process.

well the organization can take care of special customer needs and, in addition, how readily capacity can be changed to adapt to fluctuating demand patterns.

Dependability measures how well the organization delivers on its promises. This includes how well the company has met its commitments on when services are provided, such as using percentage of on-time deliveries as a measure.

5.2.1.4 Customer Loyalty   **Customer loyalty** can be one of the most important of the customer perspective measures. However, customer loyalty data can be difficult to collect, and loyalty measures are likely to be qualitative and subjective. Morgan and Hunt[3] suggested using the measures shown in Table 5-1.

5.2.2 Internal Business Perspective

The **internal business perspective** measures organizational performance in the core competency areas. The relevant questions for establishing goals, attributes, and measures under this metric are developed by investigating the answers to questions such as the following:

"What sets us apart from our competitors? What must we excel at to sustain competitive advantage? How do we cultivate customer loyalty?"

[3]Morgan, Robert M., and Shelby D. Hunt. "The Commitment-Trust Theory of Relationship Marketing." *Journal of Marketing* 58 (July 1994): 20–38.

TABLE 5-1 Measures in Relationship Marketing

Construct	Definition/Example
Relationship benefits	Compare the products you purchase from our firm with those that could be purchased from an alternative source with respect to (1) net profit derived from a product line common to both suppliers, and (2) product performance obtained from a product line common to both suppliers.
Relationship termination costs	If your relationship with our firm were terminated, what costs would be incurred with respect to (1) lack of comparable alternative suppliers, (2) relationship dissolution expenses, and (3) substantial switching costs to change to an alternative supplier?
Shared values	Indicate the degree to which you believe (A) our firm would agree to the following statements, and (B) your firm would agree with the following statements: (1) to succeed in this business, it is often necessary to compromise one's ethics; and (2) if an employee is discovered to have engaged in unethical behavior resulting primarily in personal (as opposed to corporate) gain, that employee should be promptly reprimanded.
Communication	Indicate the degree to which you agree with the following statements: In our relationship, our firm (1) keeps your firm informed of new developments, and (2) communicates well its expectations for your firm's performance.
Opportunistic behavior	Indicate the degree to which you agree with the following statements: to accomplish our firm's objectives, sometimes we (1) alter the facts slightly, and (2) promise to do things without actually doing them later.
Relationship commitment	Indicate the degree to which you agree with the following statements: the relationship that our firm has with your firm (1) is something we are very committed to, (2) is something your firm intends to maintain indefinitely, and (3) deserves your firm's maximum effort to maintain.
Trust	Indicate the degree to which you agree with the following statements: in our relationship, our firm (1) cannot be trusted at times, (2) can be counted on to do what is right, and (3) has high integrity.
Acquiescence	Indicate the degree to which you agree with the following statement: in the future, our firm will likely comply with the policies that your firm establishes for the marketing of your products by your distributors.
Cooperation	How would you characterize the cooperation between your firm and our firm regarding the following activities: (1) local/regional cooperative advertising, and (2) inventory levels.
Propensity to leave	How do you assess the chances of your firm terminating this relationship (1) within six months, (2) within one year, and (3) within two years?
Functional conflict	Indicate the degree to which you agree with the following statement: in the future, our firm will probably view differences of opinion with your firm as "just a part of doing business" that will likely result in benefits to both of us.
Uncertainty	To what extent do you now have adequate information for making future decisions regarding (1) how much you should spend on promotions and advertising, and (2) which products or brands to carry in stock?

All measures employ a seven-point scale, and the measuring tool is a carefully administered customer survey.

SOURCE: Reprinted with permission from *Journal of Marketing*, published by American Marketing Association, Morgan, Robert M. and Shelby D. Hunt, July 1994, vol. 58, 20–38.

Quality at the Source

Quality of Process

Quality at the source is **quality of process**. It is imperative that the relationship between process variables and the measures listed under customer perspective be well understood. Process measures will include such factors as output quality, cycle times and yields, employee skills and productivity, machine changeover and down times, inventory turns and levels, process throughput (flow) times, production costs, and so on. On an informal basis, some organizations choose to relegate routine quality decisions to the

**Self-Managed
Teams**

factory floor, through the use of empowered and **self-managed teams**.[4] Teams meet regularly, either at scheduled times or whenever there is a slack period in the work. Individual members are trained in the use of a variety of process improvement skills, such as the tools presented in Chapters 7 and 8. In Six Sigma companies, individuals called black belts and master black belts receive specialized training. Others receive general training in topics such as team building, process improvement, and change management.

Good ideas can be
made better by
group interaction.

5.2.2.1 Use of Teams   Teams are typically used to achieve incremental improvements.[5] On an individual basis initiative can be stifled when, after hours of tedious effort, an individual fails to muster support for a new idea. As a team member, a person's idea would be thoroughly discussed by the team and any flaws discovered at an early stage. As a result, either a good idea is turned into a more workable one or the team abandons it and moves on. In either case, an individual does not suffer the disillusionment of having wasted significant amounts of time.

Self-Policing

Self-Motivating

Teams can be more effective than individuals acting alone because teams are **self-policing** and **self-motivating**, properties that do not apply to individuals in general. The team structure itself exploits the natural inconsistencies of its membership. Not everyone gets excited, has energy, or has the inclination to carry the ball at the same time. With a team, there will always be some members who will contribute less due to personal or work conflicts; however, at such times, others will be willing to step up to the plate and keep the agenda moving.

Teams are self-
policing and self-
motivating.

**Internal Business
Objectives**

5.2.2.2 Internal Business Objectives   **Internal business objectives** are derived from corporate strategy, and performance means improving against those measures that support business purpose. Ideally, objective setting is a cascading process whereby each level sets objectives consistent with, and with greater specificity than, those of the immediate level above it. As an example, a high-level objective to reduce the total lead time for order fulfillment (called **flow time** or **throughput time**) could translate to middle-level objectives on capacity, productivity, and scheduling. Under **capacity**, a lower-level objective might be to identify and eliminate bottlenecks. The way to eliminate a bottleneck is to add capacity or rebalance the flow, and discovering feasible ways to do this could then be the focus of a process improvement team. To meet productivity objectives, improvement teams could be tasked to find ways to increase outputs and yields. Those same teams might achieve **scheduling** objectives by investigating existing procedures and determining where potential interruptions can occur.

Internal business
objectives should
originate from the
top.

Flow Time

Throughput Time

Capacity

Scheduling

5.2.3 Innovation and Learning Perspective

**Innovation and
Learning
Perspective**

The **innovation and learning perspective** focuses on the organization's ability to continuously improve. This metric is developed by considering questions such as the following:

Innovation and
learning measure
the organization's
ability to
continuously
improve.

> *"What must we do to continue to learn, improve, and create value for our customers? How can we know that we are a knowledge-driven learning organization?"*

This category might include such factors as new product and process introductions, improvement initiatives, the implementation of change, and the holistic development of personnel. The latter factor is crucial. Growing a competitive workforce is a high priority

---

[4]Clemmer, Jim. "Getting It Together." *Executive Excellence* 19, no. 4 (April 2002): 15.

[5]Townsend, Pat. "Voices from the Field: Why Can't Everyone Participate Directly in Quality Improvement?" *The Journal for Quality and Participation* 25, no. 1 (Spring 2002): 20–21.

of the top management of many major companies, who see a direct tie between success, the organization's intellectual capital, and its ability to learn. Surveys have shown that CEOs believe that people issues are becoming a more important aspect of their jobs, and that recruiting and retention strategies need to change to find and keep good employees.[6]

Such findings underscore the importance of establishing goals in HR development, a topic covered more fully in Chapter 6. The emphasis has shifted from simply providing training to facilitating learning. Some companies have found it useful to establish **communities of practice**,[7] a concept in which people with similar work interests focus on learning those things that have direct relevance to their jobs. Communities can also facilitate the exchange of knowledge. Training officers, who traditionally taught formal courses, now act as **learning counselors** who provide guidance, furnish resources, and facilitate learning to the communities. Trainers also contribute to the development of reliable measures so the **quality of learning** may be evaluated.

There is an increasing trend in the use of **e-learning** as a training medium. Using the Internet, large numbers of employees can be taught anytime, anywhere, and at a relatively low cost.[8] Online delivery programs have many advantages. Training content can be easily updated, and it has been shown that people learn faster using this medium than with conventional classroom methods. The Internet can also be used to enhance internal communications because changes can be rapidly disseminated and everyone concerned receives the same information at the same time.

5.2.4 Financial Perspective

The **financial perspective** takes a critical look at a firm's financial performance by asking questions such as the following:

> *"How do we look to our **shareholders** and other investors? Do our creditors consider us to be low risk? Would our employees be willing to invest their personal savings in our organization? What do investment counselors think of us?"*

Ultimately, the financials determine business success. Without good financial performance, **investors** will seek more attractive alternatives, and the business will eventually collapse. The assessment of financial strength depends on what measures are used and whose interests are at stake, as shown in Table 5-2. These traditional measures do not adequately measure a company's performance in achieving *profitability* (defined as the ratio of financial inputs to financial outputs). Some more relevant measures that have been suggested are discussed next.

5.2.4.1 Financial Ratios Gold and Kraus[9] recommended replacing traditional measures with a new measure: profit divided by total investment. This ratio is sensitive to changes in product pricing, production costs, resource utilization, productivity, and how

---

Margin notes:

People learn better through e-learning than with traditional methods.

Communities of Practice

Learning Counselors

Quality of Learning

E-Learning

Financial Perspective

Shareholders

Investors

Traditional financial measures do not help improve profitability.

---

[6]Oliver, Richard W. "The Return on Human Capital." *The Journal of Business Strategy* 22, no. 4 (July/August 2001): 7–10.

[7]Weintraub, Robert S., and Jennifer W. Martineau. "The Just-in-Time Imperative." *T + D* 56, no. 6 (June 2002): 50–58.

[8]Haapaniemi, Peter. "Smart Thinking." In *The CEO Guide to Innovation Delivered: Turning Ideas into Results. A Supplement to Chief Executive Magazine.* June 2002: 26–32. Also available online at http://www. chiefexecutive.net/ceoguides/june2002/p26.htm (Accessed March 26, 2005).

[9]Gold, Bela, and Ralph M. Kraus. "Integrating Physical and Financial Measures for Managerial Controls." *Academy of Management Journal* 7, no. 2 (June 1964): 109–27.

TABLE 5-2 Traditional Financial Measures

Stakeholder Risk	Financial Measures
Short-term lenders	Current assets and current liabilities
	Value of inventories and cost of sales
	Net working capital and total sales
Long-term investors	Total sales and fixed investment
	Total debt and net worth
Management performance	Return on equity

financial resources are allocated between capital goods and working capital—all things on which management should be focusing. The ratio measures management performance in internal operations (as projected through financial outcomes) and satisfies the needs of investors to ensure the security of their financial interests. It also reflects a blend between both the physical and financial nature of resource flows and is developed as follows:

$$\frac{\text{Capacity}}{\text{Total Investment}}\left(\frac{C}{TI}\right) = \frac{\text{Capacity}}{\text{Fixed Investment}} \times \frac{\text{Fixed Investment}}{\text{Total Investment}} \quad \textbf{(5-1)}$$

The C/TI ratio is a measure of the capacity that is created (expressed in units) per total dollar invested. The *fixed investment* represents the dollars allocated to creating capacity, such as investment in new machines or processes. *Total investment* is the sum of capital goods investment and working capital.

$$\frac{\text{Output}}{\text{Total Investment}}\left(\frac{O}{TI}\right) = \frac{\text{Output}}{\text{Capacity}} \times \frac{\text{Capacity}}{\text{Total Investment}}\left(\frac{C}{TI}\right) \quad \textbf{(5-2)}$$

The O/TI ratio is a measure of units produced (output) per total dollar invested. The ratio *output/capacity* is the system utilization.

$$\frac{\text{Profit}}{\text{Output}}\left(\frac{P}{O}\right) = \frac{\text{Product Value}}{\text{Output}} - \frac{\text{Total Costs}}{\text{Output}} \quad \textbf{(5-3)}$$

Profitability is only realized when output is sold.

Product Value

Profit

The P/O ratio represents unit profit contribution and may be the traditional measure or may differ in the way total costs are accumulated. For example, instead of using traditional accounting methods for allocating indirect costs, activity-based costing (ABC) methods can be used. **Product value** and output is the unit selling price. The P/O ratio is a measure of **profit** potential only because products must actually be sold before profits can be realized. A manager can make this ratio look good simply by increasing production, but actual profitability to the company is reduced if there is no demand for the extra output. If the output exceeds demand, the excess material is placed into inventory incurring additional costs.

Financial Ratio 1

$$\frac{\text{Profit}}{\text{Total Investment}}\left(\frac{P}{TI}\right) = \frac{\text{Profit}}{\text{Output}}\left(\frac{P}{O}\right) \times \frac{\text{Output}}{\text{Total Investment}}\left(\frac{O}{TI}\right) \quad \textbf{(5-4)}$$

The P/TI ratio is a measure of the unit profit contribution per dollar invested. It can be used to compute a second useful financial ratio: profit divided by equity investment (P/EI).

Financial Ratio 2

$$\frac{\text{Profit}}{\text{Equity Investment}}\left(\frac{P}{EI}\right) = \frac{\text{Profit/Total Investment}}{\text{Equity Investment/Total Investment}} \quad \textbf{(5-5)}$$

Financial Ratio 3

The *P/EI* ratio measures the unit profit contribution per shareholders' equity. The *equity* represents the assets that have been generated for investors. It is the difference between assets and liabilities, and is calculated from the firm's balance sheet. The denominator on the right side of Equation 5-5 is sometimes used as a third financial ratio. Equity investment divided by total investment (*EI/TI*) represents the proportion of the total capitalization of the business that is debt free and can be useful in tracking the effectiveness of the organization's financial structure.

**Economic Value
Added**

Economic value added measures how much is earned in excess of expectations.

5.2.4.2 Economic Value Added An alternative financial measure is **economic value added** (EVA), a term coined and trademarked in the mid-1980s by financial consultants Joel Stern and Bennett Stewart.[10, 11] In simple terms, EVA measures how much a company earns in profits as compared with investors' expectations. The minimum that investors are willing to accept is called the cost of capital and represents the threshold amount that must be earned to keep investors from taking their money elsewhere. The economics of capital[12] should always weigh heavily when contemplating process change, whether this is due to BPR, Six Sigma, TQM, lean production, and other formal program initiatives. Capital is not free (as some change advocates seem to think), is usually scarce, and can be expensive. Any contemplated changes should therefore be evaluated, giving due consideration to their capital requirements and always ensuring resources are judiciously shared among competing uses.

5.3 TQM FAILURES

During the 1990s, some organizations became disillusioned when, after spending considerable money and effort trying to implement TQM, they realized they had failed to achieve much.[13] Some reports have claimed that the rate of failed implementations were as high as 75%.[14] One survey found that only 29% of managers believed quality initiatives were directly linked to improved financial measures such as return on assets and return on investment, and only 12% believed quality had a favorable impact on stock prices.[15]

5.3.1 Major Causes for Failure

Why did some TQM implementations fail? Studies have shown that failures were not due to a flawed approach or misguided themes, but rather were due to a failed

---

[10]Stern, Joel M., and John S. Shiely, with Irwin Ross. *The EVA Challenge: Implementing Value Added Change in an Organization.* New York: Wiley, 2001, 15–26.

[11]Stewart, G. Bennett III. *The Quest for Value: A Guide for Senior Managers.* HarperCollins, 1991, 118–78.

[12]Keen, Peter G. W. *The Process Edge: Creating Value Where It Counts.* Boston: Harvard Business School Press, 1997, 57–80.

[13]Hall, Gene, Jim Rosenthal, and Judy Wade. "How to Make Reengineering Really Work." *Harvard Business Review,* November/December 1993: 119–31.

[14]Spector, Bart, and Michael Beer. "Beyond TQM Programmes." *Journal of Organizational Change Management* 7, no. 2 (1994): 63–67.

[15]Larcker, David, and Christopher Ittner. "Measuring Nonfinancial Assets." *Wharton Alumni Magazine* Winter 1997: 7–12.

implementation plan. The following is the list of top suspected causes leading to a breakdown in TQM implementation:

1. Trying to partially implement TQM by selecting some, but not all, of the key TQM principles[16]
2. Being unable to change culture or generate truthful commitment and participation[17]
3. Lack of trust in the organization's leadership[18]
4. Failing to take a holistic approach of effectively integrating quality into existing management systems[19]
5. Failing to pay sufficient attention to organizational culture, market structure, and organizational design[20]

Critics have argued that quality programs deflect energy and resources from more important activities. By focusing on internal processes, TQM creates its own bureaucracy and ironically neglects customers. This could possibly explain why some organizations achieve dramatic improvements in individual processes only to watch overall results decline.[21] It is essential that implementation plans take an open systems view of the organization.

5.3.2 Some Common Myths

There are three myths concerning the design of formal quality programs. Assuming one or more of these myths is true can be a fatal mistake that can lead to implementation failures:

1. **MYTH 1:** *Change can occur top-down, and all employees will be willing participants.*
   Change is seldom mechanical or rational, and it is often accompanied by political stratagems, vested interests, and resistance. Perhaps the most critical obstacle is the people issue. People are naturally fearful of change and do not trust that those in power will act in their best interest. A culture based on integrity and trust must be created first or any QIM implementation is doomed from the beginning.

2. **MYTH 2:** *Training and education can change individual and organizational attitudes and behaviors.*
   A common mistake that many organizations make is to greatly overestimate the strength of training as a change stimulus.[22]

---

[16]Douglas, Thomas J., and William Q. Judge, Jr. "Total Quality Management Implementation and Competitive Advantage: The Role of Structural Control and Exploration." *Academy of Management Journal* 44, no. 1 (February 2001): 158–69.

[17]Easton, George S., and Sherry L. Jarrell. "Patterns in the Deployment of Total Quality Management: An Analysis of 44 Leading Companies." In *The Quality Movement and Organization Theory,* edited by Robert E. Cole and W. Richard Scott. Thousand Oaks, CA: Sage, 2000.

[18]Ibid.

[19]Gurnani, "Pitfalls in Total," 209–28.

[20]Sameer, Jasmine Tata, and Prasad Ron Thorn. "The Influence of Organizational Structure on the Effectiveness of TQM Programs." *Journal of Managerial Issues* 11, no. 4 (Winter 1999): 440–53.

[21]Hall, Rosenthal, and Wade, "How to Make Reengineering," 119–31.

[22]Coyle-Shapiro, Jacqueline A.-M. "Employee Participation and Assessment of an Organizational Change Intervention: A Three-Wave Study of Total Quality Management." *The Journal of Applied Behavioral Science* 35, no. 4 (1999): 439–56.

3. **MYTH 3:** *All employees seek additional responsibility and prefer enriched jobs.*
Research findings suggest that personality traits determine how individuals react
to job characteristics. Not everyone is intrinsically motivated by an enriched job.[23]
This phenomenon is covered in more detail in Chapter 6.

5.3.3 Theory of Quality

Some TQM failures may have been due to the fact that although individual quality
principles are based on sound theories, no one has yet been able to articulate a coher-
ent theory of quality. As a result, implementation strategies must choose from a
plethora of loosely connected tools and philosophies, as well as disparate theories that
are rooted in economics, science, metrology, and statistics.[24] In trying to make sense of
it all, it is little wonder that some organizations became theory weary. Overwhelmed
and confused, well-intended executives inadvertently gave their blessings to system designs that were wrought with internal conflicts and incompatibilities.

5.4 TQM IMPLEMENTATION STRATEGIES: JOINING THE SECOND GENERATION

5.4.1 Is Second-Generation Quality Passé?

TQM

TOC

BPR

SCM

HIO

As organizations grappled with the transformation from first- to second-generation
quality during the 1980s and 1990s, some common themes emerged that have since become the foundations of modern management practice—even for those who profess to
have found something that works better than **TQM**. At the turn of the century, it appeared to many that second-generation programs, broadly referred to as TQM, had become passé. Attention began to turn to new more trendy concepts, such as lean
production, **TOC**, **BPR**, Six Sigma, supply chain management (**SCM**), and **HIOs**. The
proponents of these alternative approaches, largely derivatives of TQM thinking, deliberately distanced themselves from TQM in an attempt to emphasize the uniqueness
of what they professed to be new ideas. Ironically, as Table 5-3 illustrates, these new approaches are not totally new and actually have common roots to TQM.

TQM did not invent any of these themes, but it can be argued that TQM legit-
imized their usage. Through a coordinated and directed TQM framework, paradigms
have changed as quality principles became embedded in management practices.

Easton and Jarrell studied forty-four companies with mature and successful TQM
implementations.[25] The research revealed that success is evolutionary and occurs
slowly over four distinct phases. The first three of these, a predeployment phase and
two phases of deployment, represent the process required to transform a company
from a first- to second-generation quality culture, and to develop effective programs
with supporting management practices. The third deployment phase is the hallmark of
generation three, a level where quality significantly impacts business strategy. The evolution of QIM is depicted in Figure 5-4.

---

[23]Hartman, Sandra J., Anthony L. Patti, and Joseph R. Razek. "Human Factors Affecting the Acceptance of Total
Quality Management." *The International Journal of Quality and Reliability Management* 17, no. 7 (2000): 714–29.

[24]Foster, David, and Jan Jonker. "Third Generation Quality Management: The Role of Stakeholders in Integrating Business in Society." In the 7th International Conference on ISO9000 and TQM, Royal Melbourne
Institute of Technology, Melbourne, April 2002, 2.

[25]Easton and Jarrell, "Patterns in the Deployment," 89–130.

TABLE 5-3 Comparison of TQM with Alternative Approaches

TQM Theme	*Also Found in These Alternative Approaches*
Process improvement	Lean production, Six Sigma, BPR, TOC, SCM
Systems approach	Lean production, Six Sigma, BPR, TOC, SCM
Employee involvement and empowerment	Lean production, Six Sigma, TOC, HIO
Teamwork	Lean production, Six Sigma, HIO
Customer focus	Lean production, Six Sigma, BPR, SCM
Supply chain integration	SCM, Six Sigma
Emphasis on performance measurement and measures	Lean production, Six Sigma, BPR, TOC, SCM, HIO
Cycle time reduction	Lean production, Six Sigma, BPR, TOC, SCM
Value enhancement	Lean production, Six Sigma, BPR, TOC, SCM
Waste reduction	Lean production, Six Sigma, BPR

TQM, total quality management; BPR, business process reengineering; TOC, theory of constraints; SCM, supply chain management; HIO, high involvement organization.

FIGURE 5-4 Phases in TQM Implementations

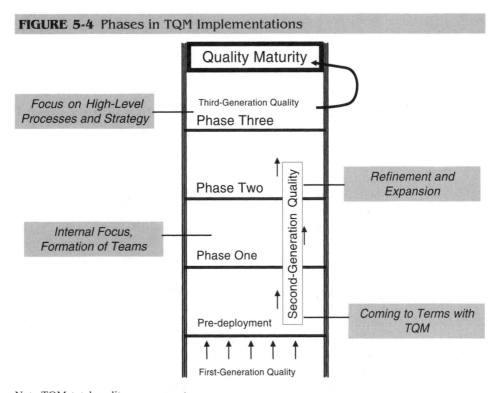

Note: TQM, total quality management.

SOURCE: George S. Easton, and Sherry L. Jarrell. "Patterns in the Deployment of Total Quality Management: An Analysis of 44 Leading Companies." In *The Quality Movement and Organization Theory,* edited by Robert E. Cole and W. Richard Scott, (89–130). Copyright © 2000 by Sage Publications. Reprinted by Permission of Sage Publications, Inc.

5.4.2 Second-Generation Predeployment Phase

Predeployment is a period of self-actualization.

An organization will typically spend two to five years coming to terms with the idea of QIM and trying to convince its employees that there is a genuine need for it. The predeployment phase is a period of corporate self-actualization, and much of what happens during this period legitimately requires time. For example, during this phase, an organization tries to make sense of its environment, to understand its internal operations, to permit open and wide debate, to align perspectives, and to grow a critical mass of support.

Activities Typical of Predeployment Phase

- *Preplanning.* Set up task committees, establish goals, determine an implementation strategy, and hold numerous meetings.
- *Expert Advice.* Engage the services of consultants to study competitive position, customer satisfaction, and product performance.
- *Benchmarking.* Benchmark other companies to learn their implementation strategies.
- *Executive Training.* Begin to train executives in quality principles.
- *Organization.* Establish a quality department; appoint a senior quality officer; and develop mission, value, beliefs, and policy statements.
- *Customer Relations.* Respond positively to customer audits or pressure.
- *Supplier Relations.* Commence supplier certification programs and reduce the number of suppliers.
- *Pilot Startup.* Pilot a quality effort on a limited scale, such as in one plant or division.
- *Statistical Process Control.* Begin using **SPC**.

SPC

5.4.3 Second-Generation Deployment Phase One

Phase one is a period of indoctrination, training, and working on easy problems.

After the predeployment phase, organizations enter a protracted period of deployment that develops over three phases. Phase one can be expected to last from one to three years. During this phase, management is internally focused, emphasizing employee involvement through companywide training and the formation of **teams**. At the end of phase one, teams have a narrow problem-specific focus, such as the elimination of a particular type of defect or the reduction of cycle time.

Teams

Steering Committee

Quality Council

A **steering committee**, or **quality council**, coordinates the grassroots team effort and guides the implementation process. Suppliers and customers become part of the overall initiative. Formal systems are engaged to help identify problem suppliers. Customer surveys are used to elicit feedback; however, during phase one, the aim is more on damage control than on a genuine attempt to better satisfy customer needs. Some preliminary goals, as well as a reporting system to track performance, are established.

Team-Based Activities

During phase one, **team-based activities** will typically show some significant improvements, as the obvious and easy problems are identified and solved. However, improvements are made within the same systems context that existed before the quality implementation. As processes are analyzed for improvement, organizations begin to understand what is required to standardize and reach statistical control. During phase one, the scope of activity has a narrow workstation focus. For example, efforts might be limited to concentrating on the elimination of certain types of defects.

Activities Typical of Phase One

- *Training.* Begin companywide training programs, starting with quality awareness and an introduction to fundamental principles. Training is then expanded to include team-based tools, such as the plan-do-check-act problem-solving methodology, Pareto diagrams, and cause and effect.
- *Organization.* Form a steering committee to guide the implementation process.
- *Customer Relations.* Use **customer surveys** to get and act on feedback.
- *Supplier Relations.* Implement a **tracking system** to monitor supplier performance.
- *Systems Management.* Establish goals and a performance tracking system.

Customer Surveys

Tracking System

5.4.4 Second-Generation Deployment Phase Two

The second phase is a period of refinement and typically requires a minimum of three years. Fundamental process changes, such as the introduction of **cellular manufacturing** and the creation of self-managed teams, occur during this period. **Employee participation** is expanded, and team training is advanced to include more rigorous analytical tools. Management becomes more aware of its responsibility for quality and begins to take a more active role. The scope of training is broadened to include the needs of managers and supervisors.

Cellular Manufacturing

Employee Participation

During phase two, the focus begins to look at systems (rather than individual operations) and starts to tackle important issues such as **cycle time reduction** and **waste elimination**. By phase two, the need to control processes and reduce defects is widely accepted throughout the organization. Although the first phase typically identified with a single quality guru (e.g., Deming's 14 points, Juran's trilogy, Crosby Quality College), by phase two an organization usually abandons a single philosophy in favor of multiple approaches drawn from a variety of sources. Phase two is the minimum entry level for Six Sigma.

Cycle Time Reduction

Waste Elimination

In phase two, the systems approach is used and managers become more involved.

Activities Typical of Phase Two

- *New product development.* Training in advanced methodologies such as quality function deployment (QFD), design of experiments (DOE), Taguchi methods, design for manufacturability (DFM), failure mode and effects analysis (FMEA) is common. Cross-functional cooperation and efforts in concurrent engineering is often commenced. Design for Six Sigma (DFSS) implementations can occur here.
- *Customer satisfaction measures.* Capturing customer satisfaction becomes systematic and routine. Customer feedback is used to focus efforts on process improvements and new product developments. Decisions are made and priorities are set based on the voice of the customer.
- *Supplier management system.* The supplier management system is formalized, and suppliers are expected to demonstrate process capability, providing evidence of SPC. The total number of suppliers is significantly reduced, and formal supplier audits are routine. Limited supplier involvement in new product development will typically occur.
- *Process improvement.* Efforts to better manage and improve processes begin in earnest. In Six Sigma companies, black and green belts will be trained and will begin to lead process improvement teams.

5.5 REACHING THE THIRD GENERATION

5.5.1 Third-Generation Deployment Phase Three

In phase three, decisions are based on how customer needs will be impacted.

Phase three marks entry into the third generation of quality maturity. At this level, managing critical process as with cross-functional teams is the norm. QIM is fully operational at all levels, and is being applied to all primary and support value streams. Quality-based strategic planning tools, such as policy deployment, are used.

Customer focus is a reality. Strategic decisions are based on metrics that anticipate and respond to future customer requirements. Customer feedback is used to develop new products, and new product development has become a core business process. The supplier management system has reached a level of sophistication with few suppliers and an integrated supply chain. All employees understand and support a common set of goals, and teams are proficient in problem solving and data analysis.

Ironically, in phase three, organizations discover that the relentless pursuit of continuous improvement is not always the best course. Foley et al. argued that "there may be times in the life of an enterprise where, to satisfy its survival criteria, it might be necessary to discontinue or slow down the rate of quality improvement activity. . . ."[26] A key idea behind the third-generation psyche is the focus on value to the total enterprise, giving due consideration to the needs of all customer groups. This insight is part of the magic of Six Sigma, in which projects are selected based on their potential value to the business.

An organization has many different stakeholders, and each one benefits in some way from the outputs and outcomes generated by the various core business processes. The balanced scorecard addresses this issue from a measurement perspective. For example, the stakeholders of a state-supported university are not just the students and their parents. Other stakeholders include the faculty, administrative staff, alumni, private benefactors, grantors, state and federal legislators, and taxpayers. At times, the needs of different stakeholder groups can be in conflict, and senior decision makers are faced with the arduous task of carefully weighing the trade-offs before major decisions can be made.

5.5.2 Stakeholder Model of Quality

Foley provides the stakeholder model of quality, shown in Table 5-4, as a framework to help third-generation organizations determine whether they are giving proper consideration to all stakeholders.[27]

The Foley model identifies all stakeholders and places them in the columns of a matrix. The rows represent those factors that drive behaviors in relation to the business. Using this model, an organization can readily identify key factors for each stakeholder. The firm can then establish a change strategy that will be acceptable to all. Because the purpose of the organization is to deliver sustained value to all stakeholders, Foley's model integrates both purpose and strategy.

---

[26]Foley, Kevin, Richard Barton, Kerry Busteed, John Hulbert, and John Sprouster. *Quality Productivity and Competitiveness: The Role of Quality in Australia's Social and Economic Development.* Strathfield: NSW Wider Quality Movement, Standards Australia, 1997.

[27]Foley, Kevin. Meta Management: A stakeholder/quality management approach to whole-of-enterprise management, *Standards Australia,* SAI Global, Sydney, 2005.

TABLE 5-4 Stakeholders and the Business Enterprise

Stakeholder Issues and Outputs	Stakeholder					
	Customers	*Management*	*Staff*	*Suppliers*	*Shareholders*	*Government*
Financial probity						
Risk						
Quality						
Health and safety						
Owner value and profit						
Environment						
Knowledge						
Ethics						
Innovation						
Strategy, plans and planning						
Data integrity						

SOURCE: From Kevin Foley, *Meta Management: A stakeholder/quality management approach to whole-of-enterprise management*, Table 1-1, Standards Australia, SAI Global, Sydney, 2005. Reprinted with permission of Kevin Foley and SAI Global.

5.6 KEYS TO SUCCESS

5.6.1 Critical Factors

An organization cannot mandate quality and expect success.

What are the critical factors for a successful QIM implementation? In a study of 193 general hospitals from across the United States, Douglas and Judge concluded that TQM is more than an "either-or" proposition.[28] The degree to which implementation has occurred matters. Rhetoric does not create quality. An organization cannot mandate QIM and expect success.

Implementations must be led and resourced from the top. Where quality has been an integral part of an organization's standard procedures, programs are more successful and financial performance is stronger. There is also strong evidence to suggest that a synergistic effect exists between control and learning. For QIM to add value to an organization, innovations that will better serve customers must come from knowledge and learning. Drawing from Douglas and Judge and other research studies, there appear to be ten key factors that have been present in successful TQM implementations.[29,30]

Keys to Success

1. Top management commitment
2. A clear and concise policy that focuses on the customer
3. Creation of a culture committed to quality
4. A steering committee that assumes the dual role of quality leadership and quality guardianship
5. A committed and empowered workforce

[28]Douglas and Judge, "Total Quality Management," 158–69.
[29]Ibid.
[30]Gurnani, "Pitfalls in Total," 209–28.

TABLE 5-5 Lessons Learned to Help TQM (QIM) Implementations Succeed

Lesson 1: Know what TQM (QIM) will mean before you start.

What is TQM, and why is it necessary?	How and when should TQM tools be used?
How will success be defined, and what metrics will be used?	What are some realistic and achievable performance goals?

Lesson 2: Establish a culture that is supportive of TQM (QIM).

A customer focus	Management by fact
A learning organization	A systems approach to improvement
A willingness by management to seek and eliminate root causes of problems	Openness to new information and recognition of importance of continuous improvement

Lesson 3: TQM (QIM) implementation must be clearly aligned with organization's strategy.

Implementation must be integrated into core values.	Congruence between TQM and organization goals and performance measures is essential.
The implementation plan must take a systems approach.	Roles and responsibilities must be clearly understood by everyone.

Lesson 4: Understand what time and effort will be required.

Do not try to accomplish too much too soon.	Allow sufficient time for the organization to adapt to and assimilate actions.
Set and communicate realistic milestones.	Provide adequate resources.

Lesson 5: TQM (QIM) implementations are unique for each organization.

Do not rely on a generic "one size fits all" program.	Implementation programs should be tailored to level of performance (low, medium, or high).

Lesson 6: Take a holistic approach.

Activities must be integrated to create synergies.	Functional barriers must be broken down.

Lesson 7: "Total" in TQM is a key word. QIM must be inclusive.

Quality is comprehensive.	"Total" applies to participation, commitment, and responsibility for everyone.

Lesson 8: TQM (QIM) is not a panacea.

There is no "magic bullet"—TQM will not necessarily quickly improve business performance.	TQM is a journey, not a destination—a means to an end, rather than an end in itself.

TQM, total quality management.

SOURCE: Reprinted with permission from Dooyoung Shin, Jon G. Kalinowski, and Gaber Abou El-Enein. "Critical Implementation Issues in Total Quality Management," *S.A.M. Advanced Management Journal* 63, no. 1 (Winter 1998): 10–14.

6. Emphasis on consistent, relevant, and application-based training with a common language set of tools
7. Continuous improvement of processes
8. Effective two-way communications
9. Management by fact evaluating performance and making decisions based on hard data
10. Adequate rewards and recognitions

5.6.2 Lessons Learned

Shin et al. compiled a list of eight lessons learned from TQM failures and successes. These lessons, summarized in Table 5-5,[31] can help an organization that is embarking on the quality journey to QIM to be able to take advantage of the experiences of others and avoid some possible pitfalls.

5.6.3 Malcolm Baldrige National Quality Award Winners

A study of each winner of the Malcolm Baldrige National Quality Award (MBNQA) can help reveal what it takes to succeed. The stories are as varied as the companies; however, these top-notch organizations all seem to share the following common characteristics:

- Visionary leadership
- An emphasis on its relationship with its customers
- High-performance work systems and development of employees
- Well-designed and managed processes for product and service delivery
- Strong financial and market results

Award recipients are profited on the MBNQA web site: http://www.quality.nist.gov/Award_Recipients.htm.

5.7 ORGANIZATIONAL READINESS

How can an organization know if it is ready for QIM? How can it adequately prepare so a second-generation quality implementation goes smoothly and is successful? Three important issues should be considered:

- Does the internal culture support change?
- Do current management practices support change?
- Is there sufficient knowledge of system behavior to support change?

The first issue has to do with HR issues and is covered in some detail in Chapter 6. The second and third issues are concerned with the organization's capability to initiate, manage, and adapt to change. The sand cone model provides a useful framework for self-assessing management readiness.

5.7.1 Sand Cone Model of Organizational Change Capability

The sand cone model shown in Figure 5-5 depicts five stages of growth toward developing a world-class change capability.

---

[31]Shin, Dooyoung, Jon G. Kalinowski, and Gaber Abou El-Enein. "Critical Implementation Issues in Total Quality Management." *S.A.M. Advanced Management Journal* 63, no. 1 (Winter 1998): 10–14.

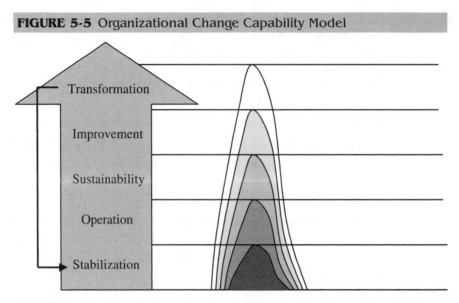

FIGURE 5-5 Organizational Change Capability Model

SOURCE: Based on *Journal of Operations Management,* 8, Kasra Ferdows and Arnoud DeMeyer, "Lasting Improvements in Manufacturing Performance: In Search of New Theory," pp. 168–84, Copyright 1990, printed with permission from Elsevier.

5.7.1.1 Stabilization Capability Before any meaningful change can commence, the senior leadership must understand its organization's building blocks—that is, the strengths available on which to build. This requires an understanding of core business processes, as well as the ability to predict outputs and outcomes. If the core business is unstable, then attention needs to be directed to stabilizing key processes before any significant effort at systems redesign can be made. This is not an easy step, and senior management cannot accomplish this in isolation. Engaging with the workforce is imperative. Attempts at stabilization will often expose the first major capability issues: what capability does the organization have to stabilize core processes?, where are the deficiencies?, and where does new capability need to be developed? **Stabilization** is a foundation capability and a good entry point for companies wanting to transition from first- to second-generation quality. Simple tools, such as those presented in Chapters 7 and 8, can be applied to identify and stabilize the most critical processes.

The foundation of change capability is stabilization.

Stabilization

The ability to operate processes in the short term is the second change capability.

5.7.1.2 Operation Capability An organization (and its quality program) advances to the second sand cone level once its key processes are stable enough to operate effectively in the short term—given the current leadership, environmental constraints, customers, suppliers, products, quality expectations, and personnel. It is essential that the operation capability exists so that value streams can function satisfactorily under static conditions before an organization can develop the flexibility to adapt to changing requirements.

Sustainability

5.7.1.3 Sustainability The third level of capability development is **sustainability**. A sustainable organization can operate effectively in the long term, and withstand changes in political, economic, and social factors, as well as the need to combat new competitors, build market share, develop new products, and adjust overall strategy. Developing a capability in sustainability requires strengthening the supporting capabilities below it

| The third change capability is sustainability—the ability to operate in the long term. |

(i.e., stabilization, operation). When an organization becomes sustainable, its quality program can take advantage of cross-functional integration and a systems view of performance. The organization can also turn a serious eye to improvement, asking such questions as, what business processes, if improved, would provide the greatest leverage in performance as reported on the balanced scorecard?, and what is the organization's capability to improve these processes?

| The fourth change capability is improvement. |

Improvement

5.7.1.4 Improvement Capability   To become sustainable, numerous incremental improvements have had to occur along the way. At the **improvement** stage, efforts are expanded from individual team-based activities to include systems improvements at the total enterprise level. This takes improvement to the strategic level, where the company will actively seek out opportunities to become more competitive, to grow, and to increase value to its customers.

| The highest change capability is transformation—the ability to reinvent systems. |

Transformation

5.7.1.5 Transformation Capability   Improvement of existing systems can only take the organization so far. There comes a point when the enterprise needs to reinvent itself. This requires a **transformation** capability—the final sand cone level. With this capability, the organization will know how to effectively incorporate transformation methodologies, such as BPR or DFSS. When the transformation has been achieved, the cycle is complete, the sand cone collapses, and the process repeats. In a new systems design, management needs to grapple with what it knows about stability of key processes, the ability to operate effectively in the short term, sustainability, improvement, and transformation.

SUMMARY OF LEARNING OBJECTIVES AND KEY OUTCOMES

1. *Demonstrate an understanding of the balanced scorecard as an integrated performance metric and how to apply its principles to develop some realistic measures for an industrial organization.* The balanced scorecard is an approach that gives appropriate performance weightings to a number of factors that are critical to success. Rather than basing business performance just on financials, the balance scorecard requires the establishment of measures in four perspective areas: customers, innovation and learning, internal processes, and financials. Under each of the four areas, a company sets specific goals that are consistent with its business plan. Attributes that are critical to the achievement of each goal are established, and specific measures are developed for each goal.

2. *Demonstrate an understanding of some of the major reasons why TQM programs fail, and discuss what steps companies can take to improve the chances for success.* Poor implementation is the major reason for TQM failures. This has been attributed to poor leadership, lack of commitment on the part of top management, a failure to prepare the culture in readiness for an implementation, and not taking an open systems approach. If QIM is to be successful, a culture based on integrity and trust must first be created.

3. *Discuss the three myths that may be responsible for many TQM failures, and defend TQM against its critics.* The three myths that have been behind many failed implementations are (1) change can be mandated from the top with little bottom-up participation in the process, (2) the way to bring about fundamental change is through rigorous training, and (3) all employees will react positively to empowerment and job enrichment opportunities.

4. *Discuss the phases necessary for a successful QIM implementation plan.* To be successful, QIM must be an evolutionary process and can take years. When a company embarks on the quality journey, a transformation begins from first- to second-generation quality. Research has demonstrated that this process requires a company to go through four distinct phases. During the first three of these, a company will be in the second generation. Phase three will take it into the third generation. Phase one is a predeployment phase during which the organization goes through a period of self-actualization, learning about itself, its operations, and its people. It may run pilot programs during this time, benchmark others, conduct training, use consultants, and start applying some statistic tools on a limited basis. During phase two, the organization begins to make quality a priority, establishing teams, proliferating training, and stressing improvement. Most of the activity is to achieve incremental improvements on existing systems. In this phase, the scope broadens to include a systems approach. Quality is extended to the design function and to include supply chain relationships. Accountability and measurement have become the norm in evaluating and improving performance. In phase three, quality is central to business strategy. Management decisions are fact based, the culture is united in a common purpose, the supply chain is integrated, and all participants up and down the chain are striving for the same goals. Customer value is the primary driver, and the organization grows by learning.

5. *Describe the characteristics of a third-generation (QIM) quality culture and how one would recognize a company with this level of quality maturity.* A third-generation culture is characterized by a committed and visionary leadership, trusting relationships with its customers, high-performance work systems, an empowered workforce that values continued learning, well-designed and managed processes, decisions that are data driven, and strong financial and market outcomes.

6. *Describe the sand cone model of change capability and how it supports a QIM culture.* The sand cone model describes the sequence of capability development that will help an organization adapt to changing conditions. Stabilization is the foundation capability that will enable a company to reliably predict its key outputs and outcomes. Next is operations followed by sustainability. Once the organization can sustain performance, it can develop a capability in improvement. The highest level is a transformation capability—the ability to reinvent value streams, infuse fresh ideas, and design new systems.

A second-generation quality program requires, as a minimum, the development of capabilities on the first three levels. The third generation requires a solid transformation capability.

To Test Your Understanding

5-1   Place yourself in the position of the president of a large public research university. Suggest some of the attributes that would be important under each of the four segments of a balanced scorecard. Suggest how these attributes might be measured. How can the balanced scorecard help the university formulate strategy and improve performance?

5-2   Reread the FPS minicase at the beginning of this chapter. Two years into the TQM, implementation management hired a consultant to evaluate progress. Do you think that management believed the program was working as intended? Why do you think the consultant found problems with the system? If you were the consultant, what would be your recommendations to FPS management?

5-3   Why is QIM an evolutionary process? Is it necessary for the implementation of quality principles to pass the test of time before taking an organization to a higher level? If a company that is at the phase two or three level merges with a company that is at the predeployment level (or below), how do you think the comingling of cultures should be handled?

5-4   Although the balanced scorecard is a useful tool in distributing management emphasis across four essential areas, a company's long-term viability depends on its financial health. Explain how QIM policies can impact each of the three financial measures in Equations 5-4 and 5-5 on page 121.

◆◆◆

Sears, Roebuck and Co.
America's Favorite Place to Shop

Sears, Roebuck and Co. (originally called the R. W. Sears Watch Company) was founded in 1886 when Richard Sears, a railway agent in Redwood, Minnesota, bought and resold a shipment of watches that had been sent in error to a local jeweler. Making a nice profit, he ordered more and thus a new business was born. In 1887, Sears moved his watch business to Chicago and recruited a qualified watchmaker, Alvah C. Roebuck, to work with him. The partnership blossomed, and in 1893, the name of the company was changed to Sears, Roebuck and Co.

In the late nineteenth century, rural farmers had to rely on nearby general stores to buy what they needed, sometimes at outrageous markups over wholesale. Sears and Roebuck saw this as a niche opportunity and started a mail-order business, offering those in rural areas a welcome alternative. Richard Sears knew farmers, understood their needs, and could write advertising copy that effectively communicated on their level.

Sears started distributing a mail-order catalog, featuring watches and jewelry. By 1895, the catalog had expanded to include general merchandise items such as shoes, women's garments, china and glassware, musical instruments, baby carriages, bicycles, saddles, firearms, fishing tackle, stoves and furniture, and buggies and wagons. Sales grew rapidly, and Sears went public in 1906. In 1925, the company opened its first retail store in Chicago. The business continued to grow, and soon became the standards

setter for retailing in the United States. The Sears catalog—America's "wish book"—became a defining element of the national culture.

By 1931, the average American family owned an automobile and needed affordable insurance. Sears seized the opportunity and established Allstate Insurance Company, named after Sears' brand of automobile tires at the time. In 1959, a second diversification move was taken with the purchase of Homart Development, a shopping center developer, and Sears retail stores became anchors in new shopping mall projects.

In 1981, Sears acquired Dean Witter Reynolds, a stock brokerage firm, and Coldwell Banker and Company, a real estate agency. The aim of what Wall Street referred to as a "socks and stocks" strategy was to create a giant supermarket of goods and services where, under one roof, consumers could buy a house, finance it, insure it, and furnish it. In 1984, Sears cofounded Prodigy, an Internet service provider, and in 1985, the company introduced the Discover Card, pioneering the "cash back" concept (refunding a small percentage of the total charges to the customer at the end of the year).

By the 1960s, the work environment within each Sears store mirrored success. Employees were loyal, energetic, and motivated. A generous incentive program made it possible for all employees to share in store profits. The climate was positive, morale was high, and everyone felt important. Most employees were full time and had expert knowledge of the products they sold. Customers grew to depend on the Sears salesperson as a source of competent advice. The company no longer referred to its personnel as "employees" or "management." Everyone had become an "associate." For nearly a century, Sears had earned the distinction of being "America's favorite place to shop."

During the 1970s and 1980s, Sears' market environment began to change. Senior management failed to take seriously the increasing competition from Wal-Mart and Kmart. Other specialty stores, such as The Limited, The Gap, and Circuit City, had also appeared on the landscape and were devouring market share. The market dominance that Sears had enjoyed for decades gradually began to slip away.

The low point came in 1990, when the company found its earnings and stock prices at 1983 levels, and discovered that Wal-Mart had eclipsed Sears as America's largest retailer. By 1992, Sears had fallen to third place behind Wal-Mart and Kmart. Financial performance spiraled downward as profits dropped. With declining profits, most internal incentive programs were eliminated.

As the market continued to falter, Sears responded with a string of initiatives that included such themes as Store of the Future, Everyday Low Pricing, Brand Central, and Stores Within a Store. Marketing programs were redirected to emphasize women's apparel and national brands. None of these ideas worked as well as hoped.

Sears Corporate also embarked on serious cost-cutting measures. One of these was to reduce the number of central support staff and to downsize the staffing in retail stores. Cash registers were relocated from the departments to central locations throughout each store. As a consequence, there were fewer product experts on the floor to help customers, and store managers who once had spent significant time merchandising and coaching staff, now found themselves immersed in paperwork and logistics. The staff at the cash register stations spent most of their time ringing up sales and little or no time on the floor learning the products and helping customers. Employee morale declined. Still, some remained optimistic because this was Sears, and Sears was an American tradition that had a history of winning.

Conditions did not significantly improve, and the customers did not return. Some believe Sears' problems stemmed from losing touch with its customers and its sense of purpose. Had Sears become irrelevant? Public confidence in Sears hit an all-time low. In 1992, Arthur Martinez, vice-chairman of Saks, was recruited to lead a turnaround of the corporation. The revitalization effort gained impetus when in May 1993, *FORTUNE Magazine* referred to Sears as a "dinosaur" that had been badly mismanaged by its executives.

In February 1993, Martinez assembled his top sixty-five executives for a three-day meeting in Phoenix. He facilitated the meeting himself, and his conduct was a surprising departure from the norm. In contrast to previous meetings when the CEO had delivered prepared speeches, Martinez rolled up his shirtsleeves and engaged his managers in frank conversation. His questions were pointed, and it was clear that he expected answers. This meeting format became an annual event. At the 1994 meeting, a turnaround strategy was developed that was based on three Cs and three Ps. The three Cs were the quintessence of a new corporate vision for Sears, which aspired to become

A *Compelling* place to *shop*,
A *Compelling* place to *work*,
A *Compelling* place to *invest*.

To achieve the three Cs, a new set of core values would be needed. The managers summarized these, using three Ps:

A *Passion* for the customer,
The belief that *People* add value,
The need for financial *Performance* leadership.

Martinez realized that achieving the Cs and Ps would require a new type of leadership—a *transformational leadership*. He outlined the following set of twelve leadership skills that would be used to rate the performance of all 15,000 managers in the Sears organization.

Sears Transformational Leadership Skills

- Change leadership
- Integrity
- Customer service orientation
- Business knowledge and literacy
- Problem solving
- Team skills

- Two-way communication skills
- Valuing diversity
- Empowerment skills
- Interpersonal skills
- Initiative and sense of urgency
- Developing associates and valuing their ideas

To determine how well the company was delivering on the three Cs, Sears developed some quantitative measures called total performance indicators (TPIs). The TPIs proved to be an effective way to link up the three Cs, and Sears dramatically changed the method for determining compensation for its top 200 executives. Using the balanced scorecard approach, a TPI bonus scheme was established in which one-third was based on "compelling place to shop" measures, one-third on "compelling place to work" measures, and one-third on "compelling place to invest" measures. All managers above the store level had some portion of their compensation tied to TPIs and the balanced scorecard.

Martinez realized that Sears had been run by managers who believed they were in the automobile and hardware business. The issue of identifying a target customer had never been addressed. A detailed analysis of customer data led to an important discovery—the demographics were different than what they had expected. Sears' typical customers were not men who were shopping for car accessories or tools for home projects. Those who made regular visits to retail stores were women, ages 25 to 54; were homeowners and parents, usually with a job outside the home; and had a medium household income of $37,500, ranging from $25,000 to $60,000. Having identified this as its target customer, the decision was made to use women's apparel as the major draw to attract more female customers. In 1993, the "Come see the softer side of Sears" nationwide advertising campaign was introduced in which an expanded selection of fashionable, affordable women's apparel and accessories were showcased.

In 1994, a "Many Sides of Sears" campaign expanded on the women's apparel focus, emphasizing that Sears fills a variety of needs during all stages of a person's life. Showcased in this campaign was a range of household and automotive products.

The three C/three P strategy worked, and Sears began to recapture market share. Revenues in 1996 increased an impressive 9.3%, representing a profit increase of 24% over the previous year. By early 1997, Sears was making indisputable progress, having gained the position as the second largest retailer in the United States, just behind Wal-Mart, and was number one as the major credit provider among retailers.

In considering growth opportunities for Sears, Martinez was inspired by the way Michael Eisner had leveraged Disney's brands and skills through a variety of formats, including licensing, retailing, new motion picture studios, and the acquisition of a major television network (ABC). Martinez believed a similar approach, which he referred to as "holistic retailing," could also work for Sears. Holistic retailing is a concept that attempts to meet a broad range of needs of middle-class homeowners. The Sears holistic strategy called for establishing a variety of retail and service formats that included

- Full-line mall department stores
- Automotive service centers
- Off-the-mall stores (Homelife furniture stores; Orchard hardware stores, which carry Sears brands; and small "dealer" stores owned and operated by independent entrepreneurs who sell Sears brand appliances, electronics, hardware, and lawn and garden products in small towns)
- Home services (HVAC, window and door replacement, pest control, replacement siding, roofing, and appliance installation and repair)

In contrast to its 1993 article, *FORTUNE Magazine* in 1997 voted Sears the most innovative general merchandise retailer, citing "the dinosaur . . . turned into a cash cow." The company's fresh approach had gained market share in almost all categories of merchandise. *FORTUNE* attributed Sears' success to a change in culture. In short, Martinez was able to change Sears because he was able to change the people within the Sears system. ∎

◆●◆

QUESTIONS FOR THOUGHT

1. Discuss how the four quadrants of Kaplan and Norton's balanced scorecard relate to the three Cs and the three Ps of Sears' turnaround strategy.

2. Was Martinez's strategy a form of QIM implementation? Explain. Where did the company appear to be consistent with total quality principles? Where were they inconsistent?

3. Is the concept of holistic retailing feasible? Given what you understand about open systems theory, strategy formulation, and implementation issues, will holistic marketing work?

4. What style of leadership did Martinez use? Why do you think he was effective?

5. What do you think of Sears' twelve transformation leadership skills? How would these skills have been effective in helping Sears deliver the three Ps and, in turn, achieve the three Cs?

6. What was the change management process Martinez used? What would you have done similarly or differently had you been in Martinez's position?

CHAPTER 6

Managing for Quality: The Human Element

If you want one year of prosperity, grow grain. If you want ten years of prosperity, grow trees. If you want one hundred years of prosperity, grow people.

—CHINESE PROVERB

Harriett's House of Horror

Empowerment or Coercion: How Do Workers Feel About QIM?

Harriett Harris has worked for the same company for ten years. Due to the early death of her mother, Harriett did not have the opportunity to attend college, although she could have easily handled the academic demands. Instead, she opted to work to support her two younger siblings. The local plant of Aztec Electronics readily employed her and trained her for their injector line, a critical process in the manufacture of electronic semiconductors. Harriett's job was to operate equipment that performed an important function in the manufacture of printed circuit boards, an operation where quality and yields are watched closely and play an important role in corporate profitability.

Harriett takes pride in her work, always striving to do a good job. Over the years, she has become one of the most highly skilled and productive workers. Her job is highly specialized and only requires a few tasks, but each must be performed with great precision and close attention to detail.

However, Harriett's world has just been turned upside down. As a result of customer pressures on Aztec for just-in-time deliveries, the company has recently hired a consultant to help transform the manufacturing plant into one that supports cellular manufacturing. New social work groups have emerged. Harriett has been moved from her line position, next to her friend Cathy, and placed in a work cell with people she does not know very well. Since her relocation, she misses the daily chats with Cathy. In addition, she is now in a new group, and has been told that her job responsibilities have changed in breadth and depth. She will have to undergo some intensive training, and her performance will not only be based on her individual achievements, but also on the collective performance of her work team. Harriett is frightened and has suddenly become overwhelmed by a sense of insecurity. Like an anchor, she feels that the tide of anxiety and frustration is slowly pulling her under. "Coming to work used to be such fun—now I dread it and look forward to the weekends." ∎

6.1 LEARNING OBJECTIVES AND KEY OUTCOMES

After studying the material in Chapter 6, you will be able to

1. Describe human resources as an open system, and explain how the HR system supports the organization's purpose
2. Describe and discuss the control theory model of human resource management
3. Describe the distinguishing features of an HPWO
4. Describe the link between culture and quality, and the process of bringing about cultural change
5. Define the five characteristics that determine the intrinsic motivating potential of a job and how this can be used in personnel assignments
6. Discuss how demographics and geographical differences affect culture
7. Describe the sand cone model of human capability and how it relates to the sand cone model of organizational change
8. Describe some approaches for measuring an organization's cultural readiness for QIM philosophies

6.2 PEOPLE: THE KEY TO QUALITY

Quality is created by inspired people who find innovative ways to solve real problems.

Process improvement is essential to good quality. However, processes do not do the work, people do. The genius of quality lies in the "informal, impromptu, often inspired ways, that real people solve real problems, in ways that formal processes can't anticipate. When you're competing on knowledge, the name of the game is improvisation, not standardization."[1] A common mistake, which could possibly be the single most important reason why some quality initiatives flounder, is to place too much faith in "hard" engineering tools, while failing to properly understand the "soft" people-related issues.

The open systems model emphasizes the important role of the human in organizational performance. The organization, as an aggregation of elements with emergent properties, is capable of collectively providing something that its individual parts alone cannot and has the ability to adapt to changing conditions. A company is a synergistic network of subsystems, each one an open system that exists to support the needs of the larger business system. One of these is concerned with the human element and is commonly called **human resources** (HR).

Human Resources

---

[1] Brown, John S., and Estee S. Gray, "The People Are the Company," *Fast Company Magazine,* Issue 01, November 1995, 78. Also available online at http://www.fastcompany.com/magazine/01/people.html (accessed April 5, 2005).

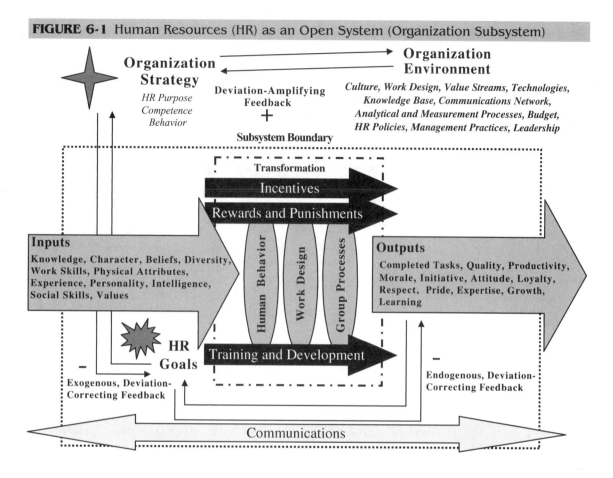

FIGURE 6-1 Human Resources (HR) as an Open System (Organization Subsystem)

6.2.1 Human Resources as an Open System

As Figure 6-1 illustrates, the HR system operates in an environment characterized by the components of the larger enterprise system, including technologies, culture, constraints, knowledge, problem-solving tools, and leadership. Inputs are those attributes that distinguish one person from another, such as knowledge, skills, experience, attitudes, beliefs, and aptitudes. Outputs can be classified in one of two ways. They either directly impact organizational **performance**, such as quality and **productivity**, or they contribute to human **behavior** (what the psychologists call the **affective domain**), such as pride and loyalty.

The transformation process is concerned with aligning individual or group behaviors with the completion of tasks in a way that supports the HR goals and is consistent with the work design. HR goals must be consistent with the organization's strategy. Incentives, rewards, and training should be carefully designed to avoid mixed signals and conflicts, and to ensure all personnel are unified behind a common purpose. Two-way vertical communications are especially important. It is essential that guidelines from a company's top echelons are clearly understood by all concerned, and conversely, senior management must actively seek input down the chain to guard against misinterpretations and noncompliance.

Performance

Productivity

Behavior

Affective Domain

Incentives should be carefully designed to avoid mixed signals or conflicts.

FIGURE 6-2 Control Theory Model of Human Resources

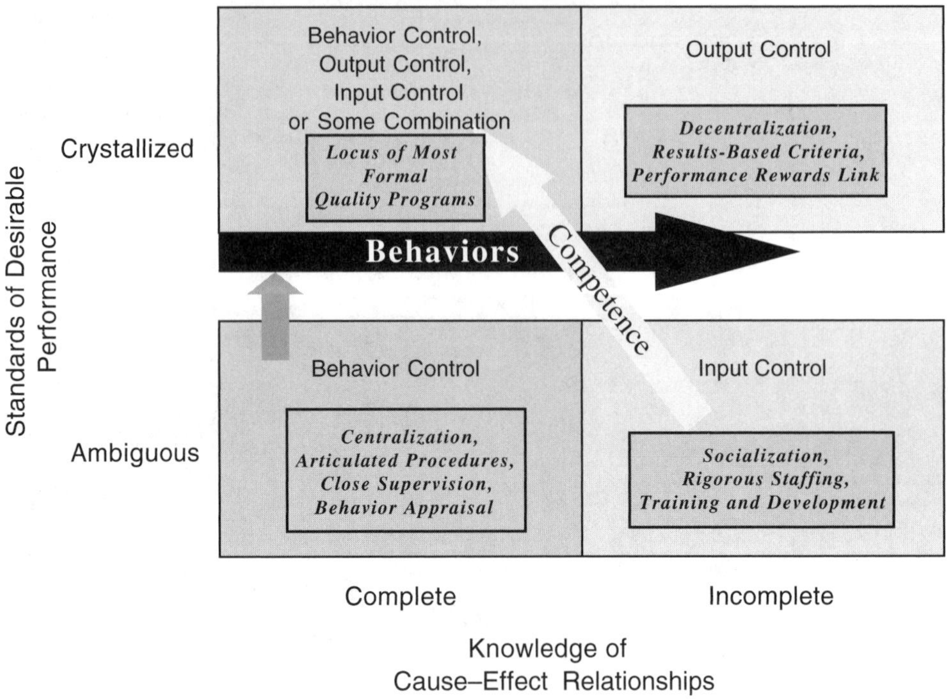

The HR system serves two primary functions: **competence management** and **behavior management.**[2] The former focuses on enriching the quality of system inputs, whereas the latter is concerned with the quality of process (the transformation). Both functions are aimed at enriching the quality of system outputs and are better understood when viewed from a control perspective.

Competence Management

Behavior Management

The primary objective of HR is to improve the quality of outputs through productive behaviors.

6.2.2 Quality and Human Resources

6.2.2.1 The Control Theory Model of HR   The control theory model (Figure 6-2), derived from open systems theory and behavioral science, advocates enhancing the quality of human resource management (HRM) through improved control mechanisms (directed toward competence management, behavior management, and output quality).

Competence management (the quality of inputs) can be controlled through recruitment and selection practices. Behavior management (transformational controls) governs the effectiveness of **training, team building**, and **behavior-based reward systems**. Output quality can be influenced by results-oriented reward systems that measure both performance and affective domains.

Training

Team Building

Behavior-Based Reward Systems

The control theory model prescribes control mechanisms based on two principal factors: how much the organization knows about its cause–effect relationships, and the

---

[2]Wright, Patrick M., and Scott A. Snell. "Toward an Integrative View of Strategic Human Resource Management." *Human Resource Management Review* 1 (1991): 203–25.

specificity of its performance standards. Cause–effect relationships are not always clear, and there is often ambiguity concerning what constitutes desirable performance standards.[3]

Standardized procedures are important to QIM as a means to ensure consistency and control. For a company to win the Malcolm Baldrige National Quality Award, employees have to demonstrate to the satisfaction of examiners that standardized procedures are in place, that they understand how to measure the quality of their work against those procedures, and in addition, that they know how their measurements support overall business performance. In mature quality programs, continuous improvement means discovering **cause–effect** relationships important to process quality. This theme is central to **Six Sigma** and is covered in more detail in Chapter 9.

Cause-Effect

Six Sigma

A core principle of all QIM philosophies is the belief that behaviors lead to (*cause*) results (*effects*), and that by influencing behaviors in a positive way, the quality of results can be improved. Problem-solving teams, which were originally called *quality circles,* are formed for the purpose of discovering and correcting the causes that inhibit excellence. Quality is made or broken at the source—that is, at the core transformation processes of the value stream. Outputs, good or bad, are largely systemic. If properly managed, the people most directly involved in the work can play an important role in influencing **quality at the source.** Team building should stress the importance of a unified approach to understanding processes, defining problems, and generating workable solutions.

Quality at the Source

The executive chairman decided to transform a Cyprian bank into a high-performing, world-class institution. Her vision was to achieve market differentiation by using the bank's employees to determine the best use of new technologies. Because financial institutions had traditionally been large, bureaucratic, and slow to change, achieving the chairman's vision was a tall order that would require a cultural shake-up. Extensive internal training was conducted to prepare personnel for their new roles. Training focused on a variety of subjects, including banking practices, quality concepts, and people skills such as communications, coaching, team facilitation, performance appraisal, the role of managers, and time and stress management. The payoff was substantial. Tapping into the intellectual capital of the bank's personnel elevated the bank to a position of market dominance. Examples of team-initiated improvements in customer service included the introduction of automated teller machines or ATMs—the first bank in Cyprus to do so—the establishment of a call center, and the introduction of Internet banking facilities.

Well-defined performance standards and good cause–effect knowledge are characteristic of the mature quality programs found in the upper left-hand quadrant of Figure 6-2. In these programs, managers are interested in simultaneously managing competence and behaviors: that is, quality of inputs (resources), outputs (performance results), and behaviors (process drivers). This is not easy. An attempt to concurrently control inputs, outputs, and behaviors can place conflicting demands on the system. As the model illustrates, **decentralization** (providing more local autonomy to the workforce) and results-based performance criteria make sense if the aim is to control output. In

Decentralization

Decentralization controls output. Centralization controls behaviors.

---

[3]Snell, Scott A. "Control Theory in Strategic Human Resource Management: The Mediating Effect of Administrative Information." *Academy of Management Review* 35, no. 2 (1992): 292–327.

Centralization

contrast, if the aim is to control behavior, **centralization** and behavior-based criteria are more effective. Input and output controls focus on the entry and exit points, respectively, and not on the process. The opposite is true in the case of behavior control. If the knowledge of cause–effect relationships is incomplete then any internal procedures aimed at resolving this dilemma more often than not result in a confused workforce.

Tension

The need to balance the use of standardized quality tools with the encouragement of creative behavior has been a source of **tension** in TQM implementations.[4] The term "control" itself implies lack of autonomy and can stifle individual initiative. An overemphasis on doing it right the first time can be a detriment to flexibility and responsiveness, whereas a willingness to accept less than perfection may in some circumstances facilitate a quick response to new opportunities or customer needs.[5]

Self-Direction

Self-Control

Shared Ownership

This does not mean that there is necessarily a conflict between the need to control quality and the desire to achieve the benefits of an empowered workforce. The key is to shift the onus from controls that are management imposed to a system that encourages **self-control**. QIM calls for a shift from control through supervision to **self-direction**, leading eventually to employee commitment through **shared ownership**. This constitutes a paradigm shift as illustrated in Table 6-1.

Either a participatory or self-management strategy can empower a workforce.

6.2.2.1 Workforce Empowerment There are two approaches that can lead to a more empowered workforce. A **participatory** strategy gives employees partial decision-making authority, while management reserves the right to judge the merits of (and reject) employee inputs. Formal suggestion schemes and **quality circles** are examples of participatory approaches. Under a **self-management** strategy—the approach favored by QIM—employees are given authority to follow through on their recommendations up to and including implementing changes. **Self-managing work teams** (SMWTs)[6] and **learning organizations** are examples of self-management strategies. When the responsibility for control is transferred to the level at which work is actually performed, the three subprocesses of the HR transformation—human behavior, work design, and group processes—are integrated.

Participatory

Quality Circles

Self-Management

Self-Managing Work Teams

Learning Organizations

Empowerment

Empowerment, which can unleash the adaptive potential in individuals,[7] requires dramatic changes in the way that managers and workers interact. Management has to be genuinely prepared to accept the consequences of an empowered workforce, and employees must be prepared to assume the new intellectual dimensions that will be added to their job responsibilities. Attempts to empower the workforce have typically failed when managers

- Are unwilling to devolve decision-making responsibilities to subordinates
- Do not listen to and act on the advice of workers
- Fail to adequately reward participatory behaviors

---

[4]Cameron, Kim S., and Carole K. Barnett. "Organizational Quality as a Cultural Variable." In *The Quality Movement and Organization Theory,* 271–94, edited by Robert E. Cole and W. Richard Scott. London: Sage, 2000.

[5]Fisher, Cynthia D., Lyle F. Schoenfeldt, and James B. Shaw. *Human Resource Management.* 5th ed, 422–78. Boston: Houghton-Mifflin, 2003.

[6]Dimitriades, Zoe S. "Total Involvement in Quality Management." *Team Performance Management,* 6, no. 7/8 (2000): 117–21.

[7]Heckman, Frank, "Designing Organizations for Flow Experience." *The Journal for Quality and Participation* 20, no. 2 (1997): 24–33.

- Are unsuccessful in matching employees to enriched jobs
- Provide inadequate training in decision-making and problem-solving skills

6.2.3 High-Performing Work Organizations

Multiskilling

SMWTs

Continuous Learning

Performance Appraisal

Mentoring

Train-the-Trainer

Organizations that stress workforce participation are called HPWOs or HIOs. The latter term is preferred by those skeptics who were unsure whether increased productivity actually led to improved profits. More recent research seems to have put that issue to rest. Studies conducted in many different countries, covering a diverse cross-section of industries, have confirmed that HPWOs are unquestionably more profitable than traditional firms with similar demographics.[8–17]

The attributes that distinguish HPWOs from traditional work cultures are employee autonomy and involvement in decision making, support for employee performance, rewards for performance, and sharing of knowledge and information.

In HPWOs, employees are autonomous, they continuously learn, and they share knowledge.

6.2.3.1 Employee Autonomy and Involvement in Decision Making   *Employee involvement* is the creation of opportunities for employees to learn and use new skills, including cross-functional **multiskilling**, the use of **SMWTs**, and the development of teaming and decision-making skills.

6.2.3.2 Support for Employee Performance   The second attribute, *performance support,* embodies work practices aimed at improved performance through **continuous learning**, and includes features such as formal **performance appraisal**, **mentoring** and coaching, and **train-the-trainer** programs.

Group-Based Performance Pay

6.2.3.3 Rewards for Performance   The third attribute, *rewards,* includes those policies and procedures designed to motivate employees and acknowledge their value, such as individual and **group-based performance pay**.

6.2.3.4 Sharing of Knowledge and Information   *Knowledge sharing,* the final attribute, signifies that systems are in place to communicate relevant and timely information

---

[8]Kling, Jeffrey. "High Performance Work Systems and Firm Performance." *Monthly Labor Review,* May 1995: 29–36.

[9]Ichniowski, Casey, Kathryn Shaw, and Giovanna Prennushi. "The Effects of Human Resource Practices on Productivity: A Study of Steel Finishing Lines." *American Economic Review* 87, no. 3 (1997): 291–313.

[10]Becker, Brian E., and Mark A. Huselid. "High Performance Work Systems and Firm Performance: A Synthesis of Research and Managerial Implications." *Research in Personnel and Human Resource Management,* Vol. 16, 53–101, edited by Gerald R. Ferris. Stamford, CT: JAI Press, 1998.

[11]Appelbaum, Eileen, Thomas Bailey, Peter Berg, and Arne L. Kalleberg. *Manufacturing Advantage: Why High Performance Work Systems Pay Off.* London: Cornell University Press, 2000.

[12]Patterson, Malcolm G., Michael A. West, R. Lawthorn, and S. Nickells. "The Impact of People Management Practices on Business Performance." *IPD Issues in People Management,* no. 22 (1997).

[13]Wood, Stephen, with Lilian de Menezes and Ana Lasaosa. "High Involvement Management and Performance." Paper delivered at Centre for Labour Market Studies. University of Leicester, England, May 2001.

[14]Betcherman, Gordon, Norm Leckie, and Katherine McMullen. *Developing Skills in the Canadian Workplace. The Results of the Ekos Workplace Training Survey.* Ottawa. Canadian Policy Research Networks, 1997.

[15]Huang, Tung-Chun. "The Effect of Participative Management on Organizational Performance: The Case of Taiwan." *International Journal of Human Resource Management* 8, no. 5 (1997): 677–89.

[16]Guthrie, James P. "High Involvement Work Practices, Turnover, and Productivity: Evidence from New Zealand." *Academy of Management Journal* 44, no. 1 (2001): 180–90.

[17]MacDuffie, John P. "Human Resource Bundles and Manufacturing Performance: Organizational Logic and Flexible Production Systems in the World Auto Industry." *Industrial and Labor Relations Review* 48 (1995): 197–221.

TABLE 6-1 The Evolution from Control to Commitment-Oriented Workforce Strategies

Human Resources Issues	Control Based (Traditional)	Transitional	Commitment to Quality-Inspired Management
Job Design	Management attention is limited to individual job performance.	Individual's responsibilities broadened to include overall system performance, partici-pative problem-solving groups formed (e.g., such quality of working life, employee involvement, and quality circle programs).	System performance and achieving organizational goals are more important than individual job performance.
	Work is standardized and fragmented; thinking is separated from doing. Accountability is focused on the individual worker. Job definitions are fixed.	Implement a systems approach to job design. Implement job enrichment strategies to add intellectual content and accountability. Implement self-managing work teams.	Job design enhances content of work, emphasizes whole task, and combines doing and thinking. Frequent use of teams as basic accountable unit. Flexible def-inition of duties, contingent on changing conditions.
Performance evaluation	Quality measurements define minimum performance. Process stability seen as desirable. Goals are estab-lished at the individual's level. Performance relative to the individual goals is re-viewed by a supervisor.	Implement problem-solving tools and statistical process control procedures as a move toward learning about processes and how to better control them. Orientation is moved from outputs to process and service.	Performance is based more on the achievement of team goals than individual achievements. Quality and service is stressed. Emphasis often placed on "stretch objectives," which tend to be dynamic and oriented to the marketplace. Evaluation is by customers, peers, and management, taking a holistic view.
Organization structure, systems, culture, and style	Structure tends to be layered, with top-down controls, emphasizing differentiation. Coordination and control depend on rigid rules and procedures. Emphasis is on power, prerogatives, and positional authority. Status symbols are distributed to reinforce the autocratic hierarchy.	Flatten organization, provid-ing more decentralization and local autonomy, im-proved communications, and a system that drives positive change based on feedback. Eliminate the rigid rules that constrain the ability to react to changing conditions. Some visible symbols are changed to signify a shift in paradigm.	Flat organization structure interconnected with a net-work of negative feedback loops with cross-functional influence capabilities. Coordination and control is based on organizationwide shared goals, values and traditions. Management has a knowl-edge orientation, emphasiz-ing problem solving, relevant information, and systems performance. Minimum status differen-tials deemphasize the levels and positional differences of the inherent hierarchy.

TABLE 6-1 The Evolution from Control to Commitment-Oriented Workforce Strategies (*continued*)

Human Resources Issues	Control Based (Traditional)	Transitional	Commitment to Quality-Inspired Management
Compensation policies	Variable pay where feasible to provide individual incentive.	Typically no basic changes in compensation concepts.	Variable rewards to create equity and reinforce group achievements: gain sharing, profit sharing.
	Individual pay geared to job evaluation.		Individual pay linked to job skills and mastery.
	In downturn, cuts concentrated on hourly payroll.	Equality of sacrifice among employee groups.	Equality of sacrifice.
Employment assurances	Employees regarded as variable costs.	Assurances that participation will not result in loss of job.	Assurances that participation will not result in loss of job.
		Extra effort to avoid layoffs.	High commitment to avoid or assist in reemployment.
			Priority for training and retraining existing workforce.
Employee voice policies	Employee input allowed on relatively narrow agenda. Attendant risks emphasized. Methods include open-door policy, attitude surveys, grievance procedures, and collective bargaining in some organizations.	Addition of limited, ad hoc consultation mechanisms; no change in corporate governance.	Employee participation encouraged on wide range of issues; attendant benefits emphasized; new concepts of corporate governance.
	Business information distributed on strictly defined "need to know" basis.	Additional sharing of information.	Business data shared widely.
Labor–management relations	Adversarial labor relations: emphasis on interest conflict.	Thawing of adversarial attitudes; joint sponsorship of quality of working life or employee involvement; emphasis on common fate.	Mutuality in labor relations; joint planning and problem solving on expanded agenda.
			Unions, management, and workers redefine their respective roles.

to all employees, and to ensure feedback from employees reaches those responsible for formulating and executing strategy. The management style that supports these four attributes is called high performing work practices (HPWPs), and represents a new way of organizing work.

QIM has little chance of success unless the internal culture supports HPWPs.[18] Just as machine theory and the open systems perspective are opposing viewpoints, the

---

[18]Detert, James R., Roger G. Schroeder, and John J. Mauriel. "A Framework for Linking Culture and Improvement Initiatives in Organizations." *Academy of Management Review* 25, no. 4 (2000): 850–63.

> The work in an HPWO is designed to help the worker learn.

difference between work in the traditional environment and in an HPWO is just as dramatic. In an HPWO, the workplace is designed to help the worker learn new skills—to tap into the worker's **tacit knowledge** and **emotional capital**—and to channel new energies into enhanced performance. The intellectual content of all jobs is enriched, and workers find themselves having to exercise discretion, decision making, and problem solving. Many workers in this environment find new job-related stress as they face a new set of responsibilities and accountabilities. Jobs that once could be performed in isolation now require interaction with coworkers, and communications that extend far beyond previous levels.

> An HPWO is an environment populated by knowledge workers.

Tacit Knowledge

Emotional Capital

Knowledge Workers

Simply committing to the idea of empowerment is not sufficient to transform a traditional workplace into a high-performing one. If ordinary employees are to be transformed into **knowledge workers**, management must be committed to workplace learning. Because there is no unanimous agreement on what constitutes a set of HPWPs, there is no universal recipe that is guaranteed to produce an HPWO. Table 6-2 depicts various practices that have come from independent research conducted in the United States and the United Kingdom.[19–21] Although there remains some lack of unanimity, what is common to all approaches is the genuine interest in the development of employees and in using the working environment as a place that fosters lifelong learning.

A study of Baldrige Award winners found that, although empowerment programs were well underway in almost all the companies, only a few had mature HPWPs, including functional SMWTs.[22] One of the reasons for this could be that formal quality programs do not usually subsume a radical overhaul of HR. This begs the question of how much more successful these paragon organizations might be with the appropriate emphasis on HPWPs. Table 6-3 provides guidance on how HR should be changed to fully support HPWPs.[23,24]

6.3 HUMAN RESOURCES—A VITAL LINK BETWEEN CULTURE AND QUALITY

6.3.1 Cultural Change

> Culture represents what the organization *is,* not what it *has.*

The term *organizational culture* does not have a widely accepted definition. Nevertheless, there is broad consensus that "culture is holistic, historically determined, socially constructed, involves beliefs and behavior, exists at a variety of levels, and manifests itself in

[19]Guest, David E. "HR and the Bottom Line: Has the Penny Dropped?" *People Management* 20 (July 2000): 26–31.

[20]Pfeffer, Jeffrey. *The Human Equation: Building Profits by Putting People First.* Boston: Harvard Business School Press, 1998.

[21]Pil, Frits K., and John P. MacDuffie. "The Adoption of High-Involvement Work Practices." In *The American Workplace: Skills, Compensation and Employee Involvement,* 137–171, edited by Casey Ichniowski, David Levine, Craig Olson, and George Strauss. Cambridge: Cambridge University Press, 2000.

[22]Blackburn, Richard, and Benson Rosen. "Total Quality and Human Resources Management: Lessons Learned from Baldrige Award-Winning Companies." *Academy of Management Executive* 7, no. 3 (1997): 49–66.

[23]Ibid.

[24]Banner, David K., W. Anthony Kulisch, and Newman S. Peery. "Self-Managing Work Teams (SMWT) and the Human Resource Function." *Management Decision* 30, no. 3 (1992): 44.

TABLE 6-2 High-Performing Work Practices

Pfeffer	Pil and MacDuffie	Guest
Employment Security	Online work teams	Realistic job previews
		Psychometric tests for selection
		Well-developed induction training
Selective hiring		Provision of extensive training for experienced employees
Self-managed teams and decentralization of authority	Offline employee involvement practices and problem-solving groups	Regular appraisals
		Regular feedback on performance from many sources
		Individual performance-related pay
Comparatively high compensation	Job rotation	Profit-related bonuses
		Flexible job descriptions
Extensive training	Suggestion programs	Multiskilling
Minimal status distinctions		Presence of work improvement teams
		Presence of problem-solving groups
		Information provided on the firm's business plan
		Information provided on the firm's performance targets
		No compulsory redundancies
Extensive sharing of financial and performance information	Decentralization of quality efforts	Avoidance of voluntary redundancies
		Commitment to single status
		Harmonized holiday entitlement

SOURCE: Data from Pfeffer, Jeffrey, *The Human Equation: Building Profits by Putting People First*, 64–98. Boston: Harvard Business School Press, 1998: Pil., Frits K., and John P. MacDuffie. "The Adoption of High-Involvement Work Practices." In *The American Workplace: Skills, Compensation and Employee Involvement*, 137–71, edited by Casey Ichniowski, David I. Levine, Craiz Olson, and George Strauss. Cambridge: Cambridge University Press, 2000; and Guest, David E. "HR and the Bottom Line: Has the Penny Dropped?" *People Management* 20 (July 2000): 26–31.

a wide range of features of organizational life."[25] The National Advisory Group for Continuing Education and Lifelong Learning in England defined culture as "that bundle of signs, symbols, beliefs, traditions, myths, ways of thinking, speaking and doing which characterize the ways of life or behavior of a given group of people."[26] Culture is not an

[25]Detert, Scroeder, and Mauriel, "A Framework for Linking," 850–63.

[26]Fryer, R. H., Chairman of National Advisory Group for Continuing Education and Lifelong Learning. *Creating Learning Cultures: Next Steps in Achieving the Learning Age.* Second report of The National Advisory Group for Continuing Education and Lifelong Learning. Sheffield, UK: Department for Electronic Education, 1999. Also available online at http://www.lifelonglearning.co.uk/nagcell2 (accessed April 5, 2005).

TABLE 6-3 Transformation of HRM to Support High-Performing Work Practices

HRM Issues	Traditional HRM	HRM to Support Quality-Inspired Management and High-Performing Work Practices
Organization culture	Individualism, differentiation, autocratic leadership; motivation is based on profits and productivity	Collective efforts, cross-functional collaboration; leadership style based on coaching and enabling; motivation is based on quality and customer satisfaction
Role of HRM department	Centralized, functional, staff auditor	Decentralized, coach, counselor, adviser
Employee participation and voice	Suggestion systems, random examples of attempts to involve employees and solicit their input	Employee participation is part of due process; organizationwide use of quality circles; vehicles such as attitude surveys are routinely used to ensure employee voices are heard at the highest levels
Communications	Top-down	Top-down, bottom-up, horizontal, lateral, and multidirectional
Recruitment, selection, promotion, and career development	Recruiting and testing, screening done by HRM development; selection by management based on narrow job skills; promotion based on individual achievements; linear career path	HRM department screening; self-managed work team (SMWT) involvement in recruiting and selection of peers (team members) based on problem-solving skills; promotion based on group facilitation; horizontal career path
Training	HRM department administers training program, which focuses on job-related technical skills, within a single function; productivity is stressed	HRM department trains the trainers in SMWT; training focuses on broad range of cross-functional skills; training emphasizes diagnostic and problem solving; productivity and quality are stressed
Job design	HRM department reviews and approves job descriptions; work is designed to achieve efficiencies and productivity; standard procedures are emphasized; span of control is narrow; each individual job is assigned a specific job description	HRM department assists in job and skill descriptions; SMWT members' jobs are defined by overlapping skill areas, stressing autonomy and empowerment; work is designed to achieve quality and customization; innovation is encouraged; span of control is wide
Wage and salary, rewards	Wage system based on skill levels, step increases, seniority, and performance; individual competition for salary increases based on merit and other benefits	Wage system includes learn to earn and some team- and group-based rewards, such as gain sharing; financial rewards are possible, as well as opportunities for nonfinancial recognition
Performance appraisal	Appraisals done by management using HRM department guidelines; performance appraised against individual goals, typically emphasizing financial measures	Peer review by SMWT members, as well as management and customers, appraise member performance based on team goals; quality and service are emphasized; SMWT is responsible for administering some discipline and rewards
Benefits administration	HRM department administers and reviews HRM process including recruitment, selection, interviewing, and termination to ensure legal compliance	SMWT members determine vacation and work times

TABLE 6-3 Transformation of HRM to Support High-Performing Work Practices (*continued*)

HRM Issues	*Traditional HRM*	*HRM to Support Quality-Inspired Management and High-Performing Work Practices HPWP*
Employment law, EEOC, wrongful discharge	HRM department administers and reviews HRM procedures including recruitment, selection, interviewing, and termination to ensure legal compliance	SMWT members follow HRM department guidelines
Health and safety	Reactive behavior, treating problems as they occur	Proactive behavior, with emphasis on prevention, conducting formal safety programs, wellness programs, and offering employee assistance concerning employee welfare
Industrial relations	Union is viewed as an adversary	Cooperative union and management relations
HR planning	HRM department plans based on business strategy including manpower and career planning	HRM department plans based on business strategy
		SMWT involved in succession, downsizing, and growth plans

HRM, human resource management; HR, human resources.

attribute that an organization *has,* rather culture represents what the organization *is.*[27] The following definition emphasizes the link between culture and quality: quality means that the organization's culture is defined by and supports the constant attainment of customer satisfaction through an integrated system of tools, techniques, and training.[28]

Because an organization's culture is woven around its people, reengineering the HR system will lead the cultural transformation. As a changing culture begins to drive toward an HPWO, the impacts can be far reaching. Team-based organizations will discover the need to learn new methods of job analysis, assessment, recruitment, and socialization.[29] A new paradigm for HRM will be required—one based on quality consciousness, HPWPs, and the alignment of culture with quality objectives.

> Cultural change is led by redesigning the human resources system.

Cultural change is slow; it will take place on many fronts and over an extended time. People must be won over to a new way of thinking and working, and begin to accept a new sense of what is normal. Old habits and conventions die hard, and cultures are particularly resistant to changes imposed on them from the outside. Therefore, it is especially important that employees at all levels participate in the change management process. The cultural transformation process has been described by Brody[30] and an example of the type of changes that are required is illustrated in Figure 6-3.

---

[27]Hawkins, Peter. "Organizational Culture: Sailing between Evangelism and Complexity." *Human Relations* 50, no. 4 (1997): 417–40.

[28]Cameron, Kim S., and David A. Whetten. "Organizational Effectiveness and Quality: The Second Generation." In *Higher Education: Handbook of Theory and Research,* 265–306, edited by J. R. Smart. New York: Agathon, 1992.

[29]Klimoski, Richard J., and Robert G. Jones. "Staffing for Effective Group Decision Making: Key Issues in Matching People and Teams." In *Team Effectiveness and Decision Making in Organizations,* 291–332, edited by Richard A. Guzzo and Eduardo Salas. San Francisco: Jossey-Bass, 1995.

[30]Brody, Pauline N. "Introduction to Total Quality Management." In *Total Quality Management: A Report of Proceedings from the Xerox Quality Forum II,* 1–24. Leesburg, VA: Xerox, August 1990.

FIGURE 6-3 Cultural Transformation

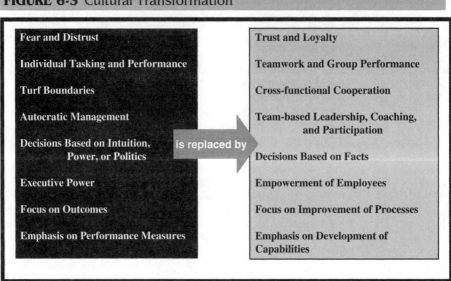

Fear and Distrust	Trust and Loyalty
Individual Tasking and Performance	Teamwork and Group Performance
Turf Boundaries	Cross-functional Cooperation
Autocratic Management	Team-based Leadership, Coaching, and Participation
Decisions Based on Intuition, Power, or Politics	Decisions Based on Facts
Executive Power	Empowerment of Employees
Focus on Outcomes	Focus on Improvement of Processes
Emphasis on Performance Measures	Emphasis on Development of Capabilities

is replaced by

Culture provides the social structure for the open system. Quality can be delivered only if all subsystems are quality conscious and share common goals. Some writers have established this linkage by describing culture as "a system of shared values defining what is important, and norms that guide members' attitudes and behaviors."[31] A quality consciousness must be intrinsic to the organizational culture. Conversely, organizational culture must foster quality consciousness. Table 6-4 shows the relationship between culture, QIM values, and the corresponding HR practices based on HPWPs.[32,33]

6.3.2 Culture and the Value Stream

Culture directly impacts the value stream. Motivation, orientation to work, and control (all of which are cultural dimensions) affect the quality of working life, work design, and productivity because employees respond in individual ways to HR policies. However, HR can only be held partially accountable for good or bad work practices. In an age of information technologies, workers at all levels are continually besieged with communications, largely via personal computers. It is not surprising that people can become confused by information overload and what at times appear to be mixed messages. Individual attitudes and values will be shaped by how data are processed and interpreted. Two people, when confronted with the same information, are likely to extract different meanings. A culture emerges when interpretations and acceptances align, leading to common values and behavioral norms.[34]

In the physical sciences, according to the second law of thermodynamics, systems will eventually self-destruct if they fail to adapt to their changing environments. This

---

[31]O'Reilly, Charles A., III, and Jennifer A. Chatman. "Culture as Social Control: Corporations, Cults, and Commitment." In *Research in Organizational Behavior,* Vol. 18, 160, edited by Barry M. Staw and Larry L. Cumming. Greenwich, CT: JAI Press, 1996.

[32]Blackburn and Rosen, "Total Quality and Human," 49–66.

[33]Detert, Scroeder, and Mauriel, "A Framework for Linking," 850–63.

[34]Jackson, Susan E., and Randall S. Schuler. "Understanding Human Resource Management in the Context of Organizations and Their Environments." *Annual Review of Psychology* 46 (1995): 237–71.

TABLE 6-4 HRM and a Quality-Conscious Culture

Dimensions of Organization Culture	QIM Core Values	Corresponding HR Practices
Truth and rationality	Decision making is knowledge based; problem solving is a process of learning and discovery, motivated by the genuine will to reveal the truth	Training, actively supported by top management, is provided to all employees; employees and teams are empowered to make decisions at their discretion; decision making and learning is an integral part of job design; management by fact is emphasized at all levels
Time and time horizon	Improvements are continuous, evolutionary, and at times, revolutionary; quality requires a long-term orientation and strategic approach	Top management is responsible for initiating, supporting, and communicating a vision of a total quality culture; systems that allow upward and lateral communications are developed, implemented, and reinforced; performance reviews are refocused from an evaluation of past performance only, to an emphasis on what management can do to assist employees in their future job-related quality efforts; HR professionals assist in implementing QIM, while making certain the HR function is transformed and managed under the same precepts
Motivation	Problems are caused by defective systems, not employees; employees are intrinsically motivated to do quality work if the systems within which they work are supportive	Autonomous work groups are not required, but processes that bring multiple perspectives to bear on quality issues are imperative; nonfinancial recognition systems at both the individual and work group levels reinforce both small wins and big victories in the quest for total quality
Stability versus change, innovation, and personal growth	Improvement is continuous and never ending; an organization must be able to adapt to changing requirements; change management is part of the evolving total quality paradigm; a quality organization is a learning organization; substantial improvements can be achieved using existing resources	Improvement and problem solving is team based; compensation systems reflect team contributions, including mastery of additional skills; employee recruitment, selection, promotion, and career development programs reflect the new realities of managing and working in a QIM environment

(continued)

TABLE 6-4 HRM and a Quality-Conscious Culture (*continued*)

Dimensions of Organization Culture	QIM Core Values	Corresponding HR Practices
Orientation to work, tasks, and personnel	Purpose is achieved by focusing on outcomes that stakeholders consider important; quality is derived from a customer focus, prevention of defects, improvement of internal processes, and introduction of new technologies	Employee participation in planning and decision making, and in the development of new initiatives, improves acceptance and implementability; safety and health issues are addressed proactively not reactively
Isolation versus collaboration and cooperation	Collaboration and cooperation are imperatives for team-based structures; cross-functional networking is important to solve problems that are of interest to customers; culture must become a community of common interests	Team building and cross-functional collaboration forms an integral part of training and job design; systems permit a free two-way flow of information, enabling employees at all levels of the organization to make known their concerns, ideas, and reactions to quality initiatives
Control, coordination, and responsibility	All employees share a common vision and ownership of organization's goals; all employees should participate in decision making and share in rewards; controls are decentralized and emphasize discipline and self-management	Controls are through empowerment strategies such as self-managed work teams; individual skills must be broadened both horizontally and vertically to include cross-training and increased intellectual content; communication systems might include suggestion opportunities with rapid response, open-door policies, skip-level policies, attitude surveys, etc.
Internal and/or external orientation and focus	All policies and procedures should be customer driven; customers are internal and external; performance is based on balanced scorecard approach rather than traditional financial measures	Customer interests are the litmus tests for all decisions; reward systems support the achievement of goals established by the balanced scorecard

HRM, human resource management; QIM, quality-inspired management; HR, human resources; TQM, total quality management.

The culture and its members must represent a good fit.

phenomenon also holds true for the HR system. To survive, HR must keep abreast of the expectations of its environment and respond appropriately to the changing roles of system members. Even the compatibility requirements for membership will be shaped as the work culture evolves. It is essential that the culture, and the individuals within it, represent a good fit. Just as a fish lying on the bank of the river is in distress, an employee who is a fish out of water is not happy. Misfit employees are likely to be unproductive and have a debilitating affect on the morale of those around them. Resolving this issue may defy traditional HR wisdom. Recruiting practices have typically allocated the greatest weight to technical skills, with the goal of matching candidates to specific jobs.

An alternative school of thought advocates assigning a heavy weighting to whether a job candidate has the potential to produce and learn in the particular work culture, and whether the job has motivating potential for the individual performing it.

6.4 MOTIVATION AND WORK DESIGN

Some workers do not want empowerment, preferring repetitive jobs.

6.4.1 Intrinsic Motivating Potential of the Job

One of Maslow's famous sayings was, if you want people to do a good job for you, then you must give them a good job to do. What is a good job? TQM fundamentals assumed employees prefer enriched jobs with autonomy and self-control. If jobs fitting these criteria are provided, people will take pride in their work, and any heroic efforts to motivate performance are unnecessary. This is exposed in Chapter 5 as one of the myths that has led to failed TQM implementations. There is contradictory evidence that some workers regard repetitive, routine work to be less stressful (and therefore more desirable) than a broader scope of responsibilities that require decision making and creativity.[35] Like Harriett Harris in the minicase introducing this chapter, job enrichment programs can have the opposite effect of what was intended. Rather than motivating the worker, additional duties (that were previously the domain of managers and supervisors) can intimidate employees who are ill prepared or unwilling to embrace new responsibilities or accountabilities. These are issues that should be kept in mind when recruiting new personnel, designing training programs, and inculcating values into the culture's consciousness.

Intrinsic Motivating Potential

Hackman and Oldham attempted to define what a good job looks like by identifying key attributes of work design that describe a job's **intrinsic motivating potential**. Their research found that work is intrinsically motivating if five characteristics are present:[36]

Skill Variety
- **Skill Variety**—the degree to which a job requires different skills, abilities, or talents

Task Identity
- **Task Identity**—the extent to which a job requires completion of a whole and identifiable unit of output

Task Significance
- **Task Significance**—the degree to which the job impacts the lives of other people, the organization, and the environment

Autonomy
- **Autonomy**—the freedom the worker has to determine the pace and sequencing of work, and the work methods used

Feedback
- **Feedback**—the degree to which the worker obtains information on the effectiveness of performance, which comes from personal observation, input from supervisors, and other sources

6.4.1.1 The MPS as a Measure of Motivating Potential   The motivating potential of work is measured using a motivating potential score (MPS) that is calculated using the following equation:

$$\text{MPS} = \frac{\text{Skill Variety} + \text{Task Identity} + \text{Task Significance}}{3} \times \text{Autonomy} \times \text{Feedback} \tag{6-1}$$

[35]Juran, Joseph, and Frank M. Gryna. *Quality Planning and Analysis (from Product Development through Use).* 3rd ed. New York: McGraw-Hill, 1993.

[36]Hackman, J. Richard and Greg R. Oldham. *Work Redesign.* Reading, MA: Addison-Wesley, 1980.

A job with a high MPS will not motivate a worker with low growth needs.

The research has revealed that jobs with a high MPS result in higher job satisfaction and productivity than jobs scoring low. Skill variety, task identity, and task significance are all related to the specific task, and together serve to provide the worker with a sense of "meaningfulness" (Why am I doing this job?, Is it important?, and Does it allow me to use my talents?). Autonomy provides the worker with a sense of "responsibility" (others are depending on me, so I better do this right.). Feedback satisfies the individual's need, as an open system, for "knowledge of results" (Did I get it right, and if not, what do I need to do differently?).

An individual's growth needs are determined from a growth needs strength questionnaire.

The MPS should be interpreted only as a crude measure because the scores assigned to the five characteristics are based on the subjective perception of an individual worker performing the job. Two workers can generate different MPS scores for the same job. It should also be kept in mind that the MPS is a measure of motivating potential. This does not mean that every job with a high MPS will motivate every worker. One needs to consider an individual's growth needs.

6.4.2 Growth Needs and Job Matching

Growth Needs

Psychological State

Hackman and Oldham found that workers with high growth needs respond to jobs with a high MPS, and those with low growth needs do not. **Growth needs** are measured by having an employee fill out a growth needs strength (GNS) questionnaire designed to measure the person's preferences concerning likes and dislikes, and what that person considers to be the ideal job. When a person is matched to a job, the job characteristics (MPS) and the employee's growth needs (GNS) combine to influence the worker's **psychological state**—that is, how the worker feels about the job. These feelings then translate into personal and work outcomes. This is illustrated in Figure 6-4.

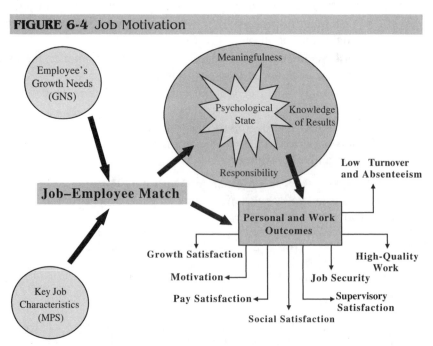

FIGURE 6-4 Job Motivation

Note: GNS, growth needs strength; MPS, motivating potential source.

6.5 REGIONAL INFLUENCE ON CULTURE

Culture is influenced by geography and demographics.

Culture can be significantly influenced by geographical location. The approach an organization takes to reform its culture depends to a large extent on national, social, political, and economic norms. The following three models[37] underscore how disparate regions of the world approach cultural change differently.

6.5.1 Nordic Model

The Nordic model is typical of Sweden, Denmark, and Finland. In the Scandanavian cultures, change is embedded within the broad context of each nation's social, economic, cultural, and political history. As a welfare society, the state is strongly committed to the development of the individual person, and government policy provides the philosophies and values that underpin education and HR practices. The concept of lifelong adult education is a core value that pervades Nordic democracies. It is not surprising that these countries lead Europe in participation rates in industrial training.

As early as the 1930s, Sweden pioneered the concept of an active labor relations policy based on cooperation rather than conflict. Today, it is common for collective bargaining agreements to include provisions for employee development. In Nordic societies, it is well understood that employers have an obligation to provide for learning and growth opportunities for workers, and to enhance their career advancement.

6.5.2 British Model

In the United Kingdom, the government provides leadership for cultural reform through comprehensive policies that link entire segments of education and training. Infrastructure and incentives are established at national and local levels, and stress the achievement of specific learning targets. Industry and the Confederation of British Industry work as a partnership to bring about cultural change on a national scale. Through broad collaboration and wide participation by a diverse cross-section of vested interests, the goal is to gradually convert Britain into a learning society.

6.5.3 American Model

In America, cultural reform is market driven and represents a complex interaction of individualism, entrepreneurialism, and community orientation. Initiatives are typically taken on a company-by-company basis. At the national level, there is substantial diversity in policies, strategies, and outcomes across industries, and even within industry groups. The federal government has not yet taken the lead to make cultural revolution a national priority.

6.6 HUMAN CAPABILITY AND ORGANIZATIONAL READINESS FOR QIM

How can an organization know if it is ready for QIM, and how can it prepare so the implementation goes smoothly and is successful? We first raised this question in Chapter 5 in the context of change management and system behavior. We now investigate this issue from the human behavior and organizational culture perspective.

---

[37]Kearns, Peter, and George Papadopoulos. *Building a Learning and Training Culture: The Experience of Five OECD Countries,* vi. Project No. NR 9015. Kensington Park, NSW: National Centre for Vocational Education and Research, June 11, 2000.

FIGURE 6-5 Human Capability Model

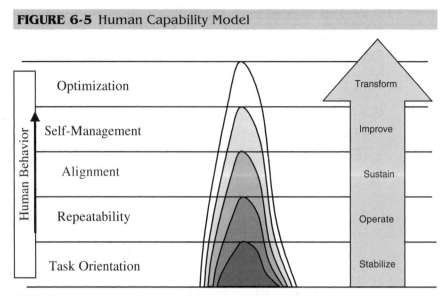

SOURCE: Based on *Journal of Operations Management,* 8, Kasra Ferdows and Arnoud DeMeyer, "Lasting Improvements in Manufacturing Performance: In Search of New Theory, pp. 168–84, Copyright 1990 printed with permission from Elsevier.

> Cultural readiness has to precede QIM implementation.

It is ironic that some quality implementations occur in a top-down manner without giving proper consideration to the organization's cultural readiness or how the workforce will be affected and its likely reaction. Assuming human resiliency will sustain the business through the transition can be risky. A more sensible approach is to introduce change in a manner that is cognizant of its impact on humans and to thereby increase the chance of success.

6.6.1 Sand Cone Model of Human Capability

> The development of human capability must occur in a prescribed sequence.

Figure 6-5 is the sand cone model of human capability, and illustrates how the sand cone model of human capability is linked with the sand cone model of organizational change presented in Chapter 5 (Figure 5-5).

> **Task Orientation**

6.6.1.1 Task Orientation Capability.   The foundation capability for this model is a **task orientation**, and defines a work environment where individuals are concerned almost exclusively with their personal job descriptions and have little appreciation for how their efforts contribute to something larger. This is the counterpart capability to the stabilization level of the sand cone model of organizational change, and showcases the basic task processes necessary for each value stream. A capability at this level is characterized by adequate descriptions and training for each task, as well as the assignment of qualified personnel. There is no encouragement for the workforce to unite behind broad business objectives. There is no emphasis on teaming, training and development, or cross-functional collaboration. If an organization remains at this level too long without advancing, personnel turnover is likely to become a problem. Talented employees, perceiving better working conditions and opportunities for growth in other organizations, may opt to leave. If this occurs, the organization cannot move forward in knowledge and skills because it will be preoccupied with the replacement of competent and experienced members of the workforce.

6.6.1.2 Repeatability Capability   The operating level of human capability, called **repeatability** has, as its objective, deriving the greatest value from the workforce, barring any fundamental redesign of the work. At the repeatability level, the focus is on instilling discipline into the workplace. This includes maximizing the efficiency and human friendliness of the work environment; establishing clear lines of communications; improving personnel selection and training, as well as matching staff with specific jobs; developing meaningful and equitable performance measures; and ensuring compensation levels are at least comparable to industry standards. When employees begin to take their job responsibilities more seriously, they will develop repeatable methods that will increase consistency of output within their specific work group, even though some significant variations in performance may still exist compared with employees in other work groups.

The effort to implement improved workforce practices begins when the organization adopts, as a core value, the continuous improvement of its workforce, targeting the key areas of knowledge, skills, motivation, and performance. Standard work practices are documented, incorporating human resource needs and broadly covering the work environment, training and development, communications, performance evaluation, staffing, and compensation. Repeatability depends on the organization's ability to institutionalize its standard work practices. A company needs to reach the repeatability level before it can consider implementing the 5-S lean production tool discussed in Chapter 9.

6.6.1.3 Alignment Capability   At the sustainability level, a human capability in **alignment** is developed. At this level, the organization strives to minimize the inconsistencies between individual workers by standardizing on best practices. Skill sets are defined for each job and matched with core business functions. Collectively, these skills represent the organization's core competencies, and programs are initiated to inculcate the core skills across the entire workforce. A common culture begins to emerge as learning and growth in core competencies are reinforced and rewarded across the board.

HR development and career planning are critical to the success of strategic planning. Creating a participatory environment enhances the growth of the culture as individuals and groups become involved in decisions regarding their work and working conditions. At the alignment level, the organization has improved its capability to predict performance due to a better understanding of the knowledge and skills of its workforce, its core competencies, the institutionalization of standardized best practices, and a culture based on unity of purpose.

6.6.1.4 Self-Management Capability   As the organization moves to the improvement level of the change model, human capabilities need to advance to a level that supports learning and self-management. The use of teams is widely emphasized to disseminate complementary knowledge between individuals with similar work interests. For the first time, the organization begins to use the management of core competencies to strategic advantage. Management strives to create internal conditions that will maximize the effectiveness of team activities. Fact replaces intuition, politics, and power as the basis for decision making. Performance is quantitatively measured, and then analyzed to determine capability and trends. Performance data are used to determine alignment at the individual, team, unit, and organizational levels, and to assess consistency with strategic goals. Mentors are provided to individuals and teams, to facilitate skills development, and to proliferate lessons learned. Because the workforce capability is known quantitatively, overall business capability can be predicted. An organization needs to be on this level before it assigns improvement projects to teams of employees.

Optimization

6.6.1.5 Optimization Capability   The final capability level is **optimization**, which is the transformation level of human resource development. The culture of an optimizing organization is relentless in its pursuit of excellence. At this level, personnel continuously strive to improve performance through increased skills, knowledge, and motivation. Improvements occur incrementally, as gradual changes in workforce practices take place, and also as quantum leaps when standard procedures are revolutionized through the introduction of breakthrough innovations.

6.6.2 Measures of Cultural Readiness

Table 6-5 is a questionnaire that has been used to measure culture.[38] The idea is to distribute the questionnaire to employees who are randomly selected from all levels of an organization. Persons selected are asked to complete the questionnaire by rating themselves on four personal attributes, each relating to **commitment**, and three dimensions of **organizational citizenship behavior—altruism**, **conscientiousness**, and loyalty. Ratings are on a 7-point scale, with 1 representing *Absolutely Disagree* and 7 representing *Absolutely Agree.* Because there are four questions in each category, aggregate scores can range from 16 to 112. An average score of 64 would signify an overall attitude of indifference. Average scores below that would assuredly signify a lack of cultural readiness, and scores above that would provide management with increasing confidence that the culture may be congruent with quality objectives, the introduction of teams, and broader employee participation.

Commitment

Organizational Citizenship Behavior

Altruism

Conscientiousness

Other survey instruments have been suggested for measuring cultural readiness.[39] Table 6-6 shows examples of the types of information that could be obtained from an organizationwide survey. When using this instrument, any areas receiving a score of 3 or less represent a deficiency that requires attention before the organization is ready for a full-scale implementation of QIM philosophies.

Questionnaires with numerical scales can be used to measure cultural change.

SUMMARY OF LEARNING OBJECTIVES AND KEY OUTCOMES

1. *Describe human resources as an open system, and explain how the HR system supports the organization's purpose.* The human resource function is an open system that operates within the larger business system. Its inputs are the attributes that distinguish one person from another, and its outputs are in the form of performance measures (e.g., quality) and behavioral attributes (e.g., feelings, emotions). The transformation process is concerned with optimizing the deployment of the human factor within the value streams to produce the best results. Communications and rewards are key determinants of optimum results. The primary purpose of the HR system is to manage inputs through better workforce competence and to improve quality through productive behaviors.

---

[38]Cardona, Pablo, and Alvaro Espejo. *The Effect of the Rating Source in Organizational Citizenship Behavior: A Multitrait-Multimethod Analysis.* Research Paper No. 474. Barcelona: University of Navarra, October 2002.

[39]Sanchez, Juan I., Eyran Kraus, Steve White, and Marie Williams. "Adopting High-Involvement Human Resource Practices." *Group & Organization Management* December 1999: 24(4) 461–78.

TABLE 6-5 Rating Organizational Citizenship Behavior

Organizational Commitment	*Absolutely Disagree*						*Absolutely Agree*
1 I would not abandon this organization, among other reasons, because my work here is sufficiently attractive to me.	1	2	3	4	5	6	7
2 Working in this organization is worthwhile, among other reasons, because my work offers me opportunities to learn and grow professionally.	1	2	3	4	5	6	7
3 I would not abandon this organization because of a sense of obligation toward my coworkers.	1	2	3	4	5	6	7
4 It will not be difficult for me to find another organization where I could feel substantially more identified.	1	2	3	4	5	6	7

Organizational Citizenship Behavior	*Absolutely Disagree*						*Absolutely Agree*
Interpersonal (OCBI)							
1 I help others who have been absent.	1	2	3	4	5	6	7
2 I willingly give my time to help others who have work-related problems.	1	2	3	4	5	6	7
3 I go out of my way to make newer employees feel welcome in the work group.	1	2	3	4	5	6	7
4 I show genuine concern and courtesy toward coworkers, even under the most trying business or personal situations.	1	2	3	4	5	6	7
5 I assist others with their duties.	1	2	3	4	5	6	7
Organizational (OCBO)							
6 I keep up with developments in the organization.	1	2	3	4	5	6	7
7 I defend the organization when other employees criticize it.	1	2	3	4	5	6	7
8 I show pride when representing the organization in public.	1	2	3	4	5	6	7
9 I frequently offer ideas to improve the functioning of the organization.	1	2	3	4	5	6	7
10 I express loyalty toward the organization.	1	2	3	4	5	6	7
Task (OCBT)							
11 I rarely miss work, even if there is a good reason for doing so.	1	2	3	4	5	6	7
12 I make few mistakes when performing my job.	1	2	3	4	5	6	7
13 I complete obligations with extreme care.	1	2	3	4	5	6	7
14 I always meet deadlines.	1	2	3	4	5	6	7
15 I am always punctual.	1	2	3	4	5	6	7

Adapted with permission from Cardona, Pablo, and Alvaro Espejo. "Effect of the Rating Source in Organizational Citizenship Behavior: A Multitrait-Multimethod Analysis." IESE Working Paper No D/474-E. October 2002. Available online at http://ssrn.com/abstract=443438, updated through personal correspondence with authors.

TABLE 6-6 Human Resource Readiness Profile

Extent to Which This Question Describes Your Organization	*Not At All*	*Poor*	*Fair*	*Good*	*Great*
Training and Development of Human Resources					
1 Company encourages continual learning by reimbursing tuition for formal studies.	1	2	3	4	5
2 Training is provided in teaming and interpersonal skills.	1	2	3	4	5
3 Employees have the opportunity to gain experience in multiple skills through job rotation or enlargement.	1	2	3	4	5
4 Skills proficiency is formally recognized through certification, increased pay, or promotion opportunities.	1	2	3	4	5
5 The effectiveness of training programs is fairly and accurately evaluated.	1	2	3	4	5
6 Employees and their supervisors are consulted on their training needs.	1	2	3	4	5
7 Employees are cross-trained on at least one other job so they can fill in or be rotated as the need arises.	1	2	3	4	5
8 Employees have the opportunity to be trained on new skills, even if these skills are not required on their current jobs.	1	2	3	4	5
9 New knowledge and skills are reinforced on the job.	1	2	3	4	5
10 Supervisors attend training in the same subject areas as their subordinates.	1	2	3	4	5
11 Mentoring is used appropriately as an informal delivery mechanism.	1	2	3	4	5
12 Employee input is sought on options for delivering education and training.	1	2	3	4	5
Selection and Promotion of Human Resources					
13 Applicants are selected based on how well they will fit into a team.	1	2	3	4	5
14 When screening applicants, skills that support the company's business strategy and purpose are taken into account.	1	2	3	4	5
15 When evaluating applicants, the ability to learn new and multiple skills is at least as important as proven proficiency in a specific skill set.	1	2	3	4	5
16 Coworkers are given the opportunity to interview applicants to assess how well they will blend into the culture and the team.	1	2	3	4	5
17 Coworkers' input is taken into account when making the final decision on who to hire.	1	2	3	4	5
18 People and team skills are as important as technical skills in deciding who gets promoted.	1	2	3	4	5
19 Selection procedures are designed to create a human resource pool that creates diversity in ideas, cultures, and thinking.	1	2	3	4	5

TABLE 6-6 Human Resource Readiness Profile (*continued*)

Extent to Which This Question Describes Your Organization	*Not At All*	*Poor*	*Fair*	*Good*	*Great*
Selection and Promotion of Human Resources					
20 A clear career progression exists for all employees throughout the organization.	1	2	3	4	5
21 Compensation and rewards support the recruitment and retention of good people.	1	2	3	4	5
22 Loyalty and core values are as important as technical performance in deciding who gets promoted.	1	2	3	4	5
Performance Evaluation of Human Resources					
23 Systems are in place to evaluate the performance of teams and the performance of individuals.	1	2	3	4	5
24 All employees know how the quality of their work is measured.	1	2	3	4	5
25 Employees are aware of how the measures they use in their individual jobs fit into the organization's overall performance measures.	1	2	3	4	5
26 Others, besides the direct supervisors, who have knowledge of the quality of work are asked for input in employee performance evaluations.	1	2	3	4	5
27 Performance evaluation procedures are designed and executed in a way that promotes employee cooperation.	1	2	3	4	5
28 Serving customers, both internal and external, is weighted heavily in evaluating performance.	1	2	3	4	5
29 Contributions to team achievements are important when evaluating individual employee performance.	1	2	3	4	5
30 Representatives of external constituencies (e.g., customers, suppliers) are asked to provide input on the performance of those employees who come in contact with them.	1	2	3	4	5
31 The ability to be an effective team player is an important component of the performance evaluation.	1	2	3	4	5
32 Employees know what is expected of them.	1	2	3	4	5
33 Employees have the resources, including information, needed to do their jobs well.	1	2	3	4	5
Design of Work for Human Resources					
34 Job descriptions are broad enough to enable flexibility in job assignments.	1	2	3	4	5
35 Employees are given opportunities to participate in tasks or volunteer for duties outside their normal job assignments.	1	2	3	4	5

(continued)

TABLE 6-6 Human Resource Readiness Profile (*continued*)

Extent to Which This Question Describes Your Organization	*Not At All*	*Poor*	*Fair*	*Good*	*Great*
Design of Work for Human Resources					
36 Work design facilitates communications and skill sharing across working units.	1	2	3	4	5
37 Employees are given the opportunity to rotate through different jobs.	1	2	3	4	5
38 Work design capitalizes on the diverse ideas, cultures, and thinking of employees.	1	2	3	4	5
39 The redesign of work is quick to adapt to changes in corporate direction and emphasis.	1	2	3	4	5
40 Employees have significant input in the design of their work systems.	1	2	3	4	5
41 Employees have the ability and are encouraged to make changes to improve the quality of their work.	1	2	3	4	5
42 Work design encourages cooperation and teamwork.	1	2	3	4	5
43 All employees have a workplace that is safe and healthy.	1	2	3	4	5
44 Individual employees believe their bosses and the organization care about them.	1	2	3	4	5
Rewards and Compensation for Human Resources					
45 The compensation of individual employees is tied to group performance (e.g., team or department).	1	2	3	4	5
46 Team efforts are rewarded in a fair and consistent manner.	1	2	3	4	5
47 Employees receive a raise in compensation when they master a new skill, complete a prescibed training course, or achieve a level of certification.	1	2	3	4	5
48 The company compensates according to the extent to which employees master particular skills.	1	2	3	4	5
49 Compensation is tied to the degree to which an employee has mastered a skills set.	1	2	3	4	5
50 Team efforts go largely unrewarded.	1	2	3	4	5
51 More employees are compensated on a salary than hourly basis.	1	2	3	4	5
52 Nonmonetary rewards contribute to good morale and employee loyalty.	1	2	3	4	5
53 Executive compensation packages are viewed by the rank and file as reasonable and appropriate.	1	2	3	4	5
54 Employees share in profit improvements.	1	2	3	4	5

SOURCE: Sanchez, Kraus, et al., *Group & Organization Management*, 24(4), pp. 473–74, copyright © 1999 by Sage Publications. Adapted by permission of Sage Publications, Inc.

2. *Describe and discuss the control theory model of human resource management.* The control theory model considers the trade-offs between how much is known about root causes that determine human behavior on the one hand, and how well defined are the expectations for human performance on the other. Quality of outputs depends on effectively managing system inputs (developing the competencies of the workforce) and managing behaviors (the transformation process). Promoting the efficiencies that can be derived from standard work methods while encouraging creative behaviors can be a source of tension. The key to resolving this conflict is through greater self-control, whereby workers become more committed through a feeling of shared ownership. There are two approaches for accomplishing this—participatory and self-management strategies. The former permits workers to make suggestions for change, but these are subject to veto by higher authority. The latter gives the workers autonomy in following through and implementing improvement ideas.

3. *Describe the distinguishing features of an HPWO.* The distinguishing features of HPWOs are employee autonomy, continuous learning, performance-based rewards, and knowledge sharing. An HPWO is an environment populated by knowledge workers using HPWPs. The purpose of HPWPs is to help workers learn and to promote lifelong learning.

4. *Describe the link between culture and quality, and the process of bringing about cultural change.* Culture is the single defining characteristic of an organization, and quality can only be achieved when the culture is unified in its desire to satisfy customers. To transform the culture, the HR system needs to be reengineered to bring it in line with corporate quality goals. A cultural change will have taken place when people accept a new sense of what is normal. In recruiting new personnel, it is more important that they be selected on their potential to fit into the new culture than on the strength of their technical skills.

5. *Define the five characteristics that determine the intrinsic motivating potential of a job and how this can be used in personnel assignments.* Intrinsic motivating potential is determined by skill variety, task identity, task significance, autonomy, and feedback. People appear to be more motivated if they can see how their contribution impacts something larger, if they think their work is important, if they have a say in how they do their work, and if they are told that they have done a good job. The five factors can be used to compute an MPS for each job. A job with a high MPS will not necessarily motivate a worker who has low growth needs. By asking personnel to complete a GNS, those with high growth needs can be matched to jobs with high MPS and vice versa.

6. *Discuss how demographics and geographical differences affect culture.* Culture is significantly influenced by geography and demographics. The accepted norms and the things that motivate people can vary dramatically with a change in location. Lifelong learning, for example, is a core value in the Nordic states, and employees expect their companies to provide opportunities for personal growth. In some countries, such as the United Kingdom, the federal government takes the lead in cultural reform. In the United States, it takes place at the company level. Even so, the process used in regions around the country may have to be different to account for diversity and bring about desired outcomes.

7. *Describe the sand cone model of human capability and how it relates to the sand cone model of organizational change.* The sand cone model of human capability shows the necessary sequence for developing a cultural readiness for QIM. At the foundation is a capability in which humans know their jobs, but perform them with little awareness of the

impact they have on something larger. This level supports the stabilization level of the change model because a process cannot be stable until its workers know what is expected of them. As change capability advances to a stage where processes can be operated in the short term, it is essential that the human tasks be repeatable. The organization reaches the next level of HR development when skills are matched to processes and inconsistencies are eliminated through best practices. When this "alignment" capability level is reached, HR can support the organization's ability to sustain performance long term. As the organization grows, human capability advances to a level of self-management, making teaming and collaboration possible. At this level, HR supports the organization's capability to improve. At the top level, an organization can only achieve a transformation capability if the culture change is complete. This is the HR optimization level.

8. *Describe some approaches for measuring an organization's cultural readiness for QIM philosophies.* Several survey tools have been devised to measure cultural change and to highlight any deficiencies that need management attention. Depending on the survey and scale used, threshold scores can be determined below which problems with the culture need to be corrected before proceeding with programs that depend on the commitment and participation of the workforce.

TO TEST YOUR UNDERSTANDING

6-1 What does culture have to do with implementing QIM principles? What are HPWPs? How would you know if you have them? Are HPWPs necessary before an organization can use teams effectively? Explain.

6-2 Place yourself in the position of someone who has just been hired to help an organization move toward an HPWO. You find that the workforce is diverse, and after testing the employees, you find that many of them have low growth needs. You also find that they mistrust management. What would you do?

6-3 Explain why the development of HR capability needs to parallel the development of change capabilities.

◆●◆
Social Security Administration
Promoting Economic Security

When evaluating performance, there is a major difference between the private and public sectors. In the private sector, market forces are the most significant drivers of change. However, government organizations are at the mercy of politicians and can be reshaped based on the ideologies of those currently in power.

In the mid-1990s, the Clinton administration made a commitment to restore public accountability to government, and a plan was implemented to introduce HPWPs into key government agencies. In 1995, the President's Management Council, recognizing the importance of human resource development (HRD) to improved performance, recommended that specific actions be taken throughout the federal government. This resulted in a change in culture and work practices for one of the largest bureaucracies in the federal government, employing in excess of 65,000 personnel—the Social Security Administration (SSA).

The mission of the SSA is "to promote the economic security of the nation's people through compassionate and vigilant leadership in shaping and managing America's Social Security programs." To

---

SSA STRATEGIC GOALS

1. To deliver high quality, citizen-centered *service*
2. To ensure superior *stewardship* of Social Security programs and resources
3. To achieve sustainable *solvency,* and ensure Social Security programs meet the needs of current and future generations
4. To strategically manage and align *staff* to support SSA's mission

---

achieve this mission, in its FY2005 Annual Performance Plan, the SSA listed four strategic goals and nine long-term strategic objectives.

Under each goal, the SSA developed nine supporting strategic objectives that add specificity and define the goal. Under each objective are long-term outcomes, which are the balanced scorecard measures that can be used to track performance against the strategic plan. There are a total of twenty of these outcomes, as shown in Table 6-7.

The SSA is responsible for three major programs: the Old Age and Survivors' Insurance, Disability Insurance, and the Supplemental Security Insurance program. SSA also provides significant support to other programs, including Medicare, Medicaid, and Food Stamps. By integrating its activities through a national delivery network, the SSA has been able to provide "one-stop shopping" to the millions of Americans who benefit from its services.

To respond to the president's mandate, SSA's HR role was expanded beyond its traditional training mission to include career and organizational development, and performance improvement. Communications became an important subrole because HR had the responsibility of clarifying business goals and ensuring personnel understood the organization's expectations of them.

HR had to identify and match technologies and people to strategic goals and scorecard metrics. Competency models were used to assess current capabilities and identify gaps. The scope of the HRD effort was expanded to include the provision and alignment of all resources, which included technologies, information, facilities, and materials, as well as people.

In the area of performance measurement, HRD manages the learning process. This translates to high levels of employee involvement, providing effective mentoring, making certain that conditions are in place to support self-improvement, and increasing the application of team building (although teaming has not been emphasized as part of the SSA culture). The SSA has set ambitious but measurable performance goals, and it is crucially important that appropriate rewards go to those who achieve them.

To maximize wide access to training materials, SSA has made use of electronic media, including interactive video training from headquarters and regional offices, stand-alone workstations at individual sites, and a "virtual campus," offering a variety of training through the agency's Web site.

The HRD function has also taken the lead in managing feedback systems. Annual satisfaction surveys, comment cards, focus groups, and special surveys have helped the SSA understand the needs and levels of satisfaction of its important customer groups.

The SSA has not emphasized the use of teams in the new culture. Notwithstanding, some teaming efforts, in collaboration with the labor union, have been piloted in each of the major service centers. Despite the lack of team activity, extensive use has been made of HPWPs in the areas of performance measurement, HRD, and improved communications.

An excerpt from the agency's FY2003 annual performance plan stated: "SSA received one of the best evaluations overall on the Federal Government's management scorecard as compared with other Departments and major Agencies."[40] The FY2004 annual performance plan contained the statement, "Of the

---

[40]Barnhardt, Jo Anne B. *FY2003 Annual Performance Plan,* Part I, 15. Baltimore: Social Security Administration, 2002. Also available online at http://www.ssa.gov/performance/2003/2003-Part1-4.pdf (accessed April 5, 2005).

TABLE 6-7 Strategic Goals, Objectives, and Outcomes

Social Security Administration Goals, Objectives, and Outcomes					
Goal		*Objectives*		*Long-Term Outcomes*	
1	To deliver high-quality, citizen-centered *Service*	1	Make the right decision in the disability process as early as possible	1	Reduce significantly the time it takes for a disability claimant to receive a final Agency decision
				2	Eliminate backlogs for disability initial claims, hearings and appeals by 2008
		2	Increase employment for people with disabilities	3	By 2008, increase by 50% from 2001 levels the number of Disability Insurance (DI) and Supplemental Security Income (SSI) disability beneficiaries who achieve employment
				4	Establish with the Department of Labor (DOL) a nationwide network of employment support staff in One Stop Career Centers to serve Social Security beneficiaries with disabilities
				5	Test the impact of early intervention and youth transition
		3	Improve service through technology	6	Eliminate backlogs for operational work by 2008
				7	Substantially increase use of electronic services
2	To ensure superior *Stewardship* of Social Security programs and resources	4	Prevent fraudulent and improper payments and improve debt management	8	By 2008, increase SSI payment accuracy to 96% (free of *preventable* error) 1. Maintain Old-Age, Survivors and Disablity Insurance (OASDI) payment accuracy at 99.8% 2. Increase the percent of outstanding debt that is in a collection arrangement 3. Remain current with DI and SSI continuing disability reviews (CDR) 4. Finish processing special disability cases 5. Reduce the backlog of workers' compensation cases
		5	Strengthen the integrity of the Social Security Number (SSN)	9	Ensure SSNs are only issued based on verified documents
		6	Increase accuracy of earnings records	10	By 2005, remove at least 30 million items from the suspense file and post them to the correct earnings record
				11	Beginning with 2005, remove 5% of the earnings items added to the suspense file each year and post them to the correct earnings record

TABLE 6-7 Strategic Goals, Objectives, and Outcomes (*continued*)

Social Security Administration Goals, Objectives, and Outcomes

Goal		Objectives		Long-Term Outcomes
		7	Efficiently manage Agency finances and assets, and effectively link resources to performance outcomes	12	Compete commercial positions suitable for study (number to be negotiated with the Office of Management and Budget (OMB)
				13	Annually receive an unqualified opinion on SSA's annual financial statements with no material weaknesses reported by the auditors
				14	By 2005, substantially complete the most significant projects in the Social Security Unified Measurement System (SUMS) and Managerial Cost Accountability System (MCAS) plan, and complete the plan by the end of 2008
				15	Increase productivity by at least 2% annually on average
				16	Get to "green" on all five President's Management Agenda (PMA) items
3	To achieve sustainable *Solvency* and ensure Social Security programs meet the needs of currant and future generation	8	Through education and research efforts, support reforms to ensure sustainable solvency and more responsive retirement and disability programs	17	Achieve reform that ensures long-term solvency
4	To strategically manage and align *Staff* to support SSA's mission	9	Recruit, develop and retain a high-performing workforce	18	By 2008, demonstrate an improvement in the retention rate of new hires
				19	Implement new performance management systems to better recognize and reward superior performance for: 1. SES executives in 2003[a] 2. GS-15s in 2004[b] 3. GS-14 and below employees by 2005, subject to contract negotiations
				20	Ensure ongoing job enrichment opportunities and training

[a] The new performance plan for SES executives was successfully implemented in FY2003.

[b] A new performance plan for non-bargaining unit GS-15 employees was implemented in October 2003.

SOURCE: Adapted from Barnhardt, Jo Anne B. *FY2005 Annual Performance Plan,* Part I. Baltimore: Social Security Administration, 2004. Also available online at http://www.ssa.gov/performance/2005/FY2005_APP_Part_I.doc (accessed April 5, 2005).

major departments and agencies, SSA is rated (by the Office of Management and Budget) among the highest in both status and progress as of December 2002."[41]

The HPWPs are working; however, the improvement process is never ending. The SSA Commissioner includes the following statement in her cover letter, transmitting the FY2005 annual performance plan: "To help meet performance goals established for FY2004 and FY2005, we must strive to resolve management challenges identified by the General Accounting Office (GAO) and SSA's Office of the Inspector General (OIG). We are addressing these challenges and have made significant progress toward meeting them. In some cases, we use numeric outcome or output goals to track our progress. For others, we use measurable milestones of initiatives tracked by our executives."[42] ∎

QUESTIONS FOR THOUGHT

1. How does establishing a culture that supports HPWPs differ between a public and private organization? Are there any barriers to cultural change that are harder to overcome in the public sector?

2. Based on the fact that the SSA has not been a great advocate of teams and self-management, is it legitimate to claim that the organization has been successful in implementing HPWPs? Explain.

3. How has the balance scorecard approach supported a commitment to introduce HPWPs throughout the SSA?

4. If you were the commissioner of the SSA, what actions would you take to ensure each job contained the five intrinsic motivating characteristics described in this chapter?

[41]Barnhardt, Jo Anne B. *FY2004 Annual Performance Plan,* Part I, 4. Baltimore: Social Security Administration, 2003. Also available online at http://www.ssa.gov/performance/2004/Part_I_312.doc (accessed April 5, 2005).

[42]Barnhardt, Jo Anne B. *FY2005 Annual Performance Plan,* Part I, 3. Baltimore: Social Security Administration, 2004. Also available online at http://www.ssa.gov/performance/2005/FY2005_APP_Part_I.doc (accessed April 5, 2005).

Quality and Process Management

CHAPTER 7

Understanding Process Behavior—Tools for Problem Solving and Decision Making

It's a funny thing about life; if you refuse to accept anything but the best, you very often get it.
—W. SOMERSET MAUGHAM

Federal Communications Commission

Positive Change through Continuous Improvement in Management and Program Operations

The Federal Communications Commission (FCC) implemented a TQM system that featured customer focus, employee involvement, and continuous improvement.[1] Quality improvement teams were formed and team leaders, facilitators, and team members were trained in problem-solving skills, quality tools, and teaming techniques. One of the early team projects was to solve the problem of backlogs in license applications received from FM radio stations. There was a nine-month backlog at

the time the problem-solving team was formed, and it was taking an average of nearly a year for each applicant to receive a license. The team decided to tackle the problem using a seven-step procedure.

The first step was to solicit ideas from branch employees and then brainstorm improvement ideas within the team. Employees were given the opportunity to vote on the team's ideas and to help narrow the list to the top five. As a second step, the team prepared preliminary cost estimates for each of the top five alternatives and developed criteria to be used in the final selection. As data were collected to support each option, the team made an interesting discovery—60% of the total applications received contained one or

---

[1]Fontaine, Daniel J., and Diane B. Robinette. "FCC Makes Dramatic Quality Improvements." *Quality Progress* 27, no. 11 (November 1994): 87–91.

more errors, significantly affecting processing time. An error-free application could be processed in an average of seven months, whereas those with errors were taking an average of fifteen months.

The third step focused on root causes. The team constructed a flowchart and cause-and-effect diagram of the licensing process. The flowchart highlighted the amount and location of rework attributable to error-prone applications. The cause-and-effect diagram helped the team to focus on two principal sources of problems: applicant responses and customer materials. Step 4 involved brainstorming ideas on how to eliminate those root causes believed to be the major drivers. This activity resulted in the design of a more user-friendly application form.

In step 5, the team developed a set of detailed instructions and piloted a new application form with a group of selected individuals within and outside the FCC. Feedback from the pilot resulted in some modification to the form design and to the instructions. Then, the team was able to move to step 6, a full-scale implementation of the new form. A public notice announced and explained the new application procedure.

Step 7 was a postaudit process, tracking the effectiveness of the implemented solution with charts to compare pre- and postsolution performance. The results were dramatic. Within nine months of implementation, the percentage of error-free applications doubled from 40% to 80%, and the backlog of applications was slashed from 600 to 16. The cycle time was reduced from one year to six months, and the cost of poor quality was reduced by 67%. ∎

7.1 LEARNING OBJECTIVES AND KEY OUTCOMES

After studying the material in Chapter 7, you will be able to

1. Describe creative tools that will stimulate new ideas and help build consensus
2. Describe process improvement planning tools
3. Describe tools to analyze and improve processes
4. Describe the seven old problem-solving tools
5. Describe six of the seven new problem-solving tools (matrix analysis excepted)
6. Describe poka-yoke and how it can be applied to prevent mistakes

7.2 TOOLS FOR CREATIVITY

7.2.1 Brainstorming

7.2.1.1 Structured and Unstructured Brainstorming Groups use this tool to generate a large number of ideas within a short period of time. The best results can usually be achieved if the participation is from a cross-section of individuals with different perspectives.

Brainstorming Rules of Conduct

- Participants should be encouraged to freely express their thoughts. This is sometimes called *freewheeling*.
- There can be no good or bad ideas, no right or wrong answers, and all ideas regardless of how ludicrous are welcomed.
- Value judgments or criticisms of any sort are strictly forbidden. The idea is to generate ideas, not critique them.

The idea behind brainstorming is to generate as many innovative ideas as possible.

The more ideas proposed, the more likely new thinking will emerge. It is essential that a climate be established where people are comfortable to freely express their opinions. The objective must be clear from the outset, and a session facilitator, guided by the steps shown in Figure 7-1, can help keep discussions focused and on purpose.

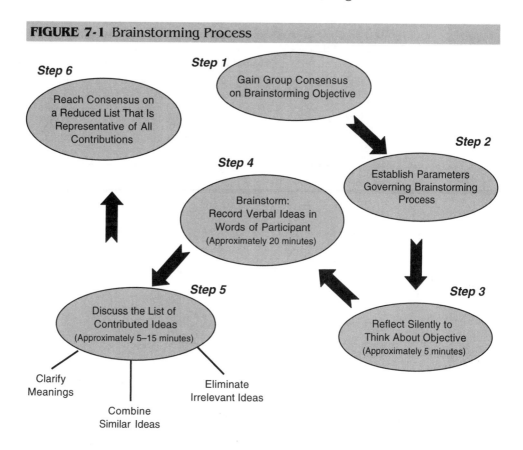

FIGURE 7-1 Brainstorming Process

Brainstorming can be structured or unstructured. Under **structured brainstorming**, the facilitator moves from one group member to the next, requiring each in turn to contribute an idea when called upon. With **unstructured brainstorming**, ideas are spontaneous and no one is forced to participate.

Structured Brainstorming

Unstructured Brainstorming

7.2.1.2 Reverse Brainstorming In **reverse brainstorming**, the group develops a list of objectives that are opposite of the ones actually desired. For example, the antithesis of the objective "improve customer satisfaction" might be "escalate the incidences of customer complaints and defections." Brainstorming then focuses on generating ideas to achieve these antigoals. The results can be startling if the ideas generated actually parallel current practices.

Reverse Brainstorming

7.2.1.3 Imaginary Brainstorming Imaginary or **creative brainstorming** is a method used to stimulate idea generation by changing all but one element (called the *essential element*) in the original brainstorm question, and then trying to apply the new ideas back to the original issue. **Imaginary brainstorming** is an eight-step process.

Creative Brainstorming

Imaginary Brainstorming

Imaginary Brainstorming Steps

Step 1. State the problem in question form, structured with three distinct elements: a subject (describing who is acting), a verb (describing an action), and an object (describing who or what is acted on).

FIGURE 7-2 Imaginary Brainstorming Replacement Question

Element	Original Problem	Suggested Replacement
	How do	How do/does
Subject	we	the president
		college students
		movie stars
		professional athletes
Verb	complete a production order	earn a million dollars
		build a house
		become famous
		get drunk
		find a mate
Object	in half the normal time[a]	in half the normal time[a]

[a]Kept as essential element.

Step 2. Perform classic brainstorming on the original question.

Step 3. Define essential elements of the problem, and identify which of the elements described in step 1 are most directly tied to a problem solution.

Step 4. Propose imaginary replacements for the other nonessential elements. An example of this step is shown in Figure 7-2.

Step 5. Formulate a new problem statement, substituting imaginary elements for the nonessential elements of the original problem.

Step 6. Have the group brainstorm the imaginary problem.

Step 7. Apply the ideas from the imaginary brainstorming back to the original problem statement.

Step 8. Analyze the ideas (real, imaginary, combined), and carry forward those of most interest.

7.2.2 Prioritization Matrix

Once brainstorming has generated a list of ideas, the group can use a prioritization matrix to sort the list in order of importance so the most critical items can receive first consideration. Brainstorming is first used to identify problems and to narrow the list to a manageable size. The team then brainstorms what criteria they will use to compare each alternative. Next, each group member ranks all items against each criterion with the largest rank being assigned to the most important. Summing the ranks across all criteria produces a group priority ranking for each item on the list.

Prioritization Matrix

Figure 7-3 illustrates a **prioritization matrix** that was produced by a team of six members. The team had identified six problems to study and agreed to rank them based on the criteria: frequency of occurrence, importance (benefits from solving), and ease of solution. Each member then ranked the problems in increasing order of importance for each criterion. Summing the ranks produced a prioritized listing. In this example, standardized methods stands out as the most important issue and problems with suppliers the least important.

FIGURE 7-3 Prioritization Matrix

Problem	Frequency						Importance						Ease of Solution						Total Points
Quality Problems from Suppliers	1	2	1	3	1	2	2	6	2	2	1	2	1	1	1	1	1	1	31
Lack of Standardized Methods	5	4	6	6	5	6	3	1	4	3	4	4	5	6	5	4	4	5	80
Poor Training	2	3	2	1	3	1	4	4	3	4	5	3	6	5	6	6	6	6	70
Insufficient Maintenance	3	1	4	2	2	4	6	5	6	6	6	6	4	4	4	5	5	4	77
Confusing or Lack of Timely Communications	4	6	3	4	4	3	5	3	5	5	3	5	3	2	3	2	2	3	65
Poor Morale	6	5	5	5	6	5	1	2	1	1	2	1	2	3	2	3	3	2	55
	WJT	ABP	RSA	TAC	AAT	NOP	WJT	ABP	RSA	TAC	AAT	NOP	WJT	ABP	RSA	TAC	AAT	NOP	

Team Members

Sum of Ranks

7.2.3 Brainwriting

During brainstorming, ideas are shared verbally. In comparison, brainwriting is a method in which ideas are generated and shared in writing. There are two types of brainwriting: nominal, in which ideas are not shared during the generation stage, and interacting, where ideas are shared openly and form the basis for stimulating additional ones. This method works well with groups of between seven and nine, with a maximum of eleven and a minimum of six. If the number of participants exceeds eleven, the group should be broken down into smaller discussion groups of between six and nine.

Nominal Brainwriting

7.2.3.1 Nominal Brainwriting A **nominal brainwriting** session typically involves four steps.

Nominal Brainwriting Steps

Step 1. Assemble the group and describe the issue at hand. The group can be sitting together or can be linked via a computer network.

Step 2. Have each person write down their ideas on 3 × 5 index cards or small sticky notes.

Step 3. After ten to fifteen minutes, collect the ideas.

Step 4. Have the group participate in organizing the ideas into groupings, then discuss and evaluate.

Interacting Brainwriting

7.2.3.2 Interactive Brainwriting A typical **interactive brainwriting** session is a four-step process.

Interactive Brainwriting Steps

Step 1. Assemble the group and describe the issue at hand. For interactive brainwriting, it is imperative that the group be in the same room and sitting together.

Step 2. Have each person write down one idea on a 3 × 5 index card or small sticky note.

Step 3. Have each person pass an idea to their person sitting to their immediate right. The person receiving the idea then has three options:

- Use the idea to stimulate a totally new idea
- Modify the idea
- Simply pass the card on to the next person in the next round

Step 4. After ten to fifteen minutes, collect the ideas. Have the group participate in organizing the ideas into groupings, then discuss and evaluate.

Brainwriting 6-3-5

7.2.3.3 Brainwriting 6-3-5 Brainwriting 6-3-5 is a variation of interactive brainwriting in which six people write three ideas on a card in five minutes. The card is then passed to the person on the left. That person develops the ideas or adds new ones in five minutes, and then passes the card to the person on the left. The process repeats until all cards are in the hands of their original owners. Then, all ideas are assembled and discussed.

7.2.3.4 Other Variations There are several other variations that add to the fun of interactive brainwriting. One version has participants write their ideas on the wings of paper airplanes and exchange them by flying them across the room to each other. Participants pick up an airplane, read the idea, write down a new one, and throw the airplane again when instructed by the facilitator. Another version has participants write ideas on a sheet of paper and tape it to their backs. The group mingles, and each participant reads comembers' ideas and adds new ones by writing on the paper taped to their backs. Then, when time is called, all ideas are collected, organized, and discussed.

Research studies have shown that, given the same group size and time period, interactive brainwriting always increases the quantity of ideas over nominal brainwriting and brainstorming.

The nominal group technique is used to build consensus.

7.2.3.5 Nominal Group Technique A brainwriting technique that results in a prioritized list of ideas or actions is the nominal group technique (NGT). The NGT method is best suited when the group is formed for the purpose of fact finding, idea generation, or the search for problem solutions. NGT sessions should be planned for one to three hours. It is better to have one long meeting than to break the time up into several shorter meetings. One member of the group is assigned the role of facilitator and another assumes the duties of group recorder. The facilitator starts the NGT session by reading the issue at hand to the group and explaining the NGT process in detail. The facilitator then leads the group through the following eight steps.

Nominal Group Technique Steps

Step 1. *Silent Generation of Ideas.* Ask participants to spend ten to twenty minutes silently and independently writing down as many ideas as they can think of relating to the issue at hand.

Step 2. *Round Robin Presentation.* Ask each participant in turn to present, but not discuss, one idea. The recorder lists each idea on a flip chart. The facilitator continues around the group, each person contributing one idea in turn, until everyone's ideas have been exhausted and recorded. This step usually takes twenty to forty minutes.

Step 3. *Discussion and Clarification.* The facilitator reads each idea to the group and asks if there is a need for clarification, interpretation, or explanation. Discussions are permitted but must be brief. If possible, similar ideas are combined, shortening the original list. At the end of this step (after approximately twenty to forty minutes), the recorder will assign a number to each item on the final list.

Step 4. *Preliminary Vote.* The facilitator asks each participant to select five to seven ideas from the list and write these on 3 × 5 index cards—one idea per card. Then participants are asked to rank the cards in order of importance and to record their rankings on each card. Figure 7-4 is an example of a format that could be used for these ranking cards. The facilitator collects the cards and records the votes on a flip chart.

Step 5. *Break.* The facilitator will call for a ten- to fifteen-minute refreshment break so the participants can reenergize.

Step 6. *Discussion of the Preliminary Vote.* The facilitator reconvenes the group and permits a discussion of up to twenty to forty minutes to discuss the preliminary vote. Collectively, the group will examine inconsistent voting patterns, and reopen discussions on ideas that have received too few or too many votes.

Step 7. *Final Vote on Priorities.* The facilitator now asks the group to take a final vote on priorities. At this point, step 4 could be repeated, asking participants to again select and rate the top five to seven ideas. An alternative is to ask participants to assign a score to all ideas on the list, with a score of 10 representing

FIGURE 7-4 Card Format for Nominal Group Technique Ranking

9 (number of idea from flip chart)

Idea Written Out

(rank order number) 3

FIGURE 7-5 Card Format for Nominal Group Technique Final Vote

Item Number	Score	Item Number	Score
1	7	14	4
2	8	15	2
3	10	16	10
4	10	17	7
5	10	18	9
6	3	19	3
7	2	20	8
8	5	21	6
9	5		
10	5		
11	9		
12	8		
13	8		

top priority and a score of 0 representing no importance. There is no limit to how many ideas a person can rate the same score (e.g., all ideas on the list could receive a score of 10 if the person believed they all merited a top priority). Figure 7-5 is a suggested format that could be used by participants to record final votes.

Step 8. *Listing and Agreement on Prioritized Items.* The facilitator collects all score-cards and calculates the aggregate score for each item. The recorder places the aggregate scores next to their corresponding item numbers on the flip chart.

7.2.4 Word Associations, Picture Associations, and Biotechniques

Word Associations

Picture Associations

Biotechniques

Word associations, **picture associations**, and **biotechniques** use words, pictures, and examples from nature to stimulate fresh ideas. These methods are intended to take a group beyond traditional thinking by comparing the attributes of seemingly unrelated items to inspire fresh perspectives. The mind is permitted to wander and bounce from one idea to another, a process that can be initiated with either a list of words or a group of pictures. Biotechniques uses biological systems (animal or plant life) as a means of breaking stereotypes and looking at problems in new ways.

The process begins with the decision group selecting a word, picture, or living thing on which to focus. The group then asks itself a series of questions, such as What ideas does the object suggest? and What is the essence of its being?

If pictures are used, the group deliberates on What is happening in this picture? If a biological system is the object of interest, the group would discuss How does the animal or plant function?, What does it represent?, and How can the appearance or behavior of the animal or plant be applied to the problem at hand?

For word associations, any word can be used. However, an *object* (e.g., horse, book, washing machine, Corvette) works best if the objective is to generate ideas for technical improvements. An *event* (e.g., garage sales, local election, graduation, running in a marathon) works best if the purpose is to get ideas leading to specific management actions.

As an example, a team in a certain health care facility selected the word "coffee" and brainstormed the question, What is the essence of coffee, and what ideas does it suggest? Team members generated numerous word associations, including pleasure, leisure, relaxation, aroma, warmth, simple to prepare, quality depends on process and recipe, and camaraderie. The team then applied these ideas to the issue at hand, which was how to improve the level of outpatient care. By examining the following sequence of questions, the team was able to develop a number of implementable suggestions for improvement:

- *How do patients feel when they enter the waiting room?*
- *Are the surroundings pleasant and inviting or fearful and intimidating?*
- *Is the procedure for processing patients simple, easy to understand, and patient friendly?*
- *How well do doctors and other staff succeed in putting the patient at ease?*
- *Do staff project an attitude of sincerity, concern, and caring?*

7.2.5 TILMAG

TILMAG

TILMAG is an acronym for the German words *transformation idealer losungselemente mit assoziationen und gemeinsamkeiten,* which translated into English means "transformation of ideal solution elements with associations and things in common." Developed by Helmut Schlicksupp, TILMAG is a structured approach that helps define ideal solutions for a problem, by creating and analyzing associations between paired combinations of ideal solution elements.[2] Figure 7-6 illustrates a TILMAG process that was used to determine how to increase market share. The first TILMAG step is a brainstorming session to generate ideas. Then, the group identifies those attributes, qualities, or properties that must be present in any solution or recommendation.

In the example shown in Figure 7-6, the group decided that acceptable solutions would have to produce superior quality, yield low cost and short cycle times, and result in happy customers. These attributes are called the problem's ideal solution elements (ISEs). Next, the group constructs a TILMAG matrix in which the ISEs are placed across the top row and down the left column, and all pairwise associations are investigated.

For each pairwise association, the group employs picture and word associations to find a person, animal, object, place, event, or activity that represents each association. The final step is to use the TILMAG matrix to stimulate ideas for an analogy chart that links back to the original issue. In this example, the team concluded that a solution based on QIM, better training, and a supportive culture with HPWPs would help increase market share.

---

[2]Ritter, Diane and Michael Brassard. *The Creative Tools Memory Jogger: A Pocket Guide to Creative Thinking,* 133–46. Salem, NH: GOAL/QPC, 1998.

FIGURE 7-6 The TILMAG Process

Issue: How to Increase Market Share

Brainstorming
- Quality at the Source
- Greater Responsiveness to Customer
- More Motivated Workforce
- Improve Value to Customers
- Shorten Cycle Times

Ideal Solution Elements → ↓	Superior Quality	Short Cycle Times	Low Cost
Superior Quality	Jeweler	A Surgical Operation	A Hike through a Rain Forest
Low Cost	Singing a Favorite Song	A Fast Food Restaurant	
Short Cycle Times	Football Team Victory		

TILMAG Matrix

Example	Core Concept	Application to Business
A Surgical Operation	Precision, Attention to Detail, High Cost of Quality	QIM Principles, Zero Defects, Six Sigma, Management by Fact
Football Team Victory	The Importance of Teamwork, Skills Development, and Practice	Training and Coaching in Teaming Skills and Encouraging the Practice of Concepts Learned
Singing a Favorite Song	Security, Familiarity, Self-Esteem	Building Culture Based on the Value of Human Resources, HPWO, HPWP

Analogy Chart

Note: HPWO, high-performing work organization; HPWP, high-performing work practice.

7.3 TOOLS FOR PLANNING

7.3.1 PDCA Cycle

PDCA is a continuous improvement model that uses rational decision making.

The plan-do-check-act (PDCA) cycle, sometimes referred to as plan-do-study-act, is a continuous improvement model, and is illustrated in Figure 7-7.

The PDCA Cycle

Plan

Plan Step.   *What do we want to know?* To emphasize its relative importance, the diagram in Figure 7-7 deliberately allocates more area to the **Plan** step than to the others. It is essential that decision makers invest enough time and energy to planning, which runs counter to the human tendency to want to get on with the "doing" and produce results. During the planning step, the problem statement should be clearly articulated and as many questions generated as possible. The group then develops a plan on how it intends to get their questions answered. This will often include a strategy for collecting data, and will specify who will do what and how it will be done.

Do

Do Step.   *What can we learn and from whom?* The **Do** step is essentially concerned with implementing the plan developed in the first step. This can entail a broad range of activities from simple data collection to performing a designed experiment.

Check

Check or Study Step.   *What did we learn?* In the **Check** step, the data are analyzed against the issues and questions raised during the Plan step. The learning that takes place will either provide the basis for action or generate a new set of issues and questions.

Act

Act Step.   *Act on what was learned.* The **Act** step can include piloting a new method, implementing new controls, solving the stated problem, or simply recognizing the team was trying to answer the wrong set of questions or the set was incomplete. In the latter case, the process cycles back to the Plan step and the process repeats.

FIGURE 7-7 PDCA Cycle

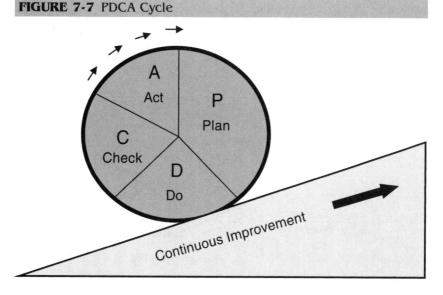

By iterating through the PDCA cycle, a team builds collective problem-solving capability, as members learn together. The quality and depth of the questions under "Plan" improve, as do the analytical skills used in "Do" and "Check." Hence, the PDCA cycle not only provides a structured process that facilitates problem solving, but it also serves as a framework for enabling the development of teaming and learning skills.

7.3.2 Radar or Spider Chart

Radar Chart

Spider Chart

A radar chart is a tool that helps decision makers visualize strengths and weaknesses.

A **radar chart**, sometimes referred to as a **spider chart**, is a tool that graphically displays the gaps and their relative magnitudes among five to ten performance areas. This chart helps a team visualize the areas of obvious strengths and weaknesses, and can be useful in strategic planning and quality improvement. An example radar chart is shown in Figure 7-8.

To construct a radar chart, a large circle is drawn and a spoke is constructed from the origin to the perimeter corresponding to each performance category. Each spoke is then labeled with the name of the category and subdivided into the number of increments the team has established for its rating scale. A Likert scale is normally used with numbers that range between 0 (serious gap) to 5, 6, or 7 (exceptional strength).

FIGURE 7-8 Radar Chart

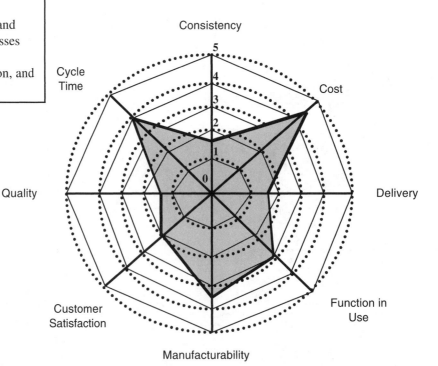

This radar chart reveals strengths in cost, manufacturability, and cycle time; weaknesses are in consistency, customer satisfaction, and quality.

FIGURE 7-9 Representative Group Norms

1. Candor
   We value the principle of expressing what is on our minds in an open environment that is conducive to furthering discussion or generating new ideas.
2. Confidentiality
   We value the principle of protecting each individual's right to privacy to remove any fears associated with free expression.
3. Equality
   We value the principle that bestows peer equity to all members of the group.
4. Truth
   We value the principle of seeking and expressing the truth, always clearly articulating any assumptions.
5. Data
   We value the principle of seeking to back up all decisions, assumptions, plans, and positions with relevant and reliable data.
6. Learning
   We value the principle of learning together; there is no such thing as a stupid question or comment.
7. Respect
   We value the principle of holding each of our fellow team members in high esteem; all opinions, including counteropinions, are welcome.
8. Listening
   We value the principle of listening to both the words and meanings of what others have to say, without being deafened by our eagerness for self-expression.
9. Constructive Participation
   We value the principle of constructive criticism, which helps solve a problem or strengthen a weakness; we are intolerant of destructive criticism, which is aimed at blocking or diverting a group momentum or discrediting or belittling individual participants.
10. Teamwork
    We value the principle of working together and forming community ideals and objectives; we value the absence of individual competition and the need to impress or succeed on an individual level.
11. Positive Attitude
    We value the principle of looking beyond the barriers and constraints, focusing instead on possibilities and opportunities.

Task Cycle

Purpose

Products

Functioning
Capabilities

A task cycle helps
plan an efficient
meeting.

7.3.3 Task Cycle

How to run an efficient meeting can be a challenge. Usually, the time available for a meeting is limited, and if unproductive, considerable resources can be wasted. It is essential to manage time so the agenda is covered, everyone has an opportunity to be heard, and the meeting ends with expected outcomes. A set of norms, such as those shown in Figure 7-9, agreed to by the team and strictly enforced, can help. The **task cycle**, illustrated in Figure 7-10, is a tool that can help keep a meeting stay on **purpose** and achieve desired outcomes within the allotted time. Using a task cycle, a meeting is pre-planned around purpose, **products**, process, and **functioning capabilities**.

FIGURE 7-10 Task Cycle for Planning an Efficient Meeting

Purpose ➡ Products

Purpose

What is the purpose of the meeting?

What does the team expect to accomplish?

A clear statement of purpose should be crafted and presented at the beginning of the meeting.

Products

What are the expected meeting outcomes?

How will the group judge whether the meeting was productive?

Functioning Capability

The functioning capability includes the resources needed for the meeting to be successful.

Resources include the meeting norms–any handouts, visual aids, flip charts, audio-visual equipment, and so on.

Process

How will the meeting be structured, and what rules will the group adopt to govern how the meeting will be conducted?

The process includes group norms, the meeting agenda, and, if appropriate, individual assignments.

7.4 TOOLS FOR PROCESS ANALYSIS

7.4.1 Flowchart

Flowchart

Map

Process

A flowchart is useful in defining a process.

A process **flowchart**, also called a process **map**, is a graphical representation of a **process** showing inputs, outputs, and all activities; how they relate; and how material or people flow through the system. When analyzing a process, it is always a good idea to construct a flowchart first. It is much easier to conceptualize process behavior and spot improvement opportunities using a visual aid rather than a written description. A flowchart is used to define an existing process (*as is*), redesign a process incorporating improvements (*could be*), and communicate standardized procedures (*operator training*). Flowcharts normally trace the path materials take through a system, but flowcharts can also be constructed to follow the movement of people. They can be constructed at two levels of detail:

1. The process as a network of subsystems (with inputs, processing steps, and outputs).
2. The process as a sequence of steps necessary for the transformation of inputs into outputs.

7.4.1.1 Process Flowchart as a Network of Subsystems Using a flowchart to map a network of subsystems can produce insight into how the components interrelate to produce a finished product or service. Sometimes called an output process chart, a system flowchart is a simple graphical tool that uses the small number of easily recognizable symbols shown in Figure 7-11.

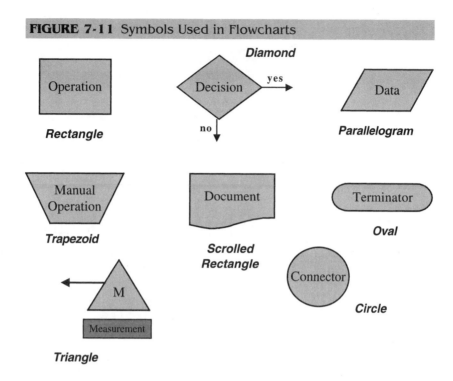

FIGURE 7-11 Symbols Used in Flowcharts

Figure 7-12 is an example of an output process chart. When constructing a flowchart, the decision has to be made as to how much detail should be shown on the chart. A good rule of thumb is to try to fit the flowchart on one side of an 8.5- × 11-inch sheet of paper. If more detail is needed than will fit on a sheet this size, then the scope is too broad. A smaller part of the overall process should be selected for study.

Deployment

A deployment flowchart assigns responsibilities for operations to individuals.

A variant of the network systems flowchart, is the **deployment** flowchart in which the process is segmented by responsibility area. For example, if three people are responsible for different steps of the process, the chart is divided into three segments, with the name of the responsible individual appearing at the top of each segment. As the chart is constructed, the steps are placed in those segments corresponding to the responsible individual. On a deployment flowchart, each line that connects steps across responsibility segments represents a customer–supplier relationship. Figure 7-13 illustrates a deployment flowchart for making breakfast. In this example, Ben has the responsibility to prepare the toast and coffee, while Alex is responsible for the eggs and the potatoes. Alice fries the bacon and assembles the breakfast tray, using the outputs provided by Ben and Alex.

Opportunity

Value Added

Cost Adding

An alternative type of chart is an **opportunity** flowchart, which separates those process steps that add value, from those that add cost (but no value). **Value-added** activities are defined to be those that are essential to the process. **Cost-adding** activities are those that are not essential to process output, but are added in anticipation that something may go wrong or because something has gone wrong. Examples of cost-adding activities are inspections, sorting out defects, awaiting approval actions, or lack of equipment availability.

FIGURE 7-12 Output Process Chart for Breakfast Preparation

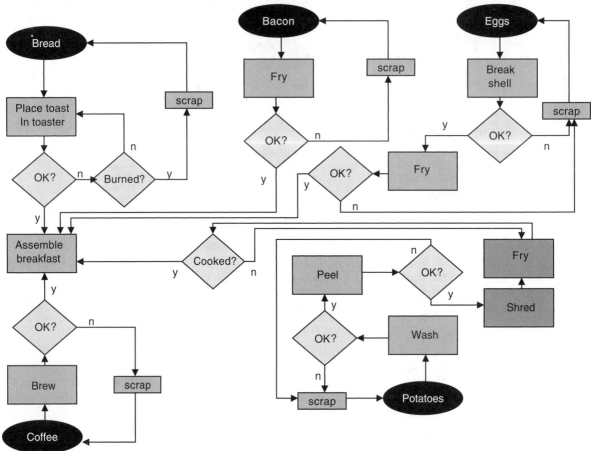

Note: y, yes; n, no.

7.4.1.2 Transformation Flow Process Charts The second level of analysis is concerned with the actual steps, or operations, required in the production system. Figure 7-14 is a template that can be used for constructing a transformation flow chart that captures the two main components of any production process—transformations (those steps that add value) and moves, called "transportations" (those steps that add place utility). In addition, the activities that add cost but not value can also be identified, and labeled as delays, inspections, or storages.

Transformation and output charts do not share a common symbology. The accepted practice in constructing transformation charts is to use the symbols adopted by the American National Standards Institute (ANSI), as shown in Figure 7-15. These are defined as follows:

- *Circle.* A circle represents an operation that transforms inputs into outputs of a higher composite value than the sum of the value of the inputs. Examples of operations include tighten nut, drill hole, seal envelope, and bus table. When analyzing

FIGURE 7-13 Deployment Process Chart for Breakfast Preparation

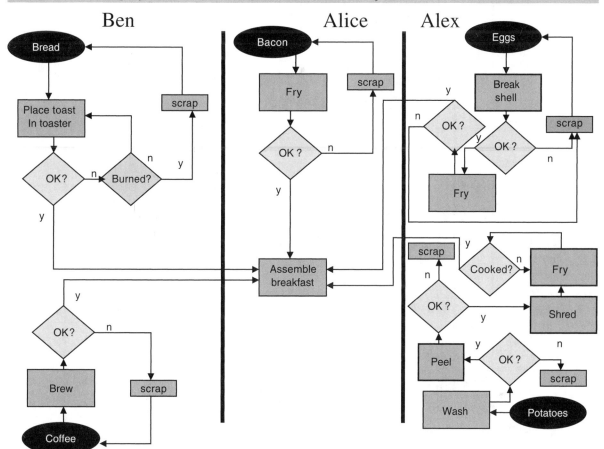

Note: y, yes; n, no.

a process, the time it takes to complete each operation is important, and this information is typically captured on the flowchart.

- *Block Arrow.* A block arrow represents a transportation whereby material is moved from one location to another by mechanical or manual means. With transportations, one is usually concerned with the total number of moves, the distance traveled, the time required, and the transportation method.

- *Inverted Triangle.* In a flowchart, the inverted triangle depicts a storage. This is defined as a system-designed delay, whereby material is deliberately taken out of the value stream for the purpose of storing it for future use. Storages would include inventory buffers, where material sits waiting to be sequenced into a subsequent operation. In an ideal process, material would flow smoothly from one operation to the next, and storage buffers would be unnecessary. Therefore, by identifying where storages exist, improvement opportunities can often be found.

- *Block Uppercase Letter D.* This symbol, an uppercase "D," identifies delays— those cases where flow is disrupted for some reason other than the explicit intent

FIGURE 7-14 Transformation Flow Process Chart

Process: _____

Subject Charted: _____

Beginning: _____

Ending: _____

			Summary		
	Activity		Number of Steps	Time (min)	Distance (m)
Operation	●				
Transport	⬆				
Inspect	■				
Delay	◗				
Store	▶				

Step No.	Time (min)	Distance (m)	●	⬆	■	◗	▶	Step Description

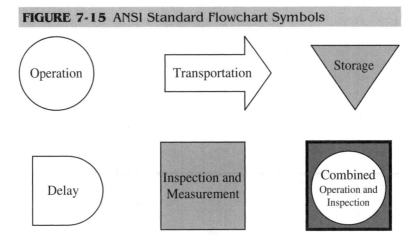

FIGURE 7-15 ANSI Standard Flowchart Symbols

Operation

Transportation

Storage

Delay

Inspection and Measurement

Combined
Operation and
Inspection

to create inventory buffers. Examples of delays are waiting for approvals, waiting for an elevator or scarce equipment, or waiting for a material handler. Once identified, delays should be carefully scrutinized to see if there are ways to reduce the duration and frequency of the delays or eliminate them altogether.

- *Square.* A square symbol represents an inspection or measurement. Examples of inspections are monitoring instrumentation or control charts, reviewing blueprints, or inspecting the quality of outputs.
- *Combined.* Two or more symbols can be combined if an activity fits more than one of the previous definitions. For example, if operators inspect the quality of their work as an integral part of performing an operation, the process step would be coded as both an operation (circle) and an inspection (square).

Figure 7-16 is a transformation flowchart for a process that manufactures table legs in a large furniture plant.

7.4.2 Knowledge Mapping

Knowledge mapping breaks down broad issues into increasing levels of detail.

Knowledge mapping is a method that is used to break down a broad issue into increasing levels of detail to gain a better understanding of existing knowledge about the issue. There are three types of knowledge maps: process, concept, and competency.

7.4.2.1 Process Knowledge Map A *process knowledge map* is a graphical representation of knowledge, and its sources, mapped to a business process. Knowledge that either drives the process or results from its operation is shown. This includes tacit knowledge (expertise, experience, and intuition), explicit knowledge (codified and documented in procedural manuals), and customer knowledge. Creating a process knowledge map requires an intense team effort, typically during a two- to three-day workshop. A suggested format for the workshop employs four distinct phases, as shown in Figure 7-17.

Knowledge process maps can be applied to planning, process improvement, training programs, the determination of intellectual capital, or tracking progress on learning

FIGURE 7-16 Flow Process Chart for Furniture Leg Production

Process: Production of Furniture Legs

Subject Charted: Material

Beginning: Operation 10

Ending: Interim Storage

Summary

Activity		Number of Steps	Time (min)	Distance (m)
Operation	●	5	4.125	
Transport	↑	6	3.11	153.2
Inspect	■	1		
Delay	◗	1	37.6	
Store	▼	1		

Step No.	Time (min)	Distance (m)	●	↑	■	◗	▼	Step Description
10	0.756							Cut lumber to 5.5" width
	0.17	4.6						Move to operation 20 by roller conveyor
20	0.797							Cut part to 11.5" length
	0.17	4.6						Move to staging area by roller conveyor
	37.6							Waiting to be transported to building D
	2.13	127						Transport to building D and operation 30 by truck
30	0.839							Drill 1.5"-diameter hole using drill press
	0.12	3.1						Move to operation 40 by roller conveyor
40	0.857							Drill 8.25"-diameter by 5/8" holes using drill press
	0.32	7.7						Move to operation 50 by belt conveyor
50	0.876							Joint edges using jointer
	0.2	6.2						Move to storage area by truck
								Inspect for defects and store

FIGURE 7-17 Constructing a Knowledge Process Map

Phase I: *Process Characterization*

Construct Process Flowchart

Phase II: *Knowledge Mapping*

Identify Knowledge Requirements and Sources

Phase III: *Analysis*

Ask:
• **What knowledge is most critical?**
• **What knowledge is missing?**
• **What knowledge contributes to the value stream, and how?**

Phase IV: *Application*

Apply the analysis to the purpose:
• **Planning**
• **Process improvement**
• **Training**

objectives. Figure 7-18 is a process knowledge map of the table leg process in the furniture plant introduced previously.

7.4.2.2 Concept Knowledge Map   A *concept knowledge map* is a useful tool for organizing and classifying content. Creating a concept map requires a deep and insightful thought process, and it is sometimes helpful to have group members write basic concepts on index cards or sticky notes so they can easily be moved around on a table or white board. Creating a concept knowledge map requires the three phases of activity shown in Figure 7-19.

Concepts

Figure 7-20 is a concept knowledge map, created by an organization that wanted to identify all the **concepts** used in the management of its operations.

7.4.2.3 Competency Knowledge Map   A *competency knowledge map* can be created for an individual or an organization. For an individual, the map is a competency profile, documenting training, skills, positions, and career path. At the organizational level, the competency map provides a broad documentation of skills, tasks, and core expertise, cross-linked to individuals who possess them. Such a map can provide a ready reference to enable anyone in the organization to seek expertise in a specific competency area.

A morphological box investigates possible relationships and practical solutions.

7.4.3 Morphological Box

Morphological analysis was pioneered by Fritz Zwicky, a Swiss-American astrophysicist and aerospace scientist at the California Institute of Technology.[3] The term "morphology" comes from the Greek word *morphe* meaning "shape" or "form." Morphology

---

[3]Zwicky, Fritz. *Discovery, Invention, Research through the Morphological Approach.* Toronto: Macmillan, 1969.

FIGURE 7-18 Process Knowledge Map for Furniture Leg Production

Process: Production of Furniture Legs

Subject Charted: Material

Beginning: Operation 10

Ending: Interim Storage

Summary

Activity	No. of Steps	Time (min)	Distance (m)
Operation ●	5	4.125	
Transport ⬆	6	3.11	153.2
Inspect ■			
Delay 🛆	1	37.6	
Store ▶	1		

Knowledge Types and Sources

- Tacit (expertise, experience, intuition)
- Explicit (codified, formal, standards, procedures)
- Customer (specifications, expectations, instructions)

Step No.	Time (min)	Distance (m)	●	⬆	■	🛆	▶	Step Description	Knowledge Required	Knowledge Source
10	0.756							Cut lumber to 5.5" width	Skill with table saw, measurement, expertise	Procedure Manual 62-507, operator experience
	0.17	4.6						Move to operation 20 by roller conveyor		
20	0.797							Cut part to 11.5" length		
	0.17	4.6						Move to staging area by roller conveyor		
	37.6							Waiting to be transported to building D		
	2.13	127						Transport to building D and op 30 by truck	Skill with fork lift truck, expertise	Procedure Manual 65-203, op experience and certification
30	0.839							Drill 1.5"-diameter hole using drill press	Skill with drill press, expertise	Procedure Manual 62-514, operator experience
	0.12	3.1						Move to operation 40 by roller conveyor		
40	0.857							Drill 8.25"-diam by 5/8" holes using drill press	Skill with drill press, expertise	Procedure Manual 62-514, operator experience
	0.32	7.7						Move to operation 50 by belt conveyor		
50	0.876							Joint edges using jointer	Skill with jointer, expertise	Procedure Manual 62-482, operator experience
	0.2	6.2						Move to storage area by truck		
								Inspect for defects and store	Specifications, perceptions, judgment	Customer, blueprints, inspector training

FIGURE 7-19 Constructing a Concept Knowledge Map

Phase I: *Create List of Main Concepts*

Ask:
• What are the main ideas relative to the goal or issue at hand?

Phase II: *Arrange Concepts from Broadest to Most Specific*

• Place broadest, most inclusive concept at top of the map.
• Add other concepts that appear to be directly linked to it.
• Work down the map adding concepts linked to second tier.
• Continue with third tier and so on until all concepts have been added.
• Limit the number of concepts linked to any one concept to three.

Phase III: *Link Concepts*

• Link concepts together using straight lines.
• On each line, write a few linking words that describe the
  relationship.

FIGURE 7-20 Concept Map for Operations Management

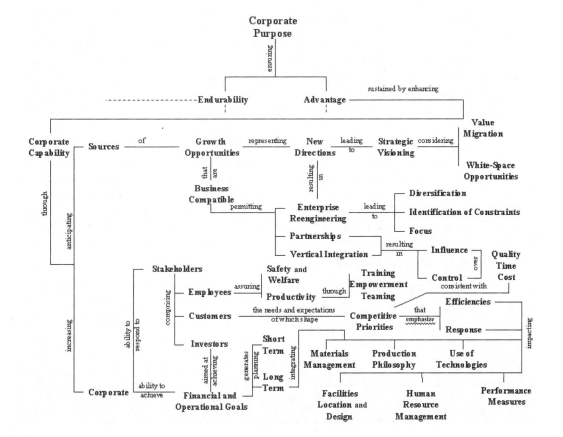

FIGURE 7-21 Morphological Box Structure

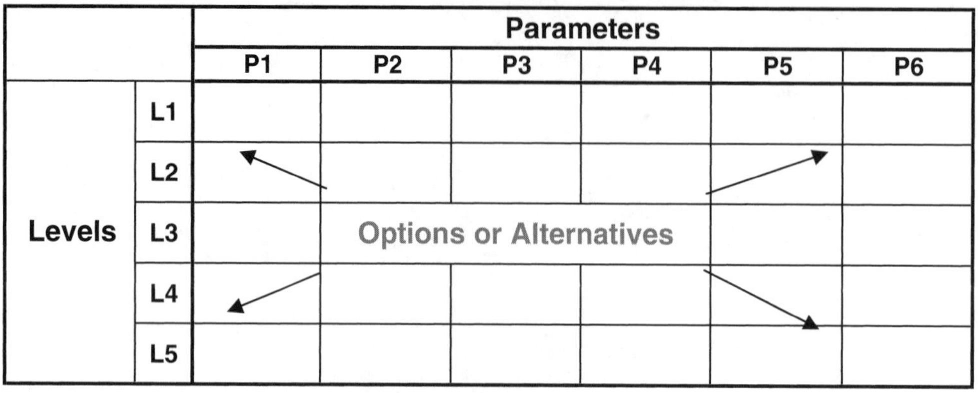

		Parameters					
		P1	P2	P3	P4	P5	P6
Levels	L1						
	L2						
	L3	Options or Alternatives					
	L4						
	L5						

is the study of patterns—how the arrangement of a system's parts interrelate to make a whole. Applied to complex decision making, morphological analysis is a method for identifying and investigating all possible relationships, configurations, or practical solutions to a given problem. Dunn used the approach to clarify the role that the Internet can play in armed conflicts,[4] and Richey applied the technique to develop a post–Cold War policy for Swedish bomb shelters.[5]

There are five steps to the process:

Parameters

- *Step 1.* Concisely formulate the problem, carefully defining all relevant **parameters**.
- *Step 2.* Under each parameter, assign all values and conditions that are likely to occur.

Morphological Box

- *Step 3.* Construct a **morphological box** (sometimes called a *Zwicky box*)—a multi-dimensional matrix that, by cross-linking parameters and values, contains all potential solutions to the problem. Figure 7-21 illustrates the general structure of a morphological box.
- *Step 4.* From the morphological box, the set of all potential solutions can be identified, analyzed, and scrutinized, and a subset of viable solutions can be extracted. The list of all possible combinations of solutions is called the *morphological field*. Figure 7-22 is a morphological box for a decision problem that contains three parameters: location (for which there are five choices), facility size (for which there are three choices), and product mix configuration (for which there are four choices). The morphological field contains $5 \times 3 \times 4 = 60$ possible solution combinations.
- *Step 5.* Optimal solutions are selected and implemented.

Figure 7-23 is a morphological box that was used to evaluate an organization's readiness to implement TQM. A total of seven parameters were selected with up to five levels under each, leading to a morphological field of 11,250 solution combinations

---

[4]Dunn, Myriam A. "The Cyberspace Dimension in Armed Conflict: Approaching a Complex Issue with Assistance of the Morphological Method." *Information and Security* 7 (2001): 145–58.

[5]Richey, Tom. "General Morphological Analysis: A General Method for Non-Quantified Modelling." Adapted from a paper presented at the 16th EURO Conference on Operational Analysis, Brussels, July 1998. Also available online at http://www.swemorph.com/pdf/gma.pdf (accessed April 6, 2005).

FIGURE 7-22 Morphological Box

Morphological Field =
5 x 3 x 4 = 60 possible solutions

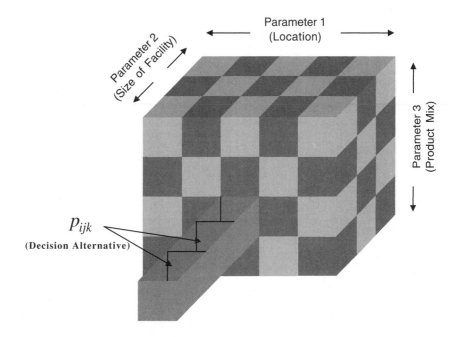

Parameter 1
(Location)

Parameter 2
(Size of Facility)

Parameter 3
(Product Mix)

p_{ijk}
(Decision Alternative)

(5 cultures $\times$ 5 commitments $\times$ 5 change capabilities $\times$ 3 communication systems $\times$ 5 reward systems $\times$ 3 customer relations scenarios $\times$ 2 supplier relations scenarios). The cells that are shaded correspond to the current solution.

7.4.4 Moment-of-Truth Analysis

Moment-of-Truth Analysis

A moment-of-truth analysis tracks how the organization responds to customer contacts.

A **moment-of-truth analysis** is a procedure for quickly analyzing the type and quality of responses resulting from instantaneous customer contacts. When used by a quality team, this tool can highlight procedures that need improvement. There are three steps to the analysis:

- *Step 1.* The team creates a list of all contacts that customers have with the organization. It is sometimes useful to construct a flowchart to help identify moment-of-truth opportunities. If feasible, involving customers in this step can sometimes provide perspectives that might otherwise be overlooked. A line of questioning similar to the following can be used to stimulate ideas:
  - What contact do customers have with the organization before they physically conduct business?
  - What contact do they have when they first walk through the door?
  - Who do they come in contact with?
  - What happens next?
  - What happens after that?

FIGURE 7-23 Morphological Box for Total Quality Management Readiness

Readiness for TQM Implementation

Supportive Culture	Committed Management	Change Capability	Communications	Rewards and Recognition	Customer Relations	Supplier Relations
Optimization level of human capability	Participatory management style	Transformation	Computer based, integrated, timely, and consistent	Team-based rewards	Customer is the boss, customer satisfaction is the number one goal	Partnerships, certification, and mentorship programs
Self-management level of human capability	Management by fact	Improvement	Timely, but not well integrated, sending mixed messages	Balanced, scorecard driven	Customer is important, but not as important as the bottom line	Relations managed by purchasing, adversarial in nature
Alignment level of human capability	Matrix management style emphasizing cross-functional interaction	Sustainability	Not timely, incomplete, disjointed, confusing	Profit sharing	Profits and costs are more important than customer satisfaction	
Repeatability level of human capability	Commitment to training of operatives, but no significant management involvement	Operation		Individual incentives		
Task orientation	Lip service to quality, but not part of measures and rewards	Stability		Compensation not tied to performance goals		

Note: Morphological Field = $5 \times 5 \times 5 \times 3 \times 5 \times 3 \times 2 = 11{,}250$ Possible Solutions.

196

FIGURE 7-24 Truth Cases Map for Hotel Service

Customer Contacts	Current Situation	Desired Situation
Speaks with agent on phone to make reservation	Busy at times, occasionally rude, customer placed on hold	Friendly, helpful, welcoming, responsive, immediate attention
First sight of hotel exterior	Some peeling paint, untidy gardens	Immaculate gardens, flowers, manicured lawns, fresh paint
Greeted by bellman	Efficient, but brusque, personal appearance could improve	Welcoming, friendly, helpful, courteous, well groomed, neat
First encounter with check-in staff	Long wait for service, appearance of staff could be improved, reservations sometimes lost or special requests not fulfilled	Immediate service, tidiness and uniformity of appearance, attention to detail, go the extra mile to satisfy any request
First sight of room	Occasional shortages, obvious shortcuts on cleaning	Meets expectations, clean, well stocked, well maintained, bathrooms spick and span
Experience with housekeeping staff	Guests staying over have to wait until late in day for room to be made	Room made up early in day, restocked, squeaky clean
Room service	Delays in service, errors in orders, cold food	Timely, courteous, accurate, food served hot and tasty
Dines in hotel restaurant	Limited menu, pricey, wait for tables, excellent food quality	Variety, competitive prices, timely service, good food
Encounter with check-out staff	Wait for check-out, mistakes in billing, discourteous at times	Express check-out, accurate account, courteous, friendly

This is continued until the customer exits the system.

- *Step 2.* From the of moment-of-truth contacts list, a truth cases map, such as the one shown in Figure 7-24, can be created.
- *Step 3.* Compare the current and desired situations, and then formulate an action plan to close the gaps.

7.4.5 Force Field Analysis

A **force field** analysis is a brainstorming tool that helps a team compare the forces that promote (or support) a mission, strategic initiative, or improvement idea with those that hinder it. As Figure 7-25 illustrates, the analysis involves constructing two columns. On the left, the team lists all those factors that contribute positively to (promote achievement of) some task. In the right column, the team lists those factors that constitute restraining

A force field analysis can generate ideas on how to capitalize on strengths.

Force Field

FIGURE 7-25 Force Field Analysis

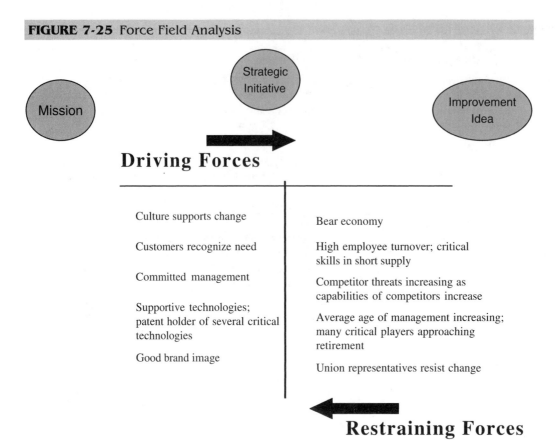

forces (those that hinder achievement). By comparing the two columns, the team can further brainstorm ideas on how restraining forces can be removed or nullified, and how driving forces can be strengthened.

7.4.6 Variance Tracking Matrix

Variance Tracking Matrix

The variance tracking matrix helps pinpoint root causes.

Figure 7-26 illustrates a **variance tracking matrix** that can help an organization focus on its core processes and trace root causes. This tool helps a group analyze all activities in the value stream, their associated sources of variability, and how these sources affect downstream processes.

The vertical axis represents the activities on the value stream—that is, the process flow through the production facility. Each major source of variation is assigned a unique number and is listed on the hypotenuse next to the process step where the source occurs. The downstream impact of each source is tracked down the matrix, and the variation number is placed next to each downstream process step where there is a likely connection.

The bottom section of the matrix represents key performance characteristics—those things that are important to the customer. The numbers in each performance row correspond to sources of variation that may affect the quality characteristic represented by that row. By tracing the number back up the column, the source of

FIGURE 7-26 Format for Variance Tracking Matrix

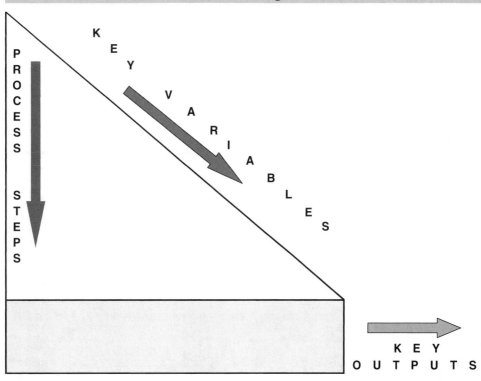

that variation is easily identified, along with the process step where the variation is created.

The variance tracking matrix is usually the product of iterative brainstorming. Once consensus has been reached, the team returns to the brainstorming mode to try to get agreement on a small subset of key variances, those that have the most significant impact on key outcomes. Once identified, each variance is targeted for reduction or elimination.

The variance tracking matrix facilitates learning. It is a dynamic tool that evolves as the knowledge base grows, the team becomes more effective, and the analytical process matures. Figure 7-27 represents a variance tracking matrix that was developed by a large paper plant.

7.4.7 Six Honest Servants and Five Whys

In 1902, Rudyard Kipling[6] unwittingly foreshadowed a learning process when he wrote,

> *I keep six honest serving-men.*
> *They taught me all I knew.*
> *Their names are **What** and **Why** and **When**, and **How** and **Where** and **Who**.*

The six honest servants can stimulate improvement ideas.

What

Why

When

How

Where

Who

[6]Kipling, Rudyard. *The Elephant's Child.* 1902 in Beecroft, John, Kipling: A Selection of His Stories and Poems, Doubleday & Company, Garden City, 1956 (383) http://www.online_literature.com/kipling/165/.

FIGURE 7-27 Variance Tracking Matrix

SOURCE: Courtesy of Thomas R. Williams, Consultant.

These six honest serving men would later become the building blocks for discovery and improvement. Ideas can often be found by repeatedly applying this tool to each step in a flowchart, with a line of questioning such as the following:

- *What is done here? Why is it done there?*
- *When is that done? Why is it done then?*
- *How is it done? Why is it done that way?*
- *Where is it done? Why is it done there?*
- *Who does it? Why is it done by those persons?*

Because each question is followed by "why," this technique is sometimes referred to as the five "whys."

The five whys can be an effective methodology for challenging convention and stimulating new thinking.

7.5 TOOLS FOR PROBLEM SOLVING

7.5.1 The Basic Toolkit: Seven Old Tools

Seven basic tools have been universally applied to the control of quality. Because these tools have been used prevalently through the first, second, and third generations of the quality movement, they have been called the "seven old tools"[7] and include

- Check sheet
- Pareto diagram
- Cause-and-effect diagram
- Histogram
- Stratification
- Scatter diagram
- Graph or chart, with specific emphasis on the control chart

Check Sheet

A check sheet is used to manually record data.

7.5.1.1 Check Sheet   Before a problem can be analyzed, it needs to be understood. A **check sheet**, usually printed on paper and used for manual recording, is used to display data in a format that can be easily understood. As an example, Figure 7-28 shows a check sheet that was used for categorizing defect types in printed materials. The inspector in this case examined 5,560 printed pages, randomly selected from production skids of a magazine produced over a six-week period.

Figure 7-29 is an example of a check sheet that was used to tally the incidences of line stoppages by machine and shift. An inspector simply made a tally notation on the form each time a stoppage occurred over a twenty-four-hour period.

Pareto

A Pareto chart helps separate the significant few from the trivial many.

7.5.1.2 Pareto Diagram   The **Pareto** principle posits that only a few causes (the vital 20%) are responsible for the majority (80%) of problems. Improvement benefits can be leveraged by focusing attention on the key issues (i.e., the 20%), and in the process, it is not uncommon for many of the less important problems to be resolved by default. When check sheet data are plotted on a Pareto diagram, the most important problems are revealed. A pair of graphs is normally plotted—a bar graph that displays item

---

[7]Ishikawa, Kaoru. *What is Total Quality Control? The Japanese Way.* Upper Saddle River, NJ: Prentice Hall, 1985.

FIGURE 7-28 Check Sheet for Defect Problems

Check Sheet for Quality Problems	
Date: *06/03/2004*	Collected By: *J. Doe*
Description of Operation: *Printing*	
Problem	**Frequency**
Density Too High—Black Ink	*13,10,9,3,2 = 37*
Density Too Low—Black Ink	*17,6,70,7,7 = 107*
Density Too High—Colors	*7,9,18,35,8. = 77*
Density Too Low—Colors	*242,168,70,21,105 = 606*
Misregister	*60,47,105,140,140 = 492*
Nip Marks	*14,11,14,14,8 = 61*
Scratches	*8,8,6,3,5 = 30*
Incorrect Fold	*2,3,4,1,1 = 11*
Wrinkles	*3,15,8,2,1 = 29*
Scumming	*13,13,9,11,4 = 50*
Piling	*3,4,3,2 = 12*
Scuffing, Belt Marks	*14,7,3,4,7 = 35*
Severe Set-Off	*14,4,7,2,1 = 28*

FIGURE 7-29 Check Sheet for Source of Downtime Problems

Tally of Downtime by Shift and Machine				
Machine	**First Shift**	**Second Shift**	**Third Shift**	**Total**
Red	/	//	JHT JHT /	14
Green		/	JHT ///	9
Blue	/		JHT JHT	11
Gold			JHT JHT //	12
Silver	//		JHT JHT JHT	17
Bronze			JHT JHT /	11
Total	4	3	67	74

percentages sorted in descending order, and a line graph that plots the cumulative percentage of items on the sorted list. These two graphs can be plotted on the same chart.

Figure 7-30 is a pair of Pareto diagrams for the printing operation data presented in Figure 7-28. Extending a horizontal line at the 80% point on the Y-axis over to the line graph, and then dropping a vertical line perpendicular to the X-axis, can separate the significant (vital) problems from the trivial ones. In the printing operation, it is clear that improvement efforts should target problems A, B, and C (i.e., low density and misregister problems).

All types of problems do not necessarily have an equal impact on quality. A variant of the Pareto procedure assigns weights to items according to their relative importance. Figure 7-31 is a weighted Pareto diagram showing the incidences of different types of defects in automobile tire manufacturing.

The tire defects have been categorized into four severity levels:

- Level 4 severity (the worst) problems result in scrapping the product. Level 4 problems have been assigned a severity index (weight) of 40.
- Level 3 defects are "blems." A tire with a blem is functional and safe, however imperfect, and must be sold at a substantial discount. Level 3 defects have been assigned a severity index of 10 or 15.
- Level 2 defects are repairable but costly. Defects in this category are assigned an index of 3 or 5.
- Level 1 defects (the lowest level) are minor repairables and therefore assigned weightings of 1 or 2.

To understand the impact of the weighted Pareto chart, consider the level 4 defect, "wrinkled fabric." This defect ranks nineteenth out of twenty-nine in frequency of occurrence, but second in weighted importance. The Pareto analysis reveals that by focusing attention on only ten of the twenty-nine types, all major sources of poor quality will be addressed.

Cause and Effect

Fishbone

Ishikawa

A cause-and-effect diagram helps a team focus.

7.5.1.3 Cause-and-Effect Diagram   The cause and effect (CE) diagram is also called a **fishbone** diagram (due to its similarity to the skeletal structure of a fish), and an **Ishikawa** diagram (in honor of its founder).[8] Once a team decides which problem it wants to solve, possibly from a Pareto analysis, the CE diagram can help it identify candidate causes.

The CE structure is illustrated in Figure 7-32. To construct a CE diagram, the problem, or *effect,* is placed in a box (analogous to the head of the fish). A horizontal line (the backbone) is drawn from the box, and from the backbone, angled fishbones are inserted that correspond to each main problem category. This forms the skeleton of the fishbone diagram.

Main categories can be anything that is relevant to the problem, but typical ones include materials, methods, personnel, and machines. From each main stem, smaller bones (or twigs) are constructed for each candidate cause, and from these, smaller bones (or twiglets) representing subcauses are drawn. The diagram can include as many sublevels as required to get to the root causes.

---

[8]Ishikawa, Kaoru. *Guide to Quality Control,* 18–29. Tokyo: Asian Productivity Organization, 1982.

FIGURE 7-30 Pareto Chart for Printing Operation

Problem	Total	Code	Percentage	Cumulative Percentage
Density Too Low—Colors	606	A	39.0	39.0
Misregister	492	B	31.7	70.7
Density Too Low—Black Ink	107	C	6.9	77.6
Density Too High—Colors	77	D	5.0	82.6
Nip Marks	61	E	3.9	86.5
Scumming	50	F	3.2	89.8
Density Too High—Black Ink	37	G	2.4	92.1
Scuffing Marks	35	H	2.3	94.4
Scratches	30	I	1.9	96.3
Wrinkles	29	J	1.9	98.2
Set-Off	28	K	1.8	100.0
Totals	1,552		100	

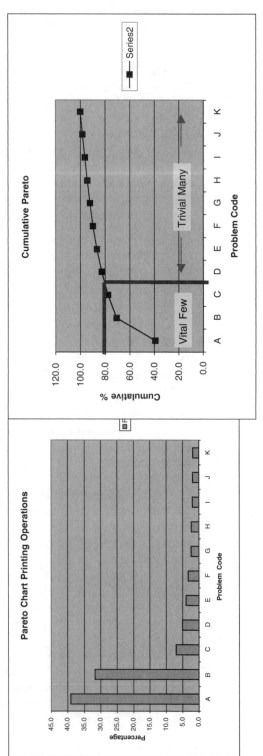

FIGURE 7-31 Pareto Chart for Tire Manufacturing

Tire Defects

Cumulative Pareto—Tire Defects

Defect Type	Total	Severity Index	Weighted Count		%	Cumulative Percent
Snaked Component	134	10	1,340	L	12.9	12.9
Wrinkled Fabric	32	40	1,280	A	12.4	25.3
Exposed First Ply	121	10	1,210	K	11.7	37.0
Wrong ID	76	15	1,140	I	11.0	48.0
Wide Liner Splice	203	5	1,015	P	9.8	57.8
Open S/W Splice	22	40	880	E	8.5	66.3
Open Liner Splice	72	10	720	J	6.9	73.2
Off Centered Bead	102	5	510	M	4.9	78.1
Wrong Component	22	15	330	H	3.2	81.3
Exposed Ply Splice	6	40	240	D	2.3	83.6
Misplaced Splice/Spotting	45	5	225	N	2.2	85.8
Humped W/W Splice	71	3	213	R	2.1	87.8
Flipback Turn-up	5	40	200	B	1.9	89.8
Foreign Material	11	15	165	G	1.6	91.4
Open Ply Splice	4	40	160	C	1.5	92.9
Wrinkled Component	68	2	136	W	1.3	94.2
Wide Ply Splice	24	5	120	O	1.2	
Open W/W Splice	34	3	102	S	1.0	
Split Ply	2	40	80	F	0.8	
Torn or Jagged S/W Edges	25	3	75	T	0.7	
No Builder Number	50	1	50	Z	0.5	
Loose Chafer	44	1	44	Y	0.4	
Air Between Plies	19	2	38	V	0.4	
Humped S/W Splice	12	3	36	Q	0.3	
Blister Under S/W	13	2	26	U	0.3	
Miscellaneous	23	1	23	AA	0.2	
Wrinkled Chafer	22		4X		0.0	
	1,242		10,362		100.0	

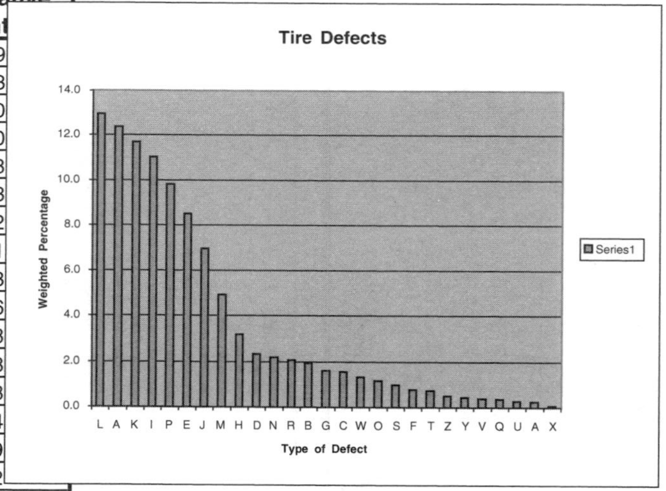

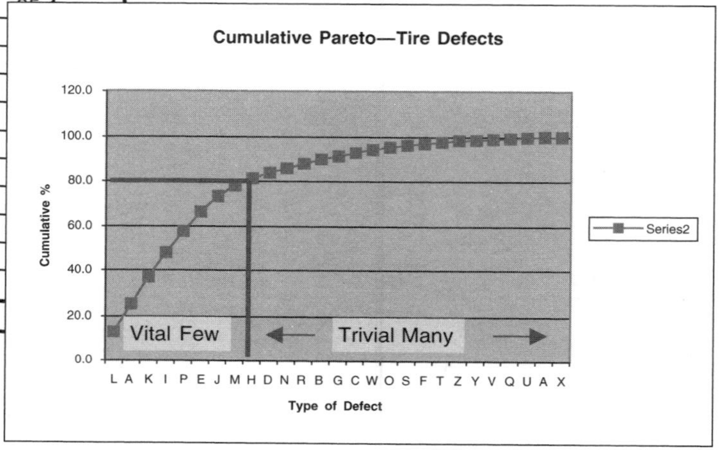

FIGURE 7-32 Fishbone Diagram Structure

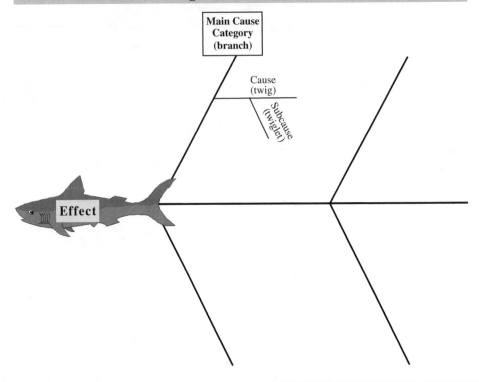

FIGURE 7-33 Fishbone Diagram for Advertising Copy Recycling Problem

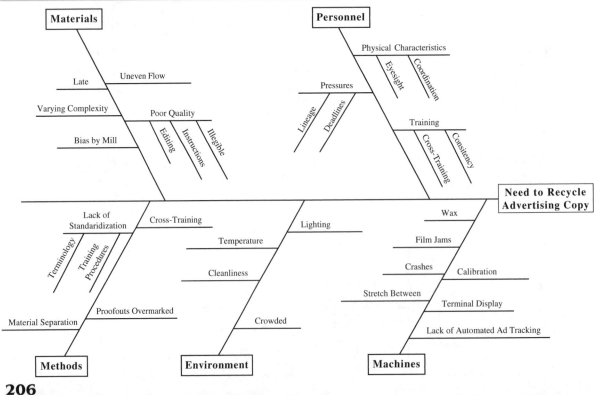

Two teams, in a large metropolitan daily newspaper, prepared the fishbone diagrams shown in Figures 7-33 and 7-34. One team was trying to find ways to reduce the number of ads that had to be reworked after the initial layout. The other team was attempting to learn why there were discrepancies between their measurements of paper basis weight and that of their suppliers.

The CE diagram adds structure to brainstormed ideas. It is important that the team understands that all "causes" shown on the diagram are merely candidates and have not been proven to be true causes of the stated effect. Consequently, it is essential that all causes suggested by team members should be listed, no matter how bazaar, zany, or unlikely.

When the team is satisfied that it has captured most of the likely causes, the next step is to narrow the list to a few for detailed study. Four guidelines can be helpful in achieving this end:

- *Guideline 1:* Separate the causes into those that the team can potentially control and those beyond its control. A team in one organization stratified its causes into two fishbones that resembled a pair of kissing fish, as illustrated in Figure 7-35. The fishbone on the right contained those causes that were beyond the group's control,

FIGURE 7-34 Fishbone Diagram for Cross-Calibration of Paper Basis Weight

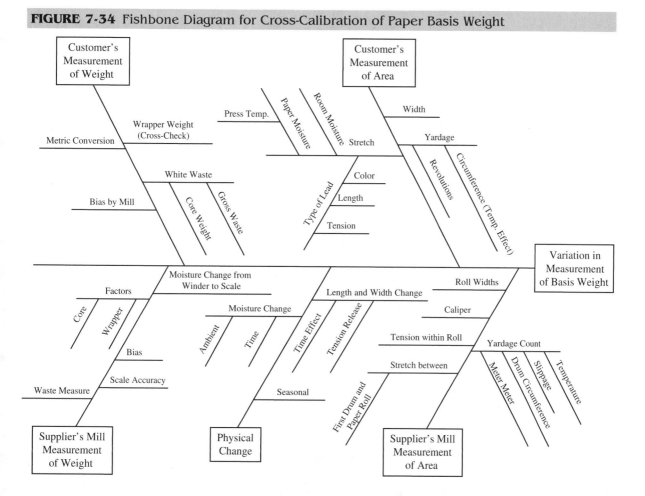

FIGURE 7-35 Dual Fishbone Diagrams

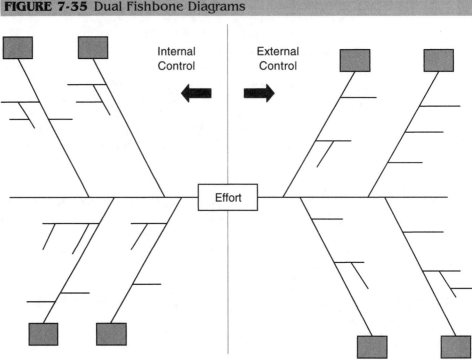

whereas those on the left were considered to be internal matters that the team could potentially influence.

- *Guideline 2.* Have each team member identify the top three causes—that is, the ones that each individual believes are likely to be major drivers. This can be done most effectively outside a formal meeting. The team will then meet, combine everyone's selections, and try to reach consensus (possibly using the nominal group technique) on a short list of three to five causes to investigate further.

- *Guideline 3.* Determine relationships. Focusing on the short list of selected causes, the team tries to understand if an association exists between the effect and each suspected cause, and also between each pair of causes. If data are available, scatter plots and statistical correlation analysis can be used to make these determinations.

- *Guideline 4.* Combine systems thinking with the cause–effect relationships. The team should question what feedback mechanisms operate between the effect and the candidate cause—that is, is the feedback loop negative (balancing) or positive (reinforcing)? As we discuss in Chapter 2, a balancing loop has a self-regulating trigger that causes a modification in behavior. When activated, the cause will induce some desired behavior or result, with respect to the effect. It will in turn have a negative influence on the cause, and in essence, the roles will reverse. In a balancing cycle, the effect will become a cause—just the opposite of how the relationship was originally perceived. In the case of a positive or reinforcing feedback

FIGURE 7-36 Feedback Fishbone Diagram for Advertising Copy Recycling Problem

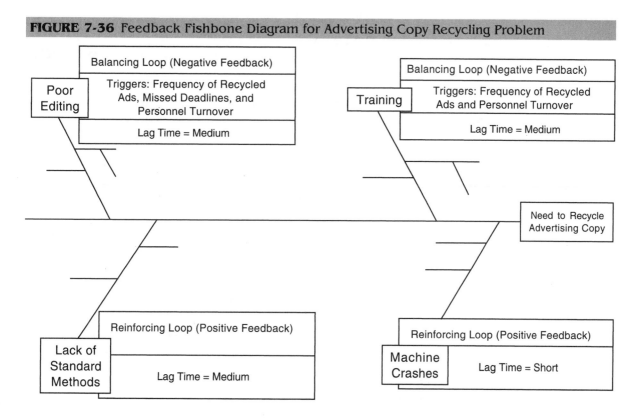

loop, the effect simply signals the cause to keep doing what it is doing. Whether positive or negative, there is usually a time lapse between when the feedback is received and when the system responds.

Figure 7-36 is an example of a fishbone diagram for the advertising recycle problem. Feedback loops have been identified together with their triggers and lag times. A feedback CE diagram is a condensed version of the original, where the main causation branches represent the small group of causes that were identified for further investigation.

To determine the type of feedback loops, the following question is directed at each causation branch: how is the behavior in the causation branch altered as a result of variability (i.e., increases and decreases) in the measured effect?

In the example, whenever the defect rate increases, the frequency of ad recycles diminishes the overall productivity of the ad preparation process. When this happens, deadlines, so vital in the newspaper industry, are jeopardized and pressure reverberates back up the value stream. Then, through the trigger mechanisms, the roles reverse. The effect now becomes the driver, activating improvement efforts in training and editing.

Triggers occur whenever there is a positive trend (or unacceptable level) of ad recycles, or experienced personnel leave and have to be replaced by inexperienced ones. As improvement efforts in training and editing begin to work, the roles reverse again, and the trend in ad recycles changes sign and becomes a negative trend. When it reaches an acceptable level, the triggers cause a slackening of the improvement efforts, representing yet another reversal of roles.

Machine crashes and lack of standard methods are representative of positive feedback loops. As the number of recycles increases, rework is comingled with new work, and the total workload grows. With increased work and tightening deadlines, workers must increase their pace just to keep up. With mounting pressures, panic sets in and workers are more likely to cut corners (looking for shortcuts) and make mistakes. Inconsistent methods across the work group become even more nonstandard, and machine crashes become more prevalent, driving the defect rate even higher.

A histogram
converts raw data
into a picture of
process output.

Histogram

7.5.1.4 Histogram   A histogram provides a graphical picture of process output. Collecting raw measurements is meaningless unless the data can be organized in a way that aids discovery and analysis. Figure 7-37a displays the measurements of 100 fifty-pound bags, selected at random, and weighed to the nearest 100th of a pound. A plot of the raw data is shown in Figure 7-37b and is difficult to interpret. Figure 7-37c is the same data organized as a histogram. With a histogram, one can gain insight into the mean (average), median (50 percentile point), **mode** (most frequent measure), and process spread (range, **variance**, standard deviation).

Mode

Variance

Standard Deviation

To construct the histogram, each of the 100 data points was assigned to one of eleven class intervals. A bar chart was then constructed by plotting the frequencies calculated in each class interval. The histogram provides an approximate picture of the

FIGURE 7-37 Bag Weight Measurements

Bag No.	Bag wt (lbs)	Bag No.	Bag wt (lbs)	Bag No.	Bag wt (lbs)	Bag No.	Bag wt (lbs)
1	49.21	26	50.57	51	50.20	76	49.07
2	50.40	27	49.35	52	49.44	77	49.57
3	50.07	28	49.29	53	49.63	78	49.18
4	50.47	29	48.92	54	49.72	79	49.03
5	50.16	30	50.15	55	50.03	80	48.64
6	50.40	31	50.14	56	49.88	81	49.23
7	50.04	32	50.82	57	50.13	82	49.45
8	50.06	33	49.27	58	49.21	83	50.49
9	49.35	34	49.41	59	49.64	84	48.99
10	49.58	35	49.89	60	50.03	85	51.45
11	50.86	36	49.78	61	49.70	86	49.28
12	49.73	37	49.40	62	49.39	87	48.72
13	49.50	38	50.47	63	49.80	88	49.14
14	49.51	39	50.24	64	51.07	89	49.75
15	50.23	40	50.12	65	50.18	90	49.40
16	50.61	41	50.17	66	50.46	91	50.54
17	50.41	42	49.94	67	50.22	92	50.12
18	50.63	43	50.01	68	50.04	93	49.43
19	49.99	44	49.24	69	50.01	94	49.23
20	50.19	45	49.39	70	49.51	95	49.77
21	49.97	46	50.45	71	50.34	96	49.66
22	51.16	47	49.87	72	49.20	97	49.25
23	49.91	48	49.69	73	48.64	98	50.35
24	48.32	49	50.31	74	50.46	99	50.43
25	50.54	50	50.02	75	49.49	100	49.43

a

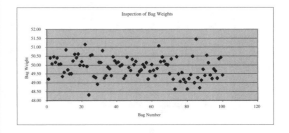

b

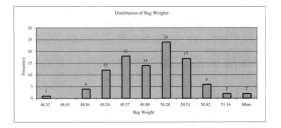

c

process distribution. In this case, it appears that the distribution of bag weights is normal, with an average close to the fifty-pound target.

The specifications for this process require a tolerance of 50 ± 1 pounds, and from the histogram, we can get an immediate insight as to how well the process is performing. It would appear that approximately 5% of the bags are underweight, and 4% are overweight. Furthermore, the natural spread of the process is wider (approximately three pounds) than the two-pound tolerance permitted. Therefore, it would appear that the process is not capable of meeting the specs unless the natural variability can be reduced.

Pattern Recognition

Through **pattern recognition**, histograms can provide valuable clues leading to improvement opportunities. Figure 7-38 illustrates eight different histogram shapes. Shape A represents a symmetrical "bell-shaped" curve that is usually referred to as a normal distribution. This is the shape of the output from many industrial processes, if they are stable and the only sources of variation present are the random fluctuations that are inherent in the system. In a normal distribution, the **mean** and **median** are equal—that is, 50% of the output lies to the left of the average (or mean) and 50% to the right.

Mean

Median

In pattern B, the distribution looks as if it may have originated as a normal distribution, but the middle of the distribution (the highest-quality product) has been carved out. This gutted normal is typical of cases where a supplier can sell product that is of the highest quality—produced near the target with small variation—at a higher price than product of a lower grade. Even though all output may fall within the allowed specification range, and the average is on target, none of the individual units are equal to the target, and the variance can be substantially greater than if the original distribution were in tact.

Normal

The augmented **normal**, shown as pattern C, could result from an inspector reclassifying output that is just below or above the specification limits. Hence, there is a "lumping" effect at the first and last class intervals where the specification cut-offs occur. Pattern D is a truncated normal. A pattern such as this could occur if a process is centered on target, its spread is wider than the tolerance limits, and the unacceptable output has not been reported in the data. A distribution can also truncate if a natural barrier is encountered, such as zero (when no negative values are possible).

Skew

Patterns E and F represent distributions that have a **skew**—that is, they lack the symmetry of the normal distribution. In a negatively skewed distribution, more than 50% of the distribution and the median lie to the right of the mean. In a positively skewed distribution, more than 50% of the distribution and the median are to the left of the mean.

Pattern G could have two possible interpretations. One scenario is that defective product was sorted from the good because the process was incorrectly targeted. Alternatively, if negative numbers are not possible (e.g., weights), truncation at a measurement equal to zero can produce this pattern.

Pattern H could be the resulting picture when several normal processes are overlaid—for example, if samples represent the output from several machines, each having a different process average.

Stratification

7.5.1.5 Stratification   **Stratification** is the process of sorting data into meaningful classifications so clues as to the what, where, when, who, how, and why relative to an issue at hand can easily be found. For example, a random selection of product at a packing operation might reveal that a certain percentage is outside the specification range, and more disturbing, the data suggests that the process is not capable of meeting specs. Stratifying the data by machine, operator, or shift could lead directly to the source of the unacceptable variability and its subsequent reduction.

Stratification sorts data into meaningful classifications.

FIGURE 7-38 Histogram Patterns

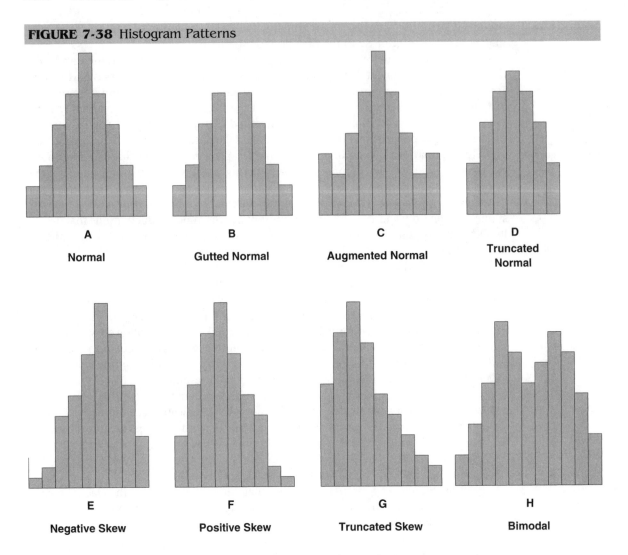

A
Normal

B
Gutted Normal

C
Augmented Normal

D
Truncated Normal

E
Negative Skew

F
Positive Skew

G
Truncated Skew

H
Bimodal

The ability to think about possible sources of variation and to design stratified data collection strategies is fundamental to continuous improvement. As an example, consider Figure 7-39. A Pareto chart for the printing operations problem is reintroduced. In this case, the defects have been classified not only by type, but also by shift. A study of this chart highlights shift 3—a good prospect for improvement.

7.5.1.6 Scatter Diagram   Like histograms, scatter diagrams aid in pattern recognition. A scatter diagram can be used to gain insight into the relationship between two factors (or variables). If a relationship is found, it cannot necessarily be inferred that one variable is the cause of the other; however, the scatter diagram can provide graphical evidence that the relationship is real and will provide some knowledge regarding the strength (**correlation**) of the relationship.

Correlation

Scatter Diagram

Relationship

Association

A **scatter diagram** is constructed by plotting the values of one variable on the horizontal (*x*) axis, and the corresponding value of the other variable on the vertical (*y*) axis. A **relationship (association)** between the two variables is evident if the resulting

FIGURE 7-39 Stratified Pareto Chart for Printing Operation

Problem	Total	Code	Shift 1	Shift 2	Shift 3	Shift 1 %	Shift 2 %	Shift 3 %	%	Cum. %
Density Too Low—Colors	606	A	100	50	456	6.4	3.2	29.4	39.0	39.0
Misregister	492	B	129	112	251	8.3	7.2	16.2	31.7	70.7
Density Too Low—Black Ink	107	C	23	34	50	1.5	2.2	3.2	6.9	77.6
Density Too High—Colors	77	D	34	12	31	2.2	0.8	2.0	5.0	82.6
Nip Marks	61	E	12	10	39	0.8	0.6	2.5	3.9	86.5
Scumming	50	F	21	12	17	1.4	0.8	1.1	3.2	89.8
Density Too High—Black Ink	37	G	7	13	17	0.5	0.8	1.1	2.4	92.1
Scuffing Marks	35	H	8	10	17	0.5	0.6	1.1	2.3	94.4
Scratches	30	I	9	8	13	0.6	0.5	0.8	1.9	96.3
Wrinkles	29	J	10	7	12	0.6	0.5	0.8	1.9	98.2
Set-Off	28	K	6	7	15	0.4	0.5	1.0	1.8	100.0
Totals	1552								100	

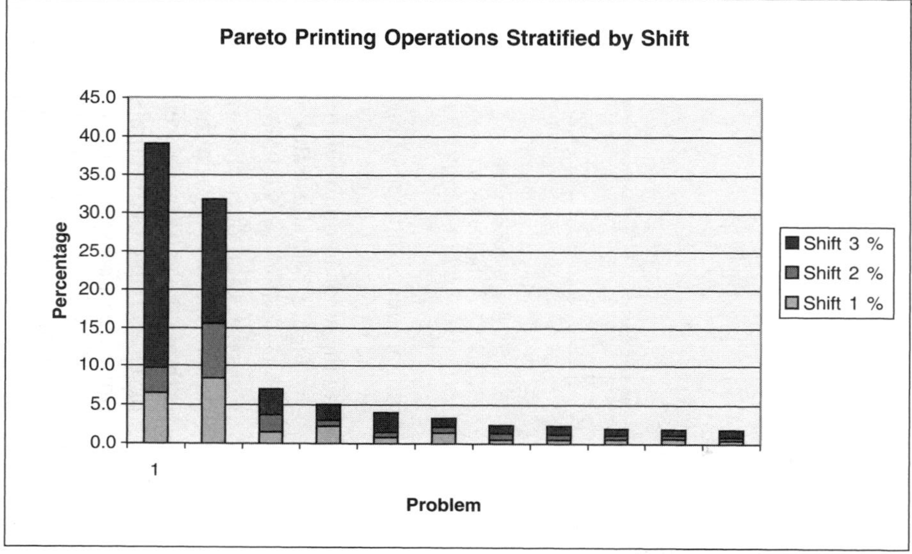

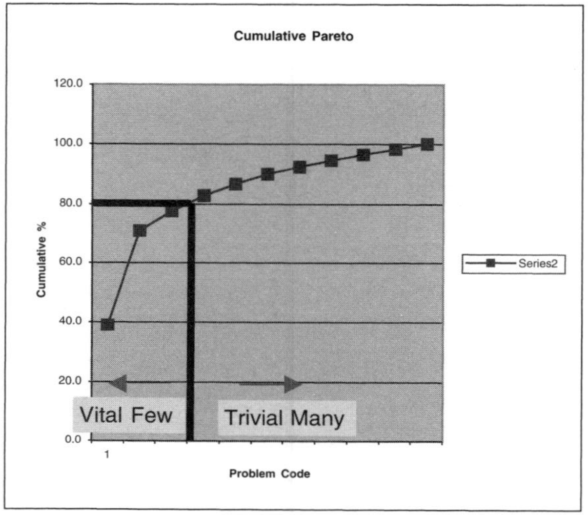

Pareto Printing Operations Stratified by Shift

Cumulative Pareto

FIGURE 7-40 Linear Relationships

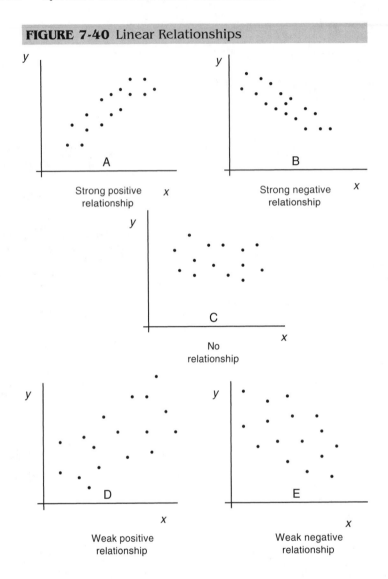

A scatter diagram
can reveal
nonrandom
relationships.

plot produces some nonrandom pattern. The strength of the relationship is determined by the variability of the cluster of points relative to a mathematical expression describing the association. A relationship can be linear or nonlinear.

Figure 7-40 illustrates some scatter diagrams that are linear. Pattern A shows a strong positive association—x and y will move in the same direction. When x increases, y increases and vice versa. The association is strong because the cluster of points is tight (low variability) around the mathematical least-squares line that fits the data. Pattern B shows the pattern in reverse—the variables move in opposite directions. An increase in one variable corresponds to a decrease in the other. Patterns D and E suggest the presence of possible but weaker relationships than patterns A and B because the cluster of points are more scattered.

In pattern C, there is no evidence of a relationship. The scatter appears to be random around an imaginary straight line with a slope of zero (i.e., a horizontal line). However,

FIGURE 7-41 Impact of Measurement Domain on Linear Relationships

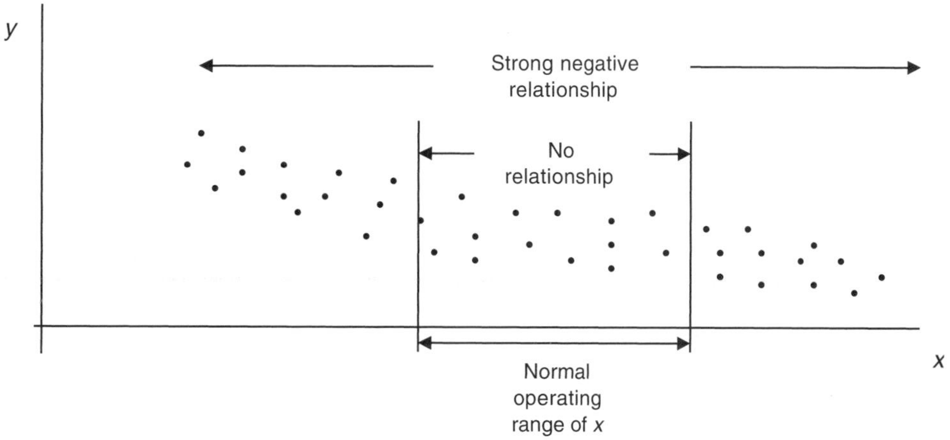

a little skepticism can sometimes pay off. The points on scatter diagrams represent data that typically come from process measurements taken when operating parameters are at their normal set points. This is because scatter diagrams almost always reflect empirical data. Even though there is no evidence to suggest a relationship between x and y in the normal range, by deliberately moving out of the operating domain one can sometimes expose a relationship, as illustrated in Figure 7-41.

Not all associations are linear. Figure 7-42 shows some typical nonlinear patterns in F, G, I, and J. Understanding the nature of a nonlinear association can provide valuable clues in discovering improvement options. Pattern H has an underlying relationship that is linear; however, the variance of y depends on the value of x—as x increases the variance of y also increases.

Charts and graphs reveal patterns in plotted points.

7.5.1.7 Graph or Chart   Graphs and charts are used to descriptively display statistical data so patterns and trends can be understood and analyzed. Histograms, Pareto diagrams, and scatter diagrams are all examples used in quality management. Other charting tools deal with how the process is affected over time. Some variable of interest is measured at various times, the data are "time ordered" and then plotted, typically with the measurement appearing on the y-axis and the time variable on the x-axis. Three tools widely used for this purpose are the run chart, the control chart, and the Gantt chart.

RUN CHART

Run Chart

Time-Ordered Chart

The **run chart** is the simplest **time-ordered chart** to plot and use. Individual measurements are plotted in the order in which they occur. Although unnecessary, it is a good idea to connect the points for ease in interpretation. Figure 7-43 shows an example run chart, representing twenty-eight measurements of a mineral product that was produced in a continuous line flow process. The average has been computed and drawn on the chart. The run chart is best used to identify sustained shifts or trends in the process average. If the process is not changing over time, approximately the same number of points should appear on either side of the average and be randomly distributed. In the mineral example, there is an equal split, but the distribution does not look random. It appears that at certain

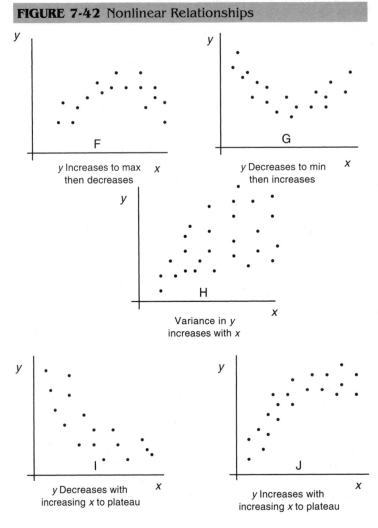

FIGURE 7-42 Nonlinear Relationships

F
y Increases to max   *x*
then decreases

G
y Decreases to min   *x*
then increases

H
Variance in *y*
increases with *x*

I
y Decreases with   *x*
increasing *x* to plateau

J
y Increases with   *x*
increasing *x* to plateau

A run chart is a time-ordered plot of individual measurements.

times the average is higher, and at other times lower, than the overall average of all twenty-eight measurements.

One way to check for a change in average is to count the number of "runs." A run is defined as a build-up of consecutive points on the same side of the average (or centerline). A run length of seven or more points provides statistical evidence that the average has changed. An alternative to the number of runs is a test for trends. Six consecutive points either increasing or decreasing with no reversal in direction provide evidence that the average is trending.

CONTROL CHART

Control Chart

A **control chart** is a run chart with control limits. These limits represent the maximum and minimum allowable values for any plotted point. Any point that exceeds these limits provides statistical evidence that the process average has changed and is no longer equal to the chart's centerline. The maximum value is

FIGURE 7-43 Run Chart

Run Chart For Mineral Mesh +20

Sample	Measurement
1	25.03
2	25.63
3	26.87
4	30.23
5	23.80
6	17.73
7	11.70
8	12.27
9	14.33
10	16.00
11	17.43
12	18.13
13	17.27
14	17.63
15	17.27
16	18.50
17	19.90
18	21.20
19	24.67
20	26.60
21	26.03
22	26.90
23	22.50
24	20.87
25	19.30
26	21.23
27	20.37
28	17.80
	577.19
	16.51

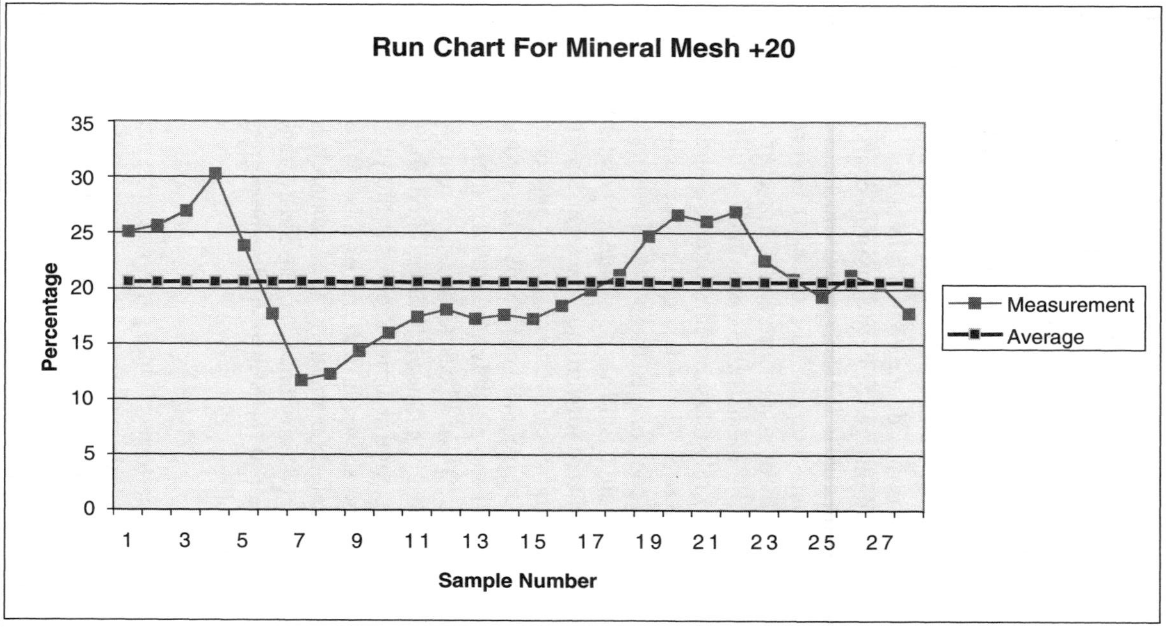

called the upper control limit, and the minimum value the lower control limit. The range of permissible values that lie between the two limits represents expected variability due to random causes. Random variability is present in all samples and is aptly called **common cause variability**. If certain sources of variability are present in some samples, but not others, one would expect the variability to exceed the bounds imposed by the control limits—such sporadic fluctuations are called **special cause variability**. The purpose of a control chart is to expose the presence of special cause variation. This can be done by detecting nonrandom patterns or observing any plotted points outside the control limits.

There is a fundamental difference between a run chart and a control chart. The points plotted on run charts typically represent individual measurements (e.g., machine downtime, percentage yields, or scrap). Control charts can also be constructed to analyze individual measurements; however, the points normally represent a statistic (e.g., the mean, range, or standard deviation) that is computed from a sample of several measurements taken at random from the process.

A control chart can be useful in understanding the underlying behavior of a process. If the process is in control (i.e., there is no statistical evidence to suggest any nonrandom patterns), it is said to be **stable**, **predictable**, and **repeatable**. Process output can be predicted forward and backward in time, and it is possible to evaluate how well it is doing relative to customer expectations.

If a process is unstable, the control chart will often provide hints as to where special causes can be found and possibly eliminated. Figure 7-44 illustrates some common control chart patterns. In all cases, the x-axis represents time. In pattern B, the plotted points appear to be randomly distributed about the centerline (average), and all lie within the control limits. Process B, therefore, is in a state of statistical control. The process shown in pattern A appears to have started at an average higher than the centerline and then, approximately half way through the sampling process, experienced a sustained decrease in average. Even though none of the points exceeded either of the control limits, the pattern is nonrandom and the process is not in control.

The process depicted by pattern C is like pattern A, except the process is undergoing a continual decrease (or trend) in average. If the trend continues unabated, a point will eventually fall below the lower control limit. Pattern D shows clear evidence of the presence of special causes. These nonrandom sources of variability are resulting in a wider pattern swing than would be expected from common cause sources alone, and consequently, points fall outside both control limits.

A control chart is the "voice of the process," but it will only provide the information it has been designed to provide. Control chart patterns are dependent on sampling strategies—how the raw data are collected. This includes sample size, frequency, and specifically how individual sampling units will be selected. An important consideration in determining the sampling plan is the intended purpose for the data. There are three basic reasons for collecting control chart data.

- *To characterize the process output.* A process in control can be used to estimate the quality of process output, including the percentage that exceeds or falls short of requirements. Such information can be valuable in communicating with customers or justifying improvement efforts.

Common Cause Variability

Special Cause Variability

The purpose of a control chart is to test the statistical stability of a process.

Stable

Predictable

Repeatable

A process is in a state of statistical control if it is stable, predictable, and repeatable.

The patterns that appear on control charts depend on how the samples were taken.

FIGURE 7-44 Control Chart Patterns

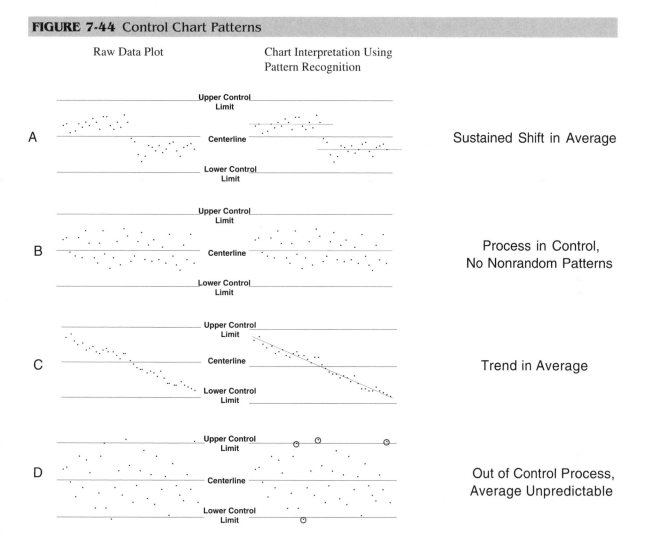

- *To monitor process performance and intervene when necessary.* A control chart can act as a tracking device and navigational aid. As a tracking device, it can validate improvements and provide early warning to an operator if the process starts to lose productivity gains. As a navigation tool, operators can use the control chart to indicate when they should intervene and "steer the process" and, just as important, when to leave the process alone.
- *To improve a process.* With a properly designed sample, a control chart can expose sources of variability—often converting common causes into special causes—in order to focus improvement efforts. For improvement, more information can often be gained from charts not in control than from data that exhibit statistical stability.

Control charts are covered in detail in Chapter 8.

GANTT CHART

Henry L. Gantt, an American engineer and social scientist, developed the Gantt chart in 1917. Originally designed for production scheduling, the Gantt chart is now frequently used by organizations to plan and track progress on projects.

Gantt Chart

A Gantt chart is used to plan and track progress.

A **Gantt chart** is constructed with the horizontal (x) axis representing time increments, and the vertical axis (y) representing the individual tasks that comprise the project. Horizontal bars (of a length corresponding to the time consumed by each task) are placed on the chart in the time slot scheduled. When two tasks can occur simultaneously, bars can overlap, but not when one task must be completed before another can commence. As a project is executed, Gantt charts can be easily adjusted to reflect actual process status. From a Gantt chart, the estimated project completion time is always readily available.

Figure 7-45 shows a pair of Gantt charts that were constructed for the manufacture of a product involving fourteen tasks. The precedence diagram shows the

FIGURE 7-45 Gantt Charts for Scheduling on Assembly Operation

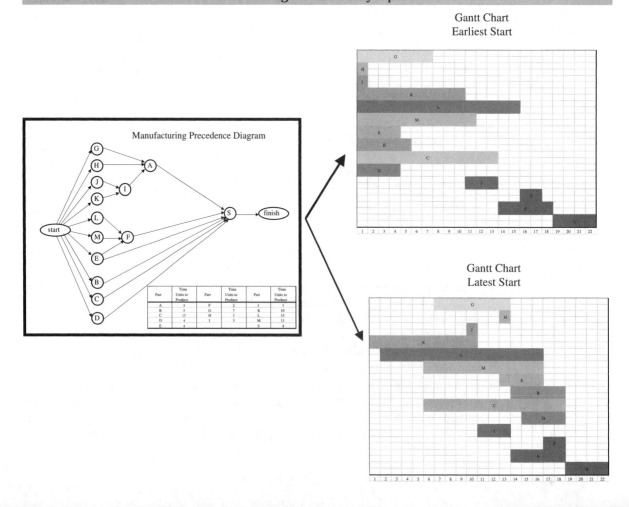

sequence of operations that must be followed, and the task times are shown in the table. One of the Gantt charts shows the earliest activity start times for each task, and the other depicts the latest. By comparing the two charts, it is easy to determine how much scheduling flexibility exists for each task. It is also clear that the critical tasks are K, I, A, and S. Any delay on these tasks will postpone the estimated overall completion time of twenty-two time units.

7.5.2 Seven New Tools for Problem Solving

The seven new tools can be used to process nonnumerical data.

In the early 1970s, it had become clear to the Japanese that the effective implementation of TQM required that managers know more than how to apply basic statistical tools. Although the tools of numerical analysis are essential, the Japanese recognized that much of the information processed by middle to senior management is nonnumerical, and often takes the form of verbal data and communications. Consequently, in 1972, a committee chaired by Yoshinobu Nayatani was established to develop new quality control tools for managerial levels. The committee's research took more than five years and resulted in a new set of techniques called the "seven new tools." In 1978, the Japanese Union of Scientists and Engineers invited Professor Shigeru Mizuno, Professor Emeritus of Tokyo Institute of Technology, and Professor Yoshio Kondo, Head of the Faculty of Engineering at Kyoto University, to guide the education and advocacy of the new set of tools. The Japanese committee did not invent the seven new tools. Most of the tools were developed in America and elsewhere, but by the late 1970s, they had not been effectively applied to quality management programs. The set of managerial tools includes

- Affinity diagram
- Relations diagram or interrelationship digraph
- Systematic diagram or dendrogram (tree diagram)
- Matrix diagram
- Matrix data analysis
- Process decision program chart (PDPC)
- Arrow diagram or activity network diagram or project evaluation and review technique (PERT) or critical path method (CPM)

Affinity Diagram

KJ Method

An affinity diagram can be used to organize a number of ideas into a small number of categories.

7.5.2.1 Affinity Diagram   An **affinity diagram**, sometimes called the **KJ method** in honor of its inventor, Jiro Kawakita (the Japanese usually write the surname first), is used to organize ideas into categories based on the perception of natural relationships or common themes. This tool is often used at step 5 of a brainstorming session or at step 4 of brainwriting, when a group has to generate a number of ideas and wants to reduce the list into a smaller number of manageable categories. The steps involved in creating an affinity diagram, depicted in Figure 7-46, include

- *Step 1.* Using a process such as brainstorming or brainwriting, participants record their ideas on sticky notes, one idea per note. All notes are placed on a white board or wall.
- *Step 2.* Participants individually try to sort the items into related groups. No discussion between participants is permitted. If a person disagrees with someone's placement of an item, they are permitted to relocate it to another category. The sorting and resorting continues until it appears the team has reached some agreement. It is important that this entire step be completed in silence.

FIGURE 7-46 Affinity Diagram

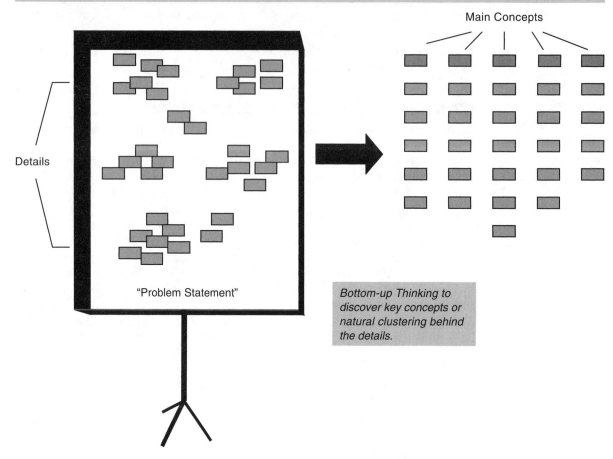

Main Concepts

Details

"Problem Statement"

Bottom-up Thinking to discover key concepts or natural clustering behind the details.

- *Step 3.* The group holds an open discussion, trying to agree on names for the categories. Header cards are created and placed on the chart above the sorted data.

Relations Diagram

Interrelationship Digraph

A relations diagram is used to help identify principal cause-and-effect relationships.

7.5.2.2 Relations Diagram or Interrelationship Digraph   A **relations diagram**, also called an **interrelationship digraph**, aids in the discovery of cause–effect relationships and in segregating major drivers from minor ones. Figure 7-47 depicts the general format for constructing an interrelationship digraph and employs the following six steps:

- *Step 1.* The team reaches consensus on some issue or problem to study. The issue is stated in clear terms that are understood by everyone.
- *Step 2.* The team then determines and lists all elements (or factors) it considers to be relevant to the issue or problem. A rectangular symbol is placed on the digraph for each element.
- *Step 3.* Each element on the digraph is compared with all others, and the team determines which ones influence and are influenced by that element.
- *Step 4.* Each element pair, where an influence relationship exists, is connected by an *influence arrow*. The element pair is connected with the arrow going from the

FIGURE 7-47 Interrelationship Digraph

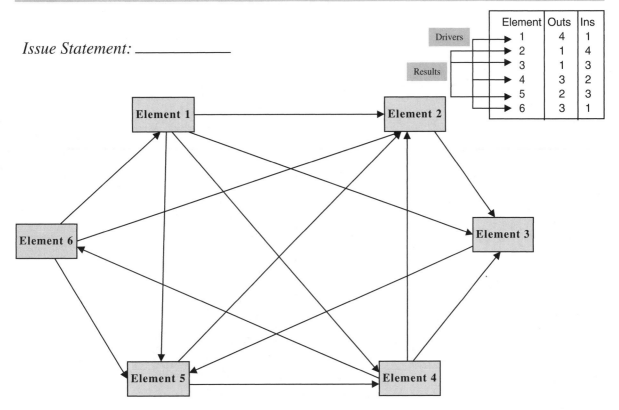

Issue Statement: _____

Element	Outs	Ins
1	4	1
2	1	4
3	1	3
4	3	2
5	2	3
6	3	1

element that influences toward the one influenced. If elements influence each other, the arrow is drawn to indicate the direction of the stronger influence.

- *Step 5.* The number of arrows pointing toward each element (called the "INS") and the number pointing away (called the "OUTS") are tallied.

- *Step 6.* The team determines which elements are drivers and which are results. If the INS > OUTS, the element is a *result.* If the OUTS > INS, the element is a *driver.* If INS = OUTS, the element is neither a result nor a driver.

Figure 7-48 is an example interrelationship digraph that a team applied to the problem of excessive employee turnover. It was discovered that the principal driver could be traced back to an autocratic management style that failed to recognize the fundamental needs of employees.

Systematic Diagram

Dendrogram

A systematic diagram can be used to link ways and means to objectives.

7.5.2.3 Systematic Diagram or Dendrogram   A **systematic diagram**, also called a **dendrogram**, is a tree diagram that displays a hierarchy of objectives that branch to lists of ways and means for accomplishing those objectives. This tool is more focused than an affinity diagram or an interrelationship digraph. At each level of the tree, the generation of the next level down is stimulated by asking questions such as

- *"How will we accomplish the objective?"*
- *"How will we implement the ways and find the means?"*

FIGURE 7-48 Interrelationship Digraph

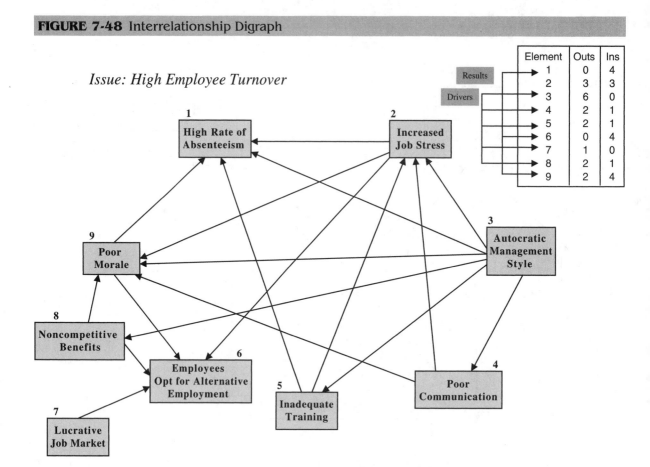

Figure 7-49 depicts the generic format for a systematic diagram. As the tree is read left to right, the logical progression goes from general to specific. Reading the chart backward (specific to general) helps clarify practical actions by answering the question "Why?" To develop an action plan, each of the ways and means is evaluated based on three classifications:

- *Practical*—The indicated ways and means are implementable and lead to clear actionable steps. This is indicated on the diagram with a circular symbol.
- *Impractical*—The indicated ways and means are not implementable, at least not at this time. This could be because they are inconsistent with overall corporate strategy, there are insufficient resources or time, or implementation could lead to some negative consequences elsewhere in the system. An impractical classification is indicated on the diagram with the symbol "x".
- *Uncertain*—The decision makers need additional information, and need to deliberate further before the implementability of the ways and means can be determined. Each uncertain classification must be carefully scrutinized in an attempt to reclassify as either practical or impractical. An uncertain classification is depicted on the systematic diagram using a triangular symbol.

FIGURE 7-49 Format for Systematic Diagram

Note: △, Uncertain; ○, practical; ✗, impractical.

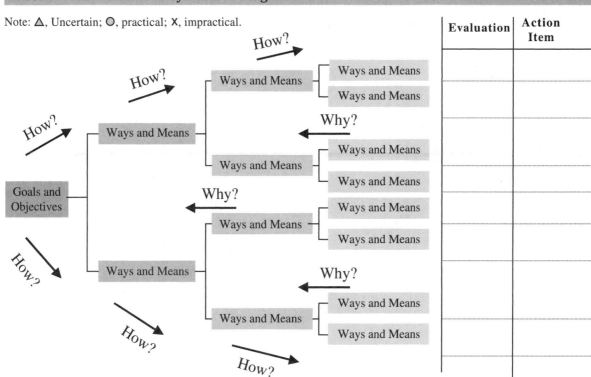

For each practical classification, the decision group specifies one or more action-able items. The collection of all actions then becomes the plan for achieving the stated goals and objectives.

Figure 7-50 is an example systematic diagram that was developed to study how a restaurant could reduce the number of customer complaints concerning eggs on its breakfast menu.

Matrix Diagram

Rows

Columns

A matrix diagram adds structure to two or more sets of data and their respective relationships.

7.5.2.4 Matrix Diagram   A **matrix diagram** is a tool that shows the relationship be-tween two or more sets of factors. A matrix is a structure that provides **rows** and **columns** that represent the factors under investigation. Each cell, where a specific row and column intersect, contains data that describe the relationship between that partic-ular pair of factors. Figure 7-51 illustrates several commonly used matrix structures. The simplest form is the "L"-shaped matrix, depicting a two-dimensional analysis that con-tains a single set of rows and columns. The other variations enable a multidimensional analysis. An example of an "L"-shaped matrix was presented in Section 7.4.6 (the vari-ance tracking matrix).

Figure 7-52 shows a "rooftop" matrix structure that is typical of the "house of qual-ity" used in quality function deployment. In this example, an organization was consid-ering several new product concepts as part of an expansion strategy. The matrix provided a useful structure for scoring and evaluating each concept, against business

FIGURE 7-50 Systematic Diagram for the Production of Eggs

Note: △, Uncertain; ○, practical; ✗, impractical.

				Evaluation	Action Item
		Improve Quality of Eggs	Tighten Quality Standards	✗	
			Change Supplier	△	
	Perfect Egg Production	Improve Cooking Method	Alter Time	○	Add 10% to Normal Time
			Alter Temp.	○	Lower Temp. 5°
Minimize Complaints Due to Defective Eggs			Change Medium	✗	
			Change Fuel	✗	
			Change Oil Type	○	Change to Vegetable Oil
		Improve Training	Tighten Specifications	○	Document Operational Definitions
			Exercise Closer Scrutiny	○	Stress Importance of Quality
	Eliminate Eggs from Menu	Promote Eggless Items	New Menus	✗	
		Focus on Omelets	Enhanced Training	✗	

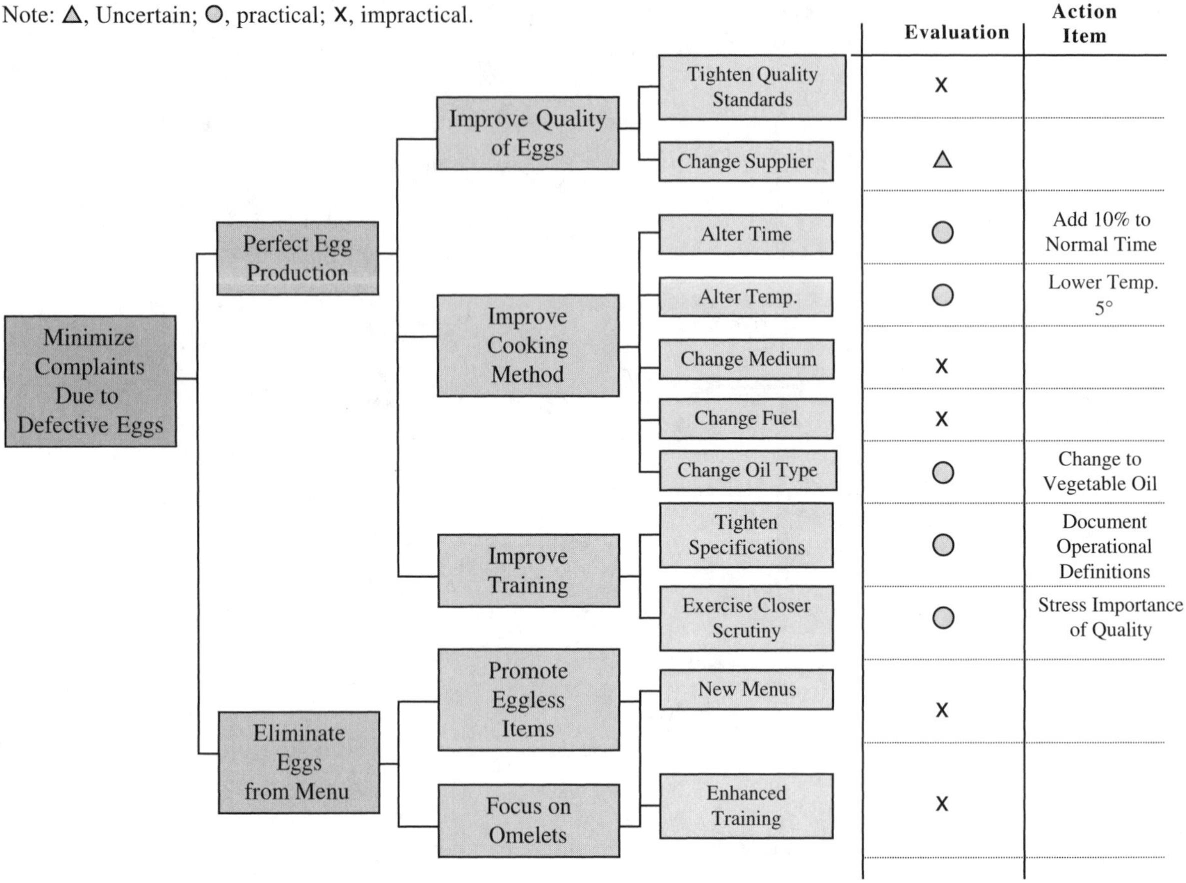

objectives and relative to each other. Each concept could also be evaluated with respect to risk. The rooftop portion of the matrix enables a pairwise analysis of interactions. For example, it would appear that concepts B and D are highly incompatible, whereas concepts D and E are compatible.

7.5.2.5 Matrix Data Analysis   The most sophisticated of the new tools, as proposed by Mizuno,[9] is called **matrix data analysis**, and is an application of principal components analysis. The idea is to take a matrix of relationships between factors and to convert it into a set of preference vectors (called *eigenvectors*) that consist of sums of fractions of those factors that significantly contribute to process variance. The vectors of composite preferences can then be used to determine which characteristics are important. Matrix data analysis can be useful in determining the product or service features that result in the most customer satisfaction, and those that can be eliminated with little or no customer dissatisfaction.

Matrix Data Analysis

Matrix analysis uses advanced statistics for cause and effect.

---

[9]Mizuno, Shigeru, ed. *Management for Quality Improvement: The 7 New QC Tools.* Cambridge, MA: Productivity, 1988.

FIGURE 7-51 Matrix Structures

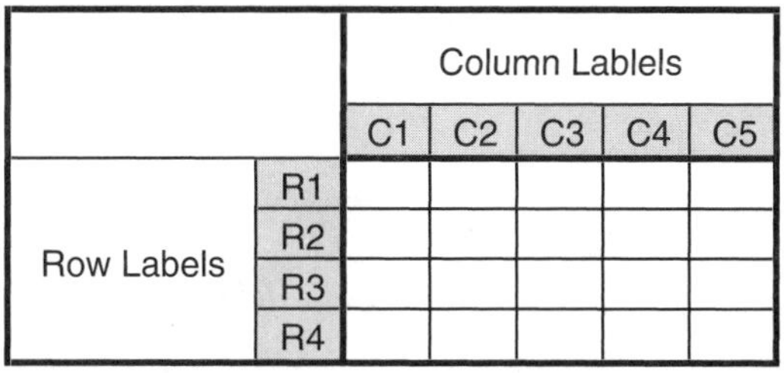

The "L" Matrix Structure

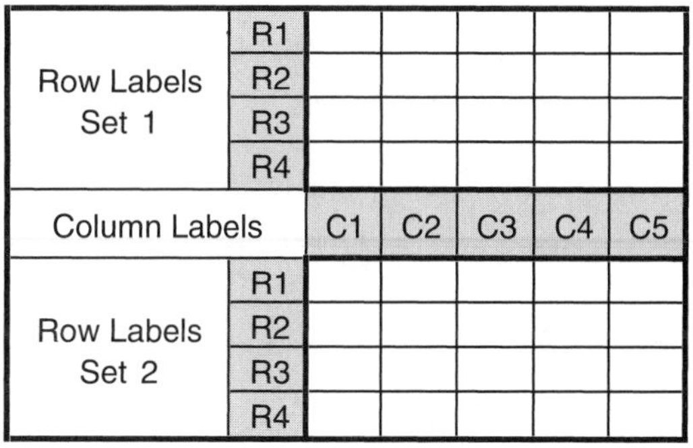

The "T" Structure

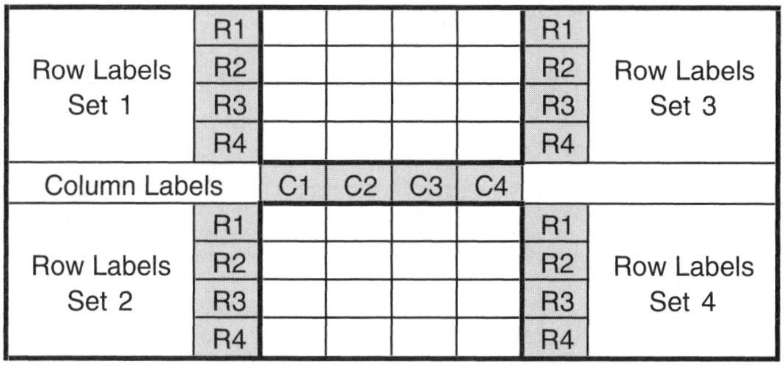

The "X" Matrix Structure

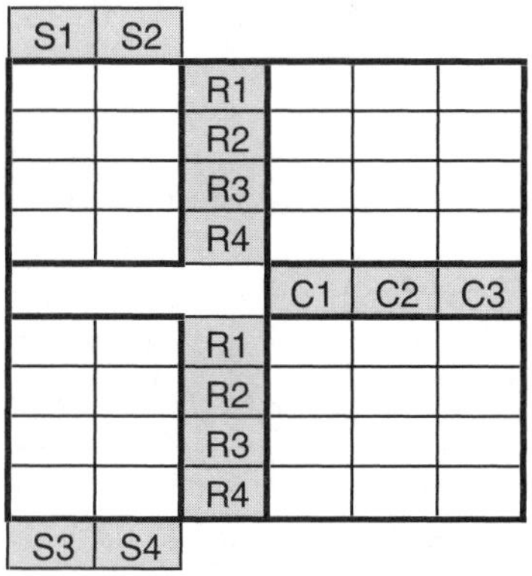

The "Y" Matrix Structure

FIGURE 7-52 Application of Matrix Diagram

Note: ◎, Score = 5, strong positive relationship; ○, score = 3, mildly positive relationship; △, score = 1, possible relationship; **X**, mildly negative relationship; **XX**, strong negative relationship.

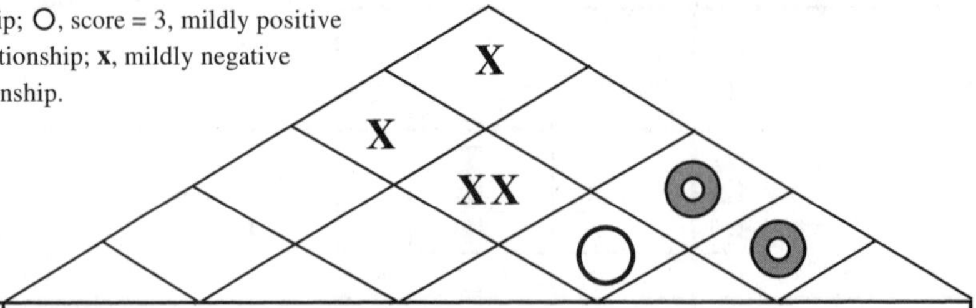

		Weight	New Product Concepts				
			A	B	C	D	E
Business Objectives	Increase Market Share	1	3 ○ 3			1 △ 1	3 ○ 3
	Establish Product Leadership	2		1 △ 2			3 ○ 6
	Good Export Potential	3			3 ○ 9	3 ○ 9	3 ○ 9
	Utilize Existing Techologies	5		5 ◎ 25			
	Good Profit Margins	4	5 ◎ 20	5 ◎ 20	3 ○ 12		3 ○ 12
Technical Risk			3	2	4	5	3
Market Risk			5	1	4	3	2
Composite Concept Score			23	47	21	10	30

Process Decision Program Chart

A process decision program chart identifies contingencies that can occur during the execution of a plan.

7.5.2.6 Process Decision Program Chart A **process decision program chart** (PDPC) is used to display the many alternative paths that can occur during the execution of a plan, including contingencies, so strategies for dealing with them can be developed in advance. There is no standard format for a PDPC. Some are shown as tree diagrams, whereas others are displayed as flowcharts. The idea is to graphically display the steps of a process or project, as well as the possible paths that are taken to complete all steps. Where things can go wrong, the path may branch at any particular step. Countermeasures (contingency plans) devised to help the process return to purpose are shown on the chart.

There are three principal uses for a PDPC:

- To identify all possible contingencies that can occur in the execution of any new plan where risks are involved

FIGURE 7-53 Process Decision Program Chart

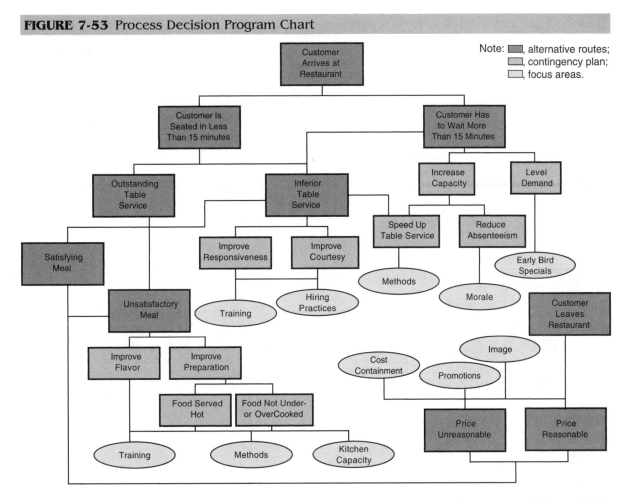

- To plan the implementation of a complex project in which the cost of failure is high
- To manage a project with an extremely tight time constraint that permits insufficient time to deal with contingencies as they occur

A PDPC should be constructed by a team that has the experience and competence to define all process steps and possible contingencies. The group places the steps on a chart in a tree diagram, or flowchart, in time and prerequisite sequence. This can be done in either a horizontal or vertical format.

The group should then scrutinize each step, asking "What can go wrong here?"

The answers to these questions are contingencies and are recorded on the chart as possible branches or diversions from the main process flow. Finally, the group determines plausible explanations or feasible countermeasures to each contingency and documents those on the chart.

Figure 7-53 is an example PDPC for customer service in a restaurant.

Arrow Diagram

7.5.2.7 Arrow Diagram   Also known as an activity network diagram, PERT, or CPM, an **arrow diagram** is a tool, borrowed from project management and used to

FIGURE 7-54 Activities-on-Arrows Diagram

Operation	Prerequisites	Time Required	Operation	Prerequisites	Time Required	Operation	Prerequisites	Time Required
A	G, H, I	5	F	E, L, M	2	K	—	10
B	—	5	G	—	7	L	—	15
C	—	13	H	—	1	M	—	11
D	—	4	I	J, K	3	S	A, B, C, D, E, F	4
E	—	4	J	—	1			

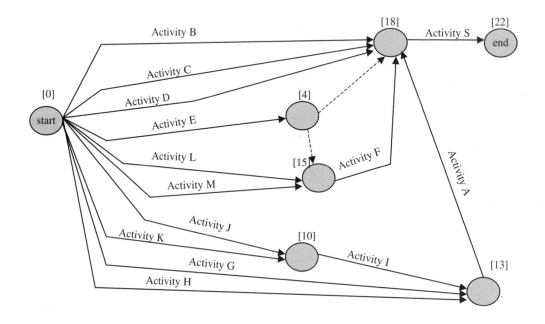

An arrow diagram is used to manage a complex project.

schedule a sequence of complex tasks. There are two conventions used for constructing an arrow diagram (AOA and AON) as illustrated in Figures 7-54 and 7-55, respectively. The first step in constructing an arrow diagram is to identify all tasks, their prerequisites, and the time required for completion. A variant procedure uses probability distributions for completion times to compute expected times and variances for each task. Another variant estimates the resources consumed by each task.

Nodes

In the activities-on-arrows (AOA) method, **nodes** are milestone events that represent the completion of all activities preceding an event and signify the earliest start time for any succeeding activity. In the activity-on-nodes (AON) representation, the nodes signify accomplishment of tasks and the arrows depict the technological linkages.

Arrow diagrams are useful in planning the schedules for each task, determining the deployment of critical resources, identifying activities that can occur simultaneously, calculating by how much individual tasks can be delayed without affecting the overall project duration, and determining the shortest total time required to complete all tasks (the **critical path**). Once the arrow diagram is constructed, the critical path can be determined by locating the shortest path through the network from start to finish.

Critical Path

FIGURE 7-55 Activities-on-Nodes Diagram

Operation	Prerequisites	Time Required	Operation	Prerequisites	Time Required	Operation	Prerequisites	Time Required
A	G, H, I	5	F	E, L, M	2	K	—	10
B	—	5	G	—	7	L	—	15
C	—	13	H	—	1	M	—	11
D	—	4	I	J, K	3	S	A, B, C, D, E, F	4
E	—	4	J	—	1			

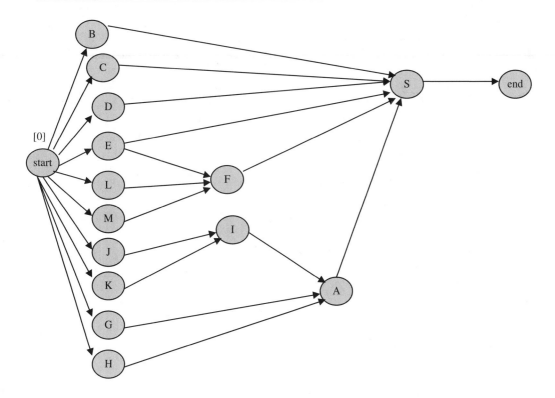

Poka-yoke incorporates mistake-proofing devices in a process design.

Applications of arrow diagrams include reengineering a production process, planning a complex business venture such as a new product development, establishing a new business unit/organizational structure, or managing a large multidimensional project.

7.5.3 Poka-Yoke

Poka-yoke

Mistake Proofing

Prevention/Detection

Poka-yoke (pronounced *POH-kay YOH-kay*) is a Japanese word that means to avoid (*yokeru*) inadvertent errors (*poka*). As a component in quality design, the use of poka-yoke incorporates **mistake-proofing** devices intended to either prevent defects from occurring, or to inexpensively inspect process output to determine, at the source, whether an error has occurred. This commonsense approach to **prevention/detection** is called *zero quality control* and was pioneered by Shigeo Shingo, a Toyota industrial engineer.[10]

---

[10]Shingo, Shigeo. *Zero Quality Control: Source Inspection and the Poka-Yoke System.* Translated by Andrew P. Dillion. Portland, OR: Productivity, 1986.

7.5.3.1 What Causes Defects?   Defects are created by one of four major sources:

- *Cultural Factors.* Chapter 6 discusses in detail human behavior and the relationship between workplace culture and quality. Such cultural factors as personal values, attitudes, motivation, commitment, rewards, and GNS can impact job performance and quality. The formation of teams, HPWPs, good communications, a committed management, and human resource practices that consistently promote the ideals of quality, all help reduce the number of defects created due to culture.

- *Variation.* Process variation can be a principal cause of defects, particularly if the process is inherently incapable of producing output that complies with design specifications. The frequency of defect occurrences can be reduced by identifying and removing special cause factors, such as differences between machines, operators, shifts, suppliers, and the like. Special cause variation can be managed and decreased using SPC techniques. Reducing common cause variation is more difficult. To do so necessitates a fundamental redesign of the process. This requires sophisticated tools such as Taguchi methods and design of experiments.

- *Complexity.* The number of opportunities for defects grows with the complexity of the product or process. Complexity can arise from the number of different product configurations (e.g., sizes, colors, options), lack of commonality of parts across products, number of processing steps, or the technological sophistication and skill levels required for critical processing steps. The complexity issue can best be addressed through an approach that integrates product and process design considerations, such as concurrent engineering and DFM.

- *Human Error.* Human mistakes can be a significant source of defects. A human error is defined as either an intention that is incorrect or a correct intention that results in unintended consequences. Human error will typically be part of the common cause system of variation, and generally will not be detected by control charts or other SPC techniques. The idea behind poka-yoke is to prevent mistakes from occurring or to detect a mistake before it becomes a defect. Poka-yoke is also known as mistake proofing, fool proofing, or fail safing. Poka-yoke is a powerful concept for four reasons:

  - *Ease of understanding.* The principal creators of poka-yoke ideas are often the operators who are closest to their processes.

  - *Poka-yoke makes sense.* It is usually easy to get buy-in because poka-yoke is grounded in common sense.

  - *Solutions are inexpensive.* Most poka-yoke ideas are easy and inexpensive to implement. No sophisticated technology or system reengineering is normally required.

  - *Poka-yoke fosters innovation.* Challenging workers to find opportunities to mistake proof their operations taps the imagination and creative juices of the human spirit.

Elimination

Replacement

Facilitation

Detection

Mitigation

As Figure 7-56 shows, poka-yoke devices generally fall into one of five categories: **elimination**, **replacement**, **facilitation**, **detection**, or **mitigation**.[11] The first three of these

---

[11]Nakajo, Takeshi, and Hitoshi Kume. "The Principles of Foolproofing and Their Application in Manufacturing." *Reports of Statistical Application Research* 32, no. 2 (1985): 10–29.

FIGURE 7-56 Categorization of Poka-Yoke Devices

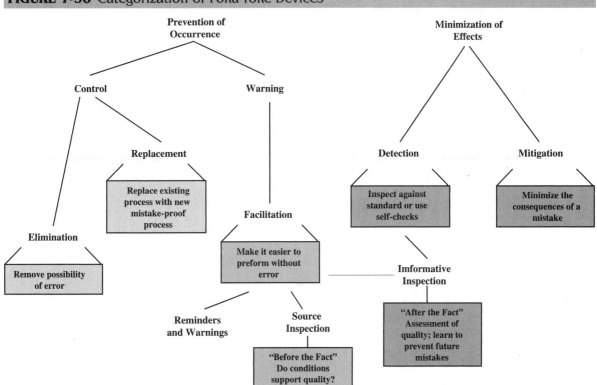

categories are aimed at preventing the occurrence of mistakes, whereas the latter two deal with minimizing the effects of a mistake once it has occurred. Where the objective is prevention of mistakes, categories can further be subdivided into control devices (those that make a mistake an impossibility) and warning devices (those that provide visual or audible symbols or reminders of the correct procedure).

7.5.3.2 Control Devices   Control devices force the worker to perform a task correctly by making it virtually impossible to make a mistake. Examples of poka-yoke control devices are evident in many of the products used every day. As an example, when new technology required unleaded fuel for automobile engines, gasoline stations had to begin stocking both leaded and unleaded products. To prevent customers from accidentally putting leaded gasoline into an unleaded vehicle, the automobile companies collaborated with the oil companies and developed a poka-yoke solution. The aperture in the gas tank on new vehicles was made small enough so the nozzle from the leaded pump would not fit. Only the smaller unleaded pump nozzle will fit into the proper gas tank opening.

Here are two other examples of control poka-yokes. Have you ever tried to put your car in gear when the key was not in the ignition or insert a floppy diskette upside-down into a computer drive? You would have had little success. The gearshift lever in automatic cars cannot be moved out of park until the key is in the ignition and turned on. Floppy discs are shaped with a beveled edge that makes it impossible to insert them incorrectly into a computer.

7.5.3.3 Warning Devices Warning devices do not force correct behavior, but rather provide visible or audible signals as a reminder. Examples are warning lights in automobiles, color-coded parts in assemblies, and clearance bars in parking garages.

7.5.3.4 Where Does Poka-Yoke Work Well? Poka-yoke is likely to work well in the following situations:

- Where labor-intensive operations require manual tasks and worker vigilance
- In tasks where positioning by the worker is critical
- In tasks where adjustments by the operator are required
- Where teams are required to generate common-sense suggestions to reduce defects caused by human errors
- Where SPC is difficult to apply, is apparently ineffective, or appears to have reached its maximum improvement potential
- Where quality is measured on a go or no-go attributes basis and not on a variables measurement basis
- Where training costs and employee turnover are high
- Where mixed model scheduling is used
- Where customers can make mistakes in the use of the product or service and place blame on the service provider
- Where special causes, although eliminated, can possibly reoccur
- Where external failure costs are much greater than internal failure costs

7.5.3.5 Where Is Poka-Yoke Unlikely to Work Well? Poka-yoke is not particularly suited for the following situations:[12]

- Where quality is determined using destructive testing
- Where production cycle time is extremely low
- Where process changes occur so frequently that the dynamics exceed the system response capabilities
- Where control charts are so effective that successive inspection and self-checks may be unnecessary

SUMMARY OF LEARNING OBJECTIVES AND KEY OUTCOMES

1. *Describe creative tools that will stimulate new ideas and help build consensus.* Creative tools help groups focus on important issues, generate fresh ideas, and then prioritize them. Consensus building is an important part of this process. There are various forms of brainstorming, brainwriting, and word and picture associations that can be tried in different situations to stimulate creativity and make the process more interesting.

2. *Describe process improvement planning tools.* Good planning can be facilitated with the use of some simple tools. A PDCA cycle is a quality management application

---

[12]Grout, John R. "Mistake-Proofing Production." *Production and Inventory Management Journal* 38, no. 3 (1997): 33–37.

of the scientific method (rational decision making) that includes planning, doing (executing the plan), checking on what was learned, and then acting appropriately.

The productivity of meetings can be improved through more thoughtful planning prior to the event. A task cycle format can help.

3.   *Describe tools to analyze and improve processes.* Process analysis usually starts with a flowchart, which can help define the overall process and identify potential problem spots. Other graphical tools that can help problem solvers visualize relationships and characteristics are knowledge mapping, morphological boxes, moment-of-truth analysis, and a force field analysis. A variance tracking matrix can help problem solvers identify major sources of variability in CTQ characteristics, and then trace those sources back up the value stream to their root causes.

4.   *Describe the seven old problem-solving tools.*

   a. A check sheet is used for manually recording data in a form that can be readily understood by everyone.

   b. A Pareto chart is a tool that is useful in separating the significant few from the trivial many so limited resources can be effectively deployed.

   c. A cause-and-effect diagram gives structure to a list of brainstormed causes to help a team focus in a root cause analysis.

   d. A histogram converts raw data into a picture of the underlying distribution of process output.

   e. Stratification sorts data into meaningful classifications so important clues concerning the data will be revealed.

   f. A scatter diagram is useful to reveal any meaningful nonrandom relationship that exists between two variables.

   g. Charts and graphs can reveal any nonrandom patterns of plotted points with respect to time. A run chart is a time-ordered plot of individual measurements that can be used to identify shifts or trends in the process average. A control chart tests the statistical stability of a process. A Gantt chart is used to plan and track progress on projects where precedence requirements must be enforced.

5.   *Describe six of the seven new problem-solving tools (matrix analysis excepted).* The seven new tools were designed to satisfy a managerial need for tools that could be used to process nonnumerical data.

   a. An affinity diagram can be used to organize a number of ideas into a small number of manageable categories.

   b. A relations diagram is used to help identify principal cause–effect relationships.

   c. A systematic diagram is a tool that helps managers link ways and means to objectives and develop realistic action plans for achieving those objectives.

   d. A matrix diagram adds structure to two or more sets of data and helps clarify the relationships between them.

   e. Matrix data analysis uses advanced statistical techniques for determining the factors that contribute the most to process variance.

   f. A process decision program chart is a tool that investigates all possible contingencies that can occur during the execution of a plan so appropriate countermeasures can be designed in advance.

g. An arrow diagram is used to schedule and manage a project that requires a sequence of complex tasks.

6.   *Describe poka-yoke and how it can be applied to prevent mistakes.* Poka-yoke incorporates mistake-proofing devices in a process design to either prevent defects from occurring or to determine, inexpensively and at the source, whether an error has occurred. There are two types of devices. Control devices prevent defects by making it impossible to create them; warning devices prevent defects by reminding the operator of the proper procedure to follow.

TO TEST YOUR UNDERSTANDING

7-1   Refer to the FCC case study at the beginning of this chapter. If you were a member of senior management, how would you use the tools presented in Chapter 7 to support initiatives to improve customer service and reduce the backlog of applications? Be specific as to what tools you would introduce and when, as the seven-step plan is implemented.

7-2   Construct a process flowchart to describe each of the following:
   a. Planning a vacation
   b. Hiring a new staff member
   c. Preparing a meal
   d. Refinishing a piece of old furniture

7-3   The Human Resources Department of AMP Vacuum, Inc., has designed a series of employee e-training courses to support its QIM program. All courses can be taken online; however, some of the courses cannot be taken until other courses are first completed as prerequisites. If all prerequisites are satisfied, an employee may enroll in multiple courses simultaneously. The following table shows the required prerequisites and duration for each training course.

	Training	*Prerequisite Course*	*Duration (days)*
A	Teaming and people skills	None	5
B	Tools for creativity	A	10
C	Tools for planning	B	5
D	Flowcharting	A	3
E	Knowledge mapping	D	5
F	Morphological analysis	A	3
G	MOT analysis	B, D	1
H	Force field analysis	B	1
I	Six honest servants and five whys	B, D	2
J	SPC: the basic toolkit	C, D, I	10
K	Seven new tools	B, J	10
L	Poka-yoke	B, D	7
M	Variance tracking	J	4

   a. Construct both an AOA and an AON network that describes the paths available to an individual employee who goes through the entire training program.
   b. Calculate the minimum number of days required for an employee to complete all courses.
   c. Construct a Gantt chart that can be used to track the earliest start times for scheduling the entire training program.

7-4   The following measurements were collected hourly from two production processes.

Process A		Process B	
6.5	9.0	9.2	4.7
4.1	9.6	6.8	8.6
5.4	9.8	10.6	9.0
5.1	8.1	13.2	10.3
5.3	8.9	13.0	9.1
3.9	9.0	14.3	9.2
5.5	7.2	4.5	9.1
6.1	7.3	9.4	13.4
3.1	8.8	12.7	9.8
5.2	8.1	7.3	9.5
7.3	9.0	8.3	8.7
4.0	5.7	5.8	14.9
4.2	8.4	5.4	12.2
6.3	6.8	7.6	15.9
4.7	7.2	8.1	8.4

a. Construct a run chart for each process.

b. What can you conclude from the pattern of points on these two charts?

7-5   Ace Jet Airlines is losing business because of late flight departures. A quality improvement team has met to discuss the issue. They have decided to construct a fishbone diagram to try to identify some possible reasons why flights fail to depart on time. They have identified five major categories they want to use to structure causes on the diagram. They are personnel, equipment, procedures, materials, and other. Using these main divisions, draft a fishbone diagram to help this team with their work.

CHAPTER 8

Statistical Process Control

Business must be profitable if it is to succeed, but the glory of business is to make it so successful that it may do things that are great chiefly because they ought to be done.

—CHARLES M. SCHWAB

Magna Minerals

Improved Customer Relations through Knowledge and the Use of Statistical Process Control

Magna Minerals Corporation (MMC) is a division of a large multinational corporation headquartered in Brussels. In the United States MMC has five facilities located across the country that mine, mill, and process a number of products that have various industrial uses, ranging from pharmaceuticals to specialized coatings. One product, XL-88, is a calcium additive that is sold to food processors and ends up in calcium-enriched fruit juices. XL-88 is packaged in fifty-pound bags with a ±one-pound tolerance. Maintaining the tolerance is important because MMC's customers use a recipe to control the percentage of calcium in each batch of juice. It is important that a fifty-pound bag of XL-88 actually contain fifty pounds of product (or close to it). Lately, there has been a rash of customer complaints concerning bag weights.

In response, the Quality Control (QC) Department at MMC introduced control charts at the bag-filling process. Five bags were selected at random each hour over a thirty-hour production period. The range chart showed good control with an average range of 1.2, and the X-bar chart showed control with an average fill weight of 50.06. Jeff Tolibar, the plant manager, was puzzled. "I do not know what customers are complaining about. On average, we are delivering fifty-pound bags as required."

Susan Alexander, the QC director, was not so certain. "Let's make some further calculations to see what is really going on." She then used the average range to estimate the process standard deviation. After making a few quick calculations, she held up the number for all to see. "The process standard deviation is a little over a half a pound! That means that our bagging process is not capable of meeting our bagging specifications." Observing some puzzled looks, she explained: "If the process standard deviation is half a pound, and the process is in control, then the natural tolerance of the process is six times this number or three pounds. Our specifications require that we hit an engineering tolerance of two pounds—that is, the difference between the heaviest bag that is acceptable (fifty-one pounds) and the lightest acceptable bag (forty-nine pounds). Our process seems to be well centered at fifty pounds, but even here we can expect to produce 50% of our bag weights outside the specification limits. The out-of-spec bags will be evenly split, with 25% too heavy and 25% too light. It is no wonder we are getting complaints from our customers."

Jeff immediately made the filling operation a plant priority. He assembled a team of engineers, operators, and equipment representatives to study the problem of fill variation. Some designed experiments were conducted to analyze the effects of various nozzle designs, pressures, and feed rates. This resulted in a number of changes to the fill line. After the changes had been fully implemented, a new set of control charts was constructed. The improvement was noticeable. The average range had dropped to 0.46. The process was still well centered, and statistical control had been maintained. Susan was happy. She convened the team and held up a card for all to see. On it she had written the estimate of the new process standard deviation—0.2 pounds. "This means we are now very capable. Our capability index has increased from 0.67 to 2.5. Anything over 1 is good. I could not be more pleased."

She added, "there's just one more thing that has me concerned. I am not sure about the accuracy of our inline scales." Susan then ordered a measurement study, using some standard test weights that had been certified by the National Institute for Standards and Technology. She discovered that when a fifty-pound standard was applied repeatedly to the scales, the scales reported an average weight of 49.5. "With this bias we have inadvertently been giving away product. Even though we have established capability, it is important that we keep our process centered on the nominal target of fifty-pounds and that our scales are accurate." Susan then ordered that the scales be recalibrated and instituted a procedure that would periodically check the calibration. Meanwhile, the use of control charts became an ongoing means for monitoring bag weights and alerting the operators when machine adjustments are warranted. ■

8.1 LEARNING OBJECTIVES AND KEY OUTCOMES

After studying the material in Chapter 8, you will be able to

1. Differentiate between nominal, ordinal, interval, and ratio scales of measurement
2. Demonstrate an understanding of the difference between special cause and common cause variability, and be able to recognize nonrandom patterns in a data set
3. Describe how sampling strategies have an impact on the ability to identify special and common cause sources of variability
4. Define statistical control and be able to construct, apply, and interpret the control charts that are appropriate for different types of data sets
5. Explain to someone in layman's terms the difference between accuracy, precision, discrimination, and resolution
6. Conduct a measurement study to identify all components of measurement error, including the calculation and interpretation of the discrimination ratio
7. Assess process capability using control charts and capability indices
8. Apply some qualitative and quantitative measures to evaluate the level of quality in a services environment

8.2 SCALES OF MEASUREMENT AND STATISTICAL PROCESS CONTROL

8.2.1 Scales of Measurement

A measurement process assigns a value to some attribute of interest, and the measured value provides a convenient means for comparing objects with respect to that attribute. The measurement process can select from four scales that form a hierarchy of increasing complexity and information:

- Nominal
- Ordinal
- Interval
- Ratio

Nominal Scale

Nominal measures assign names or values to objects that have no numerical meaning.

Attributes Data

Attributes data are measured on a nominal scale.

Ordinal Scale

An ordinal scale is used to measure relative preferences.

Interval Scale

An interval scale can measure the degrees of differences.

With a ratio scale, differences can be compared using all mathematical functions.

Variables Data

Ratio Scale

8.2.1.1 Nominal (Attributes) Scale   On a **nominal scale**, objects that are assigned equal values are considered to be the same with respect to the measured attribute. The values assigned to an individual object have no numerical meaning in the way one normally thinks about numbers. Examples of nominal measures are part numbers, go or no-go, defective or conforming, and good or bad. Counting is the only arithmetic operation that can be performed on nominal data. Nominal data that are collected for quality purposes are called **attributes data**, and the measurements that are recorded are usually a count of the number of instances, or objects, for which a certain value of the attribute (good or bad) was observed—for example, in a sample of 100 items from a production lot, an inspector might count eight defectives.

8.2.1.2 Ordinal Scale   On an **ordinal scale**, objects with a higher value have more of some attribute than objects with a lower value. With ordinal measures, one item can be judged to be greater than, equal to, or less than another. This comparative analysis is the only legitimate mathematical operation that can be performed on ordinal data. The size of the interval between adjacent values on the scale is indeterminate, so the degree of difference between objects cannot be ascertained. For example, item B and item C can both be greater than item A, and item B can be less than item C. One can deduce that item C might be the most preferred and item A the least preferred, but no information is available as to how much more benefit is derived by selecting C over B or either of these options over A. Examples of ordinal measures are items arranged on a prioritization matrix, types of defects plotted on a Pareto chart, and any rank ordering.

8.2.1.3 Interval (Variables) Scale   On an **interval scale**, the degree of difference between objects can be determined because the intervals between adjacent scale values are equal. For example, the difference between seven and six is the same as a difference between eighty-seven and eighty-six. However, ratios on an interval scale are not equivalent because there is no natural zero point. Temperature readings in degrees Fahrenheit or Celsius are measurements on an interval scale. One cannot say that if 90 degrees is twice as hot as 45 degrees, then 200 degrees is twice as hot as 100 degrees. In addition to the arithmetic operations that can be performed on nominal and ordinal data, addition and subtraction operations can be applied to interval data. When data for quality purposes are collected using interval measures, the data are said to be **variables data**.

8.2.1.4 Ratio (Variables) Scale   Most variables data are measured on a **ratio scale**, the highest level of measurement. Ratio measures are made relative to some rational "zero" point. On the ratio scale, not only are interval differences the same, but because

Variables data are measured on either an interval scale or a ratio scale.

ratios are equivalent, they can also be compared. The ratio of eight to four is the same as the ratio of fifty to twenty-five. All mathematical operations, including multiplication and division, can be applied to ratio data. Examples of ratio measures in quality management applications are lengths, distances, weights, ages, revenues, and pressures.

8.2.2 Nature of Variables Measurement

When data are collected using a variables scale (either interval or ratio), there are three characteristics of interest:

Central Tendency

Variability

Shape

- Measure of **central tendency** (what measurement is the most representative of the set of measures?)
- **Variability** (how dispersed are the data around the average?)
- **Shape** (is the distribution unimodal, symmetrical, continuous, and so on?)

Mean

Median

Range

Standard Deviation

Histograms

The arithmetic **mean** (average) is commonly used to measure central tendency, although at times the median is more useful (e.g., when the data are excessively skewed). The variance and standard deviation are statistical measures of dispersion. A simpler and alternative measure is the **range** of the data (the high value minus the low value). For large data sets, the range can introduce considerable error because all but two of the numbers are discarded in the calculation. Nevertheless, for small data sets such as samples of five or less, the range can be used to approximate the underlying **standard deviation**. As illustrated in Chapter 7, **histograms** are useful for determining the shape of data distributions.

Figure 8-1 illustrates why variability and shape are important. Processes A and B have outputs with the same averages, yet the processes are fundamentally different. These distributions represent mean time before failure of a critical electronic component, and each process appears to meet the specified requirement of 5.5. Although process A can be depended on to produce output at the specified level most of the time, process B

FIGURE 8-1 Patterns in Variables Data

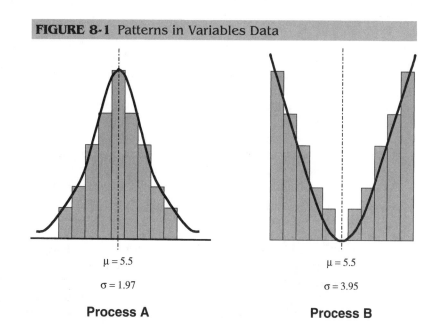

$\mu = 5.5$

$\sigma = 1.97$

Process A

$\mu = 5.5$

$\sigma = 3.95$

Process B

FIGURE 8-2 Molded Caps

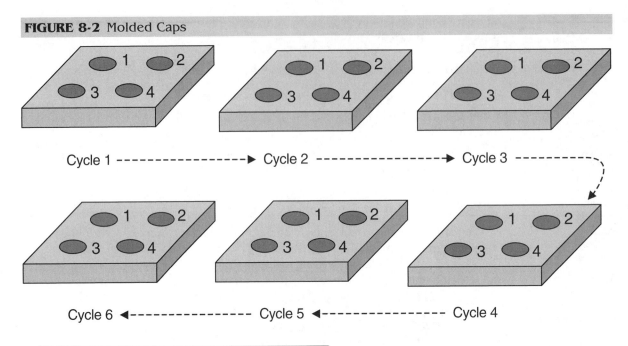

Cycle	Cavity			
	1	**2**	**3**	**4**
1	71.63	74.93	73.15	74.17
2	72.39	74.42	71.63	73.41
3	71.88	74.68	74.17	73.66
4	72.64	74.42	72.14	73.91
5	71.63	74.93	72.64	73.66
6	72.14	74.68	73.91	73.41

will rarely do so. Most of the output from process B will either fall short of or exceed the target. The measurements from process A ranged from a low of 1.5 to a high of 9.5; for process B, the measurement range is 0.5 to 10.5. However, most of process B measures are at the extremes, and no measurements were recorded at the target value. This results in a standard deviation for process B that is twice as high as that for process A.

To illustrate variables data, consider the plastic cap molding process illustrated in Figure 8-2. Each cycle of the mold produces four caps. For six consecutive cycles, the cap diameters from a representative mold were measured, resulting in a total of twenty-four measurements. Run charts for each cavity are shown in Figure 8-3 and for the combined data in Figure 8-4. Variability in the data is obvious and comes from numerous sources. As this process goes from one cycle to the next, each cavity is incapable of perfectly duplicating the product that was produced on the previous cycle. This source is called **within-cavity variability**. Another source comes from the fact that no two cavities can perfectly replicate each other's outputs. This source is called **between-cavity variability**. There also may exist numerous time-related sources that impact all cavities similarly—factors such as materials, maintenance, and personnel. In addition, samples capture any measurement variability—that is, the reality that the measurement

Pattern recognition is important to data analysis.

Within-Cavity Variability

Between-Cavity Variability

FIGURE 8-3 Run Charts of Molded Cap Data Sets

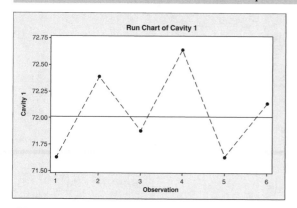

Mean = 72.05; Standard Deviation = 0.413; Range = 1.01

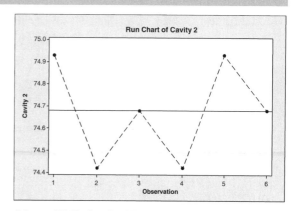

Mean = 74.68; Standard Deviation = 0.228; Range = 0.51

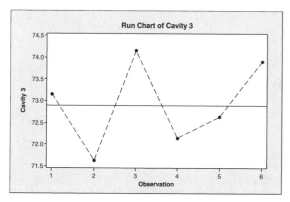

Mean = 72.94; Standard Deviation = 0.994; Range = 2.54

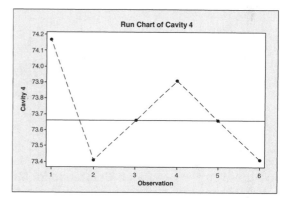

Mean = 73.70; Standard Deviation = 0.295; Range = 0.76

process is incapable of precisely and accurately revealing the ability of the true cap diameter.

A careful study of Figure 8-3 reveals that the four mold positions are different. Cavity 1 appears to have the lowest average dimension, and cavity 2 the highest. Cavity 3 has the greatest dispersion around its mean, and cavity 2 the least. If the data are plotted in strict time-ordered sequence (i.e., in the order that the measurements were taken), as shown in Figure 8-4A, the cavity-to-cavity differences might go unnoticed. Figure 8-4B reveals the apparent differences when the data are plotted by cavity. There are insufficient data to make any judgments regarding the shape of the distributions. Assuming normality, Figure 8-5 compares the distributions for these data sets.

8.2.3 Nature of Attributes Measurement

Attributes

When **attributes** data are collected (using a nominal scale), there is only a single characteristic of interest—the *central tendency* (average). For example, one might be interested in learning what percentage of a production lot is defective, on average. To

Counts

answer this question, random samples would be inspected, **counts** of the number of

FIGURE 8-4 Run Charts for the Combined Data

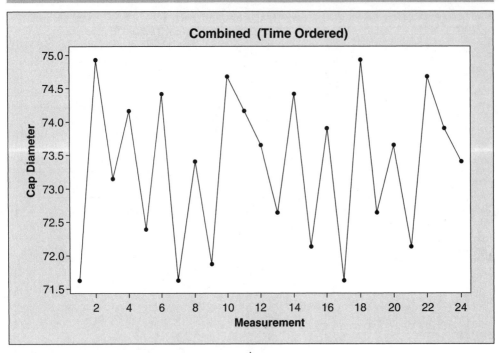

A

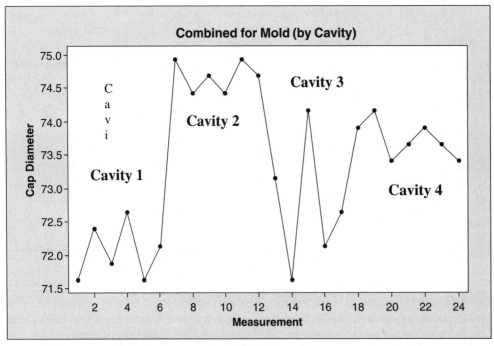

B

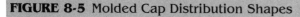

FIGURE 8-5 Molded Cap Distribution Shapes

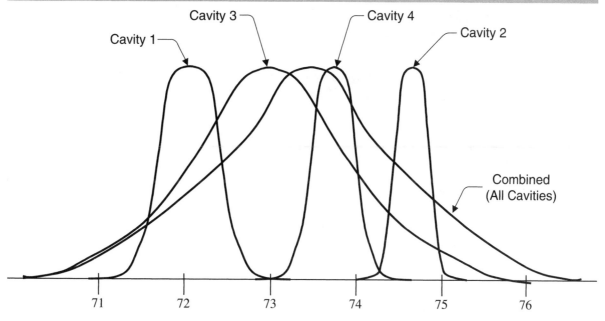

Defectives

defective units found would be carefully recorded, and the percentage of **defectives** in each sample would then be used to estimate the percent defective in the entire lot.

A simple experiment can easily be set up in a training room to illustrate some important sampling concepts (Figure 8-6). A bead box contains a total of 10,000 beads. The number is not important, provided it is large and does not change over the course of the experiment. Of the 10,000 beads, we assume that 350 are red (defective) and 9,650 are white (good). This bead box simulates a process that is 3.5% defective. Because there are only two possible states for any individual unit of output (either good or defective), the underlying distribution describing the occurrence of defectives is **binomial**

Binomial

with $\rho = 0.035$. (The distribution describing the occurrence of good product is also binomial with $\rho = 1 - 0.035 = 0.965$). One would seldom, if ever, know the true value of ρ. On occasion, it might be possible to perform a 100% inspection and learn the *truth;* however, even this approach is not foolproof because sampling error can taint the results.

Population parameters can be estimated using random samples.

Because one cannot know for sure the population mean, it can be estimated using **random samples**. As shown in Figure 8-6, we have drawn thirty-five samples of 100 beads from the bead box. It is important that we mix the beads well between each draw. To be on safe statistical grounds, we should **sample with replacement**, returning each sample to the box before selecting the next sample. However, with large populations, or if we are sampling from an industrial process, the results will not be significantly different if we **sample without replacement**; we can just set our samples aside as we collect them and tally the results, which are shown in Figure 8-7.

Random Samples

Sample with Replacement

Sample without Replacement

Even though the population is 3.5% defective, note that individual samples ranged from a low of 0% defective (sample number 29) to a high of 8% (sample number 15). So, our first observation is that any single sample can be a very poor estimate of the true population parameter. Nevertheless, the average of all thirty-five samples at 3.3%

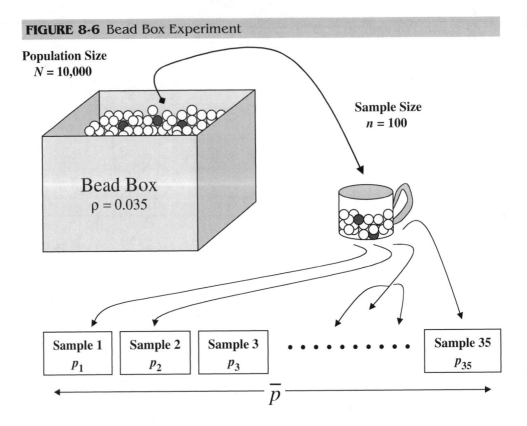

FIGURE 8-6 Bead Box Experiment

However, the average of a number of samples can come close to the true value.

Static Population

Finite Population

Dynamic Populations

Time-Ordered Data

If a process is unstable, its parameters cannot be estimated with confidence.

Common Cause

Special Cause

is much closer to the true value of 3.5%. The variable pattern across all samples is evidenced in the run chart shown in Figure 8-7. Our second observation is that the average of a large number of samples provides a good approximation of the true mean.

Because the bead box represents a **static** and **finite population**, a third observation can be made. All variation observed in sampling results is due to sampling error. This is not process variation. In the case of attributes data, unless the percentage of defectives is changing over time, the variation captured in samples is sampling error only. In the industrial world, populations are generally not finite. For example, sampling from a process is like sampling from an infinite bead box. There is no beginning or end. Industrial processes also represent **dynamic populations**. The dynamics are typically time related, so it is important to collect **time-ordered data**, if possible. Then, if the percentage of defectives is changing over time, the data will reveal a pattern of instability. When this happens, the process is said to not be in statistical control, a concept covered further in the next section. If a process is unstable, it is not possible to estimate its mean with any confidence.

8.2.4 Statistical Process Control

In Chapter 7 we introduced the two types of variability that are captured in any sampling procedure: **common cause** and **special cause**, and how these sources relate to statistical control.

8.2.4.1 Common Cause Variability Whenever samples are taken from a process, certain sources of variability are active. The active sources present in all samples are called

FIGURE 8-7 Attributes Data Generated from Bead Box

Sample	No. Defective
1	3
2	3
3	1
4	5
5	5
6	3
7	3
8	3
9	2
10	7
11	5
12	3
13	2
14	1
15	8
16	3
17	4
18	2
19	4
20	2
21	2
22	6
23	4
24	2
25	3
26	5
27	3
28	2
29	0
30	3
31	3
32	4
33	3
34	5
35	3

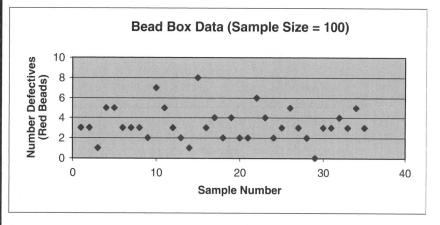

Average = 3.3 Defectives per 100 = 3.3%

Standard Deviation of Raw Data = 1.66 Defectives

Estimated Standard Deviation
(Binomial Distribution) = 1.79 Defectives

Common cause sources of variability are those that are present in all samples.

common cause variability. The observed differences in individual measures within a sample are due to the common cause sources. Examples are measurement error, operator inconsistency, and within-machine variability.

8.2.4.2 Special Cause Variability   Those sources of variability that are active in some samples and not in others are due to special causes. The observed differences between samples are due to a combination of special cause and common cause variability. Examples of special causes are shift differentials, machine-to-machine differences, operator-to-operator differences, and any time related factors such as materials, maintenance, and production mix.

Special causes are present in some samples and not in others.

8.2.4.3 Statistical Process Control   A process is said to be in a state of SPC **statistical control** when the only sources of variability present are due to common causes. This

Statistical Control

Stability

Repeatable

Predictable

A process that is in control is repeatable and predictable.

means that all active sources of variability have been captured within a sample, and each sample is statistically like every other sample. The absence of special causes means there are no additional active sources that add a between-sample component. A process in control is stable, meaning that the element of time is not a factor—a sample taken at any point in time is like a sample taken at any other time. Once a process has reached this level of **stability**, it is said to be **repeatable** and **predictable**, and important process parameters such as mean, dispersion, and shape can be estimated with confidence.

A process that is in statistical control is not necessarily producing quality output. Achieving control is simply the first step in learning how a process is behaving and what steps are needed to improve it.

8.2.4.4 Control Charts   Chapter 7 introduced the control chart calling it the "voice of the process." This chart can aid in the understanding of process behavior and can help identify improvement opportunities. To be effective, it is important that the construction of a control chart begin with a **run chart**—that is, if possible, data should be plotted in **time-ordered sequence**. Initially, it is a good idea to plot a minimum of twenty-five to thirty points. These will be used to estimate the mean and standard deviation of the process, and to compute control limits. If the chart shows a state of statistical control, the mean and standard deviation can be used to estimate process capability and quality of output.

Run Chart

Time-Ordered Sequence

Centerline

Figure 8-8 shows the generic control chart structure. Sample data points are plotted in time sequence. Each point is assumed to be a randomly selected member of a process that is normally distributed. The chart's **centerline** is equal to the average of all the data (a point estimate of the distribution mean). Upper and lower control limits are

FIGURE 8-8 Control Chart Structure

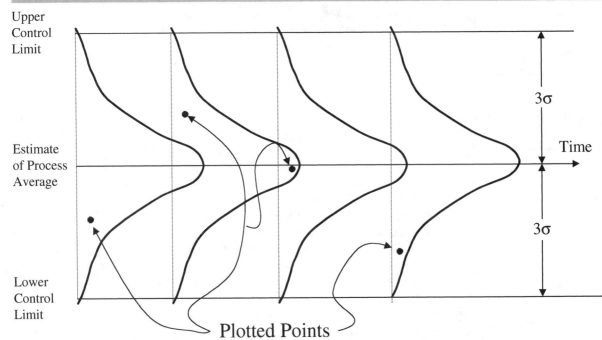

constructed equidistant from the centerline and three standard deviations away. These limits represent the largest and smallest measurements, respectively, that one would expect, assuming the hypothesized distribution (i.e., normal with mean equal to the centerline and standard deviation equal to one-third the distance from centerline to control limits) is correct and does not change over time.

Once control is established, the limits and the centerline on the control chart are fixed, and then samples are taken from the process periodically and plotted on the chart. As long as the points show no evidence of nonrandom patterns, one can assume the process mean and dispersion remain where they were when control was established. Figure 8-9 illustrates some out-of-control scenarios that can result in nonrandom patterns on a control chart. At time t_1, the process is in control with a mean equal to the centerline, and standard deviation equal to one-third the distance between the centerline and each control limit. As long as the process remains in control, any new sample has an equal chance of being above or below the centerline (i.e., higher or lower than the assumed process average). There is a very small, almost negligible, chance that a point will fall outside either of the control limits (actually about 1 in 1,000).

FIGURE 8-9 Out-of-Control Conditions

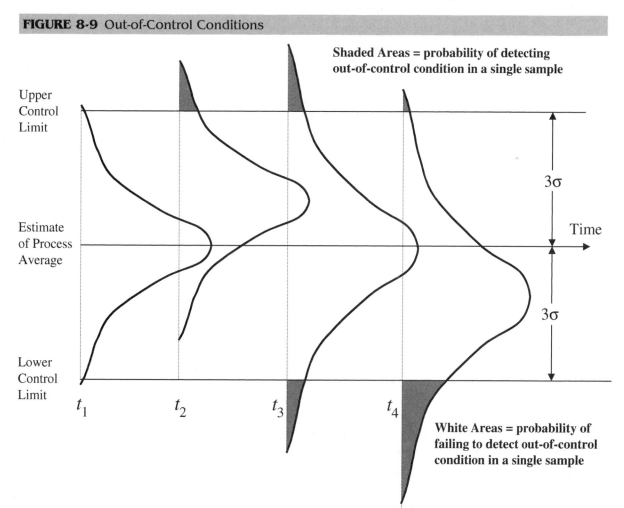

A number of
statistical tests can
be applied to a
control chart to
determine
nonrandom
patterns.

By time t_2, the process average has increased to a level that is larger than the centerline. At time t_3, the process has returned to its original mean; however, the standard deviation has increased. When the sample is taken at time t_4, the standard deviation is still at the higher level and the mean has decreased. Each out-of-control condition increases the probability of a sampling point occurring outside the control limits. Nevertheless, as Figure 8-9 shows, there is a significant probability that, even when the process changes, a sampling point will occur within the control limits and the change will go undetected. To provide some safeguards, there is a battery of statistical tests that should be employed to determine nonrandomness.

8.2.4.5 Tests for Statistical Control Statistical control must be achieved before a control chart can be used to effectively monitor a process. A chart in control can provide the basis for knowing when to intervene in a process (make adjustments) and, as important, when to leave a process alone. There are several tests for nonrandomness that should be applied, depending on whether the chart is a new startup or is ongoing.

Steps for Initiating a Control Chart

- **Step 1.** Obtain a minimum of twenty-five to thirty random samples from the process.
- **Step 2.** Calculate the mean and standard deviation of the raw data.
- **Step 3.** Plot the sample points on a chart in time sequence. Connect the points with straight lines.
- **Step 4.** Draw a centerline on the chart equal to the mean of the raw data.
- **Step 5.** Construct an **upper control limit** and **lower control limit** on the chart equal to the mean plus and minus three standard deviations, respectively.
- **Step 6.** If all plotted points are inside the control limits, proceed to step 7. Otherwise, investigate any points that are outside. If (and only if) the out-of-control points can be explained rationally, eliminate the points from the data set and return to step 2. Examples of explanations that could justify removing points from the data set are transcription errors, an unusual machine problem, or a power failure.
- **Step 7.** Count the total number of plotted points above the centerline and the total number below the centerline. Let s represent the smaller of the two counts and r represent the larger of the two counts.
- **Step 8.** Count the total number of runs. A run consists of a count of consecutive points on the same side of the centerline. The start of a new run occurs each time a line connecting the points crosses the centerline. Apply the test for **too few runs** shown in Table 8-1. If the number of runs is less than or equal to the critical value found in the table, stop because the process is not in control. Otherwise, continue.
- **Step 9.** Count and record the length of each run (i.e., the number of consecutive points comprising each run). Apply the test for **too long run** shown in Table 8-2. If the longest run is equal to or greater than the critical value found in the table, stop because the process is not in control. Otherwise, continue.
- **Step 10.** Look for any obvious nonrandom patterns in the data. Examples are
  - **Hugging the centerline**—All (or most) of the points are within one standard deviation of the chart's centerline.
  - **Hugging the control limits**—Most of the points lie between two and three standard deviations of the mean, but no points (or relatively few) are actually outside the control limits.

Upper Control
Limits

Lower Control
Limits

Too Few Runs

Too Long Run

Hugging the
Centerline

Hugging the
Control Limits

TABLE 8-1 Critical Values for Too Few Runs

r	5	6	7	8	9	10	11	12	13	14	15	16	17	18	19	20
5	3															
6	3	3														
7	3	4	4													
8	3	4	4	5												
9	4	4	5	5	6											
10	4	5	5	6	6	6										
11	4	5	5	6	6	7	7									
12	4	5	6	6	7	7	8	8								
13	4	5	6	6	7	8	8	9	9							
14	5	5	6	7	7	8	8	9	9	10						
15	5	6	6	7	8	8	9	9	10	10	11					
16	5	6	6	7	8	8	9	10	10	11	11	11				
17	5	6	7	7	8	9	9	10	10	11	11	12	12			
18	5	6	7	8	8	9	10	10	11	11	12	12	13	13		
19	5	6	7	8	8	9	10	10	11	12	12	13	13	14	14	
20	5	6	7	8	9	9	10	11	11	12	12	13	13	14	14	15

The probability of an equal or smaller number of runs than the critical value is less than or equal to .05 when the process is in control.
SOURCE: Adapted from Frieda S. Swed, and C. Eisenhart. "Tables for Testing Randomness of Grouping in a Sequence of Alternatives." *Annals of Mathematical Statistics* 14 (1943): 66–87.

TABLE 8-2 Critical Values for Longest Run

r	5	6	7	8	9	10	11	12	13	14	15	16	17	18	19	20
5	5															
6	5	5														
7	5	5	5													
8	5	5	5	5												
9	5	5	5	6	6											
10	5	5	6	6	6	6										
11	5	6	6	6	6	6	6									
12	6	6	6	6	6	6	6	6								
13	6	6	6	6	6	6	6	6	6							
14	6	6	6	6	6	6	6	6	6	6						
15	6	6	6	6	6	6	6	6	6	6	6					
16	6	6	6	6	6	6	6	6	6	6	6	6				
17	6	6	6	6	6	6	6	6	6	6	7	7	7			
18	6	6	6	6	6	6	6	6	6	6	7	7	7	7		
19	6	6	6	6	6	6	6	6	6	7	7	7	7	7	7	
20	6	6	6	6	6	6	6	6	7	7	7	7	7	7	7	7

Critical values for the length of the longest run are equal to the nearest integer to $\log_2(r + s) + 1$. Runs equal to or in excess of the critical values are extremely unlikely for processes that are in a state of statistical control. Runs equal to or less than the critical values are expected to occur frequently for processes that are in statistical control.

Stratification

- **Stratification**—When identified by machine, shift, operator, or some other criterion, the data cluster into groupings that appear to come from different distributions.

Trends

- **Trends**—Although there are no points outside the control limits and the runs test has not been violated, the data appear to be following a trend over time.

  If any nonrandom patterns are observed, stop. Otherwise, the control chart may be operationalized. To do so, the control limits are fixed at the levels where control was observed and the chart is used to plot samples taken from future production. Control limits or the centerline are not altered unless there is statistical evidence that the process has changed from the initial conditions.

As random samples are taken from the process, sampling points are plotted on the control chart. There are numerous statistical control tests that can be applied to an operational chart. These tests determine whether statistical evidence exists that would suggest a process change. They are designed so there is less than a 5% probability of being wrong and acting on a false signal. The two most common tests are shown as follows:

Out-of Control Point

- *Test 1:* **Out-of-control point.** A single point outside the control limits provides statistical evidence that the process has changed or is unstable.

Seven-Point Run Rule

- *Test 2:* **Seven-point run rule.** A run of seven consecutive points on either side of the centerline provides evidence of a process change.

8.3 CONTROL CHARTS FOR VARIABLES DATA

8.3.1 $\overline{X}$, R, and s Charts

For small samples, the R chart is used to track process dispersion.

When control charts are used to monitor variables data, a pair of charts is needed and must be read together to properly interpret data patterns. Because either the dispersion or mean, or both, of a process can be out of control, charts are needed to independently evaluate the stability of each parameter. The first control chart to be plotted and interpreted deals with process dispersion. The points on the dispersion chart represent those sources of variability that have been captured within a sample. For small sample sizes (seven or less), the range is used to estimate the within-sample variability, and the dispersion chart is called a range chart, or simply an R chart. Consider the sampling data displayed in Figure 8-10. Five measurements ($n = 5$) have been taken from one of the production processes of Acme Fastener Company. Thirty samples have been taken over three shifts for five consecutive days. For each, the average ($\overline{X}$) and the range (R) have been computed.

The constants found in Table 8-3 are used to compute upper and lower control limits three standard deviations from the centerline. When an $\overline{X}$ chart is constructed, the central limit theorem (from statistics) provides protection against overreacting to a false signal.

CENTRAL LIMIT THEOREM

If samples of size n are taken from a process with mean = μ_x and variance = σ_x^2, and the average of all n measurements, $\overline{X}$, is computed for each sample, the distribution of the $\overline{X}$s will be normal with mean $\mu_{\overline{x}} = \mu_x$ and variance $\sigma_{\overline{x}}^2 = \frac{\sigma_{\overline{x}}^2}{n}$ provided the sample size is large enough.

Experience has shown that the central limit theorem applies as long as $n \geq 3$.

FIGURE 8-10 Samples from Acme Fastener Process

Sample No.	Measurement					Range	X-bar
1	15.41	13.57	15.85	13.38	14.12	2.47	14.47
2	13.03	18.07	13.55	13.77	15.50	5.04	14.79
3	13.91	15.88	12.88	15.10	14.06	3.00	14.37
4	13.98	13.78	11.63	16.57	12.79	4.94	13.75
5	16.22	15.24	15.91	13.80	16.53	2.73	15.54
6	17.33	12.45	14.59	15.52	14.25	4.89	14.83
7	15.62	19.01	16.31	13.72	14.39	5.29	15.81
8	15.87	14.94	11.86	12.30	14.97	4.02	13.99
9	12.70	16.20	13.60	15.08	15.74	3.50	14.66
10	18.37	14.76	12.05	15.62	13.90	6.32	14.94
11	15.28	14.94	15.87	16.81	14.03	2.78	15.38
12	15.25	15.66	14.58	14.62	14.34	1.32	14.89
13	11.73	15.54	16.05	12.56	13.53	4.32	13.88
14	14.19	14.23	15.09	17.46	13.16	4.30	14.83
15	18.03	15.45	16.17	16.99	12.80	5.24	15.89
16	13.07	11.37	14.97	14.42	18.66	7.29	14.50
17	14.11	16.21	13.71	12.33	13.05	3.88	13.88
18	13.84	14.13	14.13	14.34	14.81	0.97	14.25
19	13.54	13.20	14.99	15.01	12.33	2.68	13.81
20	12.41	13.59	12.46	16.74	13.06	4.33	13.65
21	14.90	15.49	16.95	19.18	16.91	4.28	16.69
22	10.77	12.74	12.09	13.33	15.69	4.92	12.93
23	14.59	12.75	15.01	15.07	17.87	5.12	15.06
24	15.57	13.40	15.03	14.69	13.62	2.17	14.46
25	14.02	15.21	15.31	15.94	13.07	2.87	14.71
26	18.42	18.06	10.79	13.18	16.96	7.63	15.48
27	16.20	13.48	12.92	14.62	12.31	3.89	13.91
28	15.36	11.83	16.61	12.94	15.79	4.78	14.51
29	14.69	14.74	15.43	15.98	16.45	1.76	15.46
30	12.68	15.62	12.68	15.43	14.45	2.94	14.17

Totals 119.64   439.48

When analyzing a process using $\overline{X}$ and R charts, the R chart is constructed and analyzed first.

$$\text{Centerline} = \overline{R} = \frac{\sum_{i=1}^{k} R}{k} = \frac{119.64}{30} = 3.99 \tag{8-1}$$

$$UCL_R = \overline{R} + 3\sigma_R = D_4\overline{R} = (2.113)(3.99) = 8.43 \tag{8-2}$$

$$LCL_R = \overline{R} - 3\sigma_R = D_3\overline{R} = (0)(3.99) = 0 \tag{8-3}$$

Note: The D_3 and D_4 constants depend on sample size. For small sample sizes, $(n \le 7)$ $D_3 = 0$. In most cases, the $LCL_R = 0$, since, in practice sample sizes are typically less than six.

Figure 8-11 is the output from the Minitab® software. The centerline on the range chart ($\overline{R} = 3.99$) is obtained by computing the average of the ranges of all thirty samples.

TABLE 8-3 Constants for Variables Control Charts

Sample Size n	$\overline{X}$-R Control Charts			
	A_2	D_3	D_4	d_2
2	1.880	0	3.267	1.128
3	1.023	0	2.574	1.693
4	0.729	0	2.282	2.059
5	0.577	0	2.114	2.326
6	0.483	0	2.004	2.534
7	0.419	0.076	1.924	2.704
8	0.373	0.136	1.864	2.847
9	0.337	0.184	1.816	2.970
10	0.308	0.223	1.777	3.078

Sample Size n	$\overline{X}$-s Control Charts			
	A_3	B_3	B_4	c_4
2	2.659	0	3.267	0.7979
3	1.954	0	2.568	0.8862
4	1.628	0	2.266	0.9213
5	1.427	0	2.089	0.9400
6	1.287	0.030	1.970	0.9515
7	1.182	0.118	1.882	0.9594
8	1.099	0.185	1.815	0.9650
9	1.032	0.239	1.761	0.9693
10	0.975	0.284	1.716	0.9727

The chart passes the first test for control because no points are outside the control limits. There are 16 points above the centerline and 14 below. Therefore, the runs test will be applied using $s = 14$ and $r = 16$. Investigating the points on the range chart reveals that there are 16 runs. Table 8-1 provides the critical value of 11 for too few runs. Because the total number of runs exceeds the critical value, the range chart passes the test for too few runs.

> Once the R chart is in control, the within-sample variability component can be estimated.

Table 8-2 shows that the critical value for the length of the longest run is 6. Because 4 is the longest run length (obtained by points 13–16 and 21–24), the range also passes this test. Hence, one can assume for this process the range chart is in control, which means that all the variability captured within a sample is stable and repeatable. Because the range is in control, the within-sample standard deviation can be estimated using the following relationship:

$$\sigma_w \cong \frac{\overline{R}}{d_2} = \frac{3.99}{2.326} = 1.715 \tag{8-4}$$

where the d_2 constant depends on sample size and is found in Table 8-3.

Once the range chart is in control, attention can focus on the $\overline{X}$ chart. The following formulae are used to construct the $\overline{X}$ chart.

$$\text{Centerline} = \overline{\overline{X}} = \frac{\sum_{i=1}^{k} \overline{X}}{k} = \frac{439.48}{30} = 14.65 \tag{8-5}$$

$$UCL_{\overline{X}} = \overline{\overline{X}} + 3\sigma_{\overline{X}} = \overline{\overline{X}} + 3\frac{\sigma}{\sqrt{n}} = \overline{\overline{X}} + 3\frac{\overline{R}}{d_2\sqrt{n}} = \overline{\overline{X}} + A_2\overline{R} \tag{8-6}$$

$$= 14.65 + (0.577)(3.99) = 16.95$$

FIGURE 8-11 Minitab Output of **(A)** $\overline{X}$ Chart and **(B)** R Chart for Acme Fastener Process

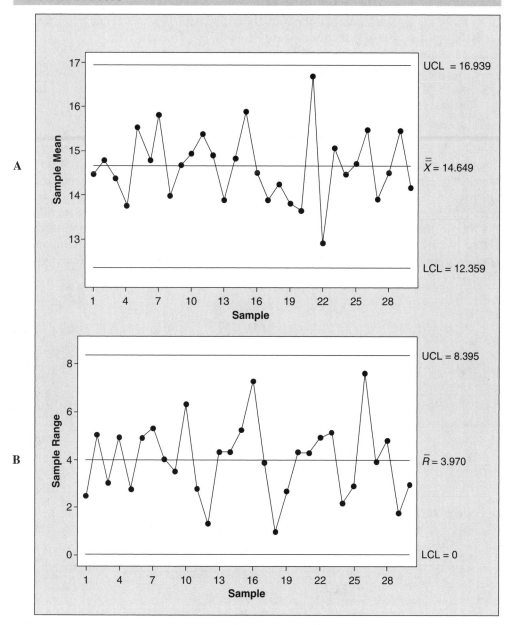

$$LCL_{\overline{X}} = \overline{\overline{X}} - 3\sigma_{\overline{X}} = \overline{\overline{X}} - 3\frac{\sigma}{\sqrt{n}} = \overline{\overline{X}} - 3\frac{\overline{R}}{d_2\sqrt{n}} = \overline{\overline{X}} - A_2\overline{R} \qquad \textbf{(8-7)}$$
$$= 14.65 - (0.577)(3.99) = 12.35$$

Note: k = the number of samples used to construct the chart. The A_2 constants depend on sample size and are found in Table 8-3.

Applying the statistical control tests to the $\overline{X}$ chart results in the following:

- All plotted points are inside the control limits.
- There are an equal number of points above and below the centerline and a total of 17 runs. The critical value for too few runs with $r = 15$ and $s = 15$ is 11. Because 17 is greater than 11, the chart passes the test for too few runs.
- The length of the longest run is 5 (points 17 – 21). The critical value for longest run is 6. Because 5 is less than 6, the chart passes the test for the length of the longest run.

Because the $\overline{X}$ and R charts each pass all tests, it can be concluded that the process is in statistical control. With the $\overline{X}$ chart in control, one can conclude that the process mean is stable and repeatable at 14.65, and that there is no between-sample variability (or it is negligible). That is, all variability was captured within the subgroup and σ_w can be used to estimate the process standard deviation, which we call σ_x for now.

The *s* chart provides an alternative to the *R* chart and is preferred when the sample size $n > 8$.

An alternative to the range chart is the s chart. The R chart and s chart provide the same information. It is never necessary to construct both. However, if sample sizes are large (greater than 8), the s chart is preferred. In Figure 8-12, the range column has been replaced with a standard deviation column. The applicable formulae for an s chart and $\overline{X}$ chart combination are as follows:

$$\text{Centerline} = \bar{s} = \frac{\sum_{i=1}^{k} s}{k} = \frac{47.71}{30} = 1.59 \qquad \textbf{(8-8)}$$

$$UCL_s = \bar{s} + 3\sigma_s = B_4\bar{s} = (2.089)(1.59) = 3.32 \qquad \textbf{(8-9)}$$

$$LCL_s = \bar{s} - 3\sigma_s = B_3\bar{s} = (0)(1.59) = 0 \qquad \textbf{(8-10)}$$

The B_3 and B_4 constants depend on sample size and are found in Table 8-3.

$$\sigma_w \cong \frac{\bar{s}}{c_4} = \frac{1.59}{0.940} = 1.691 \qquad \textbf{(8-11)}$$

where the c_4 constants depend on sample size and are found in Table 8-3.

$$\text{Centerline} = \overline{\overline{X}} = \frac{\sum_{i=1}^{k} \overline{X}}{k} = \frac{439.48}{30} = 14.65 \qquad \textbf{(8-12)}$$

$$UCL_{\overline{X}} = \overline{\overline{X}} + 3\sigma_{\overline{X}} = \overline{\overline{X}} + 3\frac{\sigma}{n} = \overline{\overline{X}} + 3\frac{\bar{s}}{c_4 n} = \overline{\overline{X}} + A_3\bar{s} \qquad \textbf{(8-13)}$$

$$= 14.65 + (1.427)(1.59) = 16.92$$

$$LCL_{\overline{X}} = \overline{\overline{X}} - 3\sigma_{\overline{X}} = \overline{\overline{X}} - 3\frac{\sigma}{n} = \overline{\overline{X}} - 3\frac{\bar{s}}{c_4 n} = \overline{\overline{X}} - A_3\bar{s} \qquad \textbf{(8-14)}$$

$$= 14.65 - (1.427)(1.59) = 12.38$$

The A_3 constants depend on sample size and are found in Table 8-3.

Figure 8-13 provides a comparison of the s chart with the R chart. The pattern of points is roughly the same. The s is a little more sensitive than the R chart to changes that occur to variability within samples. This is evidenced by point number 26 that is out

FIGURE 8-12 Samples from Acme Fastener Process

Sample No.	Measurement					X-bar	s
1	15.41	13.57	15.85	13.38	14.12	14.47	1.108
2	13.03	18.07	13.55	13.77	15.50	14.79	2.056
3	13.91	15.88	12.88	15.10	14.06	14.37	1.156
4	13.98	13.78	11.63	16.57	12.79	13.75	1.832
5	16.22	15.24	15.91	13.80	16.53	15.54	1.084
6	17.33	12.45	14.59	15.52	14.25	14.83	1.791
7	15.62	19.01	16.31	13.72	14.39	15.81	2.055
8	15.87	14.94	11.86	12.30	14.97	13.99	1.789
9	12.70	16.20	13.60	15.08	15.74	14.66	1.472
10	18.37	14.76	12.05	15.62	13.90	14.94	2.329
11	15.28	14.94	15.87	16.81	14.03	15.38	1.040
12	15.25	15.66	14.58	14.62	14.34	14.89	0.546
13	11.73	15.54	16.05	12.56	13.53	13.88	1.867
14	14.19	14.23	15.09	17.46	13.16	14.83	1.623
15	18.03	15.45	16.17	16.99	12.80	15.89	1.977
16	13.07	11.37	14.97	14.42	18.66	14.50	2.710
17	14.11	16.21	13.71	12.33	13.05	13.88	1.468
18	13.84	14.13	14.13	14.34	14.81	14.25	0.360
19	13.54	13.20	14.99	15.01	12.33	13.81	1.168
20	12.41	13.59	12.46	16.74	13.06	13.65	1.792
21	14.90	15.49	16.95	19.18	16.91	16.69	1.654
22	10.77	12.74	12.09	13.33	15.69	12.93	1.814
23	14.59	12.75	15.01	15.07	17.87	15.06	1.833
24	15.57	13.40	15.03	14.69	13.62	14.46	0.926
25	14.02	15.21	15.31	15.94	13.07	14.71	1.149
26	18.42	18.06	10.79	13.18	16.96	15.48	3.347
27	16.20	13.48	12.92	14.62	12.31	13.91	1.540
28	15.36	11.83	16.61	12.94	15.79	14.51	2.026
29	14.69	14.74	15.43	15.98	16.45	15.46	0.767
30	12.68	15.62	12.68	15.43	14.45	14.17	1.431
Totals						439.48	47.71

of control on the s chart but inside the control limits on the R chart. Nevertheless, for the small sample sizes that are typical in most applications, the convenience of the R chart (ranges are easier to compute on the factory floor than standard deviations) usually overrides any additional advantage derived from the s chart. Figure 8-14 shows that the control limits on the $\overline{X}$ chart are the same whether they are based on the sample ranges or sample standard deviations.

8.3.2 Charts for Individual Measurements—The X and *MR* Charts

An individual chart is necessary when a rational subgroup (sample) is not possible.

Certain types of data do not lend themselves to rational subgrouping (e.g., a sample that would effectively distinguish between short- and long-term sources of variability). Trying to put together a sample of multiple units would be senseless. Examples of this type of data are money and time, or when samples are drawn from a continuous process that is homogeneous at any point (e.g., flour, paint, roofing shingles, chemicals).

FIGURE 8-13 Comparison of R and s Charts

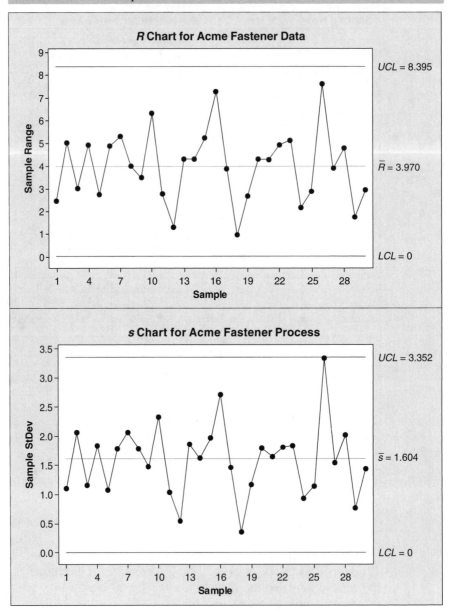

In a steel mill, iron content is important to the quality of any batch. Figure 8-15 shows measurements that were taken at half-hour intervals over a fifteen-hour period. This type of process does not lend itself to rational subgrouping. If samples of five were collected consecutively, or even at short intervals, the dominant source of variability captured within each sample would be due to measurement error and not the process. In the case of steel making, process variability is primarily due to time-related factors. As this is variables data, a pair of charts are needed to properly analyze the

FIGURE 8-14 Comparison of $\overline{X}$ Charts Using R and s Charts

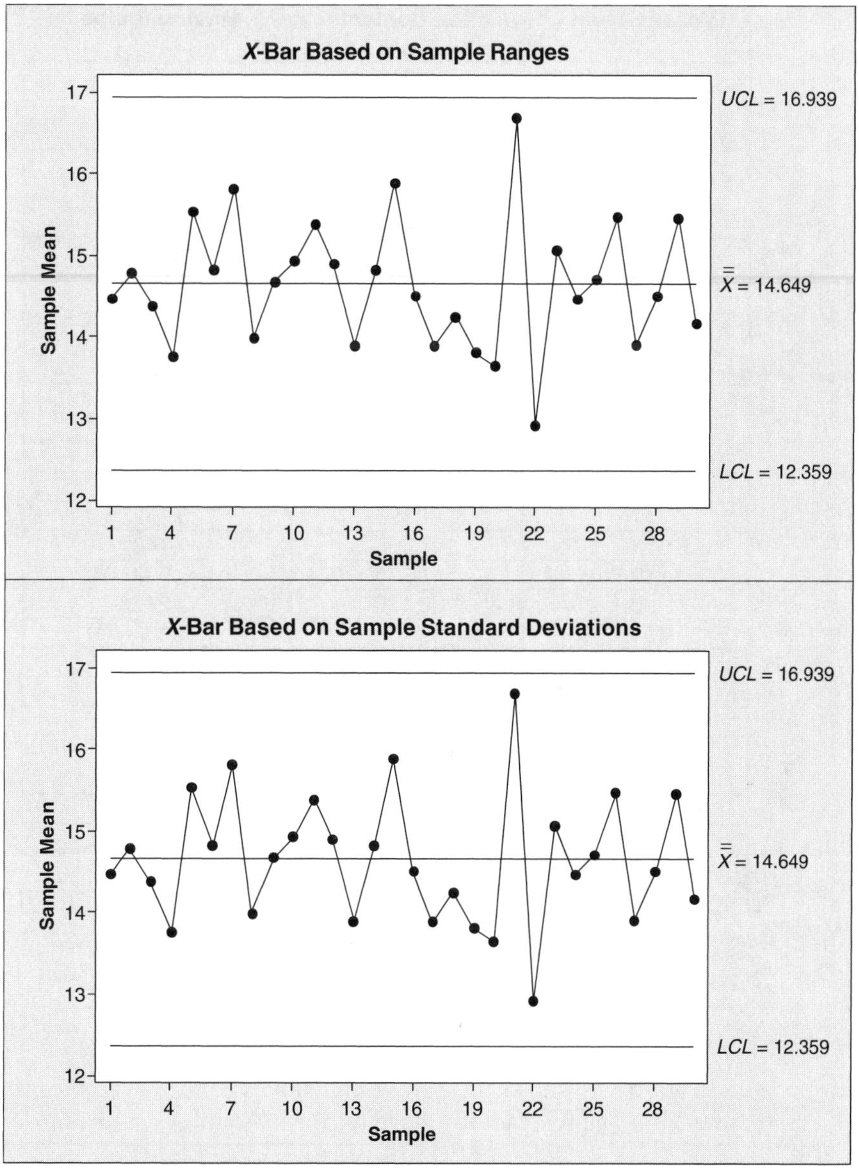
X-Bar Based on Sample Ranges
Sample Mean
Sample
UCL = 16.939
$\overline{\overline{X}}$ = 14.649
LCL = 12.359
X-Bar Based on Sample Standard Deviations
Sample Mean
Sample
UCL = 16.939
$\overline{\overline{X}}$ = 14.649
LCL = 12.359

Moving Range

process mean and standard deviation. An obstacle to this is obvious. With a sample of size $n = 1$, it is impossible to calculate a range. To overcome this difficulty, a **moving range** is used, which is the calculated difference between the high and the low of a group of measurements taken in close proximity. The most common procedure is to use a two-point moving range—that is, each range is computed as the absolute value of the difference between the two most recent consecutive measurements. Obviously, the first moving range value cannot be computed until the second measurement has been taken.

FIGURE 8-15 Individual Measurement Data in a Steel Mill

Measurement	Iron Content	Moving Range
1	2.446	
2	2.211	0.235
3	2.211	0.000
4	2.539	0.328
5	1.998	0.541
6	2.131	0.132
7	2.290	0.159
8	2.165	0.124
9	1.797	0.368
10	2.272	0.475
11	2.050	0.221
12	2.439	0.388
13	2.029	0.410
14	2.053	0.024
15	2.378	0.325
16	2.248	0.130
17	2.106	0.142
18	1.958	0.148
19	1.860	0.098
20	2.135	0.275
21	2.139	0.004
22	2.037	0.101
23	2.157	0.120
24	2.076	0.082
25	2.217	0.141
26	2.247	0.030
27	2.142	0.105
28	2.098	0.044
29	2.477	0.379
30	2.336	0.141
	65.243	5.672

Individuals

Figure 8-16 shows the pair of **individuals** control charts for the iron content measurements. The relevant formulae for the **MR** and **X** charts are

$$\text{Centerline} = \overline{MR} = \frac{\sum\limits_{i=2}^{k} MR}{k-1} = \frac{5.672}{29} = 0.1956 \tag{8-15}$$

$$UCL_{MR} = \overline{MR} + 3\sigma_{MR} = D_4\overline{MR} = (3.267)(0.1956) = 0.639 \tag{8-16}$$

$$LCL_{MR} = \overline{MR} - 3\sigma_{MR} = D_3\overline{MR} = (0)(0.1956) = 0 \tag{8-17}$$

The D_3 and D_4 constants are those for $n = 2$ from Table 8-3.

$$\sigma_s \cong \frac{\overline{MR}}{c_4} = \frac{0.1956}{0.7979} = 0.2451 \tag{8-18}$$

FIGURE 8-16 Individuals Control Charts for Steel Mill Data

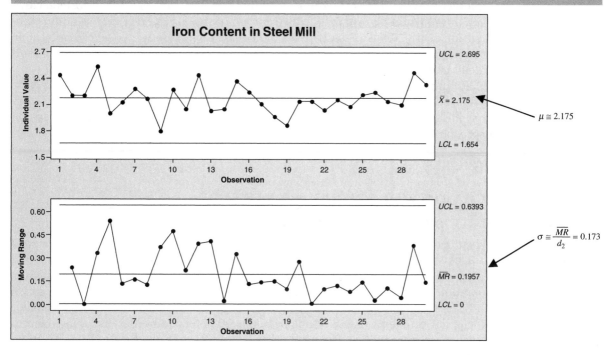

where σ_s is the short-term standard deviation, and $c_4 = 0.7979$ is the constant for $n = 2$ found in Table 8-3.

$$\text{Centerline} = \overline{X} = \frac{\sum\limits_{i=1}^{k} X}{k} = \frac{65.243}{30} = 2.1748 \qquad \textbf{(8-19)}$$

$$UCL_X = \overline{X} + 3\sigma_X = \overline{X} + 3\frac{\overline{MR}}{d_2} \qquad \textbf{(8-20)}$$

$$= 2.1748 + (3)\left(\frac{0.1956}{1.128}\right) = 2.695$$

$$LCL_X = \overline{X} - 3\sigma_X = \overline{X} - 3\frac{\overline{MR}}{d_2} \qquad \textbf{(8-21)}$$

$$= 2.1748 - (3)\left(\frac{0.1956}{1.128}\right) = 1.655$$

Evaluating statistical control in the case of individuals charts is not as straightforward as with $\overline{X}$ and R charts. In the case of the moving range chart, each point is not independent of the others because each measurement, except the first, is used in the computation of two consecutive moving range values. Therefore, the standard runs tests do not apply. Another consideration is the placement of the control limits on the X chart. Placing the limits equidistant from the centerline, three standard deviations in each direction, is based on the assumption of normality. This is statistically sound when the points plotted are averages ($\overline{X}$s) of samples because the central limit theorem ensures the distribution of the $\overline{X}$s will be approximately normal. However, this may not be true for the distribution of the Xs. In practice, it is not uncommon for distributions of individuals data (e.g., time, money) to have a noticeable skew. Given these two considerations, the standard runs tests do not apply to individuals control charts.

Standard runs tests do not apply to individuals control charts.

Returning to Figure 8-16, the control charts for the iron content data appear to be in statistical control (i.e., there are no out-of-control points and no evidence of trends or stratification), with mean approximately equal to 2.1748 and standard deviation approximately equal to 0.173.

8.4 CONTROL CHARTS FOR ATTRIBUTES MEASURES

8.4.1 *p* Charts and *np* Charts

When control charts are used to analyze attributes data, only one chart is needed to track the single parameter of interest (the mean). To illustrate, consider a plant that produces cooking oil. Bottles are filled with oil, and then proceed through an operation that applies labels. An inspector randomly selects 100 bottles from a shift's production and inspects for defective labels (e.g., missing, wrinkled, torn, or crooked) or supplier problems (e.g., printing defects). All defective bottles, including the reason code, are recorded. A **Pareto analysis** by reason code can help reduce defectives in the future.

Pareto Analysis

Figure 8-17 is a summary of inspection data that were collected over thirty consecutive shifts. For each sample of 100, the number of defective labels has been recorded. An extra column has been added to the spreadsheet that expresses the number of defectives as a proportion of sample size—for example, three defectives, when expressed as a proportion, is 0.03 of the sample. For the purpose of control charts, the proportion is given the symbol p and the number of defectives the symbol np.

Because the sample size is constant (every sample contains (proportion of defectives) exactly 100 bottles), there are two ways to chart these data. Figure 8-18 is a **p chart**, and Figure 8-19 is an **np chart** (number of defectives). There are no out-of-control points on either chart, and one can easily verify that these charts pass the statistical tests for too few and length of longest runs. Therefore, it can be concluded with a high degree of confidence that this process is in statistical control and is, on average, producing approximately 3.5% defective labels. The formulae that are used to compute the control limits on p and np charts are as follows:

p Chart

np Chart

$$\overline{p} = \frac{\text{Total Number of Defectives}}{\text{Total Number of Items Inspected}} \tag{8-22}$$

n = Sample Size

p Chart Limits:

Centerline: $\overline{p}$

$$\text{UCL}: \overline{p} + 3\sigma_p = \overline{p} + 3\sqrt{\frac{\overline{p}(1 - \overline{p})}{n}} \tag{8-23}$$

FIGURE 8-17 Inspection Summary for Defective Labels

Sample Number	Sample Size	Number of Defectives, np	Percent Defectives, p
1	100	2	0.02
2	100	2	0.02
3	100	4	0.04
4	100	3	0.03
5	100	5	0.05
6	100	4	0.04
7	100	7	0.07
8	100	5	0.05
9	100	4	0.04
10	100	7	0.07
11	100	2	0.02
12	100	4	0.04
13	100	2	0.02
14	100	2	0.02
15	100	3	0.03
16	100	3	0.03
17	100	4	0.04
18	100	2	0.02
19	100	4	0.04
20	100	2	0.02
21	100	3	0.03
22	100	6	0.06
23	100	1	0.01
24	100	2	0.02
25	100	4	0.04
26	100	5	0.05
27	100	4	0.04
28	100	3	0.03
29	100	2	0.02
30	100	3	0.03
	3,000	104	

$$\text{LCL: } \max\left\{\bar{p} - 3\sigma_p = \bar{p} + 3\sqrt{\frac{\bar{p}(1 - \bar{p})}{n}}, 0\right\} \tag{8-24}$$

np Chart Limits:
Centerline: $n\bar{p}$ (8-25)

$$\text{UCL: } n\bar{p} + 3\sigma_{np} = n\bar{p} + 3\sqrt{n\bar{p}(1 - \bar{p})} \tag{8-26}$$

$$\text{LCL: } \max\left\{n\bar{p} - 3\sigma_{np} = n\bar{p} - 3\sqrt{n\bar{p}(1 - \bar{p})}, 0\right\} \tag{8-27}$$

From the previous equations, it is obvious that the control limits depend on the size of the sample. As the sample size increases, the control limits tighten; as it decreases, the control limits widen. This makes sense when one considers that as the sample size

FIGURE 8-18 *p* Chart for Defective Labels

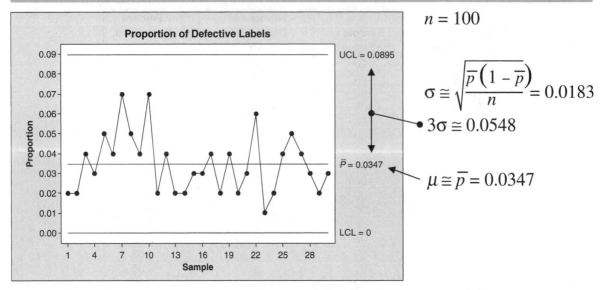

$$n = 100$$

$$\sigma \cong \sqrt{\frac{\overline{p}\left(1 - \overline{p}\right)}{n}} = 0.0183$$

$$3\sigma \cong 0.0548$$

$$\mu \cong \overline{p} = 0.0347$$

Constant Sample Size

increases, the sample average is more likely to be a better estimator of the process average than the smaller sample average. For a **constant sample size**, the formulae yield constant control limits.

What happens if the sample size is not constant? Figure 8-20 shows data collected from a plant that produces printed circuit boards. An inspection station performs a 100% inspection of all boards produced. The inspection involves a test in which a board

FIGURE 8-19 *np* Chart for Defective Labels

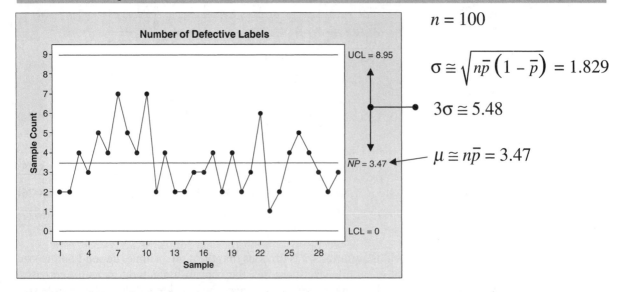

$$n = 100$$

$$\sigma \cong \sqrt{n\overline{p}\left(1 - \overline{p}\right)} = 1.829$$

$$3\sigma \cong 5.48$$

$$\mu \cong n\overline{p} = 3.47$$

FIGURE 8-20 Data for Testing an Electric Circuit

Sample Number	No Defectives, np	Sample Size, n	Proportion Defective, p
1	21	1,002	0.0210
2	27	1,109	0.0243
3	20	998	0.0200
4	27	1,234	0.0219
5	15	1,087	0.0138
6	19	1,056	0.0180
7	15	1,187	0.0126
8	16	1,108	0.0144
9	11	998	0.0110
10	26	1,007	0.0258
11	25	1,254	0.0199
12	18	1,343	0.0134
13	21	1,045	0.0201
14	19	1,253	0.0152
15	16	1,023	0.0156
16	22	987	0.0223
17	19	1,157	0.0164
18	17	1,178	0.0144
19	21	1,039	0.0202
20	12	1,039	0.0115
21	26	978	0.0266
22	21	1,167	0.0180
23	18	1,243	0.0145
24	20	1,198	0.0167
25	14	1,203	0.0116
26	15	1,180	0.0127
27	20	1,095	0.0183
28	19	1,009	0.0188
29	18	1,087	0.0166
30	8	1,165	0.0069
	566	33,429	

When n is constant, either a p chart or an np chart may be used.

Variable Sample Size

is plugged into a device that determines whether current can pass through the circuit. If current flows, the board is passed; otherwise, it is rejected as a defective. For control chart purposes, the inspection data are compiled daily. Because there is some variability in daily production rates, the sample size is not constant. When n is variable, an np chart is not an option. The p chart must be used. There are three approaches to plotting limits on a p chart with a **variable sample size**.

- *Variable Limits.* Figure 8-21a illustrates a p chart with variable limits. Using the circuit board data and Equations 8-23 and 8-24, control limits have been computed for each sample. There are several problems with this approach. One issue is that control limits need to be computed each time a new sample is collected. A second

FIGURE 8-21 *p* Charts for Variable Sample Sizes. **A,** Variable Control Limits Based on Actual Sample Size *n.* **B,** Control Limits Based on Average Sample Size $\bar{n}$

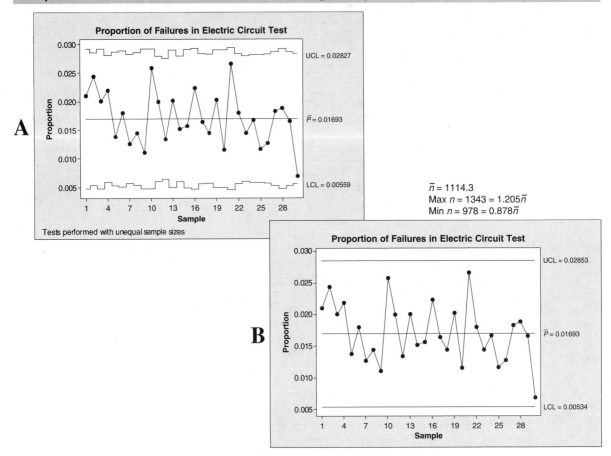

$\bar{n} = 1114.3$
Max $n = 1343 = 1.205\bar{n}$
Min $n = 978 = 0.878\bar{n}$

problem involves communications. It is sometimes difficult to explain to someone who is not familiar with control charts why a point that was in control yesterday would be out of control today (or vice versa). It could appear to the uninitiated that the limits are being arbitrarily set.

- *Limits Based on Average Sample Size.* Figure 8-21b is an alternative approach. Instead of calculating a set of control limits for each sample, constant limits have been constructed based on the average sample size $\bar{n}$. This approach works well provided sample sizes do not vary greatly. Constant limits can be used based on $\bar{n}$, provided the sample size range (maximum − minimum) is not more than ± 25% of $\bar{n}$. In the future, as samples are collected, actual limits need only be computed for points that lie close to the $\bar{n}$ limits. If a point is just inside, then the control limit (either upper or lower) needs to be computed based on the actual *n* only if $n > \bar{n}$ (i.e., the actual limits are tighter than the $\bar{n}$ limits). If a point is just outside the limits, the upper or lower control limit needs to be recomputed based on the actual *n* if and only if $n < \bar{n}$ (i.e., the actual limits are wider than those based on the $\bar{n}$ limits).

FIGURE 8-22 *p* Chart Control Limits Based on Maximum and Minimum Sample Sizes

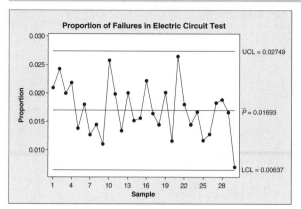

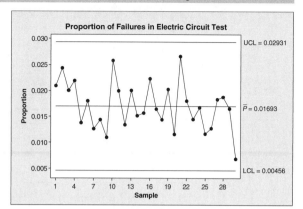

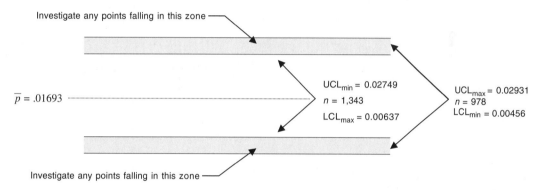

- *Maximum and Minimum Limits.* A third approach, illustrated in Figure 8-22, is to plot a pair of control limits. One set of limits is based on the largest sample size likely to be encountered. This set of limits is the tightest that might ever be expected, and any point that falls within them will be in control no matter what the actual sample size. The other set of limits is based on the smallest expected sample size, and is the widest limit that is likely to be encountered. Any point that lies outside the widest limit is out of control, regardless of the actual sample size. The zone that lies between the two sets of limits is the region where those true limits (based on actual sample sizes) would theoretically be constructed. Therefore, it is only necessary to investigate and possibly construct actual limits for those points that fall within this zone. Typically, this procedure will not involve many points, and only one control limit (either the upper or the lower) will ever have to be actually computed for any particular sample.

No points are out of control on Figure 8-21a, and the chart passes all runs tests ($s = 13, r = 17$). The critical value for too few runs is 10 (the actual number of runs is 16), and for the longest run is 6 (the actual length of the longest run is 4). As the process exhibits control, the limits shown on the chart can be used for all future samples, until there is evidence that the process has changed and the current limits no longer apply.

Figure 8-23 shows the measurements for the circuit tester collected over the next ten days. These points have been added to the control chart in Figure 8-24. The process

FIGURE 8-23 Data for Testing an Electric Circuit: The Next Ten Days

Sample Number	No Defectives, np	Sample Size, n	Proportion Defective, p
31	24	1,145	0.0210
32	32	1,098	0.0291
33	28	1,050	0.0267
34	21	1,145	0.0183
35	19	976	0.0195
36	34	1,303	0.0261
37	20	1,190	0.0168
38	27	1,200	0.0225
39	15	995	0.0151
40	33	1,115	0.0296
	253	11,217	

FIGURE 8-24 Operational p Chart with Maximum and Minimum Limits for Circuit Breaker Data

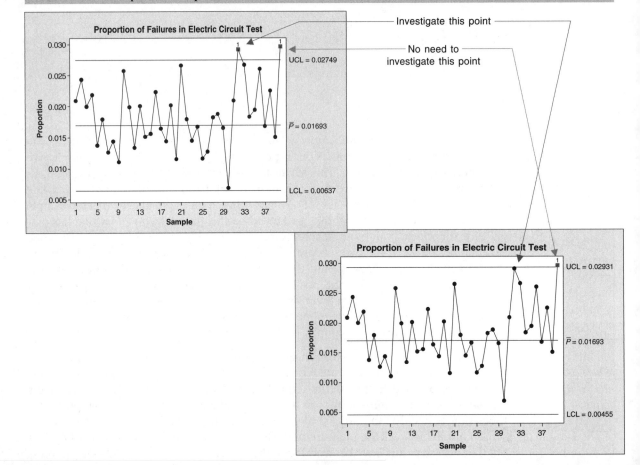

average appears to have increased. The average of the most recent ten samples is 22.5% as compared with the average of the first 30 samples of 16.9%. Point 32 falls within the investigation zone, so the exact upper control limit needs to be computed. Equation 8-23 produces an upper control limit of 0.0286; therefore, the actual measurement of 0.0291 is out of control. Point 40 at 0.0296 lies beyond the widest control limit of 0.0293, so there is no necessity to compute the exact limit. Point 40 is clearly out of control. In addition to the two out-of-control points, if point 37 had not occurred slightly below the centerline, the rule of seven would have been violated in measurements 31 through 37. The next steps would include either revising the limits to reflect the current status of the process or taking action in the short term to try to reduce the average, thereby restoring statistical control.

8.4.2 *c* Charts and *u* Charts

A defective unit may contain one or numerous defects.

Defect

A *p* chart tracks defectives. With *p* chart data, samples are taken using attributes measures, where the number of items failing to pass inspection is counted. The total count for each sample will be plotted on the *p* chart as a proportion of the sample size. An item can fail to pass inspection for any number of reasons, and each cause of failure is called a **defect**. A defect is a quality attribute, that when measured, fails to meet minimum requirements. It is an error—some flaw that creates a less than perfect condition. Some defects (imperfections) are so minor that by themselves they would not cause a production unit to be labeled as defective.

c Charts

u Charts

When the interest is in tracking (and possibly eliminating) defects rather than defectives, ***c* charts** or ***u* charts** are required. Figure 8-25 shows data that have been collected by a plant that manufactures fine-quality pool tables. Each table produced is closely inspected for any defects prior to shipment, such as blemishes in the finish, missing parts, or felt bed imperfections. The inspectors are meticulously trained in how to spot a defect

FIGURE 8-25 Data for the Inspection of Pool Tables

Table No.	No. of Defects, *c*	Table No.	No. of Defects, *c*
1	1	16	2
2	2	17	2
3	0	18	2
4	4	19	1
5	2	20	1
6	3	21	2
7	2	22	5
8	3	23	4
9	2	24	5
10	1	25	2
11	0	26	1
12	4	27	6
13	1	28	4
14	3	29	2
15	2	30	2
	30		41

and, for each table inspected, the number and type of defect are recorded. Figure 8-25 shows the total count for all types of defects for thirty consecutive tables inspected.

The sample size is defined differently for c charts than for p charts. When defects are counted, the concept of a sample size relates to the field of opportunity for a defect to occur, rather than to a discreet number of sample units. The fixed opportunity for occurrence is defined as the **inspection unit**. An inspection unit can be an item (radio, table, dozen eggs), a unit of area (100 square meters, three lineal feet), a unit of volume (1,000 cubic centimeters, fifty-gallon drum), and so on. A c chart is used when the number of inspection units is constant from sample to sample. The **Poisson distribution** is used to define the probabilities associated with c chart data, resulting in the following equations:

Inspection Unit

Poisson Distribution

$$\bar{c} = \frac{\text{Total Number of Defects}}{\text{Total Number of Inspection Units}} = \frac{\text{Total Number of Defects}}{k} \quad \textbf{(8-28)}$$

$$\frac{71}{30} = 2.37$$

$$\text{UCL}_c = \bar{c} + 3\sqrt{\bar{c}} \quad \textbf{(8-29)}$$

$$2.37 + (3)\sqrt{2.37} = 6.98$$

$$\text{LCL}_c = \max\{\bar{c} - 3\sqrt{\bar{c}}, 0\} \quad \textbf{(8-30)}$$

$$\max\{2.37 - (3)\sqrt{2.37}, 0\} = \max\{-2.25, 0\} = 0$$

Figure 8-26 shows a plot of the c chart for the pool table data. Because the chart shows a state of statistical control, one can be confident in predicting that the next pool tables produced will, on average, contain approximately 2.37 defects per table.

FIGURE 8-26 c Chart for Pool Table Defects

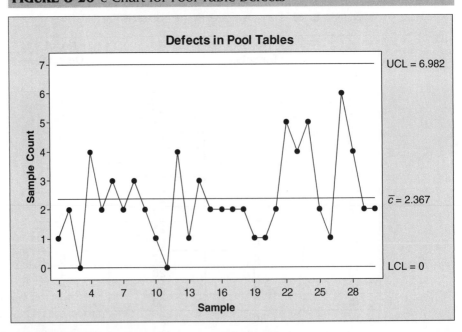

FIGURE 8-27 Errors in Purchase Orders Over a Thirty-Day Period

Day	No. of Purchase Order Errors	No. of Purchase Orders	No. of Inspection Units	Day	No. of Purchase Order Errors	No. of Purchase Orders	No. of Inspection Units
1	12	76	7.6	16	11	85	8.5
2	13	78	7.8	17	11	90	9
3	8	79	7.9	18	13	89	8.9
4	7	77	7.7	19	8	68	6.8
5	15	93	9.3	20	6	71	7.1
6	8	71	7.1	21	6	91	9.1
7	12	83	8.3	22	9	77	7.7
8	4	89	8.9	23	7	83	8.3
9	11	82	8.2	24	10	79	7.9
10	7	93	9.3	25	4	77	7.7
11	17	81	8.1	26	8	70	7
12	17	80	8	27	12	99	9.9
13	10	93	9.3	28	4	59	5.9
14	8	86	8.6	29	9	88	8.8
15	13	88	8.8	30	7	84	8.4
	162		124.9		125		121

When the number of inspection units is not the same from sample to sample, a u chart must be used. Figure 8-27 shows a summary of the data collected on errors in purchase orders over a 30-day period. The number of purchase orders processed is not the same day to day, so the opportunity for errors to occur is not constant. An inspection unit was defined as ten purchase orders. For the purpose of the u chart, the sample size n is the total number of purchase orders processed each day divided by ten. The following equations apply for constructing a u chart:

$$\bar{u} = \frac{\text{Total Number of Defects}}{\text{Total Number of Inspection Units}} \tag{8-31}$$

$$= \frac{287}{245.9} = 1.167$$

$$\text{UCL}_u = \bar{u} + 3\sqrt{\frac{\bar{u}}{n}} \tag{8-32}$$

$$\text{LCL}_u = \max\left\{\bar{u} - 3\sqrt{\frac{\bar{u}}{n}}, 0\right\} \tag{8-33}$$

As Equations 8-32 and 8-33 and Figure 8-28 show, the limits on a u chart differ for each sample. For example, on the first day, with seventy-six purchase orders (7.6 inspection units),

$$\bar{u} = 1.167$$

$$\text{UCL}_u = 1.167 + (3)\sqrt{\frac{1.167}{7.6}} = 2.343$$

$$\text{LCL}_u = \max\left\{1.167 - (3)\sqrt{\frac{1.167}{7.6}}, 0\right\} = \max\{-0.0085, 0\} = 0$$

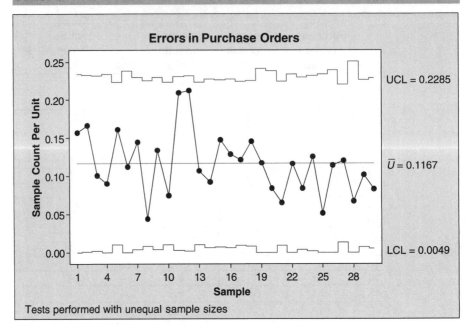

FIGURE 8-28 *u* Chart for Purchase Order Defects

On day 27, with 9.9 inspection units,

$$\bar{u} = 1.167$$

$$UCL_u = 1.167 + (3)\sqrt{\frac{1.167}{9.9}} = 2.205$$

$$LCL_u = \max\left\{1.167 - (3)\sqrt{\frac{1.167}{9.9}}, 0\right\} = \max\{0.146, 0\} = 0.146$$

Because the *u* chart shows a state of control, it can be concluded that the process is stable and is producing on average approximately 1.167 errors per ten purchase orders.

8.4.3 How to Differentiate Between *p* Chart and *c* Chart Data

It is understandable that some people get confused as to whether their data should be plotted on a *p* chart if a *c* chart is more appropriate. Figure 8-29 provides a comparison of the differentiating characteristics of the two chart types. The easiest test is to consider the possible range of values that can occur in any sample. In the case of a *p* chart, the minimum sample value is zero (i.e., no defectives). This is also the minimum value for a *c* chart (i.e., no defects). However, in the case of the *p* chart, there is a maximum (*n*)—meaning all are defective, but there is no maximum for the *c* chart (e.g., what is the maximum number of defects that can occur on a sheet of glass?). Therefore, one distinction is to determine if there is a **finite count** range. If so, the data is more likely to be *p* chart than *c* chart compatible.

Finite Count

A second test is based on the inspection objective. If the objective is to make a **final disposition** decision on the units inspected (e.g., to determine if they can be shipped or

Final Disposition

FIGURE 8-29 When to Apply a *p* Chart and When to Apply a *c* Chart

Differentiating Characteristic	*p* Chart	*c* Chart
Minimum Count in Sample	0	0
Maximum Count in Sample	*n*	No Limit
Sample Size	Discreet Production Units	Inspection Unit (Defect Opportunity)
Inspection Decision	Is Item Acceptable and Can It Be Shipped?	Are There Any Imperfections in the Inspection Unit?

forwarded to the next processing station), then the data can be tracked using a *p* chart. If, in contrast, the objective has nothing to do with whether a production unit can be shipped, instead focusing on those qualities that are less than perfect, the data are best tracked using a *c* chart.

8.5 MEASUREMENT PROCESSES

8.5.1 Measurement Is a Process

Representation

Truth

Measurements that are taken from a process are not the true value of the process attribute being measured. The measurement is simply a **representation** of the truth. If the representation is close to the **truth**, it can be said that the measurement process is good. If the error is large, the representation is not close to the truth, and it can be said that the measurement process is poor. Several issues arise concerning the quality of any measurement process.

> A measurement is only a representation of the truth.

1. *Does the process, on average, provide the true value of the attribute measured? That is, is the measurement process accurate? Figure 8-30 illustrates the concept of* **accuracy**. *If a single item is measured repeatedly, using an accurate process, the average of all measurements will come close to the true value being measured. If the average is different from the true value, the process is said to contain* **bias**. *Accuracy is a* **calibration** *issue. When the presence of bias is discovered, the problem can often be corrected by recalibrating the measuring tool.*

Accuracy

Bias

Calibration

Precision

> An accurate measurement process is not biased.

2. *Is the measurement process precise? How much variation is there in consecutive measurements of the same item? Figure 8-31 illustrates the concept of* **precision**. *A precise process has little variability around its mean. A process can be precise but inaccurate, accurate but imprecise, imprecise and inaccurate, or accurate and precise. The last condition is obviously the most desirable.*

> Precision refers to the ability of a measurement process to repeat its results.

3. *Is the measurement process consistent in its ability to represent the truth? That is, is the measurement process in statistical control with respect to accuracy and precision?*

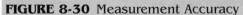

FIGURE 8-30 Measurement Accuracy

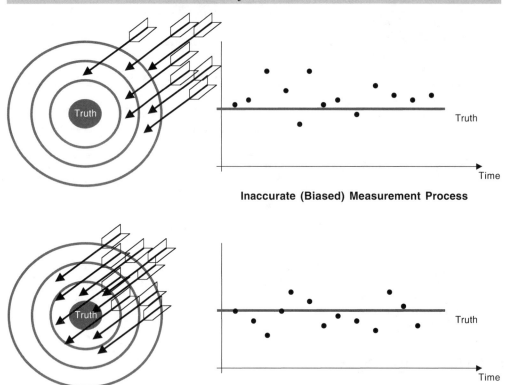

Inaccurate (Biased) Measurement Process

Accurate Measurement Process

Discrimination

4. *Is the measurement process capable of proper* **discrimination** *between different production units, batches, runs, and so on?*

5. *How much of the observed process variability is due to measurement error? How much of the design tolerance is eaten up by management error?*

Measurement is a process and can therefore be analyzed like any other, using similar tools of analysis. Before one can properly study a production process, it is important to know the capabilities of the process that will be used to evaluate quality. The following true story illustrates why.

Automobile tires pass through numerous QC checks during production. One inspection, performed early in the process, involves the collection of a rubber sample from each batch coming out of the mixing room. The sample is sent to the QC lab where it goes through a number of tests. One of these tests is on an apparatus called an oscillating disc rheometer. A certain plant has eight rheometer stations that are used to test each rubber batch for elastic modulus, viscous modulus, tangent delta, and cure rate—all important to the ultimate safety, durability, and performance of automobile tires.

The test, as shown in Figure 8-32, requires a QC technician to cut a rubber test strip and place the sample on a disc located between an upper and lower die in the rheometer machine. The machine closes and the disc begins to oscillate, placing stress on the

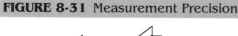

FIGURE 8-31 Measurement Precision

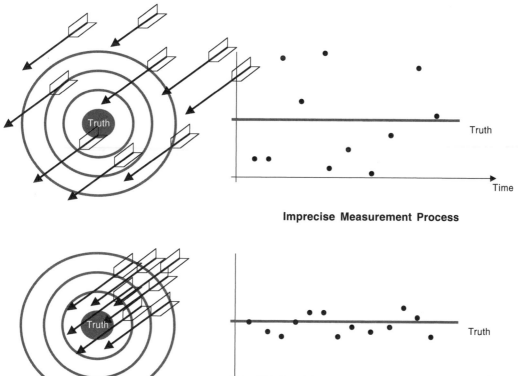

Imprecise Measurement Process

Precise Measurement Process

material. The output is a graph that plots torque as a function of time over a three-minute period. The shape of the curve for an acceptable batch, an ogive (S) curve, plots through predetermined gates in three critical zones of the ogive (lower part of S, steep upward slope, final leveling out). If the graph is not an ogive or fails to plot through the gates, the batch is rejected.

Due to the pressures of time and workload, the standard lab practice was for a technician to sheer off a sample piece of material from the master test strip. The size of these specimens varied significantly. Concerned with whether this variability would impact the test results, the QC director performed the following experiment. From the most recent batch, he had a technician cut three test specimens—a small, medium, and large size. The results shown in Figure 8-32 were enlightening. The size of the sample does matter. The production batch tested could have been either accepted (in the case of the medium-size sample) or rejected (in the case of the small or large samples) based on the size of the material specimen tested. The vendor's operation manual clearly states that a proper specimen should consist of two pieces of material, $2 \times 2 \times \frac{1}{4}$ inches, and layered. Most rheometric equipment manufacturers strongly recommend the use of sample cutters to keep samples consistent. In this case, by the next day, the plant manager had equipped the QC lab with a set of these cutters.

FIGURE 8-32 A Rheometer Test for Tire Rubber

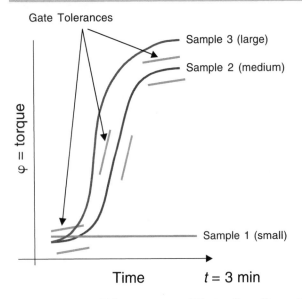

Gate Tolerances

φ = torque

Sample 3 (large)

Sample 2 (medium)

Sample 1 (small)

Time $t = 3$ min

Output Measures for an Oscillating Disc Rheometer
• Elastic Modulus
• Viscous Modulus
• Tangent Delta
• Cure Rate

Sampling Results:
Samples 1 and 3 fails test
Sample 2 passes test

Rheometer Plots for One Batch of Rubber

8.5.2 Accuracy—A Calibration Issue

Accuracy can only be determined by repeatedly measuring a standard with a known true value. Figure 8-33 shows data that have been collected to determine if a certain weighing device is accurate. The test involves placing a 454-gram **NIST** (National Institute of Standards and Technology) **certified standard** weight repeatedly on the set of scales and recording the results. A total of thirty measurements were taken, and two individuals (X) control charts were constructed. The control limits on the charts are based on a two-point moving range chart (not shown), which was in statistical control.

NIST Certified Standard

Each X chart answers a different question. The first chart is used to determine whether the process is biased. The centerline and control limits on this X chart are those that theoretically would apply under the assumption that the process average is equal to the true value of 454 grams. Because this chart is out of control, there is statistical evidence to suggest that the assumed process average is incorrect. Two points are out of control, and there is a violation of the seven-point run rule. The scales clearly need to be recalibrated, but by how much? This is the question that is answered by the second X chart.

The second chart is constructed to determine whether the process is stable and whether its operating parameters can be estimated. Figure 8-33 shows this chart to be in control with a centerline equal to 455.2. One can conclude that the scales being tested are positively biased, producing measurements that on the average are more than one gram heavier than the true value.

FIGURE 8-33 A Test for Accuracy

Measurement	Weights of 454-g Standard	Measurement	Weights of 454-g Standard
1	456.71	16	453.85
2	453.29	17	454.74
3	455.24	18	455.67
4	453.84	19	453.18
5	455.45	20	454.82
6	455.25	21	457.69
7	455.66	22	455.41
8	455.36	23	454.35
9	455.40	24	454.28
10	453.74	25	455.63
11	456.42	26	456.31
12	454.91	27	455.94
13	455.21	28	454.75
14	457.86	29	454.62
15	456.59	30	453.81

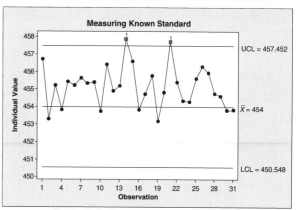

Testing Whether Average = True Value

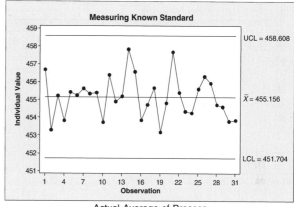

Actual Average of Process

If a measurement process is to be used to measure a range of magnitudes, it is important to test for linearity.

Linearity

Pseudostandard

Calibration of a measurement process should be performed using standards that are close to the values that are to be measured. That is, a weighing process like the one illustrated can be accurate when weighing one-pound (454 gram) units, but biased when weighing anything considerably lighter or heavier. If a measurement process is to be applied across a wide interval of values, it is important to test for **linearity**, as demonstrated in Figure 8-34. A linear process can hold its calibration across a variety of magnitudes. If a measurement process is not linear, it is advisable to restrict its use to those measures where the calibration holds.

A standard is needed to determine accuracy. However, a certified standard does not always exist. In some cases, it is possible to create an in-house **pseudostandard**. This is production material that has been set aside for the purpose of calibrating measurement processes. Use of a pseudostandard does not eliminate bias. However, the pseudostandard will ensure any bias that is present will be consistent over time.

FIGURE 8-34 Test for Linearity

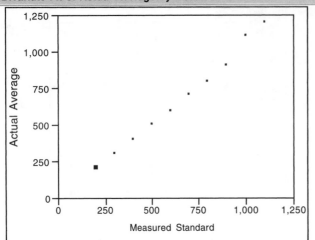

Plot of Average Measures Against Standards Measured

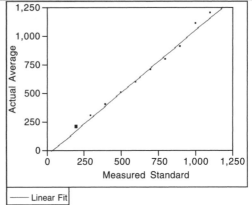

8.5.3 Precision—How to Capture Measurement Error

Figure 8-35 depicts the components of any measurement. The number that is recorded is comprised of the *true mean* of the process plus a *process variability* component plus *measurement error*. Measurement error can be further decomposed into

Measurement error consists of bias, repeatability error, and reproducibility error.

- The variability that is due to bias
- A component due to using different operators, devices, or locations called the *reproducibility effect*
- A component due to replication (or random) effects called the *repeatability effect*

Repeatability

Reproducibility

All the sources of variability combine (the variances are additive) to form the total observed variance. The concepts of **repeatability** and **reproducibility** are simple. Repeatability error means that one person who takes numerous measurements with the same measuring device will not always get the same answer. Reproducibility error

FIGURE 8-35 Anatomy of a Measurement

**Measured Value = True Mean of the Process + Process Variability
+ Measurement Bias + Operator Effect (Reproducibility)
+ Replication Error (Repeatability)**

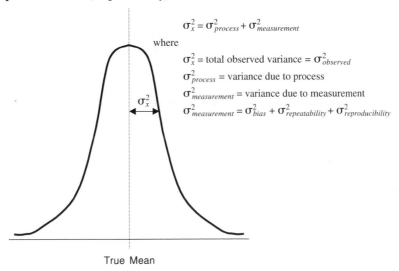

$$\sigma_x^2 = \sigma_{process}^2 + \sigma_{measurement}^2$$

where

$\sigma_x^2 =$ total observed variance $= \sigma_{observed}^2$

$\sigma_{process}^2 =$ variance due to process

$\sigma_{measurement}^2 =$ variance due to measurement

$\sigma_{measurement}^2 = \sigma_{bias}^2 + \sigma_{repeatability}^2 + \sigma_{reproducibility}^2$

True Mean

means that different people measuring the same item, or the same person using different gauges, will not always get the same answer.

The total observed variance is the variability that is captured on control charts, and is comprised of all the sources cited previously. For example, once an $\overline{X}$ chart shows a state of control, it can be assumed the R chart has captured most (if not all) the variability. Hence,

$$\sigma_x^2 = \sigma_{observed}^2 \cong \left(\frac{\overline{R}}{d_2}\right)^2 = \sigma_{process}^2 + \sigma_{measurement}^2 \tag{8-34}$$

$$\sigma_{measurement}^2 = \sigma_{bias}^2 + \sigma_{reproducibility}^2 + \sigma_{repeatability}^2 \tag{8-35}$$

What one wants is an estimate of $\sigma_{process}^2$. If a measurement process is calibrated properly, $\sigma_{bias}^2 \cong 0$ and $\sigma_{measurement}^2 = \sigma_{repeatability}^2 + \sigma_{reproducibility}^2$. If $\sigma_{measurement}^2$ can be reliably estimated, Equation 8-34 can be used to compute the value of $\sigma_{process}^2$ from $\sigma_{observed}^2$.

To illustrate how this may be done, return to the previous example of the 454-gram standard weight. Assume in the production environment two operators, Jack and Jane, are required to perform these measurements. Jack works first shift, and Jane covers the second. It is decided to conduct a measurement study as part of the routine inspection duties of these two operators. In the production environment, each operator is asked to weigh a sample four times per hour, at fifteen-minute intervals. They each record the results of thirty samples taken during a normal shift. For the measurement study, they have been asked to weigh the certified standard twice, immediately after they have taken their production sample. Special data collection

FIGURE 8-36 Measurement Study

#			#		
1	454.23	456.92	16	454.50	456.61
	455.23	452.38		453.22	454.64
2	455.82	456.35	17	453.79	454.23
	452.95	454.49		452.87	455.33
3	453.72	453.14	18	454.99	453.60
	454.01	454.25		453.08	454.54
4	454.39	452.21	19	454.00	451.94
	453.43	453.12		454.90	452.52
5	452.77	454.23	20	454.92	456.10
	454.92	454.97		453.32	452.49
6	452.61	453.81	21	455.80	452.27
	454.05	454.15		454.32	452.98
7	453.60	452.81	22	455.01	452.97
	454.89	453.55		453.59	453.43
8	453.86	455.85	23	452.93	452.86
	453.99	453.15		453.28	453.84
9	451.05	453.66	24	455.15	453.25
	454.78	453.91		453.95	456.33
10	453.66	455.31	25	452.79	453.22
	454.40	456.12		454.50	455.93
11	453.33	453.88	26	453.39	456.34
	454.51	453.40		452.66	455.84
12	453.70	452.72	27	454.53	450.89
	455.26	452.66		452.96	451.44
13	453.36	456.37	28	451.42	453.32
	455.35	451.68		452.38	453.27
14	455.33	454.64	29	452.97	455.52
	454.65	456.16		454.66	454.53
15	453.89	454.78	30	454.71	453.30
	454.05	455.79		453.01	454.74

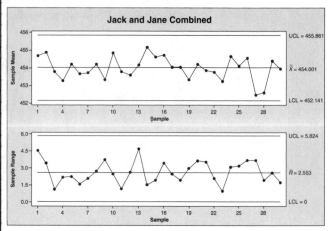

$$\sigma^2_{bias} \cong 0$$

$$\sigma^2_{measurement} \cong \left(\frac{\overline{R}}{d_2}\right)^2 = \left(\frac{2.553}{2.059}\right)^2 = (1.234)^2 = 1.537$$

forms are provided for this purpose. As Figure 8-36 shows, the range and the $\overline{X}$ chart are both in control. Because the $\overline{X}$ chart is centered at 454 grams, one can conclude that there is no bias and that the measurement process is accurate. The samples have been designed to include measurements from both operators so the ranges capture both the repeatability and reproducibility components of measurement error. Using Equation 8-35 and the fact that both charts are in control, measurement error can be estimated by

$$\sigma^2_{measurement} = \left(\frac{\overline{R}}{d_2}\right)^2 = \left(\frac{2.553}{2.059}\right)^2 = 1.537$$

The QC director was interested in learning how much of the measurement variation was due to the operator effect and how much is due to replication effect. The director decided to stratify the data collected, separating Jack's samples from Jane's. The resulting control charts are shown in Figure 8-37. From these charts it appears that, although neither Jane nor Jack are introducing any bias into the measurements, they are different with respect to their individual precision. In this case, it appears that Jane is less precise than Jack.

Observing this, the QC director decided to plot Jack's and Jane's respective data on different control charts. These charts show that Jane is not only less precise than Jack, but her chart also shows evidence that her measurement process is not stable. Refer to Figure 8-38. Jack is an experienced operator, so his results came as no surprise. The QC director therefore decided to use Jack's performance to estimate the gauge repeatability error. From this, the reproducibility error can be easily calculated using Equation 8-35.

FIGURE 8-37 Combining Two Operators on One Chart

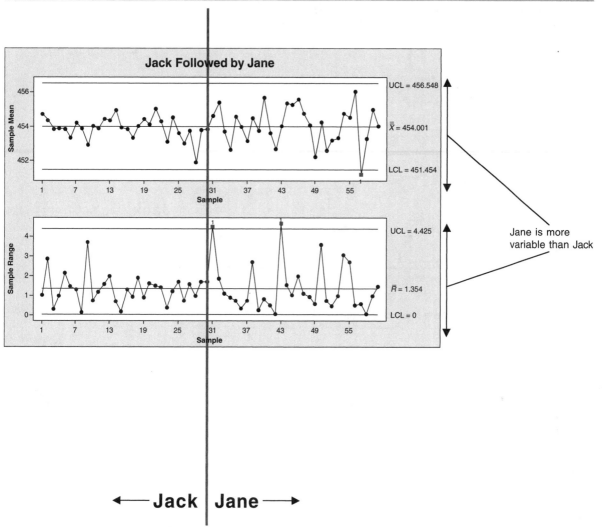

$$\sigma^2_{reproducibility} = 1.537 - (1.08)^2 = 0.371$$

$$\frac{\sigma^2_{reproducibility}}{\sigma^2_{measurement}} = \frac{0.371}{1.537} = 0.241 \tag{8-36}$$

Equation 8-36 shows that approximately 24% of the measurement error is due to differences between the operators. The next issue is whether $\sigma_{measurement} = 1.234$ should be of concern. Figure 8-39 shows some production data accumulated over time, some by Jack and some by Jane. There is no information as to who collected which sample. As both control charts are in control, $\sigma_{observed} \cong 14.60$. It is important to know whether the measurement error is a significant component of this observed variation because, if it is, one could mistake measurement variation for process variation and

FIGURE 8-38 Independent Charts for Measurement Data

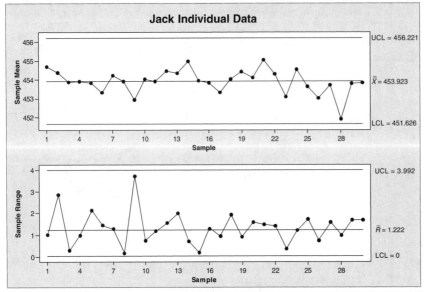

Jack $\sigma_{Jack} \cong \dfrac{\bar{R}}{d_2} = \dfrac{1.222}{1.128} = 1.08$
in control

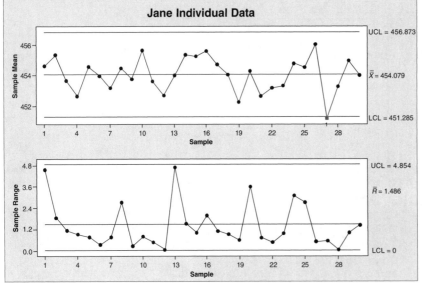

Jane $\sigma_{Jane} \cong \dfrac{\bar{R}}{d_2} = \dfrac{1.486}{1.128} = 1.32$
out of control

overcontrol the process. As a result, operators could make unneeded process adjustments and unwittingly add variability to the resulting output.

Signal-to-Noise Ratio The **signal-to-noise ratio** (SNR), Equation 8-37, is a convenient measure of the relative size of a measurement error. Another convenient measure is ρ, defined by Equation 8-38, representing the total percentage of the observed variation that is due to the process. The square of the reciprocal of the SNR, which is $1 - \rho$, Equation 8-39, represents the percentage of the observed variation that is due to measurement error. All these statistics can provide insight as to whether the size of the measurement error is large enough to cause concern.

FIGURE 8-39 Production Data

$$SNR = \frac{\sigma_{observed}}{\sigma_{measurement}} = \frac{14.60}{1.268} = 12.94$$

$$\left(\frac{1}{SNR}\right)^2 = \frac{\sigma^2_{measurement}}{\sigma^2_{observed}} = \frac{1.607}{(14.60)^2} = 0.0075 \Rightarrow$$

0.75% of observed variation is due to measurement error

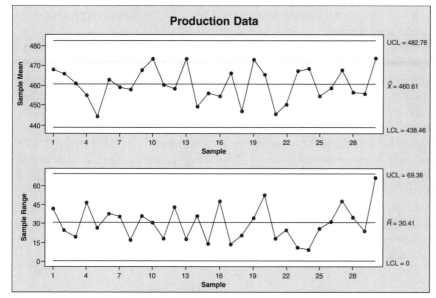

$$\sigma_{observed} \cong \frac{\bar{R}}{d_2} = \frac{30.07}{2.059} = 14.60$$

$$\sigma^2_{observed} = \sigma^2_{process} + \sigma^2_{measurement}$$

$$\sigma^2_{process} = (14.60)^2 - 1.607 = 211.55$$

$$\sigma_{process} = \sqrt{211.55} = 14.54$$

$$\text{SNR} = \frac{\sigma_{observed}}{\sigma_{measurement}} \qquad \text{(8-37)}$$

$$\rho = \frac{\sigma^2_{process}}{\sigma^2_{observed}} \qquad \text{(8-38)}$$

$$1 - \rho = \left(\frac{1}{\text{SNR}}\right)^2 = \frac{\sigma^2_{measurement}}{\sigma^2_{observed}} \qquad \text{(8-39)}$$

RULES OF THUMB

A signal-to-noise ratio greater than 10 is ideal.

If $\text{SNR} \geq 10$ $(1 - \rho \leq 0.01)$, the measurement error can be considered negligible with respect to the size of the process variation. The process variation can be estimated from the observed variation, provided the process is stable with respect to average and variability.

If $4.5 \leq \text{SNR} < 10$ $(0.01 < 1 - \rho \leq 0.05)$, measurement error may affect the ability to differentiate between dissimilar units of output. It may be advisable to take at least two measurements of each sampling unit and average them, rather than use individual measures. The measurement error should be subtracted from the observed variation to estimate the process variation.

If $\text{SNR} < 4.5$ $(0.05 < 1 - \rho)$, the measurement process has an inadequate ability to differentiate between dissimilar units of output.

If the SNR > 10, less than 1% of the total observed variation is due to measurement error. As Figure 8-39 shows, Jack and Jane's SNR is approximately equal to 13, and the measurement error represents only about three-fourths of 1% of the total observed variation. When Equation 8-34 is used to compute the process variability, it can be seen that the measurement error is negligible ($\sigma_{process} = 14.54 \cong 14.60 = \sigma_{observed}$). Once it is determined that the SNR > 10 and the measurement error is negligible, it is not necessary to subtract $\sigma_{measurement}$ from $\sigma_{observed}$ to estimate $\sigma_{process}$. It is appropriate to assume $\sigma_{observed}$ provides a good approximation to $\sigma_{process}$ if both the $\overline{X}$ and R charts are in a state of statistical control.

Discrimination

Resolution

Other considerations in determining the quality of a measurement process are **discrimination** and **resolution**. Discrimination is the ability to differentiate between units of output. Resolution refers to the smallest quantity unit that can be measured. If the resolution is low, discrimination is likely to be poor. Refer to the data in Figure 8-40. This data were collected on the diameter of twelve-inch wafers at a semiconductor plant. A total of twenty-five samples were taken of four measurements each. The first column in Figure 8-40 represents the measurements taken and recorded to the nearest 1,000th of an inch. The second column are the same measurements, but with the reduced resolution to the nearest 100th of an inch. The final column records the measurements to the nearest 10th of an inch.

Discrimination is the ability to differentiate between units of output.

Figure 8-41 provides a comparison of the charts for the three different measuring devices. Control charts (A), with resolution to the nearest 1,000th of an inch, provide good discrimination of parts. Because both (A) charts show good control, the process standard deviation can be estimated by

Resolution is the smallest quantity that can be measured.

$$\sigma_{process} \cong \frac{\overline{R}}{d_2} = \frac{0.0118}{2.059} = 0.00573 \text{ inches}$$

However, charts (B) and (C), with resolutions of 100th of an inch and 10th of an inch, respectively, are inadequate. Notable in these charting pairs are the low number of discreet values that show up on the range charts; on the (C) range chart, numerous ranges of zero appear. If the measuring process underlying charts (B) were to be used, the estimate for the process variability would be

$$\sigma_{process} \cong \frac{\overline{R}}{d_2} = \frac{0.040}{2.059} = 0.00680 \text{ inches} \Rightarrow 18.7\% \text{ higher than chart (A) results}$$

If the charts (C) process were employed, the results would be worse:

$$\sigma_{process} \cong \frac{\overline{R}}{d_2} = \frac{0.0720}{2.059} = 0.03497 \text{ inches} \Rightarrow 510.3\% \text{ higher than chart (A) results}$$

RULES OF THUMB

There is inadequate discrimination if the measurement process produces

- Three or fewer discreet values on the R chart
- Four discreet values on the range chart, and 25% or more of the ranges equal zero

---

FIGURE 8-40 Measurement Devices with Different Levels of Resolution in Measuring Wafer Diameters.

Sample	Measuring Device			Sample	Measuring Device		
	Nearest 1,000th of an inch	Nearest 100th of an inch	Nearest 10th of an inch		Nearest 1,000th of an inch	Nearest 100th of an inch	Nearest 10th of an inch
1	12.140	12.14	12.1	14	12.132	12.13	12.1
	12.146	12.15	12.2		12.144	12.14	12.1
	12.135	12.14	12.1		12.147	12.15	12.2
	12.146	12.15	12.2		12.143	12.14	12.1
2	12.146	12.15	12.2	15	12.134	12.13	12.1
	12.145	12.15	12.2		12.143	12.14	12.1
	12.137	12.14	12.1		12.138	12.14	12.1
	12.144	12.14	12.1		12.145	12.15	12.2
3	12.140	12.14	12.1	16	12.142	12.14	12.1
	12.131	12.13	12.1		12.139	12.14	12.1
	12.136	12.14	12.1		12.142	12.14	12.1
	12.137	12.14	12.1		12.146	12.15	12.2
4	12.149	12.15	12.2	17	12.137	12.14	12.1
	12.141	12.14	12.1		12.132	12.13	12.1
	12.147	12.15	12.2		12.132	12.13	12.1
	12.141	12.14	12.1		12.143	12.14	12.1
5	12.130	12.13	12.1	18	12.133	12.13	12.1
	12.149	12.15	12.2		12.135	12.14	12.1
	12.143	12.14	12.1		12.136	12.14	12.1
	12.148	12.15	12.2		12.148	12.15	12.2
6	12.133	12.13	12.1	19	12.139	12.14	12.1
	12.142	12.14	12.1		12.142	12.14	12.1
	12.140	12.14	12.1		12.131	12.13	12.1
	12.141	12.14	12.1		12.144	12.14	12.1
7	12.130	12.13	12.1	20	12.130	12.13	12.1
	12.135	12.14	12.1		12.134	12.13	12.1
	12.130	12.13	12.1		12.130	12.13	12.1
	12.141	12.14	12.1		12.132	12.13	12.1
8	12.133	12.13	12.1	21	12.135	12.14	12.1
	12.149	12.15	12.2		12.138	12.14	12.1
	12.149	12.15	12.2		12.139	12.14	12.1
	12.140	12.14	12.1		12.134	12.13	12.1
9	12.136	12.14	12.1	22	12.142	12.14	12.1
	12.131	12.13	12.1		12.148	12.15	12.2
	12.147	12.15	12.2		12.138	12.14	12.1
	12.138	12.14	12.1		12.139	12.14	12.1
10	12.135	12.14	12.1	23	12.147	12.15	12.2
	12.147	12.15	12.2		12.131	12.13	12.1
	12.137	12.14	12.1		12.140	12.14	12.1
	12.144	12.14	12.1		12.146	12.15	12.2
11	12.145	12.15	12.2	24	12.138	12.14	12.1
	12.136	12.14	12.1		12.134	12.13	12.1
	12.133	12.13	12.1		12.149	12.15	12.2
	12.131	12.13	12.1		12.144	12.14	12.1
12	12.134	12.13	12.1	25	12.145	12.15	12.2
	12.148	12.15	12.2		12.143	12.14	12.1
	12.132	12.13	12.1		12.137	12.14	12.1
	12.136	12.14	12.1		12.148	12.15	12.2
13	12.145	12.15	12.2				
	12.141	12.14	12.1				
	12.139	12.14	12.1				
	12.133	12.13	12.1				

FIGURE 8-41 Charts Showing Different Levels of Discrimination. **A,** Resolution to the Nearest 1,000th of an Inch, Thirteen Different Range Vaules. **B,** Resolution to the Nearest 100th of an Inch, Three Different Range Values. **C,** Resolution to the Nearest 10th of an Inch, Two Different Range Values—28% Zeros

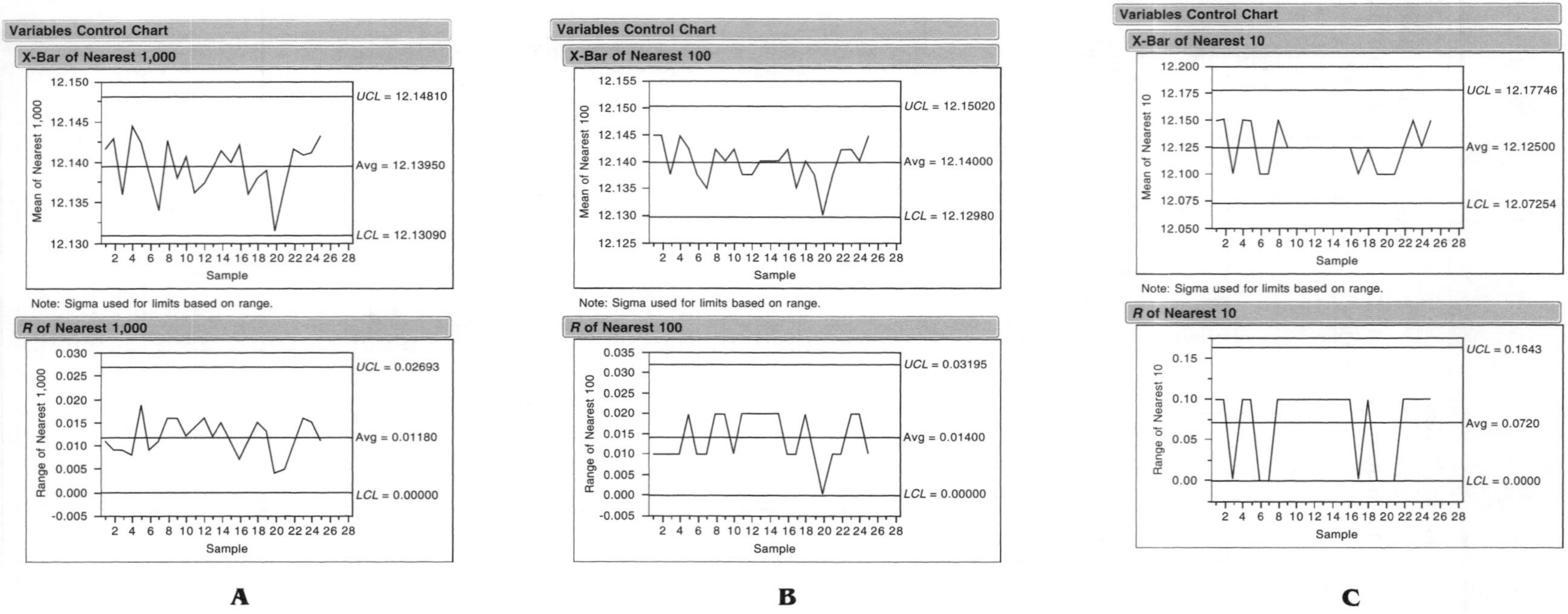
Variables Control Chart
X-Bar of Nearest 1,000
Mean of Nearest 1,000
UCL = 12.14810
Avg = 12.13950
LCL = 12.13090
Sample
Note: Sigma used for limits based on range.
R of Nearest 1,000
Range of Nearest 1,000
UCL = 0.02693
Avg = 0.01180
LCL = 0.00000
Sample
A
Variables Control Chart
X-Bar of Nearest 100
Mean of Nearest 100
UCL = 12.15020
Avg = 12.14000
LCL = 12.12980
Sample
Note: Sigma used for limits based on range.
R of Nearest 100
Range of Nearest 100
UCL = 0.03195
Avg = 0.01400
LCL = 0.00000
Sample
B
Variables Control Chart
X-Bar of Nearest 10
Mean of Nearest 10
UCL = 12.17746
Avg = 12.12500
LCL = 12.07254
Sample
Note: Sigma used for limits based on range.
R of Nearest 10
Range of Nearest 10
UCL = 0.1643
Avg = 0.0720
LCL = 0.0000
Sample
C

Discrimination Ratio

Measurement Capability

A discrimination ratio greater than 14 is ideal.

The **discrimination ratio** (DR), proposed by Wheeler and Lyday,[1] can be used to assess **measurement capability** and to compare measurement processes. The DR is calculated using Equations 8-40, 8-41, or 8-42.

$$DR = \sqrt{(SNR)^2(1 + \rho)} \tag{8-40}$$

$$DR = \sqrt{\frac{(1 + \rho)}{(1 - \rho)}} \tag{8-41}$$

$$DR = \sqrt{\frac{2\sigma^2_{process}}{\sigma^2_{measurement}} + 1} \tag{8-42}$$

RULES OF THUMB

If $DR \geq 14$, the measurement process has very good discrimination properties.

If $6 \leq DR < 14$, the measurement process has satisfactory discrimination properties.

If $DR < 6$, the discrimination ability of the measurement process is inadequate.

Returning to the Jack and Jane example,

$$SNR = \frac{14.60}{1.268} = 11.51$$

$$1 - \rho = \left(\frac{1}{11.51}\right)^2 = 0.00754$$

$$\rho = 1 - 0.00754 = 0.99246$$

$$DR = \sqrt{\frac{1 + 0.99246}{1 - 0.99246}} = \sqrt{261.153} = 16.25$$

For this process measurement discrimination is very good.

8.6 OPERATIONAL DEFINITIONS AND INSPECTOR CONSISTENCY

Operator Consistency

Lack of operator consistency can be a source of reproducibility error.

Operational Definitions

Testing Procedures

One source of reproducibility error concerns **operator consistency**. It is essential that everyone involved in the measurement process has a common understanding of how the data should be collected and the requirements. This is particularly important in the case of attributes measurements, where inspectors are often required to exercise judgments on whether a unit "passes" or "fails."

Before any measurement occurs, **operational definitions** should be developed and become part of the training for all personnel involved.

An operational definition is a clear, concise, detailed definition of what it takes for a particular measure to conform to requirements and **testing procedures** that are to be used. There can be no room for ambiguities or different interpretations. Adjectives, such as smooth, reliable, good, safe, red, and clean, are often used in the definition of

---

[1]Wheeler, Donald J., and Richard Lyday. *Evaluating the Measurement Process.* 2nd ed. Knoxville, TN: SPC Press, 1990.

Communicable Meaning

quality attributes. Such words have no **communicable meaning** unless they are operationally defined in terms of sampling and test results. For example, what does one mean by the word "clean?" What is clean enough for a table in a restaurant is unsatisfactory for an operating room or the manufacture of semiconductor wafers. How should cleanliness be measured? Will it be determined by merely taking samples from an operating surface (tabletop), or do air quality samples also need to be taken? Over what time period? One hour, one day, one week? Is cleanliness defined as an average condition or an instantaneous one (i.e., whenever a sample is taken)?

A certain printing plant has inspectors stationed at the end of a casing-in line to check finished books prior to packing. These inspectors look for problems with endpapers, covers, or trimming. With respect to endpapers, one inspection criterion is to check for wrinkles. It was found that not all inspectors could agree on what constituted a wrinkle. All had different and personal definitions. A wrinkle had never been operationally defined. Such differences in understanding can lead to operator inconsistencies, and drive up the magnitude of the measurement error.

Operational Definition

- A clear, concise, communicable written statement, including tangible examples, if appropriate, of what it takes for a particular attribute to conform to requirements.
- A set of decision criteria that can be used to determine whether an attribute conforms to requirements that include specified sampling plans, test methods, and measurement procedures.
- The ability to clearly differentiate between acceptable and unacceptable results so a clear yes or no decision can always be made on the basis of the requirements and the decision criteria.

How can inspector consistency be checked? The QC director in a certain assembly plant selected twenty parts, which she numbered and then carefully inspected herself. According to her criteria, she rejected parts numbered 1, 4, 8, 11, 14, and 16 and accepted the rest. After recording her personal results, she had three qualified inspectors independently inspect the same sample. If any part was rejected, the inspector was asked to indicate by code the reason for the rejection. Figure 8-42 shows a summary of the data that had been compiled at the end of the experiment. Needless, although disappointing, these results were enlightening to the QC director.

Two of the three inspectors rejected part number one, but for different reasons. Only inspector number one agreed with the QC director on the reason for the rejection. Inspector number three passed part number 1. Part numbers 4 and 14 were rejected by the director and accepted by all three inspectors. In contrast, part number 6 was acceptable to the director but rejected by two of the inspectors. Only one of the three inspectors agreed with the director on the unacceptability of part number 8. Inspector number three believed parts 12 and 17 should be defective, and inspector number two rejected part number 20 in error. All inspectors agreed on the rejection of part number 11, but for different reasons.

Much can be learned from studying data such as these. Misunderstandings are highlighted, and training needs can be readily identified. Even if an organization thinks that sufficient definitions are in place, it is a good idea to test them to ensure they are understood the same way by those whom the organization trusts for its quality control.

FIGURE 8-42 Inspector Consistency

Test Unit	Inspector	Accept	Reject	Reason Code	QC Reason Code
1	1		x	32	
	2		x	36	32
	3	x			
2	1	x			
	2	x			
	3		x	36	
3	1	x			
	2	x			
	3	x			
4	1	x			32
	2	x			
	3	x			
5	1	x			
	2	x			
	3	x			
6	1	x			
	2		x	23	
	3		x	23	
7	1	x			
	2	x			
	3	x			
8	1		x	41	41
	2	x			
	3	x			
9	1	x			
	2	x			
	3	x			
10	1	x			
	2	x			
	3	x			

Test Unit	Inspector	Accept	Reject	Reason Code	QC Reason Code
11	1		x	40	41
	2		x	40	
	3		x	40	
12	1	x			
	2	x			
	3		x	45	
13	1	x			
	2	x			
	3	x			
14	1	x			46
	2	x			
	3	x			
15	1	x			
	2	x			
	3	x			
16	1		x	32	32
	2		x	32	
	3		x	31	
17	1	x			
	2	x			
	3		x	25	
18	1	x			
	2	x			
	3	x			
19	1	x			
	2	x			
	3	x			
20	1	x			
	2		x	23	
	3	x			

Note: Shading means the test unit was rejected by the QC Director. QC, quality control.

289

8.7 PROCESS CAPABILITY

8.7.1 Engineering Tolerance, Natural Tolerance, and Process Capability

Engineering tolerance is the difference in specification limits.

If a process is in statistical control and producing some unacceptable output, it may be because the process average (target) is too high or too low, or it may be that the process is incapable of consistently producing output that meets requirements. Some basic definitions are necessary to properly understand the concept of process capability. The first of these is **engineering tolerance** (ET). The ET is the difference between the highest acceptable measurement, the upper tolerance limit (UTL), and the lowest acceptable measurement, the lower tolerance limit (LTL). That is,

Engineering Tolerance

$$ET = UTL - LTL \tag{8-43}$$

The tolerance limits are also referred to as specification limits. Note that the ET is established by design and has nothing to do with where the process is performing at any point in time.

Natural Tolerance

The second definition that is important is the **natural tolerance** (NT). The NT is the spread of a process that is in statistical control and is considered to be equal to approximately six process standard deviations. Then,

$$NT = 6\sigma_x \tag{8-44}$$

The natural tolerance of a process is approximately equal to six standard deviations.

A process is capable if NT ≤ ET. If NT > ET, some defective product will be produced unless some of the common cause variability sources can be identified and removed. This will usually require fundamental system improvements. Centering the process cannot eliminate defective output. However, a process that is not capable will produce the minimum out-of-tolerance product if it is centered exactly between the tolerance limits. **Process capability** is illustrated in Figure 8-43.

Process Capability

8.7.2 Capability Indices

The following indices are commonly used to evaluate capability.

1. $C_p = \dfrac{ET}{NT}$ (8-45)

C_p is a measure of whether the tolerance limits are wider than the process natural tolerance.

If $C_p \geq 1$, the process is said to be capable.

2. $C_r = \dfrac{1}{C_p} = \dfrac{NT}{ET}$ (8-46)

C_r represents what proportion of the tolerance interval is "used up" by the process spread.

3. $C_{pk} = \text{minimum } \{C_{pu}, C_{pl}\}$ (8-47)

where

$$C_{pu} = \frac{|UTL - \mu|}{3\sigma_x} \text{ and } C_{pl} = \frac{|LTL - \mu|}{3\sigma_x}$$

C_{pk} measures not only whether the ET ≥ NT, but also process centering and whether requirements are actually being met.

FIGURE 8-43 Process Capability

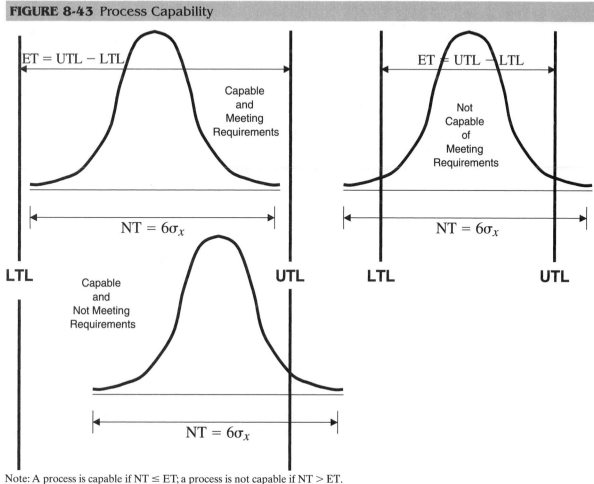

Note: A process is capable if NT ≤ ET; a process is not capable if NT > ET.

            is an index that expresses the distance from the process center (mean) to the closest tolerance limit, expressed in multiples of three standard deviations.

$C_{pk} = 1$ means that the process center lies exactly three standard deviations from the nearest tolerance limit.

$C_{pk} \geq 1$ means that there are fewer than 2,700 defective parts per million produced.

$C_{pk} \geq 1.33$ means that there are fewer than 63 defective parts per million produced.

$C_{pk} \geq 1.67$ means that there are fewer than 1 defective part per 2 million produced.

$C_{pk} \geq 2$ means that there are fewer than 1 defective part per 500 million produced.

A $C_{pk} = 2$ is the aim of Six Sigma.

    Although processes with a C_p or $C_{pk} = 1$ are generally regarded as being capable, competitiveness may demand much higher values. The object of Six Sigma programs, discussed in Chapter 9, is to achieve C_{pk}s of 2 or better for all critical processes.

Two additional capability indices are worth mentioning.

4. $C_{pm} = \dfrac{\text{ET}}{6\sigma_{\text{Target}}}$ (8-48)

where $\sigma_{\text{Target}} = \sqrt{\dfrac{\displaystyle\sum_{i=1}^{n}(x_i - \text{Target})^2}{n - 1}}$ is the standard deviation of the data with respect to the target.

C_{pm} is a measure of whether the tolerance limits are wide enough to compensate for a process center that is not equal to the target.

If $C_{pm} \geq 1$, the process is said to be capable.

5. $P_{pk} = \text{minimum}\{P_{pu}, P_{pl}\}$ (8-49)

where

$$P_{pu} = \frac{|\text{UTL} - \mu|}{3\sigma_i} \text{ and } P_{pl} = \frac{|\text{LTL} - \mu|}{3\sigma_i}$$

and

$$\sigma_i = \sqrt{\frac{\displaystyle\sum_{i=1}^{n}(x_i - \bar{\bar{x}})^2}{n - 1}} = \text{computed variability in entire data set}$$

(σ_i includes both within-sample and between-sample variability.)

P_{pk} is similar to C_{pk}. The only difference is how the process standard deviation is estimated.

The P_{pk} index is useful when it is difficult to achieve good control on sample ranges or standard deviations. Examples are new products or processes, short runs, or where control cannot be established.

For stable processes, the C_{pk} is a better measure of capability that can be sustained.

A $P_{pk} \geq 1$ means that the process center lies exactly three standard deviations from the nearest tolerance limit.

A $P_{pk} = 2$ is the aim of Six Sigma.

Figure 8-44 provides a conceptual comparison of the different capability indices.

Wizard, Inc., manufactures a certain product with a specified design tolerance of 13 ± 3. $\bar{X}$ and R charts are used to monitor the process, and both charts are in control. The $\bar{X}$ chart has a centerline equal to 13.4 and the R chart's centerline is equal to 2.45. The sample size is four. The standard deviation for the last ten samples (forty measurements) is equal to 1.29, and the standard deviation for those measurements with respect to the target is equal to 1.44.

$$\sigma_x = \frac{\bar{R}}{d_2} = \frac{2.45}{2.059} = 1.19$$

$$\text{ET} = \text{UTL} - \text{LTL} = 16 - 10 = 6.0$$

$$\text{NT} = 6\sigma_x = 6(1.19) = 7.14$$

$$C_p = \frac{\text{ET}}{\text{NT}} = \frac{6}{7.14} = 0.84 \Rightarrow \text{not capable}$$

FIGURE 8-44 Capability Indices

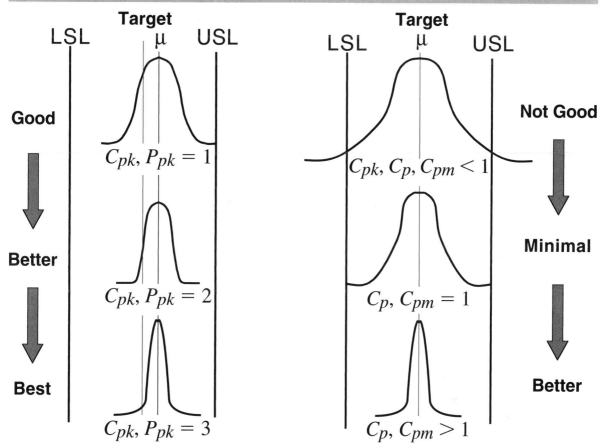

$$C_r = \frac{1}{C_p} = \frac{1}{.84} = 1.19$$

$$C_{pk} = \text{minimum}\{C_{pu}, C_{pl}\}$$

where

$$C_{pu} = \frac{|\text{UTL} - \overline{\overline{X}}|}{3\sigma_x} = \frac{|16 - 13.4|}{3(1.19)} = 0.73$$

$$C_{pl} = \frac{|\text{LTL} - \overline{\overline{X}}|}{3\sigma_x} = \frac{|10 - 13.4|}{3(1.19)} = 0.95$$

$$C_{pk} = \text{minimum } \{0.73, 0.95\} = 0.73 \Rightarrow \text{process is}$$
not capable and not meeting requirements

$$C_{pm} = \frac{\text{ET}}{6\sigma_{\text{target}}} = \frac{6}{6(1.44)} = 0.69 \Rightarrow \text{not capable}$$

$$P_{pk} = \text{minimum}\{P_{pu}, P_{pl}\}$$

where

$$P_{pu} = \frac{|UTL - \overline{\overline{X}}|}{3\sigma_i} = \frac{|16 - 13.4|}{3(1.29)} = 0.67$$

$$P_{pl} = \frac{|LTL - \overline{\overline{X}}|}{3\sigma_i} = \frac{|10 - 13.4|}{3(1.29)} = 0.88$$

$$C_{pk} = \text{minimum}\{0.67, 0.88\} = 0.67 \Rightarrow \text{process is}$$
$$\text{not capable and not meeting requirements}$$

8.7.3 Estimating Defective Parts per Million Opportunities

When a process is stable, its mean and standard deviation can be estimated with statistical confidence. Using Table A in the appendix, Equations 8-45 to 8-49 can then be applied to compute capability indices and to estimate the number of defective parts per million opportunities (DPMO). Table A is based on normal probabilities and, before accessing the table, the upper and lower z scores are computed using the following equations:

$$z_u = \frac{|UTL - \overline{\overline{X}}|}{\sigma_x} \qquad \text{(8-50)}$$

$$z_l = \frac{|LTL - \overline{\overline{X}}|}{\sigma_x} \qquad \text{(8-51)}$$

Returning to the Wizard problem,

$$z_u = \frac{|16 - 13.4|}{1.19} = 2.18$$

$$z_l = \frac{|10 - 13.4|}{1.19} = 2.86$$

Finding $z_u = 2.18$ and $z_l = 2.86$ in Table A, we discover that the process is producing 14,628 DPMO outside the upper tolerance limit and 2,118 DFMO outside the lower tolerance limit. The DPMOs can be easily converted to percentages by moving the decimal point four places to the left. Hence, the process is producing approximately 1.46% off-tolerance on the high side and 0.2% on the low side. If we subtract the total percent defective from 100, we have the process yield—in this case, yield = $100 - (1.46 + .2) = 98.34\%$. This is a short-term capability. Whether this performance can be sustained over time is questionable. In Six Sigma, long-term performance is differentiated from short-term capability through a mean-shift allowance. The assumption is that, even for a process in control, a 1.5σ drift in the mean is likely over time. In this example, the Six Sigma score would be 2.18 (select the smallest z) $-1.5 = 0.68$. Looking this revised z up in Table A, we discover that in the long term we could expect the process to produce 248,252 DFMO—nearly one defective in four. Six Sigma is covered in detail in Chapter 9.

8.8 QUALITY IN THE SERVICE SECTOR

Measuring quality in the service sector presents some unique challenges. It is often not possible to take samples of process outputs, and many of the important attributes must be measured qualitatively. When quantitative data are available, it is typically in the

Measures in a
service environment
are typically
nominal or ordinal.

form of attributes data (measured on the nominal or ordinal scales), or if variables data is nonnormal and does not necessarily address QC from the customers' perspectives (e.g., the time it takes to serve a table at a restaurant).

8.8.1 SERVQUAL

SERVQUAL

Assurance

Empathy

Reliability

Responsiveness

Tangibles

SERVQUAL is a methodology that can be used to measure service quality. It relies on a customer's ability to qualitatively "score" performance in five areas: **assurance, empathy, reliability, responsiveness**, and **tangibles**.[2] As an example, SERVQUAL has been used to determine how patrons assess desired, adequate, and perceived levels of service at four types of restaurants (Chinese, casual dining, full service, and quick service) at the Hong Kong International Airport.[3] Other applications include how to improve the quality of service in the pest control industry,[4] to bring about cultural and structural change in the Australian Public Sector,[5] to determine service levels in banking,[6] and to generate quality initiatives for the consultancy and technology transfer wing of a major educational institution in India.[7]

The idea behind SERVQUAL is that any customer in a service environment has certain expectations. The quality of service actually received is a perception relative to those expectations. If the quality does not meet expectations, the difference is called a *gap,* and the assessment of quality is based on measuring this gap.[8] The SERVQUAL measuring tool is a survey that captures what the customer expects of the service and what the customer perceives was actually delivered. Table 8-4 illustrates a typical SERVQUAL survey instrument.

Alternative criteria can be used to develop a customer questionnaire that may fit a particular application better than the SERVQUAL performance areas. For example, Singh and Deshmukh suggested what customers care the most about are[9]

Prompt Service

**Understanding of
Customer Needs**

**Undivided
Attention**

Courtesy

Interest

Helpfulness

- **Prompt service**
- **Understanding of customer needs**
- Complete and **undivided attention** by the service provider
- **Courtesy** and polite treatment
- Expression of **interest** in the customer
- Expression of proactive **helpfulness**

[2]Parsuraman, A., Leonard L. Berry, and Valarie A. Ziethaml. "Refinement and Reassessment of the SERVQUAL Scale." *Journal of Retailing* 67, no. 4 (Winter 1991): 420–50.

[3]Heung, Vincent C. S., M. Y. Wong, and Hailin Qu. "Airport-Restaurant Service Quality in Hong Kong: An Application of SERVQUAL." *Cornell Hotel and Restaurant Administration Quarterly* 41, no. 3 (June 2000): 86–96.

[4]Ninichuck, Bryan. "Service Quality Is the Key to Good Business." *Pest Control* 69, no. 9 (September 2001): 12–13.

[5]McDonnell, John, and Terry Gatfield. SERVQUAL as a Cultural Change Agent in the Public Sector, 1528–38. ANZMAC98 Conference Proceedings. Brisbane, Australia. University of Otago, 1998. Also available online at http://130.195.95.71:8081/www/ANZMAC1998/Cd_rom/McDonnell278.pdf (accessed April 6, 2005).

[6]Hussey, Michael K. "Using the Concept of Loss: An Alternative SERVQUAL Measure." *The Service Industries Journal* 19, no. 4 (October 1999): 89–101.

[7]Singh, Saurabh, and S. G. Deshmukh. "Quality Initiatives in the Service Sector: A Case." *Total Quality Management* 10, no. 1 (January 1999): 5–16.

[8]Parsuraman, A., Valarie A. Zeithaml, and Leonard L. Berry. "SERVQUAL—A Multiple-Item Scale for Measuring Consumer Perceptions of Service Quality." *Journal of Retailing* 64, no. 1 (Spring 1988): 12–40.

[9]Ibid, 5–16.

TABLE 8-4 SERVQUAL Survey Instrument

Perceptions (P)	Expectations (E)	
Directions: The following set of statements relates to your feelings about XYZ Company's service. For each statement, show the extent to which you believe XYZ has the feature described by the statement. Score the statement "1" if you strongly disagree that XYZ has that feature and a "7" if you strongly agree. Any numbers in the middle may be used to indicate how strong your feelings are. There are no right or wrong answers—we are only interested in the number that best shows your perceptions about XYZ's service.	**Directions:** Based on your experience as a customer of companies in this business, think about the kind of company that would deliver excellent quality of service. Think about the kind of company with which you would be pleased to do business. Show the extent to which you believe such a company would possess the feature described by each statement listed here. If you believe a statement is not essential for excellent companies, score the statement "1". If you believe the feature is absolutely essential for an excellent company, score the feature "7". If your feelings are less strong, provide a score somewhere in the middle. There are no right or wrong answers—we are only interested in the number that truly reflects your feelings regarding companies that would deliver excellent quality of service.	$Q = P - E$

	Tangibles	1	2	3	4	5	6	7	Tangibles	1	2	3	4	5	6	7	
1	XYZ Company has modern-looking equipment.								Excellent companies in this business will have modern-looking equipment.								
2	The facilities at XYZ Company are visually appealing.								The physical facilities at excellent companies in this business will be visually appealing.								
3	The employees of XYZ Company are neat appearing.								Employees of excellent companies in this business will be neat appearing.								
4	Materials associated with the service (such as pamphlets or statements) are visually appealing in XYZ Company.								Materials associated with the service (such as pamphlets or statements) will be visually appealing in an excellent company in this business.								
	Reliability	**1**	**2**	**3**	**4**	**5**	**6**	**7**	**Reliability**	**1**	**2**	**3**	**4**	**5**	**6**	**7**	
5	When the XYZ Company promises to do something by a certain time, it does so.								When excellent companies in this business promise to do something by a certain time, they will do so.								
6	When you have a problem, XYZ Company shows a sincere interest in solving it.								When customers have a problem, excellent companies in this business will show a sincere interest in solving it.								

	Reliability	1	2	3	4	5	6	7	*Reliability*	1	2	3	4	5	6	7	
7	The XYZ Company performs the service right the first time.								Excellent companies in this business will perform the service right the first time.								
8	The XYZ Company provides its services at the time it promises to do so.								Excellent companies in this business will provide their services at the time they promise to do so.								
9	The XYZ Company insists on error-free records.																
	Responsiveness	1	2	3	4	5	6	7	*Responsiveness*	1	2	3	4	5	6	7	
10	Employees of XYZ Company tell you exactly when services will be performed.								Employees of excellent companies in this business will tell customers exactly when services will be performed.								
11	Employees of XYZ Company give you prompt service.								Employees of excellent companies in this business will give prompt service to customers.								
12	Employees of XYZ Company are always willing to help you.								Employees of excellent companies in this business will always be willing to help customers.								
13	Employees of XYZ Company are never too busy to respond to your requests.								Employees of excellent companies in this business will never be too busy to respond to customer requests.								
	Assurance	1	2	3	4	5	6	7	*Assurance*	1	2	3	4	5	6	7	
14	The behavior of employees of XYZ Company instills confidence in customers.								The behavior of employees of excellent companies in this business will instill confidence in customers.								
15	You feel safe in your transactions with XYZ Company.								Customers of excellent companies in this business will feel safe in transactions.								
16	Employees of XYZ Company are consistently courteous with you.								Employees of excellent companies in this business will be consistently courteous with customers.								

(continued)

	Assurance	1	2	3	4	5	6	7	*Assurance*	1	2	3	4	5	6	7	
17	Employees of XYZ Company have the knowledge to answer your questions.								Employees of excellent companies in this business will have the knowledge to answer customers' questions.								
	Empathy	1	2	3	4	5	6	7	*Empathy*	1	2	3	4	5	6	7	
18	The XYZ Company gives you individual attention.								Excellent companies in this business will give customers individual attention.								
19	The XYZ Company has operating hours convenient to all its customers.								Excellent companies in this business will have operating hours convenient to all their customers.								
20	The XYZ Company has employees who give you personal attention.								Excellent companies in this business will have employees who give customers personal attention.								
21	The XYZ Company has your best interests at heart.								Excellent companies in this business will have the customers' best interests at heart.								
22	Employees of XYZ Company understand your specific needs.								The behavior of employees of excellent companies in this business will instill confidence in customers.								

Point Allocation Questions		
Directions: Listed here are five features pertaining to companies and the services they offer. We want to know how important each feature is to you when you evaluate a company's quality of service. Allocate a total of 100 points among the five features according to how important each feature is to you—the more important a feature is to you, the more points you should allocate to it. Ensure the points you allocate to the five features add up to 100.		**Points**
1	The appearance of the company's physical facilities, equipment, personnel, and communications materials.	
2	The ability of the company to perform the promised service dependably and accurately.	
3	The willingness of the company to help customers and provide prompt service.	
4	The knowledge and courtesy of the company's employees and their ability to convey trust and confidence.	
5	The caring, individualized attention the company provides its customers.	
TOTAL POINTS ALLOCATED		**100**

SOURCE: Adapted from A. Parsuraman, Valarie A. Zeithaml, and Leonard L. Berry, "SERVQUAL—A Multiple-Item Scale for Measuring Consumer Perceptions of Service Quality." *Journal of Retailing* 64, no. 1 (Spring 1988): 12–40.

	• Efficiency in the delivery of service
Accuracy	• **Accuracy** in the end result of service
Explanation of Procedures	• An **explanation of procedures**
	• Expression of pleasure in serving the customer

**Attention to
Complaints**

**Resolution of
Complaints**

**Acceptance of
Responsibility**

- **Attention to complaints**
- **Resolution of complaints** to the customer's satisfaction
- **Acceptance of responsibility** for personal or company errors

8.8.2 Use of Control Charts in a Services Environment

Where it is possible to use quantitative criteria, control charts can be used in a services environment in the same way they are used in a manufacturing setting. For example, if a measure of customer service is on-time deliveries (products or services delivered when promised), data could be collected and analyzed as shown in Figure 8-45. These data were collected from a random sample of five shipments per day over a thirty-day period. In this case, early deliveries were considered to be as bad as late deliveries. Therefore, the deviations from the target (equal to zero) were computed for each delivery selected for the samples. An analysis of the control charts shown in Figure 8-45 reveals the target of zero is being missed on the average by 0.43 days with a standard deviation of approximately 1.73 days ($\overline{R}/d_2 = 4.03/2.326$). The company has made a commitment to its customers that it will deliver on time within one day on either side of the promised delivery date. This two-day time window is a concept called **span** and represents the ET for delivery time. This is also the variability in process lead-time. With ET = 2 and NT = 10.38 (6σ), Equations 8-44 and 8-46 provide a $C_p = 0.193$ and a $C_{pk} = 0.109$, respectively. This company has much work to do if they are to live up to their commitments.

Span

Span is a measure of
variability in lead
time.

The type of data collected in service industries may not be normally distributed. For example, this is often true of data that are expressed in units of time or money. The data in Figure 8-46 were collected on transaction times for tellers at a local bank. As the histogram and scatter plot show, the data are not normal. Note how the points are more dispersed above the mean than below and how the points below hug the centerline.

The data was subgrouped into samples of five each, and the $\overline{X}$ and R charts shown in Figure 8-47a were constructed. The R chart is predictably out of control because the control limits are too narrow. Equations 8-3 and 8-4 underestimate the maximum and minimum ranges that would be expected for distributions that are not normal. The average range (the centerline on the R chart) is also an underestimate of the total process variability. Because the data set is not uniformly and randomly distributed about the process mean, an occasional sample will have a range that exceeds that which Equations 8-3 and 8-4 would predict. This source of variability will show up between samples rather than within samples. In this case, the between-sample variability is not due to special causes but is systemic. The approach shown in Figure 8-47b can be used to capture the common cause variability. In this approach, the $\overline{X}$s are treated as individuals and a two-point moving range chart is used to capture the variance. A control chart, constructed using the average moving range and Equations 8-20 and 8-21 to establish the limits on the $\overline{X}$ chart, exhibits statistical control. The following relationships can then be used to estimate the process standard deviation:

$$\sigma_{\overline{x}} = \frac{\overline{MR}}{d_2} = \frac{\overline{MR}}{1.128} \qquad \textbf{(8-49)}$$

$$\sigma_x^2 = n\sigma_{\overline{x}}^2 \qquad \textbf{(8-50)}$$

$$\sigma_x = \sqrt{\sigma_x^2}$$

FIGURE 8-45 Delivery Performance

Sample	Number of Days Promised	Number of Days Actual	Number of Days Deviation	Sample	Number of Days Promised	Number of Days Actual	Number of Days Deviation
1	20	21	1	6	20	24	4
	1	3	2		9	10	1
	20	20	0		13	13	0
	3	4	1		27	28	1
	22	20	-2		25	24	-1
2	4	2	-2	7	10	12	2
	18	20	2		1	4	3
	4	5	1		16	20	4
	5	5	0		16	16	0
	7	6	-1		13	13	0
3	14	15	1	8	14	15	1
	1	3	2		29	28	-1
	8	8	0		7	7	0
	6	6	0		20	21	1
	18	19	1		9	9	0
4	3	3	0	9	24	25	1
	8	6	-2		21	22	1
	16	16	0		22	24	2
	7	7	0		11	12	1
	3	6	3		4	5	1
5	18	14	-4	10	12	13	1
	13	13	0		3	3	0
	30	32	2		23	21	-2
	7	6	-1		2	5	3
	1	5	4		11	12	1

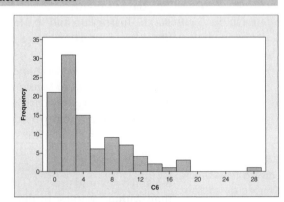

Control Charts for All 30 Days

Data for 1st 10 Days

FIGURE 8-46 Teller Transaction Times at First National Bank

Teller Transaction Times (minutes)					Range	$\overline{X}$
6.23	4.04	5.07	2.63	1.72	4.51	3.94
1.22	2.89	2.81	5.75	0.12	5.63	2.56
2.83	0.18	1.26	8.20	0.24	8.02	2.54
10.40	3.34	3.80	27.77	10.70	24.43	11.20
13.00	7.10	17.18	3.43	2.38	14.80	8.62
0.86	8.02	3.87	9.01	7.50	8.14	5.85
11.30	2.15	2.31	0.16	0.62	11.14	3.31
0.55	0.49	7.45	1.62	0.81	6.96	2.18
2.92	0.73	11.12	10.32	10.39	10.39	7.10
10.90	2.07	0.85	2.52	12.27	11.43	5.72
1.13	0.38	0.45	1.98	16.83	16.45	4.15
3.40	0.97	1.82	8.18	2.05	7.21	3.28
13.35	4.09	8.98	4.86	4.09	9.26	7.07
1.01	1.58	9.97	1.13	8.71	8.96	4.48
4.59	5.30	1.72	12.16	4.38	10.44	5.63
0.24	1.31	7.63	1.07	0.81	7.39	2.21
3.03	0.52	0.18	0.18	6.83	6.65	2.14
17.32	1.43	2.87	4.54	17.54	16.10	8.74
0.83	1.83	1.03	1.46	3.26	2.42	1.68
5.31	0.46	2.28	2.60	3.92	4.85	2.92

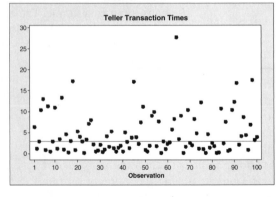

FIGURE 8-47 Teller Transaction Times. (**A**) X-bar Chart Showing Average Teller Transaction Times. (**B**) Average Teller Transaction Times Treated as Individual Measurements

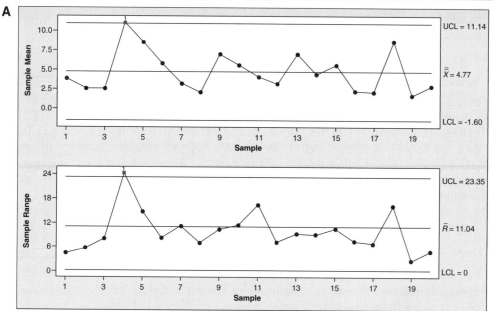

$\overline{X}$, R Charts

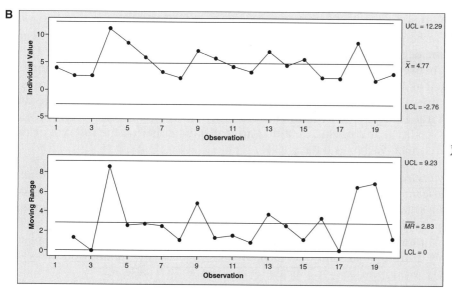

$\overline{X}$, MR Charts

$$\sigma_x = \frac{\overline{MR}}{d_2} = \frac{2.828}{1.128} = 2.507 \qquad \sigma_x^2 = \frac{\sigma_x^2}{n}$$

$$(2.507)^2 = \frac{\sigma_x^2}{5} \qquad \sigma_x^2 = 31.4276$$

$$\sigma_x = 5.606$$

This approach can be applied whenever there is reason to believe variation between samples is a natural expectation of the process, is systemic, and is not due to special causes.

8.8.3 Support Services in a Manufacturing Environment

Support Value Stream

Primary Value Stream

In a manufacturing environment, the **support value stream** exists to provide those services required by the workstations in the **primary value stream**. Many of the tools used to improve performance in the primary functions can also be applied to services. However, it is important that the right questions be asked so improvement efforts are properly focused. This often requires a shift in mind-set. Figure 8-48 shows a comparison between some old and new question sets for certain support services at a large oil refining company.

SUMMARY OF LEARNING OBJECTIVES AND KEY OUTCOMES

1. *Differentiate between nominal, ordinal, interval, and ratio scales of measurement.* Nominal, ordinal, interval, and ratio scales are listed in the order of increasing information. Nominal measures assign names or values to objects that have no numeric meaning. Quality data that are collected using the nominal scale are called attributes data. On an ordinal scale, objects with a higher value have more of some attribute than objects with a lower value. With ordinal measures, one item can be judged to be greater than, equal to, or less than another. With interval measurements, the degree of difference between objects can be determined because the intervals between adjacent scale values are equal. However, ratios cannot be compared and have no particular meaning because on an interval scale there is no natural origin, or zero point. The highest level of measurement is ratio, where there is a natural zero point. All mathematical operations can be performed on ratio data. In quality management, data that are collected either on the interval or ratio scales are called variables data.

2. *Demonstrate an understanding of the difference between special cause and common cause variability, and be able to recognize nonrandom patterns in a data set.* In any data collection scheme, a source of variation that is active in all samples is called common cause variability. A source that is active in some samples and not in others is called special cause variability. Common cause variability, for a particular sampling plan, is randomly distributed around the mean, or average, of all the samples. Special cause variability will appear on a graphical plot as a nonrandom pattern.

3. *Describe how sampling strategies have an impact on the ability to identify special and common cause sources of variability.* The sampling plan that is used will determine the common cause system. Special causes only occur in some samples and not in others. For example, if production were different in the morning than the afternoon, taking a random sample of a day's output would fail to reveal it. However, by taking separate samples in the mornings and in the afternoons, one could learn the truth.

4. *Define statistical control and be able to construct, apply, and interpret the control charts that are appropriate for different types of data sets.* A process that is in statisti-

FIGURE 8-48 Asking Relevant Questions of Support Value Chains

The Importance of Asking the Right Questions	
Accounts Payable	
Old Questions	How many checks per labor-hour are we writing?
	Can't we use temporary labor to write these checks?
New Questions	How do we know that everyone understands the procedures?
	What is the average error rate, and is it statistically stable?
	What new procedures are we going to try to lower the average error rate?
Inventory Management	
Old Questions	Can't we cut our inventories?
New Questions	What is the probability of use of the item?
	What is the cost of being without it?
	What is the optimum number to hold in inventory?
Purchasing	
Old Questions	Who has the lowest price?
	Who has the best terms?
New Questions	Is this supplier using statistical methods to ensure we get a reliable component?
	What is their capability index?
	Does their senior management use statistical thinking to make decisions?
Maintenance	
Old Questions	Can't you replace that later?
	How many people can you cut back?
New Questions	How does the cost of an online failure compare with the cost of an offline one?
	Do we have reliable data on component life?
	Is there an optimal replacement strategy?
Scheduling	
Old Questions	How long does that take, and can't you get it to us more quickly?
	What is the average delay?
New Questions	How much variability is there in that time, and what causes it?
	Is the time in statistical control?
Customer Relations	
Old Questions	What is the average number the customers will buy?
	What color do most customers buy?
	What percent of the customers prefer our product?
New Questions	How much training do the interviewers get?
	Will a postcard mail-out give us an adequate response rate?
	How complete is our sampling frame?
	What receipt control system is used?
	Are nonrespondents contacted to assess nonresponse bias?
	Do the data entry staff use a code book?
Personnel	
Old Questions	Why are those benefit checks late?
	How will we rank all these people?
New Questions	How were the procedures for paying benefit checks developed, and how do we know that everyone is following them?
	Do we have a method of identifying truly outstanding staff?
Sales	
Old Questions	Why are sales falling off?
New Questions	Have we compared the key entry error rates from the new terminals?
	Do all our sales staff understand what is meant by statistical control?
	Does our sales force receive regular updates on our statistical process control progress?

cal control is repeatable, stable, and predictable. The only sources of variability present are due to random causes that are systemic. This variability can be reliably estimated and used to determine process capability and performance. A process that is in control is one that is not significantly affected by time—process performance is the same anytime one chooses to monitor output. Practice problems are included in the problem set below to test your understanding in constructing and interpreting control charts.

5. *Explain to someone in layman's terms the difference between accuracy, precision, discrimination, and resolution.* A measuring process is accurate if repeated measurements of the same item are randomly distributed about the true value of the attribute measured. An accurate process has no bias. The process is precise if the variance of repeated measurements of the same item is small. If a single item is measured repeatedly using an accurate process, the average of all measurements will come close to the true value being measured. Discrimination is the ability to differentiate between two different items, and resolution is the smallest unit that a measuring process is capable of recording.

6. *Conduct a measurement study to identify all components of measurement error, including the calculation and interpretation of the discrimination ratio.* Measurement error consists of bias and precision error. Precision is further divided into repeatability and reproducibility errors. Repeatability is a replication error, by one operator, that can be estimated by creating a sample consisting of multiple measures of the same item. This should be repeated over time until enough samples have been generated to construct a pair of control charts. If the item measured was a known standard, the centerline of an $\overline{X}$ chart should be approximately equal to the centerline if no bias exists. If the $\overline{X}$ chart shows control, the range chart can be used to estimate repeatability error. To compute reproducibility error, a number of operators should perform the measurements described here independently, and their results should be statistically compared. The problem set that follows will test your understanding of how to isolate measurement error.

7. *Assess process capability using control charts and capability indices.* Process capability is the ability to produce within a required tolerance range, and it can only be estimated with confidence if the process is stable. There are a number of capability indices that can be used, and all convey different information. The ones that are in common use are the C_p and C_{pk}. If the C_p is greater than one, then the natural variability of the process is less than the engineering (design) tolerance, so the process is inherently capable. A C_{pk} greater than one adds the additional information that the center of the process is at least three standard deviations from the nearest tolerance limit. In this case, the process is producing acceptable product most of the time. The problem set will give you practice in computing various capability indices.

8. *To apply some qualitative and quantitative measures to evaluate the level of quality in a services environment.* Quality in a service environment may need qualitative measures using tools such as SERVQUAL. Where quantitative measures are appropriate, the tools may have to accommodate nonnormal data. In some instances, the data will

exhibit time-related (between sample) variability that is common cause. This can be handled by treating the sample averages as individuals data and constructing $\overline{X}$ and *MR* charts.

To Test your Understanding

8-1   Record the length of time it takes you to drive to work (or school) each day for twenty days. Plot the data on an individuals and two-point moving range chart. What is your interpretation of the data? Can you explain any out-of-control points?

8-2   The specifications on a certain bagged product are set at 50.5 ± 0.5 pounds. To check the consistency of the bagging operation in meeting these specs, an inspector randomly selects seven pallets from each lot number and weighs all the bags on the selected pallets. The pallets each contain forty bags. Any bag found to be either overweight or underweight is set aside and counted as a defective. The inspection results for twenty lots are recorded as follows.

Lot Number	Number of Defective Bag Wts.	Lot Number	Number of Defective Bag Wts.
1	8	11	20
2	12	12	15
3	10	13	13
4	18	14	14
5	10	15	8
6	10	16	8
7	9	17	7
8	9	18	17
9	8	19	10
10	12	20	9

a. Is the bagging process in a state of statistical control? Justify your answer by plotting a control chart appropriate to these data.

b. What is your estimate of the percentage of bag weights that do not meet specifications?

c. The next ten lots inspected yielded the following results: 11, 14, 16, 12, 16, 19, 14, 15, 15, 17. How do you interpret these new data?

8-3   The control charts that follow have been constructed for the bagging process described in problem 8-1. The centerlines on the range and averages charts are 0.3603 and 49.829.

a. What percentage of the bags produced by this process will be overweight? What percentage will be underweight?

b. If the average increases to 50.1 pounds, what is the probability of getting an out-of-control signal on the next sample after the change?

c. At the increased average, what percentage of the bags produced will be overweight? What percentage will be underweight?

d. What sample size would be required for the *p* chart in problem 8-1 to detect the change in average with the same probability as part b?

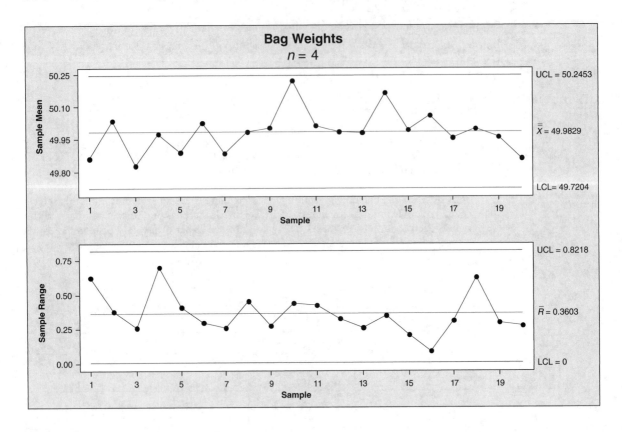

8-4   A certain manufacturing plant is having problems meeting its delivery commitments. One of the problems has been traced to purchased materials, which are frequently late or received in the wrong quantities, or the vendor ships the wrong parts in error. The purchasing director has been tasked to see whether errors in purchase orders are contributing to the problem. Ten purchase orders per day are selected at random over a twenty-day period. Each purchase order is carefully scrutinized, and the total number of errors is recorded. The aggregate total for all ten purchase orders sampled is then computed. The results are shown as follows.

	Errors in Ten Randomly Selected Purchase Orders		
Day	Errors Recorded	Day	Errors Recorded
1	8	11	15
2	11	12	11
3	7	13	10
4	19	14	13
5	7	15	16
6	12	16	13
7	11	17	16
8	6	18	7
9	10	19	15
10	6	20	13

a. Is the process of purchase order error generation stable? What is your best estimate of the number of errors that will be on the next purchase order cut? Support your answers with control chart data.

b. The following data was collected for a twenty-day period following the implementation of some improvements in the purchasing department. Using the control chart that you constructed for part a, demonstrate whether there is statistical evidence to validate the improvement.

c. Construct a control chart for the process following the improvements. Is the process in control? What is your best estimate of the number of errors in the next purchase order cut?

d. Management wants to reduce the sampling effort from ten to five per day. What centerline and control limits should be placed on the control chart?

8-5 Chip Technologies manufactures personal computers for large chain electronic retail outlets. Each day several orders are selected at random, and each computer carefully inspected against a check list. The total defects are recorded and plotted on a control chart. Because orders vary in size, the total number of computers inspected differs each day. The results for twenty days of inspection are shown in the following table.

Day	Number of Computers Inspected	Number of Defects	Day	Number of Computers Inspected	Number of Defects
1	15	35	11	18	21
2	27	27	12	16	31
3	18	70	13	32	98
4	36	69	14	16	31
5	25	78	15	17	15
6	16	14	16	37	147
7	37	71	17	19	32
8	23	65	18	37	106
9	19	41	19	32	34
10	26	82	20	36	101

a. Analyze this process using an appropriate control chart. What would be your recommendations to the plant manager?

b. A Six Sigma team was formed to investigate the defect problem. Some changes were implemented, aimed at stabilizing the process. After all workers had been thoroughly trained in the new procedures, data were collected for a twenty-day period and are summarized in the following table.

Day	Number of Computers Inspected	Number of Defects	Day	Number of Computers Inspected	Number of Defects
1	20	12	11	3	2
2	35	45	12	12	5
3	16	13	13	16	10
4	20	11	14	27	34
5	19	30	15	17	9
6	8	3	16	42	45
7	9	5	17	38	35
8	17	20	18	25	28
9	7	4	19	12	7
10	6	3	20	32	19

8-6 The controller of a large chemical refinery is concerned about the late processing of some accounts payable, thereby failing to take advantage of discounts that are available for timely payments. The following data represents performance over the most recent thirty-month period.

Number of Accounts Paid Late	Total Number of Accounts Processed	Month	Number of Accounts Paid Late	Total Number of Accounts Processed
94	1,032	April	142	856
101	1,176	May	145	1,243
44	653	June	88	766
99	1,055	July	131	1,014
97	1,110	August	150	1,163
42	640	September	151	1,099
56	768	October	103	939
78	746	November	225	1,218
64	516	December	214	1,165
89	1,153	January	220	1,104
61	571	February	100	784
133	1,031	March	63	836
181	934	April	44	555
90	575	May	85	1,199
160	947	June	39	588

a. Construct a control chart to analyze this process, using control limits based on the average sample size. Is it appropriate to use the average sample size in this case? Explain.

b. Identify the points that should be investigated based on the limits you calculated in part a. How many points did you need to investigate? Is the process in control?

c. Construct another control chart using the approach illustrated in Figure 8-22. How many points do you need to investigate using this approach?

d. Over the next few months, the controller challenged the employees to find ways to improve the process. Many suggestions were made and carried out. Data for the next thirty months is shown in the following table. Has the process improved? Where does it appear that the process has stabilized at a new level of performance? Construct a new control chart for this point onward, and estimate the average percentage of payments that are now late.

Month	Late	Processed	Month	Late	Processed
August	87	865	November	29	607
September	97	1,080	December	51	886
October	48	598	January	52	985
November	71	1,010	February	44	989
December	37	731	March	61	1,110
January	27	669	April	40	860
February	38	751	May	30	828
March	58	1,021	June	28	583
April	24	553	July	31	690
May	56	1,070	August	32	568
June	33	567	September	50	1,102
July	37	745	October	48	1,046
August	43	774	November	36	606
September	57	1,060	December	45	921
October	31	642	January	33	804

8-7   A beverage plant has a filling line that places product in twenty-ounce bottles. Consumers expect each bottle to contain twenty ounces of product, as stated on the label; however, the plant is within the legal requirements if the output is within the range nineteen to twenty one ounces. Fill volumes are monitored using random samples of five bottles, selected once each hour, and plotted on $\overline{X}$ and R charts. Both charts show good control. The $C_p = 1.23$ and the $C_{pk} = 0.69$.

   a. What is the average overfill (in excess of twenty ounces) for this process? Estimate the percentage of bottles that are above the label volume. What percentage of the output is outside the tolerance interval?
   b. What are the centerline and control limits on the R chart?
   c. What are the centerline and control limits on the $\overline{X}$ chart?
   d. If the process is centered on a target of twenty ounce, by what percentage does the fill variance have to be reduced to achieve a $C_{pk} = 1.5$? How would you recommend that the plant manager move forward to accomplish this goal?

8-8   A consumer products manufacturer has collected the following twenty-five samples of a particular composite measure. The sample size was five. The specifications for this product are 53 ± 5.5.

Sample	*Composite Reading*				
	1	*2*	*3*	*4*	*5*
1	53.1	56.6	54.9	54.7	57.8
2	56.0	53.6	53.6	55.2	55.0
3	57.5	55.6	54.8	54.7	58.2
4	53.0	53.0	54.3	51.3	56.7
5	56.0	55.8	57.7	54.2	56.2
6	55.4	54.7	52.8	56.5	54.6
7	56.0	52.9	58.9	54.7	52.8
8	53.2	51.2	56.7	56.5	57.6
9	54.8	55.0	58.0	57.1	52.3
10	55.9	50.9	57.7	57.6	57.1
11	56.4	52.9	53.7	56.0	55.7
12	56.0	55.5	55.1	53.8	55.3
13	54.0	53.2	54.1	53.3	54.8
14	54.9	52.8	57.6	54.1	56.1
15	56.7	55.1	53.8	53.1	57.1
16	53.6	53.0	55.9	57.0	52.5
17	57.3	55.1	54.0	52.8	53.6
18	58.0	53.8	56.5	55.9	56.5
19	55.8	54.7	55.0	55.3	54.3
20	53.2	55.1	57.4	53.4	58.6
21	56.1	55.4	58.7	54.1	52.4
22	55.3	55.2	53.1	56.4	55.2
23	56.0	55.3	57.5	53.5	50.2
24	55.0	54.9	55.0	53.3	54.8
25	55.4	55.3	56.2	56.2	57.2

   a. Construct a pair of control charts to determine if this process is in control. Is the process in control? Explain.
   b. Is the process on target? Explain.
   c. Is the process capable? Justify your answer by computing both the C_p and the C_{pk}.
   d. What immediate action would you recommend? What long-term action would you recommend?

8-9   Viscosity is one of the CTQ characteristics for a slurry product at a plant that produces minerals for an industrial market. The target viscosity is 1,300, and the customer has agreed to accept viscosities in the range 1,100 to 1,500. To determine how well the process is performing, an operator collects six samples per shift and sends the material to a QC lab where viscosity is determined. The data from twenty shifts are shown in the following table.

Sample No.	Measured Specimen						$\bar{X}$	R
	1	2	3	4	5	6		
1	1340	1316	1329	1343	1324	1297	1324.8	46
2	1325	1305	1322	1335	1323	1308	1319.7	30
3	1346	1326	1298	1295	1329	1307	1316.8	51
4	1376	1361	1373	1338	1349	1380	1362.8	42
5	1324	1351	1341	1337	1284	1298	1322.5	67
6	1315	1293	1319	1388	1393	1382	1348.3	100
7	1321	1298	1316	1332	1353	1322	1323.7	55
8	1305	1320	1302	1337	1288	1315	1311.2	49
9	1321	1326	1310	1333	1313	1329	1322.0	23
10	1357	1357	1356	1354	1339	1312	1345.8	45
11	1295	1318	1325	1302	1324	1340	1317.3	45
12	1357	1312	1345	1315	1295	1350	1329.0	62
13	1355	1363	1351	1358	1335	1309	1345.2	54
14	1335	1370	1372	1360	1359	1307	1350.5	65
15	1344	1346	1361	1344	1394	1372	1360.2	50
16	1354	1395	1390	1377	1362	1368	1374.3	41
17	1347	1344	1321	1330	1335	1366	1340.5	45
18	1341	1358	1328	1335	1329	1326	1336.2	32
19	1317	1310	1313	1316	1333	1306	1315.8	27
20	1297	1312	1316	1354	1358	1313	1325.0	61

a. What sources of variability are captured in the R and $\bar{X}$ charts, respectively, using this method of sampling?
b. Is this process in control? What would you recommend to management?
c. The plant manager made improvement of this process a priority. A team was assembled with representatives from process engineering, maintenance, and operators from each of the three shifts. A cause-and-effect diagram was constructed, and several possible causes were tagged for investigation. A problem with a valve in the volumetric feeder for the CMC additive was discovered. At times, intermittently and unpredictably, the valve would stick open, and the quantity of cellulose (a viscosity builder) released into the mixing tank was excessive. The feeder was repaired by replacing a part, and then the new data shown here were collected. The same sampling plan was used as before.

Sample No.	$\bar{X}$	R	Sample No.	$\bar{X}$	R
21	1310.0	45	31	1309.8	17
22	1312.0	33	32	1301.0	25
23	1293.2	40	33	1288.5	32
24	1288.8	14	34	1305.7	35
25	1302.3	12	35	1308.8	20
26	1305.8	20	36	1296.0	15
27	1308.5	35	37	1302.0	35
28	1295.0	47	38	1294.2	40
29	1300.2	30	39	1306.8	25
30	1301.2	22	40	1294.0	15

Did the replacement valve fix the problem? Is the process capable? Is the process on target? Is the process producing to specifications? Use control charts and capability indices to justify your answers.

8-10 There are two lab technicians that the plant in problem 8-4 employs to perform the viscosity tests. Sue has a total of twenty years' experience and works the day shift. Bob, who has only been performing the tests for two years, covers the night shift. For a period of thirty days, each technician has taken a sample from a pseudostandard batch, split it, and measured the viscosity for each half. Their results are shown in the following table.

	Sue			*Bob*	
Day	*Measurement 1*	*Measurement 2*	*Day*	*Measurement 1*	*Measurement 2*
1	1299	1301	1	1302	1298
2	1301	1299	2	1300	1299
3	1300	1298	3	1299	1300
4	1301	1301	4	1301	1296
5	1297	1300	5	1301	1300
6	1299	1298	6	1300	1299
7	1300	1299	7	1298	1301
8	1300	1301	8	1300	1301
9	1300	1297	9	1300	1297
10	1301	1301	10	1302	1300
11	1302	1300	11	1300	1300
12	1300	1299	12	1300	1302
13	1300	1301	13	1299	1299
14	1301	1301	14	1302	1300
15	1301	1300	15	1295	1300
16	1299	1298	16	1302	1299
17	1298	1302	17	1300	1299
18	1301	1302	18	1301	1298
19	1300	1301	19	1298	1299
20	1300	1300	20	1299	1301
21	1299	1298	21	1300	1302
22	1299	1300	22	1300	1301
23	1299	1300	23	1298	1301
24	1300	1300	24	1299	1300
25	1300	1300	25	1301	1299
26	1301	1300	26	1300	1301
27	1301	1302	27	1295	1295
28	1300	1298	28	1300	1300
29	1299	1300	29	1302	1297
30	1300	1299	30	1300	1299

a. Compute the measurement error. What proportion is due to reproducibility? What proportion is due to repeatability?
b. Compute the SNR.
c. Compute the DR.
d. Is measurement error a concern for this process? Explain.

8-11 Androx Chemicals manufactures a powdered compound that is used to coat gunite swimming pools. An important measure is the dry brightness (DB) number, and customers will not accept product that has a DB number less than 90.3. Because it is difficult to obtain a precise reading, a technician takes a grab sample of material, divides it into three parts, and then measures each part. The three measurements are then averaged and plotted on control charts. The following data represents twenty samples that were obtained from this process.

Sample No.	Dry Brightness Reading			Sample No.	Dry Brightness Reading		
1	91.50	91.30	91.20	11	91.10	91.40	91.80
2	91.70	91.50	91.30	12	91.80	91.10	91.40
3	91.50	91.70	91.50	13	91.70	91.80	91.10
4	91.60	91.50	91.70	14	91.10	91.70	91.80
5	91.70	91.60	91.50	15	91.60	90.80	90.50
6	91.90	91.70	91.60	16	92.30	91.10	90.80
7	91.90	91.90	91.70	17	92.00	91.60	91.10
8	91.90	91.90	91.90	18	91.60	92.30	91.60
9	91.90	91.90	91.90	19	91.20	92.00	92.30
10	91.40	91.80	91.10	20	91.30	91.60	92.00

a. Use control charts to analyze this process. Is it in control?
b. Does it appear that the process is meeting the minimum specification limit?
c. What would you recommend as the next step?

8-12 Krypton Ltd. manufactures silicon wafers for the semiconductor industry. The business is highly competitive with pressure from customers to design wafers with more elements per surface area. There are two ways that this can be done: larger diameter wafers and thinner lines on the wafer surface. The industry standard has been 200-mm diameters, but there is a migration by many in the industry to move toward a larger 300 mm. Such a move requires major capital and retooling.

The other alternative, thinner lines, is attractive to many customers because the chips (made from the wafers) can be smaller, the circuits operate at faster speeds, consume less energy, and generate less heat. These are attractive attributes for computers and many electronic products. The attribute, line width, is expressed microns (μM). The goal is to produce a wafer with a line width of 0.11 μM.

Wafer production is a continuous process, and the production steps create many sources of variation. On the wafer itself, the line width measure depends on where the measurement is taken. Wafers are produced in cassettes (twenty-five in a batch), and the location within the cassette can influence the measure. In addition, cassettes may be different. The following data represent line width measurements that were taken from thirty wafers. Three wafers were selected at random from ten cassettes (also selected at random). Each wafer was measured at five locations: top, left, center, right, and bottom. For ease in analysis, the results have been recorded by multiplying the micron measure by ten.

Cassette Number	Wafer Number	Wafer Line Width, Measured in Microns (μM) $\times$ **10**				
		Top	Left	Center	Right	Bottom
	1	3.20	2.25	2.07	2.41	2.39
1	2	2.65	2.00	1.86	2.14	1.98
	3	2.89	2.06	1.63	2.30	2.33
	4	3.16	2.52	2.07	2.29	2.12
2	5	2.06	2.22	1.47	1.68	1.90
	6	2.35	2.17	1.54	1.97	2.25
	7	2.20	1.73	1.36	1.67	1.43
3	8	2.23	1.56	1.52	2.07	1.78
	9	2.24	1.75	1.37	1.62	1.54
	10	2.93	2.04	1.79	1.98	2.16
4	11	2.86	2.10	1.92	2.02	2.23
	12	3.23	2.90	2.17	3.04	3.19

Cassette Number	Wafer Number	Wafer Line Width, Measured in Microns (μM) $\times$ 10				
		Top	*Left*	*Center*	*Right*	*Bottom*
	13	3.05	2.51	1.95	2.47	2.58
5	14	3.86	3.35	2.53	3.19	3.36
	15	3.69	3.40	2.96	2.95	3.47
	16	2.94	2.53	1.94	2.77	2.38
6	17	3.22	2.30	2.26	2.65	2.42
	18	3.18	2.85	1.60	2.81	2.90
	19	2.17	2.03	1.67	1.66	2.31
7	20	2.91	2.32	1.85	2.39	2.19
	21	2.20	3.32	2.70	1.96	2.51
	22	1.96	1.36	0.97	1.95	1.64
8	23	2.36	1.76	1.17	2.23	1.31
	24	2.42	1.99	1.40	2.00	2.14
	25	2.19	2.29	1.70	1.93	2.06
9	26	2.36	1.80	1.24	1.68	1.85
	27	2.01	1.52	0.79	2.00	1.35
	28	2.83	2.50	1.94	2.35	2.31
10	29	3.07	2.06	1.79	1.86	1.96
	30	3.07	2.29	1.87	2.48	2.02

Use control charts to determine the following:

a. The average of the overall process and its variability.
b. The proportion of the total variability that is due to location differences within the wafer.
c. The proportion of the total variability that is due to location differences within a cassette.
d. The proportion of the total variability that is due to different cassettes.
e. Assuming normality, what is the widest and narrowest line width that can be expected from this process?

The Third Generation: Six Sigma, Lean, and Quality-Inspired Management

CHAPTER 9

Six Sigma and Continuous Improvement

We are what we repeatedly do. Excellence then, is not an act, but a habit.

—ARISTOTLE

GE Healthcare

We Strive to See Life More Clearly

In 1981, Jack Welch became CEO of General Electric (GE) with a determination to reshape the $25 billion company. GE was not in trouble, but Welch was a visionary. He sensed that the mechanistic command-and-control structure at GE was a barrier to the company reaching its full potential. For the next decade, Jack Welch borrowed winning strategies from the world's best-managed companies to transform GE into an organic, streamlined monolith with revenues of $130 billion. Under his leadership, participation was broadened to include allowing those who were closest to an issue to make decisions.

By the mid-1990s, acting on feedback from the employees that quality was not "quite where it should be," Welch brought Six Sigma to GE. Inspired by successes at other large corporations such as Allied Signal and Motorola, aggressive targets were set five

years out, and the stage was set for Six Sigma to become an integral part of the GE culture. The impact was startling. During the first five years, returns on the Six Sigma investment were 266%, and operating margins improved from 14.4% to 18.4%.[1] In terms of dollars, the benefits attributable to Six Sigma increased from $170 million in 1996 to more than $2.5 billion in 2000. This not only pleased the stockholders, but also caught the attention of GE's customers worldwide.

As early as 1997, GE Healthcare (then called GE Medical Systems) commenced a program to take Six Sigma to its health care customers and have now successfully introduced the approach to more

---

[1]Lucier, Gregory T., and Sridhar Seshadri. "GE Takes Six Sigma Beyond the Bottom Line." *Strategic Finance* 82, no. 11 (2001): 40–47.

than 1,500 health care facilities worldwide. The inaugural effort resulted in a total benefit of $94 million in the first year, after only scratching the surface of the market. Through Six Sigma, GE is revolutionizing the way health care is delivered and administered around the world. ■

SOURCE: Data used by permission of GE Healthcare.

9.1 LEARNING OBJECTIVES AND KEY OUTCOMES

After studying the material in Chapter 9, you will be able to

1. Define Six Sigma, and describe the features that have made this approach successful in many companies
2. Describe the concept of a core business process, and determine where these processes fit in the open system and in Six Sigma
3. Discuss the five phases of the DMAIC cycle
4. Define the key roles in a Six Sigma improvement project
5. Design a training curriculum for each key player in a Six Sigma implementation
6. Describe the Six Sigma procedure for selecting projects
7. Suggest some ways in which Six Sigma projects can be generated
8. Define the lean production philosophy and how it complements Six Sigma
9. Apply Little's law
10. Describe how pull scheduling differs from a traditional push system
11. Compute takt time, and describe the significance of balancing a value stream to its takt time
12. Define andon, jidoka, and heijunka, and describe how they are used in a Lean Six Sigma environment
13. Define some changeover reduction strategies that can be used to shorten lead times
14. Explain the 5S strategy for workplace discipline
15. Explain the purpose of total productive maintenance (TPM) and how TPM is intended to operate

9.2 WHAT IS SIX SIGMA?

9.2.1 Six Sigma Defined

Six Sigma

Efficiency

Effectiveness

Six Sigma has been defined as "a comprehensive and flexible system for achieving, sustaining and maximizing business success," and "uniquely driven by close understanding of customer needs, disciplined use of facts, data, and statistical analysis, and diligent attention to managing, improving, and reinventing business processes."[2] After reading the first eight chapters, this should not sound like something new. The first eight chapters investigate how quality-inspired managers must first acquire systems knowledge

---

[2]Pande, Peter S., Robert P. Neuman, and Roland R. Cavanagh. *The Six Sigma Way: How GE, Motorola, and Other Top Companies Are Honing Their Performance*, xi. New York: McGraw-Hill, 2000.

(concerning customers, competitors, processes, and personnel) and then apply what they have learned to better adapt their business systems to meet the needs of those who depend on them. Six Sigma changes none of that. However, the best intentions are of little use if they cannot be successfully deployed. Six Sigma is the vehicle of deployment and can appropriately be thought of as an implementation strategy that has worked well in some of the top companies. The tools that are used in Six Sigma are nearly identical to those that have been applied in TQM and a good comprehensive review of these can be found in Chapters 7 and 8.

In Section 4.2.7, efficiency is defined as doing the thing right and effectiveness as doing the right thing. Six Sigma strives to improve efficiency and effectiveness at the same time, to help an organization work smarter by setting and aggressively pursuing goals that matter to customers, and to do so without error or waste.

9.2.2 Why Six Sigma Is Successful

The success of Six Sigma is due in large part to three features:

Financial Accountability

1. **Financial accountability**. Six Sigma ties project goals directly to bottom-line expectations. Expressing a project in terms of financial results is a language that senior managers understand and that stockholders will support.

Prioritization

Six Sigma requires that projects be selected that can leverage benefits to the corporation as a whole.

2. **Prioritization**. Six Sigma prescribes a method for prioritizing projects on the basis of expected benefits. Previous approaches were not as focused and tried to make quality "everyone's business." Although quality in essence is the concern of everyone, giving all personnel the responsibility to improve their individual processes fails to direct attention and resources to those areas that would leverage significant gains. All processes are not of equal importance. Assuming they are, and expecting improvements across the board, can unintentionally penalize those who have previously run "lean" processes and now have no low-hanging fruit. Those programs that proliferate the use of teams, without providing guidance and prioritizing effort, can eventually falter as teams become frustrated and demoralized. After dedicated hard work with little result, people will soon grow weary and lose interest.

Management Participation

Six Sigma requires active management participation.

3. **Management participation**. Each project has a champion and sponsor who have oversight responsibility and can direct the necessary resources where needed to achieve project objectives. Senior management selects the projects and decides who will be on the project team. Through tollgate reviews, the champion and sponsor are tied to the project from the beginning and can ensure that the team stays on purpose.

Six Sigma is about statistical analysis, perfection, and culture. It provides discipline, focus, accountability, and an implementation framework where there can be no spectators, only participants. Improvement teams set specific objectives and are held accountable for reaching them. The culture is transformed as the organization's structure aligns itself to the achievement of the Six Sigma goals. Individual responsibilities and expectations are clearly delineated, and there is a clear and widely understood training regimen to provide the skills set needed.

In preparing for Six Sigma, it is important for management to assess the cultural preparedness for the sweeping changes that will ensue.

9.3 PREPARING FOR SIX SIGMA

9.3.1 Get the Culture Ready

To prepare for any major change, it is important to prime the organization to anticipate problems, tear down barriers, and sell the idea that the change is good. Six Sigma has the benefit of being able to draw from a quarter-century of experiences on things that can go wrong and pitfalls to avoid. Section 5.3 explores a number of reasons why quality programs have failed. The first and foremost reason given was the absence of commitment by the upper echelons. It was not uncommon for past quality initiatives to result in sweeping changes—both in the way work was performed and how people worked together to get the job done. However, after intensive training and extensive rhetoric—acclaiming the virtues of customer satisfaction and zero defects—the workforce became disillusioned. Working on process improvements, attending team meetings, and keeping mountains of documentation added significantly to individual workloads.

All this might have been palatable, except for a startling realization. Despite the changes that had occurred on the shop floor, the workforce often saw little, if any, change in management. The quality efforts were not a priority, and the improvement statistics seldom made it to the pages of quarterly reports or the agendas of executive board meetings. To make matters worse, senior management often used improvements as an excuse for downsizing, "rewarding" the dedicated and loyal champions of process improvement with layoffs. Those lucky enough to keep their jobs found that their workloads had increased even more as they now had to pick up the slack for those who had been laid off.

To get the culture ready for Six Sigma, management must change first. The buy-in at the top must be complete and the commitment genuine. Managers must understand that the adoption of Six Sigma will have as big an impact on their jobs as on the lives and jobs of those throughout the organizational structure.

The impact of Six Sigma on culture depends on where the organization is on the quality journey.

The impact on the culture depends on how far an organization has come in its quality journey. If a company has reached the second or third generation of quality maturity, has previously conducted extensive training in many of the tools presented in Chapters 7 and 8, and has broadened the participation base so employees at all levels have experienced working on improvement teams, then the transition to Six Sigma should go smoothly. If the company is embarking on the quality journey for the first time, management would be wise to proceed slowly, following the steps outlined in Section 5.4.

9.3.2 Select Core Business Processes

Perhaps the most distinctive difference between Six Sigma and its forebears is that Six Sigma defines a strategy for getting work done. Management owns all primary and support value streams because these are components of the larger organizational system. Porter, in his 1985 book *Competitive Advantage*,[3] first introduced the concept of a value chain as a sequence of related work activities. This idea is expanded in Chapter 2 and is described as comprising three defining elements that must work together in harmony. These are individual attributes, group processes, and work design.

---

[3]Porter, Michael E. *Competitive Advantage.* New York: The Free Press, 1985.

The value stream can be viewed as either a fragmented chain of workstations or an integrated stream of related activities. The former view defines the value stream by function, observing that work flows from one department to the next, each contributing to the overall value of system output. This view is consistent with a traditional vertical organization chart that is also segmented by function.

Six Sigma takes an opens systems view, focusing on core business processes.

The alternative view, and the one advocated by Six Sigma, is to define a value stream as a core business process. Core business processes are those primary value streams that directly contribute to providing products or services to customers. Any activity that is not primary is part of a support value stream and does not contribute to a core business process. Under Six Sigma, support functions are of secondary importance. When the idea of value stream management was first discussed in Chapter 4, we stressed the importance of having a single person in charge—a **process owner**. Such a structure defies the traditional chain-of-command organizational structure because the primary value stream will almost always cut across functional boundaries.

Process Owner

Under Six Sigma, process owners are usually selected from management, but not always. In some cases, it might be more appropriate to appoint someone from the non-management ranks. It is most important for the process owner to be technically knowledgeable about the process, to be respected by the people who operate the process, to have a personal stake in the success of the process, and finally, to be someone who is a critical thinker and has an improvement mind-set.

Core business processes are broad in scope and are typically a list of no more than five to eight value streams that are critical to mission. These will include processes such as

- Order fulfillment
- New product/service development
- Customer service
- Customer cultivation

Support processes are those value streams that serve as enablers to the core processes, and include such areas as human resources development and acquisition, budgeting, facilities, evaluation and rewards, and information technologies.

9.4 THE DMAIC CYCLE—SIX SIGMA TACTICS

9.4.1 Improvement Models

Scientific Method

PDCA Cycle

DMAIC

A number of models have been suggested for continuous improvement. The oldest of these is the **scientific method**, and its documented use can be traced back to the ancient Greeks and Egyptians, who used logic and deductive reasoning to explain the mysteries of science. In modern times, the most popularized model is the **PDCA cycle** (plan-do-check-act) that was discussed in Section 7.3.1. First introduced by Deming in the early 1950s, the PDCA model was the centerpiece of the TQM movement. The Six Sigma version of this is **DMAIC** (pronounced duh-may-ick), an acronym that stands for the interconnected steps of define, measure, analyze, improve, and control. These models are all grounded in the same philosophy—use data to create knowledge relative to a problem and then act on the knowledge to solve the problem.

FIGURE 9-1 Improvement Models

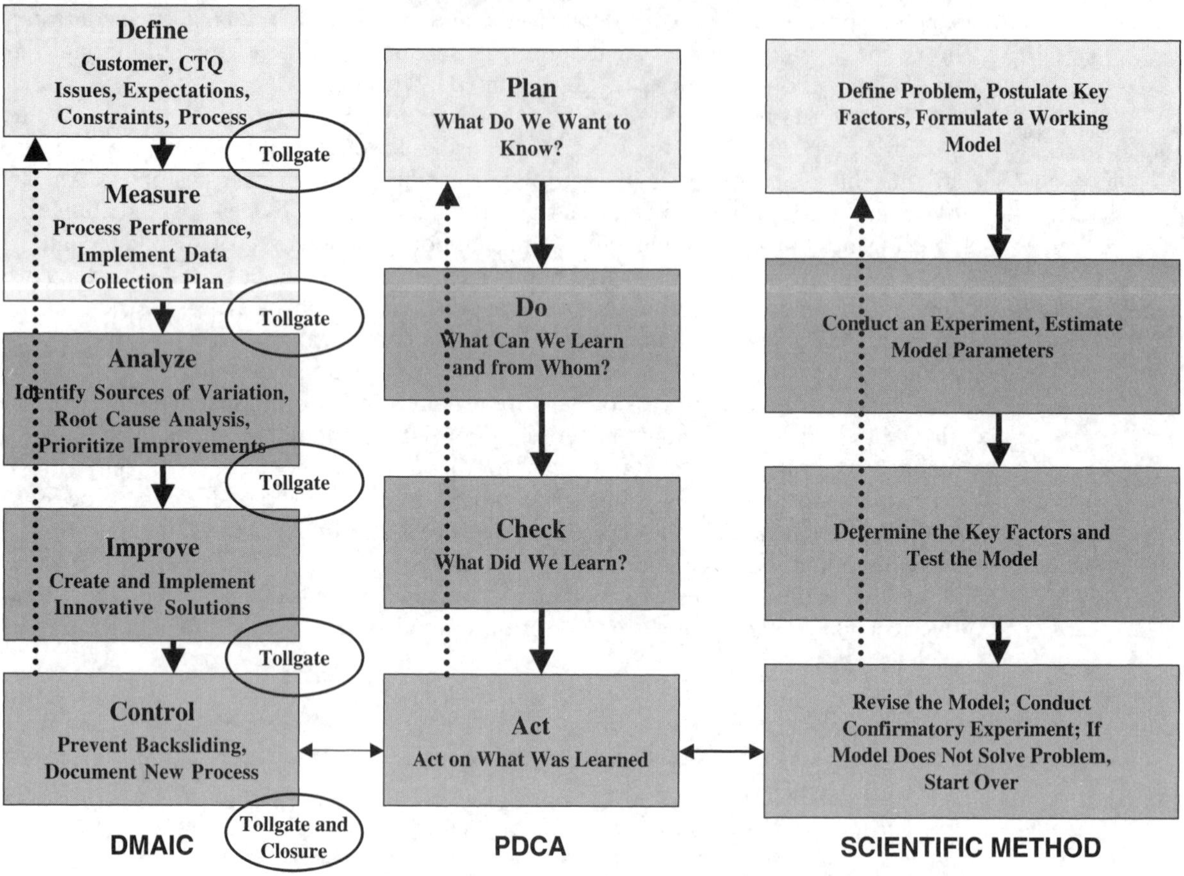

Define		
Customer, CTQ Issues, Expectations, Constraints, Process	Plan	Define Problem, Postulate Key Factors, Formulate a Working Model
	What Do We Want to Know?	

Tollgate

Measure		
Process Performance, Implement Data Collection Plan	Do	Conduct an Experiment, Estimate Model Parameters
	What Can We Learn and from Whom?	

Tollgate

Analyze		
Identify Sources of Variation, Root Cause Analysis, Prioritize Improvements	Check	Determine the Key Factors and Test the Model
	What Did We Learn?	

Tollgate

Improve		
Create and Implement Innovative Solutions		

Tollgate

Control	Act	Revise the Model; Conduct Confirmatory Experiment; If Model Does Not Solve Problem, Start Over
Prevent Backsliding, Document New Process	Act on What Was Learned	

Tollgate and Closure

DMAIC   **PDCA**   **SCIENTIFIC METHOD**

Note: CTQ, critical to quality; DMAIC, define, measure, analyze, improve, control; PDCA, plan-do-check-act.

Figure 9-1 illustrates the steps of the three models and their relationships. In Six Sigma, these steps are referred to as tactics and represent major phases that occur within the improvement process.

A feature that distinguishes DMAIC from other improvement models is the provision for "tollgates" between each phase. **Tollgate reviews** are milestones when the improvement team has the opportunity to meet with senior management and other project participants to evaluate progress and ensure the project stays on target and in alignment with corporate goals.

Tollgate Reviews

Define

9.4.2 Define Tactic

9.4.2.1 Define Phase   The **Define** tactic attempts to ask clarifying questions such as what is the problem, who is the customer, what process will be studied, and what do we expect to achieve? The Define phase sets the stage and justifies the work that is to come. In this phase, the improvement team develops a clear and communicable problem

A business case justifies a project and assigns individual responsibilities.

statement, identifies the process that will be studied, selects its key customers who define their requirements, and clearly assigns roles and responsibilities. The value of the project needs to be confirmed, and a set of project goals and boundaries drafted.

9.4.2.2 Define Tools   The tools used in the Define phase are for documenting and justifying. The first and most important of these is the **team charter**. The charter contains the business case, as well as a few sentences that explain why the project has a high priority and that link the expected outcomes to the firm's strategic plan and financial objectives. It also contains a short concise statement of the problem, written in nonthreatening terms, attaching blame to no one, and advocating no specific cause or solution. Next, the charter contains some project-specific objectives, such as a reduction in the number of defects by 50% or shrinkage of cycle time by 15%. The objectives can be revised later, if necessary. Figure 9-2 illustrates a typical team charter.

Next, the team charter contains a timeline for project completion. This can also be revised later, if necessary, but it is important that the team work to deadlines for each of the five phases. As a final component, the charter assigns roles and responsibilities. One of the strengths of Six Sigma is the clear delineation of critical roles. These roles are shown in Figure 9-3. The training requirements for "belt certification" are discussed in Section 9.5.

During the Define phase the improvement team performs a **customer needs analysis**. Each process has key customers. The particular process targeted for study will either have been explicitly identified in the charter or will be implicit in its problem statement. The first step is to obtain as much information as possible on customers and to state their expectations in unambiguous terms so each member of the team will understand process requirements. The compilation of this information is called the "voice of the customer."

The third and final step of the Define stage is to develop a high-level process chart, such as a **SIPOC map**. SIPOC is an acronym that stands for suppliers, inputs, processes, outputs, and customers. The SIPOC map expands the scope of the flowcharting tool presented in Section 7.4.1.1 to include suppliers and customers. This provides a bird's-eye view of the value stream and its linkages to the environment. Figure 9-4 is an example of a SIPOC map.

9.4.2.3 Define Tollgate   A final step is a **define tollgate** review. This is a meeting that is held to review progress. The meeting is led by the team leader (usually a black belt) and is attended by team members, the project sponsor, the project champion, a master black belt, and the process owner. The review focuses on the project goals (and whether they have changed), the project justification (with particular reference to how the project is expected to benefit the bottom line), the projected resource requirements, and the team's plans for proceeding to the next tactic—Measure.

9.4.3 Measure Tactic

9.4.3.1 Measure Phase   The **Measure** phase is concerned with designing and implementing a data collection strategy. This tactic helps the team learn as much as it can about the process they are studying. These data provide a baseline of what currently exists. Later, when the team moves to the Improve phase, the information gathered during the Measure phase can be used to evaluate the impact of any proposed changes. There are two traps that the team needs to avoid. The first is collecting too much data, compounding the task of analysis. The second is collecting too little and making inferences

Team Charter

Customer Needs Analysis

SIPOC Map

Define Tollgate

Measure

FIGURE 9-2 Six Sigma Team Charter

Grinder Gear Works

Six Sigma Team Charter

PROBLEM STATEMENT

Thirty-three percent of all MPD-5000 master cogs shipped to customers fall short of meeting requirements. Twenty percent are rejected at customers' receiving stations and are returned. These customers claim that according to their measurements the parts fail to meet specifications. Ten percent of parts shipped are technically acceptable but are delivered late. Many of our customers are scheduling production based on just-in-time deliveries and depend on orders arriving when promised. The remaining 3% are not caught, and eventually end up in products and cause failures. Grinder Gear is currently facing litigation in two major product liability cases. These quality problems are not only hurting our image in the marketplace, but also the cost of expedited delivery (when we know a shipment would otherwise be late), scrap and rework, and processing returns. Having to ship replacement by expedited means is costing the company $550,000 per month. This does not take into account the loss of goodwill or the cost if Grinder should lose either of the pending lawsuits (one suit is seeking $10 million and the other $4.5 million).

GOAL STATEMENT

Cut late deliveries in half (down to 5%) by the end of October. Reduce the number of out-of-spec parts by 75% by the end of November so results can be reported to stockholders at their annual meeting in December.

CONSTRAINTS

Team members will be expected to devote 10 to 20 hours per week to the project. The project Champion will be requested to provide backup support to team members to ensure their regular production duties are covered and that their project responsibilities are not neglected.

ASSUMPTIONS

The focus of the project will be on improving the existing processes, not on designing a new one. However, the team will not be predisposed to any specific cause or solution on the front end. All ideas will be fair game.

TEAM GUIDELINES

The team will meet on a regular schedule between 9 a.m. and 10 a.m. on Fridays. Special team meetings can be convened at other times as needed. Decisions will be by consensus, using group techniques such as brainstorming and nominal group techniques to broaden participation and buy-in. If consensus cannot be reached, the team leader will make the final decision.

Grinder Gear Works

Six Sigma Team Charter
Page 2

TEAM MEMBERS

Allan Dutwidle—Grinder Shop
Jim Walker—Black Belt and Team Leader
Kelly Peterson—Order Fulfillment
Maria Hoskins—Shipping
Robert Napoli—Engineering
Sam Nelson—Technical Sales
Ernest Childs—Machining

Other key players:

John Crenshaw—Champion and VP of Customer Service
Wayne Masterson—Master Black Belt and Technical Support Group
Judy Henshaw—IT Group

PRELIMINARY PROJECT PLAN

The team has set a project completion date of December 31. To reach that date, the team will have to work aggressively and transition smoothly through each phase of DMAIC. The team is setting the following milestone dates for tollgate meetings.

DEFINE:	July 15
MEASURE:	August 15
ANALYZE:	September 15
IMPROVE:	October 15
CONTROL:	November 15

FIGURE 9-3 Roles Critical to the Success of Six Sigma

Champion

Process Owner—Oversight responsibility to keep team strategically focused. Provides resources and removes roadblocks.

Black Belt

Team Leader—Full time responsibility to team. Sets agenda, conducts meetings, supervises daily activities. Accountable for team progress.

Green Belt

Team Leader—Part-time responsibility to team. Responsible for team activities, but has other organizational responsibilites.

Master Black Belt

Team Consultant—Part-time technical expert in improvement tools. Participates on an as-needed basis.

Team Member

Subject-Matter Experts—Responsible for conducting the actual work of the team. This is usually in addition to normal duties.

that many not be statistically sound. It is important that all data collected are relevant to the team's goals.

During the Measure phase, current performance is evaluated against the "Six Sigma scorecard." Under Six Sigma, the term sigma signifies a score, and differs from the statistical definition of a standard deviation. The Six Sigma convention used is based on the original work at Motorola in the 1980s, when it was observed that there is usually a difference between short-term process variation and that sustained over a long period of time.

As an example, Figure 9-5 represents a process that is in statistical control with a computed capability index (C_{pk}) equal to one. Under a traditional capability analysis, one would correctly estimate that the process is meeting the specification limit shown 99.865% of the time. Out of one million parts produced, 1,350 will be defective. This estimate is obtained by observing that the specification limit is 3 standard deviations from the process mean. The Six Sigma "score" computes a 1.5 standard deviation shift, adjusting for the likelihood that over time even a stable system moves around. Therefore, in this case, the Six Sigma score is $3\sigma - 1.5\sigma = 1.5\sigma$. At the adjusted score of 1.5σ, the process long-term yield is reduced to 93.3193%, or 66,807 defective parts per million produced. These numbers are taken from cumulative standard normal tables.

Six Sigma Scores   Figure 9-6 is a chart that converts computed C_{pk} into **Six Sigma scores**. To achieve quality in the defects per million opportunities (DPMO) range, it is clear from the chart

FIGURE 9-4 SIPOC Map

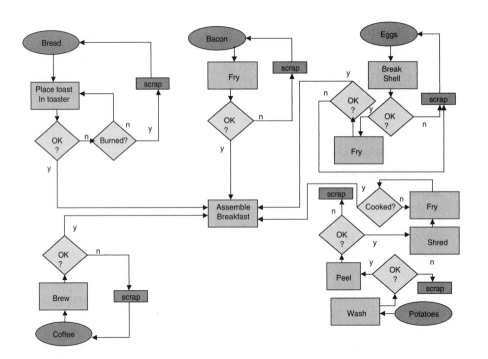

that a minimum $C_{pk} = 2$ is required. At that level, a stable process is capable of achieving a long-term yield of 99.99966%, or 3.4 DPMO. This is a near-perfect state and statistically equates to a process average that is 4.5σ from the specification limit that was used to compute the C_{pk}.

9.4.3.2 Measure Tools   The Measure tactic uses many of the tools that were described in Chapters 7 and 8 to build knowledge progressively. The team first uses some simple tools and, as information is gathered, introduces more sophisticated tools as appropriate. During the Measure phase, the team has five objectives:

1. Describe the process.
2. Focus on significant factors.

FIGURE 9-5 Six Sigma Scoring

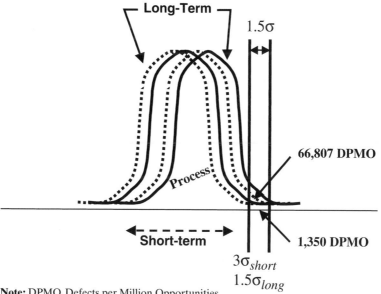

Note: DPMO, Defects per Million Opportunities.

FIGURE 9-6 Six Sigma Conversion Chart

Capability Index (C_{pk})	Short-Term Process Sigma	Long-Term Process Sigma	Process Yield	Defectives per Million
2	6	4.5	99.99966	3.4
1.83	5.5	4	99.9968	32
1.67	5	3.5	99.98	233
1.5	4.5	3	99.87	1,350
1.33	4	2.5	99.4	6,210
1.17	3.5	2	97.7	22,750
1	3	1.5	93.3	66,807
0.83	2.5	1	84.1	158,655
0.67	2	0.5	69.1	308,538
0.5	1.5	0	50.0	500,000
0.33	1	−0.5	30.9	691,462
0.17	0.5	−1	15.9	841,345
0	0	−1.5	6.7	933,193

FIGURE 9-7 Measure Tactic Tools

Understand and Reduce Variation
Runs and Control Charts
Process Capability

Collect Data and Ensure Accuracy
Check Sheets
Histograms
Operational Definitions
Scatter Diagrams

Matrix Analysis
Measurement Studies
SERVQUAL

Generate and Organize New Ideas
Six Honest Servants and Five Whys Cause–Effect Diagram
Matrix Diagram

Affinity Diagram
Stratification
Relations Diagram
Systematic Diagram
Process Decision Program Chart

Focus on Significant Factors
Variance Tracking Matrix
Pareto Diagram

Failure Modes and Effects Analysis

Describe the Process
Flowcharts
Knowledge Mapping
Morphological Box

Moment-of-Truth Analysis
Force Field Analysis

3. Generate and organize new ideas.
4. Collect data and ensure accuracy.
5. Understand and reduce variation.

Figure 9-7 illustrates these steps and the appropriate collage of tools that are applicable to each.

Measure Tollgate

9.4.3.3 Measure Tollgate   At the end of the Measure phase, the **measure tollgate** review is concerned with the justification of the sequence and set of tools selected to guide the search for information. The team must explain their logic in deciding what information to collect, how they went about collecting it, how it was analyzed, and what conclusions were drawn from the results. The review can also challenge any part of the data or the accuracy of the measurement system. After all questions concerning measurements and information are satisfactorily answered, the team will outline its plans for proceeding with the Analyze tactic.

9.4.4 Analyze Tactic

9.4.4.1 Analyze Phase   Once measurements have been made, the data collected are used to focus the team on the factors that are most likely causing the problem. Simply narrowing the scope does not prove causality. That requires additional data analysis,

Analyze

which is the objective of the **Analyze** tactic. The tools used for causal analysis can be categorized two ways: those that cause process variation, and those that cause lead time variation.

Fishbone Diagram

9.4.4.2 Analyze Tools A **fishbone diagram** is an important Analyze tool. The team brainstorms until it is satisfied that most candidate causes have been identified. Then the team might decide to investigate relationships between the effect and any number of the candidate causes, or alternatively, the interest might be whether any of the candidate causes are correlated with each other. There also may be some concerns that the stated causes are actually effects.

Causal Analysis

Control Charts

To conduct a **causal analysis**, the team can use **control charts** of selected process variables to identify and separate general sources of variability, such as machine induced, shift effect, method, and so on. Honing in on specific causes usually requires some advanced statistical tools that are beyond this text. Tools such as analysis of variance (ANOVA), correlation analysis, regression analysis, and experimental design can be conducted with the help of the team's black belt and master black belt who should be proficient in the use of such tools. The object of the Analyze tactic is to select a few causes that will be tagged for elimination in the Improve phase.

Analyze Tollgate

9.4.4.3 Analyze Tollgate The **Analyze tollgate** provides the opportunity for the team to defend the causes selected for improvement. During the review, the team presents its methodology and retraces the logic followed. It will also be called on to demonstrate how eliminating each selected cause will add value to the team's objective and to reveal how the team plans to eliminate the cause during the Improve phase.

9.4.5 Improve Tactic

9.4.5.1 Improve Phase During the Analyze tactic, cause-and-effect relationships were investigated and confirmed. The **Improve** tactic generates workable solutions that will eliminate the confirmed causes or nullify their effects. During the phases leading up to the Improve phase, the team conditions itself to think in the broadest possible terms—no idea is rejected out of hand. The emphasis is on creativity and thinking beyond accepted assumptions. In the Improve phase, the approach changes dramatically. Because the process has narrowed to a few (perhaps only one) causes, the team now must become focused and develop solutions that can be implemented. The group must therefore be able to change from an imaginative mind-set to a practical one.

Improve

Brainstorming

Nominal Group Technique

Six Honest Servants and Five Whys

9.4.5.2 Improve Tools The Improve phase is concerned with generating solution ideas, testing each idea, and finally, selecting one for implementation. Many of the tools that were useful in getting to Improve can be applied again to help with the stimulation of new ideas and to evaluate proposed solutions. For example, creative tools such as **brainstorming** and the **nominal group technique** can help. The use of flowcharts can aid in pinpointing where in the process the cause is occurring, and the **six honest servants and five whys** can sometimes result in good ideas. In some cases, it is desirable to use more advanced tools such as DOE or simulation to evaluate the impact of alternatives being considered. There are a number of tools that are part of the lean production toolkit that can also be considered at this point as a means for eliminating waste. This is discussed further in Section 9.8.

Improve Tollgate

9.4.5.3 Improve Tollgate   The **Improve tollgate** continues to focus on justification, logic, and linkages between causes. During the review, the team will present to the panel what improvements were considered, which ones were selected, and how the improvements address specific confirmed causes to help solve the problem. The team is also required to answer questions such as how the chosen improvements were tested and how the team can be certain that the benefits claimed will be achieved.

9.4.6 Control Tactic

Control

9.4.6.1 Control Phase   The **Control** tactic is about sustainability. Through the Analyze, Measure, and Improve phases, the team will have reached the point where specific defendable recommendations can be made for process improvements. The job is not complete until those improvements can be implemented and the baton of ownership passes from the improvement team to the process owner. New procedures must be carefully documented in unambiguous language and all workers, their supervisors, and the process owner need to receive consistent training in the new methods.

9.4.6.2 Control Tools   The tools that are appropriate to Control are those that can help the team document the improved method, determine the appropriate measures to monitor ongoing performance, and collect and analyze process data during implementation to validate training efforts and perform a postaudit evaluation of actual benefits. Many of the same tools that were used previously in the cycle will be used again in Control, only the emphasis will shift from problem solving to process surveillance. For example, flowcharting may be used to illustrate a revised sequence of steps to include in the new documentation. As another example, control charts may be useful in determining stability, identifying any inconsistencies in training or understanding, and validating new levels of process behavior.

Control Tollgate

9.4.6.3 Control Tollgate   The **Control tollgate** is the final review and formally closes the project. It is therefore essential that this review ensures sustainability of improvements and leverage of any learnings that took place. This final tollgate also provides senior management the opportunity to formally and publicly recognize the contributions of all team players and to express appreciation. During the Control review, there are several key issues that management will want to know. For example, it is important that the team explain what measures have been identified to track ongoing progress, their rationale, and the measurement process to be used. Individual roles and responsibilities also need to be clarified. Who will be responsible for collecting the data, how will it be analyzed, and who will take what action when the data provide what information? As for sustainability, the team describes the training program that has been carried out, including who received what training and the plan for providing this training to any new employees.

Dissemination of New Knowledge

   Dissemination of new knowledge accumulated during DMAIC is important. As a final step in the review process, the team will reflect on the lessons learned and determine whether any best practices were borrowed from others. They will then outline a plan for sharing this information outside the small circle of personnel who formed the project team. With this last step, Six Sigma becomes a vehicle to facilitate the learning process companywide so future projects do not necessarily have to start from scratch.

9.5 TRAINING REQUIREMENTS AND ROLES

9.5.1 Roles

As we mentioned previously, one of the differentiating features of Six Sigma is its clearly defined roles and responsibilities for the key players and, for each player, a pre-scribed skills set that is tied to a compulsory formal training curriculum. At the center of the Six Sigma structure are experts in process improvement tools. These people are typically referred to as **master black belts**, **black belts**, or **green belts**. As these titles suggest, (borrowed from martial arts) the belt certification requires dedication, discipline, and skill. The different belt levels, as in martial arts, indicate depth of experience and proficiency. The belt-qualified personnel act as technical experts on the Six Sigma toolkit. Oversight and management responsibilities lie with key senior managers, process owners, and project sponsors. Those who actually do the work—that is, those who must develop solutions that are implementable—are the **subject-matter experts**.

Master Black Belts

Black Belts

Green Belts

Subject-Matter Experts

Leadership Council

9.5.1.1 Leadership Council   Near the top of the Six Sigma structure is a **leadership council** comprised of senior managers. This group may go by various names, such as the Six Sigma leadership team or steering group, or the quality-inspired management council, to name a few possibilities. The members of this group are top executives who can make policy decisions and formulate strategy. They form an oversight group for Six Sigma and act as program enablers—removing roadblocks, providing resources, and helping disseminate lessons learned across the organization. The council meets regularly to discuss Six Sigma achievements, any problems, and how the program can be improved. This group will periodically review the progress on a specific project and may have a council representative attend tollgate reviews. The leadership council sets the pace and tone for Six Sigma implementation. It is the responsibility of this group to assess organizational preparedness, shape the culture, and be the committed voice of management. The frequency of their meetings and communications will influence how fast Six Sigma can move forward—the more frequent, the greater the sense of urgency and the higher priority the effort.

Champion

9.5.1.2 Champion   The **champion** is a senior manager who is usually a process owner and is not a full-time member of any team. For large processes, the process owner may appoint a direct report as the project sponsor, who then would assume the role of champion. The champion may have a number of Six Sigma teams working on projects that relate to the process and should provide broad guidance to ensure project goals are aligned with the overall business plan. The champion is a team advocate who will represent team interests before the leadership council, and will provide or find the necessary resources to support team activities, resolve any conflicts, and help remove barriers. Champions attend all tollgate reviews for active projects under their jurisdictions.

9.5.1.3 Master Black Belt   A master black belt is an internal consultant, and will normally have been a black belt first and have a track record of completed projects and significant annualized benefits. Master black belts are expected to train, mentor, and coach other personnel in Six Sigma tools, so they should have proven teaching skills, usually acquired by participating in in-house training courses for black or green belts. The master black belt is not a permanent member of any team, but is available to provide advice and training as required. Specifically, they are available to help teams design data collection strategies, analyze and interpret data, validate and communicate results, and resolve team disagreements. The master black belt attends all tollgate reviews within the assigned area of responsibility.

9.5.1.4 Black Belt   Black Belts are assigned to Six Sigma teams full time and fill the role of team leader. As such, they are responsible for the day-to-day activities of the team, run team meetings, define appropriate tools, and help other team members properly apply those tools. In addition, they must keep the team on schedule and orchestrate the team's preparation for tollgate reviews. As team leader, the black belt is also responsible for identifying and filling resource needs, and leading the tollgate review sessions. After the Control phase, the black belt assists in training personnel in any new procedures and assists with the implementation of changes.

9.5.1.5 Green Belt   A green belt is a part-time resource to the team. Having received some training in process improvement tools (usually from a black belt), the green belt may be assigned special tasks that support the project but are usually worked on independently. In some cases, a green belt may be assigned to a project as the team leader if the project is narrow enough in scope. The green belt is assigned regular production duties and may see the "extra work" as an opportunity to gain valuable experience leading to advancement to black belt or promotability on the line.

White Belt

9.5.1.6 White Belt   In martial arts, the lowest skills classification is the **white belt**. Those who hold this level, however, are more knowledgeable about the discipline than someone who has had no training. So it is with Six Sigma. It is not necessary to have white belts, but some organizations find it convenient to distinguish those individuals who have had a few hours of awareness training from those who have had none. The training can be delivered in a variety of ways, including Web-based instruction, classroom indoctrination, and independent reading. White belts form a pool of those who have been initiated into Six Sigma principles. When these individuals are selected for teams, they will have a broader understanding of what they are supposed to do, and how it is likely to benefit the company. Some of the white belts will become enthused enough to advance to green belt status. Unlike the black and green levels, the white level is generic. Some organizations will choose a company-distinctive color for this group—for example, it might be drawn from the company logo or trademark.

Team Members

9.5.1.7 Team Member   **Team members** are responsible for doing the bulk of the project work. The company depends on the team members to be thoughtful and serious in trying to solve the problem at hand, to generate creative ideas, and to work together to confirm results and design workable solutions. There is no magic number on how large or small a team should be. If the team is too large, it will become cumbersome, communications will be hampered, consensus will be difficult, and decision making will be affected. If the team is too small, the leverage that can occur through creative interactions will be restricted. As a rule of thumb, the best team size is usually between five and eight. Team members should be subject-matter experts who have an understanding of the process that will be investigated or of other relevant support processes. It is not necessary that team membership represent all relevant expertise. During DMAIC, team members can always consult experts outside the team for input as needed. The black belt normally coordinates such informational requirements.

9.5.2 Training

One of the mistakes of the TQM era was a penchant for training the masses. Hordes of people were sent through short courses for intensive training, only to return to the workplace with no clear idea of how they could use their new tools. It is no surprise that enthusiasm waned when the workforce could not see how the training was relevant to their job responsibilities. It is important that Six Sigma training be carefully planned and conducted so history is not repeated.

Two important principles should be followed. First, the training content should be clearly tied to applications that the participants can recognize, and second, the employees should be taught using methods and language that are nonthreatening and easy to understand. One size cannot fit all. Training should be tailored to the individuals and applications. Because many of the Six Sigma tools originate from TQM, many of a company's employees may have already undergone some training. If the organization has advanced to the second or third generation of quality, the Six Sigma training program should be designed to give due consideration to previous training efforts. For some employees, an abbreviated refresher course on certain topics may be all that is required. However, assuming a company is starting afresh, the following is a suggested training curriculum for each Six Sigma key role.

9.5.2.1 Senior Management Senior management training should be conducted for members of the leadership council and other executives, including process owners and project sponsors. An organization can expect the total training at this level to take an average of three to five weeks. Because these personnel have busy schedules, it is usually desirable to divide the content into small modules of one- to two-day durations. Training should begin with one or two days and cover Six Sigma awareness. This module would cover an overview of the fundamental principles of Six Sigma, how Six Sigma will benefit the company, and a description of how the program is structured, how it operates, and the key players, as well as their roles and responsibilities. The next training module might include a day or two on the specific role of the leadership council and champions, an explanation of DMAIC, and how the tollgate review process is supposed to work. The third module would introduce some basic Six Sigma tools. Three to five days should be devoted to this phase, so it might be desirable to split it into two modules. The idea is to introduce management to some of the tools, in an abbreviated form, that will be used to measure, analyze, improve, and control processes. These tools would not be covered in depth. The objective is to provide an appreciation for the type of tools that will be used, and the information that each tool can provide. The next module should be on teaming and can be scheduled for anywhere from three to five days. This module would include such topics as conducting meetings (e.g., the task cycle), applying time management, leading brainstorming sessions, facilitating discussions, building consensus, and resolving conflicts. Next, a training module should cover systems management, and include open systems theory, feedback, and performance measures. Value streams would then be taught, including the criteria for selecting core business processes, key customers, and determining critical outputs, requirements, and measures. The final module would comprise two to five days on change management. This would address such topics as formulating strategy, achieving buy-in, goal setting, promoting change, and implementation planning.

Senior managers receive three to five weeks training organized in small one to two-day modules

9.5.2.2 Black Belt Black belts require an average of four to six weeks of initial instruction. After attending the awareness training session, black belts undergo courses in teaming, tools, and change management. The teaming module incorporates the same curricula the seniors undertake and includes topics on how to conduct meetings, time management, brainstorming, how to facilitate discussions, consensus building, and conflict resolution. Tools training is in two segments—first covering basic and then intermediate tools. The segment on basic tools will take five to ten days, covering in detail the DMAIC process, and many of the soft tools of process and causal analysis. A number of the tools covered in Chapter 7 are included in this segment. After mastering the basic set, the training progresses to a five- to ten-day course covering intermediate tools of measurement and analysis. This would include the material from Chapter 8, and in addition, might cover some more advanced statistical tools such as correlation and regression analysis and DOE. When the tools segments are complete, black belts must undergo the senior management course on change management.

> Black belts must undergo four to six weeks of intensive training.

9.5.2.3 Green Belt   Green belts require an average of two to three weeks of training. This includes attending the Six Sigma awareness instruction and then two additional modules. These modules are the team training and the course covering the basic toolkit.

> Green belts go through two to three weeks of training.

9.5.2.4 White Belt   White belts may be required to attend the one- to two-day Six Sigma awareness course only. Some organizations could opt to put this course on a Web site and have participants enroll in an e-learning mode. This course might also be supplemented with required outside reading.

> White belts are given a one to two day course in Six Sigma awareness.

9.5.2.5 Master Black Belt   Normally, to become a master black belt, a person must have served first as a black belt and led a number of teams to the successful completion of improvement projects. Some organizations set minimum thresholds for advancement to master black belt, such as five to six projects and $2 to $3 million dollars in documented annualized savings. In addition to the black belt training, master black belts continue their training by enrolling in specialized training courses, usually conducted external to the organization. Examples of those topics studied are Taguchi methods, advanced DOE, advanced statistical analysis, quality function deployment, and ANOVA. The time required for this specialized training varies by topic and source.

> Master black belts must enroll in specialized training courses.

9.6 SELECTING THE RIGHT PROJECTS

Throughout this chapter, we draw comparisons with TQM to clarify how Six Sigma can correct some of the deficiencies of earlier programs. One important difference concerns the selection of projects. TQM did not have a formal project structure, so project selection was not generally an important issue. TQM acclaimed the merits of continuous improvement for all work. This was generically interpreted to mean that the road to quality was through the efforts of countless teams, continuously working together to generate improvements. These teams were patterned after the early quality circles in Japan and, in most instances, were able to achieve substantial short-term benefits. Employee motivation levels surged with new responsibilities, and teams typically did not have to look far to gain improvements in productivity or waste reduction. Notwithstanding, in some cases the TQM improvement effort failed to recognize that all improvement projects do not have the same potential, nor will all impact key performance metrics for the business. Even those that do will likely yield corporate benefits that differ significantly. It became difficult for corporate leadership to manage and respond to the multitudes of teams throughout their organization and to sift through hundreds of improvement suggestions. The Six Sigma approach is different in that the leadership council selects the projects that will go forward using criteria that include benefits, effort, resources, and time.

9.6.1   Criteria for Selection

9.6.1.1 Screening Criteria   Six Sigma projects are selected on the basis of a trade-off between the benefits that will likely occur if the project is successful, and the resources and time necessary to complete the project. A tool similar to the resource–benefit chart shown in Figure 9-8 can be used to screen ideas initially. Projects that lie in the upper left-hand corner of the chart are desirable because high benefits are expected in return for a low investment. Projects that fall in the lower right-hand corner of the chart are generally undesirable because the expected benefit is low relative to the time and effort required. Projects in the lower left-hand corner (low benefit, low resources) may be worth doing, but the benefits expected from these projects usually do not justify the use of a Six Sigma team. These low-hanging fruit opportunities are sometimes called "quick hits." If conducted, projects in this category do not require black belt skills and are usually assigned to individuals, not teams.

Projects that lie in the upper right-hand corner may or may not be worthy. The potential benefits are high, but the investment required is also high. Decisions on these projects would be guided by such criteria as business strategy (how does this project support our strategic intent?), the voice of the customer (how does this project better serve our customers?), lean strategies (how will this project reduce lead times?), or

Six Sigma project ideas are screened on the basis of trade-offs between benefits and the effort.

FIGURE 9-8 Resource Benefit Matrix

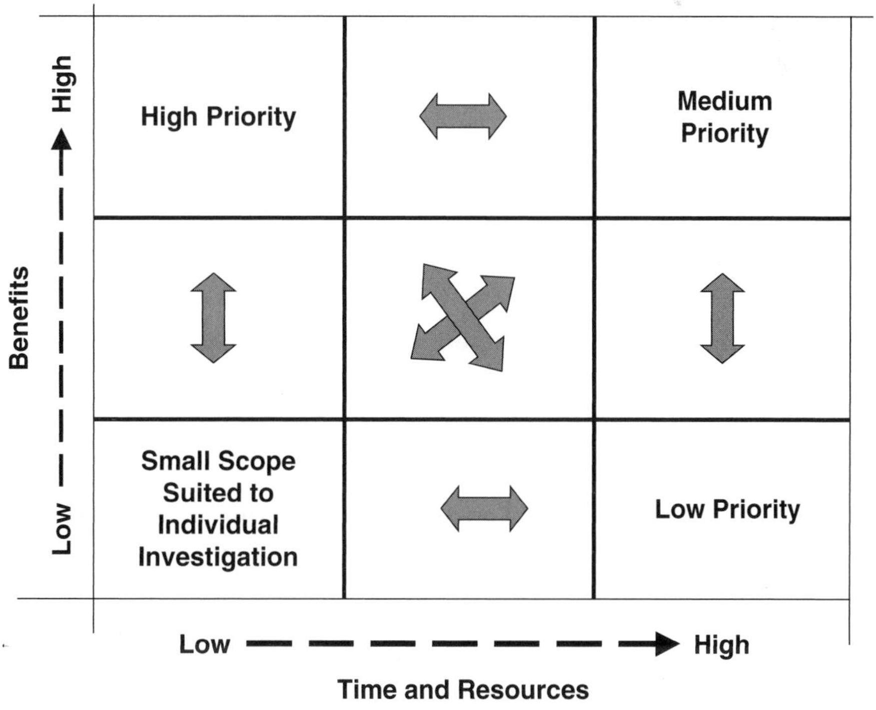

other Six Sigma projects (how will this project help the company to leverage the objectives of the project in the crimping process?).

9.6.1.2 Selection Criteria   Once project ideas have been prioritized, a decision has to be made as to which projects should be assigned to Six Sigma teams. This decision should be based on expected **benefits**, **feasibility**, and **organizational impact**.[4] Benefits should be compatible with the business plan, as well as with strategic and operational goals. Estimating project benefits is more than simply promising improved performance against some set of established measures. Gains can only be considered *benefits* if it can be demonstrated that achieving them will help the organization better execute its strategy. There are seven tests:

Benefits

Feasibility

Organizational Impact

- *Test 1: Impact on Environment*—How is the project likely to affect our customers, supply chain partners, investors, regulators, and competitors?
- *Test 2: Impact on Strategy*—How is the project likely to affect our position in the marketplace, our image, and the execution of our strategy?
- *Test 3: Impact on Capabilities*—How is the project likely to affect the development of internal capabilities? Will it help us improve relative to the sand cone and enterprise engineering scales? Is the project consistent with our core competencies?
- *Test 4: Impact on the Bottom Line*—How is this project likely to affect profits and/or costs in the short term and in the long term? How confident are we in these projections?
- *Test 5: Impact of Doing Nothing*—What will be the consequence of not performing this project? Are the symptoms of the problem getting worse? Is there any reason to believe they might get better without a formal project?
- *Test 6: Urgency*—What is the sense of urgency for this project? Is there a time window of opportunity that will disappear if the project is not selected?
- *Test 7: Dependency*—How is this project linked to other projects? Is this problem part of a larger problem? Does the solution of other problems depend on solving this problem first? Does this problem require the solution of other problems first?

The second criterion for selecting a project is *feasibility*. A project can be infeasible for a number of reasons. It is folly to set up a team for failure by assigning it an insolvable problem. It is wise to tackle the easy problems first and develop a solid track record of successes before moving on to the more complicated issues. Feasibility should be confirmed against five standards:

Resource Availability

- *Confirmation 1:* **Resource Availability**—Do we have enough people, and can we devote the necessary time and money to perform this project within the required timeframe?

Knowledge Access

- *Confirmation 2:* **Knowledge Access**—If this project is selected, will the team have access to the necessary knowledge and expertise they require?

Project Complexity

- *Confirmation 3:* **Project Complexity**—How difficult is this problem to solve? Will the problem-solving process likely be beyond the skills of the Six Sigma team? Have similar problems to this one been solved? What is the likelihood that the team will be able to produce a solution?

---

[4]Pande, Neuman, and Cavanagh, 2000, 145.

Risk of Failure

Companywide Support

- *Confirmation 4:* **Risk of Failure**—What is the probability that, if this project is selected, the team will not be successful in executing all the phases of the DMAIC cycle?
- *Confirmation 5:* **Companywide Support**—How much support will be required across the organization? Will the team likely meet resistance and lack of cooperation? How easy will it be to write a business case justifying the project?

The assessment of broader impacts is made using two impact tests:

Broader impacts are assessed using a knowledge base test and a systems test.

- *Impact 1: Knowledge Base*—How will this project contribute to learning? How will new knowledge be shared with others who could benefit from it? How will this project help improve the ability to think, analyze, and reason?
- *Impact 2: Systems View*—How will this project help remove barriers that inhibit communications and understanding across functional, cultural, and socioeconomic lines? Will the project contribute to a broader perspective of company issues? Will the project facilitate cross-functional interactions?

9.6.2 Sources for New Projects

Project ideas can be generated from the bottom or the top of the organization.

Selecting good projects is important to the success of Six Sigma. The pool of new project ideas can be generated from the top-down and the bottom-up. At the lower rungs of the organization, workers who are closest to the processes can often see problems that are transparent at higher levels. Some organizations have formal systems that encourage suggestions from the floor. These programs can include incentives, such as awarding a prize to each employee whose suggestion is selected for a project. An alternative procedure is to make the generation of project ideas a formal part of Control tollgate reviews. As a project is closed, team members can be afforded the opportunity to suggest ideas for follow-on projects.

Top-down ideas originate with the open systems view. At this level, consideration is given to projects that will support the business strategy, reflect positively in performance measures, and improve the ability to compete. The two major sources for top-down ideas are strategy and the scorecard.

9.6.2.1 Strategic Planning Cycle   The information obtained through the strategic planning process will generate many rich ideas for Six Sigma projects. Chapter 3 covers, in detail, strategic planning—an ongoing activity for senior leadership. The combination of a SWOT analysis and competitor intelligence can generate ideas that capitalize on strengths, eliminate weaknesses, take advantage of opportunities, and develop countermeasures to deal with threats. A focus on core competencies can lead to ideas for a reinvention of value streams. An environmental scan can provide important information on customer expectations and this information, together with a constraints analysis, can generate ideas for projects that will remove constraints and improve customer value. The development of internal capabilities can produce useful project ideas. Also, the sand cone model provides a framework to generate ideas that will strengthen capabilities to better support competitive priorities.

9.6.2.2 Balanced Scorecard   The state of a company's overall health is determined by the key measures contained in the four quadrants of the balanced scorecard. Ideas for projects can be generated by directing pointed questions to each quadrant: customer, internal business, innovation and learning, and financial.

The customer perspective includes measures that are intended to assess customer satisfaction. Improving those measures requires an understanding of the static and dynamic factors that customers care about. Ideas on how the organization can better respond to customer expectations, or how a more satisfying customer experience can be created would merit consideration. Coupling this with lean thinking can stimulate additional ideas by considering how response can be improved by reducing lead times.

Project ideas relating to internal processes are those aimed at improving performance along primary or support value streams, or both. As a starting point, top management could focus on those value streams that have been defined as core business processes and look for leverage points—that is, locations along the value stream that are likely to have the greatest impact on scorecard measures. An alternative viewpoint is to speculate on what process is hindering effectiveness and/or efficiencies the most. Still another criterion is to identify process areas that can be improved quickly and with relative ease.

Innovation and learning ideas are those that would strengthen the knowledge base. This could include such issues as whether to acquire new technologies, the adequacy of process documentation, and training effectiveness.

Financial measures can be improved in two ways: by increasing revenues or by decreasing costs. Business knowledge gained from projects and metrics from the other three scorecard perspectives, when applied to the financial measures, can often help management identify those areas that offer the greatest promise for gain. This could include ideas to increase sales, improve productivity, or reduce waste. Lean projects could likely contribute to the pool of ideas for eliminating waste or reducing inventories.

9.7 COMBINING SIX SIGMA WITH LEAN PRODUCTION

9.7.1 What Is Lean Six Sigma?

Speed

Lean Six Sigma

Quality

Responsiveness

Customers want to do business with companies that can provide quality and timeliness.

Just in time

Delivery Lead Times

Production Batch

Economic Batch Size

Changeover Times

The main thrust of Six Sigma is to reduce mistakes and produce an acceptable product or service on a process that is so near perfect that more than a million good experiences are witnessed before a single unsatisfactory one occurs. The main objective of lean production is the elimination of waste. Lean is also about **speed**. Putting the two concepts together results in **Lean Six Sigma**, a philosophy dedicated to rooting out and eliminating all critical **quality** problems, as well as those factors that restrict flow and create time delays.

Throughout this text, we stress the importance of **responsiveness**. Customers want to do business with companies that can deliver high-quality products and services, and do so in the timeframe required. The ability to meet expectations on shorter **delivery lead times** has become an important quality issue. Numerous companies have adopted **just-in-time** (JIT) scheduling systems and require suppliers to provide more frequent deliveries in smaller quantities. In many cases, these customers also want the option to change the order on short notice. This has presented some new challenges that manufacturers did not have to deal with in the past.

Because deliveries are scheduled just before the actual need, there is no margin for error—in the composition, quality, or quantity of the order. Some companies no longer inspect incoming shipments, trusting that their suppliers will get it right. This JIT environment has also necessitated shorter **production batch** sizes—the **economic batch size** formulae of yesteryear have now been replaced by more progressive thinking, such as looking for ways to shorten **changeover times** and designing manufacturing cells to produce a family of products.

Quality and speed are not the same thing but are closely related. Producing scrap, or even reworkable defects, has a multiplier effect and can significantly slow down a

Just in time has
required more
frequent and shorter
production batches.

factory. For example, a 90% yield (10% scrap) can double the factory cycle time. This is due to reworkable material having to buck the flow and backtrack up the value stream for tear down and repair, additional material having to be scheduled to compensate for scrap losses, operators and inspectors aborting production runs to fix quality problems, and workstation slowdowns when bottleneck operations run out of material.

Muda

Waste

Because lean thinking originated in Japan, an understanding of the lean philosophy adds a number of Japanese words to our quality lexicon. The first of these is **muda**, the Japanese word for **waste**. The object of lean production is to reduce muda, which is defined as anything that does not add value or detracts from it. One of the most obvious historical sources of waste is an excessive investment in inventories. Nothing that is produced adds benefits to the company's financials until it is sold and the customer pays for it. At that point in the transaction, the good or service is converted to revenue and contributes to cash flow. There are three categories of inventories: raw stocks, **work in process** (WIP), and finished goods. The application of sound supply chain management principles can control the levels of the former and latter categories. The WIP inventories must be carefully managed internally. WIP, as the name suggests, represents orders that were started but have not yet been completed. WIP levels can be significant. It is not uncommon to find WIP stacked around a factory that, when tallied up, is the equivalent of months of production. In addition to the investment it represents, excessive WIP can contribute to manufacturing inefficiencies. The pallets must be stacked somewhere, and this often means that aisles are blocked, line of sight is obstructed, and handlers have a difficult time moving materials in and out of workstations in a timely manner. Workers can feel claustrophobic, and not being able to see adjacent workstations means that problems may go unnoticed.

Work in Process

Excessive WIP can
be a cause of
production line
inefficiencies.

A relationship exists between WIP, cycle time, and order processing time that helps explain how large volumes of WIP can slow a factory down. First, we need some definitions:

Flow Time

- **Flow time** (FT), alternatively called throughput time, cycle time, or sojourn time, is the total time an order is in the value stream. The time starts when the order reaches the first value adding workstation and stops when the order rolls off the last station, ready for shipment. FT is expressed in time units (e.g., days, weeks).

Throughput

- **Throughput** (TP) is the average rate of output from a production process. This can apply to the entire plant or a single workstation, or even a single machine. TP is expressed in the number of units per unit time (e.g., number of units per hour).

Short Cycle Time

- **Short cycle time** (SCT) is the reciprocal of TP and can be interpreted as the time between successive output units produced. SCT is expressed in time units per unit output (e.g., number of hours per unit).

- WIP is expressed in units and represents the total number of items that have been through at least one value adding workstation, but have not completed the entire production routing that would change its status to finished goods.

Little's Law

Little's law expresses the relationship between these variables.

Little's Law

$$FT = WIP \times SCT \tag{9-1}$$

$$WIP = FT \times TP \tag{9-2}$$

An illustration of Little's law is the following. Let us assume a plant manager is interested in estimating how much WIP is scattered around the factory. An order has just begun at the first processing point. The component is marked in a location that will be visible in the finished part. The operators at the final assembly point are asked to be on the lookout for a part containing this particular component and, once they have completed it, to bring it immediately to the plant manager's office. On the twenty-first working day, an operator delivered the completed assembly to the plant manager. The flow time was then known to be equal to 21.

Meanwhile, the plant had asked one of the plant engineers to stand at the end of the line (at the last station) and study the output rate. After approximately 100 observations, the engineer reported that it appeared that the line was delivering a unit of output on the average of every thirty seconds or two units per minute. The line in question was scheduled for one eight-hour shift. Using Little's law, the plant manager was able to quickly make the following calculation, using Equation 9-2.

$$WIP = FT \times TP$$
$$WIP = (21 \, days) \times (2 \, units/min) \times (60 \, min/hr) \times (8 \, hr/day)$$
$$WIP = 20,160$$

9.7.2 The Lean Toolkit

There are likely as many lean tools in use as there are consultants trying to help companies implement Lean Six Sigma. New tools are being invented all the time for the purpose of better understanding processes, discovering causal factors, visualizing system relationships and solutions, and better providing improved documentation. Most of the tools covered in Chapters 7 and 8 fit this definition, and so are useful in the implementation of Lean Six Sigma. Our discussion here will be restricted to a few of the major tools that have not been discussed elsewhere. These are pull scheduling, autonomation, changeover reduction, workplace discipline, and TPM.

9.7.2.1 Pull Scheduling and Autonomation   In a traditional factory, individual work schedules originate with a **master production schedule** (MPS). Advanced materials and capacity plans are generated from the MPS, and these plans in turn are used to release orders to the shop floor where production is commenced. The flow of work follows a particular production routing that defines how the product is to be built. Work begins at the first activity shown on the routing and is then "pushed" from workstation to workstation until all activities are complete. Under **push** scheduling, the common procedure for releasing jobs to individual departments is to use increments called "time buckets," which are typically one week in duration. If a particular routing requires the work of nine departments, the flow time under a push system would be a minimum of nine weeks, regardless of how much value adding make time is required. A natural consequence of time bucket scheduling is the accumulation of stockpiles of inventory between departments.

In **pull scheduling**, the discipline is reversed. The triggering mechanism for work order releases is a signal from one workstation to the previous workstation that more material is needed. No workstation produces under a pull system until its output is needed further down the value stream. **Pull** is an internal requisitioning procedure that starts at the back end of the value stream and triggers orders, step by step, toward the

Master Production Schedule

Push

Time Buckets

In a push system, jobs are scheduled from the front end using time increments called buckets.

Pull Scheduling

Pull

In a pull system, work is triggered from the back end and only produced as needed.

Shop Floor Control

Kanbans

front end. Pull scheduling does not eliminate the need for advanced materials and aggregate planning—functions that are performed well by programs such as manufacturing resources planning modules.

Under the right conditions, pull scheduling can be an effective system for **Shop floor control**. Cards, called **kanbans**, are the usual means for establishing shop floor communications. Kanban is a term that is the combination of two Japanese words: Kan meaning card, and Ban meaning signal.

In a kanban system, the flow of materials is controlled using a method by which workstations can exchange signals when one is about to run out of material. By pulling rather than pushing material through the plant, work is only produced as needed. There is no longer the time bucket constraint, and an entire production batch does not need to be completed before material can be transferred to a subsequent workstation. Kanban containers, of a size that can be manually transported between workstations, permit small quantities of materials to be transported to the next operation as soon as a container is filled.

There are numerous benefits to pull scheduling. The most dramatic is a decrease in inventories. Inventory reduction does not eliminate the need for WIP, but under a pull system WIP levels can be tightly managed, and used only as required to buffer against process variability or to keep bottleneck operations fully functional.

A kanban signal need not be a card. The signaling medium does not even have to be written. Any kind of visual signal can suffice. Rolling colored golf balls down a chute, hoisting a flag, or using a semaphore-style code can be effective. One simple form of kanban involves painting a square on the floor or taping off a designated area on a workbench between two operators. When material occupies the square, the upstream operator does not produce. When the area is deplete of material, the upstream operator knows that it is okay to start producing again.

A variation of kanban incorporates a priority system. Rush jobs can be identified using a distinguishing kanban color. For example, if red indicates top priority, operators would be instructed to process red cards ahead of other colors.

Takt time is the per unit time allowed to meet the customer's timeframe.

Takt Time

Pull scheduling works best if demand is relatively stable, and maintaining a capacity balance between workstations is important. Because material will only be produced when required, an unbalanced line leads to inefficiencies. In contrast, efficiencies accrue when the entire value stream is rhythmic. When work is performed at a common pace, there is little waste, and resource utilization is high. The lean tool used to instill such rhythm is called **takt time**. Here we break from our convention of using terms that have Japanese derivatives. The word *takt* comes from the German word that is used for the baton a conductor uses to direct an orchestra. Just as the conductor uses rhythm to create precise timing, balancing a factory line to takt time puts all activities stroking to the same beat. Takt time is defined as the SCT required to meet customer demand and is computed by dividing the total available time (less any breaks, team meetings, and allowances for nonproductive downtime) by the customer demand that must be satisfied during that period. As an example, assume a plant must ship 120 of a particular product per day. Taking into account allowances for nonproductive time, there are 450 minutes available per day for production.

$$\text{Takt Time} = \frac{\text{Time Available}}{\text{Demand to Satisfy}}$$

$$\text{Takt Time} = \frac{450 \text{ Minutes}}{120 \text{ Units}} = 3.75 \text{ min/unit}$$

(9-3)

FIGURE 9-9 A Push Production Line

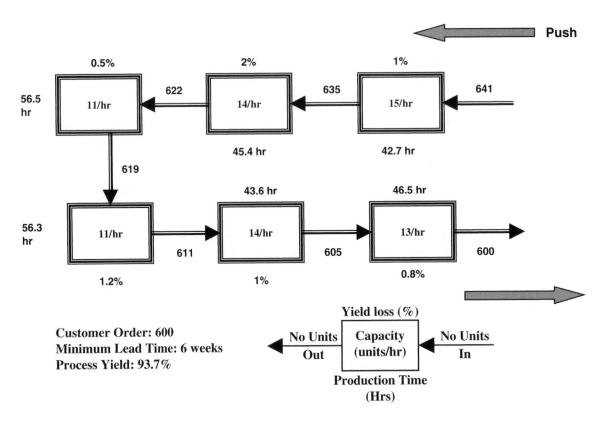

Yield Loss   Line Utilization $= \dfrac{291 \text{ Value Add Hours}}{339 \text{ Scheduled Hours}} = 85.4\%$

Customer Order: 600
Minimum Lead Time: 6 weeks
Process Yield: 93.7%

To meet this demand, one unit needs to be completed every 3.75 minutes. Figures 9-9 and 9-10 contrast two production scenarios. The first illustrates the use of a push system to fill the order in question, and the second the use of pull scheduling to fill the same order. The order received was for a total of 600 units of a part that has to pass through six departments. In the push system, the expected yield losses across the line require that the material for 641 parts be introduced into the line. The capacities, expressed as the number of units per hour, also vary and are shown for each department. These differences lead to slight line imbalances and, for this particular order, the overall utilization of the resources across the line is only 85.4%. The entire order will be produced as a batch and will show up in successive weeks on the production schedule for each department in turn. Departments are responsible for handing off the completed batch to the next department by the end of the week. Therefore, the minimum lead time for pushing the job through all six departments is six weeks.

In the pull system, the large order of 600 has been broken down into small daily kanban quantities of 120. The line has been better balanced using the takt time of 3.75 minutes as the target. One of the benefits of the pull system is its emphasis on participation and quality improvement. Teams in each of the six departments have been successful in substantially improving yields. The pull system has

FIGURE 9-10 A Pull Production Line

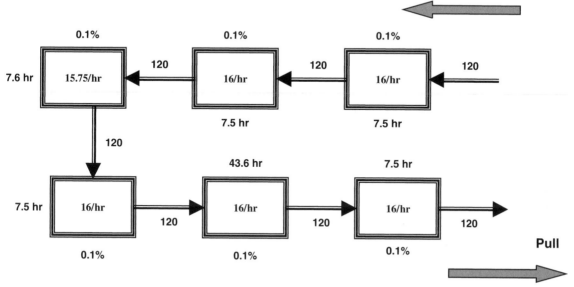

Yield Loss

$$\text{Line Efficiency} = \frac{45 \text{ Value Add Hours}}{45.6 \text{ Scheduled Hours}} = 98.6\%$$

Customer Order: 120/day
Minimum Lead Time: 5 days
Process Yield: 99.8%

$$\text{Takt Time} = \frac{\text{Time Available}}{\text{Demand to Satisfy}} = \frac{450 \text{ Minutes}}{120 \text{ Units}} = 3.75 \text{ min/unit}$$

increased line utilization to 98.6% and reduced lead time to five days—a significant improvement.

Balancing the capacities in a pull system to takt time is the ideal; however, designing to takt time will not eliminate variability. It will still exist within and between workstations due to variability in processing times and in capacity imbalances. Such variations can be smoothed out by placing small kanban quantities of WIP inventories ahead of certain workstations and by flexing capacity. **Flexible capacity** can be achieved by investing in backup machines and through multitasking (being able to move personnel to where they are needed).

Flexible Capacity

Andon

An andon is a visual signaling device.

Another tool that is useful in pull systems is called **andon**, the Japanese name for a paper lantern. Andons, used in antiquity to light the way, were like inverted lampshades with candles and were used in the same way a flashlight is today. In manufacturing plants, andons are used as visual signaling devices. A common use is a lighting system that operates similar to a traffic light with red, yellow, and green. When the light is green, production is proceeding smoothly. If something goes wrong, an operator can summon help by turning on the yellow light or stop the line by activating the red light. Andons can also be used for other purposes, such as signaling a material handler to replenish the stocks of a certain type of material.

Jidoka

Autonomation

Jidoka requires
operators to halt
production when-
ever they see a
problem.

Lean production has its roots in the Toyota production system (TPS)[5] and has two principle pillars. Pull scheduling is one, and autonomation is the other. The Japanese word for autonomation is **jidoka**, the policy that requires operators to stop a production line any time they see a problem. Jidoka is human intervention in an automated process. The English name **autonomation** comes from the two root words autonomous and automation. The idea is to empower people to autonomously detect problems and stop production. However, autonomation is more than simply stopping the line. It also means tracking down the root cause and solving the problem. This means that operators must be trained to spot problems and empowered to stop a line to fix them when they occur. It is much better to halt production than to continue to produce poor quality. Jidoka can be intimidating to some employees who are fearful of having to accept such an awesome responsibility. After all, halting an entire production line is a big deal. An answer to this is the three-color andon system described previously. If an employee is uncertain whether a problem is serious enough to warrant a shutdown, the yellow light can be activated, summoning a supervisor.

Heijunka

Heijunka helps
smooth out sporadic
demand.

Where demand is sporadic, a technique called **heijunka** can sometimes be helpful. Heijunka is a Japanese word that means to make flat and level, and this method has been used successfully to absorb fluctuations in demand without increasing inventory buffers. Heijunka smoothes out demand by breaking down the total volume of orders during some predetermined demand period (e.g., thirteen weeks) into small scheduling intervals (e.g., days). A repetitive production sequence is then calculated for a scheduling interval, and a mixed model schedule is established for a given production line. A kanban system is then used to control the correct sequence of materials through the value stream.

To understand how heijunka works, consider the following example. A consumer electronics plant produces three products—the Honker, the Wolfer, and the Squeeler. Demands are frozen six weeks out, and the aggregate demand for all three models for the next six-week-period is 36,720. Broken down into individual products this translates to 18,360 Honkers, 12,240 Wolfers, and 6,120 Squeelers. The plant operates three shifts, five days per week. The six-week demand will have to be completed over ninety shifts (6 weeks × 5 days × 3 shifts). A scheduling interval at this plant is one shift. Therefore, the demand per shift is as follows:

$$\text{Honkers: } 18,360/90 = 204$$
$$\text{Wolfers: } 12,240/90 = 136$$
$$\text{Squeelers: } 6,120/90 = 68$$
$$\text{Total Demand per Shift} = 408$$

Using Equation 9-3, takt time for a shift is computed using 450 minutes of available time.

$$\text{Takt Time} = \frac{450 \text{ Minutes Available}}{408 \text{ Items Produced}} = 1.103 \text{ Minutes per Item}$$

---

[5]Ohno, Taiichi. *Toyota Production System: Beyond Large-Scale Production.* Cambridge, MA: Productivity Press, 1988.

The ratios of each product to the total are computed as follows:

$$\text{Honker: } 204/408 = 3/6$$
$$\text{Wolfer: } 136/408 = 2/6$$
$$\text{Squeeler: } 68/408 = 1/6$$

Using the least common denominator of 68, we find that a production sequence can be designed with a cycle equal to 6 takt time units and this cycle would repeat every $(6)(1.103) = 6.618$ minutes for a total of 68 times during the shift. Within each cycle, numerous sequences are possible and permissible as long as the ratios of the product mix computed previously are maintained—it does not matter how this is done because the sequence cycle is so short. Two possible sequences are as follows:

Honker—Honker—Honker—Wolfer—Wolfer—Squeeler
Honker—Wolfer—Honker—Squeeler—Honker—Wolfer

By running small and even batches of the models over these short intervals, materials move smoothly between workstations and inventories can be maintained at low levels.

There are situations where a push system may work better than pull. However, even push systems can benefit from some of the pull features, such as andon and jidoka. Some companies have found that a combination of pull and push is necessary to accommodate product variety and different types of production processes.

9.7.2.2 Changeover Reduction When different products are manufactured on the same production line, adjustments must be made when changing over from one product to the production of another. This could involve anything from a die change to adjustments in settings, speeds, feeds, or crewing. Changeovers add cost but not value. While the machine is being set up, no output is produced. This is part of the fixed cost of a run and has been used as one of the variables in the following formula that is typically found in textbooks for calculating the **economic batch quantity**:

Economic Batch Quantity

$$\text{EBQ} = \sqrt{\frac{2(\text{Setup Costs})(\text{Demand})}{\text{Inventory Cost}\left(1 - \dfrac{\text{Demand}}{\text{Production Rate}}\right)}} \tag{9-4}$$

Equation 9-4 uses a trade-off between the fixed cost of setting up for a production run and the cost of overproducing and holding inventories to compute minimum cost batch quantity. Large inventory costs will drive the economical batch size down; large **setup** costs will drive it up. In a lean environment, the combination of flexibility and low inventories dictates small batch sizes. In many cases, the desirable batch size is less than the quantity that would result from applying Equation 9-4. For example, customers requiring JIT deliveries will likely insist on receiving their monthly requirements on a daily basis instead of all at once.

Setup

Changeover time is the sum of setup time and runup time.

With a changeover reduction strategy, it may be possible to have it both ways—that is, short batch quantities and minimal costs. First, we need to make a distinction between setup and changeover. Setup includes all the activities necessary before a production run can be commenced. **Changeover** is the total time between producing good product on the previous run and producing good product on the next run at the target speed. Changeover is the sum of setup time and runup time. Runup is the initial

Changeover

FIGURE 9-11 Changeover and Loss of Production

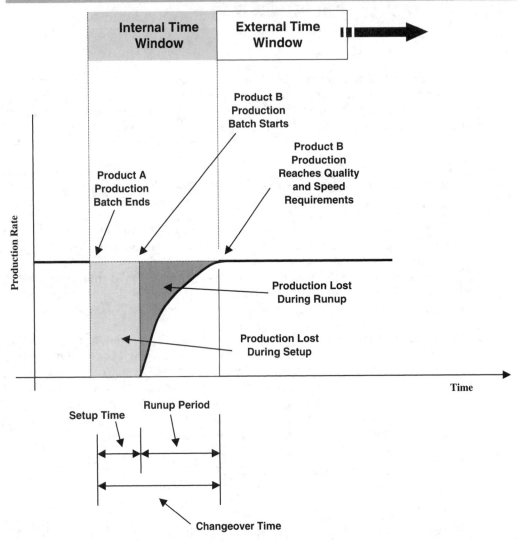

production period when the operator is fine-tuning machine adjustments and trying to get the quality right. Changeover time represents a period during which **production loss** occurs. This is illustrated in Figure 9-11.

Production Loss

Changeover reduction shrinks the time devoted to changeovers so more time is available for production. The seminal work in changeover reduction is due to Shigeo Shingo, who asserted that changeovers should take no longer than ten minutes.[6] This can be achieved by separating all those activities associated with setup time into two categories: internal and external. **External setup activities** include all the things that an operator can do to get ready for the next job while the current job is still running, such

External Setup Activities

---

[6]Shingo, Shigeo. *A Revolution in Manufacturing: The Smed System,* 25. Stamford, CT: Productivity Press, 1985.

Internal Setup Activities

as fetching the necessary tools. **Internal setup activities** are those that cannot be carried out while the line is up and running, such as changing out dies. Once all activities have been placed into one category or the other, a three-step process can be carried out to try to reduce the total changeover time:

- *Step 1—Try to convert some internal activities to external ones.* Can extra tooling be available so some time-consuming prep work can be accomplished ahead of time?
- *Step 2—Try to reduce the time required to perform the internal tasks.* Can we make use of design changes, taking advantage of such features as quick-release fasteners, keyhole slots for quick alignments, and standardized bolts?
- *Step 3—Develop a pit crew mentality.* Once changes have been made, the operators should practice and compete against themselves to better their times in much the same way that a pit crew would strive to improve performance on the race track. The crew should continually look for ways to improve how changeovers are conducted using techniques such as videotaping and critiquing actual changeovers.

Cellular Manufacturing

Mixed Model Scheduling

Group Technology

An alternative approach to changeover reduction is the widespread use of **cellular manufacturing**, in which a cell produces a family of products. The products that go through a cell are so similar that mixed model scheduling methods can often be employed. With **mixed model scheduling**, theoretically every other item can be different—that is, using a manufacturing batch size equal to one. **Group technology** (a method that groups product numbers based on manufacturing similarities) is used to form product families, and the production differences are so slight (e.g., a hole drilled in slightly different locations) that rapid changeovers are possible. Cells are autonomous work groups comprised of workers whose jobs have been enlarged and enriched. Their ability to multitask means they can flex capacity to meet changing needs and their personal sense of responsibility for quality has the effect of reducing the error rate.

The 5S workplace discipline helps achieve efficiency.

9.7.2.3 The Workplace Discipline   Workplace efficiency begins with good housekeeping. The Japanese use five words, all beginning with the letter "S," to define a workplace discipline that facilitates flow. These words are **seiri**, **seiton**, **seiso**, **seiketsu**, and **shitsuke**. Some companies use these original words and train all personnel in their meanings. Others have tried to adopt equivalent English words that also begin with the letter "S":

Seiri

Seiton

Seiso

Seiketsu

Shitsuke

- *Seiri (Sift or Sort).* The first step in establishing a workplace discipline is to go through the clutter and only keep what is necessary. What is unnecessary should be discarded. If something is not used regularly, or there is no anticipated use for it, it is best to remove it from the workplace. This includes tools or materials that have not been used for a length of time and are not likely to be needed in the future. Files and papers that have no use should also be discarded or boxed up for storage (if there is an archival purpose). The idea is to free up the space so items and materials that are needed on a daily basis can easily be located. Seiri also includes a thorough cleaning of the workplace, eliminating dust, oil, debris, and the like.

  Deciding to dispose of a specific item can be questionable, and a difference of opinion within the work group can arise. A tagging system can be a convenient procedure for making such controversial decisions. A tag is placed on the item in question with a date, usually about six months into the future. If the item is used before the date is reached, the tag is removed. Otherwise, the item is discarded.

- *Seiton (Sort or Straighten).*   An efficient workplace has a place for everything, and everything is kept in its rightful place. Human factors engineering can be used to design the workstation so that frequently used items are within easy reach to avoid bending, stretching, or even excessive walking. The need for heavy lifting can be eliminated through the use of wheeled containers or conveyors. Tools can be mounted on fixtures that hang from overhead gantries and that can be easily accessed with little effort. In tool shops, shadow boards can be constructed to ensure hand tools are returned to their proper locations. The use of labeling and compartmented drawers can also help personnel find what they need, when they need it, without wasting valuable time.

- *Seiso (Sweep or Shine).*   Seiso is about maintaining cleanliness and tidiness. Once all the clutter is gone and everything needed has been assigned a proper place, it is important that the workplace stay that way. Daily cleaning routines now become part of the job of every worker. The maintenance of a neat working environment includes keeping equipment clean and in good working order, and ensuring tools and materials are where they should be. It is a good idea to institute a daily check sheet procedure where a crew is required to sign off on each item. This procedure provides documentation that seiso is being carried out. Certain tasks may require some special skills (e.g., performing routine maintenance) and it is management's responsibility to ensure workers are properly trained to perform them.

- *Seiketsu (Spick and Span or Systemize):*   Seiketsu is the continual maintenance of seiri, seiton, and seiso. This step simply says, "maintain the routine that has been established for workplace tidiness and order." The 5S discipline becomes the new companywide standard, and it is often difficult to get all employees onboard with the new mind-set. Seiketsu is one indication of how rapidly the culture is transforming to the new order. Inspections can result in generous praise, sometimes accompanied by tangible recognition for the deserving, and suggestions for improvement in cases where standards have not been met. In the latter case, there are times when management needs to assist a workstation that is having trouble meeting organizational goals.

- *Shitsuke (Sustain):*   Shitsuke is the Kaisen of the 5S discipline. The first four steps are about establishing and maintaining a neat and organized workplace. Shitsuke is concerned with improvements—how can the state of cleanliness and order be improved? This goes beyond simple housekeeping. In this step, workers tackle the underlying causes of disorder and grime. For example, spills and leaks can be quickly cleaned, but it is far better to discover and eliminate the causes so they occur with less frequency or do not recur. Tools such as fishbone diagrams and Pareto charts can help because workers strive to identify problems. Under shitsuke, work is no longer viewed as the execution of standard methods. Workers collectively gain an improving team mind that is continually on the lookout for better methods.

9.7.2.4 Total Productive Maintenance   Research has shown that in many factories machines are only running about 60% of the time. The 40% downtime is almost equally split between personal breaks and maintenance, on the one hand, and setup time and machine breakdowns, on the other hand.[7] These numbers are alarming because they

---

[7]George, Michael L. *Lean Six Sigma: Combining Six Sigma Quality with Lean Speed*, 57. New York: McGraw-Hill, 2002.

FIGURE 9-12 Effect of Variability on Process Delays

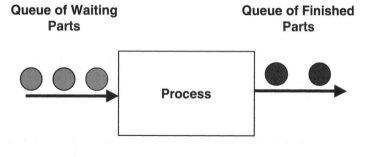

Queue of Waiting Parts   Queue of Finished Parts

Process

$$\text{Expected Delay} = \frac{\text{Utilization}}{(1 - \text{Utilization})} \times (\text{Variation in SCT})$$

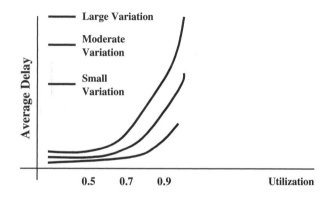

suggest a gold mine of untapped capacity. Figure 9-12 illustrates a principle drawn from queuing theory that defines the relationship between wait time, utilization, and variation. As machine utilization approaches 100%, the first term on the right of the expected delay formula approaches infinity. At that level, any variability in workstation processing time can drive the WIP (waiting in front of that workstation), and its corresponding wait time, off the planet!

A second insight from Figure 9-12 is that as processing variability increases; the waiting time climbs exponentially. Even a moderate amount of variability can introduce a waiting time that is nine to ten times the average service time. High variability can result in substantially longer delays. This is significant because wait time adds cost and no value. By increasing uptime, capacity is increased and the effect of variability on delays is reduced. As an added benefit, the actions that are taken to increase uptime sometimes also reduce the variability in processing times.

Total productive maintenance (TPM) is a lean tool that uses the operators of machines to help identify and solve problems associated with equipment downtime. TPM programs track unproductive time in six loss categories:

- Machine **downtime**
- Machine **setups**

If processing variability is high, wait times can be many times greater than processing times.

Total Productive Maintenance

Downtime

Setups

- Minor production stoppages
- Unscheduled breaks
- Production time spent in rework
- Waste

Data collected in these six categories are tied to three measures: availability (time), performance (speed), and yield (quality). The product of the losses in the three areas is a macromeasure called the overall equipment effectiveness (OEE) score. It provides a means for comparing machines and work centers, and helps teams focus on the most problematic areas for improvement.

TPM has two goals—zero breakdowns and zero defects. Simultaneously reducing downtime and production errors will improve equipment utilization and efficiency, reduce costs, and minimize inventory costs associated with spare parts. TPM involves a five-prong attack:

1. Track and document losses. Compute and evaluate the OEE for each critical workstation.

2. Involve the machine operators by allowing them to take responsibility for certain maintenance tasks, such as
   a. The performance of routine repairs and maintenance
   b. Taking proactive action to prevent problems before they occur
   c. Seeking solutions to problems to prevent their recurrence

3. Take a systematic approach to maintenance where standards are developed and preventive plans are devised. Maintenance specialists are used to oversee maintenance activities, provide assistance in problem diagnostics, and specifically train and supervise operators in carrying out routine maintenance and repair tasks.

4. Provide relevant and continuous training to all personnel in maintenance skills related to their particular work environments.

5. Achieve zero maintenance through maintenance prevention (MP). MP is a proactive approach that tracks failures to their root causes, and the information is then used to eliminate those causes at the earliest possible point in the equipment design phase. Equipment design should not only consider failures, but also take into account maintainability during the life of the machine.

TPM is important to Lean Six Sigma. It is estimated that within three years of adopting TPM, most companies can expect between 17% and 26% increases in machine uptime, 90% reduction in process defects, and up to 50% increase in productivity.[8]

SUMMARY OF LEARNING OBJECTIVES AND KEY OUTCOMES

1. *Define Six Sigma, and describe the features that have made this approach successful in many companies.* Six Sigma is a management paradigm that strives to improve the competitiveness of a company. It involves a system of setting and aggressively pursuing goals that support the organization's strategy and that matter to customers. Employee

---

[8]Nakajima, Seiichi. *Introduction to TPM: Total Productive Maintenance,* 2. Cambridge, MA: Productivity Press, 1988.

participation at all levels is encouraged, and recommendations for improvement are justified based on facts that arise from data. Six Sigma strives for perfection, and uses discipline and organization to achieve it. The three main features of Six Sigma are (1) projects must be justified based on goals expressed in financial terms that senior managers can understand, (2) projects are selected on the basis of the expected benefits to the organization, and (3) managers play an active role in selecting projects and personnel, and in monitoring the teams' progress.

2. *Describe the concept of a core business process, and determine where these processes fit in the open system and in Six Sigma.* In an open system, the process of transforming inputs to outputs consists of primary and support value streams. Those value streams that are primary are identified in Six Sigma as core business processes, and these processes are the ones that receive the major emphasis for improvement projects. A company's core business processes will be few, typically numbering between five and eight.

3. *Discuss the five phases of the DMAIC cycle.* The five phases are define, measure, analyze, improve, and control. In the Define phase, a team charter is drafted that justifies the project, projects benefits, provides a timeline for completion, and assigns responsibilities. A customer needs analysis is performed during which the team strives to learn as much as possible about the key customers of the process under investigation. Finally, during the Define phase, a SIPOC map of the process is drawn so team members can get a pictorial view of the process components and how they relate to customers and suppliers.

During the Measure phase, the team collects information to learn as much as possible about the process under investigation. Measures will be analyzed using a Six Sigma score, which is a measure that is a 1.5σ adjustment from the statistical calculation of process capability. The tools used are drawn from the toolkit that has been widely used in TQM and other quality initiatives.

The Analyze phase is concerned with proving cause-and-effect relationships, with the aim of tagging a few causes for elimination. This is the most rigorous of the phases, and may require advanced statistical tools and some help from experts outside the team structure.

During the Improve phase, the team brainstorms solution ideas. Each idea must be tested and carefully evaluated before deciding on a recommended solution. Some advanced statistical tools may also need to be used during this phase.

Finally, the Control phase implements the solution. This step requires the full documentation of any new procedures, handing off to the process owner, and training those employees that will be affected.

4. *Define the key roles in a Six sigma improvement project.* The key roles are the leadership council, the champion, the master black belt, the black belt or green belt, and the team members. The leadership council sets the tone and pace for the implementation. The members of this group are enablers, and are there to remove roadblocks, provide resources, and direct the overall effort.

The champion is a senior manager and the process owner who may have several active teams working on problems. The champion acts as a team advocate, provides resources, removes roadblocks, and resolves conflicts.

A master black belt is an internal consultant who is responsible for training, mentoring, and coaching other personnel in Six Sigma tools.

The black belt is permanently assigned to a team as the team leader and is responsible for the day-to-day activities of the team.

Green belts have had some training in Six Sigma tools, are part-time resources, are assigned to teams, and independently perform special tasks.

The white belt is someone who has received a few hours of Six Sigma awareness training. These individuals form a pool of people who have a broad understanding of expectations, benefits, and roles.

5. *Design a training curriculum for each key player in a Six Sigma implementation.* Senior managers should receive a total of three to five weeks of training to prepare them for the duties of the leadership council and champion. Suitable training topics include awareness, DMAIC, basic tools, teaming, systems management, and change management.

Black belts should receive a total of four to six weeks of training to prepare them for the duties of team leader. Training topics should include basic and intermediate process improvement tools, teaming, and change management.

Green belts should receive a total of two to three weeks of training to prepare them for team support roles. Topics should include awareness, teaming, and a course covering the basic toolkit. White belts receive awareness training only.

A master black belt must first be a black belt, and have led a minimum number of projects and achieved substantial improvements. In addition, the master black belt enrols in external specialized courses prescribed by the company.

6. *Describe the Six Sigma procedure for selecting projects.* Project ideas are initially screened on the basis of the trade-offs between benefits and the effort and time required. Once the list is narrowed, the final selection is based on benefits, feasibility, and broader impact. To qualify as a benefit, a project must pass seven tests: environment, strategy, capabilities, bottom line, doing nothing, urgency, and dependency.

Project feasibility is confirmed by testing resource availability, access to knowledge, complexity, risk, and company support. Broader impacts are assessed using systems and knowledge base tests.

7. *Suggest some ways in which Six Sigma projects can be generated.* Six Sigma projects can be generated from the top-down or the bottom-up. From the bottom, employees can be encouraged to make suggestions through a formal system that may contain an awards feature. The last tollgate review can also be a valuable source for ideas for follow-on projects.

At the top, managers can use the strategic planning cycle to stimulate good project ideas. The balanced scorecard can also be used. By reviewing the various metrics, those measures that offer the greatest potential for improvement can be selected as possible Six Sigma projects.

8. *Define the lean production philosophy and how it complements Six Sigma.* Six Sigma is aimed at improving quality and processes that produce it. Lean is about speed and the elimination of waste. Combining speed and quality improves responsiveness to customers' needs. The elimination of waste will not only speed up a production process, but it will also improve quality.

9. *Apply Little's law.* Little's law expresses the relationship between WIP, TP rate, and flow time. Using Little's law, WIP can be estimated by multiplying the flow time by the TP rate.

10. *Describe how pull scheduling differs from a traditional push system.* In a push system, orders are scheduled into production on the front end of the value stream and then pushed toward the back end. Normally, an entire order must be completed in one department before being transferred to the next. This process lengthens lead time and results in excessive WIP buildup. In a pull system, the materials control mechanism is reversed. Scheduling starts at the back end, and each workstation triggers work activity at the previous workstation by signaling when it is about to run out of material. In the pull system, work is only produced as required, thereby reducing both lead times and WIP.

11. *Compute takt time, and describe the significance of balancing a value stream to its takt time.* Takt time is computed by dividing the available production time (taking out allowances) by customer demand that must be filled during that time. When a value stream is balanced to takt time, WIP is kept to a minimum and the utilization of production resources is high.

12. *Define andon, jidoka, and heijunka, and describe how they are used in a Lean Six Sigma environment.* An andon is a visual signaling system, usually with lights, and commonly used to signal problems on the production line. Andons are often used in conjunction with jidoka, a policy that requires an operator to halt production when a problem is spotted. Heijunka is a method for aggregating uneven demand over a large period and breaking it down into small scheduling intervals, then calculating a repetitive production sequence for each interval.

13. *Define some changeover reduction strategies that can be used to shorten lead times.* One approach for shortening changeover time is to carefully define each activity required during a changeover, and then to label each activity as either external or internal. Make certain that external activities are performed during run time, leaving only the internal activities to be done during setup. Changeover time can possibly be reduced further by looking for ways to transfer internal activities to the external list, by reengineering the process to make use of standardization and quick-change devices, and by developing within the team a pit crew mentality where the group continually strives to beat its best time.

A second approach to changeover reduction is through cellular manufacturing. Using group technology to organize products into families, changeovers between different products can be almost seamless.

14. *Explain the 5S strategy for workplace discipline.* The steps of the 5S workplace discipline are seiri, seiton, seiso, seiketsu, and shitsuke. The first step, *seiri,* is to dispose of any material or equipment around the workplace that is not used or useable. The second step, *seiton,* is to give all items that are used a designated place and to make them easily accessible to the worker. The third step, *seiso,* is to make daily cleaning of the workplace part of the routine. The fourth step, *seiketsu,* is to make certain that the standards of cleanliness are working, and the last step, *shitsuke,* is to try and improve the ability of the workplace to remain orderly and tidy.

15. *Explain the purpose of total productive maintenance (TPM) and how TPM is intended to operate.* TPM has two goals: zero breakdowns and zero defects. To achieve these, TPM attacks maintenance on five fronts—track and document losses, get machine operators involved in routine maintenance and improvement, take a systematic approach, provide continuous and relevant training, and implement a proactive MP program.

TO TEST YOUR UNDERSTANDING

9-1   Imagine that you have been hired as a consultant to help a company implement Six Sigma. The company is in a highly competitive business where its customers require quality and responsiveness. Deliveries have to be made within a day on either side of the promised date and order quantities are often changed on short notice. The company has been practicing TQM for more than a decade and control charts are visible in many of the work centers. In the last five quarters, the company's market share has been trending downward as large accounts are lost to the competition. What are some of the issues that you would want to investigate first?

9-2   How does lean production support the objectives of Six Sigma? Can Six Sigma be successfully implemented without also implementing lean principles? Explain.

9-3   Visual controls, such as andon and kanban, are an important part of lean production strategies. How do such controls help achieve the objectives of Lean Six Sigma? How does the reduction in WIP facilitate the use of visual controls?

9-4   Why do you think that lean production stresses the elimination of WIP? Under what conditions is WIP advantageous? How can its levels be controlled? How can Little's formula help?

9-5   In TQM implementations, the focus is on training all employees, and instruction is provided in many of the tools presented in Chapters 7 and 8. By comparison, Six Sigma emphasized a certification program for proficiency in quality tools. Discuss the relative merits of each approach.

9-6   Are Six Sigma organizations also HPWOs? Explain.

9-7   Why is a progressive maintenance strategy important to the success of Six Sigma? How does the 5S workplace discipline support TPM?

9-8   Explain why changeover reduction is important to heijunka.

9-9   In a minerals plant, viscosity is an important quality characteristic of a particular product. The target viscosity is 1,300, and the customer has agreed to accept viscosities in the range 1,100 to 1,500. Six samples are taken per shift and sent to the QC lab for testing. The averages and ranges of all six samples are plotted on $\overline{X}$ and R charts, respectively. The $\overline{X}$ chart shows good control with a centerline $\overline{\overline{X}} = 1435$ and the range chart is in control with a centerline $\overline{R} = 46.88$.
   a. What is the Six Sigma score for this process?
   b. What is the long-term process yield?
   c. Compute the DFMO.

9-10 ABC Ltd. manufactures three parts: X, Y, and Z. Orders are on hand to deliver a total of 45,000 parts to various customers over the next four-week period. The part number breakdown is 4,500 of X, 22,500 of Y, and 18,000 of Z. The plant producing these parts works two eight-hour shifts (with a 10% allowance for downtime), five days per week. Design an heijunka production sequence for these parts, assuming cellular manufacturing and a scheduling unit of one shift. What is the takt time? What is the length of a production cycle? How many times will this cycle be repeated during a shift?

9-11 The demand for a certain customer is 50,000 gizmos to be produced during the next five days. If the factory operates a single eight-hour shift, what is the takt time for this order, allowing 10% nonproductive time for breaks and machine downtime?

◆●◆

Sertex Sealants, Inc.

The Seal of Excellence

Sertex Sealants, Inc., has been in business for thirty-three years producing sealing strips for automobiles. Sertex rubber seals can be found around door moldings, trunk lids, and windshields of many popular cars and trucks. The company operates two plants—an extrusion plant where production starts, and a finishing plant, where holes are drilled, fabric added, and fasteners attached, depending on specifications. Manufacturing cells, consisting of between six and eight workers, perform various finishing operations. A job will go through several cells before it is ready for shipment.

The extrusion operation paints a color stripe on each part that is distinctive of that particular part number. When the cell receives a batch of work they can immediately tell if this batch is reds, greens, blues, and so on. The cell team has become so proficient with the activities for each color that they can change from one color to another with minimal changeover time. Each batch comes to the cell in a kanban unit—a moveable cart on wheels that contains 150 strips. It takes the team about one hour on the average to work off a kanban batch.

All Sertex's customers require daily deliveries. Trucks start departing the loading dock at 10 a.m. each day and continue until 4 p.m., when the last truck leaves. At 4:30 p.m., Hank Dunlop, a material expeditor, receives a report on orders that for whatever reason missed the last truck. Hank then gets on the phone and arranges special shipments by air freight. In the last twelve months, Sertex paid a total of $800,000 for premium shipments by air.

Jerry Crenshaw, General Manager, cannot understand why his company does so poorly in meeting customer commitments on time. After all, advanced orders are taken right off the electronic data interchange system that provides his company with a six-week frozen production schedule for each product. Three years ago, the Sertex process improvement team—an internal consulting group consisting of three engineers—designed a kanban system to operate between the two plants. In addition, the plant manager of the finishing plant, Dick Wainwright, holds a production meeting each day at 9 a.m. to discuss any high-priority jobs in the pipeline and to finalize the day's production schedule. Each department head also conducts a weekly meeting with the team leader of each production cell to review control charts and discuss any quality problems. Nevertheless, more recently, the number of customer complaints has been increasing. Jerry has decided to bring in some experts from outside the company for advice.

A team from CPR Consulting, headed by Joyce Brady, arrived bright and early Monday morning. By noon, they were interviewing personnel and pouring over documentation. On Wednesday, they reported the following findings to the General Manager:

1. The kanban system is not working. It was designed to requisition materials from the extrusion plant for the *current* day's orders, not the *following* day's requirements. As a result, inventories build for materials that are not needed.

2. The daily production meetings are a farce. Department heads discuss the daily requirements and agree on a schedule. Then, following the meeting, some of these supervisors will check on-hand inventory levels in the warehouse and make their own decisions on what should be produced. In many cases, inventory in the warehouse has already been earmarked for shipment to customers.

3. Large discrepancies were found between physical counts in the warehouse and computer records.

4. An extraordinary number of full kanban containers were observed stacked around the plant. Consultants were told that these were orders that were in process, but no one could provide clear documentation as to the exact details of the work. A quick tally revealed that this material represents approximately six months' production.

5. Approximately 70% of the workforce has had some training in quality tools, including basic SPC and pull scheduling. However, the application of these tools appears to vary widely across the plant. There appears to be little conscientious effort at ongoing quality improvement.

6. Orders that are complete and ready for shipment are loaded onto a truck and transported to finished goods inventory in a warehouse two miles from the plant. Trucks can sit at the plant dock for hours before being moved. Completed orders are added to computerized inventory records by Mary White at the warehouse, based on receiving documentation handed to her by warehouse staff, after they have verified the material with respect to part number and quantity.

7. Sertex has six customers; four of them account for 83% of the business. Demand can be forecasted out to ten weeks in the future, and with reasonable certainty, six weeks ahead. Demand

patterns are stable. Last-minute changes sometimes occur, but this is the exception rather than the rule.

8. Even with the large annual cost for premium freight, Sertex still only met 88% of its on-time delivery commitments to customers during the last twelve months. During this same period, 5% of its shipments were returned with quality problems. Each returned shipment had to be 100% inspected and the defective material reworked. The company is losing credibility with its customers who depend on it for quality and dependability.

9. The manufacturing cells seem to be working well. Cell teams can change seamlessly from one part number to another, and all members of the team are multiskilled and can readily adjust whenever a team member is absent. The only problem is related to machine breakdowns, resulting in 15% lost production time. When a breakdown occurs, the cell has to wait for maintenance to send someone to fix the problem. ■

QUESTIONS FOR THOUGHT

1. How can Lean Six Sigma help Sertex? What would be your recommendations to Jerry Crenshaw?

2. Based on the CPR report, do you think that Sertex's culture is ready for an implementation of Six Sigma? How can Jerry know, and what can he do to prepare the organization?

3. Do you think the Sertex facility is appropriate for pull scheduling? What approach would you take to determine its appropriateness and to implement a workable system?

4. What training do you think the organization requires to prepare it for Six Sigma?

5. Why do you think there is so much WIP on the factory floor? What steps do you think can be taken to eliminate it and keep it at a minimum?

6. Do you think TPM could help address some of Sertex's problems? How?

CHAPTER 10

Materials Management: Supplier Selection and Certification, and the Procurement Cycle

Quality in a product or service … is not what the supplier puts in. It is what the customer gets out and is willing to pay for

—PETER F. DRUCKER

Harley-Davidson, Inc.

It's Time to Ride

In the early 1980s, Harley-Davidson—a name that had become synonymous with quality—was suddenly faced with an onslaught of staggering competition from Japan. Inflation, unemployment, and interest rates were high. In an effort to stay afloat, the company laid off engineering personnel in large numbers, and consequently, the number of new Harley-Davidson products on the market significantly declined. Because the lead time for new product development was four to five years, spending on research and development was not a priority.

By the mid-1990s, it had become clear that some radical changes were needed if the company was to survive. The emphasis was placed on supply chain management, giving particular attention to the procurement cycle and an expanded role for purchasing in materials management. The supplier selection process needed a major overhaul. Suppliers were chosen by the engineering department on the basis of technical competency to support designs. Due consideration was not given to all the factors that contribute to a successful buyer–supplier relationship. As a result, suppliers selected were typically low volume and did not have the capabilities to meet requirements for manufacturing and delivery. Shipments were often late, jeopardizing production schedules.

Management recognized the importance of relieving the engineering department of supplier selection responsibilities while ensuring that quality components would be purchased at the best prices. A strategic decision was made to create *purchasing engineers*—procurement experts that would work side by side with engineers throughout the design process, providing the designers with an awareness of cost and supplier issues that hopefully would then become a part of the product design. The purchasers would also become more technically savvy, which would help them better qualify suppliers based on capabilities to apply new technologies to new products.

Harley-Davidson's new approach was also aimed at helping suppliers become better suppliers. Through site visits, teams of Harley-Davidson engineers would help suppliers solve production problems, identify cost reduction opportunities, and implement lean production methods. A Supplier Advisory Council was formed to address materials issues of strategic importance. A total of sixteen delegates, selected from the supplier base, serve four-year terms.

The dogged determination of Harley-Davidson's leadership and the commitment of its people have turned the company around. Its remarkable achievements in supply chain management, summarized as follows, earned it the 2000 Purchasing Magazine Medal of Professional Excellence:

- Inventories were cut by one-third—from fifteen days to ten days.
- Costs of purchased materials were reduced by roughly $37 million, compared with a projected increase of $40 million under the old system of materials management.
- Roughly 60% of the supplier base is performing at 48 DPMO or better.
- Supply base has been cut in half.
- Sales have increased from 10% to 17% each year since 1999.
- A total of 291,100 motorcycles were shipped in 2003 compared with 177,200 in 1999.
- Net revenues have increased 13% to 20% each year since 1999. Revenues in 2003 were $4,624 million compared with $2,453 million in 1999.
- Net income for 2003 was $761 million, up 31% over the previous year.

Engaging suppliers at an early stage of design and creating solid working relationships with them has been a formula for success at Harley.

SOURCE: Data used by permission of Harley-Davidson, Inc. ■

10.1 LEARNING OBJECTIVES AND KEY OUTCOMES

After studying the material in Chapter 10, you will be able to

1. Describe the role of the purchasing function and how it can be used to ensure the quality, reliability, and timeliness of outsourced raw materials and components

2. Describe the characteristics of a buyer–supplier partnership and why it is important to the success of QIM

3. Discuss the benefits of involving key suppliers early in the product development process

4. Describe the elements of, and process for, developing an effective supplier certification program

5. Apply multicriteria decision tools to the supplier selection problem

6. Define the role of acceptance sampling in a QIM environment

7. Use Grubbs and Dodge-Romig tables to design single sampling plans with stipulated producer's and consumer's risks

8. Use Grubbs tables to design double sampling plans with stipulated producer's and consumer's risks

9. Compute AOQ, AOQL, ATI, and ASN, and use these measures to compare alternative sampling plans

10.2 THE PROCUREMENT CYCLE AND BUYER–SUPPLIER RELATIONS

Supplier Collaboration

Material Requirements Planning

The first generation of quality was characterized by little supplier collaboration.

In the 1970s, competition led to a greater emphasis on outsourcing as a means for cutting costs.

Capacity Cushion

Core Competencies

Outsourcing

By the 1980s, the focus began to shift from a cost orientation to satisfying customers.

Product Differentiation

Product Life Cycles

Offshore Competition

Solid relationships with a small supplier base are key to competitiveness.

During the first generation of the quality movement, management's primary focus was on reducing costs through mass production. Standardization left little room for flexibility in the design of products or processes. Design was not a priority and development was usually performed in-house without **supplier collaboration**. Sharing of technologies was considered an unacceptable business practice, and little attention was given to buyer–supplier relationships. During this era, purchasing decisions were based on lowest price, and order sizes were large to achieve the minimum per unit price.

During the 1970s, **material requirements planning** (MRP) was introduced and management began to see the how the large amounts of WIP inventory negatively impacted manufacturing costs, quality, product development, and delivery lead times. Intense global competition created a greater demand for more product customization, resulting in a need for more flexibility. The rapidly evolving technologies, rising input cost, and ever-changing customer preferences required organizations to develop a competitive advantage in delivery and innovation. The result was management's utilization of JIT as an effort to improve their efficiencies, reduce costs, and better meet changing customer requirements. To their dismay, management soon learned that their JIT programs often eliminated some inventories that were needed as a **capacity cushion** and to buffer against production problems. Organizations began to focus on their **core competencies** and technologies, **outsourcing** any product or component that failed to match internal capabilities.

By the 1980s, management could no longer rely on production of high volumes to reduce unit costs. It became apparent that more flexibility was needed for the increasing **product differentiation** and shortened **product life cycles** demanded by the consumer. **Offshore competition** continued to increase, putting further pressure on domestic manufacturers. The one-dimensional focus on low cost expanded to include improved quality and reliability.

Benchmark studies revealed that many of the successful Asian and European competitors had established close relationships with their key suppliers. In light of this, many U.S. manufacturers began to reduce their supply bases. These reductions were first attempted by choosing a few existing suppliers and eliminating the remainder without formal evaluation methods. Many of these efforts resulted in failure because success dictated a broadening of the supplier search, thorough evaluation and selection from the pool of potential suppliers, and then being able to transition from the traditional buyer–supplier relationship to a partnership. The role of the supplier in the procurement cycle had to change. In the past, suppliers were given a completed design and specifications, and then measured on compliance. In many industries today, the supplier receives a performance specification and interface information for the components they provide. The actual design is often the supplier's responsibility.

10.2.1 Proactive Purchasing

Traditionally, purchasing has been responsible for routine administrative transactions such as preparing requests for quote, selecting suppliers, issuing purchase orders, receiving materials, processing invoices, and verifying accounts payable. If a crisis occurred, such as a missed shipment, it was the purchasing department's responsibility to act quickly and resolve the problem. As an expeditor, purchasing played a reactive role and was evaluated based on one objective: reducing the cost of materials or services. This encouraged the practice of selecting materials or services based on price alone, but the lowest price did not always translate into the lowest total cost. Total cost includes factors that are not reflected in a price quote, including processing, process failure, inspection, warranty, rework, service, maintenance, and warehousing. Making cost the primary criterion led to multiple sourcing. The idea was that lower prices would result if suppliers were pitted against each other. This strategy often backfired, creating adversarial relationships between the purchaser and suppliers.

> The lowest price does not necessarily translate to the lowest total cost.

During the 1990s, the purchasing function began to change due to a greater emphasis on supply chain management. As the key element in the procurement cycle (refer to Figure 3-13), purchasing became accountable for selecting and qualifying suppliers; rating supplier performance; negotiating contracts; comparing suppliers on the basis of price, quality, and service; sourcing goods and service; timing purchases; executing terms of sale; evaluating the value of materials received; predicting price, service, and demand changes; and specifying the form and transportation mode for shipments. In this expanded **proactive purchasing** role, purchasing is engaged in planning and improvement activities, continuously seeking ways to save cost and improve the quality and reliability of outsourced materials.

> In the 1990s, emphasis on supply chain management led to an expanded role for the purchasing function.

> **Proactive Purchasing**

Because purchasing is responsible for choosing suppliers, it has also accepted the risks associated with a bad choice, such as poor quality, missed shipments, or late deliveries. These risks can be minimized through proactive leadership from a **systems perspective**, allowing risks to be shared across the organization.

> **Systems Perspective**

Proactive purchasing participates in the organization's planning, forecasting, decision making, and formulation of strategy. Purchasing becomes involved in activities such as reducing the supplier base, forming long-term relationships with suppliers, and encouraging early supplier involvement in new product development. Although such activities can create greater risks, purchasing's role is to reduce the risk through supplier certification programs, reduction of routine administrative tasks, and periodic supplier audits to verify that established standards are met. In turn, suppliers have a greater incentive to commit to and remain in a partnership that is not adversarial.

10.2.2 Buyer–Supplier Relationships

Purchasing is responsible for managing buyer–supplier relationships by ensuring there are direct lines of communication between critical areas, such as design, manufacturing, quality, and planning. Having long-term relationships removes the supplier's fear of losing the business on price issues, and suppliers will be more willing to invest in product and process improvements. Once the buyer and supplier agree on mutually beneficial objectives, a partnership can be forged.

> Purchasing manages supplier relationships by ensuring direct lines of communication between key players.

A few ground rules will strengthen the partnership. The buyer must provide the supplier with detailed product descriptions to ensure the supplier fully understands the requirements. Open **communications** are essential. In addition to evaluating supplier

> **Communications**

Open and honest communications with suppliers are essential.

Information Sharing

performance, the purchasing organization often plays an active role in assisting its suppliers with their quality programs. A successful partnership requires **information sharing**, and sharing of collaborative efforts to identify improvement opportunities and solve problems. This results in advantages to both parties. The supplier becomes more competitive, and the buyer benefits from quality improvements, the ability to reduce inventories, and improved flexibility and responsiveness.

It is important that top management be committed to supplier partnerships.

Top management must be committed to the creation of good supplier relations, and purchasing must be forthright in providing suppliers with information, including the direction of new product lines. This helps the supplier understand the improvements needed and where investments are necessary in new equipment and technology. A supply chain management team, consisting of representatives from operations, purchasing, design, manufacturing, quality assurance, marketing and finance, can help facilitate open communications. Relationships are based on mutual trust, and it is therefore imperative that commitments be honored from the top managements of both parties. Joint agreements covering performance measures, risks and rewards, shared education, and training are important.

10.2.3 Early Supplier Involvement in Design

Success in new product development can often be facilitated by involving suppliers early in the design process.

Although the design phase of a product life cycle typically expends only a small percentage of total product cost, as much as 80% of the total product cost directly depends on the design of the product. It becomes more difficult and costly to make changes as the product development process moves forward; therefore, it is important to bring in technical expertise as early as possible. To integrate suppliers into the product development process, organizations have many obstacles to overcome. For example, companies may be reluctant to openly share company proprietary information and process knowledge. Engineers and designers may have problems sharing control during the design phase, or suppliers may not be qualified for integration into this phase. The role of purchasing in new product development is to work closely with suppliers during the early stages and to resolve any foreseeable production difficulties. Purchasing is also responsible for assisting in design assessment and establishing reorder points, lead times, minimum stock quantities, and design alternatives.

Early collaboration with suppliers during design can help reduce costs, superior quality, and improved manufacturability.

Superior Product Designs

There are many benefits to early supplier involvement in the design of products and processes. These include the generation of new ideas, development and application of new technologies, reduction in cycle times, improvement in quality, and reduction in costs. This allows competent suppliers to incorporate their experiences into **superior product designs**, and collaboration up-front can impact the cost of the product and quality due to the supplier's process knowledge. The supplier is best suited to work with product engineers in developing the tolerances to improve assembly and manufacturability, and thereby avoid wasted time in production by fixing problems that are due to poor designs or processes. Involving the supplier in the feasibility, design, development, qualification, and support phases can minimize supply chain risks. Integrating the supplier into product development will also decrease time to market because the supplier can begin preproduction planning much earlier than would otherwise be possible.

Early supplier involvement can decrease time to market.

Purchasing will be an integral part of the cross-functional product development team, consisting of marketing, engineering, operations, and field service. During the early stages of the product development cycle, purchasing will assess supply chain risks, including technical feasibility, life cycle, viability of the supplier, material availability, and cost. Purchasing will also collaborate with the engineering department to address technology trends, select preferred suppliers, identify parts or materials with potential risks, and assist in developing alternatives.

10.3 SUPPLIER CERTIFICATION

Suppliers are part of the extended enterprise. Managing the supply chain effectively can benefit the buyer in many ways, including improved quality and reduced inventories, field service costs, and lead times. The supplier also benefits by receiving high volumes, long-term or exclusive contracts, technical assistance, financial assistance, and certification.[1]

Supply chain management focuses on the minimization of factors that adversely affect the materials flow and availability. Small disturbances can have large negative effects. Consider the impact of a customer requesting a last-minute change in requirements. Suddenly, the organization is faced with a dilemma. If the product mix remains the same, with an increase in quantity, there is a likelihood that the supplier has under-produced. Unless a special run can be organized (at additional costs), the organization may be unable to respond to the customer's request, leading to dissatisfaction and possibly lost good will and future sales. If, in contrast, the change involves either a decrease in quantity for the same mix or a change in mix, the organization may be in an over-production scenario, leading to increased inventories and associated holding costs. Such unpredictable behaviors have the effect of inducing variabilities along the supply chain. Such internally induced fluctuations can show up in inventories, ordering patterns, and costs, and are amplified as one gets further from the source. This is the bull-whip effect, discussed in section 3.3.3.2, and can offer great potential for cost improvement, through careful supplier selection and certification procedures.

Because, typically, more than half of a product's cost is in purchased materials, supplier selection is critical. An organization can only be as strong as its weakest link, so it is important that the selection process extend up the **tiered supply chain structure**, going beyond first tier (immediate) suppliers to include second tier (suppliers' suppliers), third tier (suppliers' suppliers' suppliers), and so on.

Supplier selection is influenced by whether the supply chain is to be **responsive** or efficient, as illustrated in Figure 3-14, and how competitors' supsply chains have been designed. Benchmarking can help managers learn how their supply chains measure up against those that are considered to be world class. Markets can be won and lost on the basis of how efficiently and timely materials, money, and information are exchanged up and down the chain.

Supplier certification improves supply chain performance by resolving supplier problems.[2] Management has historically shied away from formal supplier qualification programs because of the implementation costs, failing to properly recognize that such costs can be more than offset by potential savings. Certification leads to the reduction (or elimination) of receiving inspection. Incoming materials that are certified can be used without having to verify that quality requirements have been met. This saves time and costs, and results in reduced lead time, lower inventory levels, and less material handling.

Supplier selection should extend up the entire supply chain.

Supplier selection is influenced by the supply chain design.

Tiered Supply Chain Structure

Supplier Certification

Supplier certification helps improve supplier performance by resolving problems.

[1]Hutchins, Greg. *Purchasing Strategies for Total Quality: A Guide to Achieving Improvement,* 81–82. Homewood, IL: Business One Irwin, 1992.

[2]Maass, Richard, John O. Brown, and James Bossert. *Supplier Certification: A Continuous Improvement Strategy,* 49–66. Quality Press, 1990.

A certified supplier shares its customer's objectives, commitments, and risks.

A certified supplier is "one who, after extensive investigation, is found to provide material of such quality that it is not necessary to perform routine testing on each lot received" (Pharmaceutical Manufacturers Association), and one who shares their customer's objectives, commitments, and risks (ASQC Customer–Supplier Technical Committee).[3] A supplier who is certified must have formalized quality programs; strive to continually identify opportunities to improve quality; and demonstrate capability to provide the right components, on schedule, and at an acceptable quality level.

Cross-Functional Supplier Certification Team

The first step in a supplier certification process is to form a **cross-functional supplier certification team** that draws its membership from marketing, design and manufacturing engineering, operations, quality assurance, and finance.[4] The team leader should be someone from the purchasing function. The first order of business is to determine the organization's requirements based on the customer's expectations—What are we going to buy, in what condition, how much, and when do we want it? The requirements must be clear and concise to all team members, yet flexible enough for additional input from the supplier. Previous records, trade shows, conferences, magazines, and directories are some ideas for determining the potential suppliers.

Determining requirements is the first step in vendor certification.

The second step is to develop formal procedures.

The next step is to develop a supplier certification program, including procedures for measuring supplier performance and encouraging improvements. The certification process will include a supplier evaluation system that is tailored to the organization's needs and, because there are so many variables, the formalized program will vary significantly from company to company. Quality, delivery, service, and cost are typically considered. Supplier certification programs should focus on[5]

- Certifying suppliers that deliver critical items
- Choosing reasonable and realistic weights for performance factors
- Random inspections to insure consistency
- Ease of administration with minimal paperwork
- Effective feedback to supplier and offering assistance as needed for continuous improvement

Supplier Rewards

- **Supplier rewards** that are tied to performance and appropriate penalties for poor service

10.3.1 Identifying the Supplier Base

In general, the lower the number of suppliers, variation (in lead times and order quantities) will be less, supplier commitment will be greater, and internal resources will be more efficiently managed.[6] If two suppliers provide the same component, the total variation is an aggregate of the variations induced by each supplier and is greater than if either supplier were the sole source. Multisourcing leads to increased system variation. Historically, the arguments in favor of multiple vendors were that increased competition drives down costs and that multisourcing protects against unexpected problems that could disrupt supply. There is a major drawback, however. It is difficult to establish lasting buyer–supplier relationships when vendors believe they can lose the business to a

---

[3]Ibid, 2.

[4]Burt, David N., and Richard L. Pinkerton. *A Purchasing Manager's Guide to Strategic, Proactive Procurement,* 12. AMACOM, 1996.

[5]Ibid, 55, 182–83.

[6]Pyzdek, Thomas. *Quality Engineering Handbook,* 119. Marcel Dekker, 1999.

competitor. Nevertheless, there are circumstances that justify multisourcing. According to Lewis, "The optimal number of suppliers depends on the need to sustain competition, suppliers' product range, and the complexity of their products."[7]

Single Sourcing

Three alternatives to multisourcing are available for material supply: single, double, and sole sourcing.

There are three alternatives to multisourcing: single, double, and sole sourcing. **Single sourcing** means that the company can buy from other suppliers but chooses to only use one. There are risks involved with this strategy because supply can be disrupted in the event of problems, such as machine breakdowns, labor disputes, material shortages, or quality defects. Such problems can sometimes be avoided if the supplier has backup facilities that can be called on to manufacture the component, if necessary. The buyer should conduct periodic audits to ensure suppliers continue to have the capability to meet all requirements.

Double Sourcing

Sole Sourcing

Double sourcing means the buyer uses two suppliers, usually one at a significantly larger volume than the other. Double sourcing is chosen for products that have high volumes or use new technologies, or when long lead times are necessary to change suppliers. **Sole sourcing** is buying from one supplier because no one else can or will supply the product or service.

JIT requirements favor suppliers that are within a geographical proximity of the customer.

Local suppliers can often provide the best price and most reliable delivery for small quantities. Dealing with local vendors removes some of the risks associated with transportation delays. When high-priority orders require quick turnaround or shipments are rejected (due to nonconforming material), a local supplier is able to react faster than one that is distant to the plant. For this reason, local suppliers are generally preferred when the organization is operating with a JIT system. The advantages of working with larger national suppliers (nonlocal) are low prices (possible through **economies of scale**), capabilities to produce at high volumes, and less vulnerability to fluctuations in demand.

Economies of Scale

Selecting foreign suppliers can often result in low prices, but the buyer should consider problems that might be encountered due to differences in cultures, customs, language barriers, and legal systems. Buyers should also anticipate the financial impacts of currency exchange rate fluctuations and the additional administrative costs. Higher inventory levels may be required due to inconsistencies in delivery times from international carriers.

10.3.2 Supplier Evaluation and Selection

There is no best method for supplier selection; however, most approaches follow some version of the seven-step process illustrated in Figure 10-1 and start with a survey. An effective supplier survey should be comprehensive, objective, reliable, and flexible.

Supplier certification begins with a prequalification survey.

Initial screening of suppliers can commence with a self-evaluation survey similar to the one shown in Figure 10-2. These surveys are intended to cull those suppliers that are clearly not viable or financially sound. The surveys are intended to obtain information such as equipment lists, annual reports, facility descriptions, product samples, customer lists, financial statements, and background information for key personnel. The aim is to engage potential suppliers in the process of providing preliminary information so problems can be identified early and evaluations can be expedited.[8]

A cross-functional certification team reviews the surveys and determines those suppliers that exhibit the most potential. The team then makes site visits to these suppliers and completes supplier performance evaluations. In lieu of these evaluations, some organizations find it more desirable to accept a third-party certification, such as **QS9000 and ISO9000 standards**. In this case, the team should review and approve the

QS9000 Standards

ISO9000 Standards

[7]Lewis, Jordan D. *The Connected Corporation*, 56. New York: The Free Press, 1995.

[8]Mass, Brown, and Bossert, *Supplier Certification*, 49–66.

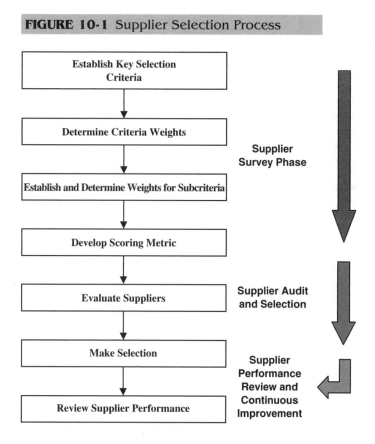

FIGURE 10-1 Supplier Selection Process

third-party certification documentation. These evaluations are intended to examine a supplier's facilities and evaluate management, operations, production capacity, experience with product, research and development capability, and existing quality systems. The team can use this data to determine whether the supplier can consistently meet requirements and to offer improvement suggestions.

The certification team should verify that an up-to-date quality system has been implemented, and that the system is complete, accurate, and regularly reviewed. There should be a well-defined procedure to control the quality system's revisions, and responsibilities should be well documented for the management of the system. Figure 10-3 is an example of a typical quality system evaluation summary, which will vary by organization.

This process is intended to quantify the strength of each potential supplier's quality system and to identify opportunities for continuous improvement. Once the performance evaluations are complete, the **supplier certification team** will get together to review the results and compile them into a weighted score **evaluation matrix**. This tool can help compare suppliers against a number of variables of differing importance.

Supplier Certification Team

Evaluation Matrix

For each supplier, a performance rating is combined with a weighting for the relative importance of each evaluation criterion. It is best if each criterion can be measured quantitatively because subjective measure can dilute the validity of the results. When the final scores are widely distributed, the matrix method can be effective in screening suppliers against numerous criteria. However, when the difference between suppliers' scores is small, it can be difficult to justify the selection of one vendor over another. The information

Quantitative criteria are generally preferred over qualitative ones.

FIGURE 10-2 Supplier Self-Evaluation Survey for Initial Screening

Survey Date _____
Supplier Name   _____
Supplier Address   _____
City/State/Zip   _____
Contact Name   _____
Phone/Fax/Email   _____
General Manager   _____
Phone/Fax/Email   _____
Quality Contact   _____
Phone/Fax/Email   _____

General Information
Description of product or service _____
Number of years in business   _____
Annual sales in dollars   _____
Number of employees (salary/hourly)   _____
Facility size in square feet   _____
Major customers   _____
Current capacity in % _____ Ability to expand?   Yes/No
Union affiliation   Yes/No
If yes, when does the contract expire?   _____
What is the patent activity?   _____
Do you have a formal Quality Assurance manual? _____
Are you QS9000 certified   _____
List laboratory test and measuring equipment (provide attachments if necessary)

_____
_____
_____
_____
_____

_____
Do you use SPC?   _____ If yes, describe where:

_____
Do you use a formal corrective action program? _____
List any customer or supplier awards: _____
_____
_____
_____

Signing this document certifies that the information is current and accurate.
Signed: _____

obtained through the evaluation process can be used to provide feedback to the suppliers, permitting them to take corrective actions as necessary. Whatever type of selection system is used, it should be clearly defined, easy to understand by both parties, and simple to update.

10.3.3 Postcertification Metrics and Decertification

Suppliers are evaluated on the basis of quality, delivery, and service.

Quality, delivery, and service are the typical performance metrics that are monitored once a certified supplier begins to ship product. A certification is not indefinite, and a supplier can be decertified if requirements are not met or if corrective actions are not taken in a timely manner.

FIGURE 10-3 Summary of Suppliers' Quality System Evaluation

Supplier:		Date:	ID #
Address:		City:	State:
City, State:		Phone:	Fax:
Evaluation Performed by:		**Weight**	**Supplier Rating**
1	Management Capability		
2	Human Resources Capability		
3	Cost Structure		
4	Quality Performance, Systems, Philosophy		
	Manufacturing/Quality Planning		
	Statistical Process Control		
	Receiving Inspection		
	In-Process Inspection		
	Corrective and Preventive Action		
	Nonconforming Material Control		
	Gauge R and R		
	Continuous Improvement		
	Final Inspection and Shipping		
5	Process, Technical, and Design Capability		
	Design Control		
	Configuration Control		
	Production Scheduling and Control		
6	Materials Management		
	Purchasing Strategies, Policies, and Techniques		
	Supplier Relations		
	Material Identification Control		
	Contract Administration		
	Document Control		
7	Environmental Regulation Compliance		
8	Financial Capability and Stability		
9	Information Systems Capability		
10	Potential for Long-term Relationship		
	Total		

Quality of Supply

The **quality of supply** can be a measure of the level of nonconformities (e.g., DPMOs), the number of supplier corrective action requests, or the number of rejected shipments due to quality problems. Acceptance sampling, discussed in Sections 10.5 and 10.6, can be used during the certification process, and then periodically applied for postcertification monitoring to help determine quality of supply.

Delivery Performance

Delivery performance can be measured as the number that are early or late, the number that were under or over the order quantity, or the number that had to be expedited

**Service
Performance**

over a certain period of time. **Service performance** can be a measure of whether documentation is complete on packing slips, invoices, certifications of compliance, shipping notices, and supplier site visits. Service is also an assessment of how well the supplier responded within required timeframes.

**Postcertification
Audits**

After certification, it is important that periodic **postcertification audits** be conducted to ensure the supplier's production and quality programs maintain compliance with the purchasing organization's standards. As a minimum, an annual review should be conducted to revalidate the supplier's capabilities, adapt the relationship to changing conditions, and identify improvement opportunities. Communications should be open, and problems should be solved as a collaborative effort between both parties.

The supplier or a particular part number can become decertified temporarily or indefinitely for reasons determined by the cross-functional team. Lack of timely response to a corrective action, unsatisfactory quality performance evaluation, poor delivery performance, withdrawal of certification from the third-party registrar, and shipment of consecutive defects are examples of reasons that could warrant **decertification**. If a problem is found as the result of an audit, the material must be contained and a material review board must decide on the disposition of the material based on the criticality of the defect. For a major nonconformity, an investigation must be performed at the supplier's facility to try to identify the problem and determine its severity. Once found, corrective action is taken, and then the team must decide if it was due to a breakdown in the supplier's quality system that could warrant decertification.

Decertification

A supplier can be decertified if performance becomes unsatisfactory.

Probationary Status

Suppliers are not normally decertified on the first appearance of a problem. They are placed on **probationary status** and evaluated on how well they responded to the problem, identifyed its cause and took corrective action. If the supplier demonstrates satisfactory performance during the probationary period, the team may reinstate the certification. If supplier performance does not improve within a predetermined length of time, the team can invoke a permanent decertification. If the team agrees that the vendor is worth recertification, more stringent sampling methods can be imposed until the supplier has proven that it is capable of meeting previous quality levels.

10.3.4 Benefits of Supplier Certification

Certification benefits both the buyer and the supplier.

Supplier certification programs are a win–win situation for the buyer and the supplier. Suppliers are rewarded for their efforts by obtaining long-term contracts, increased business potential, increased productivity, reduced scrap and rework, enhanced customer satisfaction, increased competitiveness, fewer warranty problems, and improved responsiveness. For the buyer, supplier certification minimizes inspection and testing costs, reduces the number of receiving inspectors, decreases the number of manufacturing problems and delays due to poor quality of purchased materials, and helps improve overall quality. Certification can also help with JIT implementations because manufacturers no longer need to carry inventory in quantities to buffer against quality problems, partial shipments, or late deliveries.

10.4 DECISION ANALYSIS IN SUPPLIER SELECTION

Supplier selection requires making decisions based on multiple criteria.

Supplier selection is a multicriteria decision that must use logic to decide between alternatives, which often requires considering multiple, and sometimes conflicting, factors. The decision criteria used are the independent characteristics considered important to the vendor selection process, and can be chosen through a brainstorming session to ensure all the important aspects are considered. Several techniques have

TABLE 10-1 Weighted Point Method of Supplier Selection

Criterion	Weight	Normalized Weight	Supplier 1		Supplier 2		Supplier 3		Supplier 4	
			Raw Score	Weighted Score	Raw Score	Weighted Score	Raw Score	Weighted Score	Raw Score	Weighted Score
Price	100	100/400 = 0.25	8	2.00	5	1.25	6	1.50	7	1.75
Quality	200	200/400 = 0.50	5	2.50	7	3.50	6	3.00	8	4.00
Delivery	40	40/400 = 0.10	3	0.30	10	1.00	8	0.80	5	0.50
Service	60	60/400 = 0.15	4	0.60	5	0.75	7	1.05	7	1.05
	400			5.40		6.50		6.35		7.30 ↑

Weighted Point Method

Analytical Hierarchy Process

Categorical Method

The weighted point method assigns weights to each criterion, and then ranks each supplier against each criterion on a 0 to 10 scale.

been used for evaluating suppliers against multiple criteria, including the **weighted point method**,[9] the **analytical hierarchy procedure**,[10] and the **categorical method**.[11]

10.4.1 Weighted Point Method

The weighted point method ranks criteria in order of decreasing importance and assigns weights to each based on its relative importance to the final decision. Weights are then normalized so the sum of all weights is equal to one. The alternatives are then rated on how well they satisfy each criterion using a 0 to 10 scale (0 = Poor/Unacceptable and 10 = Excellent).

A weighted score for each alternative is computed by multiplying the normalized weight by the alternative's rating for each criterion, and then summing across all criteria. The alternative having the highest cumulative weighted score is the one that is preferred.

To illustrate, assume an organization has decided to use four criteria to evaluate suppliers: price, quality, delivery, and service, as shown in Table 10-1. In this case, weights were assigned to each criteria, using price as the reference (indexed at 100). Quality was considered to be twice as important as price, so it was assigned a weight of 200. Price was considered to be 2.5 times as important as delivery, and service was considered to be 1.5 times as important as delivery. Therefore, weights of 40 (100/2.5) and 60 (40 × 1.5) were assigned to delivery and service, respectively. Summing the weights across all four criteria yields a total of 400. When each weight is divided by the total, normalized weights are obtained that sum to one.

As Table 10-1 shows, four potential suppliers are being considered. Each has been rated against the four criteria, using the 0 to 10 scale described previously. By accumulating the product of the normalized weight and the rating for each criterion, a weighted score can be computed for each supplier. The supplier with the highest cumulative weighted score is preferred—in this case, supplier 4.

10.4.2 Analytical Hierarchy Procedure

The analytical hierarchy procedure (AHP) was developed by Thomas Saaty[12] to solve complex problems involving multiple criteria. Under this method, the problem is

[9]Timmerman, Ed. "An Approach to Vendor Performance Evaluation." *The Journal of Purchasing and Materials Management* 22, no. 4 (Winter 1986): 2–8.

[10]Nydick, Robert L., and Hill, Ronald. "Using the Analytic Hierarchy Process to Structure the Supplier Selection Procedure." *International Journal of Purchasing and Materials Management* 28, no. 2 (1992): 31–36.

[11]Timmerman, "An Approach to Vendor," 2–8.

[12]Saaty, Thomas L. *The Analytic Hierarchy Process.* Pittsburgh, PA: RWS Publications, 1996.

FIGURE 10-4 Hierarchical Structure of Supplier Selection Problem

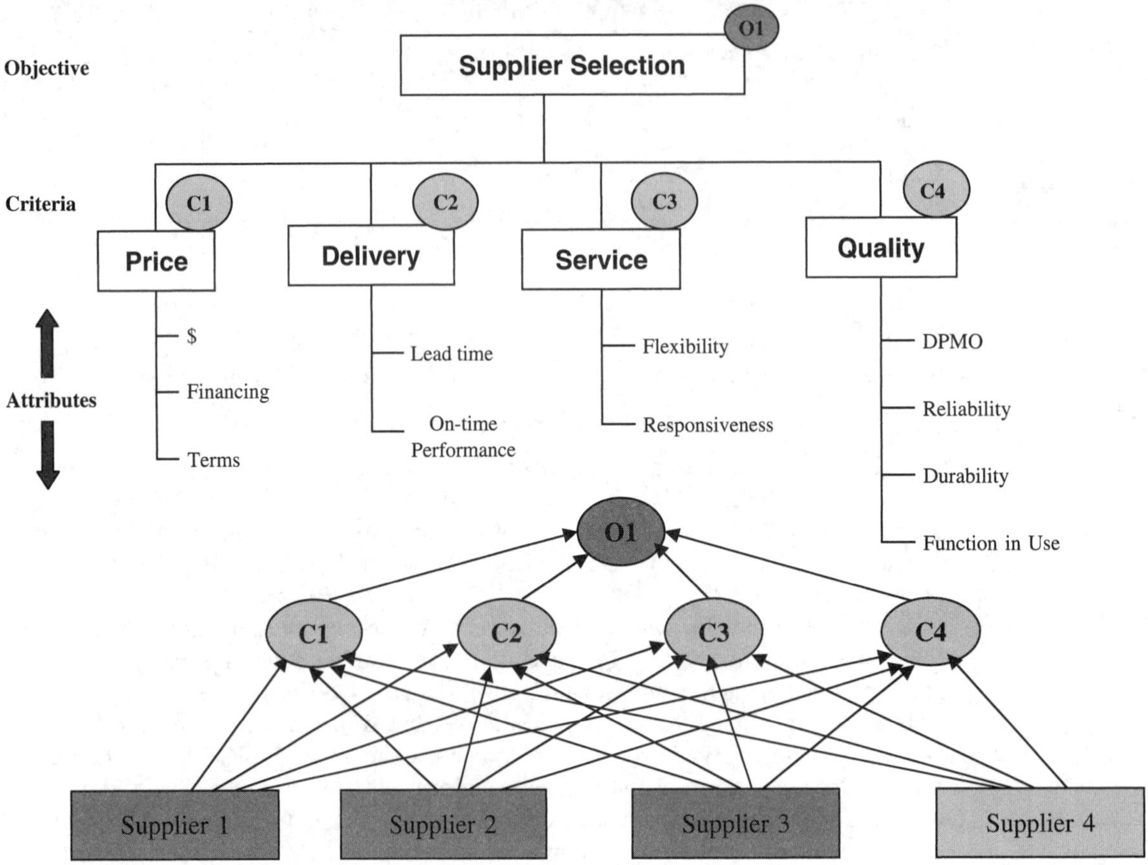

structured in the form of a **decision hierarchy**, as illustrated in Figure 10-4. At the top of
the structure is the primary objective (select a top performing supplier), and the next
level down contains the list of criteria that will be used to compare alternatives. A set of
measures, called attributes, are used to evaluate the alternatives against each criterion.

Decision Hierarchy

Under AHP
pairwise
comparisons are
used to develop
priority vectors,
which are then used
to develop a
weighted score for
each supplier.

The choice of attributes is subjective—usually the result of a group consensus—
and is critically important to the decision. The final list will be influenced by the choice
of criteria and by an intuitive feel for which attributes will effectively differentiate between alternative suppliers. The number of attributes used is critically important—too
many can result in an analysis that is unwieldy and difficult to manage, and too few can
limit an effective discrimination between alternatives. Each attribute should be able to
distinguish between at least two alternatives, and in no case should identical scores result for all alternatives. Attributes should be independent and nonredundant, and
should capture unique dimensions or facets of the problem that are assumed to be sufficient for the purpose of making the final selection.

**Pairwise
Comparisons**

AHP is a methodology for ranking alternative suppliers based on judgments concerning the importance of each criterion and how well each supplier satisfies the criteria
as evaluated through the attributes. Judgments are expressed as **pairwise comparisons**,

TABLE 10-2 Preference Ratings

Verbal Judgment of Preference	Numerical Rating
Extremely preferred	9
Very strongly to extremely preferred	8
Very strongly preferred	7
Strongly to very strongly preferred	6
Strongly preferred	5
Moderately to strongly preferred	4
Moderately preferred	3
Equally to moderately preferred	2
Equally preferred	1

using the rating scale shown in Table 10-2. In applying this table, preference is usually given to the odd numbers. The even numbers are reserved for intermediate levels where a finer level of discrimination is desired. Applying AHP to supplier selection involves five steps:

Step 1. Determine the list of criteria that will be used to evaluate suppliers.

Step 2. Develop a list of attributes for each criterion that will effectively differentiate among alternatives.

Step 3. Develop a pairwise comparison matrix for the criteria, using Table 10-2 as a guide for numerical preferences. Use the matrix to compute a priority vector for criteria. Check for **consistency**.

Step 4. Develop pairwise comparison matrices for those suppliers under review. There will be one of these matrices for each criterion. Use these matrices to compute priority vectors for suppliers against each criterion. Check for consistency.

Step 5. Use the priority vectors to compute overall weighted scores for each supplier and make the final selection.

Consistency

Tables 10-3 through 10-9 illustrate the step-by-step procedure for applying AHP to a specific supplier selection problem. A **priority vector** for the four criteria is computed

Priority Vector

TABLE 10-3 Pairwise Comparison Matrix for Criteria

	Price	Quality	Delivery	Service
Price	1.00	0.20	0.33	0.33
Quality	5.00	1.00	3.00	4.00
Delivery	3.00	0.33	1.00	4.00
Service	3.00	0.25	0.25	1.00
	12.00	1.78	4.58	9.33

Step 1: Construct preference matrix A by assigning scores to each pairwise comparison. A score s_{ij} means that criteria i is preferred over criteria j. If cell $a_{ij} = s_{ij}$, then assign $a_{ji} = 1/s_{ij}$. For n criteria, there are $[(nxn) - n/2]$ pairwise comparisons.

Step 2: Sum the values in each column. The total for column $j = t_j$.

TABLE 10-4 Normalized Pairwise Comparison Matrix for Criteria

	Price	*Quality*	*Delivery*	*Service*	*Average*
Price	0.083	0.112	0.072	0.04	0.076
Quality	0.417	0.562	0.655	0.43	0.516
Delivery	0.250	0.185	0.218	0.43	0.271
Service	0.250	0.140	0.055	0.11	0.138
	1.000	1.000	1.000	1.00	

Step 3: Normalize the preference matrix A by computing $a_{ij'} = a_{ij}/t_j$. The normalized matrix = A_{norm}.

Step 4: Compute the average of each row of A_{norm}.

$$\text{Priority vector for criteria, } w_{criteria} = [0.076 \quad 0.516 \quad 0.271 \quad 0.138]$$

TABLE 10-5 Consistency Check

Step 5: Check for consistency.

$$\text{Compute } Aw^T$$

$$\begin{bmatrix} 1.00 & 0.20 & 0.33 & 0.33 \\ 5.00 & 1.00 & 3.00 & 4.00 \\ 3.00 & 0.33 & 1.00 & 4.00 \\ 3.00 & 0.25 & 0.25 & 1.00 \end{bmatrix} \begin{bmatrix} 0.076 \\ 0.516 \\ 0.271 \\ 0.138 \end{bmatrix} = \begin{bmatrix} 0.314 \\ 2.261 \\ 1.221 \\ 0.434 \end{bmatrix}$$

Step 6: Compute λ_{max}

$$\text{Compute } \lambda_{max} = \frac{1}{n} \sum_{i=1}^{n} \frac{\text{ith element of } Aw^T}{\text{ith element of } w^T} = \frac{1}{4} \left[\frac{0.314}{0.076} + \frac{2.261}{0.516} + \frac{1.221}{0.271} + \frac{0.434}{0.138} \right] = 4.041$$

Step 7: Compute the consistency index (CI).

$$CI = \frac{\lambda_{max} - n}{n - 1} = \frac{4.041 - 4}{4 - 1} = 0.014$$

Step 8: Compute the consistency ratio (CR).

$$CR = \frac{CI}{RI}$$

n	3.00	4.00	5.00	6.00	7.00	8.00	9.00	10.0
RI	0.58	0.90	1.12	1.24	1.32	1.41	1.45	1.51

$$CR = \frac{0.014}{0.90} = 0.016$$

CR < 0.10 is acceptable

TABLE 10-6 Pairwise Comparison Matrix for Price

	Supplier 1	*Supplier 2*	*Supplier 3*	*Supplier 4*
Supplier 1	1.00	4.00	7.00	0.50
Supplier 2	0.25	1.00	3.00	0.17
Supplier 3	0.14	0.33	1.00	0.13
Supplier 4	2.00	6.00	8.00	1.00
	3.39	11.33	19.00	1.79

Step 9: Repeat steps 1 to 8 with pairwise comparisons of suppliers against each criterion. For n suppliers, there are $[(n \times n) - n/2]$ pairwise comparisons.

$$\text{Priority vector for price, } w_{price} = [0.324 \quad 0.103 \quad 0.048 \quad 0.525]$$

$$\text{Compute } \lambda_{max} = 4.047$$

$$CI = 0.016$$

$$CR = 0.017$$

TABLE 10-7 Pairwise Comparison Matrix for Quality

	Supplier 1	*Supplier 2*	*Supplier 3*	*Supplier 4*
Supplier 1	1.00	0.33	5.00	8.00
Supplier 2	3.00	1.00	7.00	9.00
Supplier 3	0.20	0.14	1.00	3.00
Supplier 4	0.13	0.11	0.33	1.00
	4.33	1.59	13.33	21.00

Step 9: Repeat steps 1 to 8 with pairwise comparisons of suppliers against each criterion. For n suppliers, there are $[(nxn) - n/2]$ pairwise comparisons.

$$\text{Priority vector for quality, } w_{quality} = [0.299 \quad 0.569 \quad 0.089 \quad 0.043]$$
$$\text{Compute } \lambda_{max} = 4.172$$
$$CI = 0.057$$
$$CR = 0.064$$

TABLE 10-8 Pairwise Comparison Matrix for Delivery

	Supplier 1	*Supplier 2*	*Supplier 3*	*Supplier 4*
Supplier 1	1.00	3.00	0.20	1.00
Supplier 2	0.33	1.00	0.14	0.33
Supplier 3	5.00	7.00	1.00	4.00
Supplier 4	1.00	3.00	0.25	1.00
	7.33	14.00	1.59	6.33

Step 9: Repeat steps 1 to 8 with pairwise comparisons of suppliers against each criterion. For n suppliers, there are $[(nxn) - n/2]$ pairwise comparisons.

$$\text{Priority vector for delivery, } w_{delivery} = [0.159 \quad 0.065 \quad 0.610 \quad 0.166]$$
$$\text{Compute } \lambda_{max} = 4.058$$
$$CI = 0.019$$
$$CR = 0.021$$

TABLE 10-9 Pairwise Comparison Matrix for Service

	Supplier 1	*Supplier 2*	*Supplier 3*	*Supplier 4*
Supplier 1	1.00	5.00	3.00	8.00
Supplier 2	0.20	1.00	0.50	5.00
Supplier 3	0.33	2.00	1.00	4.00
Supplier 4	0.13	0.20	0.25	1.00
	1.66	8.20	4.75	18.00

Step 9: Repeat steps 1 to 8 with pairwise comparisons of suppliers against each criterion. For n suppliers, there are $[(nxn) - n/2]$ pairwise comparisons.

$$\text{Priority vector for service, } w_{service} = [0.572 \quad 0.156 \quad 0.219 \quad 0.052]$$
$$\text{Compute } \lambda_{max} = 4.154$$
$$CI = 0.051$$
$$CR = 0.057$$

FIGURE 10-5 Final Selection

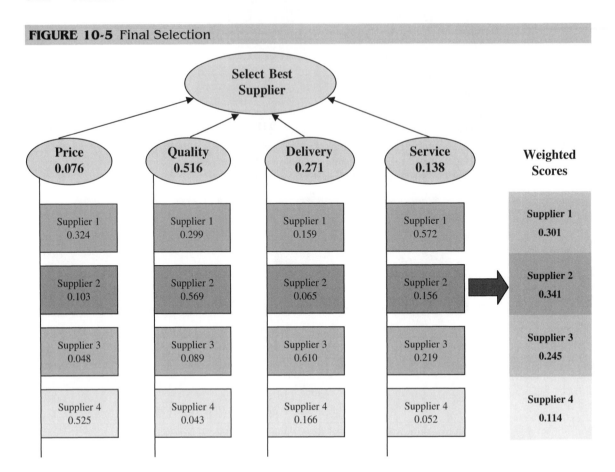

Consistency

Consistency Ratio

Consistency Index

first. In steps 7 and 8, as shown in Table 10-5, **consistency** is checked. This is a check of the logic used to assign preferences. For example, if A is preferred to B, and B is preferred to C, then A should be preferred to C. The **consistency ratio**, CR, is the ratio of the **consistency index** (based on the preferences assigned) and a random index, based on the consistency index that would be expected if preferences were assigned at random (using no logic). An acceptable CR is less than 10%.

In step 9, a priority vector for each criterion is computed. The priority vector contains elements that represent the relative rankings for the suppliers against a specific criterion. The priority vectors are used to compute weighted scores for each supplier as shown in Figure 10-5. For example, the score for supplier 1 is derived by summing the products of the weight for each criterion and the relative weight given to supplier 1 for that criterion: $(0.076)(0.324) + (0.516)(0.299) + (0.271)(0.159) + (0.138)(0.572) = 0.301$. In this case, supplier 2 would be selected with a total weighted score of 0.341.

10.4.3 Categorical Method

The categorical method is the simplest, but also the most subjective procedure for supplier selection. Personnel from purchasing, quality, production, and sales, are asked to develop criteria that are important to them. Then the groups rate each supplier against that group's criteria, using **categorical ratings** of preferred, unsatisfactory, or neutral.

Categorical Ratings

The categorical method uses ratings of preferred, unsatisfactory, or neutral to determine supplier worthiness.

All parties participate in an evaluation meeting to discuss all suppliers and the individual scores assigned by the functional groups. This meeting is led by purchasing and results in an overall score for each contending supplier.

The categorical method has its advantages. It is simple to administer, enables broad participation, and accommodates the use of disparate selection criteria. However, this technique is more subjective than other methods and rarely leads to supplier improvements.

10.5 ATTRIBUTES ACCEPTANCE SAMPLING

10.5.1 Overview and Notation

Acceptance Sampling

Acceptance sampling is a statistical tool that can be used to estimate the quality of any fixed supply of material by measuring a small representative percentage of it. This method is often used in certification programs to compare suppliers. There are two types of acceptance sampling plans—those based on attributes measures and those based on variables. The former can be applied to qualitative or quantitative characteristics, whereas the latter is only applicable to normally distributed quantitative measures. This chapter only discusses attributes plans—the most widely applied form of acceptance sampling.

In its simplest form, acceptance sampling occurs at the interface between the supplier and the customer, as described:

Sample

Nonconforming

Defectives

Accept

Reject

Company A sends a shipment of goods to company B. Rather than inspecting all the units in the entire shipment, company B takes a **sample** from the shipment and inspects it for defective (**nonconforming**) items. On the basis of the number of **defectives** found in the sample, the inspector will either **accept** or **reject** the shipment.

Acceptance sampling results in the acceptance or rejection of a shipment based on a random sample.

Some critical issues arise concerning the sampling and inspection transactions that occur between supplier and customer: How many units should be included in the sample? What number of nonconforming items in the sample will result in the shipment being accepted? What number of nonconforming items in the sample will result in the shipment being rejected? What is considered to be an acceptable fraction nonconforming? Why not inspect the entire shipment? The answers to these questions can differ dramatically, depending on whether they are posed from the producer's or supplier's point of view.

Sample Size

The producer assumes the risk that good shipments will be rejected.

The consumer assumes the risk that bad shipments will be accepted.

An acceptance sampling plan answers the first three questions by specifying the **sample size** and the maximum number of nonconforming items that can be present in a sample if the lot is to be accepted. Developing a plan that is satisfactory to the consumer (who wants to accept only shipments with 100% conformance) and also the producer (who wants to have 100% of the shipments accepted) often requires compromise. The producer must be prepared to accept some risk that a good shipment will be rejected, and the consumer must accept some risk that a bad shipment will be accepted. What differentiates a good shipment from a bad one? The following notation helps us better understand how to answer this question:

Acceptance Number

N	number of units in a shipment (or lot)
n	number of units in the sample
d	number of nonconforming units found in a sample of size n
c	**acceptance number**: the maximum number of nonconforming units that will enable a sample of size n to be accepted

	p	proportion of nonconforming units (for small, single shipments, the proportion nonconforming in the shipment; for large shipments or for a continuing series of shipments, the process average proportion nonconforming)
Acceptable Quality Level	**AQL**	**acceptable quality level**: the poorest quality that a consumer considers acceptable; expressed as a process average percent nonconforming
Lot Tolerance Percent Defective	**LTPD**	**lot tolerance percent defective**: the poorest quality a consumer will accept in a single lot; also referred to as LQL, lower quality limit, or RQL, rejectable quality level
Average Outgoing Quality	**AOQ**	**average outgoing quality**: the expected average percent nonconforming of outgoing product for a given value of percent nonconforming incoming product quality
Average Outgoing Quality Limit	**AOQL**	**average outgoing quality limit**: the worst possible average percent nonconforming in outgoing product

Using this notation, we define the risk assumed by the producer and the consumer. The producer's risk, α, is the probability that a shipment of good quality, defined to be the AQL, will be rejected. Similarly, the consumer's risk, β, is the probability that a shipment of poor quality, defined to be the LTPD, will be accepted. Note that this is consistent with the definitions of α and β for statistical hypothesis testing, where the null hypothesis is expressed as:

H_0: the shipment is of good quality

In this context, α is the type I error—the probability of rejecting H_0 when it is true. β is the type II error—the probability of failing to reject H_0 when it is false.

10.5.2 The Role of Acceptance Sampling

Acceptance sampling generally takes place at the interface between the customer and the supplier, and well after production has been completed. For this reason, it is an audit tool, used to ensure the quality of product by providing guidelines for determining acceptance or rejection based on clearly defined sampling rules. Acceptance sampling is not intended to estimate product quality. What the procedure does well is to define the probability of accepting lots at defined quality levels, either the AQL or LTPD, when applied to a series of shipments.

Acceptance sampling is not a substitute for statistical process control.

Acceptance sampling cannot substitute for the SPC tools described in Chapter 8. This technique does not measure process stability and cannot, by itself, lead to improvements. The objective of acceptance sampling is simply to determine the degree of conformance of a fixed supply of material. Acceptance sampling should not be used as a misguided attempt to inspect quality into the product. By the time a lot is presented to an acceptance sampling station, it is too late to influence the outcome. It is far better to prevent the occurrence of defects through good QC policies at the point of production, than to try and detect defectives after the fact.

It is generally unwise to rely on acceptance sampling for quality assurance. In JIT environments, there is no time for corrective actions if a shipment is rejected. If high-quality materials are not available when and where they are needed, production runs may have to be aborted, schedules altered, or commitments may be missed. Supplier certification procedures normally require SPC documentation (on an ongoing basis) to ensure suppliers are controlling quality at the source. If a supplier's process is capable, on target, and in statistical control, there is little need for incoming inspection.

So what is the role of acceptance sampling? It is essentially a middle ground between 100% inspection and no inspection. Acceptance sampling can be of value anytime there is insufficient process history to effectively use SPC—for example, in the case of new products or purchased materials from new suppliers. In such cases, acceptance sampling may be implemented as a temporary measure until adequate process history can be accumulated. Acceptance sampling can also be useful in monitoring the output from processes that are unstable, not capable of meeting requirements, or both. While such processes are being improved, acceptance sampling might offer an attractive alternative to 100% inspection so the release of defective material to customers can be controlled.

Compared with 100% inspection, acceptance sampling has some advantages. It is less time consuming and costly to inspect a small sample rather than an entire shipment. If the sampling procedure involves destructive testing, such as fracturing a structural beam, 100% sampling is not feasible. Inspector fatigue is also a factor that favors sampling inspection. The higher the workload for inspectors, the more likely the inspectors will grow weary and make errors. Acceptance sampling can also provide improvement incentives. If a lot undergoes a 100% inspection, usually it is only the defective units that are returned to the supplier. However, with acceptance sampling, if the quality is poor enough, the entire shipment is rejected and returned to the supplier. Faced with this prospect, a supplier may take greater care to ensure the quality is at least good enough to pass the acceptance criteria.

On the negative side, using acceptance sampling carries with it the producer's and consumer's risks that were mentioned previously. Under 100% inspection, there are no α and β risks, and no uncertainty because (barring any inspection error) the true fraction nonconforming is known at the conclusion of the inspection procedure. Acceptance sampling is also somewhat harder to administer than a 100% inspection procedure. Sampling schemes must be carefully planned and thoroughly documented. If entire lots are inspected, there is no need for detailed planning and the only documentation required is a count, by lot, of the numbers and types of defects encountered.

In summary, acceptance sampling is not a tool that can be used for process control or as the sole basis of QA. It can, however, be successfully applied to unstable or incapable processes to monitor output until SPC tools can be effectively implemented.

10.5.3 Randomness in Sampling

Acceptance sampling requires that inspection be performed on a **random sample**. What constitutes a random sample? Suppose a shipment consists of 2,000 identical components and that the sampling plan calls for a sample of 100 units. If the sample is truly random, each of the 2,000 components has an equal probability of inclusion in the sample, thus ensuring the sample is representative of the lot.

However, a sample may be far from representative. Humans draw samples and, if improperly trained, will seek the easiest and most efficient means to achieve results. Suppose the shipment of 2,000 components arrives on twenty pallets. The receiving agent removes the first pallet from the truck and proceeds to use the 100 units on that pallet to form the required sample of 100. If the lot is rejected, the clerk need only place the pallet back on the truck and send the entire shipment back to the supplier. Although minimizing the time and effort required at receiving, this practice may not produce random samples. The 100 components on the first pallet have a 100% probability of inclusion in the sample, but the remaining 1,900 components have 0% probability of inclusion.

If appropriate practices are not followed, acceptance sampling can produce risk factors that are dramatically different from those stipulated in the sampling design. In the previous example, if the components were known to have been thoroughly mixed prior to packaging, palletizing, and loading, a random sample could be obtained by selecting 100 units from anywhere in the lot, including taking the entire sample from the first pallet. However, in general, components are packaged and palletized in the order of their production. It is impractical to try to deliberately homogenize the product prior to shipment. Therefore, drawing all the sampling units from a single point in the shipment could result in a sample that is not representative and is biased.

Although it appears that the receiving agent could be blamed for taking a poor sample, the fault undoubtedly can be traced to the lack of proper training. Inspection personnel must be thoroughly indoctrinated on why random sampling is necessary and how representative samples can be obtained, without wasting unnecessary time and effort. It is essential that operational definitions be established to clearly communicate to all inspectors how samples should be selected, what criteria are to be used, and how conformance and nonconformance decisions are to be made.

For small lots, a true random sample can be constructed using the following procedure. Continuing with our example of the shipment of 2,000, one would assign a unique number (from 1 to 2,000), to each component in the shipment. The sample is formed using a random number generator to select 100 of the 2,000 numbers. The components corresponding to these numbers are the ones that will be pulled for inspection.

For large lots, it may be impractical to assign a unique number to each unit. In this case, the lot can be stratified into small groups with equal numbers of units in the sample taken from each group. In our example, there are 100 units on each of twenty pallets. A stratified sample of $n = 100$ would include five components from each pallet. Suppose each pallet consists of five layers each of 20 units. The lot can then be further subdivided into layers of product, with 1 unit from each layer selected for the sample. Although this stratification is not random in a pure sense, it does increase a sample's overall representation by ensuring the sample is taken from different points throughout the lot.

Acceptance sampling plans can be devised that base decisions on a single sample, two samples, multiple samples, or sequential samples.

Single Sampling

10.5.4 Types of Attributes Acceptance Sampling Plans

There are four types of acceptance sampling plans: single sampling, double sampling, multiple sampling, and sequential sampling. A **single sampling** plan requires that a sample of size n be selected from a shipment. If the number of nonconforming units in the sample, d, is less than or equal to the acceptance number, c, the lot is accepted; if $d > c$, the lot is rejected. This procedure is illustrated in the flowchart shown in Figure 10-6.

FIGURE 10-6 Acceptance Sampling Procedure

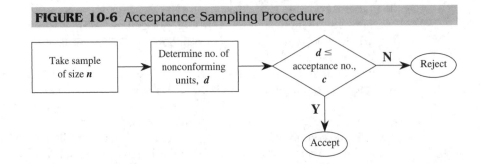

Double Sampling

Multiple Sampling

With double sampling, the decision may be deferred until a second sample is taken.

Under multiple sampling, a decision may be deferred until a predetermined number of samples have been taken, or until a prespecified number of units has been inspected.

Sequential Sampling

Sequential sampling offers the opportunity to make a decision with each unit inspected.

Double sampling plans are more complex and may require that a second sample be taken before the disposition of a lot can be determined. Under this type of plan, a shipment may be accepted, rejected, or subjected to a second sample on the basis of the results of the first sample with size n_1. If a second sample of size n_2 is required, the results of both samples are combined to determine whether the lot is accepted or rejected. Depending on the required sample sizes, a double sampling plan may require inspection of fewer units than single sampling provided a decision can be reached on the first sample. Generally, when a second sample is required, double sampling requires more inspection than a single sampling plan.

Multiple sampling extends the concept of double sampling by requiring, under certain circumstances, that more than two samples be inspected before a decision can be reached. These plans are similar to double sampling in that a decision to accept the lot, reject the lot, or take another sample is made as each subsequent sample is collected and inspected. The sampling continues until a clear decision to accept or reject can be reached or until a prespecified number of units have been inspected. Although multiple sampling plans are more complicated, they may result in the inspection of fewer units, on the average, than would be required under comparable single or double sampling plans.

Sequential sampling is another extension of double sampling. Under this type of sampling plan, individual units are inspected and, after each unit, a decision to accept, reject, or continue sampling is made. As the total number of units sampled increases, the criteria for accepting and rejecting are changed such that, theoretically, the sampling could continue until all units in the shipment have been inspected. An example of the decision regions for sequential sampling is shown in Figure 10-7.

Single and double sampling plans are discussed in detail in Sections 10.6 and 10.7. Additional coverage of multiple and sequential sampling plans is beyond the scope of this text.

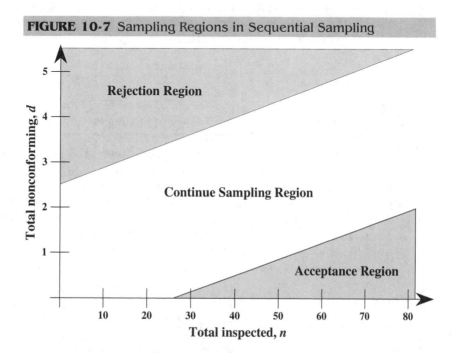

FIGURE 10-7 Sampling Regions in Sequential Sampling

10.6 SINGLE SAMPLING PLANS

Single sampling is the simplest form for lot-by-lot acceptance based on attributes. A single sampling plan requires three parameters: the shipment (or lot) size (N), the sample size (n), and the acceptance number (c). If the number of nonconforming units found in the sample, d, is less than or equal to c, the lot is accepted. If $d > c$, the lot is rejected. For example, suppose the shipment size is $N = 2,000$, the sample size is $n = 100$, and the acceptance number is $c = 2$. Under this plan, a random sample of 100 units is selected from the shipment. If the number of nonconforming units is less than or equal to 2, the shipment is accepted; otherwise, the shipment is rejected.

10.6.1 Single Sampling Plans, Producer's Risk, Consumer's Risk, and OC Curves

Operating Characteristic Curve

An **operating characteristic curve**, or OC curve, is a plot of the probability of accepting a shipment, P_A, versus the fraction nonconforming, p. Assuming the shipment is large or that it is a part of a continuing series of shipments, the binomial distribution applies, and can be used to calculate P_A over a range of values for fraction nonconforming. The formula for the binomial probabilities is shown in Equation 10-1:

An OC curve is a plot of the probability of acceptance and the quality of the lot.

$$P_A = \sum_{x=0}^{c} \binom{n}{x} p^x (1 - p)^{n-x} \tag{10-1}$$

where

$$\binom{n}{x} = \frac{n!}{x!(n - x)!}; \quad n! = (n)(n - 1)(n - 2) \cdots (3)(2)(1)$$

EXAMPLE: OC Curve for a Single Sampling Plan

Consider a single sampling plan for shipment size $N = 2,000$, sample size $n = 100$, and $c = 2$ acceptance number. Using Equation 10-1 and a fraction nonconforming $p = 0.025$, the probability of acceptance is:

$$P_A = \sum_{x=0}^{2} \binom{100}{x} (0.025)^x (1 - 0.025)^{100-x} = 0.5422$$

We assume this procedure is repeated and P_A is calculated for a number of p values, ranging from 0 to 1. The OC curve, constructed by plotting P_A versus p, is shown in Figure 10-8.

Producer's Risk

Consumer's Risk

The concepts of **producer's risk**, α, and **consumer's risk**, β, were previously defined as the probabilities of rejecting a good shipment and of accepting a bad shipment, respectively. Single sampling plans are usually designed so they simultaneously satisfy a producer's criterion, $P_A \geq 1 - \alpha$ at $p_1 = $ AQL, and a consumer's criterion, $P_A \leq \beta$ at $p_2 = $ LTPD. This requires a plan with an OC curve that passes through these two points. To achieve this, the two nonlinear equations (in two unknowns) shown as Equations 10-2 and 10-3 must be solved:

$$1 - \alpha = \sum_{d=0}^{c} p_1^d (1 - p_1)^{n-d} \tag{10-2}$$

$$\beta = \sum_{d=0}^{c} p_2^d (1 - p_2)^{n-d} \tag{10-3}$$

FIGURE 10-8 An Operating Characteristic (OC) Curve

p	P_A
0.00	1.0000
0.01	0.9206
0.02	0.6767
0.03	0.4198
0.04	0.2321
0.05	0.1183
0.06	0.0566
0.07	0.0258
0.08	0.0113
0.09	0.0048
0.10	0.0019

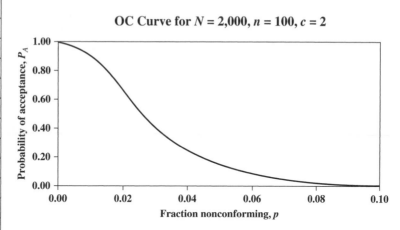

Solving this system of equations requires a complex iterative solution, where a value of c is assumed and values for n that satisfy the producer's risk and the consumer's risk are determined. If no sample size n can be found that simultaneously satisfies both producer and consumer, then it is necessary to select a larger acceptance number and repeat the process. Because the cost of sampling increases with sample size, the objective is to determine the plan with the smallest sample size that satisfies both the stipulated producer and consumer risks. The plan selected will normally meet one of the risk criteria and exceed the other.

A number of approaches have been devised to facilitate the development of such plans. A graphical technique—the binomial nomograph[13]—was developed by Larson, in which straight lines connecting the AQL to $1 - \alpha$ and the LTPD to β are overlaid. The intersection of the two lines is used to identify the sample size and the acceptance number. Another approach, developed by Grubbs, provides tables for the commonly used values of producer's risk, $\alpha = 0.05$, and consumer's risk, $\beta = 0.10$.[14] Grubbs' approach uses a ratio of LTPD/AQL to index a table for the determination of c and the calculation of n to satisfy both producer's and consumer's risk criteria. This approach is presented in Section 10.6.4. Other methods include MIL-STD-105D, developed by the military during World War II, and ANSI/ASQC Z1.4-1981.[15] Another popular approach, the Dodge-Romig tables,[16] is presented in detail in Section 10.6.5.

[13]Larson, Harry R. "A Nomograph of the Cumulative Binomial Distribution." *Western Electric Engineer* April 1965.

[14]Grubbs, Frank E. "On Designing Single Sampling Plans." *Annals of Mathematical Statistics* 20, no. 2 (1949): 242–56.

[15]American Society for Quality Control. *American National Standard—Sampling Procedures and Tables for Inspection by Attributes.* ANSI/ASQC Z1.4-1981. 1981.

[16]Dodge, Harold F., and Harry G. Romig. *Sampling Inspection Tables—Single and Double Sampling.* 2nd ed. New York: Wiley, 1959.

10.6.2 Measures of Plan Performance—AOQL and ATI

Under single sampling, an entire shipment is either accepted or rejected on the basis of one sample of n units. In an environment of JIT, lean production, or Six Sigma, a customer does not have the luxury of rejecting incoming materials. In the absence of on-hand inventories in sufficient quantities to buffer against quality problems, returning a shipment to the vendor would likely result in lost production. Some sampling plans provide for **rectifying inspection** to allow the customer to go ahead and use those units within a shipment that conform to requirements.

Rectifying Inspection

Under rectifying inspection, rejected lots undergo 100% inspection to screen out defective units.

Under rectifying inspection, if a lot is not accepted, it is subjected to a 100% screening inspection operation to separate the conforming materials from the nonconforming. Conforming material can proceed to production, whereas the nonconforming material is returned to the supplier to be replaced with good product. Further, if the shipment is accepted, but one or more nonconforming units were found in the sample, those units are also replaced by the supplier with conforming product. In most cases, the cost of the 100% inspection and all transportation costs for replacing nonconforming product are borne by the producer. This has the effect of increasing the AOQ accepted over several shipments because all rejected lots become 100% conforming following screening inspection and replacement. For shipments of size N, samples of size n, and incoming fraction nonconforming p, the AOQ for a single sampling plan is given by Equation 10-4:

$$\text{AOQ} = \frac{P_A p (N - n)}{N} \tag{10-4}$$

Substituting for P_A,

$$\text{AOQ} = \frac{\sum_{x=0}^{c} \binom{n}{x} p^x (1 - p)^{n-x} p(N - n)}{N} \tag{10-5}$$

An AOQ curve is generated by solving Equation 10-5 for several values of p, then plotting AOQ versus p. The AOQL is the maximum value of the curve, representing the worst average level of quality that the customer would receive following rectifying inspection. AOQL is one of the important metrics for evaluating alternative sampling plans. It may be determined visually from the AOQ curve or approximated by taking the maximum AOQ value from the table used to plot the curve.

EXAMPLE: AOQ Curve and AOQL for Single Sampling Plan

Consider a single sampling plan for shipment size $N = 2{,}000$, sample size $n = 100$, and $c = 2$ acceptance number. Applying Equation 10-5, the AOQ for fraction nonconforming $p = 0.04$ is:

$$\text{AOQ} = \frac{\sum_{x=0}^{2} \binom{100}{x} 0.04^x (1 - 0.04)^{100-x} (0.04)(2{,}000 - 100)}{2{,}000} = 0.0088$$

By repeating this procedure, and calculating the AOQ for a number of p values (ranging from 0 to 1), an AOQ curve can be constructed (a plot of AOQ versus p). The

AOQ curve for this example is shown in Figure 10-9, and indicates that the AOQL = 0.0130.

Average Total Inspection

The **average total inspection** (ATI) is another important tool for evaluating a sampling plan. Under rectifying inspection, the ATI represents the average number of units inspected per shipment over a series of shipments. It is calculated from the lot size, the sample size, and the probability of acceptance, and depends on sample size, fraction nonconforming, and acceptance number. Equation 10-6 is used to calculate the ATI for any given plan, given an assumed quality level p:

$$\text{ATI} = n + (1 - P_A)(N - n) \tag{10-6}$$

Substituting for P_A,

$$\text{ATI} = n + \left[1 - \left(\sum_{x=0}^{c}\binom{n}{x}p^x(1-p)^{n-x}\right)\right](N - n) \tag{10-7}$$

EXAMPLE: ATI Curve for Single Sampling Plan

Consider a single sampling plan for shipment size $N = 2{,}000$, sample size $n = 100$, and $c = 2$ acceptance number. Applying Equation 10-7, the ATI for fraction nonconforming $p = 0.025$ is approximately 970 units:

$$\text{ATI} = 100 + \left[1 - \left(\sum_{x=0}^{2}\binom{100}{x}(0.025)^x(1-0.025)^{n-x}\right)\right](2{,}000 - 100) = 969.8$$

The ATI curve is developed by plotting ATI versus fraction nonconforming over a range of values for p. The ATI curve for this example is shown in Figure 10-10.

FIGURE 10-9 An Average Outgoing Quality (AOQ) Curve

p	AOQ
0.000	0.0000
0.005	0.0047
0.010	0.0087
0.015	0.0115
0.020	0.0129
0.025	0.0129
0.030	0.0120
0.035	0.0105
0.040	0.0088
0.045	0.0071
0.050	0.0056
0.055	0.0043
0.060	0.0032
0.065	0.0024
0.070	0.0017
0.075	0.0012
0.080	0.0009
0.085	0.0006
0.090	0.0004
0.095	0.0003
0.100	0.0002

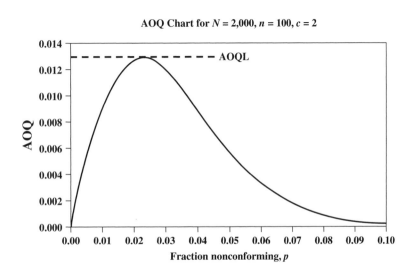

FIGURE 10-10 An Average Total Inspection (ATI) Curve

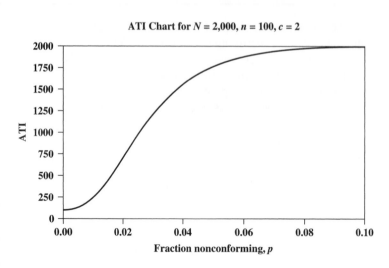

p	ATI
0.000	100.0
0.005	126.8
0.010	250.8
0.015	461.4
0.020	714.3
0.025	969.8
0.030	1202.4
0.035	1399.8
0.040	1558.9
0.045	1682.4
0.050	1775.3
0.055	1843.5
0.060	1892.4
0.065	1927.0
0.070	1951.0
0.075	1967.5
0.080	1978.6
0.085	1986.0
0.090	1991.0
0.095	1994.2
0.100	1996.3

ATI Chart for $N = 2,000$, $n = 100$, $c = 2$

The AOQL and ATI each provide different information about the performance of a sampling plan. The previous example showed that AOQ is low for lots of high quality (low p). Assuming random sampling, the AOQ can be no greater than the incoming fraction nonconforming, p. As quality decreases (p increases), the AOQ will approach p until the probability of acceptance decreases to such a level that a significant proportion of the shipments are subjected to rectifying inspection. Recall that for those lots subjected to 100% inspection, the fraction nonconforming after inspection will be zero. As p continues to increase, the number of lots subjected to rectifying inspection will increase, resulting in a decrease in AOQ. For large values of fraction nonconforming, AOQ approaches zero. The AOQL provides an indication to the customer of the worst average fraction nonconforming that would be received under a particular sampling plan, after rectifying inspection has been performed. Customers prefer low values of AOQL.

The ATI curve indicates the relationship between incoming fraction nonconforming and the average number of units that would be inspected for that fraction nonconforming, under a particular sampling plan. One of the four cost-of-quality (COQ) categories is *appraisal cost,* a portion of which is the cost of sampling. (The other three categories are prevention costs, internal failure costs, and external failure costs). An advantage of acceptance sampling (over 100% inspection) is the reduction in sampling time and cost—the larger the number of units sampled, the greater the sampling cost. Thus, a sampling plan that minimizes the number of units inspected for a particular level of incoming quality is preferred. The minimum ATI is the size of the sample, n. Shipments of 100% conformance have 100% probability of acceptance. As fraction nonconforming increases, a greater proportion of lots are subjected to rectifying inspection, where all N units in the shipment must be inspected. Thus, for $p = 0$, ATI $= n$, but as p increases, it will reach a point where ATI will approach N.

10.6.3 Curtailment Inspection for Rejected Shipments

If the sole purpose of acceptance sampling is to make decisions on acceptance or re-jection, one would cease inspection of a sample and reject the lot as soon as the ac-ceptance number is exceeded in the sample. This practice is known as **curtailment inspection** and would result in the inspection of fewer units for rejected lots. For a sam-ple of size $n = 100$ with acceptance number $c = 2$, if the third nonconforming item is found on the twenty-second item inspected, only 22 units would be inspected for that shipment, and the shipment would be rejected and returned to the supplier.

In more recent times, curtailment has fallen out of favor and is not widely prac-ticed. There are two reasons for this. First, curtailment and rectifying inspection are mutually exclusive—if inspection is curtailed after the twenty-second unit and the ship-ment rejected, the remaining $(N - 22)$ units are not inspected. Under curtailment, the shipment would be returned to the producer and none of the components would be available until the shipment is replaced. Rectifying inspection allows the customer to use all the conforming components, which are subsequently identified through 100% screening, thus avoiding a potential stock-out and the disruption of production.

The other major shortcoming is that curtailment does not provide the customer with a reliable estimate of supplier quality. For $n = 100$ and $c = 2$, suppose the third nonconforming item is found on the sixth unit inspected. Under curtailment, 50% of the units inspected are nonconforming. Using these sampling results to infer that the entire lot is 50% defective could be misleading.

10.6.4 Developing Single Sampling Plans—Grubbs' Approach

We previously demonstrated that, to simultaneously satisfy the producer's and con-sumer's risk criteria, an inspection plan's OC curve must pass through two points: $[P_A = (1 - \alpha), p = \text{AQL}]$ and $[P_A = \beta, p = \text{LTPD}]$. Rather than trying to *exactly* satisfy both criteria, a plan can be designed that meets a stipulated producer's risk and comes close to meeting the consumer's risk. Alternatively, the plan can be designed to precisely meet the stipulated consumer's risk and come close to meeting the producer's risk. Table 10-10, developed by F. E. Grubbs,[17] can be used to design single sampling plans for producer's risk of $\alpha = 0.05$ and consumer's risk of $\beta = 0.10$.

A Grubbs table is used by first computing the ratio, R_0, of the stipulated LTPD and AQL. Tabulated values of R are shown in Table 10-10 as $R_{\text{Tab}} = p_2/p_1$. Larger ratios R yield smaller acceptance numbers c, and smaller sample sizes n. A large R results from a large relative difference between AQL and LTPD. For a large R, small samples and acceptance numbers are sufficient to determine the disposition of a shipment. Smaller ratios, in contrast, require larger sample sizes and acceptance numbers.

The sampling plan is developed by locating the two tabulated $R = p_2/p_1$ values in the rightmost column that bracket the actual calculated p_2/p_1. For each, the corre-sponding acceptance number can be found in the left column of the table. If the calcu-lated ratio is near one of the tabulated R values, only one acceptance number needs to be considered. The two columns, labeled np_1 and np_2, respectively, are used to calculate a sample size corresponding to each candidate acceptance number. The np_1 column is used for calculating a sample size that meets the stipulated producer's risk, and the np_2 column is used to calculate a sample size that meets the stipulated consumer's risk.

---

[17]Grubbs, "On Designing Single," 242–56.

TABLE 10-10 Grubbs Table for Single Sampling Plans, $\alpha = 0.05$, $\beta = 0.10$

Acceptance Number, c	1 − Producer's Risk 1 − α = 0.95 np_1	Consumer's Risk β = 0.10 np_2	$R_{Tab} =$ LTPD/AQL $= p_2/p_1$
0	0.051	2.303	44.84
1	0.355	3.890	10.96
2	0.818	5.322	6.51
3	1.366	6.681	4.89
4	1.970	7.944	4.06
5	2.613	9.274	3.55
6	3.286	10.532	3.21
7	3.981	11.771	2.96
8	4.695	12.995	2.77
9	5.426	14.206	2.62
10	6.169	15.407	2.50
11	6.924	16.598	2.40
12	7.690	17.782	2.31
13	8.464	18.958	2.24
14	9.246	20.128	2.18
15	10.035	21.292	2.12

SOURCE: Grubbs, F. E., "On Designing Single Sampling Inspection Plans." *Annals of Mathematical Statistics* 20, no. 2 (1949) 256, reprinted with permission of The Institute of Mathematical Statistics.

Recall that the producer's risk is defined as the probability of failing to accept (or reject) a shipment if the process average nonconformance p is equal to the AQL (p_1), and the consumer's risk is defined as the probability of accepting a shipment if the process average nonconformance p is equal to the LTPD (p_2). For a given acceptance number, the producer favors a smaller sample size because this reduces the probability that shipments of good quality will be rejected. Similarly, the consumer favors a larger sample size because this decreases the probability that lots of inferior quality will be accepted. For calculated $R = p_2/p_1$ values falling in between the tabulated R values, the row indexed by the larger tabulated R will yield a sampling plan that meets the stipulated producer's criterion, but will have consumer's risk in excess of $\beta = 0.10$ (when the np_1 column is used to calculate n). If the np_2 column is used, the plan will meet the stipulated consumer's criterion, but will have producer's risk larger than $\alpha = 0.05$. If the smaller tabulated R is used to index the row, then both producer's risk and consumer's risk criteria can be met, but the calculated sample size and the acceptance number will be larger. The following example illustrates the use of a Grubbs table for developing a single sampling plan.

EXAMPLE: Development of Single Sampling Plan Using Grubbs Table

We want to develop a single sampling plan for shipment size $N = 1,000$ that meets the following criteria: AQL = 0.5%, LTPD = 3.0%, $\alpha = 0.05$, $\beta = 0.10$. We use Table 10-10 to determine the sample size, n, and acceptance number, c.

Step 1: Compute $R_0 = $ LTPD/AQL $= 0.03/0.005 = 6.00$.

Step 2: Identify in Table 10-10 the rows that bracket R_0.

$R_{Tab} = 6.51$, $c = 2$ and $R_{Tab} = 4.89$, $c = 3$ bracket R_0.

Step 3: Design sampling plans for each R_{Tab}.

For $c = 2$, $np_1 = 0.818$ and $n = np_1/p_1 = 0.818/0.005 = 163.6 \cong 164$.
$np_2 = 5.322$ and $n = np_2/p_2 = 5.322/0.03 = 177.4 \cong 177$.
For $c = 3$, $np_1 = 1.366$ and $n = np_1/p_1 = 1.366/0.005 = 273.2 \cong 273$.
$np_2 = 6.681$ and $n = np_2/p_2 = 6.681/0.03 = 222.7 \cong 223$.

Step 4: Compute producer's and consumer's risks for each plan, using Equation 10-1.

$\alpha = 1 - Pr\{accept|p_1\}$, $\beta = Pr\{accept|p_2\}$
For $c = 2$, $n = 164$:

For $p_1 = 0.005$, $P_A = \left(\dfrac{164!}{0!164!}\right)(0.005)^0(0.995)^{164}$

$+ \left(\dfrac{164!}{1!163!}\right)(0.005)^1(0.995)^{163} + \left(\dfrac{164!}{2!162!}\right)(0.005)^2(0.995)^{162} = 0.9501$

$\alpha = 1 - 0.9501 = 0.04990 < 0.05 \Rightarrow$ meets stipulated producer's risk

For $p_2 = 0.03$, $P_A = \left(\dfrac{164!}{0!164!}\right)(0.03)^0(0.97)^{164} + \left(\dfrac{164!}{1!163!}\right)(0.03)^1(0.97)^{163}$

$+ \left(\dfrac{164!}{2!162!}\right)(0.03)^2(0.97)^{162} = 0.12766$

$\beta = 0.12766 > 0.10 \Rightarrow$ does not meet stipulated consumer's risk
For $c = 2$, $n = 177$:

For $p_1 = 0.005$, $P_A = \left(\dfrac{177!}{0!177!}\right)(0.005)^0(0.995)^{177}$

$+ \left(\dfrac{177!}{1!176!}\right)(0.005)^1(0.995)^{176} + \left(\dfrac{177!}{2!175!}\right)(0.005)^2(0.995)^{175} = 0.94004$

$\alpha = 1 - 0.94004 = 0.05996 > 0.05 \Rightarrow$ does not meet stipulated producer's risk

For $p_2 = 0.03$, $P_A = \left(\dfrac{177!}{0!177!}\right)(0.03)^0(0.97)^{177} + \left(\dfrac{177!}{1!176!}\right)(0.03)^1(0.97)^{176}$

$+ \left(\dfrac{177!}{2!175!}\right)(0.03)^2(0.97)^{175} = 0.09738$

$\beta = 0.09738 < 0.10 \Rightarrow$ meets stipulated consumer's risk
For $c = 3$, $n = 273$:

For $p_1 = 0.005$, $P_A = \left(\dfrac{273!}{0!273!}\right)(0.005)^0(0.995)^{273} + \left(\dfrac{273!}{1!176!}\right)(0.005)^1(0.995)^{272}$

$+ \left(\dfrac{273!}{2!271!}\right)(0.005)^2(0.995)^{271} + \left(\dfrac{273!}{3!270!}\right)(0.005)^2(0.995)^{270} = 0.9509$

$\alpha = 1 - 0.9509 = 0.04941 < 0.05 \Rightarrow$ meets stipulated producer's risk

For $p_2 = 0.03$, $P_A = \left(\dfrac{273!}{0!273!}\right)(0.03)^0(0.97)^{273} + \left(\dfrac{273!}{1!272!}\right)(0.03)^1(0.97)^{272}$

$+ \left(\dfrac{273!}{2!271!}\right)(0.03)^2(0.97)^{271} + \left(\dfrac{273!}{3!270!}\right)(0.03)^2(0.97)^{270} = 0.03528$

$\beta = 0.03528 \ll 0.10 \Rightarrow$ more than meets stipulated consumer's risk

For $c = 3, n = 223$:

For $p_1 = 0.005$, $P_A = \left(\dfrac{223!}{0!223!}\right)(0.005)^0(0.995)^{223} + \left(\dfrac{223!}{1!222!}\right)(0.005)^1(0.995)^{222}$

$\qquad + \left(\dfrac{223!}{2!221!}\right)(0.005)^2(0.995)^{221} + \left(\dfrac{223!}{3!220!}\right)(0.005)^2(0.995)^{220} = 0.97349$

$\alpha = 1 - 0.97349 = 0.02651 \ll 0.05$

$\Rightarrow$ more than meets stipulated producer's risk

For $p_2 = 0.03$, $P_A = \left(\dfrac{223!}{0!223!}\right)(0.03)^0(0.97)^{223} + \left(\dfrac{223!}{1!222!}\right)(0.03)^1(0.97)^{222}$

$\qquad + \left(\dfrac{223!}{2!221!}\right)(0.03)^2(0.97)^{221} + \left(\dfrac{223!}{3!220!}\right)(0.03)^2(0.97)^{220} = 0.09597$

$\beta = 0.09597 < 0.10 \Rightarrow$ meets stipulated consumer's risk

Step 5: Select a sampling plan.

A plan with an acceptance number, $c = 2$, that meets both producer's and consumer's risk criteria cannot be achieved. The sampling plans $c = 3$ will meet or exceed producer's and consumer's risks, but the corresponding sample sizes are considerably larger. The plans that should be considered are $c = 2$, $n = 147$ (slightly exceeds producer's risk and meets consumer's risk) and $c = 3$, $n = 223$ (meets both producer's and consumer's risks). To assist in making the final decision, Equation 10-7 can be used to construct the ATI curves for the two candidate plans, as shown in Figure 10-11. Although the plan for $c = 3$ requires a larger sample size, the ATI curves for the two plans are very similar. Therefore, if rectifying inspection is to be implemented, there is little

FIGURE 10-11 Average Total Inspection (ATI) Curves for Candidate Plans

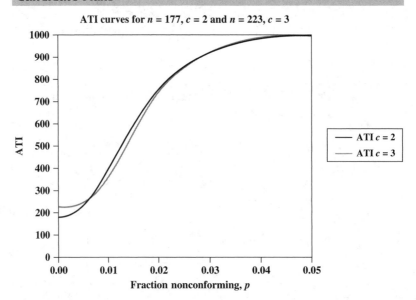

ATI curves for $n = 177$, $c = 2$ and $n = 223$, $c = 3$

difference between the two plans in the average number of units to be inspected per shipment. Either plan could be selected.

10.6.5 Developing Single Sampling Plans—Dodge-Romig Tables

Dodge and Romig developed a method for designing single and double sampling plans under rectifying inspection. Either a stipulated LTPD or AOQL can be used to enter a table and obtain a sampling plan that minimizes the ATI. These tables are based on $\beta = 10\%$ and are available for LTPD values of 0.005, 0.01, 0.02, 0.03, 0.04, 0.05, 0.07, and 0.10, and AOQL values of 0.0010, 0.0025, 0.0050, 0.0075, 0.010, 0.015, 0.020, 0.0250, 0.030, 0.040, 0.050, 0.070, and 0.100. The tables for specified LTPD values provide AOQL estimates for each sampling plan, and the tables for specified AOQL's provide estimates for LTPDs. Tables 10-11 and 10-12 are the Dodge-Romig tables for AOQL = 3.0% and LTPD = 5.0%, respectively.

The Dodge-Romig tables are entered using two parameters: the lot size and the assumed average fraction nonconforming. The quality of the incoming material can be estimated from a preliminary process qualification study or from the supplier's quality records. After a few shipments have been made, the incoming fraction nonconforming

TABLE 10-11 Dodge-Romig Single Sampling Table for AOQL = 3.0%

| | Process Average Fraction Nonconforming | | | | | | | | | | | | | | | | | |
| | 0–0.06% | | | 0.07–0.60% | | | 0.61–1.20% | | | 1.21–1.80% | | | 1.81–2.40% | | | 2.41–3.00% | | |
Lot Size	n	c	LTPD %	n	c	LTPD %	n	c	LTPD %	n	c	LTPD %	n	c	LTPD %	n	c	LTPD %
1–10	All	0	—	All	0	—	All	0	—	All	0	—	All	0	—	All	0	—
11–50	10	0	19	10	0	19	10	0	19	10	0	19	10	0	19	10	0	19
51–100	11	0	18	11	0	18	11	0	18	11	0	18	11	0	18	22	1	16.4
101–200	12	0	17	12	0	17	12	0	17	25	1	15.1	25	1	15.1	25	1	15.1
201–300	12	0	17	12	0	17	26	1	14.6	26	1	14.6	26	1	14.6	40	2	12.8
301–400	12	0	17.1	12	0	17.1	26	1	14.7	26	1	14.7	41	2	12.7	41	2	12.7
401–500	12	0	17.2	27	1	14.1	27	1	14.1	42	2	12.4	42	2	12.4	42	2	12.4
501–600	12	0	17.3	27	1	14.2	27	1	14.2	42	2	12.4	42	2	12.4	60	3	10.8
601–800	12	0	17.3	27	1	14.2	27	1	14.2	43	2	12.1	60	3	10.9	60	3	10.9
801–1,000	12	0	17.4	27	1	14.2	44	2	11.8	44	2	11.8	60	3	11	80	4	9.8
1,001–2,000	12	0	17.5	28	1	13.8	45	2	11.7	65	3	10.2	80	4	9.8	100	5	9.1
2,001–3,000	12	0	17.5	28	1	13.8	45	2	11.7	65	3	10.2	100	5	9.1	140	7	8.2
3,001–4,000	12	0	17.5	28	1	13.8	65	3	10.3	85	4	9.5	125	6	8.4	165	8	7.8
4,001–5,000	28	1	13.8	28	1	13.8	65	3	10.3	85	4	9.5	125	6	8.4	210	10	7.4
5,001–7,000	28	1	13.8	45	2	11.8	65	3	10.3	105	5	8.8	145	7	8.1	235	11	7.1
7,001–10,000	28	1	13.9	46	2	11.6	65	3	10.3	105	5	8.8	170	8	7.6	280	13	6.8
10,001–20,000	28	1	13.9	46	2	11.7	85	4	9.5	125	6	8.4	215	10	7.2	380	17	6.2
20,001–50,000	28	1	13.9	65	3	10.3	105	5	8.8	170	8	7.6	310	14	6.5	560	24	5.7
50,001–100,000	28	1	13.9	65	3	10.3	125	6	8.4	215	10	7.2	385	17	6.2	690	29	5.4

SOURCE: Harold F. Dodge, and Harry G. Romig. *Sampling Inspection Tables—Single and Double Sampling.* 2nd ed., Revised and Expanded, 202. New York, John Wiley, 1959. Reprinted with permission of Lucent Technologies Inc./Bell Labs.

TABLE 10-12 Dodge-Romig Single Sampling Table for LTPD = 5.0%

Lot Size	\multicolumn{18}{c}{Process Average Fraction Nonconforming}
	\multicolumn{3}{c}{0–0.05}	\multicolumn{3}{c}{0.06–0.50%}	\multicolumn{3}{c}{0.51–1.00%}	\multicolumn{3}{c}{1.01–1.50%}	\multicolumn{3}{c}{1.51–2.00%}	\multicolumn{3}{c}{2.01–2.50%}
	n	c	AOQL %	n	c	AOQL %	n	c	AOQL %	n	c	AOQL %	n	c	AOQL %	n	c	AOQL %
---	---	---	---	---	---	---	---	---	---	---	---	---	---	---	---	---	---	---	---
1–30	All	0	—	All	0	—	All	0	—	All	0	—	All	0	—	All	0	—
31–50	30	0	0.49	30	0	0.49	30	0	0.49	30	0	0.49	30	0	0.49	30	0	0.49
51–100	37	0	0.63	37	0	0.63	37	0	0.63	37	0	0.63	37	0	0.63	37	0	0.63
101–200	40	0	0.74	40	0	0.74	40	0	0.74	40	0	0.74	40	0	0.74	40	0	0.74
201–300	43	0	0.74	43	0	0.74	70	1	0.92	70	1	0.92	95	2	0.99	95	2	0.99
301–400	44	0	0.74	44	0	0.74	70	1	0.99	100	2	1	120	3	1.1	145	4	1.1
401–500	45	0	0.75	75	1	0.95	100	2	1.1	100	2	1.1	125	3	1.2	150	4	1.2
501–600	45	0	0.76	75	1	0.98	100	2	1.1	125	3	1.2	150	4	1.3	175	5	1.3
601–800	45	0	0.77	75	1	1	100	2	1.2	130	3	1.2	175	5	1.4	200	6	1.4
801–1,000	45	0	0.78	75	1	1	105	2	1.2	155	4	1.4	180	5	1.4	225	7	1.5
1,001–2,000	45	0	0.8	75	1	1	130	3	1.4	180	5	1.6	230	7	1.7	280	9	1.8
2,001–3,000	75	1	1.1	105	2	1.3	135	3	1.4	210	6	1.7	280	9	1.9	370	13	2.1
3,001–4,000	75	1	1.1	105	2	1.3	160	4	1.5	210	6	1.7	305	10	2	420	15	2.2
4,001–5,000	75	1	1.1	105	2	1.3	160	4	1.5	235	7	1.8	330	11	2	440	16	2.2
5,001–7,000	75	1	1.1	105	2	1.3	185	5	1.7	260	8	1.9	350	12	2.2	490	18	2.4
7,001–10,000	75	1	1.1	105	2	1.3	185	5	1.7	260	8	1.9	380	13	2.2	535	20	2.5
10,001–20,000	75	1	1.1	135	3	1.4	210	6	1.8	285	9	2	425	15	2.3	610	23	2.6
20,001–50,000	75	1	1.1	135	3	1.4	235	7	1.9	305	10	2.1	470	17	2.4	700	27	2.7
50,001–100,000	75	1	1.1	160	4	1.6	235	7	1.9	355	12	2.2	515	19	2.5	770	30	2.8

SOURCE: Harold F. Dodge, and Harry G. Romig. *Sampling Inspection Tables—Single and Double Sampling.* 2nd ed., Revised and Expanded, 184. New York, John Wiley, 1959. Reprinted with permission of Lucent Technologies Inc./Bell Labs.

can be confirmed or modified. If it is necessary to modify the estimate of p, it may also be necessary to change the sampling plan as well.

Each Dodge-Romig table contains six ranges of incoming fraction nonconforming. The ranges of p in the AOQL tables depend on the specified AOQL value—from 0.00% on the lower end to the specified AOQL value on the high end. In the LPTD tables, the p values range from a low of 0.00% to a high of one-half the stated LTPD value. The rationale for using one-half the LTPD as a maximum p is that, if the process average fraction nonconforming exceeds 50%, it is generally more economical to perform a 100% inspection rather than use acceptance sampling.

The procedure for using the Dodge-Romig tables to determine an appropriate plan is illustrated in the following two examples.

EXAMPLE: Development of Dodge-Romig Single Sampling Plan for AOQL = 3%

We want to develop a single sampling plan for shipment size $N = 1,000$ that meets the criterion AOQL = 3%. We assume the incoming process average nonconforming from the supplier is $p = 1.00\%$, and use Table 10-11 to determine sample size, n, and acceptance number, c.

Step 1: From Table 10-11, the table for AOQL = 3.0%, identify the row corresponding to a lot size = 1,000 (801 − 1,000).

Step 2:   From Table 10-11, identify the column corresponding top $p = 1.00\,(0.061 - 1.20)$.

Step 3:   The recommended sample size n and acceptance number c are found in the cell where the row and column intersect ($n = 44, c = 2$).

The estimated LTPD for the selected plan is 11.8%. This means that if the incoming process average fraction nonconforming were 11.8%, the customer would accept approximately $\beta = 10\%$ of the shipments on the basis of 2 or fewer nonconforming units in a sample of size 44. If this LTPD estimate is perceived to be too large to be acceptable, then a smaller AOQL target value (e.g., 1% or 2%) can be adopted, but this will increase the sample size.

EXAMPLE: Development of Dodge-Romig Single Sampling Plan for LTPD = 5%

We want to develop a single sampling plan for shipment size $N = 1,000$ that meets the criterion LTPD = 5%. We assume the incoming process average nonconforming from the supplier is $p = 1.00\%$, and will use Table 10-12 to determine the sample size, n, and acceptance number, c.

Step 1:   From Table 10-12, the table for LTPD = 5.0%, identify the row corresponding to a lot size $= 1,000\,(801 - 1,000)$.

Step 2:   From Table 10-12, identify the column corresponding to $p = 1.00\,(0.051 - 1.00)$.

Step 3:   The recommended sample size n and acceptance number c are found in the cell where the row and column intersect ($n = 105, c = 2$).

The estimated AOQL for the selected plan is 1.2%. This means that in the worst-case average fraction nonconforming accepted by the customer after sampling and rectifying inspection will be 1.2% under this plan.

The major difference between the Dodge-Romig approach and the Grubbs approach is that Dodge-Romig plans do not consider the producer's risk. The Grubbs sampling plans attempt to fit two points on the OC curve: producer's risk, $P_A = 1 - \alpha$ at $p =$ AQL and consumer's risk, $P_A = \beta$, at $p =$ LTPD. The Dodge-Romig approach uses a target incoming fraction nonconforming to define consumer's risk developed from the LTPD tables. For plans using the AOQL tables, consumer's risk is shown as an output of the recommended sampling plan. For the case of the sampling plan developed in the previous example, $n = 105$, $c = 2$, it is left to the reader to show that the producer's risk is $\alpha = 0.05$ at $p = 0.785\%$.

Although only the Dodge-Romig tables for single sampling plans are covered in this chapter, sets of tables for AOQL and LTPD stipulating plans for double sampling have also been developed. The procedure for using these tables is identical to the procedure for single sampling plans discussed previously.

10.7 DOUBLE SAMPLING PLANS

Double sampling plans are an extension of single sampling plans, in which an accept or reject decision can be deferred pending the results of a second sample. Rather than the binary option offered by single plans (accept or reject), double sampling provides the

FIGURE 10-12 Flowchart of Double Sampling Schemes

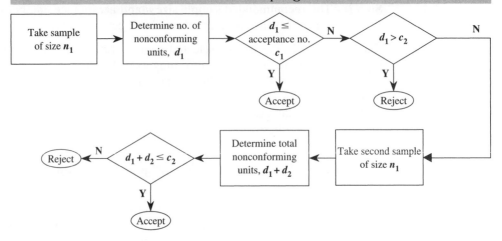

third alternative of taking a second sample. The procedure begins by collecting and inspecting the first sample of size n_1. If the number of nonconforming units d_1, in the first sample is less than or equal to the first acceptance number c_1, then the lot is accepted. If d_1 exceeds the second acceptance number c_2, the lot is rejected. If $c_1 < d_1 \le c_2$, then a second sample of size n_2 is required. The numbers of nonconforming units in both samples are added together, and if $d_1 + d_2 \le c_2$, the lot is accepted. Otherwise, the lot is rejected on the basis of the combined samples. A flowchart of the basic procedure is shown in Figure 10-12.

The double sampling plan provides a second chance for a shipment to be accepted. Because, under rectifying inspection, rejection requires 100% screening inspection, a double sampling plan often results in a lower ATI (and less sampling costs) than a single sampling plan with identical criteria.

> Double sampling can result in lower total sampling cost than single sampling.

10.7.1 Operating Characteristic Curves for Double Sampling Plans

Reduced total inspection under double sampling comes with a price—increased complexity. Rather that accepting or rejecting on the basis of a single sample, the QA inspector will (1) accept on the basis of the first sample, (2) reject on the basis of the first sample, (3) accept after taking a second sample, or (4) reject after taking a second sample. Rectifying inspection may be implemented in lieu of rejecting a sample. Before proceeding, we need to introduce some additional terminology:

$P_{A,1}$ Probability of accepting on the first sample
$P_{R,1}$ Probability of rejecting on the first sample
$P_{A,2}$ Probability of accepting on the second sample
$P_{R,2}$ Probability of rejecting on the second sample
P_A Overall probability of acceptance: $P_A = P_{A,1} + P_{A,2}$

$P_{A,1} + P_{R,1} + P_{A,2} + P_{R,2} = 1.00$ because these represent the only four possible courses of action. Further, the probability of reaching a decision on the first sample is $P_{A,1} + P_{R,1}$; thus, the probability of taking a second sample is $1 - (P_{A,1} + P_{R,1})$.

The provision for a second sample complicates the probability calculations that are required to develop OC, ATI, and AOQ curves. As Equation 10-8 shows, the probability of acceptance on the first sample is computed the same for double sampling as for single sampling:

$$P_{A,1} = \sum_{x=0}^{c_1} \binom{n_1}{x} p^x (1 - p)^{n_1 - x} \tag{10-8}$$

Determining the probability of acceptance on the second sample requires the calculation of joint probabilities—that is, the probability of acceptance on a second sample is conditioned on the requirement to take a second sample:

$$P_{A,2} = Pr\{d_1 + d_2 \le c_2 | \text{Second sample is required}\} \tag{10-9}$$

This can be restated in terms of outcomes for the first and second samples as

$$P_{A,2} = Pr\{d_2 \le (c_2 - d_1) | c_1 < d_1 \le c_2\} \tag{10-10}$$

Recall the multiplication rule from statistical theory that applies to two events, A and B,

$$Pr\{A|B\} = \frac{Pr\{A \cap B\}}{Pr\{B\}}$$

where

$Pr\{A|B\}$ = Probability of event A given that event B has occurred
$Pr\{B\}$ = Probability of event B
$Pr\{A \cap B\}$ = Joint probability of the occurrence of both A and B

$$\text{If A and B are independent, } Pr\{A \cap B\} = P\{A\}P\{B\} \tag{10-11}$$

We can let B represent the event in Equation 10-10 that a second sample has to be taken because d_1 is between c_1 and c_2, and A the event that the lot is accepted on the second sample [i.e., $d_2 < (c_2 - d_1)$]. Then, applying Equation 10-11,

$$Pr\{(\text{acceptance}|d_1) \cap d_1 \text{ nonconforming on first sample}\} = Pr\{d_2 \le (c_2 - d_1)\}Pr\{d_1\}$$

where

$$c_1 < d_1 \le c_2$$

The total probability of accepting a lot on the second sample is,

$$P_{A,2} = \sum_{d_1=c_1+1}^{c_2} \sum_{d_2=0}^{c_2-d_1} Pr\{d_1\}Pr\{d_2\} \tag{10-12}$$

This following example illustrates how these probabilities can be computed.

EXAMPLE: Probability of Acceptance for a Double Sampling Plan

A double sampling plan calls for $n_1 = 40$, $c_1 = 1$, $n_2 = 40$, and $c_2 = 3$. For fraction nonconforming $p = 0.03$, the probability of acceptance on the first sample is

$$P_{A,1} = \sum_{x=0}^{1} \binom{40}{x} 0.03^x (1 - 0.03)^{40-x} = 0.66154$$

There are a finite number of outcomes for the first and second samples that would result in acceptance on the second sample. First, we consider the outcomes for the first sample. If $d_1 = 0$ or 1, the shipment is accepted without taking a second sample. If d_1 is 4 or greater, the lot is rejected. For the intermediate numbers, $d_1 = 2$ or 3, a decision will be deferred pending the results of a second sample.

Next, consider possible outcomes for the second sample. Acceptance will result if the $d_1 + d_2$ do not exceed c_2. Therefore, if $d_1 = 2$, $d_2 = 0$ or 1 will result in acceptance; if d_2 equals 2 or more, rejection. If $d_1 = 3$, only $d_2 = 0$ will lead to lot acceptance. Considering each of the possible ways that a lot can be accepted on the second sample, $P_{A,2}$ can be calculated as

$$Pr\{d_1 = 2\} = \binom{40}{2}0.03^2(1 - 0.03)^{38} = \frac{40!}{2!38!}0.03^2(1 - 0.03)^{38} = 0.2206$$

$$Pr\{d_2 = 0\} = \binom{40}{0}0.03^0(1 - 0.03)^{40} = \frac{40!}{0!40!}0.03^0(1 - 0.03)^{40} = 0.2957$$

$$Pr\{d_2 = 1\} = \binom{40}{1}0.03^1(1 - 0.03)^{39} = \frac{40!}{1!39!}0.03^1(1 - 0.03)^{39} = 0.3658$$

$$Pr\{d_1 = 3\} = \binom{40}{3}0.03^3(1 - 0.03)^{37} = \frac{40!}{3!37!}0.03^3(1 - 0.03)^{37} = 0.0864$$

Applying Equation 10-12,

$$P_{A,2} = Pr\{d_1 = 2\}Pr\{d_2 = 0\} + Pr\{d_1 = 2\}Pr\{d_2 = 1\} + Pr\{d_1 = 3\}Pr\{d_2 = 0\}$$
$$P_{A,2} = (0.2206)(0.2957) + (0.2206)(0.3658) + (0.0864)(0.2957) = 0.1715$$

The overall probability of acceptance is the sum of $P_{A,1}$ and $P_{A,2}$:

$$P_A = P_{A,1} + P_{A,2} = 0.6615 + 0.1715 = 0.8330$$

As with single sampling plans, the OC curve for a double sampling plan is a plot of P_A versus p. The probabilities for the plan presented previously are shown in Table 10-13, and the plot of the corresponding OC curve is shown in Figure 10-13.

TABLE 10-13 Operating Characteristic Probabilities for a Double Sampling Plan with $n_1 = n_2 = 40$, $c_1 = 1$, $c_2 = 3$

p	$P_{A,1}$	$Pr\{d_1 = 2\}$	$Pr\{d_1 = 3\}$	$Pr\{d_2 = 0\}$	$Pr\{d_2 = 1\}$	$P_{A,2}$	P_A
0.00	1.00000	0.00000	0.00000	1.00000	0.00000	0.00000	1.00000
0.01	0.94016	0.05324	0.00681	0.66987	0.27029	0.05462	0.99478
0.02	0.80954	0.14479	0.03743	0.44570	0.36384	0.13390	0.94344
0.03	0.66154	0.22063	0.08643	0.29571	0.36583	0.17151	0.83305
0.04	0.52098	0.26456	0.13963	0.19537	0.32561	0.16511	0.68609
0.05	0.39906	0.27767	0.18511	0.12851	0.27055	0.13460	0.53366
0.06	0.29904	0.26746	0.21624	0.08416	0.21488	0.09818	0.39722
0.07	0.22006	0.24246	0.23116	0.05487	0.16519	0.06604	0.28610
0.08	0.15945	0.21000	0.23130	0.03561	0.12384	0.04172	0.20117
0.09	0.11397	0.17545	0.21979	0.02230	0.09097	0.02477	0.13874
0.10	0.08047	0.14233	0.20032	0.01478	0.06569	0.14410	0.22457
0.11	0.05619	0.11264	0.17635	0.00945	0.04674	0.00800	0.06419
0.12	0.03883	0.08726	0.15072	0.00602	0.03281	0.00430	0.04313

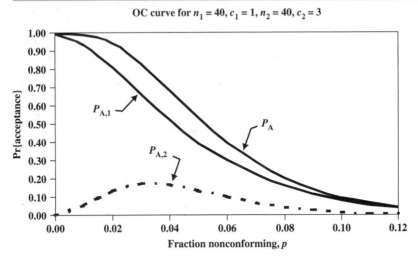

FIGURE 10-13 Operating Characteristic (OC) Curve for Double Sampling Plan

OC curve for $n_1 = 40, c_1 = 1, n_2 = 40, c_2 = 3$

10.7.2 Double Sampling Performance—ASN, AOQL, and ATI

AOQL and ATI are performance measures for single and double sampling plans.

Both the AOQL and ATI are measures of performance for single and double sampling plans. A third metric, the average sample number (ASN), is applicable to double and multiple sampling plans. The ASN is similar to the ATI in that both provide a measure of the average number of units inspected over a series of shipments (for a particular level of incoming quality). The metrics differ in that ATI calculations include the 100% screening under rectifying inspection, whereas ASN does not.

ASN measures the average number of units inspected under schemes that do not permit rectifying inspection.

Under double sampling, where the lot may be accepted on the first sample, rejected on the first sample, accepted after the second sample, or rejected after the second sample, the minimum ASN is n_1, the size of the first sample. If a decision cannot be reached on the first sample, the number of items inspected is $(n_1 + n_2)$. The majority of high-quality shipments (e.g., $p \ll \text{AQL}$) will be accepted on the first sample, resulting in ASN values near n_1. Similarly, for poor quality ($p > \text{LQL}$), most shipments would be rejected on the first sample, resulting in small ASN values. Incoming quality at intermediate levels, between the AQL and LQL, would result in a larger ASN. Equation 10-13 is the formula for computing the ASN for a double sampling plan:

$$\text{ASN} = n_1(P_{A,1} + P_{R,1}) + (n_1 + n_2)(1 - (P_{A,1} + P_{R,1}))$$
$$= n_1 + n_2(1 - (P_{A,1} + P_{R,1})) \tag{10-13}$$

EXAMPLE: Average Sample Number for a Double Sampling Plan

A double sampling plan calls for $n_1 = 40$, $c_1 = 1$, $n_2 = 40$, and $c_2 = 3$. For fraction nonconforming $p = 0.03$, applying Equation 10-13, the ASN is

$$P_{A,1} = \sum_{x=0}^{1} \binom{40}{x} 0.03^x (1 - 0.03)^{40-x} = 0.66154$$

$$P_{R,1} = 1 - \sum_{x=0}^{3} \binom{40}{x} 0.03^x (1 - 0.03)^{40-x} = 0.03140$$

$$\text{ASN} = 40 + 40(1 - (0.66154 + 0.03140)) = 52.2825$$

The ASN curve for this sampling plan is constructed by plotting the ASN versus p for various levels of incoming quality. A table of the ASN values and resulting curve is shown in Figure 10-14.

Recall that the AOQ is the average quality level that a customer will accept, following rectifying inspection and replacement, if warranted. As with single sampling plans, if the incoming lot quality is very good (e.g., low p), most shipments will be accepted on the first sample with a quality level equal to p. For the case of poor quality ($p > $ LQL), shipments will likely be subjected to 100% screening inspection and all nonconforming units replaced, resulting in a quality level near $p = 0$. If the incoming quality is between the AQL and LQL, the quality level accepted by the customer will be somewhere between 0 and p. The maximum value on the AOQ curve is the AOQL, which is the worst-case level of quality accepted by the customer for a sampling plan. Because a shipment may be accepted on either the first sample or the second, the calculation of AOQ is complicated for double sampling. Equation 10-14 is the formula used for these calculations:

$$\text{AOQ} = \frac{(P_{A,1}(N - n_1) + P_{A,2}(N - n_1 - n_2))p}{N} \tag{10-14}$$

EXAMPLE: AOQ Curve and AOQL for Double Sampling Plan

A double sampling plan calls for $n_1 = 40$, $c_1 = 1$, $n_2 = 40$, and $c_2 = 3$ for a series of shipments of size $N = 1,000$. Applying Equation 10-14 to a lot with $p = 0.03$,

$$\text{AOQ} = \frac{(0.6615(1,000 - 40) + 0.1715(1,000 - 40 - 40))0.03}{1,000} = 0.0238 \text{ or } 2.38\%$$

Table 10-14 contains the probabilities necessary to plot the AOQ curve shown in Figure 10-15. Based on the tabulated values and the AOQ curve, the AOQL is approximately 0.0261 for the case of incoming fraction nonconforming $p = 0.04$.

FIGURE 10-14 Average Sample Number (ASN) Curve

p	$P_{A,1}$	$P_{R,1}$	ASN
0.00	1.0000	0.0000	40.00
0.02	0.8095	0.0082	47.29
0.04	0.521	0.0748	56.17
0.06	0.299	0.2173	59.35
0.08	0.1594	0.3993	57.65
0.1	0.0805	0.5769	53.71
0.12	0.0388	0.7232	49.52

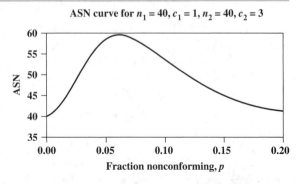

TABLE 10-14 Average Outgoing Quality Probabilities

p	$P_{A,1}$	$Pr\{d_1 = 2\}$	$Pr\{d_1 = 3\}$	$Pr\{d_2 = 0\}$	$Pr\{d_2 = 1\}$	$P_{A,2}$	P_A	AOQ
0.00	1.0000	0.0000	0.0000	1.0000	0.0000	0.0000	1.0000	0.000
0.02	0.8095	0.1448	0.0374	0.4457	0.3638	0.1339	0.9434	0.018
0.04	0.521	0.2646	0.1396	0.1954	0.3256	0.1651	0.6861	0.0261
0.06	0.299	0.2675	0.2162	0.0842	0.2149	0.0982	0.3972	0.0226
0.08	0.1594	0.21	0.2313	0.0356	0.1238	0.0417	0.2012	0.0153
0.1	0.0805	0.1423	0.2003	0.0148	0.0657	0.0144	0.0949	0.0091
0.12	0.0388	0.0873	0.1507	0.006	0.0328	0.0043	0.0431	0.0049
0.14	0.018	0.0496	0.1022	0.0024	0.0156	0.0011	0.0192	0.0026
0.16	0.0081	0.0265	0.0639	0.0009	0.0071	0.0003	0.0083	0.0013

The ATI for a double sampling plan indicates, on average, the number of units that will be inspected for a specific quality level. The ATI is important because of its implications on sampling cost. With the potential to accept or reject a shipment on either the first or second sample, calculating ATI is more complex for double than for single sampling plans. Equation 10-15 is the formula for calculating the ATI for a double sampling plan:

$$\text{ATI} = n_1 P_{A,1} + (n_1 + n_2) P_{A,2} + N(1 - P_A) \tag{10-15}$$

EXAMPLE: ATI Curve for Double Sampling Plan

A double sampling plan calls for $n_1 = 40$, $c_1 = 1$, $n_2 = 40$, and $c_2 = 3$ for a series of shipments of size $N = 1,000$. For fraction nonconforming $p = 0.03$, the ATI is

$$\text{ATI} = 40(0.6615) + (40 + 40)(0.1715) + 1000(1 - 0.8331) = 207.13$$

Table 10-15 contains the probabilities for the ATI curve shown in Figure 10-16.

FIGURE 10-15 An Example Average Outgoing Quality (AOQ) Curve

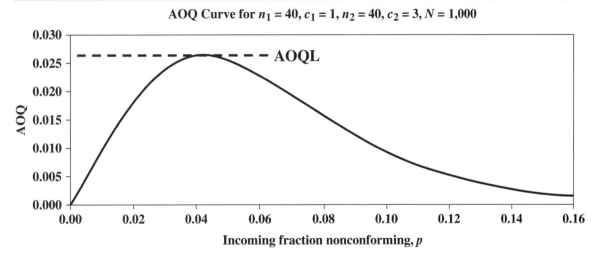

AOQ Curve for $n_1 = 40$, $c_1 = 1$, $n_2 = 40$, $c_2 = 3$, $N = 1,000$

TABLE 10-15 Average Total Inspection Probabilities

p	$P_{A,1}$	$Pr\{d_1 = 2\}$	$Pr\{d_1 = 3\}$	$Pr\{d_2 = 0\}$	$Pr\{d_2 = 1\}$	$P_{A,2}$	P_A	ATI
0.00	1.0000	0.0000	0.0000	1.0000	0.0000	0.0000	1.0000	40.00
0.02	0.8095	0.1448	0.0374	0.4457	0.3638	0.1339	0.9434	99.66
0.04	0.521	0.2646	0.1396	0.1954	0.3256	0.1651	0.6861	347.96
0.06	0.299	0.2675	0.2162	0.0842	0.2149	0.0982	0.3972	622.59
0.08	0.1594	0.21	0.2313	0.0356	0.1238	0.0417	0.2012	808.55
0.1	0.0805	0.1423	0.2003	0.0148	0.0657	0.0144	0.0949	909.48
0.12	0.0388	0.0873	0.1507	0.006	0.0328	0.0043	0.0431	958.77
0.14	0.018	0.0496	0.1022	0.0024	0.0156	0.0011	0.0192	981.66
0.16	0.0081	0.0265	0.0639	0.0009	0.0071	0.0003	0.0083	992.01

10.7.3 Developing Double Sampling Plans—Grubbs' Approach

Grubbs developed tables to assist with the determination of double sampling plans for producer's risk $\alpha = 0.05$ and consumer's risk $\beta = 0.10$. Grubbs tables cover the two most common conventions for double sampling plans, where either $n_2 = n_1$ or $n_2 = 2n_1$. The procedure for the use of these tables is similar to that for single sampling plans. The ratio $R = p_2/p_1$ is used to determine the acceptance numbers, c_1 and c_2. As with single sampling plans, the calculated R will usually fall somewhere in between two tabulated R values, resulting in two candidate sets of acceptance numbers. For an approximate R value, the column for $P_A = 0.95$ will provide an $n_1 p$ that meets the stipulated producer's risk, and the column for $P_A = 0.10$ will produce a plan that meets the specified consumer's risk. As with single sampling plans, two adjacent rows will bracket the computed p_2/p_1. The row having a tabulated $R < p_2/p_1$ will produce plans that either meet the producer's risk while having $\beta > 0.10$, or meet the consumer's risk while having $\alpha > 0.05$. The row with tabulated $R < p_2/p_1$ will produce plans that simultaneously satisfy both producer's and consumer's risk criteria, but require larger sample sizes. Tables 10-16 and 10-17 are Grubbs tables for $n_2 = n_1$ and for $n_2 = 2n_1$, respectively.

FIGURE 10-16 An Example Average Total Inspection (ATI) Curve

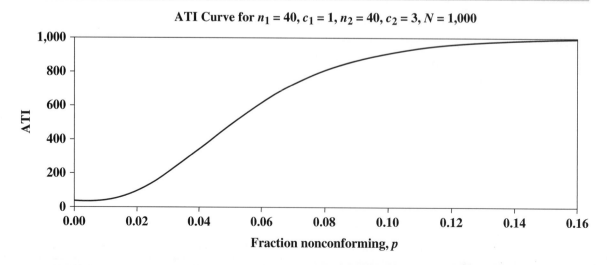

ATI Curve for $n_1 = 40$, $c_1 = 1$, $n_2 = 40$, $c_2 = 3$, $N = 1,000$

TABLE 10-16 Grubbs Table for Double Sampling Plans

Plan No.	$R = p_2/p_1$	c_1	c_2	Approx. n_1p $1 - \alpha = 0.95$	$\beta = 0.10$
1	11.9	0	1	0.21	2.5
2	7.54	1	2	0.52	3.92
3	6.79	0	2	0.43	2.96
4	5.39	1	3	0.76	4.11
5	4.65	2	4	1.16	5.39
6	4.25	1	4	1.04	4.42
7	3.88	2	5	1.43	5.55
8	3.63	3	6	1.87	6.78
9	3.38	2	6	1.72	5.82
10	3.21	3	7	2.15	6.91
11	3.09	4	8	2.62	8.1
12	2.85	4	9	2.9	8.26
13	2.6	5	11	3.68	9.56
14	2.44	5	12	4	9.77
15	2.32	5	13	4.35	10.08
16	2.22	5	14	4.7	10.45
17	2.12	5	16	5.39	11.41

SOURCE: Chemical Corps Engineering Agency. *Manual No. 2: Master Sampling Plans for Single, Duplicate, Double, and Multiple Sampling.* Edgewood Arsenal, Army Chemical Center, MD, 1953.

Note: $n_2 = n_1, \alpha = 0.05, \beta = 0.10$.

TABLE 10-17 Grubbs Table for Double Sampling Plans

Plan No.	$R = p_2/p_1$	c_1	c_2	Approx. n_1p $1 - \alpha = 0.95$	$\beta = 0.10$
1	14.5	0	1	0.16	2.32
2	8.07	0	2	0.3	2.42
3	6.48	1	3	0.6	3.89
4	5.39	0	3	0.49	2.64
5	5.09	1	4	0.77	3.92
6	4.31	0	4	0.68	2.93
7	4.19	1	5	0.96	4.02
8	3.6	1	6	1.16	4.17
9	3.26	2	8	1.68	5.47
10	2.96	3	10	2.27	6.72
11	2.77	3	11	2.46	6.82
12	2.62	4	13	3.07	8.05
13	2.46	4	14	3.29	8.11
14	2.21	3	15	3.41	7.55
15	1.97	4	20	4.75	9.35
16	1.74	6	30	7.45	12.96

SOURCE: Chemical Corps Engineering Agency. *Manual No. 2: Master Sampling Plans for Single, Duplicate, Double, and Multiple Sampling.* Edgewood Arsenal, Army Chemical Center, MD, 1953.

Note: $n_2 = 2n_1, \alpha = 0.05, \beta = 0.10$.

EXAMPLE: Development of Double Sampling Plan Using Grubbs Tables

We want to develop a double sampling plan for shipment size $N = 1,000$ that meets the following criteria: AQL = 0.5%, LTPD = 3.0%, $\alpha = 0.05$, $\beta = 0.10$, with $n_2 = n_1$. We use Table 10-16 to determine sample sizes, n_1 and n_2, and acceptance numbers, c_1 and c_2.

Step 1: Compute $R_0 = \text{LTPD}/\text{AQL} = p_2/p_1 = 0.03/0.005 = 6.00$.

Step 2: Identify in Table 10-16 the rows that bracket R_0.

R_0 falls between plan 3 and plan 4.

For plan 3, $R_{\text{Tab}} = 6.79$, $c_1 = 0$ and $c_2 = 2$

For plan 4, $R_{\text{Tab}} = 5.39$, $c_1 = 1$ and $c_2 = 3$.

Step 3: Design sampling plans for each R_{Tab}.

Plan 3:

For $P_A = 1 - \alpha = 0.95$, $np_1 = 0.43$ and $n = \dfrac{np_1}{p_1} = \dfrac{0.43}{0.005} = 86$

$n_1 = n_2 = 86$

For $P_A = \beta = 0.10$, $np_1 = 2.96$ and $n = \dfrac{np_1}{p_1} = \dfrac{2.96}{0.03} = 98.67 \cong 99$

$n_1 = n_2 = 99$

Plan 4:

For $P_A = 1 - \alpha = 0.95$, $np_1 = 0.76$ and $n = \dfrac{np_1}{p_1} = \dfrac{0.76}{0.005} = 152$

$n_1 = n_2 = 152$

For $P_A = \beta = 0.10$, $np_1 = 4.11$ and $n = \dfrac{np_1}{p_1} = \dfrac{4.11}{0.03} = 137$

$n_1 = n_2 = 137$

Step 4: Compute producer's and consumer's risks for each plan, using Equations 10-8 and 10-11.

$\alpha = 1 - Pr\{\text{Accept} | p_1\}$, $\beta = Pr\{\text{Accept} | p_2\}$

Plan 3:

For $c_1 = 0, c_2 = 2, n_1 = n_2 = 86$

At $p_1 = 0.005$, $P_{A,1} = 0.6498$ $P_{A,2} = 0.3003$ $P_A = 0.6498 + 0.3003 = 0.9501$

$\alpha = 1 - 0.9501 = 0.04990 < 0.05 \Rightarrow$ meets stipulated producer's risk

At $p_2 = 0.03$, $P_{A,1} = 0.0728$ $P_{A,2} = 0.0702$ $P_A = 0.0728 + 0.0702 = 0.1430$

$\beta = 0.1430 > 0.10 \Rightarrow$ does not meet stipulated consumer's risk

Plan 3:

For $c_1 = 0, c_2 = 2, n_1 = n_2 = 99$

At $p_1 = 0.005$, $P_{A,1} = 0.6088$ $P_{A,2} = 0.3215$ $P_A = 0.6088 + 0.3215 = 0.9303$

$\alpha = 1 - 0.9303 = 0.0697 > 0.05 \Rightarrow$ does not meet stipulated producer's risk

At $p_2 = 0.03$, $P_{A,1} = 0.0490$ $P_{A,2} = 0.0410$ $P_A = 0.0490 + 0.0410 = 0.0900$

$\beta = 0.0900 < 0.10 \Rightarrow$ meets stipulated consumer's risk

Plan 4:

For $c_1 = 1, c_2 = 3$, $n_1 = n_2 = 152$

At $p_1 = 0.005$, $P_{A,1} = 0.8233$ $P_{A,2} = 0.1272$ $P_A = 0.8233 + 0.1272 = 0.9505$

$\alpha = 1 - 0.9505 = 0.0495 < 0.05 \Rightarrow$ meets stipulated producer's risk

At $p_2 = 0.03$, $P_{A,1} = 0.0556$ $P_{A,2} = 0.0076$ $P_A = 0.0556 + 0.0076 = 0.0632$

$\beta = 0.0632 < 0.10 \Rightarrow$ exceeds stipulated consumer's risk

Plan 4:

For $c_1 = 1, c_2 = 3, n_1 = n_2 = 137$

At $p_1 = 0.005$, $P_{A,1} = 0.8497$ $P_{A,2} = 0.1141$ $P_A = 0.8497 + 0.1141 = 0.9638$

$\alpha = 1 - 0.9638 = 0.0362 < 0.05 \Rightarrow$ exceeds stipulated producer's risk

At $p_2 = 0.03$, $P_{A,1} = 0.0807$ $P_{A,2} = 0.0140$ $P_A = 0.0807 + 0.0140 = 0.0947$

$\beta = 0.0947 < 0.10 \Rightarrow$ meets stipulated consumer's risk

Step 5:   Select a sampling plan.

Plan 3, with $R = 6.79 > p_2/p_1$ yields double sampling plans that do not simultaneously meet both producer's and consumer's risk criteria. Plan 4, with $R = 5.39 > p_2/p_1$ yields plans that are capable of meeting both producer's and consumer's risk, but larger sample sizes are required.

EXAMPLE: Development of Double Sampling Plan Using Grubbs Tables

We want to develop a double sampling plan for shipment size $N = 1{,}000$ that meets the following criteria: AQL = 0.5%, LTPD = 3.0%, $\alpha = 0.05$, $\beta = 0.10$, with $n_2 = 2n_1$. We use Table 10-17 to determine sample sizes, n_1 and n_2, and acceptance numbers, c_1 and c_2.

Step 1:   Compute $R_0 = $ LTPD/AQL $= p_2/p_1 = 0.03/0.005 = 6.00$.

Step 2:   Identify in Table 10-17 the rows that bracket R_0.

R_0 falls between plan 3 and plan 4.

For plan 3, $R_{\text{Tab}} = 6.48$, $c_1 = 1$ and $c_2 = 3$

For plan 4, $R_{\text{Tab}} = 5.39$, $c_1 = 0$ and $c_2 = 3$.

Step 3:   Design sampling plans for each R_{Tab}.

Plan 3:

For $P_A = 1 - \alpha = 0.95$, $np_1 = 0.60$ and $n = \dfrac{np_1}{p_1} = \dfrac{0.60}{0.005} = 120$.

$n_1 = 120, n_2 = 2n_1 = 240$

For $P_A = \beta = 0.10$, $np_1 = 3.89$ and $n = \dfrac{np_1}{p_1} = \dfrac{3.89}{0.03} = 129.67 \cong 130$

$n_1 = 130, n_2 = 2n_1 = 260$

Plan 4:

For $P_A = 1 - \alpha = 0.95, np_1 = 0.49$ and $n = \dfrac{np_1}{p_1} = \dfrac{0.49}{0.005} = 98$

$n_1 = 98, n_2 = 2n_1 = 196$

For $P_A = \beta = 0.10, np_1 = 2.64$ and $n = \dfrac{np_1}{p_1} = \dfrac{2.64}{0.03} = 88$

$n_1 = 88, n_2 = 2n_1 = 176$

Step 4: Compute producer's and consumer's risks for each plan, using Equations 10-8 and 10-11.

$\alpha = 1 - Pr\{Accept|p_1\}, \beta = Pr\{Accept|p_2\}$

Plan 3:

For $c_1 = 1, c_2 = 3, n_1 = 120, n_2 = 240$

At $p_1 = 0.005, P_{A,1} = 0.8784 \; P_{A,2} = 0.0713 \; P_A = 0.8784 + 0.0713 = 0.9497$

$\qquad \alpha = 1 - 0.9497 = 0.0503 \cong 0.05 \Rightarrow$ meets stipulated producer's risk

At $p_2 = 0.03, P_{A,1} = 0.1218 \; P_{A,2} = 0.0011 \; P_A = 0.1218 + 0.0011 = 0.1229$

$\qquad \beta = 0.1229 > 0.10 \Rightarrow$ does not meet stipulated consumer's risk

Plan 3:

For $c_1 = 1, c_2 = 3, n_1 = 130, n_2 = 260$

At $p_1 = 0.005, P_{A,1} = 0.8617 \; P_{A,2} = 0.0756 \; P_A = 0.8617 + 0.0756 = 0.9373$

$\qquad \alpha = 1 - 0.9373 = 0.0627 > 0.05 \Rightarrow$ does not meet stipulated

$\qquad\qquad\qquad\qquad\qquad\qquad\qquad\qquad\qquad$ producer's risk

At $p_2 = 0.03, P_{A,1} = 0.0957 \; P_{A,2} = 0.0006 \; P_A = 0.0957 + 0.0006 = 0.0963$

$\qquad \beta = 0.0963 < 0.10 \Rightarrow$ meets stipulated consumer's risk

Plan 4:

For $c_1 = 0, c_2 = 3, n_1 = 98, n_2 = 196$

At $p_1 = 0.005, P_{A,1} = 0.6119 \; P_{A,2} = 0.3374 \; P_A = 0.6119 + 0.3374 = 0.9493$

$\qquad \alpha = 1 - 0.9493 = 0.0507 \cong 0.05 \Rightarrow$ meets stipulated producer's risk

At $p_2 = 0.03, P_{A,1} = 0.0505 \; P_{A,2} = 0.0146 \; P_A = 0.0505 + 0.0146 = 0.0651$

$\qquad \beta = 0.0651 < 0.10 \Rightarrow$ exceeds stipulated consumer's risk

Plan 4:

For $c_1 = 0, c_2 = 3, n_1 = 88, n_2 = 176$

At $p_1 = 0.005, P_{A,1} = 0.6433 \; P_{A,2} = 0.3199 \; P_A = 0.6433 + 0.3199 = 0.9632$

$\qquad \alpha = 1 - 0.9632 = 0.0368 < 0.05 \Rightarrow$ exceeds stipulated producer's risk

At $p_2 = 0.03, P_{A,1} = 0.0685 \; P_{A,2} = 0.0272 \; P_A = 0.0685 + 0.0272 = 0.0957$

$\qquad \beta = 0.0957 < 0.10 \Rightarrow$ meets stipulated consumer's risk

FIGURE 10-17 Average Total Inspection (ATI) Curves Comparing Double Sampling Plans

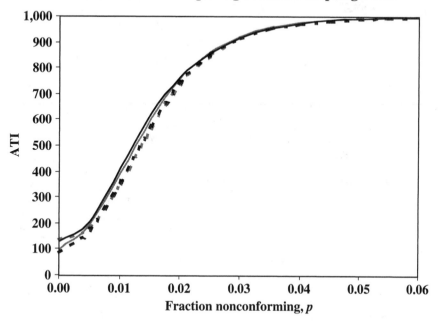

A plot of the ATI curves for the four double sampling plans developed, ($c_1 = 0$, $c_2 = 2$, $n_1 = n_2 = 99$), ($c_1 = 1$, $c_2 = 3$, $n_1 = n_2 = 137$), ($c_1 = 1$, $c_2 = 3$, $n_1 = 130$, $n_2 = 260$), and ($c_1 = 0$, $c_2 = 3$, $n_1 = 88$, $n_2 = 176$), is shown in Figure 10-17. Note that the curves for these plans are similar, but the plan with $c_1 = 0$, $c_2 = 3$, $n_1 = 88$, $n_2 = 176$ has the lowest ATI for product quality near the AQL.

10.7.4 Comparing Single and Double Acceptance Sampling Plans

The ATI and AOQL are usually used as the bases for deciding whether a single or double sampling plan is preferred. The single and double plans with the lowest ATIs (at the AQL) in the previous exercise were selected and compared using the ATI and AOQ charts shown in Figure 10-18.

Note that the double sampling plan requires fewer units to be inspected on average for superior incoming quality. However, the AOQ comparison indicates that the single sampling plan will have a lower AOQL. Ultimately, the decision will be based on a trade-off between cost—a function of the ATI and the complexity of the sampling system—and protection from poor quality—a function of the AOQL. In this case, protection from poor quality favors the single sampling plan. It is not possible without

FIGURE 10-18 Comparison of Single and Double Sampling Plans

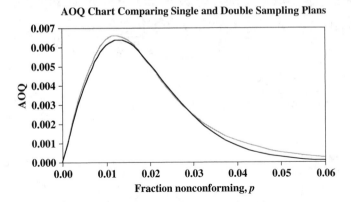

AOQ Chart Comparing Single and Double Sampling Plans

$n_1 = 88, n_2 = 176, c_1 = 0, c_2 = 3$ —— $n = 177, c = 2$

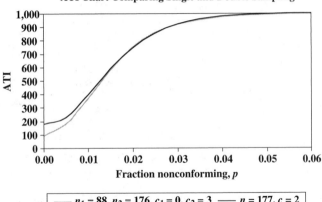

ATI Chart Comparing Single and Double Sampling

$n_1 = 88, n_2 = 176, c_1 = 0, c_2 = 3$ —— $n = 177, c = 2$

Note: AOQ, average outgoing quality; ATI, average total inspection.

further information (e.g., the actual cost of sampling and documentation costs for the two plans) to determine whether double sampling or the single plan is less costly. The ATI favors double sampling; however, record-keeping, tracking, and documentation are all simpler and less costly for single sampling.

SUMMARY OF LEARNING OBJECTIVES AND KEY OUTCOMES

1. *Describe the role of the purchasing function and how it can be used to ensure the quality, reliability, and timeliness of outsourced raw materials and components.* As the key element in the procurement cycle, purchasing participates in the organization's planning, forecasting, decision making, and formulation of strategy. It is responsible for keeping the supplier base at a manageable level, supplier certification and evaluation, and continuous improvement of the procurement function. This latter responsibility involves continuously seeking ways to save costs and improve the quality and reliability of outsourced materials.

2. *Describe the characteristics of a buyer–supplier partnership and why it is important to the success of QIM.* A good relationship between buyer and supplier is essential to

ensure purchased materials and components are of the highest quality, and are received when needed and in the quantities needed. A key to a successful partnership is the free and forthright sharing of information with suppliers, including strategic intent with respect to new products. This is a courageous move and not without risks because some suppliers will also have relationships with competitors. Therefore, it is essential that top management be fully committed to the creation of such relationships.

3.   *Discuss the benefits of involving key suppliers early in the product development process.* Involving suppliers early in the product development process enables the suppliers' technical competencies in materials and components to be incorporated into superior product designs. Suppliers may be best suited to advise on tolerances that will improve assembly and manufacturability, and avoid future production problems. Involving suppliers in design can also shorten the product development lead time because suppliers can start preproduction planning at an early stage.

4.   *Describe the elements of, and process for, developing an effective supplier certification program.* A cross-functional team is normally formed to guide the certification process, which begins by clearly determining what is purchased, when it is needed, and in what quantities. To be effective, the formal certification program should be tailored to the organization's unique needs, contain realistic and measurable performance metrics, be easy to administer, provide feedback to suppliers, and provide rewards to suppliers for taking prompt and effective corrective action, and for continuous improvements. Potential supplier lists are typically developed using prequalification surveys, followed by site visits. Certification is an ongoing process. Once certified, a supplier can face decertification for nonperformance or failure to take timely corrective action when problems arise.

5.   *Apply multicriteria decision tools to the supplier selection problem.* Three methods were presented in this chapter: the weighted point method, the AHP, and the categorical method. The most subjective of these is the categorical method, whereas the least subjective is the AHP method. The AHP approach is more structured than the others, more objective, and has the advantage of a consistency check. The review questions in the following section will test your understanding of these tools.

6.   *Define the role of acceptance sampling in a QIM environment.* Acceptance sampling is not a substitute for good QC practices in design and production processes. Acceptance sampling can be seen as a viable substitute for having to 100% inspect a lot, or shipment, to protect the level of quality that is received by the customer. Where there is good and reliable process history, there should be no need for acceptance sampling. The technique is useful where there is inadequate history, or as a temporary measure while attempts are made to stabilize a process or solve problems.

7.   *Use Grubbs and Dodge-Romig tables to design single sampling plans with stipulated producer's and consumer's risks.* The review questions in the following section will test your understanding of the design of single sampling plans.

8.   *Use Grubbs tables to design double sampling plans with stipulated producer's and consumer's risks.* The review questions in the following section will test your understanding of the design of double sampling plans.

9.   *Compute AOQ, AOQL, ATI, and ASN, and use these measures to compare alternative sampling plans.* The review questions in the following section will test your understanding of how to calculate, plot, and use AOQ, AOQL, ATI, and ASN.

10-1 A food processor sells canned vegetables to supermarket chains. The supermarkets considered dented cans to be nonconforming because consumers are reluctant to buy them. The supermarkets want to develop an acceptance sampling plan with a consumer's risk of 10% and an LTPD of 5%. The processor wants a producer's risk of 5% with an AQL of 0.75%. Shipments are made in lots of five pallets. Each pallet contains five layers of six cartons, and each carton contains forty-eight cans.

a. Design a single sampling plan using a Grubbs table.
b. Construct the OC curve for this plan.
c. Construct the AOC curve for this plan. Use the AOC curve to estimate the AOQL. What does the AOQL represent?
d. Construct the ATI curve for this plan. Use the ATI curve to estimate the average number of cans inspected per shipment. What assumptions do you make in this calculation?

10-2 Consider the food processor described in problem 1.

a. Design a double sampling plan using a Grubbs table.
b. Construct the OC curve for this plan.
c. Construct the AOC curve for this plan. Use the AOC curve to estimate the AOQL.
d. Construct the ATI curve for this plan. Use the ATI curve to estimate the average number of cans inspected per shipment.
e. Compute the ASN for this plan. Why is the ASN different from the ATI computed in part d?
f. Compare this double sampling plan with the single sampling plan designed in problem 1. Which plan would you choose? Why?

10-3 Consider the problem described in problem 1.

a. Design a single sampling plan using Dodge-Romig tables for an assumed quality level of $p = 0.3\%$.
b. What is your estimate of the AOQL for this plan?
c. Compare this plan with the plan designed in problem 1. Which plan is preferable? Why?
d. If the Dodge-Romig sampling plan were adopted, how would you suggest the inspector take each sample to ensure randomness?

◆●◆

Rollerball, Inc.

Helping Make the World Go Round

Helen Rosewald works in a branch plant of Rollerball, Inc., located in southern Louisiana. She has recently been assigned to the plant's cross-functional supplier development team (SDT). The SDT has been tasked to select a slate of suppliers that will meet current and future needs of the plant. Helen came from QA and is joined on the team with colleagues from purchasing, marketing, design and manufacturing engineering, operations, and finance.

Rollerball is an industry leader in the manufacture of bearings, principally, ball bearings, roller bearings, and thrust bearings. Its major customers include automotive, aerospace, and heavy equipment industries. These customers expect reliable, defect free components that are shipped on time. As important as delivery is, quality is not to be sacrificed for the sake of meeting delivery dates. Rollerball's customers expect these same criteria to be used in the selection of their suppliers' suppliers. Price is important, too, but is not to be used as the primary determinant of who makes the list of preferred suppliers.

The team is initially concerned with certifying suppliers for high carbon chromium alloy steel for bearing races. Acceptable material must be SAE 52100 approved, with oxygen content within 15 DPMO only. A number of supplier self-surveys have been evaluated, and the selection has narrowed to three potential steel mills. The team then examined the three prospective supplier's facilities to perform an overall evaluation of their management, operations, and quality systems.

The SDT has decided on four independent supplier selection criteria that they believe would best represent the goals and objectives of the organization: quality, price, delivery, and technology. In rating the relative importance of these criteria, the team has decided that quality is the most important and technology the least. If given a choice, the team strongly prefers quality to price, moderately prefers quality to delivery, and very strongly prefers quality to technology. Price is moderately preferred to technology, and delivery is moderately preferred to price and strongly to very strongly preferred to technology.

The team is now faced with the task of ranking the suppliers and weighting the criteria. Team meetings were convened for this purpose and consensus-building tools were employed until all team members were comfortable with the results. Much of the discussions centered on the site visit narratives.

Site Visit Narratives

Caston Millworks, a new supplier, has quoted the highest price and seems unwilling to negotiate a reduction for any reason. They blame their suppliers for their history of missed delivery dates. Caston operates a highly automated minimill that incorporates one of the world's fastest multistrand slit rolling production lines. The minimill consists of a melt shop and rolling mill, with an electric arc furnace, ladle furnace, four-strand continuous caster, eighteen-stand bar mill, and twenty-eight-strand rod mill, with an annual capacity of 600,000 tons/year. Caston prides itself on innovation and the latest technology in producing steel products that are distributed worldwide. The plant is currently operating at 75% capacity. When the equipment was inspected, it was evident that it was well maintained and validated, and that the operators were effectively using SPC to control their processes. However,

the company has not implemented Six Sigma and does not currently have a supplier certification program in place. In the interview, the company stated that it had the goal of establishing such programs in the future. The engineering department consists of experienced personnel, most of whom hold advanced degrees in mechanical engineering, material science, or metallurgy. Collectively, these engineers have earned a total of ten patents in the last year.

Belmont Steelworks, a current supplier, is a large minimill that supplies steel to all major bearing, bushing, roll, and slitter knife manufacturers in North America, as well as to a number of international customers. The Belmont mills produce in high volumes and have proposed the lowest price. With a significant investment of capital, the company has recently added a new consumable-electrode vacuum melting line. This represents the latest technology in which electrodes made from air-melted heat are remelted under vacuum by electric arcs. The remelted product is then solidified in a water-cooled copper mold under vacuum. This gives a more consistent high-quality steel than the traditional induction-melting technique. There is available capacity on the new line. Over the past five years, Belmont has not always made its delivery commitments, but their record in quality has been among the best in the industry. Belmont Six Sigma teams are continually looking for ways to improve its processes and the quality of its products. A formal supplier certification program is in place, and supplier development teams help their vendors solve problems and improve quality. The engineering department is actively involved in the introduction of new technologies, Six Sigma initiatives, and supplier certifications.

BSG, Inc., is a Mexican company that exclusively employs the vacuum-melting technology in one of its plants and has plenty of excess capacity. BSG has quoted a price that is just about midway between Caston and Belmont. There is a formal quality program in place that includes detailed operational definitions covering operations and testing. There is no formal Six Sigma program, although the management philosophy is heavily influenced by lean production principles. A QC department performs product testing; however, SPC is not used to evaluate stability and capability, or to identify improvement opportunities. BSG is committed to service and has a track record that reflects a high percentage of on-time deliveries. The engineering department is young (with the average experience of four years), but energetic and eager to make a difference. They have been preoccupied with keeping abreast of new technologies, and have not been paying enough attention to improving the quality of existing processes. ■

◆●◆

QUESTIONS FOR THOUGHT

1. Use the weighted point method to develop a relative rating for Caston, Belmont, and BSG. Based on the site visit narratives, provide your own subjective ratings for each supplier against each of the four selection criteria. Which of the suppliers should be selected on the basis of this evaluation?

2. Use the AHP method to determine the preferred supplier. Use the site visit narratives as the bases for your pairwise comparative ratings for the suppliers for each criterion. Perform and comment on consistency checks. Which of the suppliers should be selected on the basis of this evaluation?

3. Compare and contrast the methods you used in questions 1 and 2. Which procedure do you think is best? Explain.

4. Once a supplier is selected, describe the procedure that Rollerball should follow to certify the supplier.

5. Once the supplier is certified, describe the procedure that Rollerball should follow to evaluate the supplier's ongoing performance and periodically recertify it?

APPENDIX A

Quality Lexicon: The Language of QIM

Abstract Mapping
Abstract Thinking
Accept
Acceptable Quality Level
Acceptance Number
Acceptance of Responsibility
Acceptance Sampling
Accuracy
Act
Action Plans
Active Adaptation
Activity
Aesthetics
Affective Domain
Affinity Diagram
Agility
Alignment
Altruism
Analogue
Analytical Decision Making
Analytical Hierarchy Process
Analyze
Analyze Tollgate
Andon
Apostles
Applicability
Arcs
Array

Arrow Diagram
Assembly Line Manufacturing
Association
Assurance
Attention to Complaints
Attributes
Attributes Data
Automation
Autonomation
Autonomy
Average Outgoing Quality (AOQ)
Average Outgoing Quality Limit (AOQL)
Average Total Inspection (ATI)

Balanced Scorecard
Basic and Security Needs
Behavior
Behavior-Based Reward System
Behavior Management
Benefits
Between-Sample Variability
Bias
Big Q Quality
Binomial
Biotechniques
Black Belt
Boring

Bottlenecks
Boundary Judgment
Brainstorming
Brainwriting
Breakthrough
Bullwhip Effect
Business Process Reengineering (BPR)

c Chart
Calibration
Capacity
Capacity Cushion
Cash Flow
Categorical Method
Categorical Ratings
Causal Analysis
Cause–Effect
Cellular Manufacturing
Centerline
Central Tendency
Centralization
Champion
Changeover
Chaos
Chaos Theory
Check
Check Sheet

Choke Points
Circumstance
Closed System
Coevolution
Cognition
Cognitive Process
Coherence
Columns
Commitment
Commodity
Common Cause Variability
Communicable Meaning
Communications
Communities of Practice
Company-Specific Philosophy
Companywide Support
Competence Management
Competitive Factors
Competitive Intelligence
Competitive Positioning
Competitive Priorities
Competitors
Completeness
Complexity
Concepts
Conscientiousness
Consistency
Consistency Index (CI)
Consistency Ratio (CR)
Constant Sample Size
Consumer's Risk
Contingency Theory
Continuous Learning
Continuous Process Improvement
Continuous Processes
Control
Control Charts
Control Tollgate
Core Competencies
Core Values
Corporate Culture
Correlation
Cost
Cost of Quality (COQ)
Cost-Adding
Counts
Courage
Courtesy
Craft System
Creative Brainstorming
Creeping Breakeven Phenomenon
Critical Path

Crosby
Cross-Functional Supplier
    Certification Team
Current Assets
Curtailment Inspection
Customer Defection
Customer Loyalty
Customer Needs Analysis
Customer Order Cycle
Customer Perspective
Customer Surveys
Customer-Driven Quality
Customers
Customization
Cycle Time Reduction

Data
De minimus Error
Decentralization
Decertification
Decision
Decision Bias
Decision Hierarchy
Decision Maker
Defect
Defectives
Define
Define Tollgate
Delayering
Delight
Delivery Lead Times
Delivery Performance
Deming's 14 Points
Dendrogram
Dependability
Deployment
Design Issues
Desire
Detection
Determination
Deverticalization
Deviation-Amplifying Feedback
Deviation-Correcting Feedback
Discontinuities
Discrimination
Discrimination Ratio
Dissemination of New Knowledge
Divergence
DMAIC Cycle
Do
Documentation
Doing

Double Sampling
Double Sourcing
Downtime
Duplication
Durability
Dynamic Population

Earliest Start
Economic Batch Quantity
Economic Value Added
Economies of Scale
Effectiveness
Efficiency
Efficient Supply Chain
E-Learning
Elevate
Elimination
Emotional Capital
Empathy
Employee Participation
Employment Involvement
Empowerment
Endogenous Deviation-Correcting
    Feedback
Endogenous Feedback
Engineering Tolerance
Enterprise Engineering
Enterprise Redesign
Entropy
Environment
Environmental Scanning
Equity
Establishing Action Plans
Ethics
Evaluation Matrix
Exogenous Deviation-Correcting
    Feedback
Exogenous Feedback
Expectations
Experience
Expertise
Explanation of Procedures
Explicit Knowledge
Exploit
Extended Enterprise
External Customer
External Setup Activities
Facilitating Product
Facilitation
Fairness
Feasibility
Feedback

Final Disposition
Financial Accountability
Financial Perspective
Financials
Finite Count
Finite Population
Firmitas
Fishbone Diagram
Fitness for Use
Five Whys
Flexibility
Flexible Capacity
Flexible Flows
Flow Time
Flowchart
Focus
Focused Factory
Force Field
Fourteen Points
Function
Functional Silos
Functioning Capabilities
Futures

Gantt Chart
Generosity
Green Belt
Group Technology
Group-Based Performance Pay
Growth Needs

Heijunka
Helpfulness
High Involvement Organizations
   (HIO)
High-Performances Work
   Practices
High-Performing Work
   Organization
High-Tech Services
Histogram
Hollowing Out
How
Hugging the Centerline
Hugging the Control Limits
Human Creativity
Human Resources
Humility
Humor

Identify
Imaginary Brainstorming

Improve
Improve Tollgate
Improvement
Improvement Efforts
Incentives
Inconsistencies
Individuals
Information Sharing
Information Technologies
Initiative
Innovation
Innovation and Learning Perspective
Inspection
Inspection Unit
Integrity
Intent
Interactive Brainwriting
Interest
Intermediate Flows
Internal Business Objectives
Internal Business Perspective
Internal Customer
Internal Setup Activities
International Organization for
   Standardization (ISO)
Interrelationship Digraph
Interval Scale
Intrinsic Motivating Potential
Intuition
Inventory
Investment
Investors
Ishikawa Diagram
ISO9000 Standards
Isolationism

Jidoka
Job Enlargement
Job Enrichment
Job Shop Production
Job Shops
Judgment
Just in Time

Kaikaku
Kaizen
Kanbans
KJ Method
Knowledge
Knowledge Access
Knowledge Base
Knowledge Engineering

Knowledge Workers
Knowledge-Driven Leadership

Lack of Data
Lack of Experience
Latent Pathogens
Latest Start
Lattice Structure
Leadership
Leadership Council
Lead Time
Lean Production
Lean Six Sigma
Learning
Learning Counselors
Learning Organizations
Leverage
Limited Attention Span
Line Imbalances
Linearity
Little q Quality
Little's Law
Long-Term Memory
Lot Tolerance Percent Defective
   (LTPD)
Lower Control Limits
Loyalty

Machine Age
Machine Theory
Macrostructure
Make to Assembly
Make to Stock
Malcolm Baldrige National Quality
   Award
Management by Fact
Management Commitment
Management Participation
Management Principles
Management Systems
Manager Participation
Managing by Fact
Manual Operation
Manufacturing Cycle
Map
Market Share
Master Black Belt
Master Production Schedule (MPS)
Material Requirements Planning
   (MRP)
Matrix Data Analysis
Matrix Diagram

Mean
Measure
Measure Tollgate
Measurement
Measurement Capability
Measurement Error
Measurement Process
Mechanistic Structures
Median
Meeting of the Minds
Mental Imagery
Mental Models
Mental Simulation
Mentoring
Metacognition
Metaphor
Metrics
Mind Reading
Mission
Mistake Proofing
Mitigation
Mixed Model Scheduling
Mode
Moment of Truth Analysis
Moments of Truth
Morphological Box
Motivation
Moving Range
Muda
Multiple Sampling
Multiskilling

Natural Tolerance
Negentropy
Nelson Funnel
Network
Neutral Awareness
Newly Industrialized Economy
  (NIE)
Niche Markets
NIST Certified Standard
Nodes
Nominal Brainwriting
Nominal Group Technique (NGT)
Nominal Scale
Nonconforming
Normal
Normal Distribution
np Chart

Offshore Competition
Open Systems
Operating Characteristic Curve

Operational Definitions
Operations
Operator Consistency
Opportunity
Optimization
Order Qualifiers
Order Winners
Ordinal Scale
Organic Structures
Organization Citizenship
  Behavior
Organization for Economic
  Cooperation and Development
  (OECD)
Organizational Impact
Out-of-Control Point
Outcomes
Output
Outsourcing

p Chart
Pairwise Comparisons
Parameters
Pareto Analysis
Participation
Passion
Pattern Matching
Pattern Recognition
PDCA Cycle
Perception
Perceptual Filtering
Performance
Performance Appraisal
Performance Measures
Personal Mastery
Physical Product
Picture Associations
Plan
Plausibility
Pleasant
Pleasure
Poisson Distribution
Poka-yoke
Positive Feedback
Postcertification Audit
Precision
Predictable
Predicting the Future
Prevention
Primary Value Stream
Principal of Neutral Awareness
Priorities

Prioritization
Prioritization Matrix
Priority Vector
Proactive Purchasing
Probationary Status
Process
Process Capability
Process Control
Process Decision Program
  Chart
Process Owner
Process-Based Quality
  Control
Procurement Cycle
Producer's Risk
Product Differentiation
Product Life Cycles
Product Orientation
Product Value
Production
Production Batch
Production Loss
Productivity
Products
Profit
Profit Margins
Profound Knowledge
Progress Review
Project Complexity
Projecting an Ideal Future
Prompt Service
Pseudostandard
Psychoemotive Motivations
Psychological State
Pull
Pull Scheduling System
Purpose
Push
Push Scheduling System

QS9000 Standards
Quality
Quality Assurance
Quality at the Source
Quality Circles
Quality Council
Quality Gap
Quality Management
Quality of Learning
Quality of Process
Quality of Supply
Quality of Work Life

Quality-Inspired Management
  (QIM)
Quantitative Decision Modeling

Radar Chart
Random Samples
Range
Ratio Scale
Rational Analysis
Realizations
Rectifying Inspection
Reenergize
Reengineering
Reject
Relations Diagram
Relationship
Relationship Marketing
Reliability
Repeatability
Repetitious
Replacement
Replenishment Cycle
Representation
Reproducibility
Resolution
Resolution of Complaints
Resource Availability
Resources
Responsibility
Responsive Supply Chain
Responsiveness
Revenues
Reverse Brainstorming
Rework
Rightsizing
Risk of Failure
Roving Leadership
Rows
Run Chart

Sacrifices
Sample
Sample Size
Sample with Replacement
Sample without Replacement
Sand Cone Model
Satisfaction Satisficing
Scatter Diagram
Scheduling
Scientific Method
Scrap
Seeing the Invisible

Segmentation
Segregation
Seiketsu
Seiri
Seiso
Seiton
Self-Control
Self-Direction
Self-Esteem
Self-Managed Teams
Self-Management
Self-Managing Work Teams (SMWT)
Self-Motivating
Self-Policing
Self-Realization
Sequential Sampling
Serendipity
Service Delivery
Service Environment
Service Features
Service Orientation
Service Performance
Service Product
SERVQUAL
Setups
Seven-Point Run Rule
Shape
Shared Ownership
Shared Vision
Shareholders
Shitsuke
Shop
Shop Floor Control
Short Cycle Time
Signal-to-Noise Ratio
Single Sampling
Single Sourcing
SIPOC Map
Six Honest Servants and Five Whys
Six Sigma
Six Sigma Scores
Sixth Sense
Skew
Skewed Distribution
Skill Variety
Social Needs
Sole Sourcing
Span
SPC
Special Cause
Special Cause Variability
Specification Limits

Specifications
Speed
Spider Chart
Stability
Stabilization
Stable
Standard Deviation
Standard Operating Procedures
Standardized Flow
Static Population
Static Quality Factors
Statistical Control
Statistical Process Control
Statistical Tools
Steering Committee
Story Telling
Strategic Fit
Strategic Level
Strategic Visioning
Strategy Canvas
Stratification
Strengths
Structural Integrity
Structured Brainstorming
Subject-Matter Experts
Suboptimal Results
Subordinate
Subsystem Interfaces
Superior Product Design
Supplier Certification
Supplier Certification Team
Supplier Collaboration
Supplier Performance Factors
Supplier Rewards
Suppliers
Supply Chain
Supply Chain Coordination
Support Value Stream
Supportive Culture
Sustainability
System
System Boundaries
Systematic Diagram
Systems Analysis
Systems Knowledge
Systems Perspective

Tacit Knowledge
Tag Line
Takt Time
Tangibles
Targeted Policies

Task Cycle
Task Identity
Task Orientation
Task Significance
Team Charter
Team Learning
Team Members
Team Mind
Team Building
Team-Based Activities
Teams
Technical Competency
Tension
Terrorists
Testing Procedures
Theory of Constraints (TOC)
Threats
Throughput
Throughput Time
Tiered Supply Chain Structure
TILMAG
Time
Time Buckets
Time-Ordered Chart
Time-Ordered Data
Time-Ordered Sequence
Tolerance Limits
Tollgate Reviews
Too Few Runs
Too Long Run
Total Productive Maintenance

Total Quality Control
Total Quality Leadership
Total Quality Management
Toxic Waste
TQM
Tracking Systems
Training
Train-the-Trainer
Transformation
Trends
Trust
Trusting Relationships
Truth

u Charts
Understanding of Customer
    Needs
Undivided Attention
Uniformity
Unstructured Brainstorming
Upper Control Limits
Useful
Utilitas

Value
Value Adding
Value Judgment
Value Migration
Value Stream
Value Stream Reinvention
Variability

Variable Sample Size
Variables Data
Variance
Variance Tracking Matrix
Vendor
Vertical Integration
Vicious Circle
Virtuous Circle
Vision
Visionaries

Waste
Waste Elimination
Weaknesses
Weighted Point Method
What
When
Where
White Belt
White-Space Opportunities
Who
Why
Within-Sample Variability
Word Associations
Work in Process
Work Process Structure
Working Capital
Working Memory

Zero Defects

APPENDIX B

Normal Tables (DPMO)

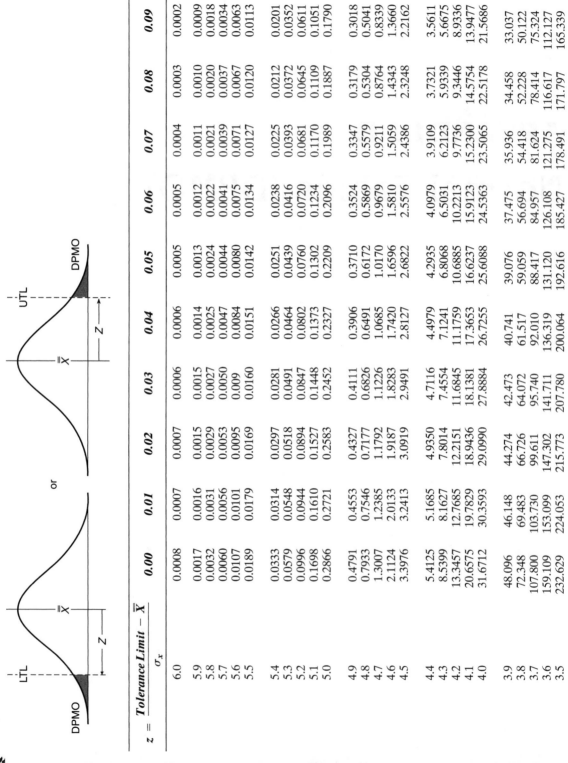

$z = \dfrac{Tolerance\ Limit - \overline{\overline{X}}}{\sigma_x}$	0.00	0.01	0.02	0.03	0.04	0.05	0.06	0.07	0.08	0.09
6.0	0.0008	0.0007	0.0007	0.0006	0.0006	0.0005	0.0005	0.0004	0.0003	0.0002
5.9	0.0017	0.0016	0.0015	0.0015	0.0014	0.0013	0.0012	0.0011	0.0010	0.0009
5.8	0.0032	0.0031	0.0029	0.0027	0.0025	0.0024	0.0022	0.0021	0.0020	0.0018
5.7	0.0060	0.0056	0.0053	0.0050	0.0047	0.0044	0.0041	0.0039	0.0037	0.0034
5.6	0.0107	0.0101	0.0095	0.009	0.0084	0.0080	0.0075	0.0071	0.0067	0.0063
5.5	0.0189	0.0179	0.0169	0.0160	0.0151	0.0142	0.0134	0.0127	0.0120	0.0113
5.4	0.0333	0.0314	0.0297	0.0281	0.0266	0.0251	0.0238	0.0225	0.0212	0.0201
5.3	0.0579	0.0548	0.0518	0.0491	0.0464	0.0439	0.0416	0.0393	0.0372	0.0352
5.2	0.0996	0.0944	0.0894	0.0847	0.0802	0.0760	0.0720	0.0681	0.0645	0.0611
5.1	0.1698	0.1610	0.1527	0.1448	0.1373	0.1302	0.1234	0.1170	0.1109	0.1051
5.0	0.2866	0.2721	0.2583	0.2452	0.2327	0.2209	0.2096	0.1989	0.1887	0.1790
4.9	0.4791	0.4553	0.4327	0.4111	0.3906	0.3710	0.3524	0.3347	0.3179	0.3018
4.8	0.7933	0.7546	0.7177	0.6826	0.6491	0.6172	0.5869	0.5579	0.5304	0.5041
4.7	1.3007	1.2385	1.1792	1.1226	1.0685	1.0170	0.9679	0.9211	0.8764	0.8339
4.6	2.1124	2.0133	1.9187	1.8283	1.7420	1.6596	1.5810	1.5059	1.4343	1.3660
4.5	3.3976	3.2413	3.0919	2.9491	2.8127	2.6822	2.5576	2.4386	2.3248	2.2162
4.4	5.4125	5.1685	4.9350	4.7116	4.4979	4.2935	4.0979	3.9109	3.7321	3.5611
4.3	8.5399	8.1627	7.8014	7.4554	7.1241	6.8068	6.5031	6.2123	5.9339	5.6675
4.2	13.3457	12.7685	12.2151	11.6845	11.1759	10.6885	10.2213	9.7736	9.3446	8.9336
4.1	20.6575	19.7829	18.9436	18.1381	17.3653	16.6237	15.9123	15.2300	14.5754	13.9477
4.0	31.6712	30.3593	29.0990	27.8884	26.7255	25.6088	24.5363	23.5065	22.5178	21.5686
3.9	48.096	46.148	44.274	42.473	40.741	39.076	37.475	35.936	34.458	33.037
3.8	72.348	69.483	66.726	64.072	61.517	59.059	56.694	54.418	52.228	50.122
3.7	107.800	103.730	99.611	95.740	92.010	88.417	84.957	81.624	78.414	75.324
3.6	159.109	153.099	147.302	141.711	136.319	131.120	126.108	121.275	116.617	112.127
3.5	232.629	224.053	215.773	207.780	200.064	192.616	185.427	178.491	171.797	165.339

z										
3.4	241.51	250.707	260.229	270.088	280.293	290.857	301.791	313.106	324.814	336.929
3.3	349.463	362.429	375.841	389.712	404.058	418.892	434.230	450.087	466.480	483.424
3.2	500.937	519.035	537.737	557.061	577.025	597.649	618.951	640.953	663.675	687.138
3.1	711.364	736.375	762.195	788.846	816.352	844.739	874.032	904.255	935.437	967.603
3.0	1,000.782	1,035.003	1,070.294	1,106.685	1,144.207	1,182.891	1,222.769	1,263.873	1,306.238	1,349.898
2.9	1,394.89	1,441.24	1,489.00	1,538.20	1,588.87	1,641.06	1,694.81	1,750.16	1,807.14	1,865.81
2.8	1,926.21	1,988.38	2,052.36	2,118.21	2,185.96	2,255.68	2,327.40	2,401.18	2,477.08	2,555.13
2.7	2,635.40	2,717.94	2,802.81	2,890.07	2,979.76	3,071.96	3,166.72	3,264.10	3,364.16	3,466.98
2.6	3,572.60	3,681.11	3,792.56	3,907.03	4,024.59	4,145.30	4,269.24	4,396.49	4,527.11	4,661.19
2.5	4,798.80	4,940.02	5,084.93	5,233.61	5,386.15	5,542.62	5,703.13	5,867.74	6,036.56	6,209.67
2.4	6,387.2	6,569.1	6,755.7	6,946.9	7,142.8	7,343.6	7,549.4	7,760.3	7,976.3	8,197.5
2.3	8,424.2	8,656.3	8,894.0	9,137.5	9,386.7	9,641.9	9,903.1	10,170.4	10,444.1	10,724.1
2.2	11,010.7	11,303.8	11,603.8	11,910.6	12,224.5	12,545.5	12,873.7	13,209.4	13,552.6	13,903.4
2.1	14,262.1	14,628.7	15,003.4	15,386.3	15,777.6	16,177.4	16,585.8	17,003.0	17,429.2	17,864.4
2.0	18,308.9	18,762.8	19,226.2	19,699.3	20,182.2	20,675.2	21,178.3	21,691.7	22,215.6	22,750.1
1.9	23,295.5	23,851.8	24,419.2	24,997.9	25,588.1	26,189.8	26,803.4	27,428.9	28,066.6	28,716.6
1.8	29,379.0	30,054.0	30,741.9	31,442.8	32,156.8	32,884.1	33,625.0	34,379.5	35,147.9	35,930.3
1.7	36,727.0	37,538.0	38,363.6	39,203.9	40,059.2	40,929.5	41,815.1	42,716.2	43,632.9	44,565.5
1.6	45,514.0	46,478.7	47,459.7	48,457.2	49,471.5	50,502.6	51,550.7	52,616.1	53,698.9	54,799.3
1.5	55,917.4	57,053.4	58,207.6	59,379.9	60,570.8	61,780.2	63,008.4	64,255.5	65,521.7	66,807.2
1.4	68,112.1	69,436.6	70,780.9	72,145.0	73,529.3	74,933.7	76,358.5	77,803.8	79,269.8	80,756.7
1.3	82,264.4	83,793.3	85,343.5	86,915.0	88,508.0	90,122.7	91,759.1	93,417.5	95,097.9	96,800.5
1.2	98,525.3	100,272.6	102,042.3	103,834.7	105,649.8	107,487.7	109,348.6	111,232.4	113,139.4	115,069.7
1.1	117,023.2	119,000.1	121,000.5	123,024.4	125,071.9	127,143.2	129,238.1	131,356.9	133,499.5	135,666.1
1.0	137,856.6	140,071.1	142,309.7	144,572.3	146,859.1	149,170.0	151,505.0	153,864.2	156,247.6	158,655.2
0.9	161,087	163,543	166,023	168,528	171,056	173,609	176,186	65,521.7	181,411	184,060
0.8	186,733	189,430	192,150	194,895	197,663	200,454	203,269	206,108	208,970	211,855
0.7	214,764	217,695	220,650	223,627	226,627	229,650	232,695	235,762	238,852	241,964
0.6	245,097	248,252	251,429	254,627	257,846	261,086	264,347	267,629	270,931	274,253
0.5	277,595	280,957	284,339	287,740	291,160	294,599	298,056	301,532	305,026	308,538
0.4	312,067	315,614	319,178	322,758	326,355	329,969	333,598	337,243	340,903	344,578
0.3	348,268	351,973	355,691	359,424	363,169	366,928	370,700	374,484	378,280	382,089
0.2	385,908	389,739	393,580	397,432	401,294	405,165	409,046	412,936	416,834	420,740
0.1	424,655	428,576	432,505	436,441	440,382	444,330	448,283	452,242	456,205	460,172
0.0	464,144	468,119	472,097	476,078	480,061	484,047	488,034	492,022	496,011	500,000

Name Index

Subject Index